T0180336

Communications
in Computer and Information Science 1532

More information about this series at https://link.springer.com/bookseries/7899

Fabián R. Narváez · Julio Proaño ·
Paulina Morillo · Diego Vallejo ·
Daniel González Montoya ·
Gloria M. Díaz (Eds.)

Smart Technologies, Systems and Applications

Second International Conference, SmartTech-IC 2021
Quito, Ecuador, December 1–3, 2021
Revised Selected Papers

 Springer

Editors
Fabián R. Narváez ⓘ
Universidad Politécnica Salesiana
Quito, Ecuador

Julio Proaño ⓘ
Universidad Politécnica Salesiana
Quito, Ecuador

Paulina Morillo ⓘ
Universidad Politécnica Salesiana
Quito, Ecuador

Diego Vallejo ⓘ
Universidad Politécnica Salesiana
Quito, Ecuador

Daniel González Montoya ⓘ
Instituto Tecnológico Metropolitano
Medellín, Colombia

Gloria M. Díaz ⓘ
Instituto Tecnológico Metropolitano
Medellín, Colombia

ISSN 1865-0929   ISSN 1865-0937 (electronic)
Communications in Computer and Information Science
ISBN 978-3-030-99169-2   ISBN 978-3-030-99170-8 (eBook)
https://doi.org/10.1007/978-3-030-99170-8

This Springer imprint is published by the registered company Springer Nature Switzerland AG
The registered company address is: Gewerbestrasse 11, 6330 Cham, Switzerland

Preface

This volume contains the papers presented at the Second International Conference on Smart Technologies, Systems and Applications (SmartTech-IC 2021) held during December 1–3, 2021, in Quito, Ecuador. The SmartTech-IC conference aims to attract researchers, scientists, and technologists from some of the top companies, universities, research groups, and government agencies from Latin America and around the world to communicate their research results, inventions, and innovative applications in the area of smart science and the most recent smart technological trends. SmartTech-IC 2021 was organized by the Universidad Politécnica Salesiana, a private institution of higher education with social purposes, nonprofit and co-financed by the Ecuadorian State. The SmartTech-IC conference was conceived as an academic platform to promote the creation of technical and scientific collaboration networks. The goal of the conference was to address topics related to smart technologies, smart systems, smart trends, and applications in different domains in the field of computer science and information systems that represent innovation in current society.

We would like to express our gratitude to all the authors who submitted papers to SmartTech-IC 2021, and our congratulations to those whose papers were accepted. There were 104 submissions. Each submission was reviewed by at least three qualified reviewers chosen from our Program Committee (PC) based on their qualifications and experience. We selected the papers based on a series of criteria including the reviewers average score and comments provided by the Program Committee members. Finally, we decided to accept 30 full papers.

We would also like to thank the PC members, who agreed to review the manuscripts in a timely manner and provided valuable feedback to the authors.

December 2021

Fabián R. Narváez
Julio Proaño
Paulina Morillo
Diego Vallejo
Daniel González Montoya
Gloria M. Díaz

Organization

Honorary Committee

Juan Cárdenas	Universidad Politécnica Salesiana, Ecuador
María Sol Villagómez	Universidad Politécnica Salesiana, Ecuador
Juan Pablo Salgado	Universidad Politécnica Salesiana, Ecuador
Tatiana Mosquera	Universidad Politécnica Salesiana, Ecuador

Organizing Committee

Fabián R. Narváez	Universidad Politécnica Salesiana, Ecuador
Julio R. Proaño	Universidad Politécnica Salesiana, Ecuador
Paulina A. Morillo	Universidad Politécnica Salesiana, Ecuador
Diego F. Vallejo	Universidad Politécnica Salesiana, Ecuador

Program Chairs

Smart Technologies

César Ferri	Universidad Politécnica de Valencia, Spain
Patricia Acosta Vargas	Universidad de Las Américas, Ecuador

Smart Systems

Teodiano Bastos	Universidade Federal do Espírito Santo, Brazil
Daniel González Montoya	Instituto Tecnológico Metropolitano, Colombia
Esteban Inga	Universidad Politécnica Salesiana, Ecuador

Smart Applications

Antoine Manzanera	ENSTA Paris, France
Angel Cruz-Roa	Universidad de los Llanos, Colombia
Gloria M. Díaz	Instituto Tecnológico Metropolitano, Colombia

Program Committee

Alberto López Delis	Medical Biophysics Center, Cuba
Alexander Águila	Universidad Politécnica Salesiana, Ecuador
Alvaro D. Orejuela	Universidad del Rosario, Colombia
Antoine Manzanera	ENSTA Paris, France

Andrés Felipe Ruiz Olaya	Universidad Antonio Nariño, Colombia
Ana Cecilia Villa	Universidad Politécnica Salesiana, Ecuador
Ángel Cruz Roa	Universidad de los Llanos, Colombia
Angélica Ramírez	Universidad Militar Nueva Granada, Colombia
Carlos Cevallos	Universidad Politécnica Nacional, Ecuador
Carlos Mera	Instituto Tecnológico Metropolitano, Colombia
Carmen Carrión	Universidad de Castilla-La Mancha, Spain
César Ferri	Universidad Politécnica de Valencia, Spain
Christian Cifuentes	Universidad de los Andes, Colombia
Daniel González Montoya	Instituto Tecnológico Metropolitano, Colombia
David Romo	Univeridad Industrial de Santander, Colombia
David Ojeda	Universidad Técnica del Norte, Ecuador
Derfrey Duque Quintero	Universidad Pascual Bravo, Colombia
Diego Carrión	Universidad Politécnica Salesiana, Ecuador
Diego Almeida	Yachay Tech University, Ecuador
Diego Vallejo	Universidad Politécnica Salesiana, Ecuador
Eduardo Pinos	Universidad Politécnica Salesiana, Ecuador
Enrique Arias	Universidad de Castilla-La Mancha, Spain
Erick Reyes	Instituto Tecnológico Metropolitano, Colombia
Esteban Inga	Universidad Politécnica Salesiana, Ecuador
Estefania Coronado	Fundazione Bruno Kessler, Italy
Fabián R. Narváez	Universidad Politécnica Salesiana, Ecuador
Fernando Urgiles	Universidad Politécnica Salesiana, Ecuador
Fernando Villalba	Yachay Tech University, Ecuador
Germán Arévalo	Universidad Politécnica Salesiana, Ecuador
Germán Corredor	Case Western Reserve University, USA
Gloria M. Díaz	Instituto Tecnológico Metropolitano, Colombia
Gustavo Caiza	Universidad Politécnica Salesiana, Ecuador
Hiram Ponce Espinosa	Universidad Panamericana, Mexico
Hugo Franco	Universidad Central, Colombia
Ignacio Larrabide	Universidad Nacional del Centro de Buenos Aires, Argentina
Israel Pineda	Yachay Tech University, Ecuador
Jack Bravo	Universidad Politécnica Salesiana, Ecuador
Jairo J. Espinosa	Universidad Nacional de Colombia, Colombia
José Ignacio Huertas	Tecnológico de Monterrey, Mexico
José Sampietro	CELEC EP, Ecuador
Jorge E. Camargo	Universidad Antonio Nariño, Colombia
Juan Pablo D'manto	Universidad Nacional del Centro de Buenos Aires, Argentina
Juan Sebastián Botero	Instituto Tecnológico Metropolitano, Colombia
Juan David Martínez	Instituto Tecnológico Metropolitano, Colombia

Juan C. Caicedo	Broad Institute of MIT and Harvard, USA
Juan C. Santillán	Universidad Politécnica del Cimborazo, Ecuador
Julio Proaño Orellana	Universidad Politécnica Salesiana, Ecuador
Leony Ortiz	Universidad Politécnica Salesiana, Ecuador
María Blanca Caminero	Universidad de Castilla-La Mancha, Spain
María Constanza Torres	Instituto Tecnológico Metropolitano, Colombia
M. Carmen Juan Lizandra	Universidad Politécnica de Valencia, Spain
María Gabriela Baldeón	University of South Florida, USA
Mauro Callejas	Universidad Pedagógica y Tecnológica, Colombia
Milton Ruiz	Universidad Politécnica Salesiana, Ecuador
Lenin V. Campozano	Escuela Politécnica Nacional, Ecuador
Lucía Rivadeneira	University of Manchester, UK
Oscar Acosta	Université de Rennes 1, France
Patricia Acosta Vargas	Universidad de Las Américas, Ecuador
Pablo Álvarez	Université de Rennes 1, France
Paula Rodríguez	Universidad Nacional de Colombia, Colombia
Paulina Morillo	Universidad Politécnica Salesiana, Ecuador
Ramón Pérez Pineda	Universidad Politécnica Salesiana, Ecuador
Ricardo Flores	Universidad San Francisco de Quito, Ecuador
Ricardo Gutiérrez	Universidad Militar Nueva Granada, Colombia
Rubén D. Fonnegra	Universidad Pascual Bravo, Colombia
Santiago Gonzáles Martínez	Universidad de Cuenca, Ecuador
Sergio Luján	Universidad de Alicante, Spain
Teodiano Bastos	Universidade Federal do Espírito Santo, Brazil
Vladimir Robles	Universidad Politécnica Salesiana, Ecuador
Villie Morocho	Universidad de Cuenca, Ecuador
Ximena López	Universidad de San Marcos, Perú

Local Organizing Committee

Tatiana Mosquera	Universidad Politécnica Salesiana, Ecuador
Janneth Pallascos	Universidad Politécnica Salesiana, Ecuador
Jessica Chávez	Universidad Politécnica Salesiana, Ecuador
Maria Belén Sánchez	Universidad Politécnica Salesiana, Ecuador
Mónica Ruiz	Universidad Politécnica Salesiana, Ecuador
Julissa Freire	Universidad Politécnica Salesiana, Ecuador
Christian Guachilema	Universidad Politécnica Salesiana, Ecuador
Byron Fernando Velasco	Universidad Politécnica Salesiana, Ecuador

Sponsoring Institutions

http://www.ups.edu.ec

https://www.itm.edu.co/

Contents

Smart Systems

Smart Technologies

Lightweight Convolutional Neural Networks Framework for Really Small TinyML Devices

César A. Estrebou[1]([envelope])[iD], Martín Fleming[2]([envelope]), Marcos D. Saavedra[2]([envelope]), Federico Adra[2]([envelope]), and Armando E. De Giusti[1,3]([envelope])[iD]

[1] Informatics Research Institute LIDI, CIC's Associated Research Center, National University of La Plata, 1900 La Plata, Argentina
{cesarest,degiusti}@lidi.info.unlp.edu.ar
[2] School of Informatic, National University of La Plata, 1900 La Plata, Argentina
{martin.fleming,saavedramarcosdavid,fedeadra}@alu.ing.unlp.edu.ar
[3] CONICET - National Council of Scientific and Technical Research, Buenos Aires, Argentina
http://www.lidi.info.unlp.edu.ar

Abstract. This paper presents a lightweight and compact framework designed to perform convolutional neural network inference on severely hardware constrained microcontrollers. A review of similar open source libraries is included and experiments are developed to compare their capabilities on several different microcontrollers. The proposed framework implementation shows at least a three-time improvement over the Google Tensorflow Lite Micro implementation with respect to memory usage and inference time.

Keywords: Machine learning · Convolutional neural networks · TinyML · Microcontrollers · Framework

1 Introduction

TinyML (Tiny Machine Learning) is an acronym that combines two very interesting areas such as machine learning and microcontrollers, something that was unthinkable not so many years ago, mainly due to the hardware limitations of microcontrollers.

TinyML technology is directly or indirectly driven by many factors. Among them we should mention the production volume of microcontrollers and IOT devices, which are constantly growing and evolving. Projections such as those made by Statista [1] and Cisco [2] estimate that the number of IoT devices connected to the Internet in 2022 will be around 11.57 billion and 12.5 billion. These numbers reveals a tremendous potential computing capacity with low costs and reduced power consumption. Another factor that has influenced TinyML technology is related to drawbacks inherent in cloud computing [3,4].

© Springer Nature Switzerland AG 2022
F. R. Narváez et al. (Eds.): SmartTech-IC 2021, CCIS 1532, pp. 3–16, 2022.
https://doi.org/10.1007/978-3-030-99170-8_1

Problems associated with computational and storage cost, power consumption, network bandwidth, response delays, privacy and security issues, caused part of cloud computing to move to edge computing. As a result, new solutions for a wide variety of devices began to emerge from different areas. But undoubtedly the biggest revolution came from the field of machine learning by enabling the execution of neural network models directly on microcontrollers [5,6].

There are online platforms available that perform the entire process of developing a machine learning solution on a microcontroller from end to end with minimal user intervention to achieve this. On the other hand, companies that manufacture microcontrollers and/or development boards have tools and libraries that allow incorporation of TensorFlow/Keras models. Unfortunately, they are only available for a limited number of microcontrollers (mainly ARM), which require 32-bit architectures with floating-point, SIMD or DSP instructions support. This limits the implementation of machine learning solutions on a large number of microcontrollers despite their popularity, low cost or additional hardware features. In particular, Tensorflow Lite Micro [7] is the most widely used development framework because it is portable, flexible and can be used on both, microcontrollers and mobile devices. However, the size of its object-based software architecture makes it an unsuitable alternative for microcontrollers with severe memory limitations. On the other hand, although it could be adapted for other architectures, it only has implementations for 32-bit microcontrollers.

In this context we have created a group to research and develop machine learning software for microcontrollers with strong hardware constraints, trying to cover as many of them as possible regardless of their architecture. This work presents EmbedIA-NN, a framework to perform Tensorflow/Keras convolutional neural network model inference for C/C++ and Arduino language platforms. We propose a simple, highly portable and lightweight solution designed to maximize the resources of microcontrollers independent of their hardware limitations.

This article is organized as follows. Section 1 contains this introduction. Section 2 describes the characteristics of microcontrollers for neural networks and the available open source software. Section 3 describes the framework proposed in this paper and its general implementation details. Section 4 describes in detail the 2 experiments to determine the performance of various frameworks/libraries. Section 5 describes and analyzes the results obtained in the experiments. Finally, Sect. 6 develops the conclusions and future work.

2   Neural Networks for Microcontrollers

2.1   Microcontroller Characteristics

A microcontroller is a chip that integrates a central processing unit, a data and program memory and a series of input/output peripherals. In the microcontroller development field there is a high level of segmentation. A wide variety of hardware characteristics can be found in these devices, such as system clock speed, number of working bits, memory size, or special instructions that increase performance through specialized hardware. Typical clock speeds can range from 8 mhz to about 500 mhz. Data memory capacity typically ranges from 8 Kib to 320 Kib, and program memory from 32 Kib to 1 Mib.

In general, microcontrollers are designed for low cost and energy consumption efficiency, so they do not provide good performance for workload-intensive tasks, such as neural networks, and in particular convolutional neural networks. Solutions to this problem can be addressed in two different ways. One is related to the microcontroller hardware and consists of integrating special DSP and/or SIMD floating-point instructions to boost computational speed. The other approach is software-related and consists of implementing efficient or optimized models [8,9] and improved techniques or libraries [10,11] to speed up the computing.

2.2   Neural Networks Software for Microcontrollers

This section briefly describes relevant and available open source libraries and frameworks for the development of machine learning and neural network applications for microcontrollers.

Tensorflow Lite Micro. [7,12] for microcontrollers requires 32-bit platforms and is coded in C++ 11. It primarily supports architectures of the *ARM Cortex-M* series and has been ported to other architectures such as *Esp32*. The framework is available as an Arduino library. It can also generate projects for development environments, such as *Mbed*. It is open source and can be included in any C++ 11 project.

μTensor [13] is a lightweight machine learning inference framework built in *Tensorflow Lite* that is optimized for ARM architecture-based microcontrollers. It takes a model generated in *Tensorflow* and produces .cpp and .hpp files containing C++ 11 code to perform the inference. It does not currently support softmax functionality.

ARM CMSIS-NN. [14] has a library for fully connected and convolutional neural networks named CMSIS-NN (Cortex Microcontroller Software Interface Standard Neural Network) that maximizes the performance of Cortex-M processors with support for SIMD and DSP instructions. It includes support for 8-bit and 16-bit data types for neural networks with quantized weights.

EdgeML. [15] is a library of machine learning algorithms for resource constrained microcontrollers. It allows training, evaluation and deployment on various target devices and platforms. *EdgeML* is written in *Python* using *Tensorflow/Keras* and supports *PyTorch* and optimized C++ implementations for certain algorithms. Convolutional neural networks are not supported at the moment.

Eloquent TinyML. [16] is an Arduino library that aims to simplify the deployment of *Tensorflow Lite* models for compatible Arduino board microcontrollers using the Arduino IDE. Starting from a model exported with *Tensorflow Lite*, this library exposes an interface to load a model and run inferences.

3   EmbedIA-NN, an Ultralight Framework for MCUs

3.1   Why a Neural Network Framework for Microcontrollers?

When considering software alternatives to incorporate into a machine learning project, it happens that these tools are of a limited use, with licenses for personal use, with paid licenses for commercial use or available for a certain type of microcontrollers. This restricts the implementation of machine learning solutions on a large number of microcontrollers despite their popularity, low cost or additional hardware features.

There are few open source library initiatives for machine learning and very few provide support for neural networks and even fewer for convolutional networks. In general, these alternatives, besides being incipient, usually lack of support and present significant limitations for the wide variety of microcontrollers available in the market. The libraries and frameworks mentioned in the Sect. 2.2, although they have their advantages, also have some important disadvantages, especially when dealing with very limited microcontrollers. In particular, Tensorflow Lite (TFL) [7] is the most widely used development framework because it is highly portable, to the fact that it can be used from microcontrollers to mobile devices. However, it is not the best alternative for microcontrollers with severe memory limitations. Although it can be adapted to other architectures, it has support for 32-bit ARM architecture microcontrollers with instructions optimized for floating point, DSP or SIMD, excluding devices with other architectures or without hardware for specialized mathematical computation. The TFL framework is developed in C++ with an interpreter that gives it flexibility and portability, interesting features for microcontrollers with significant hardware or for mobile devices. However, the object-based software architecture with inheritance and polymorphism along with the design of its interpreter consumes an amount of memory that does not allow implementing models on microcontrollers with severe memory limitations and also slows down the inference times of the algorithms.

For these reasons we decided to develop EmbedIA-NN, an open source[1], simple and ultra-lightweight framework for microcontrollers with severely limited hardware resources, which aims to minimize the size of data and program memory regardless of their architectures.

3.2   Development Process on Microcontrollers with EmbedIA-NN

Figure 1 shows a scheme of the steps involved in the development of a neural network model with EmbedIA-NN for a microcontroller. The process starts with

---

[1] https://github.com/Embed-ML/EmbedIA.

the selection of the model and the configuration of the network parameters. Then a Tensorflow/Keras model is generated using training data to finally validate the accuracy of the model with test data. If the result is not satisfactory, the process is restarted by reconfiguring the parameters.

Once the model is obtained, the parameters of the EmbedIA-NN exporter are configured. Among these you can select the type of data used in the model (floating point or fixed point variants), type of project to be generated (C, C++ or Arduino), debugging level to be included in the code, inclusion of examples for testing or checking the operation, among others. The exporter creates a folder for the project type generated including files with the necessary functions to perform the inference, files with the model, files with debugging functionalities and additional files with functionalities associated with the data type chosen for the model. Finally, the application is compiled on the platform corresponding to the project and if the executable code fits the required data and program memory size, it is deployed on the device. If the executable does not meet the memory requirements or behaves unstable, it is returned to the model optimization point or to the initial point of development to reconfigure the model parameters.

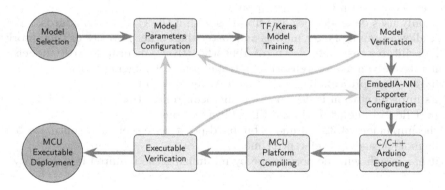

Fig. 1. Development cycle with EmbedIA-NN on Microcontrollers.

3.3   EmbedIA-NN Features

EmbedIA-NN is a compact and lightweight open source library, designed for microcontrollers that are really limited in both memory and hardware. It is implemented in C, C++ and Arduino compatible code so it can be compiled on any platform that supports these programming languages. It provides functionalities to perform inference and debugging of the models from the microcontroller. It supports different neural network layers and activation functions including convolutional, max pooling, flatten, fully connected, ReLU and softmax.

At the moment, it does not include optimizations to take advantage of advanced hardware instructions for specific microcontrollers, but there are plans to incorporate them in the future. However, some optimizations were implemented for fixed-point arithmetic in 32 bits ($Q_{14.18}$), 16 bits ($Q_{7.9}$) and 8 bits

($Q_{5.3}$). In particular, the latter version has adaptations implemented in 16 bits to improve accuracy. In general, these fixed-point implementations speed up inference, reduce program size and data memory usage for microcontrollers without specialized computational hardware. To improve data memory usage, a swap buffer was implemented to minimize the amount of dynamic memory requirements. This avoids fragmentation, something indispensable for those microcontrollers that do not implement a good management of this type of memory.

In addition, it is provided with a tool that converts a model generated in Tensorflow/Keras to C code. It also allows to generate a C, C++ or Arduino project that includes the functions to perform the inference of the converted model, including options for fixed point usage. It is also possible to include debugging functions for the model, implemented in the appropriate version of the project's target platform.

The contributions and strengths of the Embedia-NN framework can be summarized as follows:

– it is an open source framework with a simple, lightweight and efficient design.
– it facilitates the development of TinyML applications on any microcontroller architecture with C language support.
– it only uses dependencies and libraries within the C/C++ standards.
– it allows running larger models and faster than other libraries or frameworks.
– it facilitates easy deployment of Tensorflow/Keras neural network models.
– it takes advantage of Tensorflow's training and debugging tools.
– it generates projects in C, C++ and Arduino with the models.
– its implementation is designed for microcontrollers that do not natively support floating point, DSP and SIMD instructions.
– the implemented 32, 16 and 8 bit fixed-point representations optimize both memory usage and inference time.
– it has an efficient memory usage by minimizing the required functionality.

4   Experiments on Frameworks and Libraries

4.1   Description of the Experiments Performed

In order to determine the performance of the EmbedIA-NN library it was decided to perform two experiments building a convolutional neural network model [17] in Tensorflow/Keras for each one. The first experiment was designed to test different implementations on microcontrollers with very limited memory capacity. In this case, the convolutional network was trained to recognize 10-digit handwritten images with a size of 8×8. The second experiment was designed to test the limits of third-party libraries and frameworks on microcontrollers that are less limited in memory capacity. In this case, the convolutional network was trained to recognize a total of 36 classes represented by images of 26 letters and 10 handwritten digits with a size of 16×16.

With the models built, a project was developed for each experiment and replicated for each third party library and each Embedia-NN implementation

(8-bit, 16-bit and 32-bit floating-point and fixed-point). The source code for the project includes the model, the neural network functionalities and a minimum of serial communication functionality so that each microcontroller can receive a sample and send the classification result with the accuracy and time required.

As part of each experiment, each project was compiled and deployed on the selected microcontrollers. Then, each image in the test set was ranked and its result was computed to determine the performance of the microcontroller-library combination. The features considered for comparison of the different libraries were, program memory size, data memory size, inference time in microseconds (μs), and test data set hit percentage.

All the information related to both experiments has been published in a Github[2] repository. It includes the model used in the measurements, test projects for each MCU and library, as well as spreadsheets with the summary of the tests.

4.2 Microcontrollers Included in the Experiments

The decision of the microcontrollers used in the experiments was based on aspects such as local availability of development boards, low cost (US\$ 6), low to medium-low computational capacity and availability of open source software. Regarding connectivity, it was decided to incorporate both IoT and non-IoT devices, since from a machine learning and neural network point of view there are many popular and interesting devices with and without this feature.

Five microcontrollers of varying features were used for testing purpose: ATmega2560, Stm32f103c8t6 (Arm Cortex-M3), Tensilica L106, Xtensa LX6 and RP2040 (Arm Cortex-M0+). Their technical specifications are shown in Table 1.

Table 1. Technical features of the microcontrollers used in the experiments.

Development board	MCU	Clock	Memory			Flot. Pt.	Connectivity
			Bits	Data	Prog		
Arduino Mega	ATmega2560	16 MHz	8	8 KiB	256 KiB	No	No
Stm32f103c8t6	Arm Cortex-M3	72 MHz	32	20 KiB	64 KiB	No	No
NodeMCU ESP8266	Tensilica L106	80 MHz	32	80 KiB	512 KiB	Yes	Wi-Fi
ESP32-WROOM	Xtensa LX6	160 MHz	32	320 KiB	512 KiB	Yes	Wi-Fi+BT
Raspberry Pi Pico	RP2040	133 MHz	32	264 KiB	2 MiB	No	No

4.3 Experiments Datasets

MNIST Dataset. [18] (Modified National Institute of Standards and Technology database) is a dataset frequently used to evaluate image classification algorithms in areas of machine learning, neural networks and image processing. This dataset is a reduced version of the UCI [19] repository, provided by the Scikit-learn library. It comprises a selection of 1797 images from the original gray-scale dataset with handwritten digits centered in an 8×8 pixel area.

---

[2] https://github.com/Embed-ML/EmbedIA-Comparisons.

For model training and testing of experiment 1, the dataset was divided into 80% and 20%, respectively. The intensity values of the images were normalized between 0 and 1. An example of the dataset can be seen in Fig. 2a.

EMNIST Dataset. [20] is an extended version of the MNIST dataset. It is composed of a handwritten character set comprising both digits and lowercase and uppercase letters derived from the special NIST 19 database and converted to a 28 × 28 pixel grayscale image format. It is further divided into subsets of data with different combinations of digits and letters both balanced and unbalanced.

The EMNIST dataset selected for testing contains about 100800 images comprising 36 balanced classes consisting of 10 digits and 26 uppercase letters. For training and model testing of experiment 2, the dataset was divided into 80% and 20% respectively. The images were converted to a resolution of 16 × 16 pixels and the intensity values were normalized between 0 and 1. An example of the letters incorporated into the dataset can be seen in Fig. 2b.

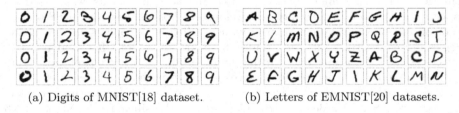

(a) Digits of MNIST[18] dataset.   (b) Letters of EMNIST[20] datasets.

Fig. 2. Datasets used in experiments for training convolutional neural networks.

4.4   Convolutional Neural Network Model for the Experiments

A convolutional neural network (CNN or ConvNet) model was used to test the experiment [17,21]. This type of networks are multi-layer artificial neural networks specialized in handling two-dimensional input data. Typically, their architecture is composed of combinations of convolutional, nonlinear, pooling and fully connected layers. The convolutional layer takes an image and decomposes it into different feature maps. The sequencing of various layers generates different levels of abstraction as the information progresses through the network. In the first layers, low level features, such as edges, are obtained, while in the last layers more complex and abstract structures, such as parts of objects, are detected. Finally, the features extracted by the convolutional layers are processed by one or more layers of fully connected neurons that end up classifying the input image.

For training models, Tensorflow/Keras for Python was used. In order to determine the architecture of the two network models of the experiments, different combinations of layers were tested in order to guarantee a good percentage of accuracy and a low number of hyper-parameters. This last feature is of fundamental importance to maintain a small byte size to ensure that the model fits on all test microcontrollers.

5   Tests and Results

5.1   Results of Experiment 1

The goal of the first experiment was developed to demonstrate two points about Embedia-NN. The first is to demonstrate that it can run convolutional neural network models on very hardware limited microcontrollers. The second is to show that it significantly outperforms other libraries with respect to memory footprint and inference speed. To perform the experiment, a test was organized for each combination between the Google Tensorflow Lite, Eloquent TinyML, μTensor (microTensor), and EmbedIA-NN (in its four versions) libraries and the ATmega2560, Arm Cortex-M3, Tensilica L106, Xtensa LX6 and RP2040 microcontrollers.

Table 2 shows a summary of the values generated by experiment 1. The breakdown of these values is omitted for space reasons and because they are similar to those shown for experiment 2.

Table 2. Summary of experiment 1. For each library/framework the ratio of the measured value to the value of the worst implementation (100%) is shown.

Library/Framework	Average values over microcontrollers for the same model				Relationship to worst case implementation (%)		
	Prog. Mem.(Kib)	Data Mem.(Kib)	Infer. Time (μs)	Acc. (%)	Prog. Mem.	Data Mem.	Inference Time
Eloquent TinyML	158.3	20.5	8789	98.89	96.8	100.0	78.3
Tensorflow Lite	145.5	18.1	7735	98.89	100.0	88.5	69.2
μTensor (Quantized)	30.2	10.7	11173	98.89	20.8	52.15	100.0
Embedia NN Flot. Pt.	15.2	6.3	5988	98.89	10.5	30.6	53.6
Embedia NN Fix Pt. 32	13.5	5.0	2865	98.89	9.3	24.6	25.6
Embedia NN Fix Pt. 16	11.7	3.1	1038	98.89	8.0	15.3	9.3
Embedia NN Fix Pt. 8	10.8	2.3	1119	89.72	7.5	11.4	10.0

In Table 2 and in Fig. 3 it can be observed how Embedia-NN outperforms the other implementations. Regarding the program memory size it occupies about 9 times less than Eloquent TinyML and Tensorflow Lite and 2.5 times of μTensor. With respect to program memory it is observed that it occupies 3 to 6 times less Eloquent TinyML and Tensorflow Lite and 0.25 to 3 times μTensor. Finally, for inference time it can be noted that EmbedIA-NN for floating point clearly outperforms other implementations and, in particular, the version of EmbedIA-NN Fixed Point for 16 bits is at least 7 times faster than other implementations.

It is important to note that the tests on the ATMega2560 microcontroller were only possible for EmbedIA-NN since, for the other libraries, the program failed to compile because memory was insufficient. As an example of the library's potential, a prototype was created for this microcontroller that recognizes handwritten digits on a 240×320 pixel graphic display with an integrated touch screen.

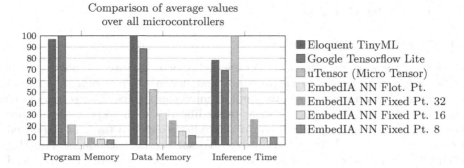

Fig. 3. Experiment 1. Comparison of the average of the variables measured in the different microcontrollers for the same model. The units are measured in percentage with respect to the worst implementation.

This example integrates the experiment model, inference functions, graphics routines code and touch screen handling code into only 24 KiB of program memory and 6 KiB of RAM (Fig. 4).

Fig. 4. ATMega2560 MCU integrating model, inference functions, graphics and touch screen functions in 24 KiB of program memory and 6 KiB of RAM.

5.2 Results of Experiment 2

The objective of this second experiment was developed to test the limits that frameworks/libraries can reach with respect to a convolutional neural network model. This model was carefully generated to maintain the memory requirements of the less efficient library/framework. The effectiveness result achieved with the 14400 images of the test dataset was 88%. We consider this value as acceptable considering the constraints posed for the libraries and that the confusion matrix showed recognition problems for only 3 groups of images with similar characteristics: number 0 and letter O, number 1 and letters L and I and number 5 with letter S. Due to the lack of context information, these symbols are often difficult to identify even by people.

To perform the experiment, a test was created for each combination between the Google Tensorflow Lite, Eloquent TinyML, μTensor (microTensor), and EmbedIA-NN libraries (in their four versions) and the Tensilica L106, Xtensa LX6, and RP2040 microcontrollers. The ATmega2560 and Stm32f103c8t6 microcontrollers were left aside because of data and program memory limitations.

It is worth mentioning that two of the libraries mentioned in the Sect. 2.2 were not considered. CMSIS-NN indicates in its official site that it is possible for the library to work with processors of earlier series than those supported. However, we were unable to compile the projects because it apparently requires SIMD or DSP instructions, that the chosen microcontrollers do not have such support. Another was Microsoft EdgeML which was also left out of the tests because it does not currently support the convolutional layers included in the test model. Regarding μTensor, it is important to clarify that since it does not support softmax layers, the latter was replaced by a fully connected layer for the tests, in order to maintain the size of the network and the speed of the inference.

The Table 3 shows the values of all tests performed. It contains the name of each microcontroller, the test target library with its variants, the values of program memory, data memory, inference time and model effectiveness. Those combinations that do not appear in the table were omitted because it was not possible to compile the test project because it does not have support for the MCU or there is a compatibility problem in the library.

Table 3. Comparison of memory footprint and inference time required by the libraries in each library-microcontroller combination.

Microcontroller/Development board	Library	Variant	Prog. M. (Kib)	Data M. (Kib)	Infer. time (μs)	Acc. (%)
Tensilica L106 NodeMCU	Eloquent TinyML	Floating Pt.	144.21	46.68	72145	88.00
	Tensorflow Lite	Floating Pt.	128.67	44.28	72280	88.00
	Embedia NN	Floating Pt.	29.98	31.15	49114	88.00
		Fixed Pt. 32 bits	27.73	31.10	34019	88.00
		Fixed Pt. 16 bits	18.39	15.90	14483	88.00
		Fixed Pt. 8 bits	13.83	11.35	16017	75.00
Xtensa LX6 Esp 32 Devkit	Eloquent TinyML	Floating Pt.	144.21	46.68	72145	88.00
	Tensorflow Lite	Floating Pt.	128.67	44.28	72280	88.00
	Embedia NN	Floating Pt.	29.98	31.15	49114	88.00
		Fixed Pt. 32 bits	27.73	31.10	34019	88.00
		Fixed Pt. 16 bits	18.39	15.90	14483	88.00
		Fixed Pt. 8 bits	13.83	11.35	16017	75.00
RP 2040 Raspberry Pico	Eloquent TinyML	Floating Pt.	91.45	31.13	78633	88.00
	Tensorflow Lite	Floating Pt.	129.75	28.99	66410	88.00
	μTensor	Cuantizado	32.47	27.37	110003	88.00
	Embedia NN	Floating Pt.	10.44	18.58	54752	88.00
		Fixed Pt. 32 bits	7.14	14.89	24228	88.00
		Fixed Pt. 16 bits	6.89	8.77	10680	88.00
		Fixed Pt. 16 bits	6.88	5.70	7829	75.00

In Table 3 and in the graphs of the Fig. 5 a, b and c we observe a notable advantage of the EmbedIA-NN implementations over the other frameworks and libraries in all the variables measured. While the 16-bit and 8-bit fixed-point implementations stand out, the former is better because it maintains the same effectiveness of the third-party implementations while the latter falls back to 13%. Nonetheless, the latter can be considered as an option for very memory limited devices as it occupies 4 to 9 times less program memory and 3 to 5 times less data memory. The Fig. 5d is a summary that averages the measurements in Table 3 on a scale expressed in percentage with respect to the library that obtained the highest value in the evaluated characteristic. A value of 50% is twice as good as the worst value (100%). Regarding the inference time, it can be noted that in general the fixed-point versions of Embedia-NN are 3 to 10 times faster than the other implementations. Regarding the amount of memory, the differences are less significant for the floating-point and 32-bit fixed-point Embedia-NN implementations. However, for the 16-bit fixed-point version an improvement of about 3 times can be observed. Finally, in the comparison of program memory we can notice in general a wide difference in favor of Embedia-NN of 3 times smaller than μTensor, 7 times smaller than Google Tensorflow Lite and 9 times smaller than Eloquent TinyML.

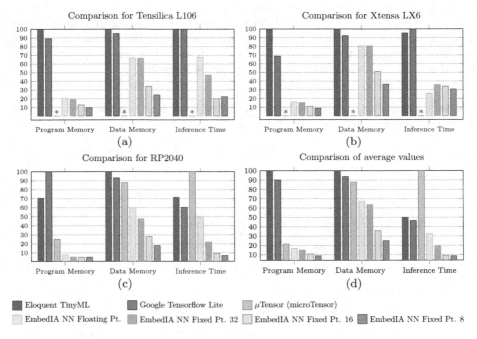

Fig. 5. Experiment 2. Comparison of memory usage and time consumption between libraries for microcontrollers. The unit is expressed as a percentage with respect to the library that had the highest value in the evaluated feature.

6   Conclusion and Future Work

This paper presented an ultralight and compact framework for convolutional neural networks, designed to run on small microcontrollers with severe hardware limitations. It consists of a library for performing inference on neural networks and a Tensorflow/Keras model conversion tool for automatic code generation for C/C++ language. It also has four implementation variants for fixed point and floating point of 8, 16 and 32 bits.

It was compared with other similar frameworks and libraries on five different microcontrollers, measuring required data and program memory size and inference time consumed. It was found that the four variants of the proposed framework clearly outperformed the μTensor, Google Tensorflow Lite and Eloquent TinyML implementations. In particular, the 16-bit fixed-point implementation achieves, on average, a 5 to 10 times improvement in inference time, about 3 times the data memory requirements and 3 to 7 times the program memory requirements.

The advantage of EmbedIA-NN lies in its combination with the model conversion tool that generates projects in C language incorporating only the strictly necessary source code, while other C++ libraries implement class-based software architectures with inheritance and polymorphism that consume a considerable amount of data memory and program memory, and slow down program execution.

EmbedIA is an open source framework available on Github[3] and is part of a new emerging project. In the future, it is planned to gradually incorporate: machine learning and neural network algorithms for really small microcontrollers; support for taking advantage of the hardware features of microcontrollers with SIMD or DSP instructions; tutorials and both practical and concrete examples of the use of the framework on different platforms, something difficult to find in other libraries.

References

1. Number of internet of things (IoT) connected devices worldwide from 2019 to 2030. https://www.statista.com/statistics/1183457/iot-connected-devices-worldwide/. Accessed 26 Aug 2021
2. Cisco annual internet report (2018–2023) white paper. https://www.cisco.com/c/en/us/solutions/collateral/executive-perspectives/annual-internet-report/white-paper-c11-741490.html. Accessed 26 Aug 2021
3. Shekhar, S., Gokhale, A.: Dynamic resource management across cloud-edge resources for performance-sensitive applications. In: 17th IEEE/ACM International Symposium on Cluster, Cloud and Grid Computing, pp. 707–710, May 2017
4. Farhan, L., Kharel, R., Kaiwartya, O., Quiroz-Castellanos, M., Alissa, A., Abdulsalam, M.: A concise review on internet of things (IoT) -problems, challenges and opportunities. In: 2018 11th International Symposium on Communication Systems, Networks Digital Signal Processing (CSNDSP), pp. 1–6, July 2018
5. Lai, L., Suda, N.: Rethinking Machine Learning Development and Deployment for Edge Devices (2018). CoRR, vol. abs/1806.07846
6. Sharma, K., Nandal, R.: A literature study on machine learning fusion with IoT. In: 2019 3rd International Conference on Trends in Electronics and Informatics (ICOEI), pp. 1440–1445, April 2019
7. David, R., et al.: TensorFlow lite micro: embedded machine learning on TinyML systems (2020). CoRR, vol. abs/2010.08678
8. Krishnamoorthi, R.: Quantizing deep convolutional networks for efficient inference: a whitepaper (2018). CoRR, vol. abs/1806.08342

---

[3] https://github.com/Embed-ML/EmbedIA.

9. Mitschke, N., Heizmann, M., Noffz, K.-H., Wittmann, R.: A fixed-point quantization technique for convolutional neural networks based on weight scaling. In: IEEE International Conference on Image Processing, pp. 3836–3840, September 2019

10. Liberis, E., Lane, N.D.: Neural networks on microcontrollers: saving memory at inference via operator reordering (2019). CoRR, vol. abs/1910.05110

11. Mocerino, L., Calimera, A.: Fast and accurate inference on microcontrollers with boosted cooperative convolutional neural networks (BC-Net). IEEE Trans. Circuits Syst. I: Reg. Papers **68**, 77–88 (2021)

12. TensorFlow Lite. https://www.tensorflow.org/lite. Accessed 26 Aug 2021

13. uTensor. https://github.com/uTensor/uTensor. Accessed 26 Aug 2021

14. Lai, L., Suda, N., Chandra, V.: CMSIS-NN: Efficient neural network kernels for arm Cortex-M CPUs (2018)

15. Dennis, D.K., et al.: EdgeML: Machine Learning for resource-constrained edge devices

16. Eloquent TinyML. https://github.com/eloquentarduino/EloquentTinyML/. Accessed 26 Aug 2021

17. Goodfellow, I.J., Bengio, Y., Courville, A.: Deep Learning. MIT Press, Cambridge (2016). http://www.deeplearningbook.org

18. LeCun, Y., Cortes, C., Burges, C.: MNIST handwritten digit database. ATT Labs, vol. 2(2010). http://yann.lecun.com/exdb/mnist

19. Alpaydin, E., Kaynak, C.: Optical Recognition of Handwritten Digits. UCI Machine Learning Repository (1998)

20. Cohen, G., Afshar, S., Tapson, J., Schaik, A.V.: EMNIST: extending MNIST to handwritten letters. In: 2017 International Joint Conference on Neural Networks (IJCNN) (2017)

21. Cun, L., et al.: Handwritten digit recognition with a back-propagation network. In: Advances in Neural Information Processing Systems, pp. 396–404. Morgan Kaufmann (1990)

Design, Implementation, and Modeling of a LoRa Network Installed in a Freshwater Body

Mateo Guerra-Londono$^{(\boxtimes)}$ ⓘ, Gustavo Urrea$^{(\boxtimes)}$ ⓘ, Juan Botero-Valencia$^{(\boxtimes)}$ ⓘ, and Erick Reyes-Vera$^{(\boxtimes)}$ ⓘ

Instituto Tecnológico Metropolitano ITM, Medellín, Colombia
{mateoguerra251449,gustavourrea314860}@correo.itm.edu.co,
{juanbotero,erickreyes}@itm.edu.co
https://www.itm.edu.co/

Abstract. Wireless communication networks with low energy consumption, a long range and with low transfer rates are used for most applications associated with the internet of things. Examples of these applications are smart cities, industrial control applications and communication of data packets in environments where commercial wireless communication networks are not available. A case of interest is the monitoring of environmental variables related with large bodies of water, as it is currently of special importance to populations both near bodies of water as well as for the public, as the stability of regional weather systems depends on those large bodies of water. However, as it is commonly found in uninhabited areas, the coverage of commercial communication networks (2G-3G-WiFi) is either limited or non-existent. Hence, chirp spread spectrum (CSS) Long range technology, known as LoRa, has become a promising and relevant alternative in recent years in these cases. LoRa allows reaching long distances with low energy consumption and it can be deployed through low-cost commercial devices. This paper presents the design and implementation of a monitoring system for environmental variables in a freshwater body through a LoRa network. A performance analysis and an estimation model of the system were performed. The system is made up of 10 nodes, 2 gateways and it uses a star connection topology. Information was acquired for 10 days. The data obtained by the sensors in the nodes were sent to the Gateways every 30 min. The RSSI value (Received Signal Strength Indicator) was stored for each node. Additionally, data of atmospheric variables in the studied area was acquired from local public databases. With the information obtained, a model was trained using Artificial Neural Networks with which it is possible to estimate the RSSI from the parameters of link distance, relative humidity, temperature, and precipitation level. The obtained results with this ANN model show that it is possible to estimate the RSSI with an error of less than 0.82 dBm. Based on this, we consider the proposed model as a useful tool for the design of wireless sensing networks or IoT applications.

Keywords: IoT · LoRa · Nodes · Gateways · Antenna · Artificial neural networks

© Springer Nature Switzerland AG 2022
F. R. Narváez et al. (Eds.): SmartTech-IC 2021, CCIS 1532, pp. 17–29, 2022.
https://doi.org/10.1007/978-3-030-99170-8_2

1   Introduction

Nowadays, wireless networks with low energy consumption, long link ranges and low bit rates are of relevance in the industrial sector, especially with the surge of the applications based on the internet of Things (IoT) [1–3]. These applications allow a direct connection with different devices for a network capable of sensing and controlling processes. Additionally, this technology has allowed for better human-machine interactions in industrial and commercial environments, optimizing processes in these contexts for cost reduction and better response times. The quality of a wireless information transfer system using IoT is evaluated throughout three fundamental criteria. First, there is how far the information can be transmitted. The second one considers a system's electric power consumption, and the third criterion is how fast the information can be transferred [11].

Different standards are currently being employed: Low Power Wide Area Networks (LPWAN), Bluetooth, Wi-Fi, 3G, 4G and LoRa (Long Range). These technologies have relative advantages and disadvantages. For the case of 3G and 4G Networks, they offer high information transmission rates even over long ranges. However, they present a continuous and considerable consumption of power, that is why communication systems based on 4G, and the even more demanding 5G, are not ideal to be used in remote field applications [2]. On the other hand, Bluetooth technology offers low energy consumption, but the link distances that can be achieved are of only a few meters. A promising and relevant alternative developed recently consists in the implementation of systems based in LoRa. This communication platform allows to reach long communication link distances with a low energy consumption. Thus, making it appealing for applications which require monitoring outdoors in or hostile environments like mountain peaks, Arctic research stations, dense forests, and large water bodies among others. Some examples of works done about monitoring in these sorts of environments can be found in [4–7] and [8]. The common factor in those applications is that they cannot rely on a power grid and thus they used solar panels or others alternative sources to power the devices. Furthermore, these applications require long distance communications. Communication systems based in LoRa are one of the best choices to monitor those environments, with a comprehensive list of the advantages would be as follows:

- Long distance connectivity.
- Secure connectivity through encryption.
- Data packets bidirectional sending.
- Ultraminimal electric consumption.
- Works in the ISM band (Industrial, Scientific, and Medical)
- High sensitivity to receive data packets

Due to the distinct advantages offered by this technology for Wireless Sensor Networks (WSN), various works studying the application of this technology have taken place. For example, in [9] an experiment was developed to observe the reliability of the received signal (using the Received Signal Strength Indicator

- RSSI parameter), the number of packets lost and an analysis of the Signal to Noise Ratio - SNR between the transmitter and receiver. The results shows that the implementation of an appropriate Spreading Factor (SF) in a LoRa device greatly improves its performance through different routes and facing signal fading.

The effects of the temperature and moisture in the radio signal intensity outdoors have consequences on data transfer as it is shown in [10]. The authors configured the physical layer (PHY) modifying parameters like bandwidth, SF, codification speed, transmission power and carrier frequency. These changes were made to evaluate the performance of this technology experimentally. They suggest faster rate configurations and the use of a signal relay instead of using slower configurations to increase signal stability. The work concludes thus that the use faster data rates and a low energy consumption relay, maximizes both packet reception rate and link quality.

This work is focused on the evaluation of performance and a neural model for the estimation of performance of LoRa networks implemented in a monitoring system for freshwater body variables. For 10 days, information like the RSSI value was sent each 30 min by the sensor nodes toward the Gateways and it was registered and stored. In parallel, data on atmospheric variables of the local area where the sensors were deployed was acquired from public databases. As a result, a training model using artificial neural networks was developed. It allows to estimate the RSSI value from the values of link distance, relative moisture, ambient temperature, and precipitation level.

This paper is organized as follows: after this introduction we have the section on methodology, it explains the implementation of the monitoring system for environmental variables of a freshwater body. The materials used, network architecture and the calculations made to get optimal radio links are described as well. We follow with the results and discussion, ending with a section on conclusions.

2   Methodology

The proposed monitoring system was employed to determine the contamination levels of a freshwater body, extracted from the measurement of different physical and chemical parameters. Thus, several sensors are used to measure turbidity, conductivity, RDO, salinity, pH/ORP, temperature and the content of chlorophyl, chloride and nitrate. The sensors were connected in twelve modules to monitor different freshwater body parameters. Eight of these modules had 4 sensors connected to each module to measure: turbidity, RDO, conductivity and pH/ORP. The remaining four modules, have 4 additional sensors which measure: chloride, nitrate, temperature and chlorophyl contents on water. Strategic points were defined to place the modules both inside and on the shore of the freshwater body at different water slopes. In total, the freshwater body was continuously monitored on 6 points inside and 6 points outside of it.

The network consists of 10 nodes and 2 gateways, which all use a Lopy4 microcontroller. This microcontroller is LoRa compatible, and it can be configured to work as a gateway. In the set of 6 modules inside the water body, we had two modules configured as gateways. The other four were network nodes. To sample water with the other 6 modules outside of the water body, a cement base was made, where a 50 mm × 50 mm square steel pipe of 2 m in length could be buried until it hit water, then the sensor would be placed into the pipe. All 6 points required burying around 50 cm of the pipe to install the modules.

2.1 Component Description

Modules: A module consists of an antenna, a battery and other 4 printed circuit boards (PCBs): a DFRobot brand Solar Power Manager, a DFRobot Multiplexer, a Gravity PCB and a Pycom. Those PCBs allow for stable powering of the module. They control the battery charge cycles and allow individual configuration of the module functions. The 12 modules used have the same base hardware, they only differ in network configuration and the case of those with extra sensor heads.

Nodes: There are 10 nodes in total, 6 outside and the rest inside the water body. All monitor the water quality of the freshwater body independently every 30 min and they store the RSSI value as well. Each node has a set of sensors, 6 of them have 4 sensors and the remaining have the same set plus an extra 4 sensors for a total of 8. There are 2 of the nodes with 8 sensors inside the freshwater body and the other 2 are located outside.

Gateways: Modules defined as a gateway are installed inside of the freshwater body because it is the central place for the information reception from their nodes and the transmission of it to their server. Each gateway has a router. The routers used were both a TP-Link-WR840N.

Power: Modules located in the platforms of the freshwater body are powered constantly. These platforms were there in fact before starting the present work. They give 110 VAC through a solar energy module that each platform has and thus, all devices installed in the platforms are switched on permanently. The modules located around the freshwater body work with solar energy as well but operated at 22 VDC. The panels used are Hersic brand, model JC-H08101-50W18MD.

2.2 Architecture

The Wireless Sensor Network (WSN) used in this work had a star topology with each node connected directly to one of the gateways.

Figure 1 shows a schematic of the implementation of this work. The first and third stages consist of the characterization of the antennas and the implementation of an ANN called multilayer perceptron respectively. The antennas used in this work are characterized to ensure their performance within the operating band of the proposed wireless network and the multilayer perceptron is used to estimate the RSSI from link distance, relative humidity, temperature, and precipitation level parameters.

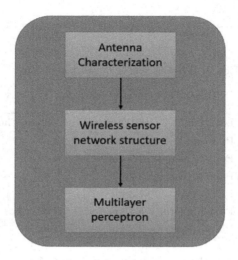

Fig. 1. Schematic of the implementation.

In the second stage of implementation is the wireless sensor network structure proposed in this work. The network schematic is observed in more detail in Fig. 2. The left side of the figure shows the connection of the end devices or nodes that send and receive information to the Gateway, which are responsible for receiving and sending information to the nodes, while the right side of the figure shows the interconnection with a client which receives all the information that the wireless network devices transmit.

Table 2 shows the location (on a platform or at the shore), the relative distance and the antenna height of each node connected to gateway 2. The other 5 nodes are connected to gateway 1 and their distance to it can be seen in Table 1. From the Tables, it can be appreciated that it was possible to link the devices over a large distance, in this case the longest link distance was of 5.4 km.

2.3 Fresnel Zones

At the beginning, the transmitted signals presented a lot of noise and significant data loss due to the lack of line of sight, which caused link problems. The vegetation and/or flora surrounding the freshwater body under study, such as: reeds, moss, ferns, among other aquatic plants, considerably reduce the received signal strength, thus increasing data loss in the communication range. When these inconveniences in the radio link were identified, a Fresnel zone analysis were made. For this analysis the Eq. 1 was used:

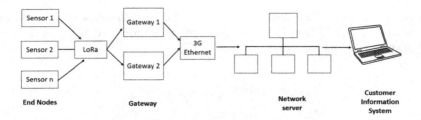

Fig. 2. Wireless sensor network structure.

Table 1. Nodes addressed to GW1

Node	Location	GW1 distance	Antenna height
GW1	Platform 2	0	3 m
1	Point 2 (shore)	3.5 km	3 m
4	Point 5 (shore)	2 km	3 m
7	Platform 4	2.3 km	3 m
9	Pint 6 (shore)	5.4 km	3 m
10	Platform 3	2.7 km	3 m

Table 2. Nodes addressed to GW2

Node	Location	GW2 distance	Antenna height
GW2	Platform 5	0	3 m
2	Point 1 (shore)	1.5 km	1.5 m
3	Platform 6	1.9 km	3 m
5	Point 4 (shore)	1.5 km	1.5 m
6	Platform 1	3.2 km	3 m
8	Point 3 (shore)	3.8 km	1.5 m

$$r = 17.32\sqrt{\frac{D}{4 \times f}} \tag{1}$$

Where r is the radius of the first Fresnel zone, 17.32 and 4 are constants, D is the distance in kilometers between antennas and, f is the transmission frequency in GHz (in this case it is 922 MHz).

The respective radius of the first Fresnel zone between each gateway and their nodes are shown in the Tables 3 and 4.

Calculations were then made to place the antennas at a better height: The 60% of the Fresnel radius is calculated because it shows the maximum recommended value where an obstacle should be. The plane connecting a module and the Fresnel radius of its gateway should not have any obstacles either above or below it. However, there were obstacles present when placing this plane at 1 m

Table 3. Analysis of the first Fresnel zone for Gateway 1 and its respective nodes

GW1 distance	Fresnel radius	60%
3.5 km	16.9 m	10.1 m
2 km	12.8 m	7.7 m
2.3 km	13.7 m	8.2 m
5.4 km	21 m	12.6 m
2.7 km	14.8 m	8.9 m

Table 4. Analysis of the first Fresnel zone for Gateway 2 and its respective nodes

GW2 distance	Fresnel radius	60%
1.5 km	11 m	6.6 m
1.9 km	12.4 m	7.5 m
1.5 km	11 m	6.6 m
3.2 km	16.1 m	9.6 m
3.8 km	17.6 m	10.5 m

above the ground level. So, the antennas should be installed at least at 6 m over the ground.

The initial height of the antennas was of 1.5 m above the ground level. Despite the results of our calculations, there were not enough resources to reinstall the antennas at height higher than 3 m from the ground. However, with LoRa was possible a good communication among gateways and nodes at 3 m above the ground level because this communication protocol offers high data transmission rates and good enough reception sensitivity due to the low weight of the packets transmitted.

As it was possible to observe in Tables 1 and 2, some antennas were placed at a height of 1.5 m from the ground. This was made by this way due to the inconsistent height of the ground around the freshwater body with respect to the water level. It was possible to get a good line of view for each of those sensors with respect to the ones placed at 3 m.

2.4   Antenna Characterization

The used antennas in the nodes and gateways were characterized to guarantee their performance within the band of operation (922 MHz) of the proposed wireless sensor network. Thus, a FSH8 vector network analyzer (VNA, Rhode & Schwartz, Germany) is used to validate the performance of the twelve antennas (ten antennas for nodes and two Gateway antennas). The characterization of these antennas was carried out from 100 kHz to 2000 MHz, while the antenna is connected to the VNA using a coaxial cable with a characteristic impedance of 50 Ω. To avoid reflections and environmental noise, the antenna was isolated using acoustic foam. Likewise, the antenna was mounted in a plastic base to eliminate reflections on the ground.

2.5 Multilayer Perceptron

A multilayer perceptron (MLP) is an artificial neural network (ANN), which is inspired by the biological nervous system. The MLP is composed of an input layer, one or more hidden layers, and an output layer. The neurons (or nodes) of each layer are connected with the neurons of the adjacent layer, so that the information can only be transmitted in one direction (forward), and it attempts to imitate the synapses in a biological brain. Usually, a MLP network is trained by a back-propagation algorithm, and commonly the number of neurons per layer and the number of hidden layers are found by trial and error. The system inputs for our application are the link distance, Fresnel height ratio and the temperature. Between the input and output layers, we change the amount and number of neurons in the hidden layers. In this experiment, the number of hidden layers were set between 2 and 4 while the number of neurons in each layer was varied between 2 and 8, in increments of 2 neurons. The expected output of the neural network is the link's RSSI.

3 Results and Discussion

First the characterization of the used antennas is carried out using the methodology described in Sect. 2.4. Figure 3 shows the obtained S11 magnitude for three node antenna and one gateway antenna (the results are limited to these four devices to improve visualization). The results show that the antenna connected to node 1 has a central frequency of 911.03 MHz, and a bandwidth of 165.96 MHz. In fact, the return losses of this antenna reached -56.84 dB at the central frequency. In addition, the impedance of the antenna was also measured using the VNA. The results reveal that this antenna has an impedance of $47.1 - j1.42 \ \Omega$. On the other hand, the Gateway antenna was characterized using the same experimental setup. In this case, the antenna has three resonant peaks at 474.89 MHz, 909.13 MHz, and 1374.36 MHz with bandwidths of 81.99 MHz, 130.31 MHz, and 170.96 MHz respectively. The antenna was configured to operate at 909.13 for our application. The same protocol was used to characterize the other antennas. Table 5 summarized the main electrical parameters for all used antennas. Therefore, these results corroborate a correct operation of all antennas used at 922 MHz as well as their individual performance. On the other hand, the results reveal that these antennas have a good impedance match with the used microcontrollers, and it allows for maximal power transmission in the wireless sensor network.

After that, the free-space path loss model (FSPL), is used to estimate the ideal propagation characteristics in the absence of obstructions and considering air as the medium. Reflections, refraction, or other common radio propagation phenomena are not considered either. Subsequently, to calculate the Link budget, it is only necessary to know the transmission power, and the power efficiency of the respective antennas. For the case presented in this work a frequency of 922 MHz was used and the RSSI was taken as a function of the distance both without taking into account the gain, that is, with a transmission power of zero and no gain for the antennas, and in the case of a practical development with a transmission power of 20 dB, and a gain of 3 dB for each antenna.

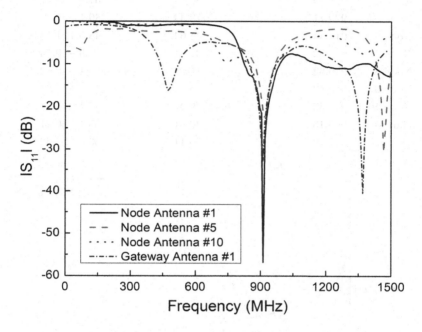

Fig. 3. Measured S11 parameter of used antennas.

The graph of each case can be seen in Fig. 4 as "Gain" with the blue colored curve and "No gain" with the red colored curve, respectively. Additionally, Fig. 4 presents the measured RSSI for each of the nodes. As mentioned above, data was taken every 30 min for 10 days, for a total of 480 RSSI and temperature data points for each node, each cluster of either asterisks or hollow squares in Fig. 4 corresponds to RSSI data taken at a given link distance. The asterisks correspond to the nodes of Gateway 1 and the hollow squares represent the nodes connected to Gateway 2. As it can be seen, there is a variability of around 5 dB for the RSSI in all cases, and all values are well below the theoretical line corresponding to the performance expected for the practical implementation. This can be explained with the fact that the required Fresnel zone height was not reached by any of the devices, paired with losses in the RF cables and coupling loses among others.

As a sample of the data, Fig. 5 shows the histogram for RSSI on node 4 of gateway 1 (G1-N4), and node 1 of gateway 2 (G2-N1). They are compared to see the dispersion of the data, the similarity of both distributions with a

Table 5. Summarized electrical parameters of the used antennas the proposed WSN.

Antenna	Center frequency (MHz)	Bandwidth (MHz)	Impedance (Ω)
Node 1	911.03	165.96	$47.1 - j1.42$
Node 2	918.97	99.644	$51.8 - j0.89$
Node 3	911.79	145.64	$48.5 - j1.13$
Node 4	918.79	135.64	$51.1 + j1.12$
Node 5	920.11	112.44	$49.1 - j1.12$
Node 6	915.44	144.64	$48.5 + j1.13$
Node 7	911.52	132.61	$51.9 - j0.76$
Node 8	919.32	115.54	$50.1 - j0.82$
Node 9	910.42	165.13	$49.1 + j1.32$
Node 10	916.33	149.42	$47.1 - j1.21$
Gateway 1	909.13	130.31	$55.1 - j0.21$
Gateway 2	911.79	155.11	$53.8 - j0.32$

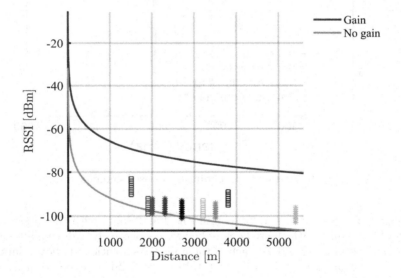

Fig. 4. Theoretical and measured RSSI (Color figure online)

normal PDF. The difference in the central value arises from the difference in link distance. G1-N4 has a link distance of 5.4 km, while G2-N1 has a link distance of 1.5 km.

To develop the RSSI estimation model, a MLP was trained in different configurations. In Table 6, the mean absolute error is shown. The network inputs are temperature, link distance and the well known as Fresnel index. Since the SF was constant, it is not part of the analysis presented in this paper. We calculate

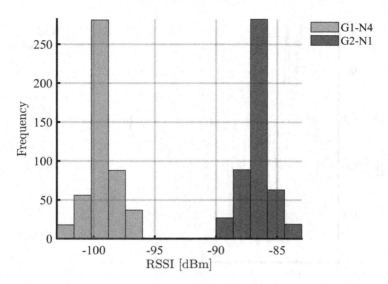

Fig. 5. Histogram RSSI

the Fresnel index by dividing the required height for each node (See the values in the Tables 3 and 4) over the actual height at which each antenna was installed. The training error reported in Table 6 is absolute, the RSSI estimate is in dBm, the rows L1, L2, L3 refer to the number of hidden layers, and the columns H2, H4, H6 and H8 give the number of neurons per hidden layer in each case. It can be seen that there is faster improvement increasing the number of neurons per layer than by increasing the number of layers.

Table 6. Absolute error

	H2	H4	H6	H8	H10
L1	1.25	1.15	0.94	0.85	0.85
L2	1.24	1.16	0.92	0.84	0.84
L3	1.26	1.14	0.91	0.85	0.82

The error in Table 6, shows that an estimate of the RSSI can be reached with an error of less than 0.82 dBm, taking the ambient temperature, the distance of the link and the Fresnel index as inputs. Finally, the estimates on a portion of the training data are presented to show the scale of the approximation's certainty in Fig. 6.

Finally, in this work it was demonstrated that it is important to characterize the antennas that are used to communicate sensors that make up the wireless sensing network to minimize losses in the transmission of information. Thus, the

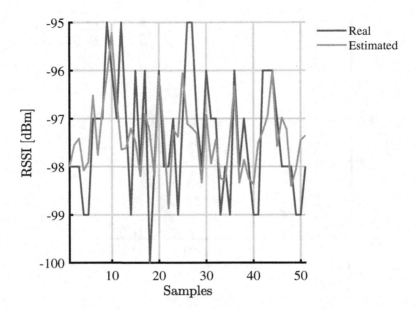

Fig. 6. Estimation error

importance of the antenna resonating at the operating frequency of the radio link and the impedance of all the elements being the same to avoid losses due to coupling was shown. On the other hand, the model presented in this work constitutes a tool that will allow the optimization of the implementation of wireless sensing networks since the errors in the RSSI are minimized. Likewise, it was demonstrated how this parameter depends on link distance, the height of the antennas and the environmental temperature.

4   Conclusions

The purpose of this work was to demonstrate that with experimental data, a simple estimation model can be adjusted to estimate important link parameters such as RSSI. As it could be seen, the difference between the theoretical model's prediction and data from the real implementation is significant, the model would have to compensate for the losses of each of the elements and other radio propagation phenomena that may occur. However, with the proposed ANN method, real link parameters can be estimated from few points of data with an error below 1 dB. Thus, showing promise for its use as a calculation tool while implementing Wireless Sensor Networks. Likewise, several common error factors were controlled as the matched between the used antennas and the microcontroller, which is very important to guarantee the quality of the obtained results.

References

1. Botero, J., Castaño, L., Márquez, D.: Trends in the Internet of Things. TecnoLógicas **22**(44), I–II (2019)
2. Reyes, E., Senior, D., Luna, J., López, F.: Advances in electromagnetic applications and communications. TecnoLógicas **21**(43), 9–13 (2018)
3. Liu, D., Hong, W., Rappaport, T.S., Luxey, C.: What will 5G antennas and propagation be? IEEE Trans. Antennas Propag. **65**(12), 6205–6212 (2017)
4. Iova, O., et al.: LoRa from the city to the mountains: exploration of hardware and environmental factors. In: Proceedings of the 2017 International Conference on Embedded Wireless Systems and Networks (2017)
5. Gaelens, J., Van, P., Verhaevert, J., Hendrik, R.: LoRa mobile-to-base-station channel characterization in the Antarctic. Sensors **17**(8), 1903 (2017)
6. Boano, C., Tsiftes, N., Voigt, T., Brown, J., Roedig, U.: The impact of temperature on outdoor industrial sensornet applications. IEEE Trans. Ind. Inform. **6**(3), 451–459 (2010)
7. Clarkson, L., Williams, D., Seppälä, J.: Real-time monitoring of tailings dams. Georisk Assess. Manag. Risk Eng. Syst. Geohazards **15**(2), 113–127 (2021)
8. Manoharan, A., Rathinasabapathy, V.: Smart water quality monitoring and metering using LoRa for smart villages. In: 2018 2nd International Conference on Smart Grid and Smart Cities (ICSGSC), pp. 57–61 (2018)
9. Rahman, A., Zaman, F., Che, A., Syahrul, A.: Performance analysis of LPWAN using LoRa technology for IoT application. Int. J. Eng. Technol. **7**(4), 212–216 (2018)
10. Marco, C., Boano, C., Römer, K.: Evaluation of the reliability of LoRa long-range low-power wireless communication. J. Sens. Actuator Netw. **6**(2), 7 (2017)
11. Botero, J., Castano, L., Marquez, D., Rico, M.: Data reduction in a low-cost environmental monitoring system based on LoRa for WSN. IEEE Internet Things J. **6**(2), 3024–3030 (2019)

Mobile Application of Registry Information for Urban Planning Context with Augmented Reality and QR Codes

María Mora-Alvarado[1,2](✉) ![ID] and Joe Llerena-Izquierdo[1,2] ![ID]

[1] Universidad Politécnica Salesiana, Guayaquil, Ecuador
mmoraa3@est.ups.edu.ec, jllerena@ups.edu.ec
[2] GIEACI Research Group and GieTICEA Educational Innovation Group, Guayaquil, Ecuador
https://gieaci.blog.ups.edu.ec/

Abstract. Augmented reality technologies present a different experience from the real thing. Using new technologies for management activities in urban environments represents a change of bet on the digital development of a city. This work presents a prototype of a mobile application for obtaining housing registry information through augmented reality and QR codes. The objective of the study is to develop a tool for the generation of authorized public information on housing in the city of Guayaquil, Ecuador, in an interactive way using a combination of new technologies as a management strategy in the context of urban planning. The research methodology is a quantitative, quasi-experimental approach. It uses the survey technique to determine the perception of the use of the mobile application and the levels of satisfaction of 400 inhabitants of the urban sector of the city of Guayaquil. With a confidence percentage of 95% and a margin of error of 4.905%, the study reveals an 88% interest in the use of the application by the participants and an 84% ease of use of the BuildingQR mobile application in its first version. The data and results are available at https://github.com/mmoraa25/Buildi ng_QR. The level of satisfaction with the proposal exceeds 90% in the medium. It is concluded that new technologies allow new experiences that complement the development of smart cities by breaking the barriers of digitization. The scope of applicability of this research work to territories or pre-divisions in rural sectors is foreseen for future works.

Keywords: Augmented reality · Mobile apps · QR code · Urban planning · Smart city

1 Introduction

Involving new technologies that allow experiences in issues concerning the development of smart cities, urban planning, architecture, cadastral management, among others, are the premises that researchers have to venture into these fields with highly innovative proposals [1, 2]. Virtual reality, augmented reality (AR), immersive reality, as well as mixed reality offer features to see reality in a different way in hybrid virtual spaces [3, 4].

© Springer Nature Switzerland AG 2022
F. R. Narváez et al. (Eds.): SmartTech-IC 2021, CCIS 1532, pp. 30–43, 2022.
https://doi.org/10.1007/978-3-030-99170-8_3

The use of mobile applications integrating new technologies such as augmented reality has crossed interdisciplinary barriers and different sectors in the educational sector [5, 6], in the sector of tourism [7, 8], in the architectural [9, 10], in health [11], and others.

The use of augmented reality in specific public information management institutions, such as municipal or metropolitan housing registries, contributes to the satisfaction of user needs when the experience of observing a virtual design and interaction are intertwined [12]. Adding other technologies, specifically the use of Quick Response (QR) codes for the identification and presentation of housing registry information results in a product that allows easier access to information [13, 14]. The importance of the use of the QR code allows the storage and management of substantial information for a specific purpose, its ability to be recognized by a reading device, its ability to regenerate and error correction are characteristics for a restoration of information data from an image [15].

The provision of public services such as the identification and presentation of housing registry information in the public administration using new technologies is an important challenge due to the opportunity to offer new solutions to citizens through services that facilitate the verification and authentication of data, its corresponding access, and the proper security of the information. Urban planning within municipal management programs would provide more focused services with standardized procedures.

The increased use of augmented reality platforms has improved experiences in terms of information management, especially in housing registry information, it should be noted that the security of visible information provided by the regulatory bodies keeps the due legal treatments for its visualization and is protected by access protocols. This area is new, and augmented reality applications have been developed for different sciences [16, 17] and the public business sector [18, 19], however, no augmented reality applications applied to the management of housing registry information have been found in Ecuador [20, 21].

It is important to use augmented reality, specifically QR codes, in housing registry information, to be able to assign property codes and license plates when carrying out censuses.

1.1 The Impact of the Use of Augmented Reality and QR Code Technologies in the Context of Urban Planning

From the point of view of technology and the concept of Augmented Reality (AR), the Quick Response (QR) codes for the identification and presentation of housing registry information based on Augmented Reality, has as a starting point the compatibility of new media (technological, physical and theoretical tools) but most importantly the interaction of these media with the users and the proper security of the information generated by these applications nowadays, as well as to assimilate the results in an accurate way. In this study, we wish to demonstrate that this technology is perfectly applicable to the housing registry information in Ecuador allowed for its visualization [22, 23].

The increased use of real estate platforms for housing, in order to link information from the Property Registry (regulatory body in the city of Guayaquil) so that the common citizen can consult the status of the property, by real estate registration or code, and represent it in a 3D model to reflect the information relating to a property, all with scanning a QR code through a mobile application, allows to improve communication between the different parties involved [24] and thus speed up the departmental processes related to the cadastres [25, 26].

Relevant work using augmented reality applications provides support to land surveyors to visualize cadastral parcels, replacing 2D maps annotated on paper when they perform field work [27]. The impact of the use of augmented reality technologies varies according to the characteristics of the applications developed and the levels of access to information (used by the regulatory body or by the common citizen), since it can range from the visualization of 3D housing models to georeferenced maps of properties, parcels and cadastres in general, in which users, cartographers, surveyors and other interested personnel, can obtain a better visual experience and help in the planning and data collection process, as long as the application allows the direct modification of the data associated with such housing.

1.2 Augmented Reality Techniques Applied to Urban Management

The key elements to make augmented reality possible are a camera, a reference marker, a monitor [29], access to a database, internet connection, hardware and augmented reality software [30].

Monitors can be of different types, there are head-mounted monitors, hand-held monitors and space monitors [31]. Head-mounted monitors are installed on the head and provide a lens at the user's eye level and use sensors that track the monitor [32]. Handheld monitors are smaller devices such as smartphones that fit in a user's hand and use the phone's camera, can use digital compasses or GPS (Global Positioning System) to add markers to the video, and nowadays it is possible to add digital information to video sequences in real time. Space monitors are made possible by digital projectors that allow the display of graphical information on physical objects to a group of users without requiring a head or handheld monitor for each user, allowing the viewing area to be enlarged, which gives it an advantage over other monitors [30]. Monitors can be combined with augmented reality hardware that allows users to have more immersive experiences.

There are three augmented reality techniques that can be applied to urban planning and management [33]. One of the most used is using position or reference markers such as QR codes that are captured by the camera of a mobile device or a computer and interpreted by an augmented reality software that activates the 3D models previously configured. Other types of reference markers like QR are Data Matrix and Maxicode that use complex and moderately complex patterns. Also, others consisting of simpler geometric shapes such as ARTag, ARToolkit, ARSTudio and Intersense, ideal for pose recognition and distance/size ratio measurement. The following technique does not use reference markers and combines technologies such as SLAM (Simultaneous Localization and Mapping) to create 3D models of real locations. It projects the 3D content and keeps it in one point without requiring prior activation [34]. The third technique is geolocation, which combines technologies such as GPS to display contextual information about specific geographic points in the outdoor environment [35].

2   Materials and Methods

The research methodology is a quantitative, quasi-experimental approach. The survey technique is used to determine the levels of interest and ease of use of the application, as well as the appreciation of the participants. From a total population of 2'698,077 inhabitants in the city of Guayaquil, 400 people were randomly selected from the urban sector of the city. With a confidence percentage of 95% and a margin of error of 4.905%.

The objective of this study is to develop a mobile application for the presentation of housing registry information through augmented reality and QR code as an informative and interactive tool in the context of urban planning that can be used by land, cadastre and land registry personnel of the Guayaquil canton, Guayas province, as well as homeowners in the urban sector.

Android Studio technology is used for QR code recognition, and Unity and Vuforia packages are used for 3D information visualization.

To acquire a more precise understanding and a complete approach to the subject, the following research questions are raised:

Table 1. Research questions

Questions	Thematic
Question 1 (Q1): -¿What are the necessary elements to develop a mobile application with augmented reality and QR code?	Development platforms, augmented reality technology, program features, user interface [36]
Question 2 (Q2) -¿What factors should be considered for the presentation of housing information?	Analysis of social, cultural and economic factors [37]
Question 3 (Q3) - ¿What development tool will be used to build the mobile application?	Augmented reality development tools according to compatibility with other platforms and their performance [44]
Question 4 (Q4) -What experience in terms of usability and satisfaction does this mobile application provide to users?	Ease of use, even if users do not have the necessary 3D modeling experience [38]. That the application meets the proposed objectives [39]

The following research questions (see Table 1) are related to the elements, factors, development tools and user experience after using the QR code augmented reality application.

In order to determine the necessary elements and factors to be considered for the development of the mobile application, a bibliographic review was carried out as part of the documentary research, using guidelines consisting of the phases of planning, conducting and reporting [40], applied as follows:

– **Planning the review:** In this phase, the need for the research is identified, the research questions are posed and the protocol to be followed with respect to the databases to be consulted, the years and the language to be consulted is drawn up.

- **Conducting the review:** In this phase, all the information obtained on the topic of interest is synthesized.
- **Revision report:** In this phase, the bibliographic review is carried out according to the interests of the study, using the search criteria "application" or "mobile" or "web" and "augmented reality" and "QR code".

The search for factors that should be considered for the representation of housing information in 3D models yields social, cultural, and economic factors. The social factors refer to the communication with the community in the implementation of the new process [37]. Cultural factors take into account the technological level of the users of the application and their ability to make use of it after training [41]. Economic factors correspond to the economic capacity of the state to finance an urban planning project using augmented reality and QR codes [42]. The agile methodology is used for the development of the mobile application [43] under which the following steps were followed:

- **Evaluation of processes and company structure:** Three departments are identified that are directly affected with the implementation of the application, the departments: Land, Cadastre and Registry. The first two departments are responsible for conducting population censuses and collecting information on site. However, when it comes to collecting information on lots, they must do it manually, opening the possibility of errors in the subsequent registration of such lots, for example, when they are registered as available lots when in fact, they do have owners, which causes conflicts with the Land Registry department; or when two cadastral codes are assigned for a single property.
- **Suggestions for process improvement and optimization:** It is determined that the implementation of the mobile application will save time for the collaborators of the three departments, since the information gathering process could be done in a faster way, by visualizing the exact information of the properties. In addition, errors and conflicts between the departments that handle this type of information are avoided.
- **Design of the application in conjunction with the client:** Users of the mobile application are constantly involved, according to their information needs and to the errors that generally occur due to the manual data collection they currently perform.
- **Construction and implementation of the application:** For the development of the mobile application, the Android Studio IDE is used, which is based on Java and provides features for the use of QR codes. Meanwhile, Unity and Vuforia were used as tools that provide features for the development of augmented reality environments, as well as a database. The process for the creation of the QR code starts with the digitalization of the image of each house to which an identifying label is assigned: house_code_1 or house_code_2. Once each image is generated, it is saved in Vuforia's database and when the QR code is read from the cell phone, it searches for the 3D model and matches it with the corresponding label. The information presented in the application includes the following fields: owner, location of the property, parish, property code, real estate registration number, registry record.
- **Evaluation and monitoring:** In this phase, the user experience of using the augmented reality software is evaluated. For this purpose, a survey is used as an instrument with questions related to the use and efficiency of the application.

As part of the materials used for the development of the mobile application, authorized official documents from the Property Registry of Guayaquil Canton, Guayas Province were used. These documents contain the process diagrams of the Land, Cadastre and Registry departments.

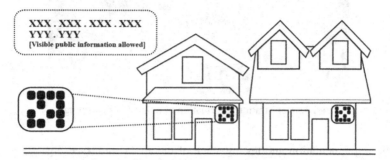

Fig. 1. Proposed cadastral information of urban dwellings using QR code

In accordance with the phases described above, and following in detail the prototype proposal, the most appropriate criteria for the development of the methodology in the description of the design of a mobile application with augmented reality, as an interactive and empowering tool for obtaining information on housing, are specifically specified. The representation of the QR code in the homes is captured by the application (see Fig. 1), where each property has a unique QR code assigned to a part of the property that is easily accessible to the cadastre staff, so that they can scan the QR code from their cell phones, using an application that activates them and shows them a 3D model of the property with all the information they need to know.

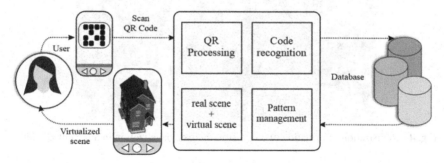

Fig. 2. Application architecture

In the architecture of the developed application (see Fig. 2) the user interacts with the application through a mobile device.

Within the application, the QR code is processed once the QR code is captured, the application recognizes the code from among those stored in the database, then interprets the pattern and displays the scene associated with that pattern on the screen.

Fig. 3. Registration information of a first-floor dwelling

In the implementation and testing stage of the application (see Fig. 3), the representation of a house can be seen when scanning the QR code corresponding to that property. The information shown on the side of the 3D model shows the owner's name, location, parish, property code, real estate registration number and latitude and longitude coordinates.

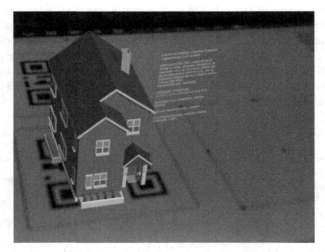

Fig. 4. Registration information of a two-story house, visualization in augmented reality

In a test carried out by the staff of the Cadastre Department (see Fig. 4), The figure shows a 3D representation of a two-story house in the property registry of Guayaquil, and on the right side the information about the property registration. The mobile device can be rotated to obtain different viewing angles of the house.

3   Results

The incorporation of informative components, specifically regarding the identification of the property or cadastre, and the need for the presentation of official information authorized by the regulatory body for display on the mobile device, has allowed a first prototype called "Building QR". The application is for mobile devices with Android systems and can be downloaded from the App Store.

The following are the results of the survey of 400 inhabitants of the city of Guayaquil who participated to obtain information to guide future improvements to the prototype.

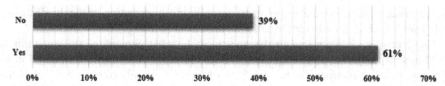

Fig. 5. Percentage of participants who have had some experience with mobile applications with augmented reality

The survey results show that 61% of respondents have had some experience using augmented reality applications, while 39% indicated that they have had no experience at all (see Fig. 5).

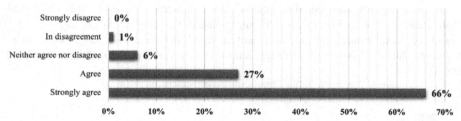

Fig. 6. Percentage of participants indicating agreement or disagreement on how augmented reality can collaborate in the management of the digitization of cadastral information of dwellings

It also shows (see Fig. 6), the percentage of respondents who agree that technologies such as augmented reality can help in the management of the digitization of cadastral information of dwellings, 66% of respondents indicated that they were "strongly agree", 27% of indicating to be "agree", 6% to indicate "neither agree nor disagree" and 1% of being "in disagreement". This shows a total acceptance rate of 93% of the population.

The participants were asked about the visual information content observed in the application, specifically, do you think this information is important for urban information management? 58% of the participants thought it was important for the management of urban information, 58% of the participants thought it was "very important", 32% thought it was "important", 8% thought it was "something important", 1% thought it was "less important" and 1% thought it was "nothing important". This shows the level

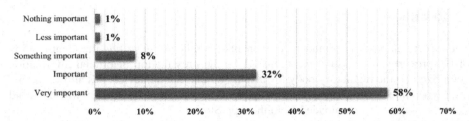

Fig. 7. Percentage of importance for the respondents of the information presented in the Building QR mobile application

of importance that the population gives to the cadastral information of the dwellings. A total of 90% believe that this information is important (see Fig. 7).

These results go according to the questions: In what percentage do you think it would benefit homeowners to have their information (only the allowed) updated in an augmented reality platform, obtaining 57% of being "strongly agree", 33% of being "agree", 9% of being "neither agree nor disagree", and 1% of being "disagree".

In addition, they were asked: If you were the owner of a house or building as shown in the examples presented in the following table, what would you do if you owned a house or building as shown in the following examples (see Fig. 3 y 4), Do you feel satisfied with the Building QR proposal after using the augmented reality application? 54% were "totally satisfied", 36% were "satisfied", 9% were "somewhat satisfied" and "1%" were "dissatisfied", reaching more than 90% of user satisfaction with the proposal presented in this work.

The participants were asked if they would recommend the use of the Building QR application for the management of urban cadastral information, obtaining that 95% would say "yes, I would recommend it" and 5% responded that "I would not recommend it", which shows the percentage of satisfaction with the prototype in its first version (see Fig. 8).

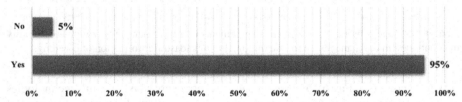

Fig. 8. Percentage of participants who would recommend the Building QR application for the management of urban cadastral information

Participants were asked about how they would identify the application according to the characteristics of: Cadastral information, Organization of the information, Visualization of the augmented images and Description of the objects found, according to the criteria of "Appropriate", "Complete", "Useful", "Accurate" and "Relevant" to determine the conformity of the proposal and the coherence with the objective sought by this research work, obtaining the results in Table 2. Being of "Appropriate" the most generalized criterion for the common citizen in the urban area that defines the Building QR application in its first version (see Table 2).

We asked: In what percentage do you think that the Building QR mobile application would benefit the urban cadastral management entities to have a representation of the information with augmented reality?, 61% believe that it would benefit them 100%, 32% believe it would benefit them 32% and 7% believe it would benefit them 50%, which means that 100% of respondents see a benefit for cadastral management entities to have the information represented with augmented reality technologies.

Table 2. Percentage of perception of the application according to the application's features

Characteristic	Appropriate	Complete	Useful	Accurate	Relevant	Total
Cadastral information	40%	30%	13%	10%	7%	100%
Organization of information	36%	35%	13%	10%	6%	100%
Visualization of augmented images	42%	30%	14%	9%	5%	100%
Description of the objects found	39%	31%	15%	9%	6%	100%

In addition, the question was asked: "How would you describe the Building QR mobile application? obtaining 49% as: "An innovative mobile application in our environment", 19.3% as: "A mobile application that opens the possibility of information management models", 13.5% as: "A mobile application that can contribute to information management", 13% as: "An informative mobile application", 4% as "A mobile application of high technological development" and 1% as: "A quality mobile application for virtual content", with this it is evident the importance of this application in an innovative information management model in our environment.

Finally, the results of the study reveal an 88% interest in the use of the application by the participants and an 84% ease of use of the Building QR mobile application in its first version.

4   Discussion

Augmented reality and QR codes are part of the current trends in the use of technologies that allow support in the field of architecture to represent 3D models of real estate for commercial purposes. In this article, an augmented reality and QR codes application was developed that can be used by personnel working in public and private institutions dedicated to the administration of urban properties and real estate cadastres in the Ecuadorian and international context, visualizing the information allowed and under the security standards provided by the applications and their technologies. The mobile application combines the representation of the houses in 3D models with information about the owner, property registration and geographic location of the houses, which can help to improve the processes related to the collection of information, census, and data updates of urban properties, carried out by the cadastral staff when they are doing field work. It is discussed that in the environment where this research work is carried out, the use of devices with Android technology are more common with medium and high performance.

The literature review found that internationally there have been few augmented reality applications in the context of urban planning for the improvement of departmental processes of cadastre in public institutions that administer it, while locally there is no evidence or evidence of development of applications for institutions such as the land registry of the different cantons belonging to Ecuador, so the development of the Building QR application is a precedent of the technological scope that allows augmented reality and the use of reference markers such as QR codes. In addition, the scope of this application could be extended to the real estate sector as an opportunity for the purchase, sale and rental of housing providing necessary information to interested parties, saving resources and time, as well as other areas that boost the productive matrix in the country. Future work foresees the availability of the mobile application for other operating environments (operating systems such as IOS or Linux, or through access for web browsers) and access devices with Raspberry or Arduino technologies.

5   Conclusion

The social, cultural and economic factors that must be taken into account for the presentation and processing of the cadastral registry information, allowed by the regulatory bodies of the state or institutions responsible for communication with the community, involves considering the technological capacity to combine improvements in information processes, and the economic capacity to finance urban planning projects with the development of an application with new technologies where users, through the use of applications with technology, have proper, reliable, fast and secure access to the information.

The prototype of the mobile application "Building QR" developed in this study uses augmented reality technologies and QR codes to represent 3D housing models together with property registry information associated with these urban properties for the improvement of departmental processes in public or private institutions that manage cadastres and urban planning.

The evaluation of the usability and satisfaction of the developed mobile application resulted in 84% of users finding it easy to use, while 95% are satisfied with the "Building QR" application in its first prototype and would therefore recommend it.

New technologies such as augmented reality and QR codes allow new experiences that complement the development of smart cities by breaking the barriers of digitization.

The scope of the applicability of this research work to territories or properties in rural sectors is foreseen for future works. As well as to make viable the proposals to other regulatory entities of cadastral information in the country as a contribution of the academy to the society.

References

1. Kitchin, R., Young, G.W., Dawkins, O.: Planning and 3D spatial media: progress, prospects, and the knowledge and experiences of local government planners in Ireland. Plan. Theory. Pract. **22**, 1–19 (2021). https://doi.org/10.1080/14649357.2021.1921832
2. Nunoo, D.C.: Smart and digital city action plan, Montreal. In: Urban Planning for Transitions. pp. 139–152. Wiley (2021). https://doi.org/10.1002/9781119821670.ch9
3. Berman, B., Pollack, D.: Strategies for the successful implementation of augmented reality. Bus. Horiz. **64**, 621–630 (2021). https://doi.org/10.1016/j.bushor.2021.02.027
4. Piga, B.E.A., Cacciamatta, S., Marco, B.: Smart Co-Design for Urban Planning: Augmented and Virtual Reality Apps in Collaborative Processes. Springer International Publishing, Cham (2021). https://link.springer.com/book/9783030678418
5. Izquierdo, J.L., Alfonso, M.R., Zambrano, M.A., Segovia, J.G.: Mobile application to encourage education in school chess students using augmented reality and m-learning|Aplicación móvil para fortalecer el aprendizaje de ajedrez en estudiantes de escuela utilizando realidad aumentada y m-learning. RISTI - Rev. Iber. Sist. e Tecnol. Inf. **2019**, 120–133 (2019)
6. Gómez Rios, M.D., Paredes Velasco, M.: Augmented reality as a methodology to development of learning in programming. In: Botto-Tobar, M., Pizarro, G., Zúñiga-Prieto, M., D'Armas, M., Zúñiga Sánchez, M. (eds.) Technology Trends. Communications in Computer and Information Science, vol. 895, pp. 327–340. Springer, Cham (2019). https://doi.org/10.1007/978-3-030-05532-5_24
7. Llerena, J., Andina, M., Grijalva, J.: Mobile application to promote the Malecón 2000 tourism using augmented reality and geolocation. In: 2018 International Conference on Information System and Computer Science 2018-Decem, pp. 213–220 (2018). https://doi.org/10.1109/INCISCOS.2018.00038
8. Han, S., Yoon, J.H., Kwon, J.: Impact of experiential value of augmented reality: the context of heritage tourism. Sustain. **13**, 4147 (2021). https://doi.org/10.3390/su13084147
9. Basu, T., Bannova, O., Camba, J.D.: Mixed reality architecture in space habitats. Acta Astronaut. **178**, 548–555 (2021). https://doi.org/10.1016/j.actaastro.2020.09.036
10. Llerena-Izquierdo, J., Cedeño-Gonzabay, L.: Photogrammetry and augmented reality to promote the religious cultural heritage of San Pedro Cathedral in Guayaquil, Ecuador. In: Botto-Tobar, M., Zambrano Vizuete, M., Torres-Carrión, P., Montes León, S., Pizarro Vásquez, G., Durakovic, B. (eds.) Applied Technologies. Communications in Computer and Information Science, vol. 1194, pp. 593–606. Springer, Cham (2020). https://doi.org/10.1007/978-3-030-42520-3_47
11. Kan Yeung, A.W., et al.: Virtual and augmented reality applications in medicine: analysis of the scientific literature. J. Med. Internet Res. **23**, e25499 (2021). https://doi.org/10.2196/25499
12. Moro, C., et al.: Virtual and augmented reality enhancements to medical and science student physiology and anatomy test performance: a systematic review and meta-analysis. Anat. Sci. Educ. **14**, 368–376 (2021). https://doi.org/10.1002/ase.2049
13. Tarng, W., Lin, Y.J., Ou, K.L.: A virtual experiment for learning the principle of daniell cell based on augmented reality. Appl. Sci. **11**, 1–24 (2021). https://doi.org/10.3390/app11020762
14. Akdag, S.G.: Small icons with wide borders: the semiotics of micro-mobility in urban space. In: Akdag, S.G., Dinçer, M., Vatan, M., Topçu, Ü., Kiris, I.M. (eds.) The Dialectics of Urban and Architectural Boundaries in the Middle East and the Mediterranean. TUBS, pp. 135–151. Springer, Cham (2021). https://doi.org/10.1007/978-3-030-71807-7_7
15. Estrada, J.C., Nacipucha, N.S., Chila, R.L.: El uso de los códigos QR: una herramienta alternativa en la tecnología educacional. Rev. Publicando. **5**, 83–106 (2018)

16. Crofton, E.C., Botinestean, C., Fenelon, M., Gallagher, E.: Potential applications for virtual and augmented reality technologies in sensory science. Innov. Food Sci. Emerg. Technol. **56**, 102178 (2019). https://doi.org/10.1016/j.ifset.2019.102178
17. Lu, W., Zhao, L., Xu, R.: Remote sensing image processing technology based on mobile augmented reality technology in surveying and mapping engineering. Soft. Comput. **3**, 1–11 (2021). https://doi.org/10.1007/s00500-021-05650-3
18. Hopkins, P.: Information and communication technologies. Debates Relig. Educ. **247**, 257 (2011). https://doi.org/10.4324/9780203813805-31
19. Bajaña Mendieta, I., Zúñiga Paredes, A., Can Sing, C., Meza Cruz, F., PurisCáceres, A.: La realidad aumentada en la publicidad, prospectiva para el mercado ecuatoriano. Cienc. UNEMI. **10**, 148–157 (2017). https://doi.org/10.29076/issn.2528-7737vol10iss23.2017pp148-157p
20. Velastegui-Cáceres, J., Rodríguez-Espinosa, V.M., Padilla-Almeida, O.: Urban cadastral situation in Ecuador: Analysis to determine the degree of proximity of the cadastral systems to the 3D cadastral model. Land. **9**, 1–20 (2020). https://doi.org/10.3390/land9100357
21. Zamora-Boza, C., ArroboCedeño, N., Cornejo-Marcos, G.: El gobierno electrónico en Ecuador: La innovación en la administración pública. Espacios. **39**, 1–10 (2018)
22. Karabin, M., Olszewski, R., Gotlib, D., Bakuła, K., Fijałkowska, A.: The New Methods of Visualisation of the Cadastral Data in Poland. FIG Work Week (2017)
23. Bednarczyk, M., Templin, T.: Mobile augmented reality application supporting building facades visualization (2020). https://doi.org/10.23967/dbmc.2020.186
24. Shojaei, D., Kalantari, M., Bishop, I.D., Rajabifard, A., Aien, A.: Visualization requirements for 3D cadastral systems. Comput. Environ. Urban Syst. **41**, 39–54 (2013). https://doi.org/10.1016/j.compenvurbsys.2013.04.003
25. Ramirez, S.: Estado del arte-Desarrollo de una aplicación móvil basada en sistemas de realidad aumentada para la validación de sistemas de información geográfica a nivel catastral (2015). https://doi.org/10.14483/2248762X.8506
26. Bydłosz, J., Bieda, A., Parzych, P.: The implementation of spatial planning objects in a 3D cadastral model. ISPRS Int. J. Geo-Inf. **7**, 153 (2018). https://doi.org/10.3390/ijgi7040153
27. Håkansson, L.: Visualizing cadastral parcels for surveyors using handheld Augmented Reality (2019)
28. Peña-Rios, A., Hagras, H., Gardner, M., Owusu, G.: A type-2 fuzzy logic based system for augmented reality visualisation of georeferenced data. In: IEEE International Conference Fuzzy System, July 2018 (2018). https://doi.org/10.1109/FUZZ-IEEE.2018.8491467
29. Harazono, Y., et al.: Development of an AR training construction system using embedded information in a real environment. In: Chen, J.Y.C., Fragomeni, G. (eds.) HCII 2021. LNCS, vol. 12770, pp. 614–625. Springer, Cham (2021). https://doi.org/10.1007/978-3-030-77599-5_42
30. Chatzopoulos, D., Bermejo, C., Huang, Z., Hui, P.: Mobile augmented reality survey from where we are to where we go. IEEE Access **5**, 6917–6950 (2017). https://doi.org/10.1109/ACCESS.2017.2698164
31. Ifrim, A.-C., Moldoveanu, F., Moldoveanu, A., Grădinaru, A.: LibrARy – enriching the cultural physical spaces with collaborative AR content. In: Chen, J.Y.C., Fragomeni, G. (eds.) HCII 2021. LNCS, vol. 12770, pp. 626–638. Springer, Cham (2021). https://doi.org/10.1007/978-3-030-77599-5_43
32. Liberatore, M.J., Wagner, W.P.: Virtual, mixed, and augmented reality: a systematic review for immersive systems research. Virtual Reality **25**(3), 773–799 (2021). https://doi.org/10.1007/s10055-020-00492-0
33. Cop, C.U., Villar, P.C., Gonzalez, D.: Realidad aumentada sin marcadores: posibilidades, librerías y prueba de concepto (2019)

34. Chen, C.W., et al.: A real-time markerless augmented reality framework based on slam technique. In: Proceedings of 14th International Symposium Pervasive Systems Algorithms Networks, I-SPAN 2017, 11th International Conference on Frontier Computer Science Technology, FCST 2017 3rd International Symposium Creating Computer ISCC 2017, November 2017, pp. 127–132 (2017). https://doi.org/10.1109/ISPAN-FCST-ISCC.2017.87

35. Nurhayati, Faridy, A., Iswara, R.P.: Implementation of Augmented Reality Geolocation Application Based on Android for Searching Hospital Location. 2019 7th International Conference on Cyber and IT Service Management, CITSM 2019 (2019). https://doi.org/10.1109/CITSM4 7753.2019.8965327

36. Pooja, J., Vinay, M., Pai, V.G., Anuradha, M.: Comparative analysis of marker and markerless augmented reality in education. In: 2020 IEEE International Conference on Innovation Technology INOCON 2020, pp. 4–7 (2020). https://doi.org/10.1109/INOCON50539.2020. 9298303

37. Sanaeipoor, S., Emami, K.H.: Smart city: exploring the role of augmented reality in placemaking. In: Proceeding 4th International Conference on Smart Cities, Internet Things Applications SCIoT 2020, pp. 91–98 (2020). https://doi.org/10.1109/SCIOT50840.2020.9250204

38. Cemellini, B., van Oosterom, P., Thompson, R., de Vries, M.: Design, development and usability testing of an LADM compliant 3D Cadastral prototype system. Land Use Policy **98**, 104418 (2020). https://doi.org/10.1016/j.landusepol.2019.104418

39. Gkeli, M., Potsiou, C., Ioannidis, C.: A technical solution for 3D crowdsourced cadastral surveys. Land Use Policy **98**, 104419 (2020). https://doi.org/10.1016/j.landusepol.2019. 104419

40. Celeste, R.K., Schwendicke, F.: Reviews systematic and meta-analysis. In: Peres, M.A., Antunes, J.L.F., Watt, R.G. (eds.) Oral Epidemiology. TCD, pp. 507–523. Springer, Cham (2021). https://doi.org/10.1007/978-3-030-50123-5_34

41. Cochrane, T., Narayan, V., Antonczak, L.: A framework for designing collaborative learning environments using mobile AR. J. Interact. Learn. Res. **27**, 293–316 (2016)

42. Tzima, S., Styliaras, G., Bassounas, A.: Augmented reality applications in education: teachers point of view. Educ. Sci. **9**, 99 (2019). https://doi.org/10.3390/educsci9020099

43. Sarlak, B.: Agile methodology for project/process management IT system infrastructure. In: 2020 11th International Conference on Computing Communication and Networking Technologies, ICCCNT 2020 (2020). https://doi.org/10.1109/ICCCNT49239.2020.9225593

End-to-End Compressive Spectral Classification: A Deep Learning Approach Applied to the Grading of Tahiti Lime

Mauricio Silva-Maldonado$^{(\boxtimes)}$ [iD], Laura Galvis [iD], and Henry Arguello [iD]

Department of Computer Science, Universidad Industrial de Santander,
Bucaramanga, Colombia
nelsonmauricio989769@correo.uis.edu.co

Abstract. Compressed sensing (CS) theory enables the reconstruction of spectral images (SI) using a lower number of measurements than the traditional Shannon-Nyquist sampling approach, through compressive spectral imaging (CSI) systems. These CSI systems rely on a dispersive-based optical setup coupled to one or more coded-apertures to capture and compress a spectral scene simultaneously. Afterward, the reconstruction of the underlying scene is obtained through computational algorithms. Then, processing tasks like classification, object detection, or segmentation are performed over the reconstructed images. However, this reconstruction process is computationally expensive, which introduces a time overhead for these tasks. In this paper, spectral classification is directly performed over compressed measurements acquired through an optical architecture following the CS framework. An end-to-end method to optimize both coded-apertures and deep learning model parameters is proposed. This approach has been applied to the grading of Tahiti lime (Citrus latifolia), but can be used for different agricultural materials. In this specific case, the classification accuracy reached 99%. In addition, for the purpose of comparison, our experiments improved up to 7% in classification accuracy over a testing database when the coded-apertures were optimized.

Keywords: Compressed sensing · Deep learning optimization · Spectral images · Spectral classification · Tahiti lime

1 Introduction

Spectral images have been used in several fields and industries such as agriculture [1], food quality [2], biomedical images [3], remote sensing [4], archaeology [5], among others. However, SI are expensive to capture due to the cost of the sensors and equipment involved [6], limiting the widespread use of this promising technology.

Many approaches have been proposed to acquire SI at a lower cost, such as those based on compressive sensing (CS) theory [7]. CS states that a signal can be recovered with a number of measurements lower than those stated

© Springer Nature Switzerland AG 2022
F. R. Narváez et al. (Eds.): SmartTech-IC 2021, CCIS 1532, pp. 44–57, 2022.
https://doi.org/10.1007/978-3-030-99170-8_4

by the Shannon-Nyquist sampling theorem, as long as the signal can be represented in a known basis such as wavelet, Discrete Cosine Transform (DCT), among others. There are several optical setups that demonstrate the CS theory, namely compressive spectral imaging (CSI) systems such as the single-pixel camera [8], the coded-aperture snapshot spectral imager (CASSI) [9], and its variants like dual-dispersion architecture (DD-CASSI) [9], single-disperser architecture (SD-CASSI) [10], and colored coded-apertures CASSI (3D-CASSI) [11]. More recently, a dual-camera compressive hyperspectral imaging system (DCCHI) was proposed by [12]. These CSI systems rely on a dispersive-based optical setup coupled to one or more coded-apertures to capture and compress a spectral scene simultaneously.

Compressed spectral images acquired with these optical systems must be reconstructed to apply further processing tasks such as classification, segmentation, and object detection. This reconstruction process is computationally expensive because an ill-posed, under-determined linear system of equations must be solved [13]. There have been different computational approaches to solve this problem, for example, the gradient projection sparse reconstruction (GPSR) [14], the orthogonal matching pursuit (OMP) [15], and the iterative hard thresholding (IHT) algorithms [16]. More recently, reconstruction algorithms make use of CNNs like the proposed by [17].

However, the reconstruction process introduces a time overhead that makes CS methods unsuitable for critical response-time applications like object detection, motion detection, etc. The reconstruction step, required as an additional process before the inference task is the main problem of CS aimed to address with this work. There have been different approaches avoiding the reconstruction step. For example, [18] successfully made motion detection, image classification, and noise filtering from compressive measurements. More recently, [19] proposed a convolutional neural network (CNN) to classify compressive measurements of the MNIST [20] database. Finally, [21] proposed a coupled deep learning architecture for coded-aperture and feature extraction optimization using both MNIST and CIFAR-10 [22] databases. The latter reporting the improvement achieved when the coded-apertures are optimized.

Nonetheless, that inference on compressive measurements has been explored by several authors. Still, to our knowledge, no approach has been proposed for spectral imaging that uses a deep learning model to optimize the coded-apertures and optical elements of the acquisition system in an end-to-end approach and for a real application, which is the hypothesis and main contribution of this work.

Traditional fruit grading has been labor-intensive, requiring lots of people to perform this task. However, advances in computer vision algorithms, like the one exposed in this work, have made the development of automatic grading and sorting machines possible.

The grading process goal is to select those fruits compliant with regulatory and market standards. These standards generally reject those fruits with diseases produced by mites, fungus, etc. Also, fruits that do not comply with market-specific characteristics like size, color, flavor, etc., are rejected.

In this work, we propose an end-to-end scheme for the classification of spectral images, which takes the SI compressive measurements as input and the categorical variable as the output of the system with no intermediate steps in the training process of the deep learning model.

A spectral database of Tahiti lime (Citrus latifoia) has been chosen to demonstrate the proposed approach. The spectral images of a set of real limes have been acquired in an optical setup implemented by the authors. Tahiti lime is a fruit that grows in tropical zones like Colombia, and it has a great potential for exporting to countries where quality products are highly appreciated. To this end, crops need to be organic, and fruits must comply with specific market standards and agricultural regulatory policies.

2   End-to-End Approach for the Tahiti Lime Classification

This section describes the proposed methodology for the classification of Tahiti lime in a compressive spectral imaging framework. The approach is divided into a learning or training process and a testing part. The learning process is proposed as an end-to-end approach that jointly optimizes the acquisition and classification tasks. A coded-aperture pattern used to modulate the scene in the compressive imaging framework is optimized for the acquisition. In the classification part, the CNN parameters are also optimized following an optimization problem described below. After the training, in the testing part, a real measurement is acquired using the coded-aperture designed, and the trained CNN classifies the lime patches in their corresponding class. A flowchart of the end-to-end approach is depicted in Fig. 1.

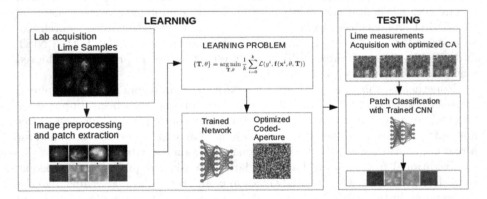

Fig. 1. Flowchart of the general steps of the proposed end-to-end model for the simultaneously coded-aperture design and lime patch classification. The two main steps are the learning and testing parts. Source: Authors.

2.1   Coded-Aperture Design

The well-known coded-aperture snapshot spectral imager (CASSI) [9] architecture is the compressive spectral system used in this work because it is suitable for the spectral classification task, as reported in the literature. The CASSI is one example of a CS sensor that captures 2D projections by multiplexing the spatio-spectral information of a scene through a coded-aperture and a dispersive element such as a prism or a diffractive device. The coded-apertures are implemented by use of a photomask, an SLM, or a digital micromirror device (DMD). The latter two provide versatility as the coding is easily modified with subsequent shots or snapshots. As a result, a multidimensional cube is generated representing the whole compressed scene.

The Coded-aperture (CA) design is a key component in the compressive acquisition system [23]. It modulates the scene spatially and/or spectrally such that an optimal image reconstruction or an optimal classification accuracy can be achieved. Scene modulation is made by applying one or multiple CA patterns or designs to the scene. A color CA is an arrangement of more than one CAs that modulates specific bands of the scene. On the other hand, a binary CA is a single CA design whose pattern is applied to every spectral band of the scene. In this work, only binary CAs will be used, resulting in only spatial modulation. The CA is defined as,

$$\mathbf{T} \in \mathbb{R}^{MN}, \tag{1}$$

where M and N are the spatial dimensions. Since only spatial modulation will be performed, the same code design $\mathbf{T}$ is applied to all the spectral bands of the scene. The acquisition of scene $\mathbf{F}$, in the CASSI system and applying the spatial modulation $\mathbf{T}$ can be expressed as,

$$\mathbf{Y}_{mn} = \sum_{k=0}^{L-1} \mathbf{F}_{m(n-k)k} \mathbf{T}_{mn} + \boldsymbol{\omega}_{mn}, \tag{2}$$

where $\mathbf{Y}$ represents the measurements, $\mathbf{F}$ is referring to the data cube, $\mathbf{T}$ defines the coded-aperture, and $\boldsymbol{\omega}$ is the noise in the system. The dimensions of the data cube $\mathbf{F}$ are $M \times N \times L$, $\mathbf{T}$ is $M \times N$, and $\mathbf{Y}$ is $M \times (N + L - 1)$. L represents the number of spectral bands. The resulting shifting in the measurements is the dispersive element effect, characteristic in the CASSI system.

2.2   Tahiti Lime Classification

The goal of the grading process of Tahiti lime is to accept or reject a whole fruit based on its healthiness and compliance with target-market standards and agriculture regulators. However, the fact that fruit has been affected by a fungus or mite or any other kind of defect does not mean that it be automatically rejected. Some levels of affectation are accepted. To reject a whole fruit, it must have affectation levels beyond the target market or regulator standards. In some cases, 10% of mite or fungus affectation is permitted. Due to this, a one-shot fruit classification will require huge quantities of training samples, which is a drawback of traditional classification systems. Instead, a patch-wise approach was implemented. This approach has two stages: the first one is used to build the training and testing database. The second to perform automated classification. In the first stage, segments of known anomalies are extracted by cropping the whole lime images with the help of a lime farmer who identifies the place, size, and type of the anomaly. Those segments are cropped again to create the patches of $16 \times 16 \times 40$ pixels using an image processing tool. Then, each patch is labeled, and finally stored as the training and testing database of the CNN classifier. In the second stage, once the CNN has been simultaneously trained and the coded-aperture optimized, it is possible to perform a whole lime classification in the patch basis. For this, a background removal algorithm [24] is applied to the lime image sample. Then, the Compact Whatersed unsupervised segmentation algorithm [25] is applied. Once the lime image is segmented, the trained network can be applied to every segment, thus resulting in a more precise and efficient classification. This image-processing workflow is depicted in Fig. 2. In this approach both anomaly and amount of surface affected can be inferred. It is up to the farmer to set the affectation allowance in order to meet its target-market requirements. Since the image processing techniques reported before have been widely studied, only the trained network used for the patch classification will be developed in this work.

2.3 Proposed Training Model

In order to optimize both the coded-aperture pattern and the parameters of the classification CNN, the training architecture depicted in Fig. 3 is proposed. The input data, which can be gray-scale, RGB, or spectral images, is pre-processed to extract the patches with some anomalies. Then, the CASSI system is simulated using an initial random coded-aperture, which spatially modulates the patches. Then, a CNN is used to find both optimal coded-aperture design and CNN parameters by solving the following optimization problem,

$$\{\mathbf{T}, \theta\} = \arg \min_{\mathbf{T}, \theta} \frac{1}{k} \sum_{i=0}^{k} \mathcal{L}(y^i, \mathbf{f}(\mathbf{x}^i, \theta, \mathbf{T})), \tag{3}$$

where $\mathcal{L}$ is a loss or cost function, $\mathbf{f}$ is the output of the trained model, $\mathbf{T}$ is the coded-aperture, θ are the CNN parameters, k is the number of training samples, y^i are the training labels, and $\mathbf{x}^i$ are the training samples.

A regularizer [26] can be added to Eq. 3 to make coded-aperture entries to converge to 1's or 0's as shown in Eq. 4,

$$\{\mathbf{T}, \theta\} = \arg \min_{\mathbf{T}, \theta} \frac{1}{k} \sum_{i=0}^{k} \mathcal{L}(y^i, f(\mathbf{x}^i, \theta, \mathbf{T})) + \mu(\mathbf{1} + \mathbf{T})^2 (\mathbf{T})^2, \tag{4}$$

where μ is a regularizer constant. This regularization is included with the aim to produce implementable coded-aperture designs.

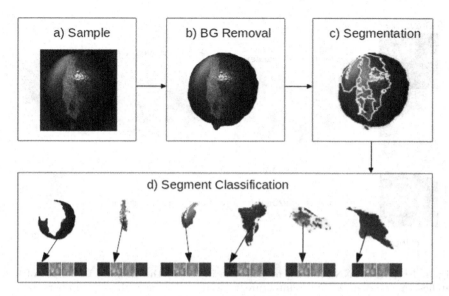

Fig. 2. Lime classification workflow. a) A lime image is acquired. b) Image background is removed. c) Image segmentation algorithm is applied. e) Segment classification using a trained network is performed over each segment. Source: Authors.

2.4   Proposed Inference/Testing Model

Once an optimal coded-aperture design and the trained network are achieved from the training stage, real lime measurements can be acquired in the lab to perform their respective classification. The CASSI system can be implemented or simulated to acquire the lime measurements in a single shot, using the designed coded-aperture obtained in the training. Then, the resulting compressive measurements are used as the input of the trained network, which classifies the observed patch. The label of the lime class is the output of the inference pipeline. Figure 4 depicts the described testing process.

3   Experimental Data Acquisition

3.1   Optical Setup

An optical setup was assembled in our laboratory to acquire the lime spectral database. The sample scene was focused by a CCD Monochrome Camera (Stingray camera F-080B) coupled with a macro lens (Tamron, Co., Ltd; 8 mm, 1.1″, C mount Lens). A tunable light source (Oriel Instruments, TLS-300XR) was used to decompose the source light in 40 spectral bands ranging from 400 nm to 700 nm. The whole setup is depicted in Fig. 5.

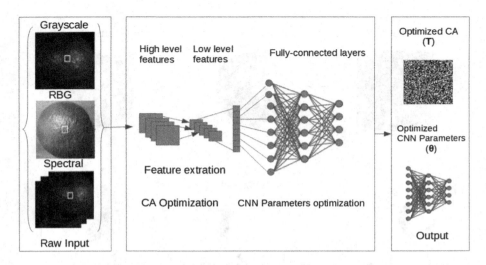

Fig. 3. Proposed CNN training model. The input for the training is the set of lime patches. A complete CNN architecture is used to optimize the coded-aperture pattern, as well as the classification CNN parameters. The output is an optimized coded-aperture and the optimized CNN parameters to be used in the testing step. Source: Authors.

3.2   Hardware and Software for the Database Acquisition

The CCD Monochrome Camera and the tunable light source were controlled by a Desktop-PC equipped with an Intel Core i7 processor and 16 GB of RAM. Matlab (The MathWorks, Inc., Natick, Massachusetts, United States.) scripts were used to control the acquisition process.

3.3   Data Acquisition and Pre-processing

Instead of using several images, a patch-wise approach has been applied to the 72 image samples acquired in the lab. The complete size of these images is $1388 \times 1038 \times 40$ pixels. This approach let us construct a spectral database of 2442 patches of $16 \times 16 \times 40$ pixels size, with which the proposed deep learning model was trained. The database spectral range is the visible spectrum from 400 nm to 700 nm. The following patch classes were defined: Healthy or European-market-ready fruits, fungus or mite-affected fruits, shadow-grown fruits, and wood-pocket affected fruits. These classes are shown in Fig. 6, and they were suggested by a Tahiti lime exporter[1], who performs manual grading of their fruits. Patch samples of both training and testing databases are shown in Table 1.

In order to tackle the category imbalance problem we have applied oversampling techniques as mentioned by [27] to the whole lime spectral database. This technique let us to copy some training and testing samples in least populated

---

[1] Orange Export S.A.S. www.orange-export.com.

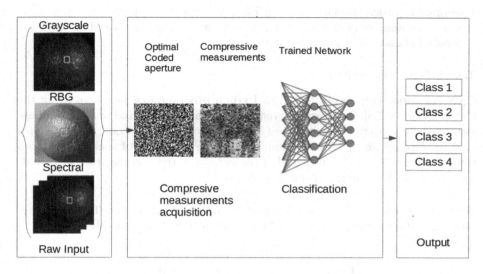

Fig. 4. Proposed CNN inference model. The input of this step is the output of the training model. Real measurements can be acquired using the CASSI system and the designed coded-aperture. Then these measurements are used to classify the lime patch in one class using the trained CNN. Source: Authors.

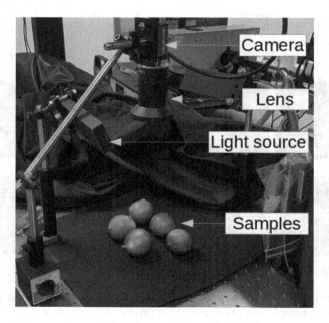

Fig. 5. Optical setup for dataset acquisition. The samples are illuminated with a tunable light source, which allows the 40 spectral bands acquisition. Source: Authors.

categories in order to match the cardinality of most populated category. This way a same number of samples per category can be achieved avoiding the most populated classes to bias the results.

3.4   CNN Implementation

CNN networks were implemented in Python programming language using the Pytorch library [28]. Lime patches required for the training and testing database were manually extracted with the Gimp (https://www.gimp.org/) image processing software and Python's Numpy library. Parameters of each CNN tested were trained with an Adam based optimizer, an initial learning rate of 0.0001, and a Cosine Annealing learning rate scheduler.

Table 1. Database of lime samples used for training and testing. The number of samples used for training and testing for each of the classes is reported.

Class name	Training	Testing
Healthy	576	100
Mite affected	488	102
Shadow-grown	484	100
Wood pocket affected	496	96
—	—	—
Totals	2044	398

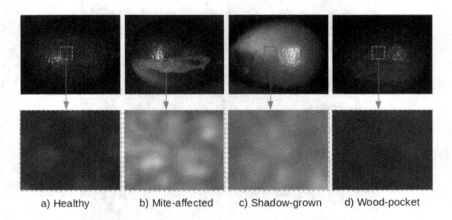

a) Healthy   b) Mite-affected   c) Shadow-grown   d) Wood-pocket

Fig. 6. Patch extraction process. For the database acquisition, several patches out of a whole fruit sample are extracted. This process is performed over lima samples belonging to the four different classes. The zoomed sections are patches examples. Source: Authors.

4   Simulations and Results

Three different CNN architectures were selected to test the accuracy of the proposed end-to-end approach: a simple CNN vanilla architecture, Alexnet [29], and Resnet34 [30]. Vanilla is a custom 7-layer architecture intended to be a baseline for bench-marking deeper architectures. Alexnet is an 11-layer, well-known, and proven deep learning architecture. Also, a state-of-the-art Resnet architecture with 34-layers was used for performance testing.

Regarding the datasets, besides the custom 40-spectral-band database of Tahiti lime aforementioned, a new database was built by selecting three spectral bands out of the 40 of the original spectral database. This experiment is intended to show the contribution of spectral information. In addition, the MNIST-Fashion database [31] also will be used for testing purposes of the end-to-end approach.

The Resnet34 architecture outperformed the vanilla and Alexnet architectures over all three datasets in up to 20% accuracy, as shown in Table 2. However, the vanilla architecture outperformed the Alexnet in the two Tahiti lime datasets, nonetheless that it was two-layer shallower. The performance of the different architectures over the MNIST-fashion dataset shows us that the deeper the network, the better the results. The performance achieved by the three CNN architectures is higher when using the 40 spectral bands, which demonstrates the advantage of using spectral instead of RGB data.

An additional set of simulations were performed to demonstrate the improvement in the classification, where the CA design is optimized. The same approach but using a random pattern instead of the designed CA is presented in Table 2. These results are referred to as Non-optimized CA in the table. As can be seen, in all the experiment combinations (CNN and dataset), the optimization of the CA design reported the highest accuracy.

Figure 7 presents the optimized coded-aperture patterns for each CNN architecture and for the 40-band lime dataset. It can be seen that patterns did not converge to a particular shape, due to the little spatial variability of the dataset. The confusion matrices also reported in Fig. 7 show the mite-affected and shadow-grown patches were the most challenging anomalies to classify. Figure 7 also presents the accuracy behavior for the different network architectures. Notice that the Resnet34 only needs 6 epochs to converge, whereas Alexnet and Vanilla need more than 10 to obtain a similar behavior.

Table 2. CNN Accuracy over test datasets. The customs 40-band and 3-band correspond to the acquired lime datasets. A comparison of the classification results with the optimized and non-optimized CA is presented.

Dataset	Coded-aperture	CNN architecture		
		Vanilla	Alexnet	Resnet34
Custom 40-band	Optimized CA	**96**%	**84**%	**99**%
	Non-optimized CA	94%	77%	97%
Custom 3-band	Optimized CA	**94**%	**80**%	**98**%
	Non-optimized CA	93%	76%	94%
Fashion MNIST	Optimized CA	**91**%	**92**%	**94**%
	Non-optimized CA	90%	91%	93%

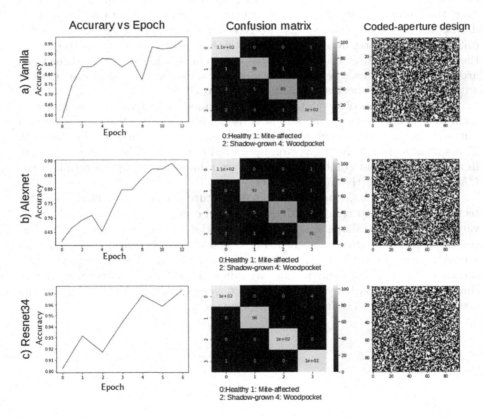

Fig. 7. Accuracy, confusion matrix, and CA design for each CNN architecture selected using the 40-band lime dataset. Source: Authors.

5   Conclusions

A compressive spectral classification method using an end-to-end optimization pipeline was proposed and evaluated. The end-to-end approach optimizes the coded-aperture design used for compressive acquisitions and the parameters of a classification network at the same time. The joint design of the coded-aperture and the CNN network was validated using an acquired real dataset of Tahiti lime. Three different CNN architectures were used to show the advantages of using the proposed approach. It was also demonstrated that a CNN can be trained with samples generated following a patch-wise approach instead of the traditional whole-image approach, hence, requiring a reduced database for training. Finally, the experiments showed that accuracy achieved with the 40-bands Tahiti lime dataset outperformed the 3-band dataset by up to 4%, showing the contribution of the spectral information, and therefore the advantages of using compressive spectral frameworks.

Acknowledgment. The authors acknowledge the support by the Sistema general de regalías de CTeI - Colombia (BPIN 2020000100415, "Desarrollo de un sistema óptico - computacional para estimar el contenido de carbono orgánico de suelos agrícolas a través de imágenes espectrales e inteligencia artificial en cultivos cítricos de Santander." with UIS code 8933). Laura Galvis was supported by the postdoctoral program of the VIE-UIS.

We also acknowledge Orange Export S.A.S. for supplying the classified lime samples studied in this work.

References

1. Nandhini, A., Hemalatha, S., Radha, R., et al.: Web enabled plant disease detection system for agricultural applications using WMSN. Wirel. Person. Commun. 102, 725–740 (2018)
2. Draganić, A., Orović, I., Stanković, S., Zhang, X., Wang, X.: Compressive sensing approach in the table grape cold chain logistics. In: 2017 6th Mediterranean Conference on Embedded Computing (MECO), pp. 1–4 (2017)
3. Yang, Y., Qin, X., Ruan, S., Tian, D.: A new compressed sensing model based on median filter with application to reconstruct brain MR images. In: 2018 IEEE 3rd International Conference on Signal and Image Processing (ICSIP), pp. 116–120 (2018)
4. Mirrashid, A., Beheshti, A.A.: Compressed remote sensing by using deep learning. In: 2018 9th International Symposium on Telecommunications (IST), pp. 549–552 (2018)
5. Zhang, Y., Orfeo, D., Huston, D., Xia, T.: Compressive sensing based software defined GPR for subsurface imaging. In: 2021 IEEE Radar Conference (Radar-Conf21), pp. 1–6 (2021)
6. TE-Cooled Fluorescence Spectrometer—Edmund Optics. https://www.edmundoptics.com/p/te-cooled-fluorescence-spectrometer/28866/
7. Donoho, D.L.: Compressed sensing. IEEE Trans. Inf. Theory **52**(4), 1289–1306 (2006)

8. Duarte, M.F., et al.: Single-pixel imaging via compressive sampling. IEEE Signal Process. Mag. **25**(2), 83–91 (2008)
9. Gehm, M.E., John, R., Brady, D.J., Willett, R.M., Schulz, T.J.: Single-shot compressive spectral imaging with a dual-disperser architecture. Opt. Exp. **15**(21), 14013 (2007)
10. Wagadarikar, A., John, R., Willett, B., Brady, D.: Single disperser design for coded aperture snapshot spectral imaging. Appl. Opt. **47**(10) (2008)
11. Lin, X., Liu, Y., Wu, J., Dai, Q.: Spatial-spectral encoded compressive hyperspectral imaging. ACM Trans. Graph. **33**(6) (2014)
12. Wang, L., Xiong, Z., Shi, G., Wu, F., Zeng, W.: Adaptive nonlocal sparse representation for dual-camera compressive hyperspectral imaging. IEEE Trans. Pattern Anal. Mach. Intell. **39**(10), 2104–2111 (2017)
13. Xingyi, C., Yujie, Z., Rui, O.: Block sparse signals recovery algorithm for distributed compressed sensing reconstruction. J. Inf. Process. Syst. **15**(2), 410–421 (2019)
14. Figueiredo, M.A., Nowak, R.D., Wright, S.J.: Gradient projection for sparse reconstruction: application to compressed sensing and other inverse problems. IEEE J. Sel. Top. Signal Process. **1**(4), 586–597 (2007)
15. Tropp, J.A., Gilbert, A.C.: Signal recovery from random measurements via orthogonal matching pursuit. IEEE Trans. Inf. Theory **53**(12), 4655–4666 (2007)
16. Blumensath, T., Davies, M.E.: Iterative hard thresholding for compressed sensing. Appl. Comput. Harmon. Anal. **27**(3), 265–274 (2009)
17. Zhao, C., Zhang, J., Wang, R., Gao, W.: Cream: CNN-regularized ADMM framework for compressive-sensed image reconstruction. IEEE Access **6**, 76 838–76 853 (2018)
18. Davenport, M.A., Boufounos, P.T., Wakin, M.B., Baraniuk, R.G.: Signal processing with compressive measurements. IEEE J. Sel. Top. Signal Process. **4**(2), 445–460 (2010)
19. Kulkarni, K., Lohit, S., Turaga, P., Kerviche, R., Ashok, A.: ReconNet: Noniterative reconstruction of images from compressively sensed measurements. In: Proceedings of the IEEE Computer Society Conference on Computer Vision and Pattern Recognition, vol. 2016-December, pp. 449–458 (2016)
20. LeCun, Y., Cortes, C.: MNIST handwritten digit database (2010). http://yann.lecun.com/exdb/mnist/
21. Bacca, J., Galvis, L., Arguello, H.: Coupled deep learning coded aperture design for compressive image classification. Opt. Express **28**(6), 8528–8540. http://www.opticsexpress.org/abstract.cfm?URI=oe-28-6-8528
22. Krizhevsky, A., Nair, V., Hinton, G.: Cifar-10 (Canadian Institute for Advanced Research). [Online]. http://www.cs.toronto.edu/~kriz/cifar.html
23. Galvis, L., Mojica, E., Arguello, H., Arce, G.R.: Shifting colored coded aperture design for spectral imaging. Appl. Opt. **58**(7), B28–B38 (2019). http://www.osapublishing.org/ao/abstract.cfm?URI=ao-58-7-B28
24. Sobral, A., Vacavant, A.: A comprehensive review of background subtraction algorithms evaluated with synthetic and real videos. Comput. Vis. Image Underst. **122**, 4–21 (2014). https://www.sciencedirect.com/science/article/pii/S1077314213002361
25. Neubert, P., Protzel, P.: Compact watershed and preemptive SLIC: on improving trade-offs of superpixel segmentation algorithms. In: 2014 22nd International Conference on Pattern Recognition, pp. 996–1001 (2014)

26. Higham, C.F., Murray-Smith, R., Padgett, M.J., Edgar, M.P.: Deep learning for real-time single-pixel video. Sci. Rep. **8**(1), 2369 (2018). https://doi.org/10.1038/s41598-018-20521-y
27. Buda, M., Maki, A., Mazurowski, M.A.: A systematic study of the class imbalance problem in convolutional neural networks. Neural Netw. **106**, 249–259 (2018). https://www.sciencedirect.com/science/article/pii/S0893608018302107
28. Paszke, A., et al.: Pytorch: an imperative style, high-performance deep learning library. In: Wallach, H., Larochelle, H., Beygelzimer, A., d'Alché-Buc, F., Fox, E., Garnett, R. (eds.) Advances in Neural Information Processing Systems, vol. 32, pp. 8024–8035. Curran Associates Inc. (2019), http://papers.neurips.cc/paper/9015-pytorch-an-imperative-style-high-performance-deep-learning-library.pdf
29. Krizhevsky, A., Sutskever, I., Hinton, G.E.: ImageNet classification with deep convolutional neural networks. In: Pereira, F., Burges, C.J., Bottou, C.L., Weinberger, K.Q. (eds.) Advances in Neural Information Processing Systems, vol. 25. Curran Associates Inc. (2012). https://proceedings.neurips.cc/paper/2012/file/c399862d3b9d6b76c8436e924a68c45b-Paper.pdf
30. He, K., Zhang, K., Ren, S., Sun, J.: Deep residual learning for image recognition. CoRR, abs/1512.03385 (2015) http://arxiv.org/abs/1512.03385
31. Xiao, H., Rasul, K., Vollgraf, R.: Fashion-MNIST: a novel image dataset for benchmarking machine learning algorithms. CoRR, abs/1708.07747 (2017). http://arxiv.org/abs/1708.07747

Data Mining Applied to a Serious Game of Memory and Attention Training

Marcos Orellana[1]([✉]) [ID], Juan-Fernando Lima[1] [ID], María-Inés Acosta Urigüen[1] [ID], Andrés Patiño[1] [ID], Nicolás Álvarez[2], and Juan Cordero[2]

[1] Laboratorio de Investigación y Desarrollo en Informática - LIDI, Universidad del Azuay, Cuenca, Ecuador
{marore,flima,macosta,andpatino}@uazuay.edu.ec
[2] Universidad del Azuay, Cuenca, Ecuador
{nicolas.alvarez,juanchocordero}@es.uazuay.edu.ec

Abstract. Serious games are software applications developed to achieve learning objectives during the user's performance. One of the fields where these games are developed is the psychological domain, where applications to measure cognitive attention are widely developed. Multiple kind of data can be collected while it is running, and these data are related not only to demographics users' variables but to performance indicators of the game. The controlled environment makes possible that different data mining techniques are applied to extract relevant information, features, or patterns. This work shows the application of data mining techniques on data collected from a serious game to describe patterns among players, the analyzed attributes were the game level and the responsive time; the results show a hidden pattern based on gender among players and their behavior across the different levels.

Keywords: Serious game · Data mining · Psychological · Patterns

1 Introduction

A serious game can be considered as a software application that captures not only the full attention of the player, but at the same time, it contributes with an educational purpose associated with its execution [1, 2]. In the process of developing a serious game application, the modeling process is important, as well as the application design stage, the purpose of the game, the accessibility, the game usability, and the user's performance [3, 4]. Several serious games are developed, for example a group of them are designed for cognitive training to process speed, attention and memory [5]. Memory Match Game is a serious game that consists of a card game with images in which all the cards are placed face down on a surface; and the objective is to turn over pairs of equal cards with the fewest possible attempts [6]. During the execution of a serious game, it is possible to collect data related user's personal information, user progress with respective achievement and certification of capabilities [3]. This information can be stored in a database and analyzed.

© Springer Nature Switzerland AG 2022
F. R. Narváez et al. (Eds.): SmartTech-IC 2021, CCIS 1532, pp. 58–68, 2022.
https://doi.org/10.1007/978-3-030-99170-8_5

The application of data mining in the information obtained from serious games has had an important contribution in areas such as defense, education, scientific exploration, health care, among others more. Educational games has been developed, focusing on identify problems and improve strategies at different levels, adapting them to particular situations [7, 8]. For instance, in health area, data mining techniques analyze patterns for detection of disorders such as Alzheimer [9]. Additionally, the application of data mining techniques provides relevant information that can be used in processes of continuous improvement of game mechanics. Our purpose on this work is to apply data mining techniques on data that comes from a serious game developed for training the cognitive memory and attention, in order to identify patterns between male and female groups related to the user's performance in the game.

This work is organized as follows: Sect. 2 describes the related works for serious games and data mining techniques. Section 3 details the methodology implemented for detect patterns, Sect. 4 offers a discussion on the achievements of this work and Sect. 5 presents the conclusions.

2 Related Work

The term "serious games" can have different connotations, but it is assumed as the use of computer games whose main purpose is not pure entertainment [10]. Serious games are software applications developed with a specific purpose such as attention, motivation, knowledge or skill acquisition, process support, joy/playfulness or information [10, 11]. On this context, a subgroup are games designed for cognitive training which include logic challenging for humans and problem solving skills [12].

In this context, [13] presented a serious game based on virtual reality for cognitive training including attention and memory tasks of daily life activities. The game promotes the improvement in memory and attention functions thought cognitive stimulation with mobile technology. The cognitive functions such as: working memory tasks, visual-spatial orientation tasks, selective attention tasks, recognition memory tasks and calculation were set gradually increasing demands on memory and attention abilities. The results showed that the comparisons between the experimental group and control ones have different values between when attention and general memory ability are measured.

Another example is a serious game designed for diagnosis and training of children with cognitive disabilities whose objective is to propose a system that creates different scenarios according to the user's conditions [14]. The game includes hidden many being that should be found for the player in order to complete levels, and testing the attention and memory are needed to perform it. The results presented a prototype that generates dynamically adapt scenarios.

In some studies, data mining techniques have been used over data collected in learning-oriented games with the aim of finding patterns that are not identifiable simply by looking at them. In [7], a game called ELISA oriented to medical training, it was applied to a group of Biology students learning about the immunological technique for determination of anti-HIV antibodies. The results obtained from the game were used as input for the application of clustering techniques, such as K-Means or Expectation Minimization algorithms, from which the existence of five clusters associated with learning effectiveness was determined. This made it possible to identify those clusters where the students did not demonstrate solid knowledge, and therefore required the support of an expert to explain the process in detail.

Halim et al. [15] propose the use of data mining techniques to correlate information with the five major personality traits. For this, data sets from games such as World of WorldCraft, Age of Empire II and Starcraft, the same ones on which clustering techniques were applied (k-means, kmedoids, fuzzy c-mean, and hierarchical clustering) were used; they allowed to identify groups of users, whose quality was tested using cluster validation indices. Based on these data, classifiers of personality traits were trained, from which the super vector machine technique obtained the highest precision (98%).

Although there are applications of data mining in the cognitive area, there are no studies that analyze data from serious games for cognitive training of attention and memory. For this reason, the present study seeks to apply these techniques to determine if there is a relationship between the variables that describe the user's profile (age, gender, etc.) and the variables that record the performance of the game. The results that are intended to be obtained will allow the identification of age groups or types of disability that may show specific behaviors in the data.

3   Methodology

This work is focused on evaluate data collected from a serious game, and try to describe hidden features into the response times collected throughout the levels of the game. The SPEM2.0 speciation [16] is used to represent each stage in this methodology. In Fig. 1, is possible observe the main processes until to bring to light the features of people when they played the game.

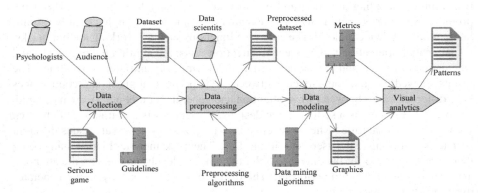

Fig. 1. Methodology used to obtain patterns about time response over the serious game.

3.1   Data Collection

The game named "Picture pairing" is an online game focused on guess pairs of pictures, it was designed from psychologists seeking to reinforce the brain areas of attention and memory, the game has four levels and each level has a matrix of pairs from 2×2 until 5×5 giving complexity and demanding more comprehensiveness for each level. And it measures the response time of individuals when them guess a new pair and when they pass to a new level.

Demographical data of users is collected when a user signs in, and before the game execution the guidelines are showed seeking to inform and grant the same level of knowledge about the game rules. The users could attempt any number of times, if they consider necessary, in Ecuador, people with access to a computer was take into account to play the game, also like, people who has any impairment. A total of 97 people played the game and Table 1 shown the features collected throughout the game. The user profile features such as dni and name were no included for data analysis.

Table 1. Description of dataset variables.

Feature	Datatype	Description
DNI	String	User DNI – Private for user profile
Name	String	User's name – Private for user profile
Birthday	Date	User's birthday – Private for user profile
City	String	City where user lives
Phone number	String	Phone number as a user contact field
Gender	Categorical	[Male, Female]
Laterality	Categorical	[Right-handed, Left-handed, Ambidextrous]
Educational stages	Categorical	[Primary, Secondary, Tertiary]
Has impairment	Boolean	Used to warn if user has to choose an impairment type
Impairment type	Categorical	[Visual, Hearing]
Game time	Number	Total time from game starts until level 4 is over
Time level 1	Number	Global start time and end time measured in level 1
Time level 2	Number	Global start time and end time measured in level 2
Time level 3	Number	Global start time and end time measured in level 3
Time level 4	Number	Global start time and end time measured in level 4
Game points	Number	Total points earned

3.2 Data Preprocessing

Techniques used prior to the application of a data mining methods is known as data preprocessing. Data will likely be imperfect, containing inconsistencies and redundancies. The data collected require sophisticated mechanisms to analyze it. Preprocessing techniques are able to adapt the data to the requirements posed by each data mining algorithm, and it allows to enable process data that would be unfeasible otherwise [17].

Dataset Preview. Before application of preprocessing techniques, data was analyzed seeking to understand how it was collected, we can highlight: a) The 86.45% of data was collected around the Cuenca, Ecuador city, and only the rest of records were collected from other cities, it creates a requirement of data extrapolation to the rest of cities, however, this technique can create bad results due to the statistical estimation [18], and b) the elapsed time for each level is an accumulative value, therefore, is required to extract the proper values.

Derivation of Columns. It is possible to derive some relevant data from fields: from birthday is obtained the age field, however, there were people who typed the present date (dd-mm-2021) as birthday creating inconsistencies into data. On the other hand, times of levels was derived by the subtraction of level time and previous level time.

Drop Non-relevant Data. In the first stage, wrong typed data as birthday was dropped, even though some imputing methods were taking into account to maintain the collected data, it does not mirror the true fields and finally it was dropped. In addition, was dropped: name, phone, birthday due to age was obtained, city due concentration, based on they do not contribute to this work.

Data Scaling. Prior to data modeling, the min-max scaler $(-1, 1)$ was used to normalize data [19], the posterior stage includes the application of a grouping algorithm and it is considered as an isotropic technique that commonly requires data normalization [20].

3.3 Data Mining Modeling

This stage is focused on build and assess the data mining techniques until to get the proper set of steps, algorithms, and parameters whose can contribute and display results without issues caused by a fast algorithms application [21].

Modeling Techniques. From the article written by Bauckhage et al. [22], we can extract that games have been boarded from multiple analytic views mainly how they are played, it allows a better understanding of player behavior, and it is commonly used to help improving a game's design, or ensure the best user experience, or identifying valuable players, or those at risk of leaving a game. The authors provide a tutorial on cluster analysis for game behavioral data. The clustering technique is focused on group a set of objects such that similar ones are assigned to the same group. In this context, players or artificial agents can be grouped via finite sets of features.

K-means algorithm is commonly used in game analytics, due to the simplicity and popularity. However, in centroid methods is necessary to define the number of clusters; hence, algorithms then determine the centers and assign the objects to the nearest one, but different distance techniques are possible and lead to different variants of clustering [22]. The PCA technique was used as complement the clustering, it was focused on dimensional reduction and allow to plot the clusters created by the k-means, the variance of dimensional reduction was used as real representation indicator [19].

Test Design Generation. A test stage was designed to get the best grouping parameters, and according to the algorithm the needed preprocessing techniques. The first issue is the number of groups required to run the algorithm, a variant of k-means named x-means was used, unlike k-means this variant uses two parameters (start number of groups and end number of groups) to calculate the suitable number of groups. In this stage, multiple executions from starting from 02 until 50 groups were tested. The number of groups to get a proper grouping application was between two and four groups. and, the total amount of PCA variance was closely to 1.

Building the Data Mining Model. This data mining approach aims to discover patterns hidden in groups of players among the game levels. This is based on two stages: a) The clusters are going to be create using variables such as: age, gender, start time, end time for each level. And the stage b) The times are evaluated according to centroids of groups of players, and the radar plots are used to achieve this evaluation.

Data Mining Model Assessment. To get the assess of this approach, multiple executions of algorithms are evaluated approximate 20 times until to obtain results that we indicate a real human behavior.

3.4 Visual Analytics

This technique consists on transforming different data types into visual representations. The most important feature of this technique is the incorporation of human capabilities for data analysis [23]. This strategy is used to evaluate data labeled by different clusters. In this subsection, we recommend the most useful graphics to define the scenarios, and detect the patterns. The commonly visualization methods are: Line chart, Bar chart, Pie chart, Scatter plot, Bubble Char, Parallel Coordinates, and TreeMaps [24]. However, based on the visualization methods, the below methods are described to search patterns in the game of pairs:

- Bar Chart: It is considered as columns plot, and is used to examine multiple aspects of the data. It is helpful to visually quantify the demographical data.
- Scatter plot: Is considered as two dimensional plot showing the relation between the two variables. It focuses in showing how the data is spread over the two-dimensional plane. Complementary to this chart, the PCA is used as dimensional reduction until get two dimensions and generate the 2D plot.
- Radar (spider or web) chart: It is a two-dimensional chart type designed to plot one or more series of values over multiple quantitative features [25].

4 Results and Discussion

After the methodology applied, below we present the results obtained with the use of the visual analytics for detecting hidden patterns in times of players.

4.1 Clustering Analysis by Time of Level

The Fig. 2 shows the clustering approach applied for each level, as above is describe each level has collected two variables (start time and end time), in addition the age feature was added to the clustering.

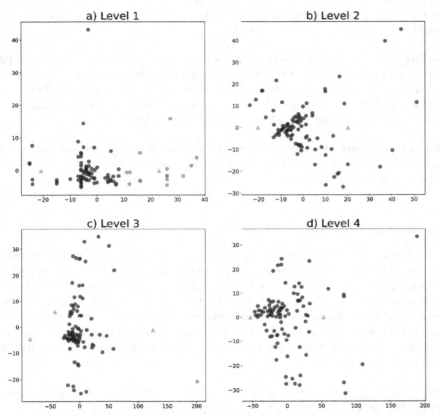

Fig. 2. K-means clustering, the red points represent the centroids for each group. (Color figure online)

From Fig. 2, part a) Level 1 shows three groups and each group has a similar density, based on this, it is possible to describe that it is caused by the start time is too similar for all players. In part b) Level 2 there are two groups well defined, however, a big part of data is only in one cluster, it leads us to interpretate that there are many similarities of time among players when they solve the level 2. In part c) shows k-means clustering created three groups where two of them are catching data, so it leads us to pay a special attention to this data, and try to discover patterns of time among players in level 3. Finally, Figure d) shows a similar behavior that part c) therefore, this is also selected to deep about features of grouping in the below subsection.

4.2 Analysis of Centroids by Radar Plot

The centroids of groups help to decrease the complexity of analysis, due to a centroid is a vector created by one number for each feature. Each number is the mean of the feature for the observations in that cluster [26].

Analysis by Game Levels. The centroids of clusters are evaluated for each level aiming to collect patterns of players' behavior (Fig. 3).

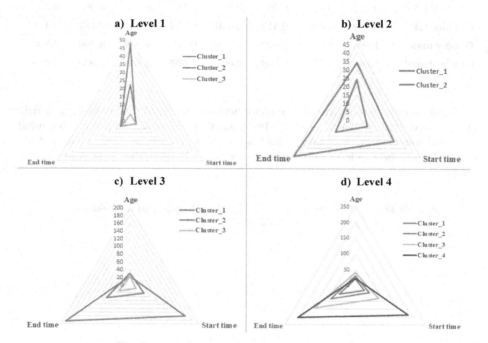

Fig. 3. Clustering centroids analysis by game levels.

The first part of the figure shows a complete normal general behavior of players due to start time and end time are no showing distortions in the series.

Analysis of Players Behavior by Gender. In addition to the above analysis, features were added and removed using the wrapped method, this method normally is used in feature selection tasks, when features of age, game points, levels and gender was used then the x-means technique created eight groups, however, the groups were spitted into four for male, and four female groups. The centroids of x-means are showed in Table 2. This leads us to determinate an existence of special groups of behavior by gender players.

Table 2. Centroids of clustering after adding gender features.

Feature	C1	C2	C3	C4	C5	C6	C7	C8
Age	0.644	0.317	0.252	0.583	0.430	0.337	0.306	0.569
Points	0.763	0.905	0.603	0.190	0.740	0.880	0.998	0.369
End time L1	0.019	0.027	0.032	0.083	0.025	0.022	0.014	0.026
End time L2	0.061	0.070	0.092	0.196	0.082	0.067	0.040	0.103
End time L3	0.162	0.145	0.200	0.374	0.188	0.148	0.096	0.261
End time L4	0.329	0.280	0.412	0.690	0.374	0.281	0.187	0.476
Gender male	**1.000**	**1.000**	**1.000**	**1.000**	**0.000**	**0.000**	**0.000**	**0.000**
Gender female	**0.000**	**0.000**	**0.000**	**0.000**	**1.000**	**1.000**	**1.000**	**1.000**

Figure 4 describes a particular behavior between male and female players, female players have similar times to pass each level, due they are solved the pairs with normal time, and some ladies lose game points but they try to reduce the time in pairing task. Unlike ladies, the gentlemen do not try to reduce time when they lose points across levels.

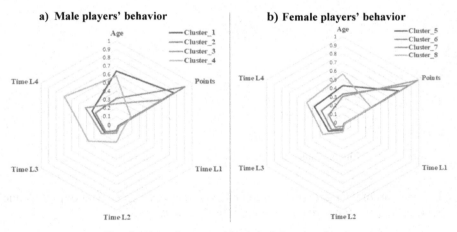

Fig. 4. Clustering centroids analysis by game levels.

5   Conclusions

This work is focused to discover hidden patterns in data collected from a serious game, this game was created to improve the skills of attention and memory of the users, the features collected when using the game allowed to apply data mining processes, allowing analyzing hidden patterns among players. Data mining was based in include the iterative application of preprocessing techniques, and evaluation of results. This allows us to demonstrate the natural human behavior. Also, the evaluation of the final model showed us that results do not change in another execution.

We detect a strong relevance of age and gender features among patterns of players, being these patterns were clearer when players were faceted to high levels. This approach allows us knowledge of human behavior while they are face to solve games. In future work, we will include other set of serious games, with the purpose of generate a comparison with results obtained for detecting if exists patterns are general among players or if exists patterns are emerging in the game in isolation.

References

1. Michael, D.R., Chen, S.L.: Serious games: games that educate, train, and inform (2005)
2. Torrente, J., Freire, M., Moreno-Ger, P., Fernández-Manjón, B.: Evaluation of semi-automatically generated accessible interfaces for educational games. Comput. Educ. **83**, 103–117 (2015). https://doi.org/10.1016/j.compedu.2015.01.002
3. Spyridonis, F., Daylamani-Zad, D.: A serious game to improve engagement with web accessibility guidelines. Behav. Inf. Technol. **40**(6), 587–596 (2020). https://doi.org/10.1080/014 4929X.2019.1711453
4. Jaramillo-Alcazar, A., Lujan-Mora, S., Salvador-Ullauri, L.: Accessibility assessment of mobile serious games for people with cognitive impairments. In: Proceedings - 2017 International Conference on Information Systems and Computer Science, INCISCOS 2017, November 2017, pp. 323–328 (2018). https://doi.org/10.1109/INCISCOS.2017.12
5. Chi, H., Agama, E., Prodanoff, Z.G.: Developing serious games to promote cognitive abilities for the elderly. In: 2017 IEEE 5th International Conference on Serious Games and Applications for Health, SeGAH 2017, pp. 1–8 (2017). https://doi.org/10.1109/SeGAH.2017.793 9279
6. Khenissi, M.A., Essalmi, F., Jemni, M., Kinshuk: A learning version of memory match game. In: Proceedings - IEEE 14th International Conference on Advanced Learning Technologies, ICALT 2014, pp. 209–210 (2014). https://doi.org/10.1109/ICALT.2014.67
7. Slimani, A., Elouaai, F., Elaachak, L., Yedri, O.B., Bouhorma, M.: Learning analytics through serious games: data mining algorithms for performance measurement and improvement purposes. Int. J. Emerg. Technol. Learn. **13**, 46–64 (2018). https://doi.org/10.3991/ijet.v13i01. 7518
8. Alonso-Fernández, C., Pérez-Colado, I., Freire, M., Martínez-Ortiz, I., Fernández-Manjón, B.: Improving serious games analyzing learning analytics data: lessons learned. In: Gentile, M., Allegra, M., Söbke, H. (eds.) GALA 2018. LNCS, vol. 11385, pp. 287–296. Springer, Cham (2019). https://doi.org/10.1007/978-3-030-11548-7_27
9. Valladares-Rodríguez, S., Anido-Rifón, L., Fernández-Iglesias, M.J., Facal-Mayo, D.: A machine learning approach to the early diagnosis of Alzheimer's disease based on an ensemble of classifiers. In: Misra, S., et al. (eds.) ICCSA 2019. LNCS, vol. 11619, pp. 383–396. Springer, Cham (2019). https://doi.org/10.1007/978-3-030-24289-3_28
10. Rego, P., Moreira, P.M., Reis, L.P.: Serious games for rehabilitation: a survey and a classification towards a taxonomy. In: Proceedings 5th Iberian Conference on Information Systems and Technologies, CIST 2010, pp. 1–6 (2010)
11. Söbke, H., Streicher, A.: Serious games architectures and engines. In: Dörner, R., Göbel, S., Kickmeier-Rust, M., Masuch, M., Zweig, K. (eds.) Entertainment Computing and Serious Games. LNCS, vol. 9970, pp. 148–173. Springer, Cham (2016). https://doi.org/10.1007/978-3-319-46152-6_7

12. Bockholt, M., Zweig, K.A.: Why is this so hard? Insights from the state space of a simple board game. In: Göbel, S., Ma, M., Baalsrud Hauge, J., Oliveira, M.F., Wiemeyer, J., Wendel, V. (eds.) JCSG 2015. LNCS, vol. 9090, pp. 147–157. Springer, Cham (2015). https://doi.org/10.1007/978-3-319-19126-3_13

13. Gamito, P., et al.: Cognitive training on stroke patients via virtual reality-based serious games. Disabil. Rehabil. **39**, 385–388 (2017). https://doi.org/10.3109/09638288.2014.934925

14. Sehaba, K., Mille, A., Hussaan, A.M.: Tailoring serious games with adaptive pedagogical scenarios a serious game for persons with cognitive disabilities (2011). https://doi.org/10.1109/ICALT.2011.152

15. Halim, Z., Atif, M., Rashid, A., Edwin, C.A.: Profiling players using real-world datasets: clustering the data and correlating the results with the big-five personality traits. IEEE Trans. Affect. Comput. **10**, 568–584 (2019). https://doi.org/10.1109/TAFFC.2017.2751602

16. Menéndez Domínguez, V.H., Castellanos Bolaños, M.E.: SPEM: Software Process Engineering Metamodel. Rev. Latinoam. Ing. Softw. **3**, 92 (2015). https://doi.org/10.18294/relais.2015.92-100

17. García, S., Ramírez-Gallego, S., Luengo, J., Benítez, J.M., Herrera, F.: Big data preprocessing: methods and prospects. Big Data Anal. **1**, 1–22 (2016)

18. Forbes, V.E., Calow, P., Sibly, R.M.: The extrapolation problem and how population modeling can help. Environ. Toxicol. Chem. **27**, 1987–1994 (2008). https://doi.org/10.1897/08-029.1

19. Buitinck, L., et al.: API design for machine learning software: experiences from the scikit-learn project. In: ECML PKDD Workshop: Languages for Data Mining and Machine Learning, pp. 108–122 (2013)

20. Wu, X., et al.: Top 10 algorithms in data mining. Knowl. Inf. Syst. **14**(1), 1–37 (2008). https://doi.org/10.1007/s10115-007-0114-2

21. Chapman, P., et al.: CRISP-DM 1.0: step-by-step data mining guide. SPSS inc. **9**, 13 (2000)

22. Bauckhage, C., Drachen, A., Sifa, R.: Clustering game behavior data. IEEE Trans. Comput. Intell. AI Games. **7**, 266–278 (2015). https://doi.org/10.1109/TCIAIG.2014.2376982

23. Chen, W., Guo, F., Wang, F.: A survey of traffic data visualization. IEEE Trans. Intell. Transp. Syst. **16**, 2970–2984 (2015). https://doi.org/10.1109/TITS.2015.2436897

24. Santhi, K., Reddy, R.M.: Critical analysis of big visual analytics: a survey. In: 2018 IADS International Conference on Computing, Communications & Data Engineering (CCODE) (2018)

25. Saary, M.J.: Radar plots: a useful way for presenting multivariate health care data. J. Clin. Epidemiol. **61**, 311–317 (2008). https://doi.org/10.1016/j.jclinepi.2007.04.021

26. Leisch, F.: A toolbox for K-centroids cluster analysis. Comput. Stat. Data Anal. **51**, 526–544 (2006). https://doi.org/10.1016/j.csda.2005.10.006

Indoor Smart Walker Based on Artificial Vision for the Autonomous Movement of Seniors with Mobility Problems and Reduced Vision

José Guamushig-Laica[1], Miguel Jerez-Gavilánez[1], Darío Mendoza-Chipantasi[1(✉)], and Jessica Mariño-Salguero[2(✉)]

[1] Universidad de Fuerzas Armadas ESPE, Quijano y Ordoñez, Latacunga 050102, Ecuador
djmendoza@espe.edu.ec
[2] Technische Universität Darmstadt, Dolivostraße 15, 64293 Darmstadt, Germany
marino@fnb.tu-darmstadt.de

Abstract. The usual solution to mobility problems for the elderly lies in the use of conventional canes and walkers. However, when the older adult also has vision problems, these devices are not sufficient to provide safe walking, and the senior suffers from constant falls. This article proposes a smart walker based on artificial vision for indoor use in nursing homes that safely enables autonomous mobility for visually impaired seniors. The walker has been equipped with activation switches on the handlebars, ultrasonic sensors, a Kinect visual sensor, traction motors, and a controller. The control algorithm is based on reactive navigation, odometry and artificial vision and is designed to avoid obstacles and detect dangerous situations such as stairs. The control unit is a Raspberry Pi running Raspbian and relies on message passing between processes and visualization. The prototype of the smart walker is implemented in the nursing home "Luis Maldonado Tamayo" (Pujilí-Ecuador), where tests are being carried out with elderly persons who still have motor skills and some partial vision impairment. The walker can effectively detect obstacles in a distance range from $50 - 86$ cm. Almost 90% of small, 96% medium, and 98% dynamics obstacles are avoided. The demonstration video is available at https://youtu.be/MJzvzIily4k.

Keywords: Intelligent walker · Senior – mobility · Machine vision · Image processing · Mobile robotics

1 Introduction

In the last decade, many seniors have lost their ability to see because of aging, which in turn has reduced their ability to move around independently [1]. Seniors are aware that a lack of vision can cause accidents to themselves and others [2], so they limit their mobility or do so under the supervision of a caregiver. According to the WHO, approximately 28–35% of people over 65 years old suffer falls each year. This problem increases to 32–42% for those over 70 years of age. Approximately 30–50% of the older

© Springer Nature Switzerland AG 2022
F. R. Narváez et al. (Eds.): SmartTech-IC 2021, CCIS 1532, pp. 69–83, 2022.
https://doi.org/10.1007/978-3-030-99170-8_6

people live in nursing homes, and around 40% of them lose their balance and fall each year [3].

To reduce the problem of falls, in recent years, the use of walkers has increased as they provide support, help to maintain balance, and improve the independent mobility of seniors [4, 5]. There is a wide range of conventional walkers on the market, which can be classified into standard, two-front-wheeled, and four-wheeled types. The standard walker is a four-legged aluminum frame that must be lifted and moved forward while walking [6]. The two-wheeled front walker is designed for people with weaker upper extremities or the ones who tend to fall backward when the equipment is lifted. The four-wheeled walker does not need to be lifted and has systems that allow it to roll and pivot smoothly and with little effort. However, they provide less stability, as a save motion control of the device depends on the user's quick reaction time for braking. Therefore, using a walker requires muscle strength, coordination, and reaction capacity [7].

Smart walkers are similar to four-wheeled walkers, but in most cases, they are equipped with two motorized wheels and two caster wheels to ease the movement [8, 9]. Furthermore, they include electronic and robotic components, thus promoting better walking assistance [8, 10, 11], especially in terms of navigation [12, 13], gait monitoring [14, 15], and partial body weight support [16]. Navigation and obstacle detection employs vision, ultrasonic, and infrared sensors capable of detecting obstacles even while moving [10, 17]. The control system helps the user avoid obstacles by sound or vibration signals and directly changes the motor trajectory [18]. This feature is essential for people with progressive vision loss or to help navigate environments with multiple dynamic obstacles. Other functionalities include automatic navigation and localization inside buildings and outdoors [10, 15], which help people with cognitive and related memory and location problems [19].

Some current indoor smart walker models are detailed: FriWalk [20] is a commercial walker with a guidance system that can guide the user through locations along a planned path. A webcam detects QR-codes placed on the flour, and in combination with incremental encoders, control the movement of the brushless motors installed in the rear wheels. The AGoRA Smart Walker [8] measures the walker's ego-motion with two encoders and an Inertial Measurement Unit (IMU) while sensing the obstacles with a 2D Light Detection and Ranging Sensor. The low-rise and dynamic obstacles are detected by two ultrasonic boards and an HD camera. The Smart Walker V [21] is an indoor walker that senses the surrounding with RGB and depth sensors. This walker creates a graph-based simultaneous localization and mapping (SLAM) using Real-Time Appearance-based Mapping (RTAB-Map) and gets the odometry with a Robotic Operating System (ROS). The indoor smart robotic walker presented in [22] is based on a deep neural network. It tracks users in the front and predicts the movement of the user using different sensors. An infrared temperature sensor and a lidar sensor mounted on the walker in front of the user's knee and foot detect the lower limb gait. A soft-robotic interface [23] on the handle monitors abnormal force pressure to activate the emergency brake to prevent falls. Four microphones locate sound sources, and the walker navigates toward it using the RL-based SSL technique when the users say specific keywords. The odometry is based on an IMU and encoders.

Despite the remarkable technological development in these devices, they are still not free of problems, and some situations instigate the user to fall. Further, such aid tools are still not affordable for everyone, and many of the control techniques used are still only applicable in laboratories. These problems motivate us to seek a viable solution and develop a walker with sufficient intelligence and interaction to ensure safe mobility for seniors, especially with progressive impairment of vision due to aging.

In this article, we propose a novel smart walker that helps seniors with motor and vision problems to walk safely indoors in nursing homes. The device detects dangerous situations (unseen obstacles or uneven floors) indoors with the help of artificial vision techniques introduced in the control algorithm of the intelligent walker. Thus, it avoids sedentary lifestyles in people with reduced vision who fear injury due to accidents caused by collisions with objects present inside nursing homes.

2   Smart Walker Design

The smart walker is designed to meet the mobility needs of seniors in nursing homes with reduced mobility and visual problems. Table 1 summarizes the most important design conditions, while Fig. 1 shows the 3D model of the proposed smart walker and its three modules: mechanical system, electrical/electronic system, and control system.

Table 1. Smart walker design requirements

Concept	Necessity	Parameter
Application	Indoor design, accessibility	Distance between wheels 60 cm
	Lower speed than the average elderly walking speed 0.81 m/s [24] for safe walking	Max speed 0,5 m/s
	Extended operating period	Min 2 h
	Obstacle avoidance	Max perception distance 3 m; min camera resolution and focus of 640 × 480 Mpx
	Simple graphical interface	Touchscreen size 7 Inch^2
	30% body weight support	Average elderly weight 60 kg
Manufacturing	Adjustable hand support height	Minimum height 80 cm
	Lightweight	Max 100 N
	Static and dynamic stability	4 wheels
	Brake system	
Control	Simple and effective motion	2 motors and 2 support wheels
	Open-source technology	Linux platform
	Sensor-driven	Distance from user to sensors 10 cm
Cost	Low cost	

2.1 Mechanical System

Structure. The device consists of four castor wheels to facilitate mobility and avoid back propulsion problems and an aluminum structure frame with adjustable armrests. The electronic components are encapsulated in an acrylic housing with a rigid aluminum base installed directly on the wheels to balance the structure's weight and increase the wheels' grip. In addition, the walker has a height-adjustable aluminum base that supports the minicomputer for the user interface and the vision sensor. **Drive system.** Two DC motors with gearboxes, the Gear Turbo Motor 12V model with high torque at 110 RPM, are installed on the rear wheels. This selection considered the displacement speed of 0.5 m/s, wheel diameter of 173 mm, a friction coefficient of 0.5, approximate weight of the walker of 100 N, and the 30% of body support. **Displacement mechanism.** A differential drive is selected to combine standing support and an effective control strategy [22]. It consists of two front active split wheel offset casters wheels, and two rear caster wheels mounted parallel to the structure. The caster wheels have a good grip on surfaces, thus avoiding slipping and responding quickly [9].

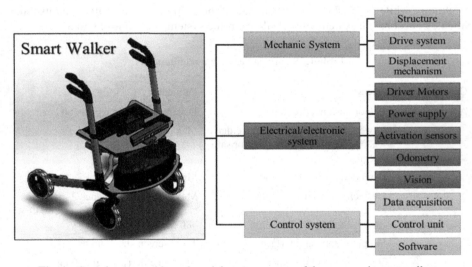

Fig. 1. Complete assembly and modular components of the proposed smart walker.

2.2 Electrical/Electronic System

Driver motors. We use a Mosfet IRF3205 controller module. **Power supply.** Two lithium-polymer batteries, LIPO PRO-7600 mAh with a nominal voltage of 11.8 V, are used. One for the control system and the other for the motor power supply. **Activation sensors.** An ultrasonic sensor HC-SR04 is placed at the user's waist height, and two force sensors FSR402 are installed on the device's handles. The ultrasonic sensor detects the presence of the person at the rear for actuation. The force sensors need to be pressed by the user to start the operation. Thus, the dual activation control prevents accidental activation of the walker. **Odometry.** Two encoders and a low-cost and highly accurate inertial measurement unit MPU-6050 measure the parameters to determine the position and orientation of the walker during navigation. The walker also has rotation direction pushbuttons incorporated in the handles of the walker device that allow rotation in the direction of the sensor that is actuated. The inclusion of these pushbuttons allows the user a small percentage of control, but with the ever-present condition of obstacle avoidance. **Vision.** The vision sensor is an Xbox 360 Kinect unit. It can generate depth maps from an infrared sensor and an RGB camera. The camera position on the walker reduces the mapping angle, which hinders the detection of objects at close range. So, we installed 3 HC-SR04 ultrasonic sensors on the walker's front left, center, and right to detect nearby obstacles properly.

2.3 Control

Data acquisition. We acquire data from the Kinect sensor and an embedded Arduino Mega 2560 system with 16 digital pins and 2 analogue pins. The Arduino receives data from motors, pushbuttons, force, and ultrasonic sensors. **Control unit.** The walker motion is controlled by a Raspberry Pi 3 card connected to a touchscreen that facilitates interaction with the user. **Software.** The control program is developed on the Raspbian Jessie platform. It uses the *pyserial* library to communicate the Arduino, Raspberry Pi 3 and OpenCV (Open-Source Computer Vision) library for real-time image processing. Fig. 2 shows the flowchart of the control program. For the serial communication between the Raspberry Pi 3 embedded system and the Arduino controller board, the COMSERIAL script belonging to the Raspberry Pi programming files is used. This script, written in Python, specifies the communication parameters, encodes the data to be sent to the Arduino, decodes the data received from the Arduino, and closes the communication ports once the system is finished.

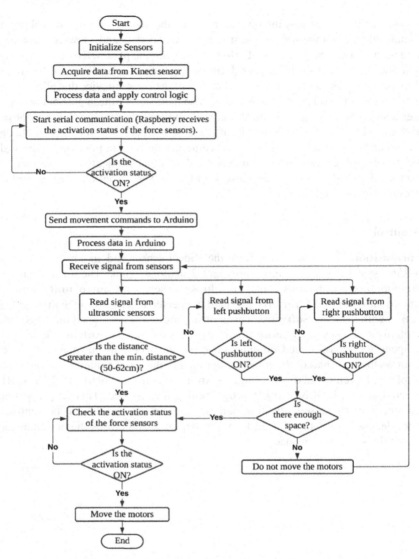

Fig. 2. Block diagram of the walker control program

3 Object Detection Algorithm

The object detection algorithm identifies obstacles present at a certain distance and emits control signals to the motors. The algorithm for digital image processing consists of 5 stages: capture, preprocessing, segmentation, feature extraction, and object identification.

3.1 Capture

The acquisition data from the RGB camera of the Kinect sensor is complemented with the depth image-based plane provided by the infrared sensor of the same. Therefore, two functions are implemented. The first one obtains the data from the RGB camera, and the second one the information from the infrared depth sensor. The information is received in real-time and stored in variables to be processed in the following stages or visualized (see Fig. 3).

The default image depth image-based plane format is an 11-bit depth map. It contains much information to distances but is inadequate to be visualized with the *imshow* method of OpenCV, so the image is converted to an 8-bit format to visualize and understand the information captured by the sensor graphically.

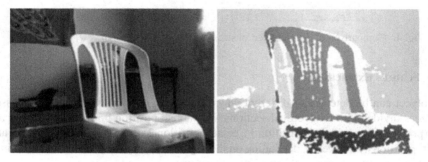

Fig. 3. Acquisition functions output images

3.2 Preprocessing

As shown in Fig. 3, small white areas represent the noise in the data acquisition. For this reason, filtering processes must be applied to obtain a clear image and avoid the erroneous detection of objects.

The filtering process is given by *erode* and *dilate* states. *Erode* stage removes black spaces within the region of interest, and *dilate* stages magnify white regions in areas that should be black. For the *dilate* stage, the initial definition of the kernel size is critical before applying morphological transformations. The kernel is the matrix used to apply the *dilate* convolution. A comparison of the image with different kernel sizes is shown in Fig. 4. Insufficient kernel size captures blobs or objects of smaller areas, mostly noise present in the data acquisition. These are false positives present in the displayed scene due to the range limitations of the Kinect sensor.

3.3 Segmentation

To create a distance segmentation function, we placed the Kinect sensor in front of a wall and sampled from 0 m to 3.5 m considering an approximate viewing angle of 70°. The results (see Table 2) were used to find a correlation between distance and value in the depth map.

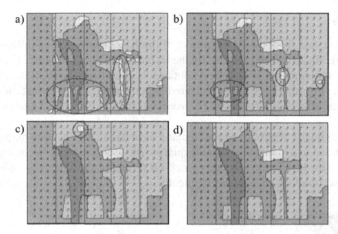

Fig. 4. Comparison of different kernel sizes a) 3 × 3, b) 5 × 5, c) 7 × 7, and d) 9 × 9

3.4 Feature Extraction

An object can be detected in different ways depending on its position. The processed image is divided into five vertical sections to establish position limits. The sections are left (position 0), center-left (position 1), center (position 2), center-right (position 3), and right (position 4). However, depending on the object's size, the object can share sections and thus generate more possibilities of occupancy.

The algorithm checks if an object is within one of the five sections. The function is called occupancy status indicator and returns a logical value of 0 or 1. Value 0 returns if the object is within the ranges of that section. Otherwise, it returns value 1.

Table 2. Correspondence of distance on the depth map from 0 m to 3.5 m.

Analogy	Distance (cm)	Depth map value
0	Less than 50	80
1	50–62	100
2	62–74	120
3	74–86	140
4	86–98	160
5	98–110	180
6	110–122	200
7	More than 122	220

4 Object Identification

The following process is the control logic based on the occupancy status indicator function and the depth map value resulting from the segmentation. This process generates a truth table with 25 possible cases and activates the parameters: *move* and *show*. The *move* sends information to the Arduino to control the motors and *show* displays the direction in the output image to avoid possible objects.

Figure 5 represents an output format of the resulting image. The vertical lines indicate the division of the sections, and the numbers, the analogy corresponding to the depth. The area of higher intensity marked with the number 2 is the area that is processed within the code to avoid the obstacle.

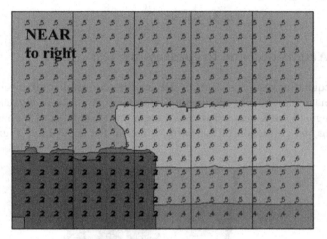

Fig. 5. Output processing format

5 Stairs Detection Algorithm

For accurate stairs detection, we consider the geometric configuration shown in Fig. 6. The Kinect unit's tilt motor angle is 20°, and the distance from the sensor to the ground plane is about 80 cm.

Since the acquisition plane of the Kinect sensor has an angle, its projection to the floor plane is used. It is assumed that the floor is fixed and has no representative inclination. We extract the lower pixels of the image to create a region of interest (ROI) that allows us to detect the floor. If the distance acquired from the depth map increases, the walker is in front of a staircase and movement in that direction is disabled.

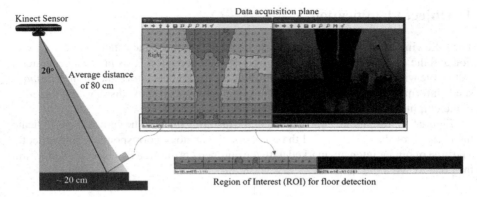

Fig. 6. Stair detection process.

6 Image Acquisition and Preprocessing Test

The image acquisition test consisted of verifying the acquisition of the RGB and depth data of the image individually and then unifying them. In this test, we determined the optimal tilt angle of the Kinect sensor and the appropriate number of frames per second for processing and correction of the mirror effect in the acquisition. Figure 7 shows

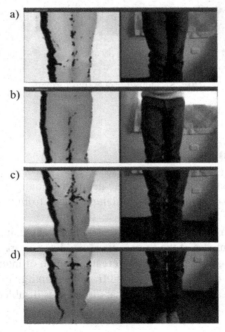

Fig. 7. Testing data acquisition at different tilt angles of the Kinect sensor: a) 30°, b) 25°, c) 20°, and d) 15°.

the images acquired at four different tilt angles towards the floor of the Kinect sensor. The most appropriate angle was 20°, which voids detection of the floor in the walking direction and optimizes the detection of small objects in front of the walker.

7 Results and Discussion

This smart walker was designed for indoor use in nursing homes. Therefore, its objective is the avoidance of obstacles in a controlled environment that generally has everyday static objects such as chairs, tables, and others and dynamic actions such as crossing people.

The prototype is tested in the nursing home, HOGAR DE VIDA "Luis Maldonado Tamayo", located in the Canton Pujilí-Ecuador. The center houses 45 older people, 50% of whom have progressive vision loss and lack of mobility in their lower limbs to move freely within the home. The population used for the functional tests was 30 seniors who still have motor skills and partial vision impairment. The tests consisted of assisted walking using the smart walker within the nursing home facilities. The tests were performed during the day in the periods set aside for the physical activity. The duration of each walk depended on the time required for each user to walk around the nursing home facilities.

7.1 Distance Detection

Fifty obstacle detection tests were performed. Each test consisted of detecting four obstacles located at different distance ranges measured from the user's position to validate the acquisition of the depth image. Table 3 summarizes the test results. At distances less than 50 cm, a 78% detection rate is achieved, while at distances between 50 and 62 cm 90%, and for distances greater than 62 cm 94%. We observed that the Kinetic unit does not detect correctly small objects at a distance less than 50 cm. So, in the detection algorithm, the ultrasonic sensors are mandatorily activated at distances less than 50 cm.

The algorithm has an effective response for a distance of more than 62 cm. However, there is a possibility that dynamic objects may quickly position themselves very close to the walker; therefore, a safety measure within the algorithm is included for distances between 50 and 62 cm.

Table 3. Distance detection test

	Depth detection range (Analogy)			
	<50 cm (0)	50–62 cm (1)	62–74 cm (2)	74–86 cm (3)
Detect	38	45	47	47
No detect	12	5	3	3

7.2 Detection and Avoidance of Small Objects

We placed boxes of $(17 \times 6 \times 6)$ cm^3 at different positions in front of the walker for this test, as shown in Fig. 8. A visualization image of the depth map is obtained with the identifiers according to analogies of Table 2. The word "Left" triggers the movement to the left to avoid the obstacle.

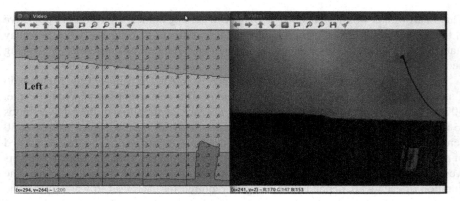

Fig. 8. Detection of small objects and actions

Table 4 summarizes the number of small objects detected during 40 tests with different users. At each test, the device follows different paths hindered by a varying number of boxes (from 1 to 5). The effectiveness of detection of small objects was about 89%.

Table 4. Small object detection and avoidance test

Test	Total objects	Detect	No detect	Effectivity
40	83	74	9	89,16

7.3 Detection and Avoidance of Medium-Sized Objects

Similarly, at the previous test, a box of $(50 \times 45 \times 6)$ cm^3 is placed in different positions in front of the walker. Table 5 shows the number of detected and undetected medium-sized objects resulting from 40 tests with different users and following paths hindered from 1 to 3 objects. The effectiveness of detection of medium-sized objects is about 96%.

7.4 Dynamic Object Detection

Dynamic objects are people or objects that, for some reason, are in motion. For this test, one or two people move quickly and spontaneously towards the walker. The algorithm detects the person and sends instructions to avoid her/his, as shown in Fig. 9.

Table 5. Medium object detection test

Tests	Total objects	Detect	No detect	Effectivity
40	80	77	3	96,25%

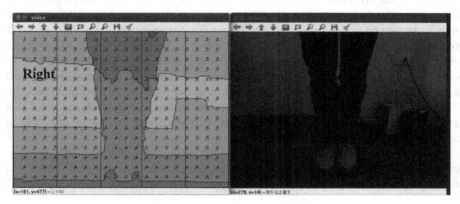

Fig. 9. Detection and evasion of persons

Table 6 collects the results of 40 tests, of which half of the assisted walks had to evade one person, and the remaining had to evade two people. The results show more than 98% effectiveness in this scenario.

Table 6. Dynamic object detection and avoidance testing

N. Tests	N. objects	Detect	No detect	Effectivity
40	60	59	1	98,33%

8   Conclusions

A smart walker has been designed and built for indoor use in nursing homes, which with the help of the depth images provided by the Kinect and the use of the OpenCV library, can avoid obstacles. The depth images obtained by the Kinect unit are processed in real-time, using various filters and sectioning. The image was divided into five vertical sections, and within the control algorithm, an occupancy state was implemented to optimize the object detection stage.

In addition, given that the Kinect acquisition range is from approximately 50 cm, it was decided to complement the object avoidance with ultrasonic sensors distributed in three directions and thus obtain better results. However, the data acquisition time of the ultrasonic sensors adds time delay in the serial communication between the Raspberry

Pi 3 control board and the Arduino. For this reason, a separate Arduino nano was used to acquire the distances of these sensors and avoid obstacles in real-time.

The control algorithm also includes stairs detection and immediately stops the device if these are detected.

Comparing the proposed smart walker with some of the models developed by the references as the FriWalk [20] or AGoRA [8] smart walkers, our device has significantly fewer sensors and components and offers similar walking assistance to the reference models. According to the functionality tests, our device can avoid almost 90% of small, 96% medium, and 98% dynamics obstacles. Besides, the present smart walker is not based on commercial robotic prototypes with high-cost laboratory sensors as the mentioned models. Our smart walker uses free software, allowing it to be easily replicated and uses low-cost components which are easy to acquire but are still accurate enough. The approximate device cost is around 2,145 US dollars. Another advantage of this device is its light weight and its geometry suitable for the size percentiles of people in the Latin America region, allowing easy mobility.

During the operation tests, it was observed that objects with characteristics of transparency or reflectance cannot be detected or are partially detected, so solutions to this problem will be investigated in future works.

References

1. Schwanen, T., Páez, A.: The mobility of older people – an introduction. J. Transp. Geogr. **18**, 591–595 (2010)
2. Whelan, M., Langford, J., Oxley, J., Koppel, S., Charlton, J.: The elderly and mobility: a review of the literature (2006)
3. Organization, W.H., Ageing, W.H.O., Unit, L.C.: WHO global report on falls prevention in older age. World Health Organization (2008)
4. Tagawa, Y., Shiba, N., Matsuo, S., Yamashita, T.: Analysis of human abnormal walking using a multi-body model: joint models for abnormal walking and walking aids to reduce compensatory action. J. Biomech. **33**, 1405–1414 (2000)
5. Gell, N.M., Wallace, R.B., Lacroix, A.Z., Mroz, T.M., Patel, T.M.: Mobility device use in older adults and incidence of falls and worry about falling: findings from the 2011–2012 national health and aging trends study. J. Am. Geriatr. Soc. **63**(5), 853–859 (2015). https://doi.org/10.1111/jgs.13393
6. Costa, N., Caldwell, D.G.: Control of a biomimetic" soft-actuated" 10dof lower body exoskeleton. In: The First IEEE/RAS-EMBS International Conference on Biomedical Robotics and Biomechatronics, BioRob 2006, pp. 495–501 (2006)
7. Mundt, M., Batista, J.P., Markert, B., Bollheimer, C., Laurentius, T.: Walking with rollator: a systematic review of gait parameters in older persons. Eur. Rev. Aging Phys. Activity **16** (2019)
8. Sierra, M., Jimenez, S.D., Frizera-Neto, A., Munera, M., Cifuentes, C.A.: Control strategies for human–robot–environment interaction in assisted gait with smart walkers. In: Interfacing Humans and Robots for Gait Assistance and Rehabilitation, pp. 259–286. Springer, Cham (2022). https://doi.org/10.1007/978-3-030-79630-3_10
9. Page, S., Saint-Bauzel, L., Rumeau, P., Pasqui, V.: Smart walkers: an application-oriented review. Robotica **35**(6), 1243–1262 (2017). https://doi.org/10.1017/S0263574716000023

10. Aristizabal-Aristizabal, J., Ferro-Rugeles, R., Lancheros-Vega, M., Sierra M., S.D., Múnera, M., Cifuentes, C.A.: Fundamentals for the design of smart walkers. In: Interfacing Humans and Robots for Gait Assistance and Rehabilitation, pp. 121–141. Springer, Cham (2022). https://doi.org/10.1007/978-3-030-79630-3_4
11. Alves, J., Seabra, E., Caetano, I., Santos, C.P.: Overview of the ASBGo++ Smart Walker. In: ENBENG 2017 – 5th Portuguese Meeting on Bioengineering, Proceedings (2017)
12. Morris, A., Donamukkala, R., Kapuria, A., Steinfeld, A., Matthews, J.T., Dunbar-Jacob, J., Thrun, S.: A robotic walker that provides guidance. In: 2003 IEEE International Conference on Robotics and Automation (Cat. No. 03CH37422), pp. 25–30 (2003)
13. Werner, C., Moustris, G.P., Tzafestas, C.S., Hauer, K.: User-oriented evaluation of a robotic rollator that provides navigation assistance in frail older adults with and without cognitive impairment. Gerontology **64**, 278–290 (2018)
14. Andre, J., et al.: Markerless gait analysis vision system for real-time gait monitoring. In: 2020 IEEE International Conference on Autonomous Robot Systems and Competitions, ICARSC 2020, pp. 269–274 (2020)
15. Gill, S., Nssk, S., Seth, N., Scheme, E.: Design of a smart IoT-enabled walker for deployable activity and gait monitoring. In: 2018 IEEE Life Sciences Conference, LSC 2018, pp. 183–186 (2018)
16. Frizera, A., Ceres, R., Pons, J.L., Abellanas, A., Raya, R.: The smart walkers as geriatric assistive device: the simbiosis purpose. In: Proceedings of the 6th International Conference of the International Society for Gerontechnology, pp. 1–6 (2008)
17. Mostofa, N., et al.: A Smart Walker for People with Both Visual and Mobility Impairment. Sensors **21**(10), 3488 (2021). https://doi.org/10.3390/s21103488
18. Wachaja, A., Agarwal, P., Zink, M., Adame, M.R., Moller, K., Burgard, W.: Navigating blind people with a smart walker. In: IEEE International Conference on Intelligent Robots and Systems, pp. 6014–6019 (2015)
19. Cortés, U., et al.: A SHARE-it service to elders' mobility using the i-Walker. Gerontechnology **7**, 95 (2008)
20. Ferrari, F., et al.: Human–robot interaction analysis for a smart walker for elderly: the ACANTO interactive guidance system. Int. J. Soc. Robot. **12**(2), 479–492 (2020)
21. Ramachandran, S., Sahin, F.: Smart Walker V: implementation of RTAB-Map Algorithm. In: 2019 14th Annual Conference System of Systems Engineering (SoSE). IEEE (2019)
22. Zhao, X., et al.: A smart robotic walker with intelligent close-proximity interaction capabilities for elderly mobility safety. Front. Neuroroboti. **14** (2020)
23. Chowdhary, G., Gazzola, M., Krishnan, G., Soman, C., Lovell, S.: Soft robotics as an enabling technology for agroforestry practice and research. Sustainability **11**(23), 6751 (2019)
24. de Busch, T., et al.: Factors associated with lower gait speed among the elderly living in a developing country: a cross-sectional population-based study. BMC Geriatrics **15** (2015)

Integrating Medical Information Software Using Health Level Seven and FHIR: A Case Study

Kevin Maxi$^{(\boxtimes)}$ and Villie Morocho

Universidad de Cuenca, Cuenca, Ecuador
`kevin.maxi@ucuenca.edu.ec`

Abstract. This article describes the architecture of a framework for integrating medical information using Health Level Seven and FHIR. An iterative programming methodology was followed along with the incremental approach. The following steps have been done in order: the exchange format type is established, the terminologies, code systems and value sets, to be used are established, mappings that will be used are established, set the RESTful API over HTTP, gather all the FHIR resources required, set URLs for the search, set URLs for the operations, establish asynchronous usage, Design of communications with rest of systems, coding and testing and establish profiling. In conclusion, a framework was designed and developed to enable interoperability in different medical information systems, all this through the use of the international standards HL7 and FHIR, and taking into account certain lessons learned from previous works related to the area.

Keywords: HL7 · FHIR · Interoperability · Web services · E-Health · Integration · Middleware · Integrated care

1 Introduction

About this time, the key requirement to improve the quality of healthcare is interoperability [1]. With the rapid increase in the diversity of models and the scale of health-related data, more and more problems are generated to comply with this characteristic.

For this reason, *Electronic Health Records* (EHR), which make a large amount of data available to diverse actors, have become widely accepted.

These actors include executives, doctors, researchers, inter alia, for various purposes [2].

However, databases that contain this type of information are difficult to consult, given the multiplicity of their relational tables and the lack of standardization, which significantly complicates interoperability between systems [2].

1.1 Motivation and Context

The interoperability problems derive in: patients restricted to a single provider of medical services, poor efficiency of resources, and, indirectly, the universality of medical services.

© Springer Nature Switzerland AG 2022
F. R. Narváez et al. (Eds.): SmartTech-IC 2021, CCIS 1532, pp. 84–98, 2022.
https://doi.org/10.1007/978-3-030-99170-8_7

Other countries, such as India, have dramatically improved public safety with the implementation of appropriate interoperability standards, as accurate patient information can be accessed anytime, anywhere. Available standards can provide the semantic and syntactic meaning of the correct information [1].

Among existing health information standards, the Fast Healthcare Interoperable Resources (FHIR; HL7 standard that has been rapidly adopted by the healthcare community) framework appears to be the likely candidate to overcome this challenge. In addition, it is also compatible with an enriched information model that allows for achieving semantic interoperability of clinical data [3].

Furthermore, these standards are necessary to comply with objective 6 of the Sustainable Health Agenda of the Americas 2018–2030 (ASSA) [4] to allow the technical integration of the information subsystems.

Instead of the traditional document-oriented approach, HL7 FHIR accepts a modular approach and represents atomic/granular health data as separate modular entities as *Resources*. FHIR resources are managed through APIs and RESTful interface, two common terms of modern web applications [5].

But why FHIR? FHIR offers a strong focus on implementation, multiple implementation libraries, is free, interoperability out-of-the-box, evolutionary development path from HL7 version 2 and CDA, strong foundation on web standards, support RESTful, concise and easily understood specifications, and human-readable serialization [6].

This manuscript is organized as follows: Sect. 2 discusses the related works, Sect. 3 presents a brief result of determining the implementation of FHIR that was used, Sect. 4 presents the applied methodology, Sect. 5 shows a case study in Ecuador, Sect. 6 details about obtained results, and Sect. 7 detail the conclusions.

2 Background and Significance

Hereby, a lot of research has been carried out to integrate the different data models from the different medical information systems, Saripalle et al. [5] explore and make a critical analysis of the use of FHIR to achieve interoperability in health of patient history to design and realize a mobile interoperable prototype of patient health history that corresponds to the functional model HL7 PHR and enables bidirectional communication with OpenEMR.

On the other hand, Kilintzis et al. [7] present a methodology for the implementation of a data management framework for telemedicine, to support integrated care services for chronic and multi-morbid patients. This framework makes use of an ontology built on FHIR resources, to provide storage and representation of semantically enriched electronic medical record data following Linked Data principles, it should be noted that this solution was implemented within the framework of the *EU project WELCOME for managing data in a telemonitoring system for patients with COPD and co-morbidities* and was successfully implemented.

Kamel and Nagy [8] illustrate how FHIR can be used to offer radiology better clinical integration and a user-centered system. In Latin America, several efforts have also been made, such as the case of Argentina with Lopez et al. [9] where FHIR is being used to develop and implement a web platform for telemedicine for electronic consultations.

However, these constant investigations around the health, have been focused on solving the problem of data integration from the different medical information systems, centering on solutions where what is required is new information that follows the standard used (in this case FHIR), leaving aside all the existing information that is in a specific format for each region, country and even each medical service provider. Finding this type of problem is common in Latin America where adaptation to these international standards is relatively new, such is the case in Ecuador where efforts to achieve interoperability of medical information systems are just beginning.

With this approach, Kiourtis et al. [10] propose to solve this problem by mapping data from the medical industry to FHIR through an alignment of ontologies. Besides authors focuses on a mechanism that can take full advantage of the data-intensive environment without losing the complexity of health.

However, these results are not entirely accurate due to their automatic processing and without human supervision, so the authors recommend it for real-time data flow scenarios since it is better and more efficient compared to others. Additionally, Mandirola et al. [11] explicitly conclusion the following statement:

The lack of policies on standards increases costs and errors in system interoperability processes. Therefore, before defining the systems to be used, it is necessary to define the frameworks and policies that will allow the interoperation of the systems that are implemented. This includes messaging standards, terminology, identifiers, master tables, and integration engines.

2.1 Proposed Solution

For this reason, the proposal of this paper is developing a framework in which this transformation is carried out through the experts of each of the systems, they also, defines the policies of the systems, to establish the maximum precision of the transformation and can be used to exchange data with those of other medical organizations.

The mapping proposed in this paper is much more rigid than in other cases, which allows medical service providers to work directly with this correlation.

The reason why this middleware is necessary in the current era is due to the lack of expressiveness in the attributes of the data schemas, since these are often generated in an illegible way for any human being, thus avoiding any possible meaning semantic making impossible the idea of automatic process on them.

3   Implementation of FHIR

Currently, there are numerous implementation options for the HL7 FHIR standard, so this section will present a brief comparison with which the best implementation for this case was determined. This comparison took into account 5 key attributes:

- Cloud deployment models: it describes the way the models are displayed.
- FHIR models: this attribute refers to all FHIR models that the implementation accepts, actual list is:

– DSTU1, DSTU2, DSTU2.1, DSTU3, R4, R5

- Based on open source: this attribute describes whether the implementation is based on open source.
- Elastic server options: this attribute refers to whether the implementation has elastic server options.
- Serverless: this attribute describes whether the implementation can do without a server or not.

Of all the available options, 5 fit provisionally with the objective of this paper, these are:

- HAPI FHIR[1]: is a complete implementation of the HL7 FHIR standard for healthcare interoperability in Java.
- SMILE CDR[2]: Smile CDR is a complete, purpose-built clinical data repository designed around the HL7 FHIR standard that is used for storing health records.
- FHIR AZURE[3]: Azure API for FHIR enables quick connection to the current data sources, such as electronic health record systems or research databases.
- CLOUD HEALTHCARE API GOOGLE[4]: The Cloud Healthcare API enables data to be exchanged in a simple and standardized way between healthcare applications and solutions compiled on Google Cloud.
- OPEN SOURCE FHIR API AWS[5]: open-source software toolkit that can be used to add capabilities of an FHIR interface to existing healthcare software.

Table 1 presents a summary of the functionalities of the different options proposed. It should be noted that SMILE CDR is built on HAPI FHIR, which is a complete repository of clinical data and specially designed according to the HL7 FHIR standard that is used to store medical records. In addition, this together with HAPI FHIR require a later phase where the place of hosting is determined, which entails a series of additional steps. On the other hand, Azure, Google Cloud, and AWS offer these services in a managed way, which facilitates their development and maintenance.

With the results of the comparison, HAPI FHIR was decided as the best implementation for this case, since it houses the majority of FHIR models together with SMILE CDR, but HAPI FHIR is free to use while SMILE CDR has a cost associated with its use.

---

[1] https://hapifhir.io/.

[2] https://www.smilecdr.com/.

[3] https://azure.microsoft.com/es-es/services/azure-api-for-fhir/.

[4] https://cloud.google.com/healthcare.

[5] https://aws.amazon.com/es/blogs/opensource/using-open-source-fhir-apis-with-fhir-works-on-aws/.

Table 1. Comparison between the different implementation options.

Attribute	Platform				
	HAPI FHIR	SMILE CDR	FHIR AZURE	CLOUD HEALTH-CARE API GOOGLE	OPEN SOURCE FHIR APIS AWS
Cloud deployment models	Needs server	Needs server	Cloud	Cloud	Cloud
FHIR models	DSTU1, DSTU2, DSTU2.1, DSTU3, R4, R5	DSTU1, DSTU2, DSTU2.1, DSTU3, R4, R5	R4, STU3	R4, STU3, DSTU2	STU3 and R4.0.1
Based on open source	Yes	Yes	Has an open-source option to deploy in their servers	No	Yes
Elastic server options	Depends on server	Depends on server	Yes	Yes	Yes
Serverless	No	No	Yes	Yes	Yes

4 Methodology

For this reason, proposal is the development of a framework to allow the integration of medical information software using Health Level Seven and FHIR where the data will be accessed and served through BlockChain [12], architecture is presented in Fig. 1.

The system consists of two main parts: the first is one that is hosted on a server and will be in charge of handling the data and conversions, and the second, which is data extractor and provider, on which security layer is applied.

On the server side, there will be two controllers, one HL7 and the other FHIR, both of which will be in charge of transformation and interpretation of the different data stored in the databases of the external applications. The data will be exchanged through REST and XML endpoints. For HL7 controller it was decided to use as a HL7-FHIR translator, since this task is easily automatable, and since all framework communicates its data in FHIR standard.

For the elaboration of this paper, an iterative programming methodology was followed along with the incremental approach, this includes certain concepts concerning the development of systems with FHIR standards. For this, the required process Business Process Model and Notation (BPMN) must be taken into account, as well as its minimum data set that contains the minimum information to establish interoperation in any organization.

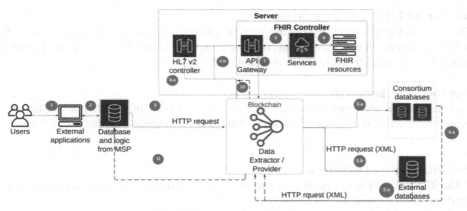

Fig. 1. Framework architecture.

The reason why it was decided to use this methodology over others is that it maintains its center in the FHIR standard as well as with the FHIR development process [6] and has been mentioned in [1], which is established in the official standard description page. Figure 2 describes the proposed methodology.

Following this methodology, the following steps have been done in order:

Exchange Format Type is Established
In this step the type of format for the exchange is chosen, possible ones include XML, JSON, and RDF.

Terminologies, Code Systems, and Value Sets, to Be Used are Established
In FHIR the descriptions of certain attributes, such as diseases or family roles, among others, must be described in terminologies, which must be described on the public website.

Establish Mappings that Will Be Used
In this step, the mappings necessary are defined for the conversion to other standards such as HL7 V2 and other data schemas.

Set RESTful API Over HTTP
Because FHIR is a standard, it is based on the standardization of resource structures and interfaces. This can be seen as a violation of REST principles, but it is critical to ensuring consistent interoperability between different systems. The same interactions are defined for each "resource type", with which resources can be managed in a very granular way [13].

Gather All FHIR Resources Required
In this step, the resources used in the medical information system are aligned with the FHIR resources, in this way a conversion scheme is obtained that will be used in the implementation of FHIR for the conversion of the data.

Set URLs for the Search
The search for resources is fundamental to the mechanics of FHIR. Lookup operations traverse an existing set of resources filtered by parameters supplied to the lookup operation [14].

Set URLs for the Operations
"The RESTful API defines a set of common interactions (read, update, search, inter alia.) performed on a typed resource repository" [15].

Establish Asynchronous Usage
The RFC 7240-based asynchronous requirement standard is adapted for this application and applies to all defined interactions and operations, although it does not take advantage of many of these applications. Servers can choose which interactions should support the pattern (if any), and servers can only support some operations that use the asynchronous pattern [16].

Design of Communications with Rest of Systems
In this step, the communications with the systems with which the framework will be connected for the extraction and sending of data are designed.

Coding and Testing
Finally, all the schemes and data obtained in the previous steps are encoded.

Establish Profiling
The FHIR specification describes a number of basic functions, frameworks, and APIs that are used in many healthcare contexts. However, there are large differences between jurisdictions and across the health ecosystem where practices, requirements, regulations, training, and interventions are feasible and/or beneficial. For this reason, the FHIR specification is a *platform specification*: it creates a common platform or foundation upon which a variety of different solutions are implemented. [17].

5 Case Study

In the introduction has mentioned that finding this type of problem is common in Latin America because of that it was decided to take Ecuador as the case study. Ecuadorian Ministerial Agreement NO. 00001190 [18] mention universality where it is defined as: extend the coverage of the benefits of the health system to the entire population.

On the other hand, in the Ecuadorian ministerial agreement NO. 00001190 [18] the agreement for the approval of the use of HL7 and its implementation in all the institutions of the national health system is detailed.

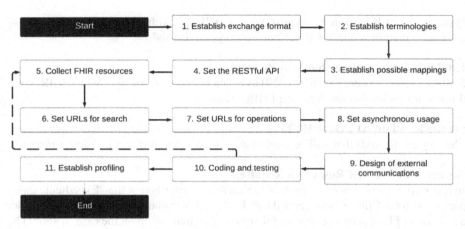

Fig. 2. Methodology proposed

Since the methodology is to be applied to the health-related data stored in a country, it is necessary to have a description of each of these resources. This description can be obtained from the document: *Expediente único para la Historia Clínica* issued in 2007 through Ministerial Agreement NO. 0000116 of Ecuador from which the following documents were obtained:

- "Anamnesis"
- "Consulta Externa – Anamnesis y Examen Físico"
- "Consulta Externa – Evolución"
- "Evolución y prescripciones"
- "Examen Físico"

The Exchange Format Type is Established
In this case, the format chosen for the exchange will be XML because this type uses human language and is readable and understandable. Another reason to use this format is its compatibility with Java, which is the development language of this framework.

The Terminologies, Code Systems, and Value Sets, to Be Used Are Established
As in the previous step, in this case, you can find several options that are valid for development, however, taking into account that the framework is focused on being deployed in Latin America and specifically in Ecuador, it has been decided to use the

system code of ICD10 in its Spanish version (CIE10). Although to define the roles of the family members, the V3-RoleCode code system is used.

Establish the Mappings that Will Be Used
For this case, it was decided to use [19] as a data converter from HL7 V2 to FHIR, since this document focuses on obtaining FHIR resources.

Set the RESTful API Over HTTP
The request methods that will be used mainly are the get, post, put and delete methods.

Gather All the FHIR Resources Required
In this step, the conversion of each of the attributes described in the "Expediente único para la Historia Clínica" was carried out. Each of the attributes was aligned with either a field of an FHIR resource or a complete resource, depending on the case. It should be noted that if the required information is not specifically found, FHIR presents the option of making extensions to each of its resources, so if this is the case, this option should be chosen.

In Fig. 3 we present a software process engineering model (SPEM) of the action to add a new Medical Service Provider (MSP) to the framework. In this process only developer of external system (the one who wants to be added) and framework administrator (called middleware admin). In correlation phase, all information defined in previous steps (like the alignment obtained of FHIR resources) was an input. This to represent our obtained EHR that represents all information of the list of documents declared in the third paragraph of this section. This information let, to the developer, build a list of conversion documents representing the data of his system in terms that the framework can understand. The rest of the process is done by the framework administrator. Administrator is responsible of insert this data to the MDE process, MDE that was built for this purpose, and to insert the obtained files in the framework, enabling its use within our proposal.

With this, the objective is to is to be able to reach the possibility of including any MSP proprietary software, but at the time of writing this article, we can communicate with all MSPs that have enabled endpoints for accessing its data.

In this case, an example would be vaccines of a patient, these correspond to form 002 – "Anamnesis – consulta externa", to the subcategory of "Antecedentes personales", initially the name of the vaccine and a description would go, however, the medical information systems add the ICD10 code, plus an ID.

In FHIR the vaccines are under the Immunization resource so that the alignment would be as follows (Table 2):

Additionally, the resource specifies that the status of the vaccine and the number of doses must be established since this is history, for the vaccine to be listed it must have been completed, so this field must always go to complete, and if the number of doses does not exist, the number 1 will be specified.

For the case in which the alignment is not possible, as is the case of the maternal surname of a patient, extensions should be used, an example is presented in Table 3.

If no extension matches the field, one must be defined somewhere accessible on the internet and it can be used within FHIR.

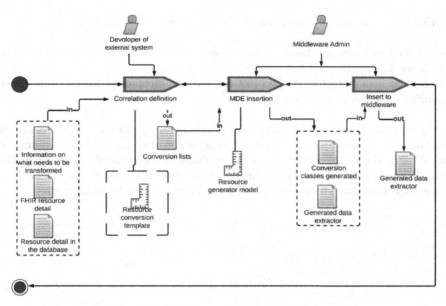

Fig. 3. Process to add a new MSP

Table 2. Alignment of resources

Vacuna (Anamnesis)	Immunization
Id del paciente	patient
Fecha	occurrence
Id	identifier
Nombre	vaccineCode
Descripción	note
Código	vaccineCode

Table 3. Alignment of non-basic fields of resources

Paciente (Registro de Primera admisión)	Patient
Apellido Materno	patient-mothersMaidenName (extension of patient)

In this phase, each one of the files required by the middleware is generated to include a new medical service provider in the conversion. For this, it was decided to use the model-based engineering (MDE) approach. Here new medical service provider enter the information of the conversion, previously obtained, list within the model generated for the resource.

This phase has as input the conversion list document and as output to:

- Generated conversion classes: The classes necessary for the operation of the middleware
- Generated data extractor: A class that has the specification of the endpoints from which the data will be extracted

Figure 4 shows the model generated for the case of the patient; this model is similar to one of classes. Each organization can have a definition of a patient within its system. In turn, these two entities describe each of the attributes necessary for the conversion. The medical service provider inserts the name of the equivalent attributes into its database. This process is repeated for each of the resources obtained for the middleware.

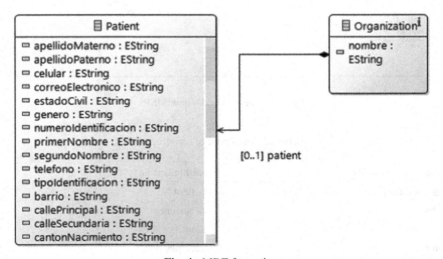

Fig. 4. MDE for patient

Set the URLs for the Search
The structure of the URLs for the search used is the one suggested by FHIR [14] and implemented by HAPI FHIR. This can be summarized in the following string:

```
GET [base]/[type]?name=value&...{&_format=[mime-type]}}
```

Where [base] is the base URL of the server, [type] is the name of the FHIR resource and the parameters are a series of name-value pairs encoded in the URL. On the other hand, for the POST method, it can be summarized as follows:

```
POST [base]/[type]/_search{?[parameters]{&_format=[mime-type]}}
```

In this case, the server is the one that determines the set of resources that matches the specified criteria and returns the results in a bundle with all the resources.

Following our example of the vaccine, the URL would be:

```
http://localhost:8080/fhir/Immunization?patient:Patient:1
```

Set the URLs for the Operations

Since the operations, in this case, are not an essential part of the functioning of the system, what was taken into account was that "Operations are executed using a URL derived from the FHIR endpoint, where the name of the operation is prefixed by a" dollar sign "('$') character" [15]. An example is:

```
POST http://fhir.someserver.org/fhir/Patient/1/$everything
```

The rest of the extended operations used in this case follow what is stated by FHIR [15]. Following the example case, it would be:

```
http://localhost:8080/fhir/Immunization/1/$evertything
```

Establish Asynchronous Usage

For this case, the use of the System is intended to be synchronous, for all resources, given that the amount of information is not too much and not too much processing will be carried out by the server, so asynchronous use is not defined for this case.

Design of Communications with the Rest of the Systems

In this case, the communication design is the one presented in Fig. 1. In this way, the data extraction from the different databases is modeled and encoded.

Coding and Testing

The framework was coded and tested with various types of data structures from local medical information systems in Ecuador. Additionally, each resource was tested with Instance Validator[6], which is the HAPI FHIR instance validator.

Establish Profiling

In this case, all the restrictions inferred from the *Expediente único para la Historia Clínica* are established, that is, only the resources obtained through this process will be used, without the possibility of adding the rest of the resources specified by FHIR, in addition to the use of The API will be restricted by two levels of access, the first will show information related to an external query, while the second level of access will show the rest of the details of each patient. As previously stated, ICD10 will be used in its Spanish version.

---

[6] https://hapifhir.io/hapi-fhir/docs/validation/instance_validator.html.

6 Discussion

The developed framework presents a viable flow to establish the necessary policies to enable the interoperation of medical information systems, which is one of the main problems in the area, exactly this occurs in step 11 of the proposed methodology, were once with all the necessary resources, the restrictions to be used in the systems are established. In addition, the proposed methodology allows the experts of each system to be part of the process, being they who ensure successful interoperability through the alignment of the resources used in the different systems. On the other hand, when developing the framework certain aspects of the area began to become more and more evident, as is the case of the difficulty that currently exists for medical personnel with the use of the ICD10, as it is a code system, it certainly adds an extra complexity when using the system during the day.

6.1 Limitations and Upcoming Improvements

One of the main limitations of the proposed methodology is the missing resources in both cases, for this reason, the proposed solution is a first step in the transition from the different data schemes of the different medical information systems, to the use of the FHIR standard, for. On the other hand, the alignment of the resources translated to FHIR must be available to each of the users of the Framework since certain labels do not coincide between FHIR and the resources of the medical information systems. Therefore, an immediate improvement to this methodology would be to automate this process of obtaining alignment documents.

7 Conclusion

A framework was designed and developed to enable interoperability in different medical information systems, all this through the use of the international standards HL7 and FHIR, and taking into account certain lessons learned from previous works related to the area. All this fulfills all the proposed methodology so that the systems that are part of the framework can exchange information between them safely and reliably.

However, when making this middleware, as in other documents, the existing difficulty in the correlation of the data has been found.

Likewise, the expressiveness of the attributes of the database schemas is very complex, which is why the use of this middleware is important, since this would eliminate this inconvenience through a much more rigid mapping that allows the medical service providers work directly with this correlation.

For the case study, the difficulty of interpreting the names of the fields of the database used was demonstrated, as well as the complexity of standardization in relation to FHIR, despite the fact that the example started from an implementation of the single Ecuadorian clinical history. However, it is demonstrated through the generated process that the middleware allows the understanding of the entities correlated with the FHIR schema. In the case study, we worked specifically with a subset of documents of *Expediente único para la Historia Clínica* of Ecuador, documents that had been specified at Sect. 5.

For the attributes like neighborhood, zone, occupation, among others it was necessary to use the extensionality provided by FHIR, since it does not correspond to specific fields of the document of the *Expediente único para la Historia Clínica*. This complexity solved in the case presented, would multiply exponentially with the complete digital medical record, but the middleware can be extended mechanically and would allow the integration of other sources with the EHR of each one of them in a simpler way.

Acknowledgment. We thank the company INNTRATEC S.A. for allowing us to be part of the development of this project. In addition, we also express our gratitude to the Telemedicine Laboratory of the University of Cuenca that has given us their collaboration in the development of the project.

References

1. Sharma, M., Aggarwal, H.: HL-7 based middleware standard for healthcare information system: FHIR. In: Krishna, C.R., Dutta, M., Kumar, R. (eds.) Proceedings of 2nd International Conference on Communication, Computing and Networking. LNNS, vol. 46, pp. 889–899. Springer, Singapore (2019). https://doi.org/10.1007/978-981-13-1217-5_87
2. Boussadi, A., Zapletal, E.: A Fast Healthcare Interoperability Resources (FHIR) layer implemented over i2b2. BMC Med. Inform. Decis. Mak. **17**(1), 1–12 (2017). https://doi.org/10.1186/s12911-017-0513-6
3. Leroux, H., Metke-Jimenez, A., Lawley, M.J.: Towards achieving semantic interoperability of clinical study data with FHIR. J. Biomed. Semantics **8**(1), 1–14 (2017). https://doi.org/10.1186/s13326-017-0148-7
4. Organización Panamericana de la Salud: "Agenda de Desarrollo Sostenible para las Américas 2018–2030, Objetivo 6: Fortalecer los sistemas de información para la salud" (2017). https://www.paho.org/hq/index.php?option=com_content&view=article&id=14601:sustainable-health-agenda-for-the-americas-2018-2030-goal-6-information-systems-for-health&Itemid=42350&lang=es
5. Saripalle, R., Runyan, C., Rusell, M.: Using HL7 FHIR to achieve interoperability in patient health record. J. Biomed. Inform. **94**, 103188 (2019). https://doi.org/10.1016/j.jbi.2019.103188
6. HL7.org: Introducing HL7 FHIR (2021). https://www.hl7.org/fhir/summary.html#status
7. Cáceres, C., Peralta, D.: Propuesta de Identidad Digital para Historial Clínico Unificado utilizando tecnología Blockchain. Universidad de Cuenca (2021)
8. Kilintzis, V., Chouvarda, I., Beredimas, N., Natsiavas, P., Maglaveras, N.: Supporting integrated care with a flexible data management framework built upon Linked. J. Biomed. Inform. **94**, 103179 (2019). https://doi.org/10.1016/j.jbi.2019.103179
9. Kamel, P.I., Nagy, P.G.: Patient-centered radiology with FHIR: an introduction to the use of FHIR to offer radiology a clinically integrated platform. J. Digit. Imaging **31**(3), 327–333 (2018). https://doi.org/10.1007/s10278-018-0087-6
10. Lopez, E., et al.: Results of the use of the teleconsultation platform after 2 months of implementation. Stud. Health Technol. Inform. **270**, 1377–1378 (2020). https://doi.org/10.3233/SHTI200450
11. Kiourtis, A., Mavrogiorgou, A., Menychtas, A., Maglogiannis, I., Kyriazis, D.: Structurally mapping healthcare data to HL7 FHIR through ontology alignment. J. Med. Syst. **43**(3), 1–13 (2019). https://doi.org/10.1007/s10916-019-1183-y

12. Mandirola Brieux, H., Guillen, S., La Rosa, F., Moreno, C.: Integrating medical applications with HL7: lessons learned MIRTH CONNECT ONLINE COURSE (2017). Available: https://www.hl7latam.org/HL7LATAMNews/N7/N7E.pdf. Accessed 16 June 2021
13. HL7: RESTful API (2021). https://www.hl7.org/fhir/http.html
14. HL7: Search (2021). https://www.hl7.org/fhir/search.html
15. HL7: Extended Operations on the RESTful API (2021). https://www.hl7.org/fhir/operations.html
16. HL7: Asynchronous Request Pattern (2021)
17. HL7: Profiling FHIR (2021). https://www.hl7.org/fhir/profiling.html
18. Ministerio de Salud Pública: Ley Orgánica del Sistema Nacional de Salud. Desarro. Soc., pp. 3–4 (2002). Available: http://www.desarrollosocial.gob.ec/wp-content/uploads/downloads/2013/10/ley-sis-nac-salud.pdf
19. LinuxForHealth hl7v2-fhir-converter [Source code] (2020). https://github.com/LinuxForHealth/hl7v2-fhir-converter

A Machine Learning Approach for Blood Glucose Level Prediction Using a LSTM Network

Nayeli Y. Gómez-Castillo[1,4]([⊠]) [iD], Pedro E. Cajilima-Cardenaz[2,4] [iD],
Luis Zhinin-Vera[2,4] [iD], Belén Maldonado-Cuascota[1,4] [iD],
Diana León Domínguez[3,4] [iD], Gabriela Pineda-Molina[1,4] [iD],
Andrés A. Hidalgo-Parra[4] [iD], and Fernando A. Gonzales-Zubiate[1,4] [iD]

[1] School of Biological Sciences and Engineering, Yachay Tech University,
100119 Urcuqui, Ecuador
{nayeli.gomez,fgonzales}@yachaytech.edu.ec
[2] School of Mathematical and Computational Sciences, Yachay Tech University,
100650 Urcuqui, Ecuador
[3] School of Biochemistry and Pharmacy, University of Cuenca,
010112 Cuenca, Ecuador
[4] MIND Research Group-Model Intelligent Networks Development,
Urcuqui, Ecuador

Abstract. Diabetes is a chronic disease characterized by the elevation of glucose in blood resulting in multiple organ failure in the body. There are three types of diabetes: type 1, type 2, and gestational diabetes. Type 1 diabetes (T1D) is an autoimmune disease where insulin-producing cells are destroyed. World Health Organization latest reports indicate T1D prevalence is increasing worldwide with approximately one million new cases annually. Consequently, numerous models to predict blood glucose levels have been proposed, some of which are based on Recurrent Neural Networks (*RNNs*). The study presented here proposes the training of a machine learning model to predict future glucose levels with high precision using the OhioT1DM database and a Long Short-Term Memory (*LSTM*) network. Three variations of the dataset were used; the first one with original unprocessed data, another processed with linear interpolation, and a last one processed with a time series method. The datasets obtained were split into time prediction horizons (*PH*) of 5, 30, and 60 min and then fed into the proposed model. From the three variations of datasets, the one processed with time series obtained the highest prediction accuracy, followed by the one processed with linear interpolation. This study will open new ways for addressing healthcare issues related to glucose forecasting in diabetic patients, helping to avoid concomitant complications such as severe episodes of hyperglycemia.

Keywords: Blood glucose level prediction · Long short-term memory · Machine learning · Linear interpolation · Time series

F. R. Narváez et al. (Eds.): SmartTech-IC 2021, CCIS 1532, pp. 99–113, 2022.
https://doi.org/10.1007/978-3-030-99170-8_8

1   Introduction

Diabetes is a serious, long-term condition characterized by the elevation of glucose in the blood, which causes severe damage to the heart, kidneys, eyes, and nerves. *The World Health Organization and the American Diabetes Association (ADA)* classify diabetes as one of the world's greatest health threats [3,23].

The estimated number of people with diabetes has increased by 88%, from 246 million in 2006 [12] to 463 million in 2019, and it is estimated to increase to approximately 700 million in 2045 [14,24]. The last estimate reported that 4.2 million adults among 20–79 years of age died from diabetes and its complications in 2019, representing the 11.3% of mortality rate [25]. In the long-term, hyperglycemia can cause complications such as cardiovascular disease, nerve damage (neuropathy), kidney failure (diabetic nephropathy), and damage to the retina blood vessels (diabetic retinopathy) with consequent blindness. Moreover, untreated hyperglycemia can become severe and finally cause a diabetic coma [1]. Therefore, therapy with insulin administration has become crucial in the prevention of hyperglycemia with the use of multiple daily injections or insulin infusion using insulin pumps.

The three main types of diabetes are Type 1 diabetes (*T1D*), Type 2 diabetes mellitus (*T2D*), and Gestational diabetes mellitus (*GDM*). *T1D* is an autoimmune disease characterized by the destruction of pancreatic beta-cells resulting in insulin deficiency and, in consequence, high levels of glucose in blood. The occurrence of *T1D* is increasing worldwide, with approximately one million cases annually [13].

Although insulin can be delivered by multiple daily injections, monitoring of glucose levels is essential for diabetes treatment. Blood glucose monitoring can be performed by self-monitoring of blood glucose (*SMBG*) using improved blood glucometers [5], continuous glucose monitoring (*CGM*) devices [2], and newer insulin pumps with integrated sensor-augmented systems [22].

There have been numerous models used to predict blood glucose levels, some of which use neural networks and have been shown to be accurate [16,18,20,21,30]. In this work, a Machine Learning model is trained to predict future glucose levels in a very precise and accurate manner. The data used come from the OhioT1DM database and comprise the data of twelve *T1D* patients on insulin pump therapy with continuous glucose monitoring (*CGM*) during eight weeks. After a deep analysis of different prediction models and an arduous data preparation process, data sets were created and the Machine Learning was put for training with a Long Short-Term Memory logarithm. To sum up, we were able to improve the capacity of a machine learning model to predict future glucose levels with a very high precision.

2   Related Works

Many prediction models have been used for blood glucose forecasting and, recently, neural network has been incorporated for this purpose. In fact, some researchers reported promising results with the implementation of neural networks for blood glucose forecasting on Ohio T1DM (2018) dataset, these results are shown in Table 1. In this table, the performances of the previous prediction models are measured based on Root Means Square Error ($RMSE$) and, in some cases, the time lag for 30 min and 60 min horizons (PH). The time lag is an approach to measure the similarity between the original and predicted signal using cross correlation coefficient [16]. By this way, in contrast to their results, some researches trained their model with more than one dataset [7,16,30]. The literature reviewed fall into two kinds of input data; they are either working with a single input or use multiple inputs.

Rabby and collaborators present a multi-layered $LSTM$ based on a RNN model and a Kalman Smoothing for preprocessing obtaining an average RMSE value of only 6.45 mg/dL for a 30 min horizon and 17.24 mg/dL for a 60 min horizon, being until now the leading average prediction accuracy for the OhioT1DM dataset (2018) [21]. On the other hand, Martinsson et al. obtained mean $RMSE$ values for 30 min and 60 min horizons of 18.867 mg/dL and 31.043 mg/dL respectively, by using a RNN with glucose levels as the only input data [18].

Despite authors in [31] also include several input fields such as carbohydrate intake and insulin doses, they obtained the highest average $RMSE$ value cited for a 30 min horizon (PH = 30 min, 21.72 mg/dL).

Meanwhile, authors in [30] trained their model for a 30 min horizon and obtained similar results to those of [18,29]. They evaluated their datasets using different algorithms such as; auto-regressive model (ARX), support vector regression (SVR), and conventional neural networks with predicted glucose ($NNPG$). These authors obtained lower $RMSE$ values in each of the algorithms using the $UVA\ Padora$ simulator dataset than using the OhioT1DM dataset [30].

Midroni and collaborators have performed a study with many feature sets and recurrent neuronal network variants to predict glucose at a 30 min time horizon. They depicted performance for RNN, $XGBoost$, and RF with an average $RMSE$ of 23.48, 16.11, and 28.59 respectively [20].

At this time, only two papers from the presented literature calculated the time lag [16]. Among them, the lower time lag result for a 30 min horizon using Ohios dataset is the one obtained by Li et al. (8.03 min), which is close to that of [30] (8.10 min).

3   Dataset

In this work, the OhioT1DM dataset was used [17]. The data consists of blood glucose level measurements for twelve people with type 1 diabetes ($T1D$) obtained and realeased in 2018 and 2020 (six patients per year). All patients were on insulin pump therapy with either Medtronic 530G or 630G. A continuous glucose monitoring (CGM) device, Medtronic Enlite, was used to collect data during eight weeks, at 5-min intervals, for each individual. Physiological data was obtained from a fitness band while other life-event parameters, such as meal information, time of exercises and time of work, were reported by the

Table 1. Related works, literature models using Ohio T1DM (2018) dataset.

Input	Method	Dataset	Mathematical accuracy				Reference
			30 min horizon		60 min horizon		
			RMSE [mg/dL]	Time lag [min]	RMSE [mg/dL]	Time lag [min]	
Glucose levels	RNN	Ohio T1DM	18.867	-	31.403	-	[18]
Glucose levels, meal, bolus step counts	DRNN	Ohio T1DM	6.45		17.24	-	[21]
Glucose levels, meal, bolus, time index	CNN	Ohio T1DM	21.72	-	-	-	[31]
Glucose levels, meal, bolus, time index	DCNN	Ohio T1DM ABC4D T1D UVA/Padova T1D simulator	Ohio: 19.28 ABC4D: 19.19 UVA/Padova: 8.88	Ohio: 8.03 ABC4D: 11.34 UVA/Padova: 0.83	Ohio: 31.83 ABC4D: 31.78 UVA/Padova: 19.90	Ohio: 17.78 ABC4D: 30.28 UVA/Padova: 16.43	[16]
For IDIAB, Ohio and T1DMS: Glucose levels, meal, bolus	Fully CNN	Ohio T1DM IDIAB T1DMS	Ohio: 20.10 IDIAB: 20.32	-			[7]
Glucose levels, meal, bolus	DRNN SVR ARX NNPG	Ohio T1DM UVA/Padova T1D simulator T1DMS	**Ohio T1DM** DRNN: 18.9 SVR: 21.7 ARX: 20.1 NNPG: 22.9 **UVA** DRNN: 7.8 SVR: 11.9 ARX: 11.3 NNPG:13.1	**Ohio T1DM** DRNN: 8.1 SVR: 15.3 ARX: 13.6 NNPG:16.4 **UVA** DRNN: 0.4 SVR: 6.8 ARX: 4.8 NNPG: 9.3		-	[30]
Many feature sets	RNN XGBoost RF	Ohio T1DM	RNN: 23.48 XGBoost: 16.11 RF: 28.59	-		-	[20]

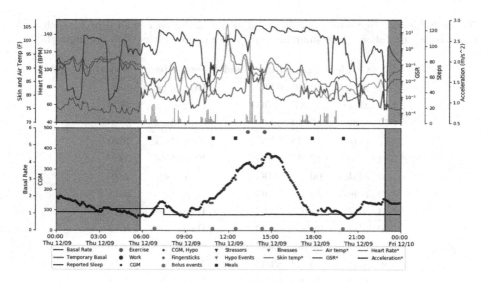

Fig. 1. OhioT1DM viewer data sample for patient with ID 591. This tool was designed by the authors to show a visualization by dates of the variables present in the dataset. Source: [17].

patient via a custom mobile app. There were 7 male and 5 female patients. In total, eight patients were between 40–60 years old, three were between 20–40, and one was between 60–80. Table 2 shows patient data, insulin pump model, and sensor band type, by cohort. The patients have been anonymized and are referred to by random ID numbers. Figure 1 shows an example of the data collected for patient with ID 591 on a single day using the OhioT1DM Viewer tool.

The dataset includes: a *CGM* blood glucose level; insulin doses, both bolus and basal; self-reported data such as blood glucose levels (finger-sticks), meal time on carbohydrate estimates, time of sleep, work, and exercise; and data obtained on the Basis Peak or Empatica Embrace band. In Table 3, the different variables for OhioT1DM dataset are compared regarding the sensor band types used in each cohort and their data fields.

In the 2018 cohort, the patients wore the Basis Peak band, which includes the following data: 5-min aggregations of heart rate, galvanic skin response (*GSR*), skin temperature, air temperature, and step count. In the 2020 cohort, Empatica Embrace band was used, and the data includes 1-min aggregations of *GSR*, skin temperature, and magnitude of acceleration. Both bands detected when the patient was asleep, nonetheless, not all participants wore the band overnight [17].

Table 2. Gender, age range, insulin pump model, and sensor band type for each data contributor, by cohort. This summary data corresponds to the Ohio database [17].

ID	Gender	Age	Pump model	Sensor band	Cohort
540	Male	20–40	630G	Empatica	2020
544	Male	40–60	530G	Empatica	2020
552	Male	20–40	630G	Empatica	2020
567	Female	20–40	630G	Empatica	2020
584	Male	40–60	530G	Empatica	2020
596	Male	60–80	530G	Empatica	2020
559	Female	40–60	530G	Basis	2018
563	Male	40–60	530G	Basis	2018
570	Male	40–60	530G	Basis	2018
575	Female	40–60	530G	Basis	2018
588	Female	40–60	530G	Basis	2018
591	Female	40–60	530G	Basis	2018

Table 3. Comparison between sensor band types and their data fields obtained from OhioT1DM dataset. *These parameters are expressed in hours and minutes (00:00).

Data fields	Sensor band type	
	Empatica embrace	*Basis peak fitness*
CGM blood glucose level	Every 5 min	Every 5 min
Finger sticks	Periodic self-monitoring	Periodic self-monitoring
Insulin doses	Bolus and basal	Bolus and basal
Self-reported Meal information*	Times and carbohydrate estimates	Times and carbohydrate estimates
Times of exercise (min)	Self-reported intensity on a scale of 1 to 10 (10 for most physically active)	Self-reported intensity on a scale of 1 to 10 (10 for most physically active)
Times of sleep*	Self-reported numeric estimate of sleep quality and asleep times	Self-reported numeric estimate of sleep quality and asleep times
Times of work*	Self-reported intensity on a scale of 1 to 10 (10 for most physically active)	Self-reported intensity on a scale of 1 to 10 (10 for most physically active)
Times of stress*	Self-reported stress	Self-reported stress
Times of illness*	Self-reported illness	Self-reported illness
Heart rate	Not available	5-min aggregations
Galvanic Skin Response (GSR)	1-min aggregations	5-min aggregations
Skin temperature (F)	1-min aggregations	5-min aggregations
Air temperature	Not available	Every 5 min
Step count	Not available	Every 5 min
Magnitude of acceleration	Every 1 min	Not available

4 Methodology

4.1 Long Short-Term Memory Network

Recurrent Neural Networks (*RNNs*) come from the neural network family and differentiate from their counterpart, Feedforward Neural Networks (*FNN*), by receiving feedback from the outputs of their basic building blocks. *RNNs* possess a memory able to store information that has been registered until a specific moment. *RNNs* are also effective models for sequential data (time series) [11], as they forecast the future output based on the preceding one. The networks themselves have repeating loops in this situation [4]. The *LSTM* network used in this work is a special case of a *RNN* that tackles the problems of long-term dependency of *RNN* in which the *RNN* cannot estimate the words stored in the long-term memory, but they can give more accurate predictions from the recent information [26, 27].

In this sense, the novel, efficient, gradient-based method, *LSTM*, incorporates nonlinear trainable data-dependent controls into the *RNN* to ensure that the gradient of the objective function with respect to the state signal does not vanish. *LSTM* centers its operations on two main objectives: data and control of data, while its standard formulation includes a cell, input gate, output gate, and usually a forget gate. The input and output gates regulate the incoming and outgoing data, protecting the memory cell, while the forget gate can be used to clear the memory cell when its data is no longer needed. These three components of the *LSTM* cooperate to accomplish the main goal of this neural network, which is to store data for an arbitrary amount of time. This architecture can be seen in Fig. 2.

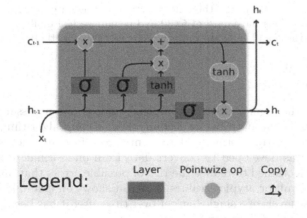

Fig. 2. Structure of LSTM where the LSTM cell can process data sequentially and keep its hidden state through time. Author: Guillaume Chevalier

The proposed machine learning system requires the database to be in the best conditions in order to make a reliable prediction of the data. Therefore, after pre-processing each dataset, distinct treatments and tests were applied which allow for the exploration of a variety of possible outcomes. A flowchart of the general methodology implemented is shown in Fig. 3. It shows that the Ohio database first goes through a pre-processing process where cleaning of data and common errors are done. Then begins the Data Treatment phase in which datasets are created according to different criteria. Finally, training sets with 5, 30 and 60 min horizon intervals are created and trained with a *LSTM* algorithm.

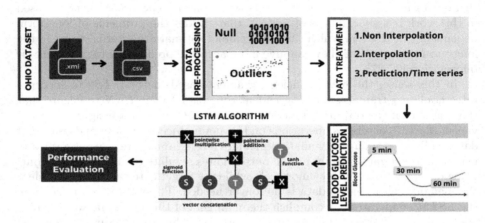

Fig. 3. Flowchart of the proposed machine learning algorithm. First the Ohio database was transformed from *.xml* to *.csv* format and the data was preprocessed (outliers, nulls). Then three versions of the same data were created: non-interpolated, interpolated and time series. Then, the three new versions are again divided into three each. These new sub-versions have data of 5, 30 and 60 min each. Finally, LSTM was used to train each of these and evaluate the performance of this method.

4.2   Preprocessing

After choosing the algorithms to be implemented, it was necessary to perform a preprocessing of the data before feeding them to any algorithm. For this, it was fundamental to transform the data from a *.xml* format to a *.csv* format. A Python script was developed to convert data from one format to another one. Then, they were cleaned to reduce the risk of possible errors that may arise from the presence of null or atypical values. Figure 4 shows an example of a *.csv* file with the glucose levels of a single patient over time after it has been preprocessed where existing gaps of data can be seen.

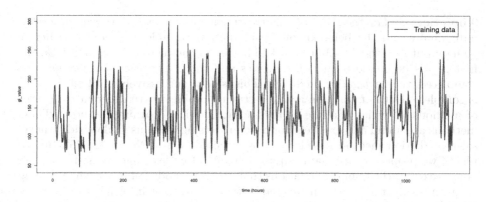

Fig. 4. Preprocessed training data: due to technical errors in sampling, the patient 596 showed absence of glucose level data at certain points [17]. In the following sections it is shown how the lack of data was corrected.

Before feeding the training dataset into the models, it was treated with three methods separately to compare the resulting precision of each method. One variation was treated with a time series prediction method, another with an interpolation method, and the last one did note receive any treatment. Time horizons of 5, 30, and 60 min were then taken from each data file to determine which *PH* would result in the best precision. The variables of these resulting files which were missing a large amount of data were filled with null values, while the values that were missing were relatively small amounts.

Three variations of the dataset were used; the first one with original unprocessed data, another processed with linear interpolation, and a last one processed with a time series method.

Non Interpolated. There are various studies that used the Ohio database without previously interpolating the data and have obtained good prediction results [6,19]. For this reason, this methodology is repeated with the objective of having a good base for comparing the results obtained once a treatment method is applied.

Interpolated. Linear interpolation searches for straight line that passes through the end points x_A and x_B [10]. This approach worked quite well for this database and was proposed in order to evaluate the impact of the absence of data for prolonged periods of time and to check if, by performing a simple interpolation, the results showed a significant variation. A simple formula is shown below:

$$X_i = \frac{x_A - x_B}{a - b}(i - b) + x_B \tag{1}$$

Time Series. For the focus of this treatment method, the data was processed individually and the behavior of the prediction variable was predicted before being input into the *LSTM* network. That is, to complete the missing data, the first gap is predicted using a time series and then, with that part of the data completed, the next gap is predicted. This is done successively until all the data is complete. Data imputation is a well-studied problem with different categories of methods, of which the latest of these include deep learning methods. These methods are useful and excellent for data processing when used alongside a novel sales prediction method based on Convolutional Neural Networks [28]. In this phase, we propose to use data imputation with deep learning methods that are able to extract the temporal relations that other methods fail to see when dealing with time-sequential data. In this paper we use a variant implementation of the GRU-D method [8].

4.3   Training and Testing

In this section, the resulting datasets of the three treatment methods were used separately: interpolated, non-interpolated and time series. The *LSTM* algorithm maintained the same hyperparameters used in [6], 200 *LSTM* cells, for the encoder and decoder to maintain an ideal scenario for comparison. This layer was followed by 2 dense layers containing 150 and 1 units, respectively, wrapped in a *TimeDistributed* layer. The model was trained for 80 epochs with batch size of 40. The Adam optimizer [15] was used with a learning rate of 0.01 and MSE as the loss function.

The training datasets from both 2018 and 2020 were sent to the algorithm with the purpose of evaluating its behavior when using data which have certain differences between some variables. Then, the testing datasets that are included by default in the Ohio database are used to evaluate the performance and accuracy of the algorithm.

5   Results

In order to calculate the amount of deviation of the predicted data from the real data, Root-Mean-Square-Error (*RMSE*) and Mean-Absolute-Error (*MAE*) were calculated for each predicted data file. The formulas of each metric are shown below:

$$RMSE = \sqrt{\frac{1}{N}\sum(y - \hat{y})^2} \tag{2}$$

$$MAE = \frac{1}{N}\sum|y - \hat{y}| \tag{3}$$

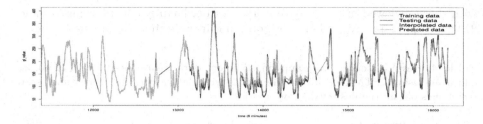

(a) This result corresponds to data with a PH 5 minutes.

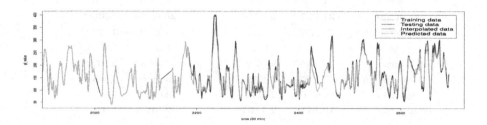

(b) This result corresponds to data with a PH 30 minutes.

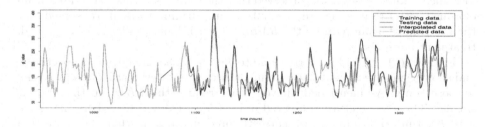

(c) This result corresponds to data with a PH 60 minutes.

Fig. 5. Comparison of test data with predicted data of patient 540. In addition, a part of the interpolated training data is displayed to visualize where the prediction starts.

After which the mean *RMSE* and *MAE* are calculated and used as performance measures for a given dataset treatment and *PH*. The results of these mean performance measures are shown in Table 4. From the three data treatments, time series method obtained the best prediction performance (lowest *RMSE* and *MAE* values) while the not interpolation method resulted in the weakest prediction performance (highest *RMSE* and *MAE* values). The *RMSE* values obtained in the present work for *PH* of both 30 and 60 min are quite competitive with those reviewed in the relative works section, having only 14.24 mg/dL and 21.98 mg/dL respectively. This work does not include time lag measurements.

Table 4. Resulting errors from applying different data treatments to data of 60, 30 and 5 min using LSTM algorithm. The results with data processing using time series techniques obtain the best evaluation metrics.

Time	Data treatment	Mean RMSE	Standard deviation RMSE	Mean MAE	Standard deviation MAE
60 min	*Not interpolated*	36.2730	6.1625	26.8833	4.6336
	Interpolated	33.9189	3.8244	24.9613	3.4702
	Time series	**21.9772**	**2.5514**	**20.0383**	**2.3893**
30 min	*Not interpolated*	32.3213	5.2312	24.1232	3.3277
	Interpolated	24.3728	3.6721	21.3122	3.1883
	Time series	**14.2389**	**2.9283**	**14.0831**	**2.9733**
5 min	*Not interpolated*	13.2037	3.4759	10.3112	2.5154
	Interpolated	12.8597	2.7113	10.0538	1.8988
	Time series	**12.6145**	**2.1157**	**9.8954**	**1.4171**

As expected, the lowest the prediction horizon the better the prediction performance is. In all cases it was observed that the datasets with a PH time of 5 min obtained better results than those of 30 min and 60 min. It was also observed that the *PH* time of 5 min reduced the *RMSE* and *MAE* mean difference between all treatment methods.

Figures 5(a), (b) and (c) correspond to data for 5, 30 and 60 min, respectively, and show a small section of the training dataset with interpolated data for visual purposes only. As mentioned above, as we reduce the *PH* time the error is smaller. This can be clearly observed in Figs. 5(a), (b) and (c), where the graph with *PH* time of 60 min has less correctly predicted regions than the one with a PH time of 5 min.

6   Conclusions

The proposed algorithm shows promising results for the prediction of blood glucose levels using data collected in a period of 5 min that are treated using time series prediction method. It is also evident that non-interpolated data significantly affect the correct prediction of glucose levels, therefore a pre-treatment of the data is necessary. Our results show a better performance with respect to previous papers [6,9,19] which do not interpolate data and others which interpolate with similar techniques but nevertheless do not obtain better results than those derived from a time series treatment.

This machine learning approach will help establish a reliable system able to detect possible episodes of hyperglycemia, hypoglycemia, and other concomitant complications in diabetic patients and help the user to prevent to enhance insulin administration decision-making and deliver effective therapy. This model represents an innovative alternative to predict glucose levels in real-time for patients suffering from type 1 diabetes ($T1D$).

6.1 Future Perspectives

According to recent works, accuracy is usually calculated over the entire glycemic range which may lead to deceptive conclusions. In future work it is necessary to segment the glycemic range into significant parts and analyze each subrange separately similar to the study carried out by Mayo et al. [19].

In addition to the Ohio database, our group currently working with a database of Ecuadorian patients which was provided by the research department of a national hospital. Some variables are similar to those found in the Ohio database, while others are completely different due to the nature of the data. We will apply the same methodology with some significant improvements in data preprocessing and build on top of the work done in this project. The relation between variables of the data needs to be investigated in depth, especially in countries where there is no culture of correct data handling and storage. This work is intended to be a first step in a project that in the future will improve the prediction of glucose levels in Ecuadorian patients and allow specialists to make life-saving decisions.

References

1. Hyperglycemia in diabetes. https://www.mayoclinic.org/diseases-conditions/hyperglycemia/symptoms-causes/syc-20373631
2. Continuous glucose monitoring and intensive treatment of type 1 diabetes. New Engl. J. Med. **359**(14), 1464–1476 (2008)
3. ADA: classification and diagnosis of diabetes: standards of medical care in diabetes. Diabetes Care **44**, S15–S33 (2020)
4. Apaydin, H., Feizi, H., Sattari, M., Colak, M.S., Band, S., Chau, K.W.: Comparative analysis of recurrent neural network architectures for reservoir inflow forecasting. Water **12**(5), 1500 (2020)
5. Benjamin, E.M.: Self-monitoring of blood glucose: the basics. Clin. Diabetes **20**(1), 45–47 (2002)
6. Bhimireddy, A.R., Sinha, P., Oluwalade, B., Gichoya, J., Purkayastha, S.: Blood glucose level prediction as time-series modeling using sequence-to-sequence neural networks. In: KDH@ECAI (2020)
7. De Bois, M., El Yacoubi, M.A., Ammi, M.: Adversarial multi-source transfer learning in healthcare: application to glucose prediction for diabetic people. Comput. Methods Prog. Biomed. **199**, 105874 (2021)
8. Che, Z., Purushotham, S., Cho, K., Sontag, D., Liu, Y.: Recurrent neural networks for multivariate time series with missing values (2016)
9. Chen, J., Li, K., Herrero, P., Zhu, T., Georgiou, P.: Dilated recurrent neural network for short-time prediction of glucose concentration. In: KDH@IJCAI (2018)
10. Gnauck, A.: Interpolation and approximation of water quality time series and process identification. Anal. Bioanal. Chem. **380**(3), 484–492 (2004). https://doi.org/10.1007/s00216-004-2799-3

11. Graves, A., Mohamed, A.R., Hinton, G.: Speech recognition with deep recurrent neural networks. In: 2013 IEEE International Conference on Acoustics, Speech and Signal Processing, pp. 6645–6649 (2013)
12. International Diabetes Federation: Diabetes Atlas, 3rd edn. International Diabetes Federation, Brussels (2006)
13. International Diabetes Federation: Diabetes Atlas, 6th edn. International Diabetes Federation, Brussels (2013)
14. International Diabetes Federation: Diabetes Atlas, 8th edn. International Diabetes Federation, Brussels (2017)
15. Kingma, D.P., Ba, J.: Adam: a method for stochastic optimization (2017)
16. Li, K., Liu, C., Zhu, T., Herrero, P., Georgiou, P.: GluNet: a deep learning framework for accurate glucose forecasting. IEEE J-BHI **24**(2), 414–423 (2019)
17. Marling, C., Bunescu, R.C.: The OhioT1DM dataset for blood glucose level prediction: update 2020. In: Proceedings of the 5th International Workshop on Knowledge Discovery in Healthcare Data Co-Located, vol. 2675, pp. 71–74. CEUR-WS.org (2020)
18. Martinsson, J., Schliep, A., Eliasson, B., Mogren, O.: Blood glucose prediction with variance estimation using recurrent neural networks. J. Healthc. Inform. Res. **4**(1), 1–18 (2020). https://doi.org/10.1007/s41666-019-00059-y
19. Mayo, M., Chepulis, L., Paul, R.G.: Glycemic-aware metrics and oversampling techniques for predicting blood glucose levels using machine learning. PLoS ONE **14**(12), 1–19 (2019)
20. Midroni, C., Leimbigler, P., Baruah, G., Kolla, M., Whitehead, A., Fossat, Y.: Predicting glycemia in type 1 diabetes patients: experiments with XG-Boost. In: KHD@ IJCAI (2018)
21. Rabby, M.F., Tu, Y., Hossen, M.I., Le, I., Maida, A.S., Hei, X.: Stacked LSTM based deep recurrent neural network with Kalman smoothing for blood glucose prediction. BMC Med. Inform. Decis. Making **21** (2021). Article number: 101. https://doi.org/10.1186/s12911-021-01462-5
22. Riemsma, R., et al.: Integrated sensor-augmented pump therapy systems [the MiniMed® paradigm™ Veo system and the Vibe™ and G4® PLATINUM CGM system] for managing blood glucose levels in type 1 diabetes: a systematic review and economic evaluation. Health Technol. Assess. **20**(17), 1–252 (2016)
23. Roglic, G.: Who global report on diabetes: a summary. Int. J. Non-Commun. Dis. **1**, 3–8 (2016). https://doi.org/10.4103/2468-8827.184853
24. Saeedi, P., et al.: Global and regional diabetes prevalence estimates for 2019 and projections for 2030 and 2045: results from the International Diabetes Federation Diabetes Atlas. Diabetes Res. Clin. Pract. **157**, 107843 (2019)
25. Saeedi, P., et al.: Mortality attributable to diabetes in 20–79 years old adults, 2019 estimates: results from the International Diabetes Federation Diabetes Atlas, 9th edition. Diabetes Res. Clin. Pract. **162**, 108086 (2020)
26. Shajun Nisha, S., Mohamed Sathik, M., Nagoor Meeral, M.: 3 - application, algorithm, tools directly related to deep learning. In: Balas, V.E., Mishra, B.K., Kumar, R. (eds.) Handbook of Deep Learning in Biomedical Engineering, pp. 61–84. Academic Press (2021)
27. Sherstinsky, A.: Fundamentals of recurrent neural network (RNN) and long short-term memory (LSTM) network. CoRR abs/1808.03314 (2018)
28. Velastegui, R., Zhinin-Vera, L., Pilliza, G.E., Chang, O.: Time series prediction by using convolutional neural networks. In: Arai, K., Kapoor, S., Bhatia, R. (eds.) FTC 2020. AISC, vol. 1288, pp. 499–511. Springer, Cham (2021). https://doi.org/10.1007/978-3-030-63128-4_38

29. Xie, J., Wang, Q.: Benchmark machine learning approaches with classical time series approaches on the blood glucose level prediction challenge. In: CEUR Workshop Proceedings, vol. 2148, pp. 97–102 (2018)
30. Zhu, T., Li, K., Chen, J., Herrero, P., Georgiou, P.: Dilated recurrent neural networks for glucose forecasting in type 1 diabetes. J. Healthc. Inform. Res. 4(3), 308–324 (2020). https://doi.org/10.1007/s41666-020-00068-2
31. Zhu, T., Li, K., Herrero, P., Chen, J., Georgiou, P.: A deep learning algorithm for personalized blood glucose prediction. In: KHD@ IJCAI, pp. 64–78 (2018)

Real-time Social Distancing Detection Approach Using YOLO and Unmanned Aerial Vehicles

Darwin Merizalde[1] and Paulina Morillo[1,2(✉)] [iD]

[1] Universidad Politécnica Salesiana, Quito, Ecuador
pmorillo@ups.edu.ec
[2] IDEIAGEOCA Research Group, Quito, Ecuador

Abstract. The current COVID-19 pandemic has undoubtedly brought new challenges to society and the constant search for solutions to control and reduce its effects. In this sense, the use of technology has become essential to cope with the situation. Thus, this work proposes a real-time social distancing detection system using Deep Learning algorithms and carrying out the monitoring through a UAV. This system consists of two fundamental blocks. The first one consists of convolutional neural network training to detect people using the YOLO object detection system while the second one consists of real-time video acquisition and analysis. Practical applications involves detecting people and calculating the distances between them to determine whether social distancing measurements are being obeyed or not. By increasing surveillance capabilities, authorities and security forces may control and prevent possible outbreaks of massive COVID-19 infections. The experiments were made in three different flight scenarios with altitudes of 15, 30, and 50 m. According to the results, the detection system's recall reaches values close to 90%, although the highest values were obtained in flights at 30 m high. Regarding the calculation of the distances, in the three scenarios, the average relative error did not exceed 5%. Thus, the video transmission showed a high performance during the experiments. Hence, the system returns reliable results to control compliance with measures such as social distancing.

Keywords: COVID-19 · UAV · CNN · YOLO · Computer vision · Deep learning

1 Introduction

Currently, society is facing one of the greatest challenges caused by COVID-19 [11]. Despite the rapid vaccination rates worldwide, the use of masks and the practice of social distancing are still required, forcing society to adapt to a new reality. All levels of society and the different disciplines of science have been

Supported by IDEIAGEOCA Research Group.

F. R. Narváez et al. (Eds.): SmartTech-IC 2021, CCIS 1532, pp. 114–127, 2022.
https://doi.org/10.1007/978-3-030-99170-8_9

focused on finding solutions to control and mitigate the effects of the pandemic. In this way, in the field of Artificial Intelligence (AI), algorithms for detection, monitoring, recognition, location, and counting of people [7] have taken center stage, in order to control crowds, detect sources of contagion, and offer health security to society.

Similarly, according to [15], it is necessary to use technological tools to control massive COVID-19 infections and prevent the spread of the virus [2]. Actions such as social distancing and the reduction of crowds are essential for this purpose, but, in many cases, these measures are difficult to control, so new tools must be available to verify their compliance [12]. The AI algorithms are very effective for this task. However, they do not work alone, they go hand in hand with video surveillance systems, which obtain images of the regions of interest. Its operation is based on the use of cameras fixed or integrated into mobile points [18], the latter facilitate monitoring, especially in areas of difficult access or high risk. In this sense, technological devices such as drones or unmanned aerial vehicles (UAVs) have proven to be very useful in monitoring the health crisis caused by COVID-19, managing to cover large areas, and determining infection focus [13]. Its integration with IA algorithms has made it possible to monitor the population in an almost automated way [8], facilitating the biosafety control measures. Additionally, the most current video surveillance systems act actively through optical sensors, which gives them the ability to identify signals, segment them, separate them, recognize them, and interpret a scene, in most cases in real-time. All of this, thanks to the development of Computer Vision and wireless communications [20].

Recent works show the effectiveness of Artificial Vision and Deep Learning algorithms to determine places with crowds of people, the body temperature of a person, the use of masks, social distancing, among others. For example, [5] shows the use of pre-trained convolutional neural networks (CNN) such as AlexNet and videos captured by drones to determine areas of a high density of people and measure social distancing. The algorithm they implement achieves more than 80% accuracy for the first phase of classification and close to 100% for the distance calculation. Similarly, in the article [3], UAV equipped with cameras and thermal sensors are used to capture information related to body temperature and determine possible COVID cases. Likewise, it presents a face detection scheme and use of the mask, obtaining accuracies greater than 99%. In another article [21], an implementation that involves the people detection is carried out, also through the use of convolutional neural networks in this case YOLO it (You Only Look Once). The distance tracing between the people of the scenario, with the detection of those who are violating social distancing, is made on virtual environments, using the platforms Gazebo and Robotic Operative System (ROS), their functions facilitate the real-environments virtualization in 3D.

As evidenced in the literature, there are several studies with different approaches that seek effective control of the measures taken during the pandemic. Likewise, this article proposes an automatic social distancing detection system, but in real-external environments, in scenarios captured by a camera incorporated into a UAV, with an effective angle of 0 to 45 °. To identify the objects of interest (people), an important Computer Vision algorithm and previously trained convolutional neural networks such as YOLO were used. After, the distance calculation was performed using Euclidean geometry in space. Thus, the methodology used is described in greater detail in Sect. 2, the experimental results of the implementation are presented in Sect. 3. Finally, in Sect. 4, the conclusions and prospects of this work are shown.

2   Methodology

The methodology followed in the development of the system consists of two blocks, as shown in the diagram in Fig. 1. The first block consists of the setting and training of the convolutional neural network used to detect people. It also includes the labeling images for training and model evaluation. The second block consists of the video analytic that involves communication with the UAV device, the acquisition and processing of the video in real-time, and the distances estimations between people. The results of the analysis were visualized in a user interface, which facilitates control and decision-making.

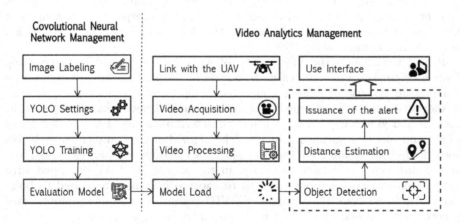

Fig. 1. General outline of the methodology

2.1   Setting and Training YOLO

Object detection is one method in Computer Vision that aims to localize objects in an image that contains more than one object. YOLO is an algorithm that uses a convolutional neural network model to detect objects [21]. This CNN performs the detection by adjusting the image pixels to an $S \times S$ matrix. If the class or object to be detected is within one of the generated grids, it is in charge of predicting by associating a probability value (Fig. 2).

The architecture of the convolutional neural network used in this work is the optimized version YOLO called "Tiny-Yolo-v2 version" [22], this version is the second of YOLO with a file model slightly trained weights to only consider a single type of objects, which in this case are people. It is similar to the full version but with a lower number of layers and filters since it consists of 3×3 convolutional layers and 1×1 reduction layers [16] plus fully connected layers, thus avoiding the use of a complete network that uses a total of 24×24 layers, which generates a high computational cost and in turn makes the implementation more expensive [14].

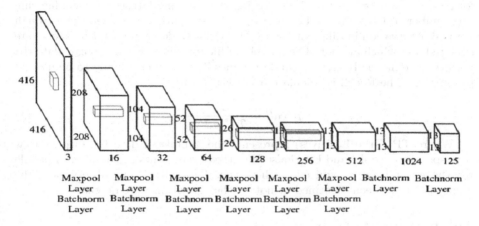

Fig. 2. Architecture tiny yolo V2 for image classification [22]

All convolutional neural network settings were carried out in the multifunctional Python language, thanks to its intuitive programming characteristics and its adequate CNN libraries support. Also, it is widely used by many application developers of Deep Learning. The used algorithm is fully adaptive and allows modifications in the layers to improve the performance of the model.

For the training of the convolutional neural network, a set of labeled images is required. In this case, there is a base of 1600 images obtained from UAV flights with cameras with 4k definition, captured in flights at heights from 15 to 50 m, with a camera whose resolution is 14 megapixels and its field of view (FOV) is up to 45 °. For a greater angle up to the zenith perspective, another training is required [19]. The labeling process of each image consists of manually drawing the desired objects (people), using free software based on Python called *LabelImg*, which saves the points that make up the drawn rectangle (which represents the object) and their positions. In this way, the CNN identifies the position of the object and then can classify it. Subsequently, a file .xml is generated with annotations of the location of each class and object within the image [11], these objects are the detection boxes that each scenario contains and that the algorithm learns to detect. As a result of this process, the machine will learn to classify the objects and mark their position in the scene with a detection box [9].

After labeling, the model is created and trained using these images as input. The input image is integrated with the labeling matrix, and then it is normalized, resulting in a unitary matrix that contains the same information. Then these images are passed by the different convolutional layers to extract the characteristics that will allow their classification. The training generates a model with the least amount of loss in object detection. Once the model is created, a test is carried out with images that were not part of the training set. In this way, its real performance can be evaluated. If the model does not have a good performance, it can be fine-tuned, debugging the training dataset or re-configuring the number of CNN layers. In this work, the evaluation is carried out through manual observation in different frames of a video to determine which objects are detected and which are not. The number of hits or misses is used to calculate the performance metric Recall, which determines if the model is ready to be used in production. The Recall is calculate using Eq. 1 [16].

$$Recall = \frac{TP}{TP + FN} \tag{1}$$

Where TP (True Positives) represents the number of detected objects that correspond to people, and FN (False Negatives) represents the number of people who have not been recognized at the scene. Through manual observation, the items that have been identified or not by the algorithm were detected.

2.2   Real-time Video Analytics

To begin with, the video is acquired through cameras incorporated in the UAV. in which certain parameters of hardware usage are previously initialized such as GPU activation (Graphical Process Unit) and the height values and camera angle during the flight. These variables will be crucial for the distance calculation. Once the frames are captured, they become the input of YOLO, which detects the objects (people) into the scene in real-time.

Video Acquisition via a UAV. The communication between the drone and the video analytics system uses the video transmission protocols through a streaming server called Real Time Multiple Message (RTMP). This protocol allows obtaining the video in real-time [6].

Then, in order for the computer and the UAV to maintain communication with each other, it is necessary to create an internal network with an intranet video server that captures the vision of the UAV locally from any computer, and in the best possible resolution depending on the network bandwidth and the video transmission rate. Optionally, the system allows the use of screen transmission tools to the WAN such as OBS (Open Broadcaster Studio), which only redirected the video to the public transmission server [10], to transmit the video processing to an external user.

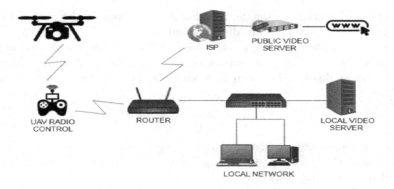

Fig. 3. System communication diagram.

Social Distancing Calculating. After the people are identified in the video and before calculating the distances between them, the number of objects (n) detected in the scene is determined, thus creating a $n \times 4$ matrix (M), where the columns contain the four coordinates of the rectangle that surrounds each object, then the centroid of each rectangle is calculated, which will be used to determine the distance of that object to all the others. With the centroids of each object, we proceed to calculate a matrix of Euclidean distances $(D_{n \times n})$ where each element d_{ij} represents the distance from the object O_i to the object O_j $(i = j = 1, 2, .., n)$. Finally, each distance is compared with a threshold value, that according to the World Health Organization, varies from 1.5 to 2 m [11]. In this way, compliance with social distancing is verified. Those people who do not comply with the expected distance will be framed in red to facilitate monitoring and issue a violation alert to this measure.

To obtain the separation between two objects, first, the rectangles that define the detection objects are obtained, each rectangle is defined through four vertices with which the centroid [8] is calculated through the Eq. 5. It will locate the object's center of gravity at each detection.

$$\bar{I}_x = \frac{bh^3}{12} \tag{2}$$

$$\bar{I}_y = \frac{b^3 h}{12} \tag{3}$$

$$\bar{I}_{xy} = 0 \tag{4}$$

$$C = (\bar{I}_x, \bar{I}_y) \tag{5}$$

Where $\bar{I}_x$ represents the point of inertia on the x axis, $\bar{I}_y$ represents the point of inertia on the y axis, $\bar{I}_{xy}$ would be the inertia at both points, which would generally be zero, b is the value of the base of the rectangle, h represents the height of the detection rectangle, and finally, C represent the centroid of the rectangle, all these variables are dimensioned in pixels.

Once the centroids or centers of gravity of the objects have been obtained, the value for both x and y of each detection rectangle is taken as a reference, and a Euclidean distance is drawn between each of the centroid points using the Eq. 6 [2]

$$d = \sqrt{(x_1 - x_2)^2 + (y_1 - y_2)^2} \tag{6}$$

Where d represents the distance, x_1 is the position of the first point in x, x_2 is the value of the second point in x, y_1 and y_2 are the positions in and at the first and second point, respectively.

For marking the distance based on the real-high and the measurement of the height frame, a calibration based on the similarity of triangles was performed by auto-calibration method [17], taking as reference the angle of the camera and the height of flight from the UAV using Pythagorean rule 7.

$$f_d = \frac{a}{h * cos(\gamma - \alpha - \beta)} \tag{7}$$

Where f_d represents the distance adjustment factor that will be applied at the distance within the analyzed scenario, a represents the image height in pixels, h represents the UAV height, γ represents the maximum angle of vision of the camera that can cover, α, represents the intermediate reference angle from the position of the camera to the minimum angle that the camera can observe [4] and for the last β is the dead angle, which the camera is no longer able to observe. These parameters consider a frontal perspective with a camera angle greater than 45 ° because when the camera is located in a zenithal view, the panorama changes completely, being α equal to zero, and the rest of the angles are uniformly distributed with a view towards both sides. It is important to mention that the YOLO detection system improves its object recognition performance with camera angles ranging from 45 to 90 ° [1].

Evaluation of the distances calculus, two metrics are used (Eqs. 8 and 9) that represent the absolute error and the relative error, respectively. The term X_e is the measurement estimated by the system, also called the estimated distance, and X_r represents the actual distance measured in the field where the experiments were performed.

$$E_a = \mid X_e - X_r \mid \tag{8}$$

$$E_r = \frac{E_a}{X_e} = \frac{\mid X_e - X_r \mid}{X_r} \tag{9}$$

To define the global error of the algorithm used to calculate the distances, proceed to calculate the mean of both errors E_a and E_r (Eqs. 10 and 11), adding the individual errors and dividing by the total number (n) of objects found in each frame.

$$\overline{E_a} = \frac{\sum_{i=1}^{n} |X_e - X_r|}{n} \tag{10}$$

The Eq. 11 is available for the mean of the relative error.

$$\overline{E_r} = \frac{\sum_{i=1}^{n} \frac{E_a}{X_r}}{n} = \frac{\sum_{i=1}^{n} \frac{|X_e - X_r|}{X_r}}{n} \tag{11}$$

3   Experiments and Results

The system's people detection block, used by YOLO, is mounted on Darknet and CUDA, while openCV is used for processing videos and images. Table 1 shows the hardware and software specifications of the system implementation.

In the experimentation phase, ten frames of three different scenarios have been randomly selected, taken at 15, 30, and 50 m high (Scenario 1, Scenario 2, Scenario 3, respectively). The metrics considered in the experiments were the sensitivity of the algorithm in the detection of people, the error in the calculation of the distances, and the latency times in the transmission of the video.

Fig. 4. Frame example showing people detection results, the camera was at 15 m high and 45 ° angle of vision.

People Detection Model Performance. Figure 4 shows the detection of people in a frame of a video in real-time. The camera high was at $15m$ and $45°$ angle of vision. The detection was made over a frame, which is one of the thousands that are captured in a video. The values of Table 2 were obtained with a random sample of ten frames in different time intervals. Despite the fact that the video frequency is 60 Hz, for the processing (people detection and distance calculation), only four frames per second are taken. The experiment was carried out in the same way for the three scenarios.

Table 1. Hardware and software specifications.

Item	Specification
Drone	Bebop-2 Parrot
Camera	Bebop 14 Mpxls Native
Computer	Laptop
Processor	Intel Core i7
Memory	16 GB RAM
GPU	NVIDIA, Geforce GTX-960
Operating System	Windows 10
Python	v. 3.7
OpenCV	v. 4.1
CUDA	v. 10
Darknet	v. 1.0

As shown in Table 2 the Recall is higher in flights of 30 m high. It is because the resolution of the UAV camera improves at that distance and that the trained neural network better determines the characteristics of the object and recognizes them as such.

Table 2. Summary object detection model performance

Frames	Scenario 1 (15 m)				Scenario 2 (30 m)				Scenario 3 (50 m)			
	Objects	VP	FN	Recall	Objects	VP	FN	Recall	Objects	VP	FN	Recall
F1	20	18	2	0,9000	7	7	0	1,0000	6	6	0	1,0000
F2	21	20	2	0,9524	9	9	0	1,0000	2	2	0	1,0000
F3	22	20	2	0,9091	8	7	1	0,8750	8	6	2	0,7500
F4	19	16	3	0,8421	8	8	0	1,0000	6	5	1	0,8333
F5	21	20	1	0,9524	7	6	1	0,8571	6	6	0	1,0000
F6	22	19	3	0,8636	7	6	1	0,8571	8	7	1	0,8750
F7	19	18	1	0,9474	7	6	1	0,8571	5	5	0	1,0000
F8	20	18	2	0,9000	7	6	1	0,8571	6	5	1	0,8333
F9	22	20	2	0,9091	7	6	1	0,8571	3	2	1	0,6670
F10	17	16	1	0,9412	7	6	1	0,8571	5	5	0	1,000
Mean	20	18,5	1,8	0,9117	7	6,7	0,7	0,9018	6	4,9	0,6	0,8958

Error Estimation in the Distance Calculus. The distances measured in the frames of the different scenarios are contrasted with the real measurements of the distance manually through a mechanical odometer, allowing compare the error made for the algorithm.

Fig. 5. Frame example showing the estimating distances between people, the camera was at 30 m high and 45 ° angle of vision.

Table 3. Summary average errors in the distance calculus of each frame

Frames	Scenario 1			Scenario 2			Scenario 3		
	n	$\bar{E}a$	$\bar{E}r$	n	$\bar{E}a$	$\bar{E}r$	n	$\bar{E}a$	$\bar{E}r$
F1	20	0,1700	0,0170	7	0.1800	0.0178	6	0,3100	0,0163
F2	21	0,0500	0,0250	9	0.3200	0.0321	2	0,0500	0,0250
F3	22	0,0500	0,0250	8	0.3100	0.0312	8	0,3900	0,0780
F4	19	0,0800	0,0160	8	0.2400	0.0243	6	0,4300	0,0253
F5	21	0,2600	0,0200	7	0.2900	0.0289	6	0,3200	0,0363
F6	22	0,1300	0,0433	7	0.1800	0.0178	8	0,3500	0,0463
F7	19	0,2500	0,0500	7	0.2300	0.0229	5	0,4500	0,0023
F8	20	0,1800	0,0200	7	0.3100	0.0311	6	0,2000	0,0133
F9	22	0,3100	0,3100	7	0.2900	0.0288	3	0,3100	0,0155
F10	17	0,1400	0,0467	7	0.3200	0.0317	5	0,1100	0,0069
Media	**20**	**0,1620**	**0,0573**	**7**	**0,2670**	**0,0267**	**6**	**0,2920**	**0,0265**

Figure 5 shows an example of the distances between people calculated by the system (blue lines) in Scenario 2, at a 30 m high. In each frame, the values calculated by the system are compared with the respective real values measured by the odometer. So, the absolute and relative error is calculated (Table 4). In the end, the average error made in each frame is calculated, and this process is repeated in the other two scenarios. The results and the average errors of each frame are summarized in the Table 3.

Table 4. Example of error distance estimation - Scenario 3

d	Estimated	Real	E_a	E_r (%)
1-2	10,03	10,35	0,32	0,03
2-3	5,81	6,12	0,31	0,05
1-3	9,48	9,32	0,16	0,02
Mean			**0,26**	**0,03**

In the first scenario, at 15 m height, an average of absolute error was obtained 0.1620 m, an average relative error of 0.0573, which is lower than the other two scenarios. On the other hand, in the second and third cases at 30 and 50 m height, respectively, the average relative error was very close.

Performance in Video Transmission. A fundamental aspect in a system that works in real-time is the video transmission latency, since the rest of the processes such as detection, distance calculation, and the delay time of the video. The communication tests with the UAV were made from a *Bebop 2* drone of the PARROT brand with a mobile application called *Larix Screencaster* that allows communication with any type of RTMP video server. This protocol allows video to be transmitted in Streaming. In the case of more robust UAVs such as *DJI*, it can be transmitted through its native applications. Connection tests have been carried out by this transmission method, during the test period, more than 100 video transmission connections have been achieved, and none had failures. Hence, in general, the communication system was stable, and it did not have major connective problems since the server is the one who performs the calculations to configure the most suitable transmission frequency to avoid latencies during transmission.

Table 5 shows the performance of captured video about other parameters such as frequency, transmission speed, etc. The results show the performance is proportional to the speed of the available network, for example, if the performance transmission is 50%, it means that the server will let one pass for every two frames that is half the frames sent by the UAV. The camera resolution used for the experiment was 740×480 Megapixels.

About the transmission frequency, the server provides 30 to 25 frames per second, thus obtaining a natural and real-time transmission. However, the object detection and distance calculation require additional time that could cause transmission delays and latency. To solve this problem, the detection is made every ten frames, thus giving enough time to perform the analytics video and that the results be properly synchronized on the screen.

Table 5. Video streaming parameters

Frequency	Transmission speed	Network speed	Fps	Performance (%)
60 Hz	20 Mbps	10 Mbps	30	50
30 Hz	10 Mbps	10 Mbps	30	100
15 Hz	5 Mbps	10 Mbps	60	200

4   Conclusions and Future Work

The resulsts of the proposed real-time social distancing detection system shows that the Recall of the detection model of people was close to 90% with errors in the estimation of the distances lower than 3%. As a result, the system may be used to issue alerts to people who are violating the COVID-19 distancing restrictions in order to prevent possible new COVID-19 infections.

According to the flight tests carried out at heights of 15 m, 30 m, and 50 m, the flight altitude that achieved the highest Recall was 30 m. This length is suitable for control purposes of social distancing. Heights less than 15 m, in addition to obtaining less sensitivity, it has a greater risk of the instrument beings sabotaged from the ground.

As shown in the introduction, several works, including this, use convolutional neural networks to detect with high precision the compliance with measures such as social distancing, use of a mask, or detecting crowds in the context of COVID-19. However, in future works, it would be interesting to analyze and compare the performance of these models and their computational cost, as these are two significant parameters for systems to be successful in real-time applications.

References

1. Aghaei, M., Bustreo, M., Wang, Y., Bailo, G., Morerio, P., Del Bue, A.: Single image human proxemics estimation for visual social distancing. In: 2021 IEEE Winter Conference on Applications of Computer Vision (WACV), pp. 2784–2794 (2021). https://doi.org/10.1109/WACV48630.2021.00283
2. Ahamad, A.H., Zaini, N., Latip, M.F.A.: Person detection for social distancing and safety violation alert based on segmented ROI. In: 2020 10th IEEE International Conference on Control System, Computing and Engineering (ICCSCE), pp. 113–118 (2020). https://doi.org/10.1109/ICCSCE50387.2020.9204934
3. Barnawi, A., Chhikara, P., Tekchandani, R., Kumar, N., Alzahrani, B.: Artificial intelligence-enabled internet of things-based system for covid-19 screening using aerial thermal imaging. Future Gen. Comput. Syst. **124**, 119–132 (2021)

4. Bhambani, K., Jain, T., Sultanpure, K.A.: Real-time face mask and social distancing violation detection system using yolo. In: 2020 IEEE Bangalore Humanitarian Technology Conference (B-HTC), pp. 1–6 (2020). https://doi.org/10.1109/B-HTC50970.2020.9297902

5. Bouhlel, F., Mliki, H., Hammami, M.: Crowd behavior analysis based on convolutional neural network: social distancing control covid-19. In: VISIGRAPP (5: VISAPP), pp. 273–280 (2021)

6. Chalmers, C., Fergus, P., Aday Curbelo Montanez, C., Longmore, S., Wich, S.: Video analysis for the detection of animals using convolutional neural networks and consumer-grade drones. J. Unman. Veh. Syst. **9**(2), 112–127 (2021). https://doi.org/10.1139/juvs-2020-0018

7. Chan, A.B., Liang, Z.S.J., Vasconcelos, N.: Privacy preserving crowd monitoring: Counting people without people models or tracking. In: 2008 IEEE Conference on Computer Vision and Pattern Recognition. pp. 1–7 (2008). https://doi.org/10.1109/CVPR.2008.4587569

8. Degadwala, S., Vyas, D., Dave, H., Mahajan, A.: Visual social distance alert system using computer vision amp; deep learning. In: 2020 4th International Conference on Electronics, Communication and Aerospace Technology (ICECA), pp. 1512–1516 (2020). https://doi.org/10.1109/ICECA49313.2020.9297510

9. Dobrea, D.M., Dobrea, M.C.: An autonomous UAV system for video monitoring of the quarantine zones. Rom. J. Inf. Sci. Technol. **23**, 53–66 (2020)

10. Doull, K., Chalmers, C., Fergus, P., Longmore, S., Piel, A., Wich, S.: An evaluation of the factors affecting 'poacher' detection with drones and the efficacy of machine-learning for detection. Sensors **21**(12) (2021). https://doi.org/10.3390/s21124074,

11. Gawde, B.B.: A fast, automatic risk detector for covid-19. In: 2020 IEEE Pune Section International Conference (PuneCon). pp. 146–151 (2020). https://doi.org/10.1109/PuneCon50868.2020.9362389

12. Gupta, S., Kapil, R., Kanahasabai, G., Joshi, S.S., Joshi, A.S.: SD-measure: a social distancing detector. In: 2020 12th International Conference on Computational Intelligence and Communication Networks (CICN), pp. 306–311 (2020). https://doi.org/10.1109/CICN49253.2020.9242628

13. Kumar, A., Sharma, K., Singh, H., Naugriya, S.G., Gill, S.S., Buyya, R.: A drone-based networked system and methods for combating coronavirus disease (covid-19) pandemic. Future Gen. Comput. Syst. **115**, 1–19 (2021)

14. Madane, S., Chitre, D.: Social distancing detection and analysis through computer vision. In: 2021 6th International Conference for Convergence in Technology (I2CT), pp. 1–10 (2021). https://doi.org/10.1109/I2CT51068.2021.9418195

15. Naqiyuddin, F.A., Mansor, W., Sallehuddin, N.M., Mohd Johari, M.N.S., Shazlan, M.A.S., Bakar, A.N.: Wearable social distancing detection system. In: 2020 IEEE International RF and Microwave Conference (RFM), pp. 1–4 (2020). https://doi.org/10.1109/RFM50841.2020.9344786

16. Paredes, M., Calderón, M., Riquelme, J., Darwin, M.: Multipurpose unmanned system: an efficient solution to increase the capabilities of the UAVs. In: 2020 IEEE ANDESCON, pp. 1–6 (2020). https://doi.org/10.1109/ANDESCON50619.2020.9272196

17. Pizarro, D.A., Campos, P.: Comparación de técnicas de calibración de cámaras digitales **13**(1), 57–67 (2005)

18. Rashied Hussein, M., Shams, A.B., Hoque Apu, E., Abdullah Al Mamun, K., Shahriar Rahman, M.: Digital surveillance systems for tracing Covid-19: privacy and security challenges with recommendations. arXiv e-prints arXiv:2007.13182, July 2020

19. Shao, Z., Cheng, G., Ma, J., Wang, Z., Wang, J., Li, D.: Real-time and accurate UAV pedestrian detection for social distancing monitoring in Covid-19 pandemic. IEEE Trans. Multim. **99**, 1–1 (2021). https://doi.org/10.1109/TMM.2021.3075566
20. Siriwardhana, Y., De Alwis, C., Gür, G., Ylianttila, M., Liyanage, M.: The fight against the Covid-19 pandemic with 5g technologies. IEEE Eng. Manag. Rev. **48**(3), 72–84 (2020)
21. Somaldo, P., Ferdiansyah, F.A., Jati, G., Jatmiko, W.: Developing smart Covid-19 social distancing surveillance drone using yolo implemented in robot operating system simulation environment. In: 2020 IEEE 8th R10 Humanitarian Technology Conference (R10-HTC), pp. 1–6 (2020). https://doi.org/10.1109/R10-HTC49770. 2020.9357040
22. Wai, Y.J., Yussof, Z.b.M., bin Salim, S.I., Chuan, L.K.: Fixed point implementation of tiny-Yolo-v2 using OpenCL on FPGA. Int. J. Adv. Comput. Sci. Appl. **9**(10), 506–512 (2018). https://doi.org/10.14569/IJACSA.2018.091062, www.ijacsa.thesai.org

An Approach to Estimate the Orientation and Movement Trend of a Person in the Vicinity of an Industrial Robot

Vanessa Morales, Adriel Machado, Mauricio Arias$^{(\boxtimes)}$ ⓘ, Carlos Sánchez, Wilfer Nieto, and Yorman Gómez

Vision and Photonics Lab, Instituto Tecnológico Metropolitano Calle 73 No. 76A - 354 Vía Al Volador, Medellín, Colombia
mauricioarias@itm.edu.co

Abstract. Implementation of industrial robots worldwide -not only typical caged robots, manipulating heavy machinery and performing repetitive tasks, but also collaborative robots-, comes with the challenge of guaranteeing the safety of human operators, whether they work aside from the robot or in its vicinity. The UNE-EN ISO10218 safety standards for industrial robots set that robots and people can work in common spaces if robots have safety devices or are supported by them, to avoid hurt human operators. This paper introduces an approach that allows estimating the orientation and movement trend of a person in the vicinity of a robotized industrial task, aiming to avoid the collision between human and robot. As a previous requirement of the approach, a PointNet architecture was trained with the point clouds obtained from Depth images of a proprietary RGB-D image dataset. This task, in turn, required detecting people in the corresponding RGB images, through the application of a pre-trained saliency algorithm. To estimate the orientation of the detected person, a modified Biternion network was trained with the resized images from the same proprietary database. At evaluating the system, depth images captured by a Kinect sensor were used as inputs, then, for a set of four iterations (four frames), the movement trend was calculated since the orientation of the person was known for every frame. The prediction capability of the proposed approach was evaluated with three groups of images and resulted in a general precision greater than 0.5.

Keywords: Convolutional neural networks · Orientation estimation · Industrial robot safety · RGB-D images · Collision detection

1 Introduction

According to data from the International Federation of Robotics (IFR), by the end of 2019 there were 2.7 million industrial robots operating in factories around the world (an increase of 12% compared to 2018). At a global level, COVID-19 pandemic has had a great impact on production in 2020, however, it has also made clear the advantages of implementing industrial robots in different production tasks. Such automation is

F. R. Narváez et al. (Eds.): SmartTech-IC 2021, CCIS 1532, pp. 128–142, 2022.
https://doi.org/10.1007/978-3-030-99170-8_10

not only done by typical caged robots, manipulating heavy machinery, and performing repetitive tasks, but also by collaborative robots. As proposed by Industry 4.0, there is an increasing number of tasks in which humans and robots combine their skills in collaborative work, therefore previously existing barriers (separating human and robot workspaces) have disappeared [1–3]. Nevertheless, in collaborative environments the safety of human operators is a constant challenge and therefore it is required that during the execution of the robot's tasks, possible collisions with humans be avoided [3, 4]. According to the UNE-EN ISO10218 safety standard, robots and people can work in collaborative spaces if the robots have safety devices or are supported by them, to avoid hurt the human operators [5].

Computer vision techniques have been widely used in the workspace of industrial robots. In [6], an autonomous intelligent system with environmental awareness ready for human/robot interaction, uses the information retrieved from the machine vision system during path planning stage to detect obstacles and re-plan motion paths to enable pick-and place operations while interacting with a dynamically moving obstacle in the robot workspace. A system that uses ROS (Robot Operating System) and an RGB-Depth sensor to acquire objects and humans in the surrounding environment, is introduced in [7]. This implementation allows to replan the robot's movements, avoiding collisions while guaranteeing the execution of tasks. A self-identification method developed for a dual-arm robot, based on the 3D point cloud and the robot skeleton, demonstrates in [8] that the collision prediction system can avoid the collision even if the obstacle is close to the robot, and at the same time, prevent unnecessary robot movements when the obstacle is far enough from the robot. The method is supported by images acquired with an RGB-Depth sensor (Kinect). Due to the level of risk presented by the interaction of robotic arms with humans, in [9] the authors modelled safe scenarios using stereo cameras. Both humans, and robots were modelled in 3D and safe trajectories were calculated from these models. This also made possible to determine risk areas and safe passage areas for people. Other works combine artificial vision techniques with haptic devices installed on the operator's body, that provide information to the robot controller about the operator's location in relation to the robot's work volume -and its trajectory- [10]. Nevertheless, the system is neither practical nor safe. Once possible collisions have been detected, it is possible to avoid them by means of trajectory and speed control algorithms [11] or through devices that redirect the impact force such as variable impedance actuators [12].

An approach to estimate the orientation and movement trend of a person in the vicinity of a robotic industrial task, with the aim of avoiding the collision between human and robot is proposed in this work. The approach uses a saliency algorithm and RGB-Depth images from a proprietary dataset [13] to train a people´s detector based on PointNet architecture. Once the detection has been carried out, an estimation of orientation is made by means of a modified Biternion architecture [14]. The operation is iterated, and the movement tendency of a person is obtained. The remainder of this paper is organized as follows: Sect. 2 presents relevant related work to our approach. In Sect. 3, the dataset's creation and PointNet based human detector training is presented. Section 4 introduces the proposed approach consisted of a human detection pre-trained network, a modified Biternion network to estimate the orientation angle of the detected person and a person's movement trending estimation. Section 5 presents experimental results; finally, we conclude this paper in Sect. 6.

2   Related Work

Related to the orientation of people and the detection of movement trends, we found [15] in which neural networks with multi-scale graphs are used to learn the characteristics of people's movements and predict their movement. In [16] multiple sequences of people's movement postures are predicted through 3D images using a skeleton, which is generated by means of an RGB-D sensor. A novel neural network model to predict the human trajectory and future activity -simultaneously- in public spaces, by means of enriched visual characteristics, is presented in [17] with very good results for pedestrians in an environment surveilled by cameras. The movement characteristics of people are used to train recurrent neural networks (RNN) in [18], yielding the prediction of movement because of the approximation. Predicting the trajectory of people in environments designed for humans is a critical task for both social robots and autonomous vehicles and the analysis of the behavior of the agents involved in the movement is the basis of the prediction of trajectory in the work of [19], where the authors introduce a recurrent generative model that exploits a neural network based on double attention, to collect information about the mutual influences between the different agents and predicts the trajectory of people.

The orientation of a person moving in the vicinity of a robotic task is a useful attribute for different human-robot interaction (HRI) tasks [20]. Depth images have been shown to have greater advantages for orientation estimation than RGB images -or a combination of both- [14]. In our work, it is relevant to estimate the movement orientation of a person and his movement trend when moving in the vicinity of a robotic industrial task. With such information, it can be known whether the person is moving in the direction of the industrial robot's workload (imminent collision).

To estimate the orientation of a person's upper body as a continuous angle around the axis perpendicular to the floor, modern Deep Learning (DL) techniques are used, usually convolutional neural networks [14, 20, 21]. This is achieved from direct estimation on RGB images, or by deriving the orientation from skeleton-like images. In the second case, the calculation of the body's joints is required, and the orientation is subsequently derived by means of a vector perpendicular to the chest. There are several approaches to skeleton estimation and therefore to extract orientation [22, 23], however, skeleton estimation is computationally expensive and requires inference in real time.

In direct estimation, the features extracted from the input image are mapped to an orientation value, as presented in [24], but deep neural networks can also be trained to estimate the orientation, either to obtain a regression or a classification. Viewed as a multiclass classification problem, the orientation estimation yields discretized outputs in the range of $0°$ to $360°$ in a fixed set of eight classes (typically) where each class covers $45°$ [25–27], which yields errors of -at least- $11.25°$. A larger number of classes would increase the computational cost and the amount of data needed for training. On the other hand, when the orientation estimation problem is treated as a regression problem, the angles are calculated continuously and therefore the result is more exact as presented in [28].

The orientation's estimation performance treated as both: a regression and classification problem (multi-class) are presented in [21], where the classification is extended to the continuous domain with very low execution times. Authors based their approach on the attribute estimation of [29], and both, color and depth images obtained from a Kinect sensor are transformed into colored point clouds representing people. Mean angular error (MAE) is 12.2° with 79.8 ms runtime from a consumer CPU.

On the other hand, in [14], the authors estimate the orientation of the trajectory of people from RGB and Depth images using Biternion networks as a baseline in their experiments, which resulted in an estimation of the orientation of the upper body with mean absolute errors (MAE) between 3° and 12° and estimation speeds (including detection) of up to 13.43 frames per second.

Estimating the orientation of the head is a process like estimating the orientation of the upper body, but in the first case, the result also provides information regarding the direction of a person's gaze [30]. To determine the pose of a person's head in degrees using periodic intervals from 0° to 360°, an approach is proposed in [20] based on convolutional neural networks (CNN) with an output layer that integrates an angle in two dimensions. The architecture is called biternion networks and its effectiveness for continuous periodic orientation regression is demonstrated through validation with different datasets.

Based on the review of orientation algorithms, we chose to work with the biternion architecture to estimate the orientation of a person's body in the vicinity of a robotic task and subsequently determine its movement trend. Estimating the orientation of the head is not considered a sufficiently robust characteristic to contribute to determining the movement trend of a person, because a person could be looking at a different place to which he is directing.

3 Human Detection Training with RGB-d Dataset

A human detector based on PointNet architecture was trained with point clouds obtained from Depth labelled images, which have been mapped from correspondent RGB labelled images. Automatic labelling in RGB images begins at applying a pre-trained saliency algorithm, to an RGB-D dataset. The process is explained in this chapter.

3.1 RGB-d Dataset

People detection systems in robotic environments based on RGB-D images require large datasets for their training [31]. One of the most popular devices for acquiring RGB-D images is Microsoft's Kinect sensor, due to its low cost, the resolution of its depth images (640px × 480px in its first version) and the ease of implementation [32].

In [31, 33, 34] datasets acquired with the Kinect sensor are presented, consisting of images of office objects, utensils, furniture, household goods, and cleaning implements. There are also datasets obtained indoors, consisting of images of bedrooms, bathrooms, study rooms, and kitchens, which are very useful in machine vision-supported mobile robot navigation tasks [35–37], but are different from datasets used to apply the simultaneous localization and mapping (SLAM) technique of mobile robots [38, 39]. Other datasets with RGB-D images have been created for human activity detection and recognition tasks [40], in which both men and women assume different positions with their hands. In [41], a pair of Kinect sensors were installed (facing each other) to acquire images of groups of people engaged in recreational activities such as raising their hands, clapping, throwing objects, and moving. Gestures as well as body posture are of particular interest in [42]. In this work there are RGB-D images related to finger movements, lip movements and other facial expressions classified in 20 categories of gestures stored as depth images, skeleton images and RGB images. A dataset of RGB-D images of the human body performing different activities of daily life is presented in [43], which is particularly interesting due to the different types of occlusions in the human figure.

Table 1. Classification of acquired RGB-Depth images. Source: [13]

Class	Type	Quantity of images
One person	RGB + Depth	562 + 562
Two people	RGB + Depth	1174 + 1174
Three to four people	RGB + Depth	3548 + 3548
No person	RGB + Depth	5260 + 5260

In [13], a review of 20 RGB-D datasets available on the web is presented. Some of these datasets, containing images of household objects, offices, people tracking, and people in daily activities -among others-, however, the authors did not find any RGB-D image dataset related to people moving in the vicinity of a robotized industrial task (or robotic industrial process) and that is their main reason to introduce a dataset called RGBD DHaRIo. The dataset comprises images of people moving around a robotized industrial task known as dishware pick and place task. The images were obtained by means of a Kinect sensor. The robotized industrial task was performed by a 6 DOF rotational manipulator robot, a conveyor belt, and operators. Both the RGB images and Depth images acquired by the Kinect have a resolution of 640 × 480 pixels and have been classified according to the number of people present in the image as shown in Table 1. In Fig. 1, examples can be seen of images for one, two and more than two people.

3.2 Salient Detection

In computer vision the detection of relevant elements (saliency or salient detection), is a concept that refers to the simultaneous performance of two stages: the stage of detection of relevant objects in an image and the stage of precise segmentation of the regions corresponding to those objects. These stages are clearly differentiated in the works of [44–46], while in [47], a top-down model based on the HED (Holistically-nested Edge Detection) architecture but introducing additional connections that allow the network to precisely locate the positions of salient objects, is designed. A pre-trained model from [47] has been used in our approach to perform a good detection of relevant elements in RGB images, which are part of the RGBD- DHaRIo dataset. The output of the algorithm

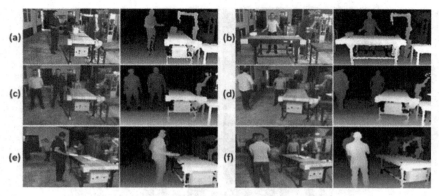

Fig. 1. RGB and Depth images for: (a) 1 person; (b) 1 person with occlusion; (c) 2 people; (d) 2 people with occlusion; (e) and (f) 3 people. Source: [13].

consists of a labelling file which has the coordinates of the regions of interest (ROI) in the images (green regions representing the people), as seen in Fig. 2.

The coordinates of the generated ROIs (saved in a labelling file) constitute the input to another algorithm, in charge of mapping the ROIs in the corresponding Depth images of the database (i.e., the images that were obtained simultaneously through the Kinect.

The ROIs of relevant elements in the RGB images have been mapped to their corresponding Depth images, therefore, for an *RGBi* image in which there are m relevant elements with m bounding boxes of x, y, w, h coordinates each; the same m squares can be obtained in the corresponding Di image (for the same relevant elements), in depth values.

It must be clear that the output of the saliency algorithm not only detects people as "relevant objects", but it can also detect some of the machines -or even the robot- that are part of the process. It can also happen that a relevant region includes both a human and a machine. To avoid that the ROIs in the images correspond to machines or non-people, a human detector based on PointNet was trained, using the point clouds generated from the depth images.

3.3 Human Detection

PointNet [48] an approach based on CNN for object classification, works directly with point clouds without previous treatment, that is why in our work PointNet receives the point clouds corresponding to the segmented regions of depth images (from our dataset) and yields the number of people present in the image as a class. In our work, PointNet has been trained with 19597-point clouds and the evaluation was carried out with 4899. The training with 250 epochs presented an accuracy of 96% and the loss function was: 0.096735. The whole procedure since the RGB-D are loaded as inputs until the obtained output as a classification result is shown in Fig. 3.

Like the procedure presented in [13], the detection of people in the vicinity of robotic industrial tasks using the RGBD- DHaRIo dataset images, consist of the following steps: obtaining the ROIs in the RGB images by applying saliency; mapping the coordinates of

Fig. 2. Detection of relevant elements in RGB images in which 1 person appears. The OpenCV library for Python was used to apply filters, obtain contours, highlight in green and generate the ROI rectangles. The algorithm has been applied to images in the RGBD- DHaRIo dataset that contain only one person.

ROIs to Depth images and obtaining the corresponding point clouds from the boundaries. Then the point clouds become inputs to the PoinNet classifier -previously trained- to determine if there are people in the image (one person, two person or three people). The images in which the presence of one person is detected are separated and grouped in a file of Depth positive images to feed the next process, which consists of the orientation estimation.

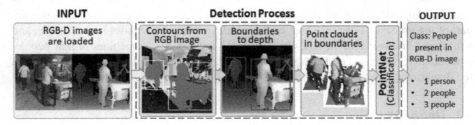

Fig. 3. Procedure carried out for detecting people in RGBD images.

4   Estimation of Orientation and Movement Trend

The proposed approach receives as input Depth images that are processed by the previously trained PointNet architecture, to send resized images (images with one person) to a modified Biternion network and thus obtain the estimated orientation angle of the person present in the image. Every four consecutive frames, this procedure is repeated, and the person's movement trend is determined. If the trending's result is an imminent collision between the person and the robot -as the central tool of the robotic task-, then an output consistent with the values stipulated by the ISO/TS 15066 standard (slow down or stop the robot) is generated. Details of the proposed approach are presented below.

4.1 Estimating Orientation

The estimation of the orientation of people in the vicinity of robotic industrial tasks, required training of the modified biternion network architecture proposed in [14], with images from the RGBD-DHaRIo dataset.

The biternion network architecture is inspired by the ImageNet winning VGG architecture [49], which consist of two stages, the first develops a features extraction using multiple convolutional layers followed by a max-pooling layer. In the second stage, two fully connected layers are used to carry out the orientation estimation task. In [20] modifications to the network architecture were proposed according to the size of the input images, but due to orientation estimation errors in images in which people were very close to the edges of the images, another modification was proposed in [14] which consisted of replacing all convolutions (except the last two close to the fully connected layers) and adding a third pooling layer to all networks as compensation. This architecture, designed for input images with a size of 96 × 96, is what has been called a modified biternion network.

It's very important to state, that in our job, we are using the same modified biternion network architecture that was designed, proposed, and evaluated in [14], but our biternion network has been trained with re-sized images (96 × 96) from RGBD DHaRIo dataset (70% of the dataset). During the learning process we worked with different learning rates, and it was possible to establish experimentally that 5° was the lowest error obtained in orientation with a rate of 0.05 in 600 epochs.

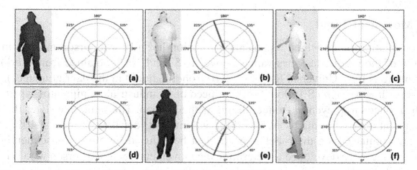

Fig. 4. Graphic representation of the orientation of a person through the evaluation interface designed to evaluate the training results of the modified biternion network. (a) 357° orientation of a person, (b) 201° orientation, (c) 270° orientation, (d) 90° orientation, (e) 340° orientation, (f) 225° orientation.

A graphic interface was developed to evaluate the training results. The graph representing the degrees of orientation of the person detected in the image has been designed as a circumference with 0° at its lowest point, which represents a full-frontal view of a person (the person is facing the camera). If the person is facing away from the camera, then an angle of 180° should be indicated on the interface. When the person is facing to the right side the interface will indicate an angle of 90° and when the person is facing to the left side, then the interface will indicate an angle of 270°. Any other orientation will be indicated between these angular values, as can be seen in Fig. 4. Based on this orientation measurement system, the robotic task in the images acquired for the dataset (and the robot itself), is located at 90°.

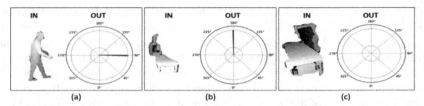

Fig. 5. Modified biternion network training evaluation interface. In (a) we can see the result in degrees as an out, and corresponding image as an input to the network. In (b) a false positive is presented in which the output indicates 180° for an input image without people present. In a similar input image (no-humans present), the output in the graphic interface does not display any value in degrees.

Among the results of the evaluation, false positives were presented when images of equipment and machines were used as inputs (or images with no-humans present), as well as unexpected problems such as images that did not resulted in degrees when there weren't humans present in the image (which is attributed to a rendering problem in the interface), as shown in Fig. 5.

4.2 Movement Trend

The orientation range which represents a collision hazard for a person moving in the vicinity of the robotic task has values between 75° and 105°, obtained from workload computations for a Universal Robot's UR10 (robot featured in the dataset images).

According to ISO/TS 15066 [50], the speed of an industrial manipulator-type robot can be reduced to prevent it from colliding with a human. The same rule states that if a person is at 40% from the robot's working volume (Vt) distance (it means: 40% more than the volume), then the robot's speed must be reduced by 50%. Consequently, an algorithm has been developed to determine the movement trend of a person who is in the vicinity of the robotic task. This trend is calculated based on the person's direction of advance in consecutive frames, so that, the persistence of direction in 4 frames indicates his direction of advance. If that direction is between 75° and 105° and the person is at 0.4 Vt of the working volume, a risk collision alarm will be activated, and the speed of the robot will be reduced. If the limit distance in the direction of the task has been exceeded (below 0.4 Vt), then the robot will be stopped.

There are three steps of the proposed approach to estimate the orientation and determine the movement trend of a person in the vicinity of a robotic industrial task as shown in Fig. 6. In step (1) with Depth images as inputs to the -previously trained- PointNet network, people are detected and the images containing people are automatically cropped and resized. In step (2) those images resized to 96x96, become inputs to the modified Biternion network which in turn yields the estimated orientation (angle in degrees), for the person present in the image. Then in (3), from the estimated orientation for each frame in a sequence of 4 frames, the movement trend is determined.

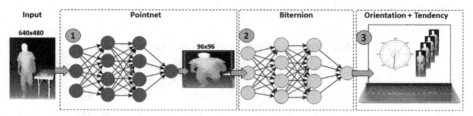

Fig. 6. Proposed methodology for the estimation of orientation and determination of the movement trend of a person in the vicinity of a robotic industrial task. (1) Detection of people with Pointnet from Depth images, (2) estimation of orientation with modified Biternion network, in (3), the movement trend is determined in a sequence of 4 iterations (4frames).

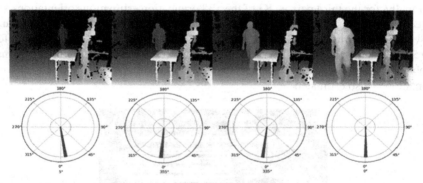

Fig. 7. Orientation estimation and movement trend for a person in the vicinity of a robotic task that does not represent a risk of collision.

If the trending of the person is moving in direction of the robot's work volume (between 75° and 105°), an alarm is activated in a graphic interface (developed to display the performance of the approach) as effect. The alarm's effect is whether "reduce speed" or "stop" the robot, according to the values stipulated by the ISO/TS 15066 standard. If -on the other hand-, the person tends to move in a direction that will not generate a collision with the robot's work-volume (and therefore with its task), then no alarm will be activated (as can be seen in Fig. 7) and the process will begin again to the next 4 frames.

5 Results

The ability of the proposed approach to effectively determine the movement trend was evaluated with three groups of images, each group corresponding to one person (three different people). As shown in Table 2, for the first person 131 orientation estimations were obtained, 97 of them were correct with a representative precision of 0.7405. For the second person, 136 orientation estimations were obtained, 76 of them resulted in a successful prediction with a precision of 0.5588.

Table 2. Results obtained from the validation process.

	Person 1	Person 2	Person 3
Confusion matrix	34/97	60/76	55/83
Accuracy	0.7405	0.5588	0.6014
Recall	0.7405	0.5588	0.6014
Precision	1	1	1

Finally, for the third person, 83 of the 138 orientation estimations orientations were correct with a precision of 0.6014. In all cases, a precision greater than 0.5 was obtained and variations are due to the differences in shape and size between people, which affects the results obtained during the segmentation process (required for the algorithms to make a good estimation). These results are satisfactory compared to [51] and [14] in which orientation is also estimated.

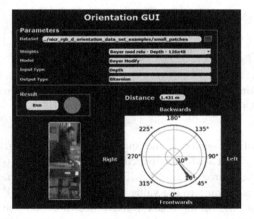

Fig. 8. Graphic interface for the proposed approach.

The graphic interface designed to display the results of the approach can be seen in Fig. 8 (Orientation GUI), it explicitly presents the distance to the volume of the robot (in meters), the estimated orientation angle for the detected person in the vicinity of the robot and an alarm constituted by a circle whose colors -like traffics lights- is green, to indicate no collision risk between the person and the robot; yellow circle indicates a possible collision and therefore the robot's speed must be reduced according to the ISO/TS 15066 standard. Finally, if the circle is red, the collision is intended as imminent, and the robot's task must be stopped.

6 Conclusions

In this paper an approximation that allows estimating the orientation and movement trend of a person in the vicinity of a robotic industrial task is introduced, aiming to avoid the collision between human and robot.

Prior to the development of the system a pre-trained saliency algorithm was used for detecting relevant elements (mainly persons) in the RGB images. Then, a PointNet person detector was trained with Depth images by means of the RGBD- DHaRIo dataset. As the output of the saliency algorithm could be a person or equipment or even the robot, the training of the PointNet network resulted a few affected with some false positives in the detection of people (we decided that it was not enough to reprocess the training). To estimate the orientation of the person detected, an orientation estimator based on a modified Biternion network was trained with images of the same dataset, resized to 96x96. The system was evaluated by creating a graphic interface with a different set of RGB-D images captured with a Kinect sensor. The predictability of the proposed approach was evaluated with three groups of images (a different person for each group). In all cases, a general precision greater than 0.5 was obtained.

Our approach contributes to compliance with safety regulations in activities that involve safe human-robot interaction.

References

1. Guerry, M., Bieller, S., Mueller, C., Kraus, W.: IFR Press Conference 24th September 2020 Frankfurt. Int. Fed. Robot. IFR. (2020)
2. Villani, V., Pini, F., Leali, F., Secchi, C.: Survey on human–robot collaboration in industrial settings: safety, intuitive interfaces and applications. Mechatronics **55**, 248–266 (2018). https://doi.org/10.1016/j.mechatronics.2018.02.009
3. Robla-Gómez, S., Becerra, V.M., Llata, J.R., Gonzalez-Sarabia, E., Torre-Ferrero, C., Perez-Oria, J.: Working together: a review on safe human-robot collaboration in industrial environments. IEEE Access **5**, 26754–26773 (2017)
4. Wang, L., Schmidt, B., Nee, A.Y.C.: Avoidance for human-robot vision-guided active collision collaborations. Manuf. Lett. **1**, 5–8 (2013). https://doi.org/10.1016/j.mfglet.2013.08.001
5. Bothe, K., Winkler, A., Goldhahn, L.: Development of a robot-human-interface using an RGBD camera. In: 59th Ilmenau Scientific Colloquium, Technische Universität Ilmenau, 11–15 September 2017
6. Zabalza, J., et al.: Smart sensing and adaptive reasoning for enabling industrial robots with interactive human-robot capabilities in dynamic environments—a case study. Sensors **19**(6), 1354 (2019)
7. Brito, T., et al.: Dynamic collision avoidance system for a manipulator based on RGB-D data. Iberian Robotics conference. Springer, Cham (2017)

8. Wang, X., Yang, C., Ju, Z., Ma, H., Fu, M.: Robot manipulator self-identification for surrounding obstacle detection. Multimed. Tools Appl. **76**(5), 6495–6520 (2016). https://doi.org/10.1007/s11042-016-3275-8

9. Corrales, J.A., Candelas, F.A., Torres, F.: Safe human-robot interaction based on dynamic sphere-swept line bounding volumes. Robot. Comput. Integr. Manuf. **27**, 177–185 (2011). https://doi.org/10.1016/j.rcim.2010.07.005

10. Huang, S., Ishikawa, M., Yamakawa, Y.: An active assistant robotic system based on high-speed vision and haptic feedback for human-robot collaboration. In: Proc. IECON 2018 - 44th Annu. Conf. IEEE Ind. Electron. Soc., pp. 3649–3654 (2018). https://doi.org/10.1109/IECON.2018.8592810

11. Zardykhan, D., Svarny, P., Hoffmann, M., Shahriari, E., Haddadin, S.: Collision preventing phase-progress control for velocity adaptation in human-robot collaboration. In: IEEE-RAS Int. Conf. Humanoid Robot, pp. 266–273 (2019). https://doi.org/10.1109/Humanoids43949.2019.9035065

12. Vanderborght, B., et al.: Variable impedance actuators: a review. Rob. Auton. Syst. **61**, 1601–1614 (2013). https://doi.org/10.1016/j.robot.2013.06.009

13. Nieto, W., Arias-Correa, M., Madrigal-González, C.: Acquisition and evaluation of depth data from humans, in robotized industrial environments. J. Phys. Conf. Ser. **1547**, 7 (2020). https://doi.org/10.1088/1742-6596/1547/1/012016

14. Lewandowski, B., Seichter, D., Wengefeld, T., Pfennig, L., Drumm, H., Gross, H.M.: Deep orientation: fast and robust upper body orientation estimation for mobile robotic applications. IEEE Int. Conf. Intell. Robot. Syst. **2**, 441–448 (2019). https://doi.org/10.1109/IROS40897.2019.8968506

15. Li, M., Chen, S., Zhao, Y., Zhang, Y., Wang, Y., Tian, Q.: Dynamic multiscale graph neural networks for 3D skeleton based human motion prediction. In: Proc. IEEE Comput. Soc. Conf. Comput. Vis. Pattern Recognit., pp. 211–220 (2020). https://doi.org/10.1109/CVPR42600.2020.00029

16. Barsoum, E., Kender, J., Liu, Z.: HP-GAN: Probabilistic 3D human motion prediction via GAN. In: IEEE Comput. Soc. Conf. Comput. Vis. Pattern Recognit. Work, pp. 1499–1508 (2018). https://doi.org/10.1109/CVPRW.2018.00191

17. Liang, J., Jiang, L., Niebles, J.C., Hauptmann, A., Fei-Fei, L.: Peeking into the future: Predicting future person activities and locations in videos. In: IEEE Comput. Soc. Conf. Comput. Vis. Pattern Recognit. Work, pp. 2960–2963 (2019). https://doi.org/10.1109/CVPRW.2019.00358

18. Martinez, J., Black, M.J., Romero, J.: On human motion prediction using recurrent neural networks. In: Proc. - 30th IEEE Conf. Comput. Vis. Pattern Recognition, CVPR 2017, pp. 4674–4683 (2017). https://doi.org/10.1109/CVPR.2017.497

19. Monti, A., Bertugli, A., Calderara, S., Cucchiara, R.: DAG-Net: double attentive graph neural network for trajectory forecasting. In: 2020 25th International Conference on Pattern Recognition (ICPR), pp. 2551–2558. IEEE (2021)

20. Beyer, L., Hermans, A., Leibe, B.: Biternion nets: continuous head pose regression from discrete training labels. In: Gall, J., Gehler, P., Leibe, B. (eds.) GCPR 2015. LNCS, vol. 9358, pp. 157–168. Springer, Cham (2015). https://doi.org/10.1007/978-3-319-24947-6_13

21. Wengefeld, T., Lewandowski, B., Seichter, D., Pfennig, L., Gross, H.M.: Real-time person orientation estimation using colored pointclouds. In: 2019 Eur. Conf. Mob. Robot. ECMR 2019 - Proc. 2 (2019). https://doi.org/10.1109/ECMR.2019.8870914

22. Zimmermann, C., Welschehold, T., Dornhege, C., Burgard, W., Brox, T.: 3D human pose estimation in RGBD images for robotic task learning. In: Proc. - IEEE Int. Conf. Robot. Autom. 1986–1992 (2018). https://doi.org/10.1109/ICRA.2018.8462833

23. Schnürer, T., Fuchs, S., Eisenbach, M., Groß, H.M.: Real-time 3D pose estimation from single depth images. In: VISIGRAPP 2019 - Proc. 14th Int. Jt. Conf. Comput. Vision, Imaging Comput. Graph. Theory Appl., vol. 5, pp. 716–724 (2019). https://doi.org/10.5220/000739 4707160724

24. Fitte-Duval, L., Mekonnen, A.A., Lerasle, F.: Combination of RGB-D features for head and upper body orientation classification. In: Blanc-Talon, J., Distante, C., Philips, W., Popescu, D., Scheunders, P. (eds.) ACIVS 2016. LNCS, vol. 10016, pp. 591–603. Springer, Cham (2016). https://doi.org/10.1007/978-3-319-48680-2_52

25. Kawanishi, Y., Deguchi, D., Ide, I., Murase, H., Fujiyoshi, H.: Misclassification tolerable learning for robust pedestrian orientation classification. In: Proc. - Int. Conf. Pattern Recognit., pp. 486–491 (2016). https://doi.org/10.1109/ICPR.2016.7899681

26. Choi, J., Lee, B.J., Zhang, B.T.: Human body orientation estimation using convolutional neural network. arXiv preprint arXiv:1609.01984 (2016)

27. Raza, M., Chen, Z., Rehman, S.U., Wang, P., Bao, P.: Appearance based pedestrians' head pose and body orientation estimation using deep learning. Neurocomputing 272, 647–659 (2018). https://doi.org/10.1016/j.neucom.2017.07.029

28. Kohari, Y., Miura, J., Oishi, S.: CNN-based human body orientation estimation for robotic attendant. In: IAS-15 Workshop on Robot Perception of Humans (2018)

29. Linder, T., Arras, K.O.: Real-time full-body human attribute classification in RGB-D using a tessellation boosting approach. In: IEEE Int. Conf. Intell. Robot. Syst., pp. 1335–1341 (2015). https://doi.org/10.1109/IROS.2015.7353541

30. Ahn, B., Park, J., B, I.S.K.: Real-Time Head Orientation from a Monocular, vol. 1, pp. 82–96. Springer (2015)

31. Aldoma, A., Tombari, F., Di Stefano, L., Vincze, M.: A global hypotheses verification method for 3D object recognition. In: Fitzgibbon, A., Lazebnik, S., Perona, P., Sato, Y., Schmid, C. (eds.) ECCV 2012. LNCS, vol. 7574, pp. 511–524. Springer, Heidelberg (2012). https://doi.org/10.1007/978-3-642-33712-3_37

32. Han, J., Shao, L., Member, S., Xu, D., Shotton, J.: Enhanced computer vision with microsoft kinect sensor: a review. IEEE Trans. Cybernetics 43, 1318–1334 (2013)

33. Janoch, A., et al.: A category-level 3-D Database: putting the kinect to work. In: ICCV 2011 Work. Consum. Depth Cameras Comput. Vis. (2011)

34. Lai, K., Bo, L., Fox, D.: Unsupervised Feature Learning for 3D Scene Labeling. In: IEEE (ed.) 2014 IEEE International Conference on Robotics and Automation (ICRA), pp. 3050–3057 (2014)

35. Anand, A., Koppula, H.S., Joachims, T., Saxena, A.: Contextually guided semantic labeling and search for 3D point clouds. arXiv preprint arXiv:1111.5358 (2011)

36. Couprie, C., Farabet, C., Najman, L., LeCun, Y.: Indoor semantic segmentation using depth information. arXiv preprint arXiv:1301.3572 (2013)

37. Karpathy, A., Miller, S., Li, F.F.: Object discovery in 3D scenes via shape analysis. In: Proc. - IEEE Int. Conf. Robot. Autom., pp. 2088–2095 (2013). https://doi.org/10.1109/ICRA.2013. 6630857

38. Engelhard, N., Colas, F., Cremers, D., Siegwart, R., Burgard, W., Engelhard, N., Colas, F.: Towards a benchmark for RGB-D SLAM evaluation. In: RGB-DWorkshop Adv. Reasoning with Depth Cameras Robot. Sci. Syst. Conf. (RSS), (2011)

39. Glocker, B., Izadi, S., Shotton, J., Criminisi, A.: Real-time RGB-D camera relocalization. In: 2013 IEEE Int. Symp. Mix. Augment. Reality, ISMAR 2013, pp. 173–179 (2013). https://doi.org/10.1109/ISMAR.2013.6671777

40. Sung, J., Ponce, C., Selman, B., Saxena, A.: Unstructured human activity detection from RGBD images. In: 2012 IEEE International Conference on Robotics and Automation, pp. 842–849. IEEE (2012)

41. Ofli, F., Chaudhry, R., Kurillo, G.: Berkeley Multimodal Human Action Database (MHAD). In: IEEE Workshop on Applications of Computer Vision (WACV), pp. 53–60 (2013)
42. Escalera, S., et al.: Multi-modal gesture recognition challenge 2013: dataset and results. In: Proceedings of the 15th ACM on International Conference on Multimodal Interaction, pp. 445–452 (2013)
43. Diby, A., Charpillety, F.: Pose estimation for a partially observable human body from RGB-D cameras. In: IEEE Int. Conf. Intell. Robot. Syst., pp. 4915–4922 (2015). https://doi.org/10.1109/IROS.2015.7354068
44. Borji, A.: What is a salient object? a dataset and a baseline model for salient object detection. IEEE Trans. Image Process. **24**, 742–756 (2015). https://doi.org/10.1109/TIP.2014.2383320
45. Yin, L., Xiaodi Hou, C.K.: The secrets of salient object segmentation supplementary materials. In: 2014 IEEE Conf. Comput. Vis. Pattern Recognit. (CVPR), pp. 4321–4328 (2014)
46. Liu, T., et al.: Learning to detect a salient object. IEEE Trans. Pattern Anal. Mach. Intell. **33**(2), 353–367 (2010)
47. Hou, Q., Cheng, M.M., Hu, X., Borji, A., Tu, Z., Torr, P.H.S.: Deeply supervised salient object detection with short connections. IEEE Trans. Pattern Anal. Mach. Intell. **41**, 815–828 (2019). https://doi.org/10.1109/TPAMI.2018.2815688
48. Qi, C.R., Su, H., Mo, K., Guibas, L.J.: PointNet: Deep learning on point sets for 3D classification and segmentation. In: Proceedings - 30th IEEE Conference on Computer Vision and Pattern Recognition, CVPR 2017, pp. 77–85 (2017). https://doi.org/10.1109/CVPR.2017.16
49. Simonyan, K., Zisserman, A.: Very deep convolutional networks for large-scale image recognition. In: 3rd Int. Conf. Learn. Represent. ICLR 2015 - Conf. Track Proc., pp. 1–14 (2015)
50. Rosenstrauch, M.J., Kruger, J.: Safe human-robot-collaboration-introduction and experiment using ISO/TS 15066. In: 2017 3rd Int. Conf. Control. Autom. Robot. ICCAR 2017, pp. 740–744 (2017). https://doi.org/10.1109/ICCAR.2017.7942795
51. Soni, A.N.: Human detection using RGBD images and parallel regional convolutional networks. J. Innov. Dev. Pharm. Tech. Sci. **2**(8) (2019). ISSN (O) 2581-6934

A Novel Algorithm for Greatly Accurate Electrical Fault Detection and Classification Based on Haar Wavelet

Milton Ruiz[ID] and Manuel Jaramillo[⊠][ID]

Universidad Politécnica Salesiana, Quito, Ecuador
{mruizm,mjaramillo}@ups.edu.ec

Abstract. The present investigation presents an algorithm for fault detection and classification in transmission lines using the Haar-type wavelet mother transform. Voltage and current signals contain all the information of the power system, therefore when a fault occurs in the electrical power system, these signals present disturbances in their amplitude, phase changes and presence of harmonics. Mathematically, all mother wavelets respond with an impulse when there is an abrupt change in the signals, this property allows to detect when a fault has occurred (in the time domain). Experimental results have shown that with frequencies above 100 kHz it is possible to detect a fault with 100% accuracy by taking only 4 samples of the signal and applying the Haar wavelet. The fault detection times vary between 0.31 ms and 1.15 ms and the fault classification times vary between 0.94 s and 1.31 s.

Keywords: Fault detection (FD) · Fault-type classification (FC) · Fault location (FL) · Fault diagnosis · Wavelet transforms

1 Introduction

Power systems have been a fundamental part of human development since the past decades; due to the complexity in these systems, there is always the possibility of unwanted currents and voltages (caused by disturbances in the network). Power Quality in a power system is a study trend among researches mainly because its study focuses on guaranteed the network operation closer to its stability margins [2,3].

Among the most common disturbances that can modify voltage and currents to unwanted values, this research centres its analysis in faults. A fault is an unexpected phenomenon that when occurred modifies the power system main characteristics (voltage, current) and it modifies system reliability causing accidents, damages to equipment and especially undesired blackouts. Over the years, researchers have developed advances regarding fault detection, fault diagnosis, and fault progression, which as a whole improves the system Power Quality [3,5].

In a power system, faults can be classified according to their physical nature and how they are produced. Physical contact between transmission lines conductors or between transmission lines and ground are the most common causes

© Springer Nature Switzerland AG 2022
F. R. Narváez et al. (Eds.): SmartTech-IC 2021, CCIS 1532, pp. 143–157, 2022.
https://doi.org/10.1007/978-3-030-99170-8_11

for faults in a power system. Specifically, in a three-phase power system, there are four fault types: Single line to ground faults (LG), Line to line faults (LL), Double line to ground faults (LLG) and three-phase symmetrical faults (LLLG or LLL) [2,8].

When an electrical fault occurs in a power system, the consequences for the end-user is the loss of reliability in electricity supply, which imposes economic losses in households and businesses. The economic loss is produced due to damage to equipment made with sensitive electronic circuits that are affected by voltage spikes, spoilage of food that needs electricity for being kept under controlled temperature conditions, wasted and unproductive time for workers with temporarily stopped activities in factories or businesses [2].

Thus, faults diagnosis methods are always a subject of research and analysis, which is the focus on the present paper. Regarding fault detection methods, the following can be found in the literature review:

In [7] the detection method that the author proposes is a Fuzzy-neuro based one, it is tested in 50 Hz 220 kV system and it analyzes fault current and various voltage samples. This method is based on back-propagation and fuzzy control theory, the high harmonic components are removed via FFT and as results, the fault detection is done in less than 10 ms.

In [10] the fault is detected through a method that is based on the Discrete Wavelet Transform and Artificial Neural Networks, it is tested in 60 Hz 230 kV system and it analyzes current and voltage signals. This method normalizes voltage and currents signals to values in a range from -1 to 1 and a Wavelet Db4 is implemented. This method can obtain an accuracy of 100% for fault detection and a 99.83% accuracy for fault classification.

In [13] the fault is detected through a method that is based on linear discriminant analysis (LDA) and Wavelet transform. The algorithm is tested in 50 Hz 400 kV system and it analyzes only current signals. This method uses Wavelet transform to process the current samples up to three levels then the relays are set-up to 90% of the transmission line. This method can obtain 100% of accuracy for both fault detection and fault classification.

In [6] the author uses Superimposed sequence components based integrated impedance (SSCII). The algorithm is tested in 50 Hz 400 kV system and it analyzes current and voltage profiles at the beginning and end of the transmission lines. This method is reliable for low and high resistance faults and the algorithm is suitable for high-speed communication channels. This method can detect the fault in less than 20 ms.

Henceforth, this article is organized as it follows. Section 2 presents the formulation of the problem. Section 3 presents the results. Section 4 analyzes the results of the model and its simulation. Finally, in Sect. 5 presents this research conclusions.

2   Problem Formulation

Different works regarding methods for detection, classification and localization of faults are of great interest to researchers. These areas of study usually require advanced data signal processing, which translates as considerable time processing. Nowadays, thanks to current computing power, it is possible to use advanced techniques of signal processing, artificial intelligence, machine learning, global positioning systems and communication systems and getting results in a fraction of the time it would be required years ago. Thus, allowing researchers to carry out studies in greater detail and depth, improving traditional techniques used in electrical protection systems.

Measurement data is acquired by current transformers, intelligent electronic devices or phasor measurement units, depending on the measurement equipment there are restrictions on the transmission rates determined by the technology used by the measurement equipment. After data is acquired, the next difficulty the researcher has to deal with is the processing of a large amount of information collected.

As for measured signals, researches centre their focus in current and voltage signals, because they allow identifying the vast majority of characteristics from the electrical power system and the nature of its faults. Finally, there are restrictions related to telecommunication system itself. Even though the current and voltage signals have all the information about the electrical power system, it is impossible to frame all fault types that exist in the electrical power systems in a set of rules and criteria.

There are various techniques to extract information from electrical signals, for example, information about their fundamental frequency component and the harmonic components can be extracted from the signals in the time domain. It is important to take into consideration the data dimension since a large size of data can decrease the performance of the algorithms, however, it also provides more accurate results in the detection, classification and location of faults.

Among the most used techniques to detect faults in a power system, the most common approach consists in sensing small changes in electrical signals (usually current). For this purpose, the mathematical tools apply are Fourier transform, wavelets and transformed into S domain.

This methodology is used by protection equipment in electrical power systems. The Fourier transform is applied in half-cycles or complete cycles, the difference between one and the other is the time it takes for the equipment to detect a fault. For example, if the fault occurs at the beginning of the positive edge using the complete cycle the algorithm will take $(1/50)$ or $(1/60)$ s, on the other hand, if the transform is applied in every half cycle the algorithm will take $(1/25)$ or $(1/30)$ s.

The fault detection based on the extraction of characteristics of the signals is one of the most used techniques, fault detection is the first task carried out by the protection equipment, followed by the fault classification and finally the fault location. Dependent or independent methods can be used for the detection, classification and location of electrical faults in transmission lines. The fault detection must have a high degree of reliability and discriminate an electrical fault from other power systems defects, allowing the safe operation of the protections.

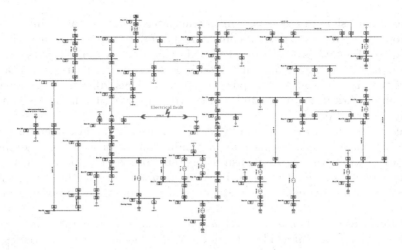

Fig. 1. Electrical fault in power system

Nowadays the process to transform analogue signals to digital signals is carried out by several secondary smart digital devices knows as Phasor Measurement Unit (PMU), these devices perform several tasks as controlling, metering, protecting, supervising and communicating with other modules of the system. The large amount of data that is acquired by sensors installed in the different points of the electrical network produces a large consumption of energy, however, this consumption is necessary in order to process information as a consequence of the large volume of data traffic [9].

For the present study, the IEEE 39-bar model has been selected as a case study. This is a model that shows the arrangement of a transmission line and it is widely used in the study of electrical power flows and fault analysis as well. A fault in a circuit is any kind event that interferes with the normal flow of current. Most transmission line failures are caused by lightning strikes that result in opening insulators. The high voltage between a conductor and the grounded tower that supports it causes ionization, this phenomenon provides a path to ground to atmospheric discharge. Additionally, when switches are opened to isolate the failed portion of the line from the rest of the system, this system condition interrupts current flow in the ionized path, thus allowing de-ionization in the circuit.

Generally, in transmission lines operation, a re-connection of the switches is highly successful after a fault. In Fig. 1, the red line shows the presence of a fault, this event will generate several post fault voltage and current signals which will be used later as the base of the signal reconstruction.

Algorithm 1 presents the steps to detect faults; the signals can be current or voltage. The first step is to acquire the signals, which would simulate acquiring data from a CT or PT. In the second step, four samples are taken from the signal, that is, we compare the present sample with three past samples and apply the Haar level one wavelet transform. Step 3 extracts the characteristics of the coefficients. When applying the wavelet transform, the coefficients contain half the data as the original, therefore in step 4, the coefficients are interpolated until the dimension of the signal is obtained from the original. Finally, in step 5, the maximum value is searched, it indicates the time when the fault starts. The amplitude of a fault must be greater than a threshold established based on the electrical power system. Finally, the value of the fault time and the amplitude are saved.

Algorithm 1. Fault detection

1: Step 1: Acquire data from .csv file
2:          $OS = load('filename.csv')$
3: Step 2: Wavelet coefficients calculations
4:          $for\ i = 1 : length(OS)$
5:          $[c, l] = wavedec(OS(1 : 4), level, wavelet\_type)$
6: Step 3: Extract detail coefficients
7:          $d1 = detcoef(c, l, level);$
8: Step 4: Interpolation using FFT method
9:          $FD = interpft(d1, 2 * length(d1));$
10: Step 5: Finding of Maximum values and comparison with established limits
11:          $MV = max(abs(FD))$
12:          $if\ MV > threshold$
13:          $TF = i + 1$
14:          $AF\ MV$
15:          end
16:          end

In order to investigate all the possibilities, the 11 possible types of failures that can occur in transmission lines are simulated; as a consequence, it has been verified that the results obtained and validated in a three-phase fault include the signals of the remaining 10 types of failures. The three-phase fault produces an electromagnetic phenomenon that can be evidenced in the current and voltage signals that are recorded by the PMU phasor measurement units at both ends.

Algorithm 2 allows to identify the type of failure, in TF the instant in which a fault occurs is saved; if there is no fault TF saves the value of zero. In the first step, the TF values that are zero are replaced by NaN, then the position of the minimum value and the TF mode are searched, these two values are used to discriminate if it is a fault or is a disturbance produced by a fault in another phase. A threshold must be established, the values entered within this parameter indicate that the phase is in failure. Finally, a comparison is made to establish the type of failure and the phases that the failure presents.

Algorithm 2. Fault classification

1: Step 1: Replace zeros by NaN
2:         $TF(TF == 0) = NaN$
3: Step 2: Finding minimum value and mode
4:         $[Am, Bm] = min(TF)$
5:         $[AM, BM] = mode(TF);$
6: Step 3: Finding values within the threshold
7:         $amax = max(AF) * 0.45$
8:         $[row, col] = amax > (max(AF) - AF)\&amax <= (max(AF))$
9:         $[C, D] = size(col)$
10: Step 5: Fault Classification
11:         $if\ D == 1$
12:         $Single - phase\ fault$
13:         $phase\ col(1)$
14:         end
15:         $if\ D == 2$
16:         $if\ BM == 1$
17:         $Single - phase\ fault$
18:         $phase\ Bm$
19:         $else$
20:         $Two - phase\ fault$
21:         $phase\ col(1)$
22:         $phase\ col(2)$
23:         end
24:         end
25:         $if\ D == 3$
26:         $cont = 0;$
27:         $if\ BM == 1\ \&\&\ Bm == 1\ \&\&\ Standard deviation\ (TF) > 0.6$
28:         $Single - phase\ fault$
29:         $phase\ Bm$
30:         $cont = 1;$
31:         end
32:         $if\ BM == 1\&\&\ Bm == 2\ \&\&Standard deviation\ (TF) > 0.6$
33:         $Single - phase\ fault$
34:         $phase\ Bm$
35:         $cont = 1;$
36:         end
37:         $if\ cont == 0$
38:         $Three - phase\ fault$
39:         end
40:         end

---

3   Results

Based on the experiments carried out, it has been verified that the minimum sampling frequency should be 100 kHz, this, by considering that the measurement equipment today can achieve sampling rates of up to 1 MHz, processing data every microsecond at 18 bits of resolution, for example, the SEL-T401L relay with response times from 1 ms to 5 ms.

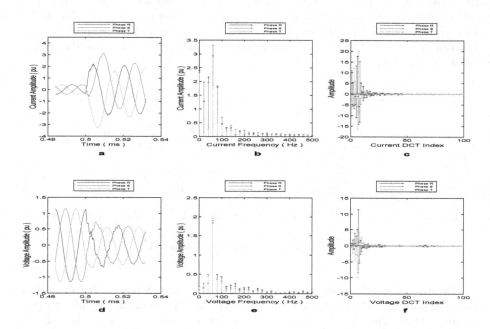

Fig. 2. Time signals, frequency spectrum, DCT index for both current and voltage

The fault detection is carried out by taking at least 4 samples of the signal (current or voltage), this allows to improve detection times since many algorithms perform the detection for each cycle or in the best of cases every half cycle. In other words, with a sampling rate of 100 kHz, there are 1666 samples per cycle at a network frequency 60 Hz and 2000 samples per cycle at a network frequency 50 Hz. At 100 kHz, each sample is acquired every 10 μs, thus measuring the 4 minimum samples for fault detection will take 40 μs. To test the effectiveness of the algorithm, the model has been tested on the 11 types of faults with resistances varying from 0 Ω to 20 Ω using the IEEE 39 bars test model. Finally, the computer equipment used in the experiment development has the following characteristics: Processor (Intel (R) Xeon (R) E-2176M CPU @ 2.70 GHz), and 64 GB RAM.

In Fig. 2, top left corner, the three-phase current signals taken from Bus 4 are shown, and it is noted that there are a phase and magnitude disturbance. The frequency spectrum that is the result of the electrical fault is shown in Fig. 2 top centre. In this figure, the frequency with greater amplitude is the fundamental one 60 Hz, however, new frequency components have been included due to the electrical failure.

In Fig. 2 d, the voltage signal presents phase disturbances and magnitude decrease. The frequency spectrum that is the result of electrical fault is shown in literal e. In this figure, also the frequency with greater amplitude is the fundamental one 60 Hz, however, new frequency components have been included due to the electrical failure. In part f, the discrete cosine transform is shown, it can be seen that the energy of the signal is concentrated in a few data allowing to create a sparse matrix.

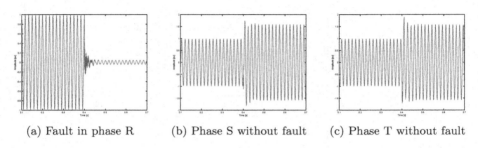

(a) Fault in phase R   (b) Phase S without fault   (c) Phase T without fault

Fig. 3. Single phase fault at phase R

Figure 3 shows the voltage signals in three phases R, S and T. It can be seen that the fault occurs in a single phase because the voltage in the R phase reduces its magnitude. The S and T phases present disturbances due to the failure in the R phase; it is evident that the voltage magnitudes in these two phases increases due to the response of the system to maintain the supplied power. It is important to consider that the fault detection method must have the ability to discriminate a fault from a possible disturbance since the protection equipment must open only the faulty phase.

Figure 4 shows the response of the wavelet Haar level 1 transformation. It can be noted that in steady-state, the response of the wavelet does not present any alterations. However, when a failure or disturbance occurs, it can be visualized how an impulse is created at the exact moment of the abrupt change on the signal. The amplitude of the response of the wavelet in steady-state varies between 0.002 and 0.005 [up]; when a fault occurs the amplitude of the impulse varies between 0.08 and 0.18 [pu] and when a disturbance occurs the amplitude of the impulse varies between 0.045 and 0.055 [pu]. To discriminate a fault from a disturbance, a threshold is set and a comparison is made between the amplitudes obtained.

Figure 5 shows the frequency vs. time representation in a single-phase fault. When the voltage or current signals are in steady-state, there is only the fundamental frequency as it is shown in the red boxes. When a fault occurs as in Fig. 5a, several additional frequencies are created apart from the fundamental, each with a different amplitude and with a different duration in time, in addition, it can be noted that the fundamental frequency disappears. Figure 5 Literals b and c show that for the other two phases, frequencies are added at the

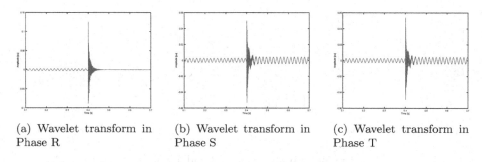

(a) Wavelet transform in   (b) Wavelet transform in   (c) Wavelet transform in
Phase R   Phase S   Phase T

Fig. 4. Wavelet transform applied in a single phase fault scenario

same instant when the fault occurs in phase R, but the fundamental frequency does not disappear. Therefore it is possible to discriminate from a fault and a disturbance by simply analyzing the frequency response of the signal.

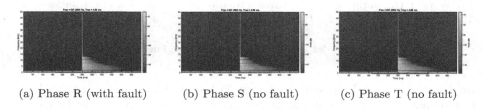

(a) Phase R (with fault)   (b) Phase S (no fault)   (c) Phase T (no fault)

Fig. 5. Single phase R fault, frequency vs time analysis

Figure 6 shows the voltage signals in three phases R, S and T. It can be seen that the fault occurs in two phases, specifically in phases R and T because their voltage reduces their magnitude. S phase presents disturbances due to the failure in phases R and T; in this phase, the voltage magnitude increases its value due to the response of the system to maintain the supplied power.

Figure 7 shows the response of the wavelet Haar level 1 transformation applied to a two-phase fault. For the phases R and T (fault condition), the amplitude of the response of the wavelet varies between 0.14 and 0.15 [pu]. While phase S that does not experience any fault has an amplitude of 2.6×10^{-3} [pu].

Figure 8 shows the frequency vs. time representation in a two-phase fault scenario. When the voltage or current signals are in steady-state, there is only the fundamental frequency as it is shown in the red boxes. When a fault occurs as in Fig. 8 a and c, several additional frequencies are created apart from the fundamental, each with a different amplitude and with a different duration in time, in addition, it can be noted that the fundamental frequency disappears. Figure 8 Literals b shows that for the S phase (no-fault), frequencies are added at the same instant when the fault occurs in phases R and T, but the fundamental

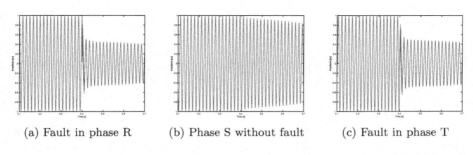

(a) Fault in phase R   (b) Phase S without fault   (c) Fault in phase T

Fig. 6. Two phase fault, R and T phases

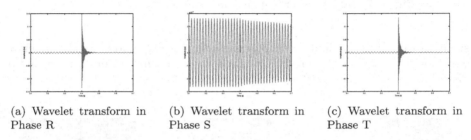

(a) Wavelet transform in   (b) Wavelet transform in   (c) Wavelet transform in
Phase R   Phase S   Phase T

Fig. 7. Wavelet transform for a two phase fault scenario

frequency does not disappear. Therefore, in this scenario, it is also possible to discriminate from a fault and a disturbance by simply analyzing the frequency response of the signal.

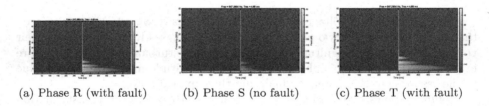

(a) Phase R (with fault)   (b) Phase S (no fault)   (c) Phase T (with fault)

Fig. 8. Two phases R and T fault, frequency vs time analysis

Figure 9 shows the voltage signals in three phases R, S and T. It can be seen that the fault occurs in the three phases. In this scenario, phases R, S and T reduce their respective voltage magnitude which of course occurs due to the fault in the three phases.

Figure 10 shows the response of the wavelet Haar level 1 transformation applied to a three-phase fault. For all the phases, R, S and T, the amplitude of the response of the wavelet varies between 0.08 and 0.2 [pu].

Figure 11 shows the frequency vs time representation in a three-phase fault scenario.

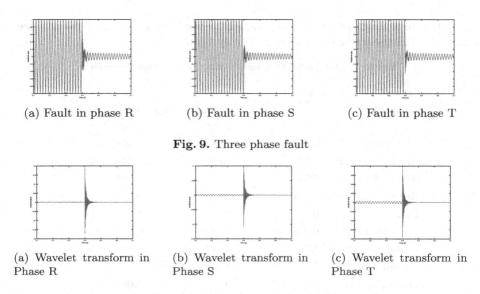

(a) Fault in phase R   (b) Fault in phase S   (c) Fault in phase T

Fig. 9. Three phase fault

(a) Wavelet transform in   (b) Wavelet transform in   (c) Wavelet transform in
Phase R   Phase S   Phase T

Fig. 10. Wavelet transform for a three phase fault scenario

When the voltage or current signals are in steady-state, there is only the fundamental frequency as it is shown in the red boxes. When a fault occurs as in Fig. 11 a, b and c, several additional frequencies are created apart from the fundamental, each with a different amplitude and with a different duration in time, in addition, it can be noted that the fundamental frequency disappears. Therefore, in this scenario, it is also possible to discriminate from a fault and a disturbance by simply analyzing the frequency response of the signal.

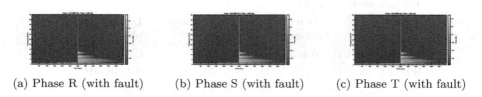

(a) Phase R (with fault)   (b) Phase S (with fault)   (c) Phase T (with fault)

Fig. 11. Three phases fault, frequency vs time analysis

4   Analysis of Results

Table 1 summarizes the results from this work for fault detection and classification in transmission lines for the proposed case of study (IEEE 39 bus-bar transmission system). The precision of the algorithm developed for fault detection is 100%, however, it is important to take into consideration that when there is a fault in a single-phase and depending on the fault resistance, disturbances may occur in the other two phases of the system.

Table 1. Fault detection results achieved in this research

Present work summary			
Fault type	Absolute error phase R	Absolute error phase S	Absolute error phase T
Single-phase 0 Ω	0	2.20E−05	2.20E−05
Single-phase 5 Ω	NFD	NFD	4.20E−05
Single-phase 10 Ω	NFD	3.10E−0.5	NFD
Single-phase 20 Ω	2.10E−0.5	NFD	NFD
Two-phase 0 Ω	0	0	NFD
Two-phase 5 Ω	6.20E−05	NFD	6.20E−05
Two-phase 10 Ω	NFD	3.10E−0.5	3.10E−0.5
Two-phase 20 Ω	1.42E−0.4	1.22E−0.4	NFD
Three-phase 0 Ω	0	0	5.00E−06
Three-phase 5 Ω	2.120E−04	2.22E−05	2.20E−05
Three-phase 10 Ω	1.220E−04	1.12E−05	2.12E−05
Three-phase 20 Ω	1.64E−04	1.42E−04	2.92E−04

As a consequence, Table 1 shows that when a single-phase fault occurs, the fault is also detected on the other two lines. The results also indicate when there is no fault detected (No fault detected NFD).

Table 2. Fault detection times achieved in this research

Present work summary			
Fault type	Detection time phase R	Detection time phase S	Detection time phase T
Single-phase 0 Ω	0.382E−03	0.411E−03	0.3350E−03
Single-phase 5 Ω	0.338E−03	0.356E−03	0.335E−03
Single-phase 10 Ω	0.362E−03	0.315E−03	0.373E−03
Single-phase 20 Ω	0.417E−03	0.296E−03	0.290E−03
Two-phase 0 Ω	0.374E−03	NFD	0.338E−03
Two-phase 5 Ω	0.366E−03	NFD	0.348E−03
Two-phase 10 Ω	NFD	0.373E−03	0.336E−03
Two-phase 20 Ω	0.387E−03	320E−03	NFD
Three-phase 0 Ω	0.345E−03	0.312E−03	0.2831E−03
Three-phase 5 Ω	0.322E−03	1.477E−03	0.3171E−03
Three-phase 10 Ω	0.467E−03	0.344E−03	0.619E−03
Three-phase 20 Ω	0.316E−03	0.278E−03	0.567E−03

Table 2 shows the time in milliseconds that takes for the algorithm to detect a fault in the test system. Table 3, shows the time in seconds that takes for the algorithm to classify a fault according to its type. This fault classification algorithm has an accuracy of 100%.

From the literature review in Sect. 1, the best results achieved in previous works with similar methodologies are summarized in Table 4.

As it can be seen in Table 4, previous works were able to accomplish high accuracy for fault location or fault classification, however, it is also important to analyze how long did it take for those research works to accomplish those results.

From Table 4, the best results for fault detection achieved were 99.7% and 100% accuracy with detection times that varied from 10 ms to 20 ms. In this research with the algorithm developed, it was possible to achieve 100% accuracy for fault detection in all the analyzed scenarios and the best detection time was 0.278 ms which is by far better than previous works.

Table 3. Fault classification times achieved in this research

Present work summary			
Fault type	Fault classification time	Phases with electrical fault (proposed scenario)	Fault classification results
Single-phase 0 Ω	0.98387	R	R
Single-phase 5 Ω	1.64782	S	S
Single-phase 10 Ω	0.86177	T	T
Single-phase 20 Ω	1.08435	R	R
Two-phase 0 Ω	0.90893	R, T	R, T
Two-phase 5 Ω	0.89210	R, T	R, T
Two-phase 10 Ω	0.93385	S, T	S, T
Two-phase 20 Ω	0.93911	R, S	R, S
Three-phase 0 Ω	0.97855	R, S, T	R, S, T
Three-phase 5 Ω	0.93298	R, S, T	R, S, T
Three-phase 10 Ω	0.90478	R, S, T	R, S, T
Three-phase 20 Ω	0.92153	R, S, T	R, S, T

Following the results from Table 4, the best results for fault classification achieved were 97%, 99% and 100% accuracy with classification times that varied from 6 ms to 10 ms. This research achieved 100% accuracy for fault classification in all the analyzed scenarios and the best detection time was 0.86177 s. By analyzing both parameters, accuracy and classification time, this work exceeds previous ones.

Table 4. Fault detection and classification best results in literature review

Best Results from previous works: Fault detection		
Technique	Accuracy	Detection times
Wavelet and Fuzzy-neuro based [12]	High but not 100%	10 ms
Discrete Wavelet transform and Artificial Neural Networks [11]	100%	Not specified
Wavelet transform and a self-organized artificial neural network, [4]	99.7%	Not specified
Best Results from previous works: Fault classification		
Technique	Accuracy	Detection times
Back-propagation network classifier [1]	99%	Not specified
Fuzzy-logic and WT based method [14]	99%	10 ms

5   Conclusions and Future Works

Among the different types of electrical faults in a transmission system, single-phase faults are the easiest to detect because the amplitude of the wavelet transform response is large compared to the response of two-phase and three-phase faults. Therefore, the algorithm thresholds must be set depending on the specific electrical power system and as a function of the three-phase system responses.

The minimum sampling rate required for correct fault detection and classification is 100 kHz, with lower frequencies, it has been found that the error in both detection and classification increases and is not reliable.

Finally, it has been found that the algorithm is 100% reliable in both detection and classification with response times in detection of less than 1 ms and response time in the classification of around 1 s.

References

1. Aggarwal, R.K., et al.: A novel fault classification technique for double-circuit lines based on a combined unsupervised/supervised neural network. IEEE Trans. Power Deliv. **14**(4), 1250–1256 (1999)
2. Aleem, S.A., Shahid, N., Naqvi, I.H.: Methodologies in power systems fault detection and diagnosis. Energy Syst. **6**(1), 85–108 (2014). https://doi.org/10.1007/s12667-014-0129-1. ISSN 18683975
3. Barik, Md.A., et al.: A decentralized fault detection technique for detecting single phase to ground faults in power distribution systems with resonant grounding. IEEE Trans. Power Deliv. **33**(5), 2462–2473 (2018). https://doi.org/10.1109/TPWRD.2018.2799181. ISSN 08858977
4. Elangovan Cheng Hong, S.: A B-spline wavelet based fault classification scheme for high speed protection relaying. Electr. Mach. Power Syst. **28**(4), 313–324 (2000). https://doi.org/10.1080/073135600268289

5. Gonzalez, C., et al.: Directional, high-impedance fault detection in isolated neutral distribution grids. IEEE Trans. Power Deliv. **33**(5), 2474–2483 (2018). https://doi.org/10.1109/TPWRD.2018.2808428. ISSN 08858977
6. Gupta, O.H., Tripathy, M.: An innovative pilot relaying scheme for shunt-compensated line. IEEE Trans. Power Deliv. **30**(3), 1439–1448 (2015)
7. Wang, H., Keerthipala, W.W.L.: Fuzzy-neuro approach to fault classification for transmission line protection. IEEE Trans. Power Deliv. **13**(4), 1093–1104 (1998)
8. Raza, A., et al.: A review of fault diagnosing methods in power transmission systems. Appl. Sci. (Switzerland) **10**(4) (2020). https://doi.org/10.3390/app10041312. ISSN 20763417
9. Ruiz, M., Montalvo, I.: Electrical faults signals restoring based on compressed sensing techniques. Energies **13**(8) (2020). https://doi.org/10.3390/en13082121. ISSN 19961073
10. Silva, K.M., Souza, B.A., Brito, N.S.D.: Fault detection and classification in transmission lines based on wavelet transform and ANN. IEEE Trans. Power Deliv. **21**(4), 2058–2063 (2006)
11. Silva, L.R.M., et al.: Gapless power-quality disturbance recorder. IEEE Trans. Power Deliv. **32**(2), 862–871 (2017). https://doi.org/10.1109/TPWRD.2016.2557280. ISSN 08858977
12. Wang, X., et al.: Analysis of power quality disturbance signal based on improved compressed sensing reconstruction algorithm. In: 2017 IEEE Transportation Electrification Conference and Expo, Asia-Pacific, ITEC Asia-Pacific 2017, pp. 1–5 (2017). https://doi.org/10.1109/ITEC-AP.2017.8081002
13. Yadav, A., Swetapadma, A.: A novel transmission line relaying scheme for fault detection and classification using wavelet transform and linear discriminant analysis. Ain Shams Eng. J. **6**(1), 199–209 (2015). https://doi.org/10.1016/j.asej.2014.10.005. ISSN 20904479
14. Youssef, O.A.S.: Combined fuzzy-logic wavelet-based fault classification technique for power system relaying. IEEE Trans. Power Deliv. **19**(2), 582–589 (2004)

Smart Systems

Weather Recognition Using Self-supervised Deep Learning

Diego Acuña-Escobar[1] , Monserrate Intriago-Pazmiño[1(✉)] ,
and Julio Ibarra-Fiallo[2]

[1] Departamento de Informática y Ciencias de la Computación,
Escuela Politécnica Nacional, Quito, Ecuador
{diego.acuna,monserrate.intriago}@epn.edu.ec
[2] Colegio de Ciencias e Ingenierías, Universidad San Francisco de Quito,
Cumbayá, Ecuador
jibarra@usfq.edu.ec

Abstract. The automatic recognition of weather in images has many important applications in different fields, such as: land and air traffic control, autonomous vehicles, road safety warnings, crop control, improvement of images taken in outdoor areas, among others. Despite the great applicability, this field of study has not yet been explored in detail, primarily due to the great challenge and difficulty involved in extracting deterministic features for each type of weather. Several works have focused their efforts on designing binary classifiers that allow determining just two classes. A difficulty lies especially in the fact that the target classes are not completely exclusive in an image. Different classes can share the same features. Another difficulty that previous work has faced is the need for a large number of labeled images to model the various weather states. In this work, we propose an approach called self-supervised deep learning applied to weather recognition in order to reduce the requirement of the huge amount of labeled images. Our architecture, a ResNet-50 implementation, is responsible for obtaining the representations of each unlabeled image with a self-supervised approach for both pre-training and fine-tuning steps. It has been used transfer learning for sharing the architecture between these steps. Our results reached an average accuracy of 0.8833. Based on this result, it can be concluded that self-supervised learning is a convenient solution to obtain high performance in the weather recognition task from digital images.

Keywords: Weather recognition · Self-supervised deep learning · Residual learning · Transfer learning · Fine tuning

1 Introduction

The weather's state is one of the most important variables to be considered when deciding on doing one activity or another. It is so important that it can even influence our mood and the consequences that derive from it. Knowing

© Springer Nature Switzerland AG 2022
F. R. Narváez et al. (Eds.): SmartTech-IC 2021, CCIS 1532, pp. 161–174, 2022.
https://doi.org/10.1007/978-3-030-99170-8_12

the different weather states in relation to the time has allowed to determine the biodiversity of species, ecosystems, and natural places generated from them. Places can be habitable or completely uninhabitable due to the weather [1]. Technological advances have initially allowed the design of analytical systems that seek to predict the state of the weather based on historical information on the behavior of the weather over time using variables such as temperature, atmospheric pressure, winds, humidity, and precipitation.

Currently, with the advancement of machine learning for automatic image processing, it has been possible to model the state of the weather based on graphical data extracted from training images containing the different weather states: cloudy, foggy, rainy, shine and sunrise [18]. These models have allowed solving problems ranging from approaches as simple as walking or riding a bicycle in a city to more complex solutions such as autonomous driving assistants [8].

According to the authors in [19], rainstorms, blizzards, and fog are three kinds of the most studied extreme weather. Figure 1 shows four types of extreme weather conditions from the Multi-class Weather Dataset(MWD) [18], which will lead to reduced visibility and friction coefficient of road, resulting in tremendous potential dangers. For that reason, automatically recognizing weather is essential for many applications, such as highway traffic condition warnings, automobile auxiliary driving, climate analysis, and so on.

Fig. 1. Extreme weather conditions from the MWI dataset [18]

Many approaches and methodologies have been proposed in the field of weather recognition, like multitask learning [9], dictionary and multiple kernel learning [18], convolutional neural networks, and others. All these approaches have a problem balancing the efficiency of the solution and the number of images required to train the algorithm in a supervised model.

Training a model with a fully deep learning supervised approach requires a synergistic effort to obtain adequate and especially correctly labeled training images that allow the algorithm to learn. The training images require the maximum amount of, making it very difficult to apply deep learning when labeled data is scarce, as in the case of weather recognition. It varies by case, but in most cases, training a deep learning model requires thousands, hundreds of thousands, millions, even billions of training images to learn accurate representations of the images [7].

Once the training images difficulty is solved, another common problem in Deep Learning approaches is the well known *vanishing/exploding gradients*, which is a cause of increasing the depth of a deep learning model. It is essential to understand that the network depth is of crucial importance. The leading results in the ImageNet challenge [12] implement *"very deep"* models with a depth of sixteen to thirty stacked layers [16]. The degradation problem is attributed to an increased depth while the accuracy gets saturated. This is not caused by overfitting, and while adding more layers the training and test errors get higher (See Fig. 2).

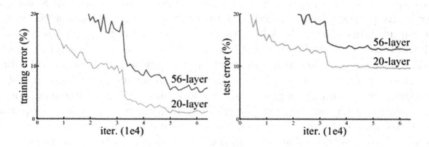

Fig. 2. Training and test errors in plain deep networks [6]

In this work, we will deal with the weather recognition problem focused on five weather types: cloudy, foggy, rainy, shine and sunrise. To extract relevant information from the training images, we follow a "very deep" neural network architecture following a ResNet-50 implementation for a self-supervised pre-training and a supervised fine tuning.

The rest of this paper is organized as follows. Section 2 provides fundamental details of related works. In Sect. 3, the datasets and the method are described. Next, results, a comparison with other works, and a discussion are stated in Sect. 4. Finally, some conclusions are presented in Sect. 5.

2   Related Works

In [18], the authors propose a method to classify the weather among sunny, rainy, snowy, and haze images. The method is based on multiple weather features, learning dictionaries, and kernel learning algorithm. Sky, shadow, rain streak, snowflake, and dark channel are extracted as local characteristics. These features are processed using several algorithms, for example, shadow and rain are represented using Histogram of Gradient (HOG), snowflake is described as a kind of noise. Then, multi-feature and class specific dictionaries are created. However, the dictionaries are shared for all weather classes. Finally, the decision is performed by feature fusion. The multiple kernel learning approach is used to obtain the best weights for all features. The proposal was evaluated using their own public dataset, Multi-class Weather Image (MWI), which is composed of 20K images. The method performance was 0.7139 on the accuracy average.

Images can also be associated with other rich image-weather association data, like temperature and humidity. In [3], the authors associate visual data with heterogeneous metadata to build a more robust weather classifier to estimate weather properties from single images. The authors target the properties: weather types (sunny, cloudy,snowy, rainy, and foggy), temperature (between $-25\,^{\circ}$C and $45\,^{\circ}$C), and humidity (between 0% and 100%). Regarding weather types, the proposal computes several features and creates a random forest classifier. This proposal was trained and tested using Image2Weather dataset. It is a public dataset, and the whole targets obtained in this work are included on its website. The results report 0.766 on average accuracy classifying weather types. Other interesting work presented in [8], achieved an accuracy of almost 90%, training a CNN model with the Image2Weather dataset which consists of more than 180000 images of global landmarks of four weather categories, such as sunny, cloudy, rainy, snowy, and foggy. They introduce a framework of parallel deep CNN models to recognize weather and visual conditions from street-level images of urban scenes using four deep CNN models to detect dawn/dusk, day, night-time, glare, rain, snow, and fog.

The implemented models refer to: 1) NightNet detects the differences between dawn/dusk, day and night-time. It aims to understand the subtleties of street-level images despite the dynamics of weather conditions and urban structure, 2) GlareNet detects images with glare regardless of its source (sun or artificial light) for both dawn/dusk, day and night-time of various weather conditions.

Different network architectures have been proposed to face image recognition in general tasks. They have been divided into two general groups: plain and residual architectures. As plain network implementation, we can mention the VGG nets [15] with convolutional layers mostly of 3×3 filters. These implementations follow two simple design rules: (i) for the same output feature map size, the layers have the same number of filters; and (ii) if the feature map size is halved, the number of filters is doubled to preserve the time complexity per layer. Figure 3 illustrates the general groups for different network architectures.

Residual Learning methods have achieved the highest results in the Imagenet Dataset challenge [12]. Residual Learning asymptotically approximates residual functions in the form, $H(x) - x$, where x denotes the inputs in the first layer and $H(x)$ represents the underlying mapping function for some stacked layers. So rather than approximate $H(x)$, this layers will approximate $F(x) := H(x) - x$. The original function thus becomes $F(x) + x(1)$. This way, if adding more layers as identity mappings, a deeper model should have a training error no greater than its shallower counterpart.

In experiments, Fig. 4, it has been shown that the learned residual functions in general have small responses. It suggests that identity mappings provide reasonable preconditioning.

$$y = F(x, Wi) + x \tag{1}$$

To reduce the amount of labeled samples, a method called self-supervision has been proposed, which is one of the most future promising frameworks that improve the accuracy of the prediction models, not only for image recognition tasks, also for time-series signals recognition [13]. For image processing, in [4], it was achieved 85% top-1 accuracy by using only the 10% of the Imagenet data. Common image transformations or corruptions (see Fig. 5) have been applied to generate the auto labeled data [11], like: Gaussian Noise, Shot Noise, Impulse Noise, Defocus Blur, Frosted Glass Blur, Motion Blur, Zoom Blur, Snow, Frost, Fog, Brightness, Contrast, Elastic, and Pixelate.

These transformations have been tested for image classifier robustness. It standardizes and expands the corruption robustness topic while showing which classifiers are preferable in safety-critical applications. It also evaluates performance on common corruptions and perturbations, not worst-case adversarial perturbations.

Self-supervised learning has also been proved to be successful in other critical tasks like medical image classifications. The authors in [2], introduce a novel Multi-Instance Contrastive Learning framework that uses multiple images of the underlying pathology per patient case for medical image classification. In this work, three steps are proposed: (1) supervised pretraining on a large labeled dataset such as ImageNet. (2) self-supervised pretraining using contrastive learning on unlabeled data. (3) Supervised fine-tuning on labeled medical images.

Finally, the study of transfer learning (see Fig. 6) also assumes significance for this study as it is motivated by the fact that people can intelligently apply knowledge learned previously to solve new problems faster or with better solutions [10].

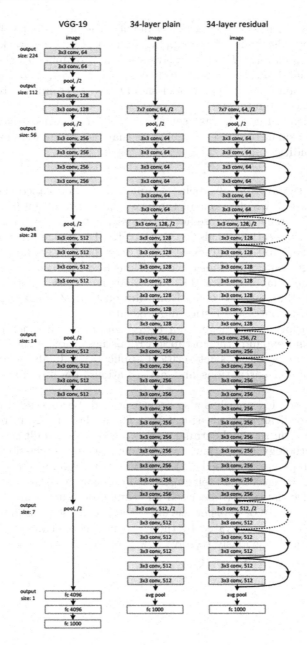

Fig. 3. Example network implementations for image recognition [6]

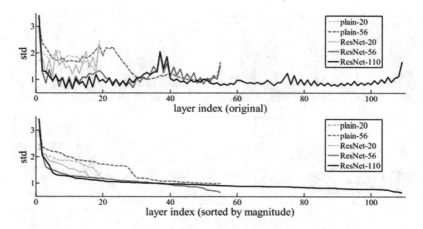

Fig. 4. Standard deviations(std) of layer responses on CIFAR-10 [6].

3   Materials and Method

3.1   Dataset

The data was extracted from the public dataset called weather dataset [5], which is available and was used for other weather recognition studies. This data was analyzed, pre-processed, and then fed to the artificial neural network for the self-supervised pre-training task. This dataset contains 300 training images for each class: cloudy, foggy, rainy, shine, and sunrise, along with other 30 images for testing and validation. These images are in different sizes and utilize the RGB model for the color description. The images need to be resized to an input size of 224 × 224 × 3 to have the required size for the ResNet architecture. These images will be applied to common transformations as shown in Fig. 5 in order to build a binary classifier model. In the first step, the model must learn to distinguish if an image was previous transformed (class 1) or not transformed (class 0). To discriminate between these two classes, the model must extract some general features of each image. In this step, it does not matter which real class the image belongs to. It is just a pre training step.

Once the self supervised model is pre-trained, it needs a fine tuning process for which we used other random images from a different weather public dataset called Multi-Class Images for Weather Classification [14]. From this dataset, we extracted 200 random images for each class for the fine tuning and 100 other random were used for validation.

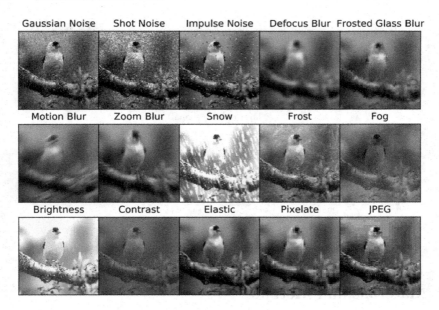

Fig. 5. Common image transformations [11]

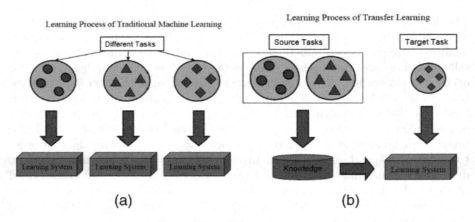

Fig. 6. Traditional machine vs transfer learning

3.2 Method

Figure 7, shows a general overview of our proposed method, which is composed by three main features: pre-training, transfer learning and fine tuning.

We implemented a residual learning architecture with 50 layers depth as suggested in [6]. Residual learning minimizes the gradient vanishing problem which is common while training. Deep neural networks uses shortcuts connections or identity mappings to connect the features in the building blocks (see Fig. 8a).

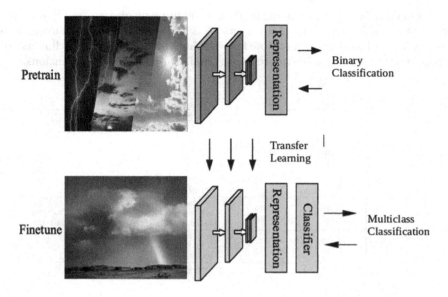

Fig. 7. General overview of the proposed method

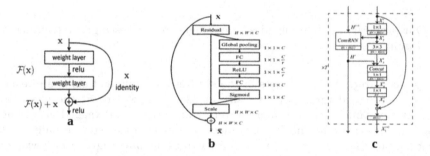

Fig. 8. Residual learning: a) building block [6] b) SE-ResNet block [7] c) RegNet block [17]

One variation made to the default ResNet architecture is adding Squeeze and excitation blocks (SE) [7], which aim to improve performance and increase model complexity. SE blocks adaptively recalibrate channel-wise feature responses by explicitly modeling interdependencies between channels (see Fig. 8 b). Finally, we added a regularization module [17], to capture the spatio-temporal dependency between building blocks while constraining the speed of parameter increasing (see Fig. 8).

For each residual function, in the ResNet 50 implementation (see Fig. 9), it is used a stack of 3 layers. The three layers are 1×1, 3×3, and 1×1 convolutions, where the 1×1 layers are responsible for reducing and then increasing dimensions, leaving the 3×3 layer a bottleneck with smaller input/output dimensions.

layer name	output size	18-layer	34-layer	50-layer	101-layer	152-layer
conv1	112×112	7×7, 64, stride 2				
		3×3 max pool, stride 2				
conv2_x	56×56	$\begin{bmatrix} 3\times3, 64 \\ 3\times3, 64 \end{bmatrix}$×2	$\begin{bmatrix} 3\times3, 64 \\ 3\times3, 64 \end{bmatrix}$×3	$\begin{bmatrix} 1\times1, 64 \\ 3\times3, 64 \\ 1\times1, 256 \end{bmatrix}$×3	$\begin{bmatrix} 1\times1, 64 \\ 3\times3, 64 \\ 1\times1, 256 \end{bmatrix}$×3	$\begin{bmatrix} 1\times1, 64 \\ 3\times3, 64 \\ 1\times1, 256 \end{bmatrix}$×3
conv3_x	28×28	$\begin{bmatrix} 3\times3, 128 \\ 3\times3, 128 \end{bmatrix}$×2	$\begin{bmatrix} 3\times3, 128 \\ 3\times3, 128 \end{bmatrix}$×4	$\begin{bmatrix} 1\times1, 128 \\ 3\times3, 128 \\ 1\times1, 512 \end{bmatrix}$×4	$\begin{bmatrix} 1\times1, 128 \\ 3\times3, 128 \\ 1\times1, 512 \end{bmatrix}$×4	$\begin{bmatrix} 1\times1, 128 \\ 3\times3, 128 \\ 1\times1, 512 \end{bmatrix}$×8
conv4_x	14×14	$\begin{bmatrix} 3\times3, 256 \\ 3\times3, 256 \end{bmatrix}$×2	$\begin{bmatrix} 3\times3, 256 \\ 3\times3, 256 \end{bmatrix}$×6	$\begin{bmatrix} 1\times1, 256 \\ 3\times3, 256 \\ 1\times1, 1024 \end{bmatrix}$×6	$\begin{bmatrix} 1\times1, 256 \\ 3\times3, 256 \\ 1\times1, 1024 \end{bmatrix}$×23	$\begin{bmatrix} 1\times1, 256 \\ 3\times3, 256 \\ 1\times1, 1024 \end{bmatrix}$×36
conv5_x	7×7	$\begin{bmatrix} 3\times3, 512 \\ 3\times3, 512 \end{bmatrix}$×2	$\begin{bmatrix} 3\times3, 512 \\ 3\times3, 512 \end{bmatrix}$×3	$\begin{bmatrix} 1\times1, 512 \\ 3\times3, 512 \\ 1\times1, 2048 \end{bmatrix}$×3	$\begin{bmatrix} 1\times1, 512 \\ 3\times3, 512 \\ 1\times1, 2048 \end{bmatrix}$×3	$\begin{bmatrix} 1\times1, 512 \\ 3\times3, 512 \\ 1\times1, 2048 \end{bmatrix}$×3
	1×1	average pool, 1000-d fc, softmax				
FLOPs		1.8×10^9	3.6×10^9	3.8×10^9	7.6×10^9	11.3×10^9

Fig. 9. ResNet architectures [6]

Our proposed method includes three stages: preprocessing, pre-training, and fine tuning.

Preprocessing. All the images in the dataset have different sizes, and each of them was cropped randomly to a size of $224 \times 224 \times 3$ to fit the input layer size. At the same time, the images were transformed and tagged accordingly. Labels transformed and not transformed were used in this step. Finally, all the images were saved in a single file with extension .$h5$. Figure 10 shows some transformations applied to all the images for the self-supervision pre-training.

Pre-training. Pre training a self-supervised model includes using the image common transformations [11]. It allows the model to learn and predict if an image is transformed or if it is not. This step is implemented as a binary classification. Image is transformed class 1 and image is not transformed class 0. Here we use the ResNet-50 architecture implemented. Figure 11 shows the architecture and the results for the binary classification pre-training.

Fig. 10. Transformations applied

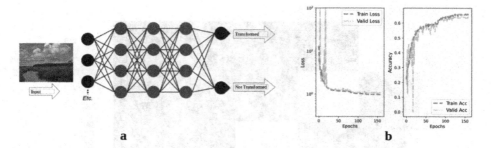

Fig. 11. a) Pre training network. b) Pre training process

Fine Tuning. We fine tuned the model using 200 random labeled images for each weather class. Transfer learning is used at this stage, so we can reuse part of the pre-trained model and just change the dense layer for using the real weather classes. Figure 12 shows the process for the fine tuning.

4   Results and Discussion

The model was implemented in python, and using the TensorFlow machine learning framework from Google. It was tested in three different hardware for getting the best hyperparameters such as: epochs, batch size, learning rate, performance metrics, and execution time. In most cases, it took three days for pre-training the model and six hours for the fine tuning.

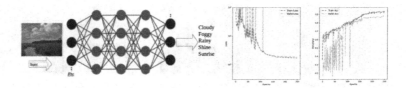

Fig. 12. Fine tuning process

- 64 GB ram, i7 cpu, Ubuntu.
- 32 GB ram, 8 GB GPU, i7 cpu 4 vCPUs, Windows 10.
- azure virtual machine: 32 GB ram, 4 vcpus, Ubuntu.

We used the confusion matrix (see Fig. 13), to demonstrate the results obtained by our proposed method in the validation predictions. Then, we calculate precision, recall and F1 to measure the performance of our algorithm, see Table 1.

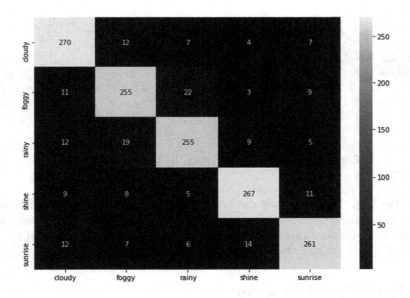

Fig. 13. Validation confusion matrix

The experiments achieved an average accuracy of 88%. It is graphically reported in Fig. 12. Table 2 shows a comparison with other related works that have been detailed in a previous section.

As shown below, the results obtained by our proposed method improve the results obtained by other related works that focused on fully supervised methods, considering that we drastically reduced the number of labeled images used in the

Table 1. Metrics obtained by our experiments

	Cloudy	Foggy	Rainy	Shine	Sunrise
Precision	09	0.85	0.85	0.89	0.87
Recall	0.86	0.85	0.86	0.9	0.89
F1	0.88	0.85	0.86	0.86	0.88

Table 2. Performance of the proposed method and other works

Method	Year	Classes	Accuracy
[18]	2016	Sunny, rainy, snowy, haze	0.7139
[3]	2017	Sunny, cloudy, snowy, rainy, foggy	0.7660
Proposed self-supervised	2021	Cloudy, foggy, rainy, shine, sunrise	**0.8833**

training stage and were faced with a great limitation in computational resources. Our results can be further improved by solving the hardware issues to be able to do a pre-training with a multi-class approach instead of adopting a binary classification.

5 Conclusions

In this research work, a convolutional neural network has been implemented with the addition that it is not fully supervised and it introduces self-supervised learning.

Experiments showed that pre-training a model with self-supervised learning can help achieve better results compared with some related works about weather recognition with fully supervised training.

The results achieved are promising. However, it is necessary to recognize that more computational resources are fundamental in order to derive a convenient model. It is really important to plan the resource requirements when training with big images since it might require high physical memory availability.

The network architecture should consider the size of the images and the computational resources available to get good training and validation results.

In view of the above, there are several suggestions for future works. Among them, it is required that the model grows and self-learns using a greater number of rotations. Images can be included from other datasets in the self-supervised learning phase to find a more generalized solution and to evaluate the model with a higher number of images.

References

1. Why is weather important in people's lives?. http://scienceline.ucsb.edu/getkey.php?key=4580

2. Azizi, S., et al.: Big Self-Supervised Models Advance Medical Image Classification, January 2021. https://arxiv.org/abs/2101.05224v2
3. Chu, W.T., Zheng, X.Y., Ding, D.S.: Camera as weather sensor: estimating weather information from single images. J. Vis. Commun. Image Representation **46**, 233–249 (2017). https://doi.org/10.1016/j.jvcir.2017.04.002
4. Goyal, P., et al.: Self-supervised pretraining of visual features in the wild, Technical report (2021)
5. Gupta, V.: Weather dataset—Kaggle. https://www.kaggle.com/vijaygiitk/multiclass-weather-dataset
6. He, K., Zhang, X., Ren, S., Sun, J.: Deep residual learning for image recognition. In: Proceedings of the IEEE Computer Society Conference on Computer Vision and Pattern Recognition, December 2016, pp. 770–778 (2016). https://doi.org/10.1109/CVPR.2016.90
7. Hu, J., Shen, L., Albanie, S., Sun, G., Wu, E.: Squeeze-and-excitation networks. IEEE Trans. Pattern Anal. Mach. Intell. **42**(8), 2011–2023 (2020). https://doi.org/10.1109/TPAMI.2019.2913372
8. Ibrahim, M.R., Haworth, J., Cheng, T.: WeatherNet: recognising weather and visual conditions from street-level images using deep residual learning. ISPRS Int. J. Geo-Inf. **8**(12), 549 (2019). https://doi.org/10.3390/IJGI8120549. https://www.mdpi.com/2220-9964/8/12/549/htmwww.mdpi.com/2220-9964/8/12/549
9. Li, X., Wang, Z., Lu, X.: A multi-task framework for weather recognition. In: Proceedings of the 2017 ACM Multimedia Conference, MM 2017, pp. 1318–1326 (2017). https://doi.org/10.1145/3123266.3123382
10. Pan, S.J., Yang, Q.: A survey on transfer learning. IEEE Trans. Knowl. Data Eng. **22**(10), 1345–1359 (2010). https://doi.org/10.1109/TKDE.2009.191
11. Rudy, J., Ding, W.G., Im, D.J., Taylor, G.W.: Benchmarking neural network robustness to common corruptions and perturbations, pp. 1–9 (2015)
12. Russakovsky, O., et al.: ImageNet large scale visual recognition challenge. Int. J. Comput. Vis. **115**(3), 211–252 (2015). https://doi.org/10.1007/S11263-015-0816-Y
13. Saeed, A., Ozcelebi, T., Lukkien, J.: Multi-task self-supervised learning for human activity detection. Proc. ACM Interact. Mob. Wearable Ubiquitous Technol. **3**(2), 1–30 (2019). https://doi.org/10.1145/3328932
14. Sharma, S.: Multi-Class Images for Weather Classification—Kaggle. https://www.kaggle.com/somesh24/multiclass-images-for-weather-classification
15. Simonyan, K., Zisserman, A.: Very deep convolutional networks for large-scale image recognition. In: 3rd International Conference on Learning Representations, ICLR 2015 - Conference Track Proceedings, September 2014. https://arxiv.org/abs/1409.1556v6
16. Srivastava, R.K., Greff, K., Schmidhuber, J.: Highway Networks, May 2015. https://arxiv.org/abs/1505.00387v2
17. Xu, J., Pan, Y., Pan, X., Hoi, S., Yi, Z., Xu, Z.: RegNet: self-regulated network for image classification, pp. 1–6 (2021). http://arxiv.org/abs/2101.00590
18. Zhang, Z., Ma, H., Fu, H., Zhang, C.: Scene-free multi-class weather classification on single images (2016). https://doi.org/10.1016/j.neucom.2016.05.015
19. Zhu, Z., Zhuo, L., Qu, P., Zhou, K., Zhang, J.: Extreme weather recognition using convolutional neural networks. In: Proceedings - 2016 IEEE International Symposium on Multimedia, ISM 2016, pp. 621–625 (2017). https://doi.org/10.1109/ISM.2016.81

Software to Assist Visually Impaired People During the Craps Game Using Machine Learning on Python Platform

Nicolás Hernández Díaz[1]([✉]) [iD], Yersica C. Peñaloza[2] [iD], Y. Yuliana Ríos[1] [iD],
and Luz A. Magre Colorado[1] [iD]

[1] Universidad Tecnológica de Bolívar, Parque Industrial y Tecnológico Carlos
Vélez Pombo, Km 1 Vía Turbaco, Cartagena de Indias, Colombia
{nihernandez,yrios,lmagre}@utb.edu.co
[2] Universidad de Pamplona, Ciudadela Universitaria, Km 1 Vía Bucaramanga,
Pamplona, Colombia
yersica.carrillo@unipamplona.edu.co
https://www.utb.edu.co/, https://www.unipamplona.edu.co/

Abstract. Pattern recognition is a prominent area of research in computer vision, where different methods have been proposed in the last 50 years. This work presents the development of a Python API to identify the result of two six-sided dice used in the game called "Craps" as a no-controlled environment to help visually impaired people. The software is structured in four stages. The first one is capturing images through a device with a digital camera connected to the web via IP address. The second stage corresponds to the captured image processing; it is necessary to establish a standard image size and resize and equalize the digitized image. The third stage seeks to segment the object of study by artificial vision techniques to identify the result of the dice after being thrown. Finally, the fourth stage is to interpret the result and play it through a speaker. The expected possible result is a system that integrates the four stages mentioned above through an intuitive and accessible low-cost Python API, mainly aimed at visually impaired people.

Keywords: Craps game · Visually impaired people · Non controlled environment · Python API · Artificial vision techniques · Image processing

1 Introduction

Human beings acquire information from the environment through the senses, from which sight is one of the most important. The impairment or absence of this sense generates a disadvantage for the individual in their daily life.

Craps is one of the most played games by people of all ages. Due to the game's characteristics, blind people cannot play, generating a problem of exclusion that

---

Supported by Universidad Tecnológica de Bolívar & Universidad de Pamplona.

F. R. Narváez et al. (Eds.): SmartTech-IC 2021, CCIS 1532, pp. 175–189, 2022.
https://doi.org/10.1007/978-3-030-99170-8_13

inhibits this part of the population from accessing this type of recreation or social interaction.

Many proposals have been developed with similar objectives and using different techniques or tools to ensure the implementation of each project. In [4], an approach to identify cards and count chips in a poker game environment is presented, using Template Matching as their chosen computer vision technique. A system of automatic recognition of a deck card located on a table was developed in [10]. The focus, in this case, is to assist blind people in the game of chance called "forty". The k-means algorithm was used, and the data set was obtained under controlled lighting conditions. In [11], machine learning is used to classify card images by suit and number, for which a model is trained using Tensor-Flow (Python) to detect the card suit and number given in an image. Also, a convolutional neural network was used to classify the images from a database.

A novel identification method based on a computer vision system for dice score recognition is proposed in [8]. The system employs image processing techniques and a modified gray unsupervised clustering algorithm (MUGCA) to identify the point number accurately. This method works well only in a controlled and filtered environment. The publications cited above have developed low-cost systems for different purposes. However, only the last one presents an adequate solution for the problem addressed in this paper.

This paper is organized as follows: in Sect. 2, the craps game, the preliminaries of image processing, and the deep learning technique are presented. The proposed methodology is described in Sect. 3. In Sect. 4, the collected data process and analysis are formulated. Section 5 exposes the dice result identification. Finally, conclusions are addressed in Sect. 6.

2   Preliminaries

2.1   Craps Game

Craps is a game of chance that deals with putting diverse wagers on the result that the players believe that they will get when tossing two dice within the next roll or in an entire round.

Rules. The fundamental bet in craps is the Pass line bet, which is a bet for the shooter to win. This bet must be at least the table minimum and at most the table maximum [12].

– If the come-out roll is 7 or 11, the bet wins.
– If the come-out roll is 2, 3, or 12, the bet loses (known as "crapping out").
– If the roll is any other value, it establishes a point.
– If, with a point established, that point is rolled again before a 7, the bet wins.
– If, with a point established, a 7 is rolled before the point is rolled again ("seven out"), the bet loses.
– The Pass line bet pays even money.

2.2 Morphological Operations

Mathematical morphology is a widely used tool in image processing, which includes dilation, erosion, opening and closing [6].

- **Binary Dilatation.** *The dilation operation causes an object to increase in size* [13].
- **Binary Erosion.** *It is the complement of the dilation operation in context with the effect of the operation* [13].
- **Opening.** *It is a combination of an erosion followed by a dilation always with the same structural element* [6].
- **Closing.** *It consists in the connection of a dilation followed by an erosion* [6].
- **Morphological Structuring Element.** *A structuring element is an array that identifies the pixel in the image being processed and defines the neighborhood used in the processing of each pixel* [6,13].

2.3 Image and Region Properties

Image regions, also called objects, connected components or blobs, have properties such as area, center of mass, orientation and bounding box [17].

- **Area.** Actual number of pixels in the region, returned as a scalar.
- **Centroid.** Center of the region, returned as an array.
- **Remove Small Objects From The Binary Image.** It removes all connected components having fewer pixels from the binary image.
- **Label Connected Components In a 2-D Binary Image.** A connected component of a binary image is a set of pixels that form a connected group.

2.4 Deep Learning

It is a type of machine learning that teaches the computer to perform something natural to humans: learning from experience which is essentially a neural network with three or more layers.

Neural Networks. Neural networks are composed of simple elements operating in parallel. They are used to perform complicated tasks in many subjects, such as classification, identification, etc. [14].

A deep learning neural network consists of multiple nonlinear processing layers: an input layer, several hidden layers and an output layer. The layers are interconnected through neurons, and each hidden layer uses the output of the previous layer as input [16].

Convolutional Neural Networks. Convolutional neural networks (CNN) are often used for deep learning techniques, especially those using images as input data. A convolutional neural network consists of different types of layers: convolutional layers, maximum clustering or average accumulation layers and fully connected layers that uses activation functions like (Softmax) [15,18].

The convolutional layer of CNNs is the main factor of these convolutions, because it allows receiving the pure pattern to be classified and not features extracted from it.

2.5   The L*a*b* Color Space for Color-Based Segmentation

This color space is a mathematical transformation of the XYZ space in which a reference target is fixed and whose tristimulus values are (X_n, Y_n, Z_n).

The three axes of the CIELAB system are indicated by the names L*a*b*. They represent Luminosity, red-to-green and yellow-to-blue hue respectively [1].

Conversion Generality. To obtain an image in L*a*b* color space, its necessary to convert from sRGB color space to (X, Y, Z) color coordinates [2] and from (X, Y, Z) color coordinates to L*a*b* color space of interest [3].

Where X_n, Y_n, Z_n are the XYZ tristimulus values of the reference target point. For an $Observer = 2°, Illumination = D65$,

$$X_n = 95.047, \qquad Y_n = 100.000, \qquad Z_n = 108.883 \tag{1}$$

Euclidean Distance. The Euclidean distance between two points in the plane measures the length of a segment connecting the two points. A generality for a matrix, can be written as seen in the Eq. 2, [5]

$$d^2_{(i,j)} = \sum_{k=1}^{k} (X_{ik} - X_{jk})^2 \tag{2}$$

Minimum Elements of a Matrix. If A is a multidimensional matrix, then $\min(A)$ is the minimum argument across all dimensions [9].

$$\left(\mu_k, Z_k^i\right) = argmin\left(Z_k^i, \ \mu_k\right)^J \tag{3}$$

3   Methodology

Craps is a gambling game in which players make a round of bets to predict the future result of the dice before rolling them. Once the bets are placed, players take turns rolling the dice. Visually impaired people cannot be sure of the correct result due to:

– Other players that could be manipulating the reported score.
– Distrust from the visually impaired player towards the other players.

As described above, implementing a sound system that offers an accurate result when rolling the dice by a person with low vision is a strategy to provide security to users during the game. The proposed methodology described in Fig. 1 is given by:

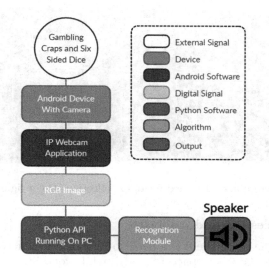

Fig. 1. Methodology.

– **Step 1.** The external signal state is instantly acquired and digitized when the player's dice stops rolling using an Android device with a camera.
– **Step 2.** Once the Android device is turned on, a local Hotspot and the IP Webcam application is configured and installed to send the digital signal to the Python software, running with $Windows$ 10×64 and linked to the local Hotspot.
– **Step 3.** The information is processed in order to extract the data results and play them through a speaker.

A similar methodology is detailed in [7].

4   Capture, Processing and Analysis of the Data Collected

This section is divided in two sections, the data collection, and steps to process and analyze the data collected.

4.1   Data Collection and Work Environment

The working environment images, as seen in Fig. 2, were acquired through a routine of 1200 iterations (for a total of three sessions). TCP/IP communication with the webcam server initialized on a cell phone with the Android operating system through the IP Webcam application is used; this routine was conditioned to changes between iterations.

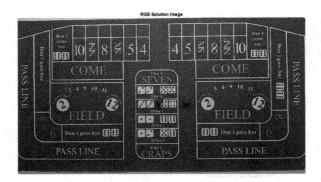

Fig. 2. Environment designed for data collection (Color figure online)

4.2   Data Processing and Analysis

After collecting the data, there is a need to identify the different colors on the mat by analyzing the color space L*a*b*, mainly focusing in the color of the dice.

Step 1: Acquire the Image. Initially an image like Fig. 2 is read via Python through a TCP/IP request to the camera server initialized on the Android device, this image is in .jpg format and is processed by Python as a Uint8 type RGB image.

Step 2: Define the Number of Sample Colors in the RGB Color Space. If you look closely at Fig. 2 you can see six main colors in the image: the background color (green), white, black, orange, yellow and red. Certainly identifying each color visually is a very simple task for a human being, so advantage is taken of such explicit knowledge to quantify these visual differences using the L*a*b* color space.

Step 3: Sample Region Selection. To perform this step, the image in Fig. 2 is treated with a loop of a size that is equal to the number of colors intended to be classified, in this case a total of 6. Thus, a small sample region is extracted at each iteration and labeled according to the corresponding color. Figure 3, illustrates the colors of interest according to the polynomial region plotted by color.

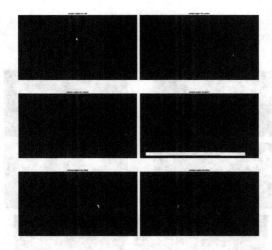

Fig. 3. Regions sampled for the different colors in Fig. 2

Step 4: Calculation of Sample Colors in L*a*b* Color Space for Each Region. To perform the calculation of the sample colors or color markers, the conversion of the sRGB color space to L*a*b* of the image in Fig. 2 is performed. Then the a*b* components described by the previously plotted regions or coordinates are taken and the average value of each extracted region is calculated. These values serve as color markers in the 'a*b*' space. Table 1 presents the color markers obtained as a result of the calculations performed.

Table 1. Color markers in L*a*b* space.

Colors	a	b
red	175.7013	166.0833
green	98.4234	149.2245
yellow	109.0128	186.4487
orange	144.1282	172.6666
white	127.3409	131.0965
black	130.8	127.6857

Step 5: Sort Each Pixel Using Nearest Neighbor Rule. Since each color marker now has an 'a*' and a 'b*' value, we proceed to classify each pixel in the original image converted to the L*a*b* color space by calculating the Euclidean distance of each pixel in the image with respect to each color marker. The minimum distance of a pixel (meaning RGB value) between a specific color marker determines how much similarity there is between the two data.

Step 6: Display Nearest Neighbor Classification Results. The label matrix obtained after applying the minimum between each pixel and the different color markers present in the original image, allows developing the desired segmentation by object color, as seen in Fig. 4.

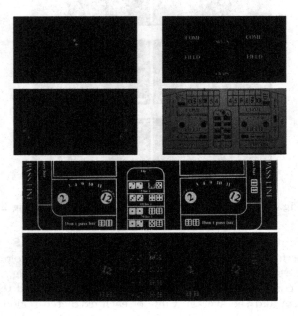

Fig. 4. Segmentation of objects by color, red, yellow, orange, green, white and black, respectively. (Color figure online)

Step 7: Display the 'a*' and 'b*' Values of the Labeled Colors. The matrix of labels to be classified for representation in the L*a*b* color space is shown in Table 2. As seen in Fig. 4, the nearest neighbor classification is very effective, since they separated the different color populations with a very small percentage of observable error.

Step 8: Returned Data. This procedure returns only a binary image representing the positioning of the dice which is illustrated in Fig. 5. The above steps guarantee the detection of the position of the dice on the mat or work surface with a percentage of effectiveness of approximately 100%, this facilitates the extraction or cutting of the dice by means of a comparison between a binary image like the one in Fig. 5, that represents the positioning and its original image in RGB.

5   Identification of the Dice Result

This section presents the methodology applied to identify the player's result after throwing the dice in the Craps game environment.

Table 2. Color - label relationship

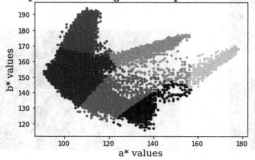

Colors	Colors_Labels
red	r
green	g
yellow	y
orange	tab:orange
white	c
black	k

Fig. 5. BW positioning image of the object of interest

5.1 Post-processing of the Binary Image and Cutouts

The images in Fig. 6, share the same interpretation problem: at the moment of verifying the number of the objects present in any of these images, a total of three can be appreciated, but there are only two of them. This supposes a problem in segmentation, for the authors is named Segmentation Error 1.

In images processing, some techniques allow, without deforming the information in the binary image, to group or ungroup objects close to each other. These techniques are applied to avoid the Segmentation Error 1 as follows,

1. Filling operation by flooding in background pixels.
2. Morphological closure with structuring element of 7×7 rectangle type.
3. Removal of small objects with less than 30 pixels.
4. Dilation of objects in the image with structuring element of 5×5 rectangle type.

Although the Segmentation Error 1 was solved, a second problem occurs when the two objects of interest are very close, forming a single object, as shown in Fig. 7, this problem is named Segmentation Error 2.

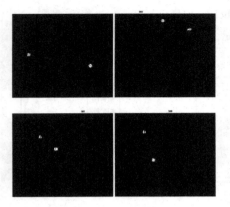

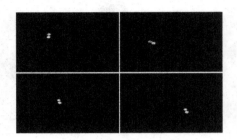

Fig. 6. Segmentation error 1   **Fig. 7.** Segmentation error 2

  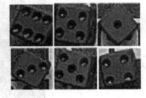

Fig. 8. Case, Extraction error 1 On the left. On the center the solution (Extraction error 1), left CDC unmodified, right CDC modified. On the Right, Style of clippings obtained.

In this case, it is necessary to consider a second stage that guarantees that at least two objects are perceived using the following methodology,

1. Acquisition of the binary image obtained by the process explained in Subsect. 4.2.
2. Filling operation by flooding in background pixels.
3. Morphological aperture with structuring element type rectangle of (gr x gr) through a loop with gr in range 1:18
4. Removal of small objects with less than 30 pixels
5. Dilation of objects in the image with 5 × 5 rectangle structuring element

It is observable that through the solution previously proposed, this set of interconnected elements are separated into two objects. However, the morphological opening process for cases like the one observed in the left side of Fig. 8 is too rough when performing the segmentation; situation that is reflected at the time of extracting in the RGB image the area of interest described by the binary image (For the purposes of the document, this problem is called Extraction Error 1).

This last error can be solved by modifying the property constructor of the objects present in a binary image after being labeled and characterized by their centroid, area and contour bounding box (CDC). For this, it is enough to identify the dimensions of each object and by means of a threshold, in this case, obtained in a heuristic way of size less than 35, resize the contour bounding box as shown in Fig. 8, in the center. The result as a set of examples of the types of cuts made can be verified in Fig. 8, on the right.

Now that the sequential process of image processing for the clipping of the data of interest is defined, the process of classification and storage of the clippings is performed manually. At this stage of the database initially built (a total of 1200 images) 40% was taken to be labeled one by one in a supervised manner through a keyboard input. Thus, building a vector of 1000 labels and a 4D type variable of 1000 dimensions containing in each dimension an image, all this with the intention of training the CNN network architectures described below. The same procedure was performed with the remaining 60% of the data, obtaining a vector of 1400 labels and a variable type 4D of 1400 dimensions, which will be used as validation test data.

5.2 Network Creation and Configuration

During the development of the project different approaches were tested in order to implement a multi-class classification system. However, low complexity techniques such as high-pass filters, adaptive filters, histogram equalization and HSV filters were not very suitable to address the basic problem of the project which roughly consists of identifying 6 possible classes or faces of a dice that is subjected to fine variations in brightness, contrast and intensity, especially under non-standardized observable perspectives (i.e. rotations, deformations, scaling, mirroring on both axes and light reflection), an example of the type of situation described here is shown in Fig. 9.

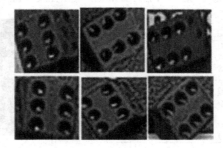

Fig. 9. Sample of the number 6 and its different variations.

Based on the behavior of the recorded training data, the use of CNN (Convolutional Neural Networks) is chosen as the artificial intelligence technique to ensure a robust classification of a multiclass data set.

Once the training data and the artificial intelligence technique for classification to be used have been identified, the network to be evaluated throughout the project are configured.

Since there is indeed no clear methodology on how a CNN should be built, it is verified in the literature that a good starting point is the general architectural principles of the VGG models. This is because they achieved top performance in the ILSVRC 2014 competition and because the modular structure of the architecture is easy to understand and implement (For more details on the VGG model, see paper [14]).

The architecture proposed below is configured with the following parameters: Image size in height (H = 28), width (W = 28) and depth channels; the number of filters that can be learned (F = [32, 64, 128]); the batch size (B) (default 128), the filter size (S = [3 3]) and finally the number of desired classes as parameter (C = 6).

5.3   Applied Architecture

Using techniques such as DropOut and DataAugmentation allow to improve the accuracy of the network, both in the training adjustment and in the testing process. However, in this particular case, it was observed that out of the two techniques, it was preferable to apply DataAugmentation instead of DropOut, since a percentage disconnection between layers to avoid OverFiting is not the problem to be corrected. The architecture in the Fig. 10 corresponds to the final architecture developed in this work.

After evaluating the architecture of Fig. 10 containing four VGG blocks, the results can be seen in the Table 3 where the accuracy of the trained network for all classes is shown in bold, and by columns the accuracy of the same according to class.

Table 3. Test results of the Fig. 10 and its matrix confusion for test data.

	precision	recall	f1-score	support
T1	1.00	1.00	1.00	217
T2	0.99	1.00	1.00	224
T3	0.98	0.97	0.98	176
T4	0.98	0.98	0.98	227
T5	1.00	1.00	1.00	269
T6	0.99	0.99	0.99	287
accuracy			0.99	1400
macro avg	0.99	0.99	0.99	1400
weighted avg	0.99	0.99	0.99	1400

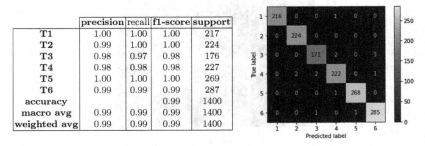

Figure 11 illustrates the training history mediated by the architecture of Fig. 10, using the training and test data provided, although this architecture is indeed able to classify about 100% of the training data, when classifying the

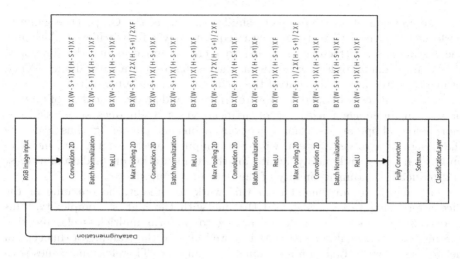

Fig. 10. Fourth CNN architecture configured with $F = [BloqueVGG1 = 32, BloqueVGG2 = 64, BloqueVGG3 = 128$ y $BloqueVGG4 = 128]$

test data it reaches a maximum accuracy of 99%, which although still not desired for the system to be developed, a tolerance of 1% is acceptable, considering that 1% of 1400 images are 14 misclassified images.

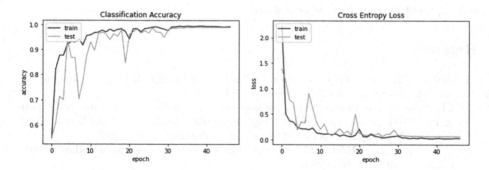

Fig. 11. Training monitor for Fig. 10 architecture.

6 Conclusions

The aforementioned allows us to conclude that it is possible to include blind or visually impaired people in games with similar characteristics to the Craps game. Therefore, the reader or interested parties are encouraged to use the methodology presented in this paper as a tool for identifying the outcome of a pair of dice in this type of environment.

The creation of an environment similar to that of the Craps Dice game to perform the respective tests and data acquisition was fully achieved. Although the research is satisfactory in trying to recreate and evaluate the developed system in an uncontrolled environment, the results present a natural uncertainty, probably correctable if we control the environment a little bit more.

The algorithm developed to capture, process, and analyze the data of interest present in an image makes use of artificial vision techniques such as filters, morphological operations, color space conversions and clustering, thus achieving the design of a robust system, with low computational consumption, intuitive and user friendly, and mainly facilitating the segmentation of the data of interest and reducing the dimensionality of the data to its output.

The algorithm implemented in this work to predict the outcome of the dice after being thrown is indeed the one with the highest complexity. This is because it makes use of deep learning to perform multiclass classification through convolutional networks. As it is well known, the training of this type of networks requires a high computational consumption. Therefore, machines with low resources take too much time to adjust a model that satisfies the input data. In this work, it took around 3 min with a PC (Intel Core i3 5th, 4 cores, 4 ram and SSD) for the proposed architectures. However, after obtaining such a model the classification process is less expensive and quite fast (5 s per result).

Evidently the results obtained with the project have not been completely the expected ones (100%), considering that the system presents a natural error of 1% in relation to the constructed database. However, it is an acceptable tolerance for this type of Python API considering that it is a first approach to a possible development and final implementation.

References

1. Boscarol, M.: El espacio de color L*a*b*—Imagen digital. http://www.gusgsm. com/el_espacio_de_color_lab. Accedido 11 June 2021
2. CIE: Colour measurement and management in multimedia systems and equipment (1998). https://web.archive.org/web/20050105122556/. http://www.colour. org/tc8-05/Docs/colorspace/61966-2-1.pdf. Accedido 11 June 2021
3. CIE: ISO/CIE 11664–4:2019 (2019–06). https://www.iso.org/standard/74166. html. Accedido 11 June 2021
4. Cisneros Navarrete, S.K., Medina Encalada, L.P.: Reconocimiento automático de cartas de barajas ubicadas sobre una mesa. Technical report, Universidad Politécnica salesiana sede quito (2017). http://dspace.ups.edu.ec/handle/ 123456789/14564. Accedido 11 June 2021
5. Danielsson, E.P.: Euclidean distance mapping. Comput. Graph. Image Process. **14**(3), 227–248 (1980). https://doi.org/10.1016/0146-664X(80)90054-4. Accedido 11 June 2021
6. EDMANS: Técnicas y algoritmos básicos de vision artificial. https://publicaciones. unirioja.es/catalogo/online/VisionArtificial.pdf. Accedido 11 June 2021
7. Hernández Díaz, N., Suarez, O.J., Pardo Garcia, A.: A real-time pattern recognition module via Matlab-Arduino interface, August 2020. https://doi.org/10.18687/ LACCEI2020.1.1.646. Accedido 16 Nov 2021

8. Huang, K.Y.: An auto-recognizing system for dice games using a modified unsupervised grey clustering algorithm. Sensors **8**(2), 1212–1221 (2008). https://doi.org/10.3390/s8021212. Accedido 11 June 2021
9. Moore, H.: MATLAB para ingenieros 1st edn. Pearson Prentice Hall (2007)
10. Ortega, H., Tufiño, R., Estévez, J.: Hacia la construcción de un dispositivo de asistencia para personas no videntes en el juego de cuarenta. Enfoque UTE **8**(4), 27–40 (2017). https://doi.org/10.29019/enfoqueute.v8n4.170. Accedido 11 June 2021
11. Rohlfing-Das, A.: Image Classification for Playing Cards. https://medium.com/swlh/image-classification-for-playing-cards-26d660f3149e. Accedido 11 June 2021
12. Roto, R.: Casino Craps: Simple Strategies for Playing Smart, Lowering Risk, and Winning More. Skyhorse Publishing (2016). https://books.google.com.co/books?id=X5sgDAAAQBAJ
13. Ruiz Fernández, L.Á.: Aplicación de filtros morfológicos en imágenes. Technical report, Universitat Politècnica de València, June 2020. https://riunet.upv.es/bitstream/handle/10251/145903/Ruiz%20-%20Aplicaci%C3%B3n%20de%20filtros%20morfol%C3%B3gicos%20en%20im%C3%A1genes.pdf?sequence=1. Accedido 11 June 2021
14. Simonyan, K., Zisserman, A.: Very deep convolutional networks for large-scale image recognition. In: 3rd International Conference on Learning Representations, ICLR 2015 - Conference Track Proceedings. International Conference on Learning Representations, ICLR, September 2015. https://arxiv.org/abs/1409.1556. Accedido 11 June 2021
15. The MathWorks, I.: Learn About Convolutional Neural Networks - MATLAB & Simulink - MathWorks Italia. https://it.mathworks.com/help/deeplearning/ug/introduction-to-convolutional-neural-networks.html. Accedido 11 June 2021
16. The MathWorks, I.: MathWorks Introducing Deep Learning with MATLAB (2021). https://it.mathworks.com/campaigns/offers/deep-learning-with-matlab.html. Accedido 11 June 2021
17. Thompson, C., Shure, L.: Image processing toolbox: For use with MATLAB [user's guide] (2017)
18. Yuan, B.: Efficient hardware architecture of softmax layer in deep neural network. In: International System on Chip Conference, pp. 323–326. IEEE Computer Society, April 2017. https://doi.org/10.1109/SOCC.2016.7905501. Accedido 11 June 2021

A Novel Technique for Forest Height Estimation from SAR Radar Images Using the Omega K Algorithm

Jhohan Jancco-Chara[1], Facundo Palomino-Quispe[1],
Roger Coaquira-Castillo[1], and Mark Clemente-Arenas[2]([✉])

[1] Escuela Profesional de Ingeniería Electrónica, Universidad Nacional de San Antonio
Abad del Cusco, Cusco, Peru
[2] Grupo de Circuitos y Sistemas Electronicos ECS-HF, Universidad Nacional
Tecnologica de Lima Sur, Lima, Peru
mclemente@untels.edu.pe

Abstract. The height of forest canopy is a valuable information to estimate or predict of aboveground live biomass in places such as natural
reserves or parks. Many of these sites use satellite data based on Lidar
or radars to run carbon stock models. The parks in low income countries can not afford to use these expensive solutions. Airborne and small
radars tailor made for a given specific area can be deployed as alternative
solution. In this paper, we present an algorithm that contains a complete
technique for the signal processing needed to estimate canopy height. The
algorithm includes a simulator of SAR raw data and SAR images based
on impulse response. This algorithm enable testing of focus algorithms
and generate three-dimensional images. We use a rigorous and extensive
method to implement the SAR image processing part of the algorithm
based on the Omega-k algorithm. To confirm the validity of the algorithm we use Quad polarized images of trees from a Polarimetric SAR
simulator. Finally, we use SAR raw data acquired by the ERS-2 satellite
to test and validate the overall process. The technique is shown to be
effective and simple, since even signals with only one and two polarization are sufficient. Height results were compared with Range Doppler
based techniques available in the literature.

Keywords: Synthetic aperture radar · Impulse response · Omega-K ·
Forest height estimation

1 Introduction

Radar imaging has been widely used in civil and military applications for remote
sensing since it is possible to achieve high-resolution imagery independent of
weather and time. Furthermore, synthetic aperture radar SAR has also a wide

Supported by Cienciactiva-UNSAAC.

F. R. Narváez et al. (Eds.): SmartTech-IC 2021, CCIS 1532, pp. 190–203, 2022.
https://doi.org/10.1007/978-3-030-99170-8_14

variety of applications since it offers many advantages compared to other technologies when it is implemented on a low/medium scale, especially for low income countries. Thus, SAR have been used in a handful of technologies going from topography, glaciology, agriculture, geology [1], earthquake monitoring [27] and volcanic activity [28], environmental monitoring [15], reconnaissance [34], etc. One area that is particularly sensible for tropical countries is the carbon stock inventory to support sustainable forest management [31]. Up to date information of forest height and accurate measurements of tree attributes are crucial to create models for forest inventory. Technologies such as Lidar and radars are employed with this purpose. In the case of Lidars, they are convenient for on point measurement or small area mapping, while SAR radars are used in large scale. SAR sensors often are mounted on small planes[10] or satellites[16,21].

The equipment and facilities required to mount SAR radar on small planes make this technology highly expensive[14]. In the other hand, satellite radars involve even bigger budgets only available to rich countries [6]. Environmental entities dedicated to the amazon forest conservation must look to alternatives for its activities that require remote sensing technology. One approach is to use available data from satellite sensors, although sometimes they are not optimized for any location or each case of study. Another approach is to implement a basic small SAR radar with specific user requirements, that could be attached to a drone to cover small and medium size areas [20]. In this case, the systems have to be implemented from scratch, from both, the hardware and software point of view. In the case of the software for image processing, it is possible to find diverse signal processing algorithms in literature such as: The range-Doppler algorithm [22], the Chirp Scaling algorithm [24], the Omega-k algorithm [8]. They are used to focus on SAR raw data, raw signals, which results in SAR images to be used in height estimation. Other specialized algorithms aim to enhance the spatial resolution of SAR images [29], extract uniformity information of SAR images [19], super-resolution techniques [33], etc. Some frequency-domain algorithms, like Omega-k, cut the link between range and azimuth. Then, they perform the compression independently along each direction with high efficiency. Although, the Omega-k algorithm has shown to be effective in focusing the SAR raw signal relative to other algorithms [8]. State of the art SAR systems use more sophisticated versions of algorithms [12] that were implemented more than 2 decades ago, however many contributions [23], have confirmed its validity these days.

Even for the software side of the SAR systems required some licensing rights that also can became costly [17]. Thus, as previously said, there is a need to produce simple and lightest versions of the algorithm to simulate, focus raw data and calculate forest canopy height, while optimizing resources for small embedded systems. In this work, we present a simple but complete algorithm for simulating, focusing and estimate height in forest canopy. The algorithm includes: a modified version of the Omega-k algorithm to focus master and slave SAR raw signals; an interferometric SAR simulator to generate raw signals; a digital elevation model that unwraps the phase to estimate height. Many contributions in the literature have focused on only one of the tasks described above, since SAR systems are large in size and complexity. For example, some previous works are related to the process and results of producing and focusing SAR images from raw data [4,23], other contributions have focused on the extraction of vegetation height from images [2,3] also available in the literature. Not much effort has been put into implementing or presenting the implementations of the whole process from raw data to forest canopy height estimation. Many contributions focus on one part or stage of the SAR image processing and how this stages are improved individually. This contribution aims to cover the whole process to present an efficient method to estimate forest canopy.

The paper is organized by first presenting the ways to obtain the signals needed for testing and validating our algorithm. Then, a overall view of our algorithm including math related details are presented in Sect. 2. Section 3 presents the results of the proof of concept and the test that we run to validate the algorithm.

1.1   Basic Definitions for SAR Radars

A synthetic aperture radar (SAR) is an active sensor installed onboard an aerial or space platform with a height H, which moves with a uniform rectilinear movement V_S. The onboard antenna, with a given radar beam, transmit and receive chirp signals perpendicular to the direction of movement called azimuth. The radar directs the beam to a point target inside the antenna footprint on the ground plane, depending on the squint range, azimuth angle, and slant range, as seen in Fig. 1a.

The SAR system has a direction of rectilinear motion called azimuth and the direction of wave propagation towards the surface of interest is called the range. The area illuminated by the radar system is also commonly called the antenna footprint, the graphic description is shown in Fig. 1a.

SAR raw signal depending on radar azimuth time u and transmitting time t is described by Eq. 1. It is a sum of echoes reflected from the surface of the target and it is not used directly in any application [7,26,32].

$$s(t, u) = \sum_{1}^{N_b} \sigma_o \text{rect} \left[\frac{t - \frac{2R_k(u)}{c}}{T_p} \right] \cdot \exp \left[\frac{-j4\pi R_k(u)}{\lambda} \right] \cdot \exp \left[j\pi k_r \left(t - \frac{2R_k(u)}{c} \right)^2 \right]$$

$$(1)$$

Where: f_0 is frequency of the chirp signal, T_p is pulse duration, k_r is chirp signal modulation rate, c is speed of light, N_b is the number of targets, λ is the wavelength and R_k is slant range. Figure 1b shows the locations of these variables in a simplified representation geometry of the simulator used to generate the point targets. Interferometry is a useful technique to generate the digital elevation modeling that is obtained from an interferometric phase [25]. In other words, it goes from the phase of a master and slave image. Where: B is the baseline vector, B_y is horizontal baseline, B_z is vertical baseline, H is SAR platform height, θ is angle of incidence, $\Delta\theta$ is phase difference, α is baseline angle, R_1 and R_2

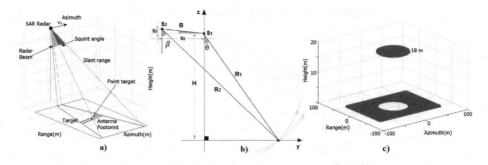

Fig. 1. a) SAR geometry, b) InSAR geometry, c) Location of 14805 simulated point targets.

are slant ranges corresponding to master and slave antenna signal $s_{r1}(u,t)$ and $s_{r2}(u,t)$.

A general representation of interferometry that uses two antennas s_1 and s_2 for the acquisition of backscattered signals. The phase of these signals is $\varphi = -\frac{4\pi\Delta R}{\lambda}$. Where: the difference between slant range is $\Delta R = R_2 - R1$. Besides, φ represents the interferometric phase expressed as a function of the sloped range difference R with values from a few meters to hundreds and thousands of meters. The interferometric phase is obtained through the processing of SAR images. Figure 1c, shows how 14805 isotropic point targets are generated to simulate an artificial SAR signal. These points are conveniently grouped in a matrix with dimensions 105×141, emulating the shape of a cylinder with a radius of 30 m and a height of 18 m.

1.2   SAR Signal Simulator

For a SAR vehicle that is moving with a velocity V_s for a given time t is located at $X_m = V_s t$. The slant ranges are $R_1 = \sqrt{y_o^2 + (x_o - x_m)^2 + (H - z_o)^2}$ and $R_2 = \sqrt{(y_o + B_y)^2 + (x_o - x_m)^2 + (H + B_z - z_o)^2}$ for a point target located at (x_o, y_o, z_o) for both signals S_{r1} and S_{r2}. Then, A custom made algorithm called InSAR has been implemented in Matlab using Eq. 1 to generate the chirp signals for antennas $s_{r1}(u,t)$ and $s_{r2}(u,t)$.

The master and slave SAR raw data are simulated taking into account the initial parameters shown in the Table 1 and Fig. 1b. This SAR raw data is used to test the Omega-k algorithm when it generates SAR images.

The simulation considers an airplane located at a height of 3000 m. The antenna footprint is a rectangle, whose dimensions are 104.760740 and 140.760740 m respectively.

Table 1. InSAR initial parameters (E-SAR)

Parameters	Symbol	Description
Frequency	f_o	1.3 GHz
Angle of incidence	θ	45°
Horizontal baseline	B_y	10 m
Vertical baseline	R_{az}	1 m
Azimuth resolution	R_{rg}	1 m
Slant range resolution	B_z	1 m
Height	h	18 m
Matrix rows	M	105
Matrix columns	N	141

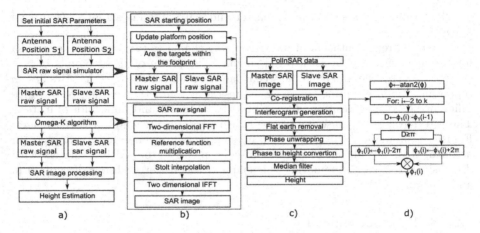

Fig. 2. a) SAR signal processing algorithm, b) InSAR simulator, c) Omega-k algorithm, d) Algorithm for reading binary data from PolInSar, e) Phase unwrapping.

1.3   SAR Signal Simulator Algorithm

SAR signal processing technique to estimate digital elevation is based on the block diagram presented in Fig. 2a. As mentioned before, simulated SAR raw data are used for this part of the study. Therefore, the process starts by acknowledging the target point and both antenna positions s_1 and s_2. Figure 2a, also shows how other parameters are also initialized, such as frequency, bandwidth, pulse duration, pulse repetition frequency and the system's speed. Antennas s_1 and s_2 are responsible for the acquisition of the back-scattered signals over the surface. They capture the raw master and slave signal data. Then, the Omega-k algorithm is applied to generate SAR images (InSAR). These procedure will allow to calculate the height by digital processing of SAR images. Figure 2b shows the flowchart of the InSAR raw data simulator, presented in Sect. 1.2.

In this algorithm, SAR raw data is generated only when the targets are within the footprints of the antennas. Otherwise no raw data is generated. The data is generated by the InSAR simulator when the SAR system is in motion to capture master and slave signals, then the Omega-k algorithm is applied. Figure 2c presents the flowchart of the Omega-k algorithm. In this part of the algorithm, the Fourier transform is applied in two dimensions transforming the SAR raw data into two-dimensional frequency domain (f_t, f_n), as described in Eq. 2 and Eq. 3.

$$S(f_t, u) = \int_{-\infty}^{\infty} s(t, u) exp(-j2\pi f_t t) dt \tag{2}$$

$$S(f_t, f_n) = \int_{-\infty}^{\infty} S(f_t, u) exp(-j2\pi f_n u) du \tag{3}$$

Then, general focusing is performed by multiplying by the reference function, whose phase is described by Eq. 4.

$$\theta_{2Df}(f_t, f_n) = -\frac{4\pi R_o}{c} \sqrt{(f_0 + f_t)^2 - \left(\frac{cf_n}{2V_r}\right)^2} - \frac{\pi f_t^2}{k_r} \tag{4}$$

After that, differential focusing is performed using Eq. 4. This process is also known as stilt interpolation, which consists in the exchange of variables ft by ft'.

$$f_t' = \sqrt{(f_0 + f_t)^2 - \left(\frac{cf_n}{2V_r}\right)^2} - f_0 \tag{5}$$

$$\theta_{Stolt}\left(f_t', f_n\right) = 4\pi \frac{(R_o - R_{ref})}{c}\left(f_0 - f_t'\right) \tag{6}$$

This process is depicted in Fig. 2c, which is used for cell migration correction in range. As a final step of this process, the inverse Fourier transform is applied in range and azimuth to obtain a SAR image. This process also considers the response of the impulse when using the focusing algorithm. The response of a point target is used to calibrate and calculate the quality parameters such as spatial resolution, Peak Sidelobe Ratio PSLR and Integrated Sidelobe Ratio ISLR.

1.4 PolSARproSim

Once the simulated SAR signals were simulated and prepossessed by the Omega-K algorithm, we need to validate them with proven tools. One of them is the PolSARproSim, which is an open source software developed by Dr Mark L. Williams for educational and scientific research purposes from the European Space Agency (ESA) [30]. In this tool master and slave signals are represented by Eq. 7.

$$s_1 = \begin{pmatrix} s_{hh}^1 & s_{hv}^1 \\ s_{vh}^1 & s_{vv}^1 \end{pmatrix}, \quad s_2 = \begin{pmatrix} s_{hh}^2 & s_{hv}^2 \\ s_{vh}^2 & s_{vv}^2 \end{pmatrix} \tag{7}$$

Where s_1 is master Sinclair matrix and s_2 is slave Sinclair matrix whose elements are: s_{hh}, s_{hv}, s_{vh} and s_{vv}, images with HV, VH and VV polarization respectively. It is defined that H is horizontal polarization and V is vertical polarization. A SAR image such as s_{11} or s_{hh} is a complex variable in binary format that contains M $\times$ N $\times$ 2 $\times$ 4 bytes [9]. A reading function for SAR data is implemented on MatLab, taking into account Eq. 7. This is useful for interpreting complex values of the Sinclair matrix [18] in the algorithm. The Quad-Pol SAR images are simulated in PolSARproSim configured by default with the data in Table 1 corresponding to the E-SAR sensor.

2   Method for Image Processing

The SAR image processing is based on the technique of SAR interferometry [11]. To model the digital elevation, we use SAR images generated by the Omega-k algorithm and Quad-Pol or PolInSAR data. The image processing algorithm is described by Fig. 2d. In Fig. 2d also shows that the PolSARpro software is part of the PolSARproSim simulator, which is used to generate Quad-Pol SAR images in binary master and slave format ".bin". The initial parameters are presented in Table 1. These data are interpreted by the readout algorithm developed in Matlab because it does not import directly. In the case of PolInSAR data, the SAR images are calibrated using Eqs. 8 and 9 [5]:

$$s_1 = w_1^1 \frac{s_{hh}^1 + s_{vv}^1}{\sqrt{2}} + w_1^2 \frac{s_{hh}^1 - s_{vv}^1}{\sqrt{2}} + w_1^3 \sqrt{2} s_{hv}^1 \tag{8}$$

$$s_2 = w_2^1 \frac{s_{hh}^2 + s_{vv}^2}{\sqrt{2}} + w_2^2 \frac{s_{hh}^2 - s_{vv}^2}{\sqrt{2}} + w_3^3 \sqrt{2} s_{hv}^2 \tag{9}$$

Where: s_1 represents a master image and s_2 represents a slave image, and the vectors of the weights for the calibration are given by the following expression:

$$w = \begin{bmatrix} w^1 & w^2 & w^2 \end{bmatrix} = \begin{bmatrix} \cos \alpha & \sin \alpha \cos \beta e^{j\varepsilon} & \sin \alpha \sin \beta e^{j\mu} \end{bmatrix}^T \tag{10}$$

Where ε, β, α and μ are angles of polarization. PolSARproSim generates binary files, which are interpreted in Matlab. The digital processing algorithm of SAR images initiates with PolInSAR data that are available in Matlab in ".mat" format, for fully polarimetric master and slave data are also available. Then, co-registration and image calibration is performed using Eqs. 8 and 9, and then to calculate the correlation coefficient which determines the compatibility of the images to determine the interferogram. After that, the phase is removed of the curvature of the earth (flat Earth). Followed by the phase unwrapping to avoid high phase shifts or discontinuity. Finally, the phase is converted to height using Fig. 2e and the median filter. The generated matrix has elements that are complex numbers, therefore, the magnitude is called the SAR image which is shown in Fig. 3, which are calibrated.

The correlation coefficient measures the degree of coherence between master and slave SAR images [5,13], and it can be expressed as in Eq. 11:

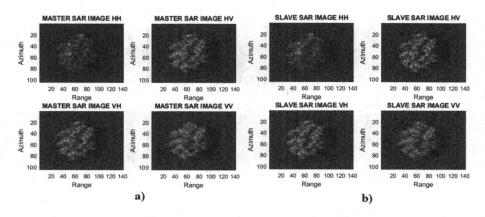

Fig. 3. a) Master SAR images in Matlab, b) Slave SAR images in Matlab.

$$\gamma = |\gamma| \, exp(j\varphi) = \frac{\sum_{i=1}^{L} s_{1i} s_{2i}^*}{\sum_{i=1}^{L} s_{1i} s_{1i}^* \sum_{i=1}^{L} s_{2i} s_{2i}^*} \tag{11}$$

Where: $0 \le |\gamma| \le 1$ and $-\pi \le \varphi \le -\pi$, in which $|\gamma| = 1$ indicates a degree of optical coherence.

The interferogram is determined by multiplying the master SAR image and the conjugate of the slave SAR image [5,13], [?]. The phase of this interferogram is φ, where the signal processing is performed. Then flat earth removal routine is implemented by first using Eq. 12, [?], [5].

$$\phi_{fe} = \frac{4\pi}{\lambda}(R_2 - R_1) \tag{12}$$

Then, the phase of the flat-earth can be removed by multiplying directly to the complex interferogram.

$$s_a = s_1 s_2^* exp(-j\phi_{fe}) \tag{13}$$

The phase unwrapping, in this stage, the phase is expressed in multiples of 2π to avoid discontinuity or sudden phase changes. In Fig. 2e, the one-dimensional phase unwrapping development block diagram is shown. It applies in range and azimuth directions.

3 Algorithm Results

First the algorithm was tested with the simulated InSAR images, then a real SAR image was used to validate the algorithm in a real use case.

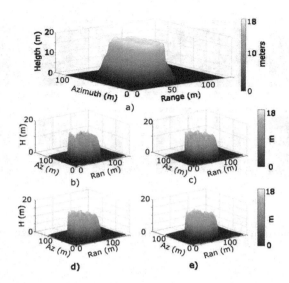

Fig. 4. a) Digital elevation modeling (DEM) for 30 m radius cylinder. DEM results of forest height using PolInSAR data for all polarization combinations b) HH, c) HV, d) VH and e) VV. (Color figure online)

3.1   Simulated InSAR Images

The Omega-k algorithm is used to focus master and slave SAR raw signal of a point target isolated and isotropic. Then, this generated raw SAR data and Omega-k algorithm is used to determine the SAR images. After that, the inter-ferometry technique is used to produce the digital elevation modeling or forest canopy estimation which has directions such as: range, azimuth and height shown in Fig. 4.

On the other hand, the SAR image processing algorithm was also validated using interferometric polarimetric SAR (PolInSAR) images known as Quad-Pol SAR images. This allows to obtain the height of the forest as shown in the color bar in Fig. 4 from 0 m (blue) to 18 m (yellow) where the trees are located in the center of the scene area with a radius of 30 m. The results of digital elevation algorithm shown in Fig. 4b for their non-diagonal components are similar because the radar system is monostatic.

3.2   Real SAR image

A synthetic aperture radar with a chirp signal frequency of 5.4 GHz and a bandwidth of 15.5 MHz $\pm$ 0.1 MHz is installed on board an ERS-2 satellite. The Tests for the Omega-k algorithm are performed using the real SAR raw data, which is a matrix of dimensions are 4096 and 4800. For this testing, SAR raw data is used with dimensions 4096 and 8192, that is, powers of 2 to avoid spectrum leakage. Figure 5a shows the magnitude of the SAR raw data in the

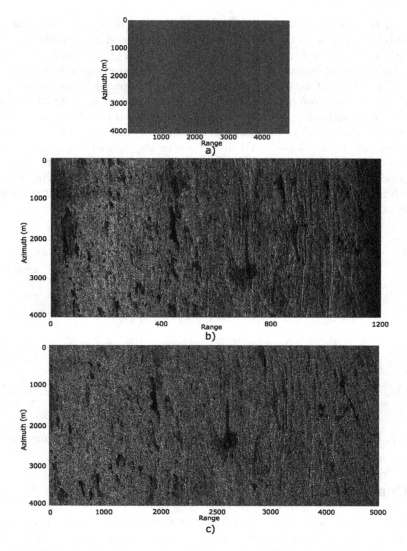

Fig. 5. a) SAR raw signal acquired by ERS-2 satellite, b) SAR image using the Omega-k algorithm, c) SAR Training Processor v1.1 (range-Doppler algorithm).

time domain. This SAR raw signals is processed by the Omega-k algorithm to generate a SAR image whose magnitude is shown in Fig. 5b using multilook filter. Figure 5-c) shows the result of the SAR image generated by the SAR training Processor v1.1 software which uses the range-Doppler algorithm. Comparing Fig. 5b) and Fig. 5-c) the validation of the implemented Omega-k algorithm is confirmed since they are similar, in addition, with the implemented Omega-k algorithm it is possible to observe some areas of the surface not noticed with the SAR training processor v1.1. Both Figs. 5-c and d, do not share the same horizontal range, due to the nature of the algorithms used on each of them. Both images start from the same raw signal, presented in Fig. 5-a. However, through both algorithms, they change in size, as the matrix are invariant and different inside in the algorithm. Both algorithms can be compared by assigning meters to each row and column of the image. Nevertheless, the range-Doppler algorithm (SAR training software) generates an image, which is a matrix.

Figure 6 shows the comparison of the forest height profiles in range and azimuth from the developed SAR image processing algorithm compared to the results obtained in PolSARpro. The maximum value of the height of the forest canopy exceeds the 18 m limit when PolSARpro tool is used. The proposed algorithm in red curve is efficient since it does not exceed this 18 limit initially established.

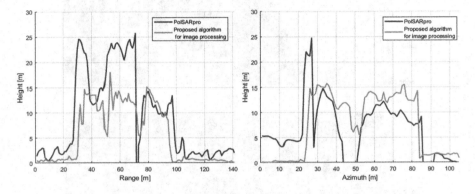

Fig. 6. Comparison of height profiles in range and azimuth. (Color figure online)

4 Conclusion

A comprehensive methodology of a InSAR raw signal simulator and image processing algorithm was implemented in the L band. The process followed a simple and computationally light way to optimize resources for a embedded SAR system. It begins by locating point targets in three dimensions such as the range, azimuth and height with azimuth resolution of 1.5 m and a slant range resolution 1.06066 m. The point targets are located at 0 m height to simulate the surface and 18 m to simulate the forest canopy. Those target points represented in 3 dimensions to simulate InSAR raw data. Then, InSAR raw signals were processed by the proposed Omega-k algorithm generating master and slave SAR images. After that, a SAR image processing algorithm was implemented generating the digital elevation modeling of a cylinder whose height variation goes from 0 to 18 m. Thus, an extensive SAR signal processing algorithm was completed from initial steps such as obtaining SAR images from raw data to the forest canopy height estimation step. Other intermediate steps were also validated. For example, the Omega-k algorithm implemented was validated using real SAR raw data acquired by the ERS-2 satellite. Likewise, the final SAR image generated by the algorithm was compared with the results of the range-Doppler algorithm used by SAR Training Processor v1.1 tool. Finally, the SAR image processing was tested using the Quad-Pol data obtained with PolSARproSim with the initial default parameters. The result is a fully polarimetric InSAR image digital processing algorithm that allows digital elevation modeling. This algorithm has shown to be effective to estimate forest canopy height that goes from 0 to 18 m. In addition, the image processing technique used by PolSARpro determines the forest canopy height with Quad-Pol data. Meanwhile, the proposed image processing algorithm can determine the forest height using only one polarization, or Duad-Pol or Quad-Pol. A single polarization was also used in the master and slave InSAR raw data to focus the cylinder with the Omega-K algorithm.

References

1. Amitrano, D., Di Martino, G., Iodice, A., Riccio, D., Ruello, G.: Unsupervised rapid flood mapping using sentinel-1 GRD SAR images. IEEE Trans. Geosci. Remote Sens. **56**(6), 3290–3299 (2018)
2. Antropov, O., et al.: Tropical forest tree height and above ground biomass mapping in Nepal using tandem-x and alos palsar data. In: IGARSS 2018–2018 IEEE International Geoscience and Remote Sensing Symposium, pp. 5334–5336 (2018). https://doi.org/10.1109/IGARSS.2018.8519190
3. Babu, A., Kumar, S.: Tree canopy height estimation using multi baseline RVOG inversion technique. Int. Arch. Photogram. Remote Sens. Spat. Inf. Sci. **XLII-5**, 605–611 (2018). https://doi.org/10.5194/isprs-archives-XLII-5-605-2018, https://www.int-arch-photogramm-remote-sens-spatial-inf-sci.net/XLII-5/605/2018/
4. Bamler, R.: A comparison of range-doppler and wavenumber domain SAR focusing algorithms. IEEE Trans. Geosci. Remote Sens. **30**(4), 706–713 (1992). https://doi.org/10.1109/36.158864
5. Cloude, S.R.: Pol-insar training course. Radio Sci. (2005)
6. Covello, F., et al.: Cosmo-skymed an existing opportunity for observing the earth. J. Geodyn. **49**(3–4), 171–180 (2010)
7. Cumming, I.G., Wong, F.H.C.: Digital Processing of Synthetic Aperture Radar Data: Algorithms and Implementation. Artech house, Norwood (2005)
8. Cumming, I., Neo, Y., Wong, F.: Interpretations of the omega-k algorithm and comparisons with other algorithms. In: IGARSS 2003. 2003 IEEE International Geoscience and Remote Sensing Symposium. Proceedings (IEEE Cat. No. 03CH37477), vol. 3, pp. 1455–1458. IEEE (2003)
9. ESA: Polarimetric data standard format. https://step.esa.int/main/toolboxes/polsarpro-v6-0-biomass-edition-toolbox/
10. Fatoyinbo, L., et al.: The 2016 NASA AfriSAR campaign: airborne SAR and lidar measurements of tropical forest structure and biomass in support of future satellite missions. In: 2017 IEEE International Geoscience and Remote Sensing Symposium (IGARSS), pp. 4286–4287 (2017). https://doi.org/10.1109/IGARSS.2017.8127949
11. Ferretti, A., Monti-Guarnieri, A., Prati, C., Rocca, F.: InSAR Principles: Guidelines for SAR Interferometry Processing and Interpretation. ESA Publications, Auckland (2007)

12. Franchi, I., Zozaya, A.: Focusing of ASAR raw data of the ENVISAT satellite using the omega-k algorithm. IEEE Latin Am. Trans. **100**(1e) (2020)
13. Hein, A.: Processing of SAR Data. Springer, Heidelberg (2004). https://doi.org/10.1007/978-3-662-09457-0
14. Jones, C.E., Holt, B.: Experimental l-band airborne SAR for oil spill response at sea and in coastal waters. Sensors **18**(2), 641 (2018)
15. Krieger, G., Hajnsek, I., Papathanassiou, K.P., Younis, M., Moreira, A.: Interferometric synthetic aperture radar (SAR) missions employing formation flying. Proc. IEEE **98**(5), 816–843 (2010)
16. Krieger, G., et al.: Tandem-x: a satellite formation for high-resolution SAR interferometry. IEEE Trans. Geosci. Remote Sens. **45**(11), 3317–3341 (2007)
17. L3Harris: l3harrisgeospatial (2021). https://www.l3harrisgeospatial.com, Accessed 19 Nov 2021
18. Lee, J., Pottier, E.: Polarimetric Radar Imaging From Basics to Applications. CRC Press, Boca Raton (2009)
19. Li, W., Zou, B., Zhang, L.: Ship detection in a large scene SAR image using image uniformity description factor. In: 2017 SAR in Big Data Era: Models, Methods and Applications (BIGSARDATA), pp. 1–5 (2017)
20. Moreira, L., et al.: A drone-borne multiband dinsar: results and applications. In: 2019 IEEE Radar Conference (RadarConf), pp. 1–6 (2019). https://doi.org/10.1109/RADAR.2019.8835653
21. Morena, L., James, K., Beck, J.: An introduction to the radarsat-2 mission. Can. J. Remote Sens. **30**(3), 221–234 (2004)
22. Neo, Y.L., Wong, F.H., Cumming, I.G.: Processing of azimuth-invariant bistatic SAR data using the range doppler algorithm. IEEE Trans. Geosci. Remote Sens. **46**(1), 14–21 (2007)
23. Rahman, S.: Focusing moving targets using range migration algorithm in ultra wideband low frequency synthetic aperture radar (2010)
24. Raney, R.K., Runge, H., Bamler, R., Cumming, I.G., Wong, F.H.: Precision SAR processing using chirp scaling. IEEE Trans. Geosci. Remote Sens. **32**(4), 786–799 (1994)
25. Rosen, P.A., Hensley, S., Zebker, H.A., Webb, F.H., Fielding, E.J.: Surface deformation and coherence measurements of kilauea volcano, hawaii, from sir-c radar interferometry. J. Geophys. Res. Planets **101**(E10), 23109–23125 (1996)
26. Khwaja, S.: Fast Raw Data Generation of Realistic Environments for a SAR System Simulator. Thesis 3727, Université Rennes 1 (2008)
27. Tzouvaras, M., Kouhartsiouk, D., Agapiou, A., Danezis, C., Hadjimitsis, D.G.: The use of sentinel-1 synthetic aperture radar (sar) images and open-source software for cultural heritage: an example from paphos area in cyprus for mapping landscape changes after a 5.6 magnitude earthquake. Remote Sens. **11**(15) (2019). https://doi.org/10.3390/rs11151766, https://www.mdpi.com/2072-4292/11/15/1766
28. Valade, S., et al.: Towards global volcano monitoring using multisensor sentinel missions and artificial intelligence: the MOUNTS monitoring system. Remote Sens. **11**(13) (2019). https://doi.org/10.3390/rs11131528, https://www.mdpi.com/2072-4292/11/13/1528
29. Wang, Z., Wang, S., Xu, C., Li, C., Yue, B., Liang, X.: SAR images super-resolution via cartoon-texture image decomposition and jointly optimized regressors. In: 2017 IEEE International Geoscience and Remote Sensing Symposium (IGARSS), pp. 1668–1671 (2017)
30. Williams, M.L.: A coherent, polarimetric SAR simulation of forests for polsarpro. Technical Report, ESA, Nordwijk, The Netherlands (2006)

31. Wulder, M.: Optical remote-sensing techniques for the assessment of forest inventory and biophysical parameters. Progr. Phys. Geogr. **22**(4), 449–476 (1998)
32. Zeng, T., Hu, C., Sun, H., Chen, E.: A novel rapid SAR simulator based on equivalent Scatterers for three-dimensional forest canopies. IEEE Trans. Geosci. Remote Sens. **52**(9), 5243–5255 (2013)
33. Zhang, J., Wu, D., Zhu, D., Jiang, P.: An airborne/missile-borne array radar forward-looking imaging algorithm based on super-resolution method. In: 2017 10th International Congress on Image and Signal Processing, BioMedical Engineering and Informatics (CISP-BMEI), pp. 1–5 (2017)
34. Zhao, Z., Ji, K., Xing, X., Zou, H., Zhou, S.: Ship surveillance by integration of space-borne SAR and AIS-review of current research. J. Navig. **67**(1), 177 (2014)

Air Pollution Software Architecture Design and Modeling: A Peruvian Case

Félix Melchor Santos López[1(✉)], Edgar Luis Cáceres Angulo[2],
Jhon Manuel Portella Delgado[1], and Eulogio Guillermo Santos de la Cruz[3]

[1] School of Science and Engineering, Pontifical Catholic University of Peru Lima,
Lima, Peru
{fsantos,jportella}@pucp.edu.pe
[2] Faculty of Mathematical Sciences, National University of San Marcos, Lima, Peru
ecaceresa@unmsm.edu.pe
[3] Faculty of Industrial Engineering, National University of San Marcos, Lima, Peru
esantosd@unmsm.edu.pe

Abstract. In Peru, the public sector of environmental regulatory agencies still presents enormous challenges in data connectivity, due to its geographic complexity. Remote air quality monitoring stations need to achieve interoperability in order to transmit raw data from remote data loggers to centralized data centers. Proper microservices software architecture and other design patterns (API REST) were developed with the formal Attribute Driven Design (ADD) method version 3 to achieve scalability, interoperability, and proper performance. For regulatory purposes, testing and validation stages were achieved through an asynchronous data quality process that was performed in an Enterprise Service Bus (ESB). Then, for analytic purposes, data simulation was executed on an Autoregressive Integrated Moving Average (ARIMA) model built on real data of sulfur dioxide and particulate matter with a diameter of less than 2.5 and 10 μ (year 2020). The simulation of the model and the dashboards were coded in the R language. A Peruvian government agency in charge of environmental assessment tasks and the national standards of environmental quality air are taken as a reference case.

Keywords: Software architecture · ADD · Microservices · Air pollution · ARIMA

1 Introduction

One of the mission objectives of environmental assessment agencies is the monitoring and surveillance of air quality in territories adjacent to economic activities such as mining, oil extraction, hydrocarbons, electricity, and industry in general. Therefore, these specialized government agencies must deploy monitoring stations in areas close to economic activities, usually in remote areas, to carry out their environmental assessment work [19]. However, in the initial stages, this work is usually conducted without including technological requirements that

© Springer Nature Switzerland AG 2022
F. R. Narváez et al. (Eds.): SmartTech-IC 2021, CCIS 1532, pp. 204–218, 2022.
https://doi.org/10.1007/978-3-030-99170-8_15

involve an online transmission of the data under an architecture that promotes real-time processing, scalability and high availability.

In developing countries, government agencies still present enormous challenges in interoperability. For instance, in Peru, various initiatives have recently been promoted to develop low-cost monitoring systems, in partnership with universities [11]. In addition, a peruvian entity such as the Environmental Assessment and Control Agency (OEFA) only has 12 stations nationwide [17], while in countries such as South Korea (a country with less extension of territory), the number rises to 209 [15]. Therefore, in developing countries, it is still a challenge to carry out end-to-end integration, i.e. a holistic solution including data capture, processing, storage, and analytical dashboards.

This technical paper describes the software architecture implementation for the on-real time data capture and processing at an environmental agency in Peru. The document explains the current non-connections among stations and a data center, the analysis of the architectural drivers, and the requirements. It also illustrates the software design that applies Attribute Driven Design (ADD) rationalized on microservices architecture (independent Fat Jars coded in Spring Boot 2.3), API REST, Eureka Server (registry), Zuul as a load balancer and API Gateway pattern, and asynchronous message processing for data quality in interoperability with an Enterprise Service Bus (ESB). On-premise and legacy platforms are reused and interconnected to achieve architectural drivers. Additionally, the stage of statistical data quality is developed based on Peruvian national standards and an Autoregressive Integrated Moving Average (ARIMA) model that elaborates on R language programming.

2   Characterization of the Problem

2.1   Analyzing the Off-Line Technology Architecture

The data capture from the air quality monitoring stations was not available via online transmission. Instead, a set of technical professionals specializing in the management of data loggers needed to travel to the stations every 15 to 20 days, where they extracted the data directly to an external hard disk. This procedure caused the government agency significant time lags in obtaining the necessary data; the monitoring stations were not interconnected with the agency's data center, as shown in Fig. 1.

The gas analyzer is responsible for transforming electrical signals into numbers, i.e., data capture from the sensors. Then, the dataset is sent to the data logger for consolidation and adequate user manipulation [10].

Extracting data from isolated environmental stations requires constant visits by technical personnel to extract data. Additionally, those stations which are located in remote areas with poor internet connections-some with no static IP available from Asymmetric Digital Subscriber Line (ADSL) providers. This complicates proper interoperability with a data center. Figure 2 shows an isolated station in the Andes of Peru.

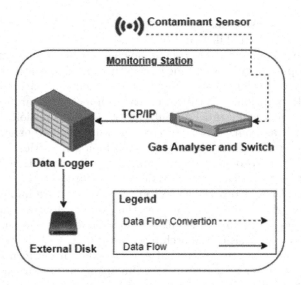

Fig. 1. Deployment view of the off-line architecture.

Fig. 2. Environmental station without internet connection.

2.2   Data Logger Characteristics

Data loggers are technology devices capable of collecting data and obtaining environmental measurements [4]. This implementation used the Campbell Scientific brand data logger, whose model is CR1000. Table 1 explains some relevant features [3] for software.

Table 1. Data logger characteristics

Characteristic	Description
Communication port	TCP/IP, email, FTP, web server
CRBasic	Language programming compatible with HTTP
JSON	Readable data format generated from Strings
Internet protocol	FTP, HTTP, XML, SMTP, Telnet, NTCIP
Operating temperature	$-25\,°C$ to $+50\,°C$
Beta Gauges sensor	For particulate matter of 2.5 and 10 μ
Support software	LoggerNet, PC200, PC400, RTDAQ
Clock accuracy	±3 min per year
Sulfur dioxide gas	Ultraviolet fluorescence technique

2.3 Data Validation

Due to the lack of ability to perform real-time processing of the data, they were validated late. The process was completed manually in Excel spreadsheets, which are prone to human error.

3 Software Architecture

For the design of the target software architecture, ADD version 3, which is based on seven steps, was used as a formal method [7]. This process has five architectural driver inputs (design goal, quality attributes, primary functionality, architectural concerns and architectural concerns), which are validated in step 1. The first seven steps could be executed iteratively, depending on whether or not the architectural design was concluded.

3.1 Architectural Drivers

The validation of the five architectural drivers for this methodology is shown in the following list:

Design Goal. Establish interoperability between the environmental monitoring station and the government agency data center, a scalable and highly available architecture, run data quality asynchronously, and reuse the legacy database. All this, in a single iteration.

Quality Attributes. Table 2 lists the quality attributes considered in the design.

Table 2. Quality Attributes (QA)

Code	QA	Description	Priority
QA1	Interoperability	Data must be transmitted from the remote station data logger to the central data center located in Lima city. The data logger must be able to send data frames	High
QA2	Availability	The sending flow must be continuous, and the architecture must propose a solution that guarantees the continuity of the reception service of the measurement frames	High
QA3	Performance	The software component in charge of receiving data must respond to the monitoring station in the shortest possible time. Time is critical to avoid generating rejection in processing	Medium

Primary Functionality. For this methodology, the primary functionality can be associated with use cases or user stories. This explains the functional behavior of the system. Table 3 provides a brief description of the main functional requirements included in the design.

Architectural Concerns. This driver defines all the concerns presented by the stakeholders regarding both the software architecture and the project [8]. Table 4 provides a brief description of the architectural concerns (optional) included in the design.

Architectural Constraints. They are mandatory considerations that must be included in the design process. These can be legal, standard, regulatory, among others [2]. Table 5 briefly lists the architectural constraints (compulsory) included in the design.

4   Design Process

The ADD design process will be executed taking into consideration the five previously mentioned architectural drivers. The seven steps are outlined below.

Table 3. Functional Requirements (FR)

Code	Description	Priority
FR1	Implement a software component capable of receiving the data frames sent by the data logger in JSON format and following HTTP protocol. The data shall be stored in a relational database	High
FR2	Implement an automatic data quality mechanism based on Peruvian environmental regulations. This procedure shall not affect the response time reception from the data center to the remote station	High
FR3	Implement statistical reports for the contaminants	Medium

Table 4. Architectural Concerns (CON)

Code	Description
CON1	The Java programming language is the organizational standard
CON2	REST API should be the interoperability standard
CON3	Legacy infrastructure and virtual machines should be used

Table 5. Architectural Constraints (CRN)

Code	Description
CRN1	A scalable architecture is mandatory due to the incremental number of environmental quality stations in the future
CRN2	The process of receiving and responding to the data frames should not exceed 5 s
CRN3	The legacy database, Oracle, must be used and no other can be created

Step 1. Reviewing the entries and validating that they match the parameters described in the previous section.

Step 2. Establishing the objective of the iteration, which is to develop an interoperable, scalable architecture with an adequate response time.

Step 3. Choosing the elements of the system to refine - in this case the data logger - primarily, the current (AS-IS) architecture shown in Fig. 1.

Step 4. Selecting the following design concepts and patterns, to solve the purpose of the architecture:

REST API. Representational State Transfer is a hybrid network-based architecture established in a uniform connector interface (QA1). The Client-Server style, the stateless characteristic, and the HTTP verb POST contribute to the purpose of the communication between the station and the data center (FR1). Hence, REST API was selected as an interoperability standard for data register (CON2), which at the same time allows the use of the JSON format.

API Gateway. This pattern works together with REST API. API Gateway provides a single entry point for defined back-end APIs and microservices. This is a fully managed service for forwarding and coordinate messages [22].

Horizontal Scalability. Due to scalability requirements, it was necessary to establish three host nodes (organizational restrictions) in high availability that were managed by a load balancer (QA2). This mechanism allows horizontal scalability; more nodes can be added subsequently.

Microservices Pattern. Scalability needed to be achieved through a pattern which allowed swift responses to increases in requests. Sam Newman [16] proposed the architectural pattern of microservices based on small, autonomous, self-discoverable, and decoupled services.

Event-Driven Pattern. To achieve high performance, an event-driven integration pattern with an asynchronous process was required [13] (QA3 and FR2). This pattern implements the data quality process based on messages delivered in an event channel.

Shared-Data Pattern. This pattern applies in the context where different components or devices require access, whether for reading or modifying, to a common data store platform (FR1). A slight variation in this pattern is that it is allowed to handle a clustering scheme where multiple nodes act as one. In the case of databases, the mirror scheme-instant and automatic data replication-is mandatory to ensure real-time data updates. A load balancer is required to implement this scheme.

Step 5. The following rationale was used to instantiate the elements according to the described patterns and design concepts:

Remote Connection. First, a satellite internet connection was established between the remote station and the data center, as shown in Fig. 3. Then, as the first point of entrance, an Apache Server acted as a reverse proxy. This in turn was protected by a firewall, and redirected the message to a Zuul server that implemented the API Gateway pattern [21]. This pattern hid the final address of the microservices, and balanced the load with the three host nodes based on the virtual machines of the Red Hat Enterprise Linux (RHEL) 7.1 operating system (CON3). It is worth noting that the organization already has a technological capacity installed, not yet a cloud-based solution, but with a robust on-premises solution.

Scalability Application. The microservices discovery service was performed by the Eureka server; this received the signals of new scaled services, registered and validated them using the architectural heartbeat tactic, and notified the Zuul server to balance them, as illustrated in the component view of Fig. 4. The available microservices recorded air-quality monitoring data in a highly available database, so the microservice's server is connected to a load balancer first.

Asynchronous Processing. The microservice, named Vigamb, as a final component, sent an asynchronous message to a message queue implemented under MQ technologies on an ESB Red Hat JBoss Fuse 6.3. Server, which performs data quality automatically (CRN2). The results are recorded in the high availability database, so the ESB is connected to a load balancer first.

Legacy Database. The organization has an Oracle 11G R2 relational database of RAC architecture (mirrors) in a single schema (FR1 and CRN3). Therefore, it is proposed to maintain this solution and not implement an additional database. A personalized schema for this design must be implemented.

Visualization. Data analytics, reporting and dashboards were performed on a stand-alone Shiny Server in the R programming language (FR3). The data will be extracted from the legacy Oracle database.

Framework for Development. Java language programming and Spring Boot 2.3 framework were used (CON1). A single jar per virtual machine [20] is the strategy for deployment. The FAT Jars are shown in the deployment view of Fig. 4.

Step 6. The entire sketch view is depicted in Fig. 3, and Fig. 4 shows two architectural views regarding components and deployment.

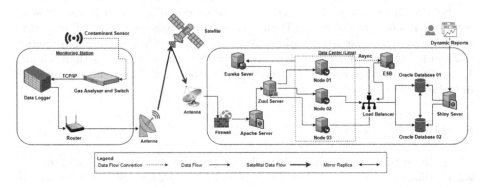

Fig. 3. Physical component view architecture (TO-BE).

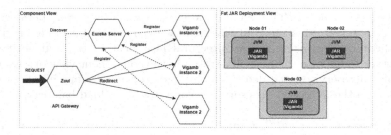

Fig. 4. Microservices architecture (TO-BE).

Step 7. A review of Steps 1 through 6 established that the three quality attributes were achieved, as were the constraints, architectural concerns, and each primary functionality. Thus, all process inputs have been met, and no additional iterations are required; the software design process is complete. The elaboration of a Kanban board was omitted. The agile board will be useful in scenarios where some architectural drivers are not covered or are partially reached.

Step 8. This step does not apply. It is not necessary to refine to carry out a new iteration, since all the drivers were satisfied and the requirements were fulfilled in just one iteration.

5   Application Case

After elaborating on the architecture design, this proposal was implemented with a monitor station located in the La Oroya region, at an altitude of 4781 meters. The technical conditions of the place required the hiring of a satellite internet service. In addition, the microservices were implemented at Lima city, as well as the virtual machines. The FAT Jars were deployed and load balancers were configured. The reuse of the ESB and the database was completed. The quality attributes and the system operations were satisfactory. The measured parameters were sulfur dioxide and particulate matter with a diameter of less than 2.5 and 10 μ. The data were collected throughout the year 2020, and subsequent data modeling was achieved.

6   Data Standards

The pollutants monitored are sulfur dioxide (SO_2) as well as particulate matter with a diameter less than 2.5 μ ($PM_{2.5}$) and 10 μ (PM_{10}). SO_2 is measured in parts per billion units (ppb) and, $PM_{2.5}$ and PM_{10} are measured in microgram per cubic meter ($\mu g/m^3$). For SO_2, converting ppb to $\mu g/m^3$ amounts to 2.62

for normal conditions (25 °C). The gas analyzer uses fluorescence technology to measure SO_2. Particulate matter is measured with airborne particulate detection equipment. Both types of automatic equipment a reused to perform this type of sampling. The sufficiency to calculate the arithmetic average is 75% according to the current air quality protocol [12]. The internal coherence of hourly data was validated, considering the following relationships:

$$\frac{PM_{2.5}}{PM_{10}} \leq 1 \tag{1}$$

In Peru, the Ministry of the Environment (MINAM) is the government agency which regulates air quality protocols and standards. This organization provides the national standards of environmental quality air, based on the parameters of measurement periods, values, evaluation criteria, and analysis methods [12]. Table 6 provides the details of the standard for SO_2, PM_{10} and $PM_{2.5}$.

Table 6. National standards of environmental quality for air in Peru

Parameter	Period	Value $\mu g/\mathrm{m}^3$	Evaluation criteria	Analysis method
SO_2	24 h	250	DNE[a] > 7 times/year	UF[b]
PM_{10}	24 h	100	DNE[a] > 7 times/year	Inertial
	Annual	50	Annual arithmetic mean	Separation/ Filtration (Gravimetry)
$PM_{2.5}$	24 h	50	DNE[a] > 7 times/year	Inertial
	Annual	25	Annual arithmetic mean	Separation/ Filtration (Gravimetry)

[a]Do not exceed
[b]Ultraviolet Fluorescence (Automatic Method)

7 ARIMA Model and Simulation

7.1 SO_2 and PM_{10} Estimation

A methodology to identify, estimate and diagnose dynamic time series models in which the time variable plays a fundamental role, is required to reduce the specification of the model [18]. Thus, for the air quality data modeling process, real data were used to obtain the coefficients of the ARIMA model for SO_2 and PM_{10} parameters. The implementation of ARIMA models begins with stochastic trend series. The methodology consists of differentiating the series d times until obtaining another stationary series in covariance, identifiable by an Autoregressive Moving Average (ARMA) model, and estimating the parameters of the model [6].

Definition: (ARIMA process (p, d, q)). A time series Y_t, $t\epsilon Z$ follows an ARIMA (p, 1, q) model, with a trend, if (1-L)Y_t follows an ARMA (p, q) process stationary in covariance, with a non-zero mean. In other words, if:

$$\varphi(L)(1 - L)Y_t = \delta + \theta(L)\varepsilon_t, \quad \varepsilon_t \sim RB(0, \sigma^2) \tag{2}$$

and $\varphi(z) = 0$ has the roots outside the unit circle. A time series follows an ARIMA (p, d, q) model if:

$$\triangle^d Y_t = (1 - L)Y_t, \quad d = 1, 2, \ldots \tag{3}$$

It is an ARMA (p, q) process stationary in covariance. The $PM_{2.5}$ model was built based on PM_{10} model. The parameters are listed in Table 6 and the R report is shown in Fig. 5.

7.2 SO_2 and PM_{10} Simulation

Based on the real data, a preliminary estimate was made to enable simulation of an ARIMA model for SO_2 and PM_{10}. The ARIMA model was the only source of error for data generation. The number of observations was 8784 and the number of series generated was 100 for each contaminant. Based on an analysis of these series, the one that provided the best fit was sought and; therefore, the one in position 52 was selected for the variable SO_2, and position 77 for PM_{10}.

Table 7 shows the estimation of the coefficients of the ARIMA models for variables SO_2 and PM_{10}, except for variable $PM_{2.5}$ which used a model regression to preserve the condition related to the variable PM_{10}.

Since the variable $PM_{2.5}$ presents a condition related to the variable PM_{10} (1), $PM_{2.5}$ simulation starts with a regression model with the original variables to estimate a λ_0 (0.225) which can be seen through a Box-Cox power graph illustrated in Fig. 6. Regression coefficients β_0 (2.427) and β_1 (0.0147) were estimated to finally reconstruct the pollutant $PM_{2.5}$ taking as base pollutant PM_{10} simulated above, which is shown below the identity line of Fig. 7.

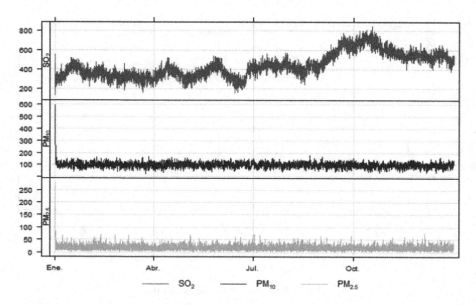

Fig. 5. ARIMA model simulation results for 2020.

Table 7. Simulation

Contaminants	Model	AR(1) AR(2) AR(3)	MA(1) MA(2) MA(3)
SO_2	ARIMA (3, 1, 3)	−0.1945 −0.6255 0.42	−0.3414 −0.2557 −0.8858
PM_{10}	ARIMA (3, 0, 3)	0.8491 −0.0494 0.1015	−0.4805 −0.0235 0.0365
$PM_{2.5}$	$z = 2.427 + 0.0147\ PM_{10}$ $PM_{2.5} = (0.225\ z+1)^{(1/0.225)}$	Does not apply	Does not apply

The use of both models is harnessed when all the data is transformed into an ARMA model, starting from an ARIMA model. Other authors also followed the ARIMA model to analyze the trend of sulfur dioxide (SO_2) for air pollution [1,9,14]. The United States Environmental Protection Agency (US EPA) environmental report on acid rain and related programs [5] was also a clear example of the application of ARIMA to the SO_2 trend.

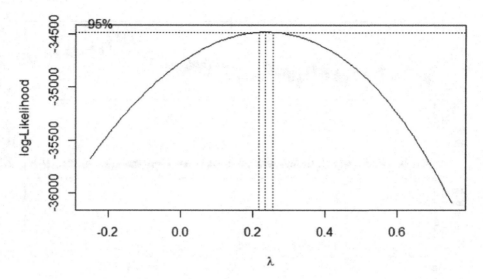

Fig. 6. Box-Cox power for λ_0 estimation.

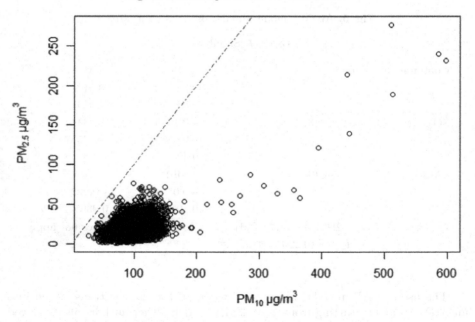

Fig. 7. Relationship between $PM_{2.5}$ and PM_{10}.

8   Conclusions

The 7-step ADD v.3 methodology was effective in achieving a robust, interoperable, scalable, high-performance, and orderly architecture in its design process.

Each pattern contributed to achieving part of the architectural drivers. For data analysis, we were able to simulated an ARIMA model for SO_2 and PM_{10} parameters, based on the fact that the time series can be established as stationary models in covariance. For the relationship between $PM_{2.5}$ and PM_{10} a linear regression model was tested.

This governmental experience is intended to serve as a guide for the design and implementation of a holistic solution, i.e. to convert an off-line solution into one in real-time, including data analytics. Developing countries with low budgets can take this experience and results as a feasible solution, especially in contexts where sophisticated telemetry mechanisms may not be available. In addition, the ARIMA model demonstrated that the data and its relationships meet the national standards of Peru.

References

1. Abhilash, M.S.K., Thakur, A., Gupta, D., Sreevidya, B.: Time series analysis of air pollution in Bengaluru using ARIMA model. In: Perez, G.M., Tiwari, S., Trivedi, M.C., Mishra, K.K. (eds.) Ambient Communications and Computer Systems. AISC, vol. 696, pp. 413–426. Springer, Singapore (2018). https://doi.org/10.1007/978-981-10-7386-1_36
2. Baptista, G., Abbruzzese, F.: Hands-On Software Architecture with C# 8 and .NET Core 3: Architecting software solutions using microservices, DevOps, and design patterns for Azure Cloud. Packt Publishing Ltd. (2019)
3. Campbell Scientific: Cr1000 measurement and control datalogger. https://www.campbellsci.com/cr1000. Accessed 20 June 2020
4. Carre, A., Williamson, T.: Design and validation of a low cost indoor environment quality data logger. Energy Build. **158**, 1751–1761 (2018). https://doi.org/10.1016/j.enbuild.2017.11.051
5. EPA: Acid rain and related programs: 2008 environmental results. https://www.epa.gov/acidrain/acid-rain-program-results. Accessed 10 Nov 2021
6. Giraldo, N.: Notas de clase series de tiempo con r. Universidad Nacional de Colombia (2006)
7. Ingeno, J.: Software Architect's Handbook: Become a Successful Software Architect by Implementing Effective Architecture Concepts. Packt Publishing, Birmingham (2018)
8. Khalid, L.: Software Architecture for Business. Springer, Cham (2020). https://doi.org/10.1007/978-3-030-13632-1
9. Lohani, D., Barthwal, A., Acharya, D.: Modeling vehicle indoor air quality using sensor data analytics. J. Reliab. Intell. Environ. **125**, 1–11 (2021). https://doi.org/10.1007/s40860-021-00137-2
10. Makhija, S., Khatwani, A., Khan, M.F., Goel, V., Roja, M.M.: Design implementation of an automated dual-axis solar tracker with data-logging. In: 2017 International Conference on Inventive Systems and Control (ICISC), pp. 1–4 (2017). https://doi.org/10.1109/ICISC.2017.8068708
11. MINAM: Minam y senamhi brindan asistencia técnica sobre el uso de sensores de monitoreo de la calidad del aire a bajo costo. https://www.gob.pe/institucion/minam/noticias/61292-minam-y-senamhi-brindan-asistencia-tecnica-sobre-el-uso-de-sensores-de-monitoreo-de-la-calidad-del-aire-a-bajo-costo. Accessed 20 Feb 2021

12. MINAM: Supreme decree approving environmental quality standards for air. https://sinia.minam.gob.pe/download/file/fid/59018. Accessed 15 June 2020
13. Monteiro, D., Gadelha, R., Maia, P.H.M., Rocha, L.S., Mendonça, N.C.: Beethoven: an event-driven lightweight platform for microservice orchestration. In: Cuesta, C.E., Garlan, D., Pérez, J. (eds.) ECSA 2018. LNCS, vol. 11048, pp. 191–199. Springer, Cham (2018). https://doi.org/10.1007/978-3-030-00761-4_13
14. Naseem, F., et al.: An integrated approach to air pollution modeling from climate change perspective using ARIMA forecasting. J. Appl. Agric. Biotechnol. 2(2), 37–44 (2018)
15. National Air Pollution Network: Air quality monitoring. http://nationalatlas.ngii. go.kr. Accessed 21 Apr 2021
16. Newman, S.: Building Microservices: Designing Fine-Grained Systems. O'Reilly Media Inc., Sebastopol (2015)
17. OEFA: Environmental survillance. https://publico.oefa.gob.pe/Portalpifa/. Accessed 6 Apr 2021
18. Pérez Ramírez, F.O.: Modelos ARIMA-ARCH. Algunas Aplicaciones a las series de tiempo financieras. Sello Editorial de la Universidad de Medellín (2008)
19. Prinsloo, J., Mathews, M., du Plessis, J., Vosloo, J.: Development of a software-based monitoring and information system for industrial telemetry applications. South Afr. J. Ind. Eng. 30(1), 54–68 (2019)
20. Puripunpinyo, H., Samadzadeh, M.: Effect of optimizing java deployment artifacts on AWS lambda. In: 2017 IEEE Conference on Computer Communications Workshops, pp. 438–443. IEEE (2017)
21. Siriwardena, P.: Edge security with an API gateway. In: Advanced API Security, pp. 103–127. Apress, Berkeley (2020). https://doi.org/10.1007/978-1-4842-2050-4_5
22. Zuo, X., Su, Y., Wang, Q., Xie, Y.: An API gateway design strategy optimized for persistence and coupling. Adv. Eng. Softw. 148, 102878 (2020)

Automatic Recognition of Pictograms with Convolutional Neural Network Approach for Literacy

Ayleen Reyes[1] and Diego Vallejo-Huanga[2](✉) iD

[1] Department of Computer Science, Universidad Politécnica Salesiana,
Quito, Ecuador
areyesr@est.ups.edu.ec
[2] IDEIAGEOCA Research Group, Universidad Politécnica Salesiana,
Quito, Ecuador
dvallejoh@ups.edu.ec

Abstract. Literacy is a fundamental and intrinsic right for every person; therefore, government agencies, NGOs, and private donors seek to implement sustainable and long-term plans that allow citizens to access quality, inclusive, and equitable education. But despite their efforts, illiteracy has not yet been fully eradicated, so educational programs and tools have been created to work to solve this problem. In this research, a web application is developed that takes the resources of the Google QuickDraw API to generate an interactive image interpretation tool, which aims to support the learning of reading and writing in people with illiteracy. The tool allows an illiterate person to draw pictograms that are interpreted by the software and through convolutional neural networks with deep learning, a prediction of the image is generated. The result is presented in a graphical user interface, which displays a real image corresponding to the prediction together with text and audio assistance, essential for user learning. The results show a performance of 75% accuracy in the training and 56% in the test. The performance tests yielded indicate that the tool meets the minimum software requirements for its future implementation in institutions that work in the education of people with illiteracy.

Keywords: Illiteracy · QuickDraw · LeNet CNN architecture · Deep learning · Image processing

1 Introduction

Since 1946 the United Nations Educational, Scientific and Cultural Organization (UNESCO) has been one of the forerunners of literacy processes worldwide [1]. This organization is one of the main defenders of this competence as a fundamental and intrinsic right in the educational field for every human being. In this sense, it has developed global efforts to promote a vision that aims to achieve a

© Springer Nature Switzerland AG 2022
F. R. Narváez et al. (Eds.): SmartTech-IC 2021, CCIS 1532, pp. 219–231, 2022.
https://doi.org/10.1007/978-3-030-99170-8_16

literate world for all. In addition, it argues that literacy is capable of empowering peoples, thus allowing them to form and participate in society [2].

Literacy is an essential part and integral axis of lifelong learning, an idea that is strongly supported and is part of the 2030 Agenda for sustainable development of UNESCO [3]. This agenda proposes 17 objectives to achieve the sustainable development of all countries and their inhabitants that include topics such as ending poverty, ensuring health equity, reducing inequality among countries, achieving gender equality, combating climate change, etc. The fourth goal advocates an inclusive, equitable quality education that promotes lifelong learning opportunities.

Despite the advances in the last decade, around 260 million children were still not in school in 2018, representing a fifth of the world's population. In the COVID-19 pandemic, several countries conditioned the operation of schools, which caused a considerable impact on more than 91% of students worldwide. This caused the most vulnerable and marginalized children to be the most affected in learning [3].

School-age children are not the only ones affected by this problem. The problem of literacy especially affects people with considerable levels of poverty, women, and marginalized groups. Despite the great efforts promoted by UNESCO, at least 750 million young people and adults have not acquired the skills to read and write, causing exclusion in their social environments. According to the results of the 2010 census of population in Ecuador, the illiteracy rate for that year was 6.8% at the national level, with the indigenous community being the most affected with 20.4% [4]. Ergo, it is necessary to implement innovative technological solutions to solve problems related to access to information and the development of basic skills in the context of literacy.

The widespread use of mobile devices in all social strata, access to the Internet, and the facilities to obtain these services at low costs, have allowed the development of support applications for people with illiteracy. These circumstances mitigate problems of deficiency in the educational development of children, adolescents, and anyone who does not have the possibility of accessing formal education systems.

Advances in the scientific field of Artificial Intelligence (AI) have made it possible to create projects that use mechanisms to perform tasks normally developed by humans, with an extensive information storage capacity. One of these projects was launched by Google in November 2016 under the name Google QuickDraw [5]. This is an online game whose objective is to challenge the players to draw an object and test whether a neural network is capable of identifying the pictogram. The API uses Machine Learning (ML) algorithms and could allow illiterate people to have an accessible tool to understand certain words through drawings.

The use of Google QuickDraw in literacy projects has been little explored, so this scientific article aims to develop a web application for literacy with a user interface adapted to the Ecuadorian context.

1.1 Related Work

One of the biggest challenges in a digital world with persistent illiteracy problems is finding an efficient and effective methodology with a set of procedures and actions for rapid learning [6]. Each implemented methodology must generate a comprehensive training to support each didactic strategy composed of recreational activities, participatory tasks and different procedures that help assimilation in the teaching and learning process [7]. One of these learning methods is the use of pictograms as a pedagogical resource to develop reading comprehension skills.

In the article of Guaicha et al. [8], 45 students were used divided into two groups. The first one of 22 was the experimental group, and the other one of 23 persons was the control group, where an improvement in comprehension skills was evidenced after applying a stimulus through pictograms.

In [9], pictograms were analyzed as a means for language development in children with autism. The research results show that the methodology can be implemented as a psychoeducational resource for the development of children with expressive language and comprehension disabilities. This research also indicates that the use of pictograms helps the development of tasks, thus reducing symptoms of anxiety and fear.

Most strategies and methodologies are implemented in the physical classroom, but for virtual environments, other mechanisms should be considered in the learning process in the digital age. Thus, new research incorporates information technologies as a dynamic and effective tool. In [10], pictograms were integrated into a web using a communication board. This instrument was used as an expression tool for the learning of children with Down syndrome. The results showed that web tools are essential learning instruments and contribute to cognitive and affective development.

In the literature, there is no consensus or clear definition to measure illiteracy since it is a concept that has evolved by changes in society and education [11].

Thus, UNESCO defines illiteracy as people who cannot read or write, or understand a simple text, and the way to measure this lack is through statistical from official sources of each country. For the United Nations Economic Commission for Latin America and the Caribbean (CELAC) an illiterate is the individual who cannot read or write and is identified in population censuses. On the other hand, the Organization of Ibero-American States for Education, Science, and Culture (OEI) defines illiteracy as the lack of literacy and basic arithmetic notions that have no studies, and this parameter is measured by official statistics from each country.

The difference between the alphabet and illiterate people is not only governed by a minimum set of reading and writing skills but in the activities that people can carry out. So three central aspects have been taken into account for the comprehensive evaluation of a person with illiteracy. The first aspect measures the level of comprehension in reading, writing, and mathematics. The second aspect focuses on the functional perspective as an individual, i.e., integration to social or work demands and personal development. Finally, the third aspect considers the conditions of a dignified life that not only implies reading comprehension [12].

So, there are different levels and indicators to assess the level of illiteracy of a person. Thus, it has been divided into absolute illiteracy, which corresponds to a person who cannot read or write and whose data was taken from a population census, being the proxy indicator for this variable at zero schooling; and functional illiteracy, defined as the lack of ability to function in society due to various social, geographical, and educational factors [13].

Depending on the definition and type of illiteracy, the internal and external variables of a person can be grouped according to the dimension of the problem and its relationship with the central problem. So, absolute illiteracy occurs when a person not has completed the basic school first year, and the indicator is the comparison between matrices, approvals, failures, and withdrawals from educational establishments. On the other hand, functional illiteracy refers to people who cannot read or write, and the metric is collected through questions used in population censuses.

For this research, several pictogram drawing software has been analyzed, and QuickDraw has been chosen due to its versatility and its large dataset. Quick-Draw is a neural network integrated into a web application created by Google and its AI Experiment development team [14]. It allows drawing pictograms, and the algorithm predicts the drawing class from a collection of more than 50 million instances divided into 345 categories. Its database is updated in real-time with each new drawing. The raw data is available on Google Cloud as category-separated *ndjson* files. QuickDraw allows drawing precise diagrams and is easy, intuitive, and interesting software to draw different geometric sketches.

Stephenson et al. used QuickDraw to demonstrate the agility and ease of use of this tool through an experiment involving first-year schoolchildren. The experiment involved introducing computer graphics and multimedia applications, allowing them to create visually appealing programs with minimal complexity [15].

2   Materials and Methods

2.1   Software Architecture and Design Parameters

The web application for literacy implemented used ISO/IEC 25000 standards to have quality guidelines for the software developed under a SCRUM work methodology. An architecture Model View Controller (MVC) was used. The Model where the data of the web application is encapsulated; the View, for the interaction with the user; and the Controller, responsible for relating the view and the model [16], as shown in Fig. 1.

The Model component contains the prediction function called *predictv2*, where a variable and the 64-bit image sent from the view by the controller are stored. In this component, a normalization of the image obtained is carried out, and the value of the category that will be used for the classification algorithm is determined. After comparing the image with the corresponding model, it returns

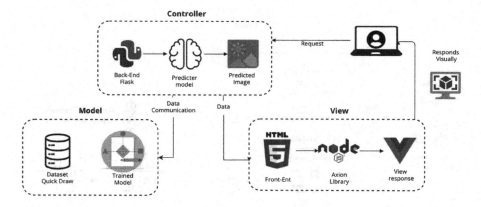

Fig. 1. Model view controller system for the web application

the result that represents the maximum probability obtained between the user's pictogram and the response of the trained model.

The view represents the user interface, which allows interaction with the software. The dynamic functionality of the user interface was made with Javascript Vue.js. In this section, the calls to the API and the rendering on the web of the information from the model are made. Bootstrap was used for the predefined and optimized styles of the responsive web.

The controller is responsible for connecting the view and the model. Also, send the category and the image in Base64 to the model. For this, it uses the REST service based on the HTTP Flask protocol to obtain and generate data in JSON format, thus allowing communication between the view and the predictor of the model layer.

2.2 Image Acquisition and Data Pre-processing

Before the training of the neural network, the images obtained from the Quick-Draw dataset have been pre-processed to facilitate the training of the model [17]. After acquiring the .npy images and resizing them to 28 × 28 pixels, the data were transformed to 32-bit floating and is divided for the maximum value of one byte, i.e., 255. In this way, it is ensured that the input data of the model take a value between zero and one for the learning rate to work properly.

Then, the dataset was divided into arrays, with 56% for training, 14% for validation, and 30% for testing, as shown in the schema of Fig. 2.

Xtrain is the dataset to train, and ytrain are the labels of the dataset that are entered in the algorithm. Xval and yval are used to tune the hyperparameters of the classifier and evaluate the performance of the neural network in several iterations during training. Finally, xtest and ytest will be used to test the performance of the neural network.

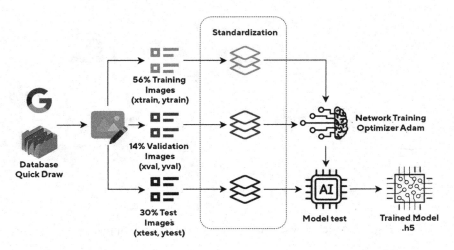

Fig. 2. Image processing block diagram and training model methodology

The dataset partitioned is normalized [18] before starting the training to increase the number of stored images. The normalized dataset decreases training time and the probability of error [19].

2.3   Definition of the Prediction Model

For the training model, a deep learning neural network architecture was implemented, based on a supervised machine learning model with LeNet CNN architecture [20]. This architecture has two feature extraction layers implemented with the Conv2D class constructor from the Keras library. In the first layer, it has a total of 6 filters and 16 filters for the second, with a kernel dimension (3, 3). In addition, it has a Rectified Linear Unit (ReLu) activation function to activate a single node if the input is above a certain threshold. For our case, the value is zero but if the value is greater, the function assigns the value of one.

At the end of each convolution, the activations of the previous layer of each batch are normalized again, i.e., a transformation is applied that keeps the mean activation close to zero and the activation standard deviation close to one. In addition, the *Flatten()* method was invoked to convert the elements of the input image array to a flat array, and in the classification layer, are added to a group of densely connected hidden layers with the *Dense* declaration.

In the hidden layer of classification, three layers trained with the Back-Propagation learning algorithm were defined. This implements a multi-layer perceptron [21] with 120 and 84 densely connected neurons for the first two layers with a ReLu activation function, and 10 neurons in its last layer composed of a softmax-like activation function of 84 inputs and 10 densely connected neurons, as shown in Fig. 3.

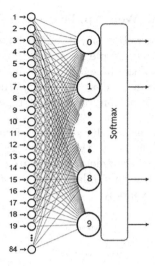

Fig. 3. Image recognition training model architecture.

The perceptron returns a matrix of 10 possible data points that is the image membership probability. The output of the softmax activation function is a vector of values that represents the probability of each image obtained on all the images that belong to that category. The sum of the probabilities must equal one, and the probability of belonging to an image is expressed by Eq. 1.

$$\sigma(z)_j = \frac{e^{z_j}}{\sum_{k=1}^{k} e^{z_k}} \tag{1}$$

Where the k values are all real numbers between zero and one, e^{z_j} is the calculation of the evidence of belonging of the image, and $\sum_{k=1}^{k} e^{z_k}$ is the sum of each of the images belonging to a category.

In the training, the *fit()* method of the model was called, and the Short Adaptive Moment Estimation (Adam) optimizer was used. Adam calculates the learning rate that combines the properties of Adadelta and RMSprop [22] and, therefore, tends to work best for training. In addition, the cross-entropy loss function and the hit rate were used for the metrics.

Once the training architecture was chosen, the parameters were initialized with a set of 10 categories made up of 170,800 images for training representing 56% of the dataset. For the validation, 42,700 images were taken corresponding to 14% of the data, and the remaining 30%, 91,500 images, for the test.

Random weights were implemented to break symmetry and thus prevent neurons in the same layer from training in a similar way. The algorithm was configured with 40 epochs, a learning rate of 0.003, and the Adam optimizer introduces a random batch sample, in each epoch, of 128 image fragments.

2.4 Development of the Web Application

For the development of the web application, specific categories were selected, grouped by the familiarity that people have with the concepts that these images represent. The abstraction of the image in the mind of the person was used for the user to draw a pictogram as close to reality. In this way, it is estimated that the retention of the information, represented together by the image and the word, is successful.

Another factor that influenced the selection of categories was the relationship between the classes belonging to the QuickDraw dataset. The categories in Fig. 4 met the minimum number of elements required for the development of the application, i.e., 10 elements with similar characteristics could be completed to classify them in the same taxonomy.

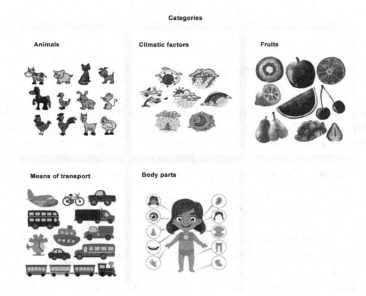

Fig. 4. GUI categories for the image classification model.

A canvas was embedded in the web application for the user to draw the pictogram. This drawing is transformed to Base64, to represent binary data from the image using an ASCII string, ensuring that your data remains unchanged and is stored and transferred through the Axios library. This library allows to perform operations as an HTTP client, and through the GET method, obtain the encoding scheme of the image and link it with the prediction function *predictv2*.

In this function, the trained model is loaded using the Python Flask framework, and the Base64 image is obtained, which will be decoded and transformed into an image in PNG format. This image is processed according to the methodology described in Fig. 1 so that the model makes the prediction and returns the result to the user.

The front-end shows the result of the prediction of the tool model, in the middle left part of the interface is the canvas, where the user drew the pictogram to be predicted. Also, an actual image of the prediction is displayed at the same height on the right side of the screen. At the bottom of this image, the text that represents the image is shown, and the user can see their characters. Next to the text, there is a button that plays audio of the pronunciation of that word.

Finally, at the bottom, there is a text box where the user can enter the characters corresponding to the resulting word using the keyboard to compare their writing with that displayed by the web application, as shown in Fig. 5.

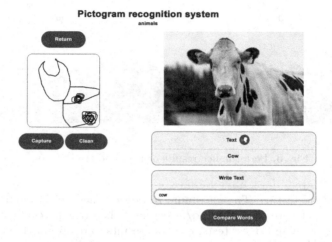

Fig. 5. User view of the result of drawing the pictogram of a cow.

The application is stored under Cloud Computing technology in a PaaS infrastructure with a cloud architecture of a CPU, 2 GB of RAM, 50 GB hard disk, Linux operating system, and CENTOS 8 distribution. The URL to access the application is http://167.99.115.136//.

3   Results and Experiments

The experiments were conducted in two ways, the first for the evaluation of the web system and the second for the validation of the prediction model.

To evaluate the behavior of the system, the web application was subjected to non-functional tests to identify potential risks of poor performance in production environments. So, load and stress tests were carried out with a certain number of requests to analyze the behavior of the application in front of a large number of concurrent users. In the case study, 50 Virtual Users (VU) were used.

The software was analyzed by the open-source web tool K6, designed for performance testing. This tool, built-in JavaScript, supports local and remote

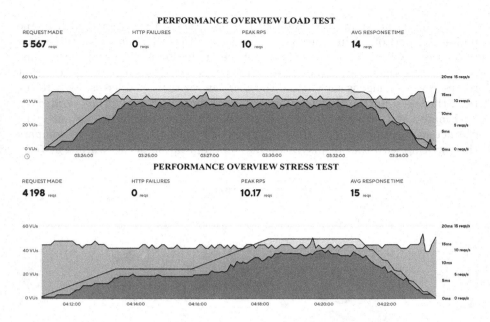

Fig. 6. Performance results of load and stress tests.

modules for load testing. The maximum response times, the standard deviation [msec], the number of requests [req/msec], and the error percentage were analyzed. For the load and stress tests, the final results were obtained in area graphs as shown in Fig. 6. Table 1 summarizes the results of the software test values.

Table 1. Response times and errors of stress and load tests in the web application

URL	Number of samples		$\mu \pm \sigma$ [sec]		Performance [req/sec]		Error [%]	
	Load	Stress	Load	Stress	Load	Stress	Load	Stress
http://167.99.115.136:81/	50	50	64 ± 16	133 ± 17	10	10	0	0
http://167.99.115.136:81/v2/predict	50	50	64 ± 17	133 ± 18	5	5	0	0
.../static/img/bus.6281a70.jpg	50	50	19 ± 11	23 ± 15	0.83	0.83	0	0
.../static/img/speak.6a4f488.png	50	50	12 ± 9	22 ± 12	0.83	0.83	0	0

On the other hand, to check the operation of the algorithm that was later implemented in the web system, experiments were carried out that allowed the performance of the prediction model to be measured.

Thus, in the training set, the performance of the model obtained a precision of 0.7450, recall of 0.74, and an F1 score of 0.74. The experiments were carried out in the five previously selected taxonomies with different elements for each category. As an example, the confusion matrix of the category transport in the training set is shown in Fig. 7.

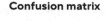

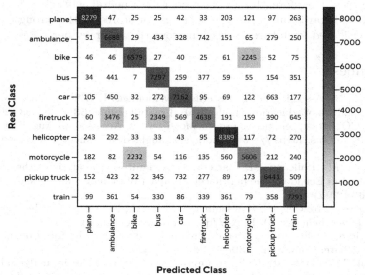

Fig. 7. Confusion matrix for the category transport in training set.

Then the CNN trained and validated was implemented in the web application. In the web environment a total of five experiments were carried out for each category. The result is represented in a Boolean way, i.e., if the prediction was correct, the value of one is assigned to the test, but if the result was incorrect, the value zero is assigned.

For the animal category, the accuracy was 80%. In the categories climate, fruits, and transport, the software was able to correctly predict three of the five pictograms. Finally, for the human body parts category, CNN had an accuracy of 20%. The results of the experiments show that the software has a mean accuracy of 56% for all taxonomies.

4 Conclusions and Future Work

In this article, an educational support web tool for illiterates was developed using simple and eye-catching pictograms, in order to help people expand their vocabulary and develop their written communication. The machine learning algorithm used achieved an accuracy of 75% in training and 56% in the test, which showed that the application can be used in real educational environments but needs some improvements before taking it to an environment of production.

During the development of the web tool, errors were found corresponding to the data stored in the Quickdraw dataset. Several of the pictograms in the dataset were identified as being incomplete or not corresponding to their respective categories. Therefore, the use of a more robust neural network, a data preprocessing that discards incomplete pictograms (or stored in the wrong category), will be considered for future work to improve the accuracy percentage.

References

1. Matasci, D.: Assessing needs, fostering development: UNESCO, illiteracy and the global politics of education (1945–1960). Comput. Educ. **53**(1), 35–53 (2017)
2. UNESCO. https://en.unesco.org/themes/literacy. Accessed 30 Aug 2021
3. United Nations. https://www.un.org/sustainabledevelopment/. Accessed 30 Aug 2021
4. Orellana, M., Raileanu, M., Barrera, D.: A multilevel analysis of the returns to education in Ecuador. The multifaceted impact of human capital. Sci. Ann. Econ. Bus. **63** (2017)
5. Jongejan, J., Rowley, H., Kawashima, T., Kim, J., Fox-Gieg, N.: The quick, draw! - A.I. experiment (2016). https://quickdraw.withgoogle.com/
6. Valdivieso, S.: Functional literacy, functional illiteracy: the focus of an ongoing social debate. Convergence **39**(2), 123–129 (2006)
7. Cabral, J.: Didactic strategies to improve the competencies in analytical reading and academical writing of future teachers and teachers in service. Eur. J. Multidisc. Stud. **3**(1), 155–166 (2018)
8. Guaicha, K., Delgado, J.C., Coello, A., Rivera, A., Yaure, A., Quevedo, H.: Use of digital pictograms as a teaching strategy to strengthen the reading process of students in basic general education. In: Proceedings of EDULEARN20 Conference, vol. 6, p. 7th (2020)
9. Herrera, G., et al.: Pictogram room: natural interaction technologies to aid in the development of children with autism. Annu. Clin. Health Psychol. **8**, 39–44 (2012)
10. Centeno, H.D., Bautista, J.L., Díaz, J.C., Román, G.E.: Inclusion of pictograms with the alternative augmentative methodology in the development of a communication board for children with down syndrome. Rev. Digit. Novasinergia **1**(1), 51–58 (2018)
11. Horning, A.: Defining literacy and illiteracy. Read. Matrix **7**(1), 69–84 (2007)
12. Torres, R.: Illiteracy and literacy training in Latin America and the Caribbean. Prospects **20**(4), 461–468 (1990)
13. Thengal, N.: Social and economic consequences of illiteracy. Int. J. Behav. Soc. Move. Sci. **2**(2), 124–132 (2013)
14. Ha, D., Eck, D.: Neural representation of sketch drawings. In: 6th International Conference on Learning Representations (ICLR) (2018)
15. Stephenson, B., Taube-Schock, C.: QuickDraw: bringing graphics into first year. In: Proceedings of the 40th ACM Technical Symposium on Computer Science Education, pp. 211–215 (2009)
16. Chen, S.: Understanding of the management information system based on MVC pattern. In: AIP Conference Proceedings, vol. 1955, no. 1, p. 040014. AIP Publishing LLC (2018)
17. Padmaja, G.M., Nirupama, P.: Analysis of various image compression techniques. ARPN J. Sci. Technol. **2**(4), 371–376 (2012)
18. Ioffe, S., Szegedy, C.: Batch normalization: accelerating deep network training by reducing internal covariate shift. In: International Conference on Machine Learning PMLR, pp. 448–456 (2015)

19. Jayalakshmi, T., Santhakumaran, A.: Statistical normalization and back propagation for classification. Int. J. Comput. Theory Eng. **3**(1), 1793–8201 (2011)
20. Bouti, A., Mahraz, M.A., Riffi, J., Tairi, H.: A robust system for road sign detection and classification using LeNet architecture based on convolutional neural network. Soft. Comput. **24**(9), 6721–6733 (2020)
21. Rosenblatt, F.: Principles of neurodynamics. Perceptrons and the theory of brain mechanisms. Cornell Aeronautical Lab Inc., Buffalo (1961)
22. Kingma, D., Ba, J.: Adam: a method for stochastic optimization. In 3rd International Conference for Learning Representations (2017)

Pose Conditioned Human Motion Generation Using Generative Adversarial Networks

Andres Aguilar Luhrs, Saúl Tovar Arriaga⊙, Jesús Carlos Pedraza Ortega⊙, and András Takács⁽✉⁾ ⊙

Universidad Autónoma de Querétaro, 76000 Querétaro, QRO, Mexico
andras.takacs@uaq.mx

Abstract. This work proposes a model that allows for the generation of human pose sequences represented by points in the 3D space based on artificial intelligence algorithms. A GAN framework AC-GAN variant uses pose-based labels with a simple discriminator and two auxiliary classifiers, one based on unsupervised k-means labels and the other on the 3DPCK metric. This model focuses on the emulation of the human body movement while cooperatively performing various activities. It successfully models human interaction behavior, achieving a 0.1507 in the Kolmogorov-Smirnov metric, 45.55 3DPCK of 150 mm, 4.4019 for the FID metric, and 0.0487 for the MMD metric, all for unseen motion data.

Keywords: Motion synthesis · Generative adversarial network · Deep learning

1 Introduction

Human-machine interaction is a long-time studied topic, the goal is to achieve a human-like level of realism for actions performed by virtual agents [1], so they can serve as companions [2, 3], coworkers [4], or caretakers [5] to achieve the desired results. On the topic of human-like companions, there are many problems to be resolved, like emulation of emotions and feelings [6], language [7], appearance [8], and others; some of these problems have already been addressed, especially the ones related to language and emotions modeling.

There also have been works related to the creation of appropriated responses to external stimuli from different elements of the environment, especially the interaction with objects and natural features [9], some others between agents, and a few with human beings trying to emulate naturally feeling movements, even fewer related to the generation of such actions to emulated human behavior based on probability distribution instead of directly learned poses [10].

This work offers a method that allows the generation of movements based on a known distribution of actions learned by the discriminator and auxiliary classification networks. These movements serve as a base to generate adequate responses for the input movements of the generator network. We assessed the model using a quantitative approach to measure the level of pertinence between the distribution of the expected and the generated motion.

© Springer Nature Switzerland AG 2022
F. R. Narváez et al. (Eds.): SmartTech-IC 2021, CCIS 1532, pp. 232–246, 2022.
https://doi.org/10.1007/978-3-030-99170-8_17

We use the Kolmogorov-Smirnov (K-S) statistic [11] to measure the level of fitness between the real and generated poses, the Euclidian distance to measure the space between generated data, and the ground truth in mm [12, 13]. 3DPCK (3D Percentage of Correct Key points) with a 150 mm threshold [14], Maximum Mean Discrepancy (MMD) [30], and Fréchet inception distance (FID) [29].

The novel contributions in this paper are:

- The use of continuous pose-based conditional labels for 3D pose generation using an AC-GAN framework,
- The use of K-means and 3DPCK as labels for the auxiliary classifier of the AC-GAN discriminator,
- Two novel models for both the generative and discriminative networks.

2 Related Work

Many human motion syntheses works exist. Some works utilize the activity levels over time to emulate the movements of a human being while in a conversation [1] or speech to upper-body gesture generation [15]. Others use the beat obtained from music [16], text, and audio [17], except for the last, and most of these approaches use a 2D articulatory model like the open pose skeleton for the motion capture and generation and are then limited to a 2D projection of their resulting poses.

Other work focused on using pseudo images of the values of angles in the skeleton joints to generate movements from a latent space, using a classical convolutional GAN [10].

Some methods to generate synthetic single subject pose sequences, for example:

- Bayesian adversarial approach for human motion synthesis [18].
- Pose sequence generation based on style transfer using mixtures of autoregressive models (MAR) [33].
- Captured human motion variation using Dynamic Bayesian Networks [34].
- And Hierarchical Hidden Markov models for pose generation and motion modeling [19].

Finally, some other works take a trajectory to generate a feasible sequence of movements as it moves through a given environment [20].

Still, there is not much information about methods that can use poses to generate a response pose, lacking the possibility of the human interaction factor based on body language offered in this work. It is not possible to directly compare most of the described methods since they depend on different types of inputs, datasets, and objectives, even if they are all human motion generation models because they all have different purposes; the same happens with this work as there is no other work modeling a two subject interaction using point-based poses data as input.

3 The Methodology

We suppose that the non-verbal communication through body language represented as point-based poses holds enough information in the captured motion from a first subject [21], given in R3 cartesian coordinates as shown in Fig. 1, to infer the points-based information response of a second subject. The method used in this work models the distribution from the ground truth of the motion capture dataset where two subjects are recorded performing various activities interpreted as point clouds. A Generative Adversarial Neural Network (GAN) that uses a recurrent generator model provides responses to unknown data while preserving a low Euclidean distance between actual and generated samples. Five ensembled networks trained in the GAN with differently initialized weights are used to increase the network coverage and obtain even higher precision in the predictions.

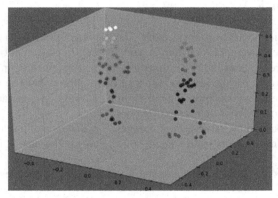

Fig. 1. Normalized point cloud representation of subject motion capture both subjects are walking to each other. Values are scaled by 1/s.

3.1 Preprocessing

It is necessary to identify its structure, clean it from missing values, standardize its values and define the new shape they will take, if necessary, as its dimensions and type of data passed to the neural network.

Data comes as c3d formatted files from the CMU dataset [28], which contain clouds of 3D points for two given subjects that are separated by the internal name of the subject ("Justin" and "Rory"). The lost points on the first frames are replaced by zeros to avoid NAN values. However, as some points are not equally labeled between motion sequences, 41 points have been identified to appear on each one of the motion captures files, so only those points are used for every poses. There are 11 pose sequences to be processed, labeled on the CMU dataset as on the actions 18_01,18_03, 18_05, 18_07, 18_08, 18_09, 18_10. 18_12, 18_13, 18_15 and 19_01.

When both subjects' data are separated, it is necessary to standardize the subject's height. The maximum height of each subject in each pose sequence is obtained and utilized to standardize the subject's statures. When both characters have the same 1681 mm height on all sequences, the points axes are separated at each time step and then concatenated to form a 3×123 matrix.

The flattened coordinates chunks will then be saved as pickled NumPy arrays to be loaded in the python training script later, and both subjects' pose sets are split into their training and test sets.

After loading the data into the training section, the data will be divided by a constant s representing the maximum radius of the motion. The purpose of this is to limit the range of the data to be between -1 and 1, which is convenient for the GRU input layer, without distorting the motions, and the total scale factor is $s = 2 \times 1681$ mm.

The resulting data is a set of 3×123 matrices, where every row is a time step, and every column represents an axis X, Y, or Z, such that every three columns represent a point whose values range from -1 to 1.

3.2 Network Details

The framework used in this work is a GAN proposed by Ian J. Goodfellow [22]. This framework aims to model the probability of a distribution in a neural network called a generator while a discriminator learns to distinguish generated and actual samples. This process continues until the generated samples cannot be distinguished from the real ones. The generator and discriminator play this min-max game following the function on Eq. (1).

$$\min_{G} \max_{D} V(D, G) = \mathbb{E}_{x \sim p_{\text{dat}}(x)}[\log D(x)] + \mathbb{E}_{z \sim p_z(z)}[\log(1 - D(G(z)))] \quad (1)$$

Where D is the discriminator and G the generator, z input noise distribution, x the actual data, and p_{dat} the ground truth distribution.

A GAN is used as generative because it allows us to parameterize the output using labels as inputs; in this case, those labels represent sequences of human poses. There are currently many different types of GAN like the original GAN [1], AC-GAN [23], Conditional GAN [35], Wasserstein GAN [36], and others.

GANs can be tailored for the needs of each problem; in this case, we use the 3DPCK metric and unsupervised clustering to generate classes to control the position of the generated pose and how it is from the original points. A GAN also allows us to experiment with his components, by changing types of layers, optimizers, activation functions, and cost functions, for a more delicate tunning process.

GANS are groups are neural networks, and it is known that backpropagation can be costly if there are many parameters to train, but thanks to model GPU technology, it turned into an advantage as this process can be heavily parallelized in comparison with other methods that are CPU intensive as most CPUs have fewer cores than GPUs.

For this work we used a modified version of this min-max game function, which uses an auxiliary discriminator to reduce mode collapse and conditional labels that will allow control of the desired output by parametrizing the generator inputs, the model in question is called auxiliary classifier GAN [23] (AC-GAN), which loss function $\mathcal{L}$ is described in Eqs. (2), (3) and (4) where $G_a(z_i, Y_i)$ is the generator and $D_{a(a)}(X_i, Y_i)$ is the discriminator, z_i is the latent space distribution and Y_i the conditional label.

$$\mathcal{L}_a^a\big(D_{a(a)},G_a\big) = \frac{1}{n}\left(\sum_{i=1}^n \log\left(\begin{array}{c} D_{a(a)}(X_i; Y_i) \\ + \log\big(D_{a(a)}(G_a(z_i,Y_i); Y_i)\big)\end{array}\right)\right) \tag{2}$$

For the discriminator

$$\mathcal{L}_d^a(D_a,G_a) = \mathcal{L}_d^u\big(D_{a(rf)},G_a\big) + \mathcal{L}_a^a\big(D_{a(a)},G_a\big) \tag{3}$$

And for the generator

$$\mathcal{L}_g^a(D_a,G_a) = \mathcal{L}_g^u\big(D_{a(rf)},G_a\big) + \mathcal{L}_a^a\big(D_{a(a)},G_a\big) \tag{4}$$

The proposed generator network consists of a deep network with 5 GRU [32] layers and a dense layer for the latent representation. The model is, in fact, a simple recurrent encoder-decoder, where GRU layers operate to reduce the dimensionality of the input from the data steps concatenated with the GAN latent space. A compressed representation is obtained from the dense layer, and then the dimensionality is increased by the GRU layers to achieve the desired size of 3×123. The models are shown in Fig. 2.

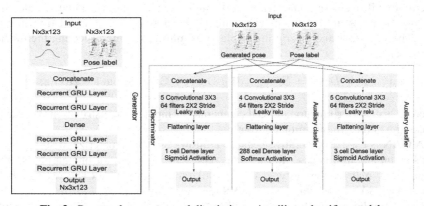

Fig. 2. Proposed generator and discriminator/auxiliary classifier models

The latent space representation of the GAN, which is the same size as the input array, is to maximize the number of possible distributions that the generator could learn at the cost of less stability on the generated motions.

The GRU recurrent layers are intended to maintain coherence through time and reduce jittering movements and sudden position changes in the point cloud.

The proposed discriminator and auxiliary classifier networks consist of a purely convolutional binary classifier. This auxiliary convolutional classifier will learn to categorize the real and generated samples between N number of classes obtained by a k-means classifier to represent the possible locations in a discrete manner represented as categorical values. The other auxiliary classifier determines which points are compliant with the 3DCPK@0.5 condition of proximity for each timestep of the generator output and real samples, as shown in Fig. 2.

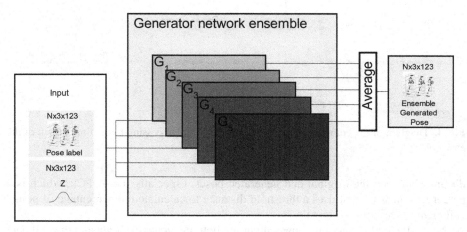

Fig. 3. Averaged generator ensemble

It was observed experimentally that a single neural network could achieve good results to make valuable predictions. However, this project uses an ensemble to increase the coverage and reduce the Euclidean distance loss between the generated data and the ground truth. In this case, five neural networks get trained under the technique known as different weight initialization, as shown in Fig. 3, where the networks are trained with different random starting values for the weights of each neural network [24]. The networks are trained and then combined on an average ensemble, where the output of each network is collected and then averaged to improve the results.

Every network took 12 h of training on a computer with an Intel Core i7 4770 processor with four cores at 3.40 GHz and an Nvidia Tesla K40c with 12 GB GDDR at 1502 MHz and 2880 cores at 745 MHz.

Other measures were implemented to reduce mode collapse, including adding noise to the input pose sequence labels [25], soft labels [26], and noisy labels [27].

3.3 Training Setup

The data was split into 80/20 train/test sets, which means 2225 unshuffled samples for training and 796 samples for testing. Then the algorithm executed 6000–12000 iterations. When the patience limit of 2000 was reached, the patience starts counting, and the weights for the last neural network will be kept in a variable and then saved if patience reaches 0. Then the algorithm will repeat until the stop conditions are reached if the loss value improves. A diagram explaining the process is detailed in Fig. 4.

3.4 Metrics

There are various aspects of the generated poses we must measure. First, how similar are the individually generated poses to the real poses? They must keep a certain level of resemblance to the original poses, even if the objective is to generate new movements. For this reason, the Euclidean distance and 3DPCK metrics are used to measure the

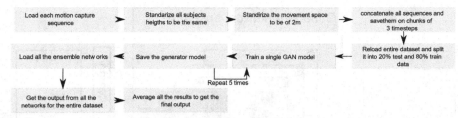

Fig. 4. Diagram of the complete model workflow, from preprocessing to the final output of the ensemble.

distance between the original and generated poses, especially the 3DPCk, which is a perceptual measure that uses a threshold distance to calculate the percentage of points sufficiently near to the originals.

Second, we must measure how similar are both the generated data and the real data in general, by joint and for all the joints. For each join, the Kolmogorov-Smirnov metric is adequate as the join information is not normally distributed, as shown in Fig. 6. For all joints, the Maximum Mean Discrepancy test and FID let us observe how similar they are to the distribution of the actual poses and the generated data.

Kolmogorov-Smirnov Metric

The Kolmogorov Smirnov (K-S) test measures the fitness between 2 univariate, non-normal distributions. This metric was selected to measure the fitness level between individual features of the generated movement sequences, using the worst-performing feature of the movement axis as a reference. The value returned by this test is the supremum of the distance between the cumulative distribution of 2 samples $F(x)$. The following formula calculates the K-S score:

$$D_{n,m} = \sup_{x} |F_{1,n}(x) - F_{2,m}(x)| \tag{5}$$

Where $F_{1,n}(x)$ and $F_{2,m}(x)$ are the cumulative distribution functions of the generated data and the actual data and $D_{n,m}$. Is the K-S statistic that represents the level of fitness between two distributions.

Euclidian Distance

The Euclidean distance is an essential measure of the performance, representing the distance between 2 given points. In this case, it represents the mean of the Euclidean distance [13] between each point of the point cloud that represents each pose for each timestep, given by Eq. (6).

$$\frac{1}{f_n} \sum\nolimits_{j=1}^{f_n} \frac{1}{p_n} \sum\nolimits_{i=1}^{p_n} \sqrt{\left(P_{x_{1_{ij}}} - P_{x_{2_{ij}}}\right)^2 + \left(P_{y_{1_{ij}}} - P_{y_{2_{ij}}}\right)^2 + \left(P_{z_{1_{ij}}} - P_{z_{2_{ij}}}\right)^2} \tag{6}$$

Where f_n is the number of time steps of the sample, p_n the number of points in the pose, P_{x_1} is the pose of the first subject y P_{x_2}. Is the pose of the second subject. In this, we compare the results of the different neural networks to show that the ensemble performed better for the train data and the complete dataset, as we can see in Table 2.

As the value of Euclidean distance becomes smaller, the generated data is geometrically closer to the actual data.

Percentage of Correct Key-Points
The problem with Euclidean distance is that it does not correctly represent other finer features on the movement and depends on the shape of the skeleton. An alternative measurement called 3DPCK is more robust in detecting incorrect joins, as it uses a threshold, in this case of 150 mm, to determine if it is adequately positioning for its objective joint position; 3DPCK is calculated by equation seven as follows:

$$CPK = 100 * \frac{1}{f_n} \sum\nolimits_{j=1}^{f_n} \frac{1}{p_n} \sum\nolimits_{i=1}^{p_n} \left[\begin{cases} 1 \ if \ D_e(P_{x_{1_{ij}}}, P_{x_{2_{ij}}}, P_{y_{1_{ij}}}, P_{y_{2_{ij}}}, P_{z_{1_{ij}}}, P_{z_{2_{ij}}}) \geq 150 \, mm \\ 0 \ if \ D_e(P_{x_{1_{ij}}}, P_{x_{2_{ij}}}, P_{y_{1_{ij}}}, P_{y_{2_{ij}}}, P_{z_{1_{ij}}}, P_{z_{2_{ij}}}) < 150 \, mm \end{cases} \right]$$

(7)

Where:

$$D_e\left(P_{x_1}, P_{x_1}, P_{y_1}, P_{y_2}, P_{z_2}, P_{z_2}\right) = \sqrt{\left(P_{x_1} - P_{x_2}\right)^2 + \left(P_{y_1} - P_{y_2}\right)^2 + \left(P_{z_1} - P_{z_2}\right)^2} \quad (8)$$

Fréchet Inception Distance
The Fréchet Inception Distance (FID) [29] is an improved version of the Inception score (IS). The problem with IS is that it cannot compare the statistics of the actual sample with the generated or synthetic samples. On the other side, FID uses the Wasserstein-2 distance to measure the two first moments or polynomials, the covariance, and average, for the equality expectations $p(.) = p_w(.)$, that hold only for $\int p(.)f(x)dx = \int p_w(.)f(x)$, where $f(x)$ are such polynomials for the given data, then x is substituted for one of the coding layers of the Inception v3 model [31] to get relevant features. FID is represented by Eq. (9), where m is the mean and C is the covariance of the inception coding layer for each input.

$$d^2((m,C), (m_w,C_w)) = \|m - m_w\|_2^2 + \text{Tr}(C + C_w - 2(CC_w)^{1/2})$$

(9)

Maximum Mean Discrepancy
The Maximum Mean Discrepancy (MMD) [30] is a metric that represents the distance measure between feature means, given by the Eq. (10).

$$MMD(P, Q)^2 = \mathbb{E}_{X \sim P}[k(x - x')] + \mathbb{E}_{Y \sim Q}[k(y - y') - 2\mathbb{E}_{X,Y \sim P,Q}[k(x, y)]] \quad (10)$$

In this case, we are going to be using the Gaussian kernel such that $k(X, Y) = \langle \varphi(x), \varphi(y) \rangle_{\mathcal{H}}$ where MMD will be defined as shown by Eq. (11).

$$MMD(P,Q)^2 = \langle \mathbb{E}_{X \sim P}\varphi(X), \mathbb{E}_{X' \sim P}\varphi(X') \rangle_{\mathcal{H}} + \langle \mathbb{E}_{Y \sim Q}\varphi(Y), \mathbb{E}_{Y' \sim Q}\varphi(Y') \rangle_{\mathcal{H}}$$
$$-2\langle \mathbb{E}_{X \, P}\varphi(X), \mathbb{E}_{Y' \sim Q}\varphi(Y') \rangle_{\mathcal{H}}$$

(11)

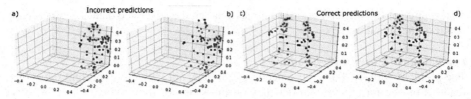

Fig. 5. Comparison of 2 poses performing different actions, a) represents the real pulling action, b) represents the result from the ensemble, which is inadequate for that case, c) represents the real speaking action, d) represents the result from the ensemble which is adequate in this case. Values scaled is $1/s$

4 Experimental Evaluation

The used dataset consists of trials 1 to 15 obtained from CMU Graphics Lab Motion Capture Database [28] on the category of human interactions and subcategory two subjects. Data acquired from this section contains enough information to prove our network's concept while preserving a reasonable training time of 12 h per network.

As we can see in Tables 1,2 and 3, we have the results for both the ablation test and the metrics for the complete dataset and the train and test splits. In the ablation test, we can see that the model that only has a simple discriminator performs worse than any of the models that use an auxiliary discriminator. It is possible to appreciate the function of each one of the auxiliary discriminators. The 3DPCK discriminator increases the PCK metric percentage reduces the error for the worst behaving articulation for the K-S test. On the other hand, the K-means auxiliary classifier improves the Euclidian distance loss and the MMD and FID metrics.

For the sake of having a global understanding of the results, the entire dataset compared was to their respective split by calculating the FID between the split and the complete data, as seen in the first row of Tables 2 and 3.

Our proposal ensemble and individual model performs better than the baseline method, even on test data, as shown in Table 3. Perhaps the results can be further improved by using a weighted average instead of a simple averaged ensemble because one network, specifically net two, sometimes produces better results concerning the FID and mean K-S metrics. These results could also mean that for some cases could be better to use a single network instead of a single ensemble. The two best results for each test are in bold.

A conditional beta variational autoencoder that similarly used a sequence of poses as a label to generate the corresponding sequence was used as baseline on all the experiments conducted.

The motion produced by the method is not perfect for every sample. However, it offers an excellent solution for specific scenarios like greeting and handshaking, pulling actions, and sitting, mainly when near the point $P = (0, 0, a)$ where a is any given height. As shown in Fig. 5 a), it can have problems performing interactions where it must emulate actions at the edge of the borders of the space as shown in Fig. 5 b).

Overall, the distribution produced by the generator has a good level of the resemblance of the learned actions as shown in Table 2, and as demonstrated by the comparison

Table 1. Results for the complete dataset

Model	3DPCK (%)	Euclidian distance (mm)	FID	MMD	MMD STD	Kolmogorov-Smirnov mean	Kolmogorov-Smirnov max
Real Data Full	0.00	0.00	0.0000	0.9490	0.0493 + -	0.0000	0.0000
Full Model	80.18	143.05	0.8284	0.0031	0.0027 + -	0.1041	0.2844
Vanilla Model	66.20	191.91	1.2583	0.0053	0.0063 + -	0.0967	0.4196
No-Labels Model	12.33	689.64	36.5965	0.2461	0.0977 + -	0.6248	0.9448
Only K-Means Model	71.15	163.81	0.9309	0.0033	0.0027 + -	0.0873	0.3565
Only PCK Model	69.32	199.91	1.1166	0.0046	0.0052 + -	0.0939	0.3142
Ensemble Model	**87.29**	**103.69**	**0.4703**	**0.0025**	0.0029 + -	**0.0708**	**0.2447**
Network 1 Model	83.76	130.75	**0.5319**	0.0028	0.0028 + -	0.0798	0.2505
Network 2 Model	**83.92**	**124.45**	0.5417	**0.0026**	0.0024 + -	**0.0675**	0.2607
Network 3 Model	80.18	143.05	0.8284	0.0031	0.0027 + -	0.1041	0.2844
Network 4 Model	79.51	145.01	0.7801	0.0032	0.0028 + -	0.0901	0.2543
Network 5 Model	81.52	141.08	0.7225	0.0041	0.0038 + -	0.0820	**0.2255**
CVAE Model	0.02	1080.75	21.0437	0.3216	0.0779 + -	0.5888	1.0000

Table 2. Results for the train dataset split (80%)

Model	3DPCK (%)	Euclidian distance (mm)	FID	MMD	MMD STD	Kolmogorov-Smirnov mean	Kolmogorov-Smirnov max
Real Data	0.00	0.00	0.2057	0.9644	0.0300 + -	0.0000	0.0000
Ensemble Model	**97.73**	**47.48**	**0.1844**	**0.0003**	0.0002 + -	**0.0650**	**0.2441**
Network 1 Model	94.44	70.84	0.3649	**0.0006**	0.0006 + -	0.0759	0.2590
Network 2 Model	**94.55**	**70.44**	0.3322	0.0007	0.0009 + -	**0.0674**	0.2520

(*continued*)

Table 2. (*continued*)

Model	3DPCK (%)	Euclidian distance (mm)	FID	MMD	MMD STD	Kolmogorov-Smirnov mean	Kolmogorov-Smirnov max
Network 3 Model	90.24	86.32	0.6635	0.0010	0.0004 + -	0.1006	0.2729
Network 4 Model	89.25	90.12	0.5828	0.0009	0.0003 + -	0.0923	0.2763
Network 5 Model	91.45	81.51	0.5501	0.0009	0.0003 + -	0.0788	**0.2388**
CVAE Model	0.05	1204.05	20 .3325	0.4243	0.1906 + -	0.5904	1.0000

Table 3. Results for the test dataset split (20%)

Model	3DPCK (%)	Euclidian distance (mm)	FID	MMD	MMD STD	Kolmogorov-Smirnov mean	Kolmogorov-Smirnov max
Real Data Test	0.00	0.00	2.0791	0.9535	0.0632 + -	0.0000	0.0000
Ensemble Model	**45.55**	**326.30**	4.4019	**0.0487**	0.0665 + -	0.1507	0.3095
Network 1 Model	41.21	367.43	**4.0150**	0.0583	0.0793 + -	0.1544	**0.2802**
Network 2 Model	**41.51**	**337.17**	4.4734	**0.0428**	0.0516 + -	**0.1428**	0.3032
Network 3 Model	39.81	368.09	4.1165	0.0546	0.0615 + -	0.1519	0.3455
Network 4 Model	41.02	362.69	4.2693	0.0521	0.0680 + -	**0.1404**	0.3023
Network 5 Model	41.43	378.39	4.3279	0.0640	0.0791 + -	0.1470	**0.2641**
CVAE Model	0.04	1631.88	52.1564	0.5661	0.3071 + -	0.7328	1.0000

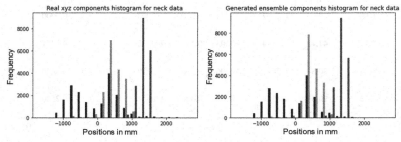

Fig. 6. Histogram compares the ensemble and actual distribution for a neck point data for the x y and z axes in blue, red, and green, respectively.

distributions on the histogram of Fig. 6, which indicates that the generated movements will correspond to a similar distribution compared with the ground truth.

Training of GAN can be an unstable process due to the need to have equilibrium between the generator and discriminator. However, taking advantage of the methods shown in the methodology, it was possible to converge to a specific Euclidian distance loss. Figure 7 can be appreciated the values of the losses for the 3DPCK metric through the training. The training results rely primarily on the initial values and conditions of the GAN model of each trained network.

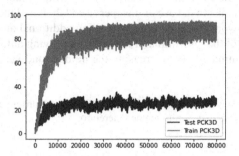

Fig. 7. 3DPCK@0.5 during the generator training

The time complexity for the training algorithm was obtained empirically as many of the steps are different algorithms on their own (k-means inference, 3DPCK calculation, backpropagation of dense/RNN, forward pass to obtain a sample from the generator) and involve the use of GPU or CPU processors separately, making the analytical calculation of the time complexity difficult. The experiment determined that the time complexity is linear, as shown in Fig. 8 because even if it has a better fitness value for a cubic estimator, this is caused by the interpolation overfitting the minor variations caused by the TensorFlow memory allocation process. Hence, the time complexity is approximately equal to $\mathcal{O}(n)$.

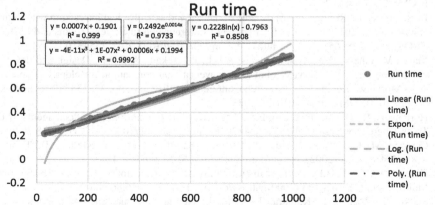

Fig. 8. Results of the time complexity experiments show that even when the polynomial complexity R2 value is closer to 1, it is overfitting the runtime curve, while the linear curve better describes the algorithm time complexity behavior.

5 Conclusion

Human motion generation is an important field of research today, as it is fundamental for human-machine interaction, from robotics to virtual agents.

Generative approaches that specialize in the simulation of the interaction of human beings while focusing on the quality of the sample and fitness between the real and the produced data distributions are essential goals that will advance other fields.

We used an AC-GAN in this work to model the actual data distribution while maintaining variability in the movements between runs, which made the results look less rigid and unnatural, thanks to the use of unsupervised labels and the 3DPCK metric. The results shown in this work could be improved using additional auxiliary classifiers and improving the design of the discriminator network, employing online optimization using the pre-trained discriminators and increasing the number and variety of the ensembled networks.

Acknowledgment. This work was supported in part by the Consejo Nacional de Ciencia y Tecnología and the Universidad Autónoma de Querétaro.

References

1. Nishimura, Y., Nakamura, Y., Ishiguro, H.: Human interaction behavior modeling using generative adversarial networks. Neural Netw. **132**, 521–531 (2020). https://doi.org/10.1016/j.neunet.2020.09.019
2. Dautenhahn, K.: Robots we like to live with?! - a developmental perspective on a personalized, life-long robot companion. In: RO-MAN 2004. 13th IEEE International Workshop on Robot and Human Interactive Communication (IEEE Catalog No.04TH8759), pp. 17–22. https://doi.org/10.1109/ROMAN.2004.1374720
3. Mori, Y., Ojima, Y., Ishida, M., Kubota, N.: Autonomous behavior generator for a companion robot 'SELF' with which humans do not get bored. In: 2007 IEEE/ICME International Conference on Complex Medical Engineering, pp. 1216–1220 (2007). https://doi.org/10.1109/ICCME.2007.4381937
4. Beetz, M., et al.: Robotic agents capable of natural and safe physical interaction with human coworkers. In: 2015 IEEE/RSJ International Conference on Intelligent Robots and Systems (IROS), pp. 6528–6535 (2015). https://doi.org/10.1109/IROS.2015.7354310
5. Malith Manuhara, G.W., Muthugala, M.A.V.J., Jayasekara, A.G.B.P.: Design and development of an interactive service robot as a conversational companion for elderly people. In: 2018 Moratuwa Engineering Research Conference (MERCon), pp. 378–383 (2018). https://doi.org/10.1109/MERCon.2018.8421933
6. Hortensius, R., Hekele, F., Cross, E.S.: The perception of emotion in artificial agents. IEEE Trans. Cogn. Dev. Syst. **10**(4), 852–864 (2018). https://doi.org/10.1109/TCDS.2018.2826921
7. Cavazza, M., Charles, F., Mead, S.J.: Character-based interactive storytelling. IEEE Intell. Syst. **17**(4), 17–24 (2002). https://doi.org/10.1109/MIS.2002.1024747
8. Cosatto, E., Graf, H.P.: Photo-realistic talking-heads from image samples. IEEE Trans. Multimedia **2**(3), 152–163 (2000). https://doi.org/10.1109/6046.865480
9. Starke, S., Zhang, H., Komura, T., Saito, J.: Neural state machine for character-scene interactions. ACM Trans. Graph. **38**(6), 1–14 (2019). https://doi.org/10.1145/3355089.3356505

10. Xi, W., Devineau, G., Moutarde, F., Yang, J.: Generative model for skeletal human movements based on conditional DC-GAN applied to pseudo-images. Algorithms **13**(12), 319 (2020). https://doi.org/10.3390/a13120319
11. Chakravati, I.M., Laha, R.G., Roy, J.: Handbook of Methods of Applied Statistics, vol. 1, 1st ed., pp. 392–394. John Wiley and Sons, New York, 1967
12. Moreno-Noguer, F.: 3D human pose estimation from a single image via distance matrix regression. In: Proceedings - 30th IEEE Conference on Computer Vision and Pattern Recognition, CVPR 2017, vol. 2017, pp. 1561–1570 (2017). https://doi.org/10.1109/CVPR.2017.170
13. Sarafianos, N., Boteanu, B., Ionescu, B., Kakadiaris, I.A.: 3D Human pose estimation: a review of the literature and analysis of covariates. Comput. Vis. Image Underst. **152**, 1–20 (2016). https://doi.org/10.1016/j.cviu.2016.09.002
14. Chen, C., Zhuang, Y., Nie, F., Yang, Y., Wu, F., Xiao, J.: Learning a 3D human pose distance metric from geometric pose descriptor. IEEE Trans. Visual Comput. Graphics **17**(11), 1676–1689 (2011). https://doi.org/10.1109/TVCG.2010.272
15. Wu, B., Liu, C., Ishi, C.T., Ishiguro, H.: Modeling the conditional distribution of co-speech upper body gesture jointly using conditional-GAN and unrolled-GAN. Electronics **10**(3), 228 (2021). https://doi.org/10.3390/electronics10030228
16. Lee, H.Y., et al.: Dancing to music. *arXiv*, no. NeurIPS, pp. 1–11 (2019). https://doi.org/10.4135/9781446251409.n4
17. Yu, L., Yu, J., Ling, Q.: Deep neural network based 3D articulatory movement prediction using both text and audio inputs. In: Kompatsiaris, I., Huet, B., Mezaris, V., Gurrin, C., Cheng, W.-H., Vrochidis, S. (eds.) MMM 2019. LNCS, vol. 11295, pp. 68–79. Springer, Cham (2019). https://doi.org/10.1007/978-3-030-05710-7_6
18. Zhao, R., Su, H., Ji, Q.: Bayesian adversarial human motion synthesis. In: Proceedings of the IEEE Computer Society Conference on Computer Vision and Pattern Recognition, pp. 6224–6233 (2020). https://doi.org/10.1109/CVPR42600.2020.00626
19. Zhao, R., Ji, Q.: An adversarial hierarchical hidden Markov model for human pose modeling and generation. In: 32nd AAAI Conference on Artificial Intelligence, AAAI 2018, pp. 2636–2643 (2018)
20. Kania, K., Kowalski, M., Trzciński, T.: TrajeVAE -- Controllable Human Motion Generation from Trajectories. http://arxiv.org/abs/2104.00351 (2021)
21. Knapp, M.L., Hall, J.A., Horgan, T.G.: Nonverbal Communication in Human Interaction, 8th Ed., Cengage Learning (2013)
22. Goodfellow, I., et al.: Generative adversarial networks. Commun. ACM **63**(11), 139–144 (2020). https://doi.org/10.1145/3422622
23. Sricharan, K., Bala1, R., Shreve, M., Ding, H., Saketh, K., Sun, J.: Semi-supervised conditional GANs, *arXiv*, pp. 1–23 (2017)
24. Li, H., Wang, X., Ding, S.: Research and development of neural network ensembles: a survey. Artif. Intell. Rev. **49**(4), 455–479 (2017). https://doi.org/10.1007/s10462-016-9535-1
25. Arjovsky, M., Bottou, Ĺ.: Towards principled methods for training generative adversarial networks. *arXiv*, pp. 1–17 (2017)
26. Salimans, T., Goodfellow, I., Zaremba, W., Cheung, V., Radford, A., Chen, X.: Improved techniques for training GANs. In: Advances in Neural Information Processing Systems, pp. 2234–2242 (2016)
27. Sønderby, C.K., Caballero, J., Theis, L., Shi, W., Huszár, F.: Amortised map inference for image super-resolution. In: 5th International Conference on Learning Representations, ICLR 2017 - Conference Track Proceedings, pp. 1–17 (2017)
28. University, C.M.: CMU Graphics Lab Motion Capture Database. http://mocap.cs.cmu.edu/
29. Heusel, M., Ramsauer, H., Unterthiner, T., Nessler, B., Hochreiter, S.: GANs trained by a two time-scale update rule converge to a local Nash equilibrium. In: Adv. Neural Inf. Process. Syst., vol. 2017-December, no. Nips, pp. 6627–6638 (2017)

30. Gretton, A., Borgwardt, K.M., Rasch, M.J., Schölkopf, B., Smola, A.: A kernel two-sample test. J. Mach. Learn. Res. **13**, 723–773 (2012)
31. Szegedy, C., Vanhoucke, V., Ioffe, S., Shlens, J., Wojna, Z.: Rethinking the inception architecture for computer vision. In: Proc. IEEE Comput. Soc. Conf. Comput. Vis. Pattern Recognit., vol. 2016, pp. 2818–2826 (2016). https://doi.org/10.1109/CVPR.2016.308
32. Cho, K., et al.: Learning phrase representations using RNN encoder-decoder for statistical machine translation. In: EMNLP 2014 - 2014 Conf. Empir. Methods Nat. Lang. Process. Proc. Conf., pp. 1724–1734, 2014. https://doi.org/10.3115/v1/d14-1179
33. Xia, S., Wang, C., Chai, J., Hodgins, J.: Realtime style transfer for unlabeled heterogeneous human motion. ACM Trans. Graph. **34**(4), 1 (2015). https://doi.org/10.1145/2766999
34. Lau, M., Bar-Joseph, Z., Kuffner, J.: Modeling spatial and temporal variation in motion data. ACM Trans. Graph. **28**(5), 1 (2009). https://doi.org/10.1145/1618452.1618517
35. Mirza, M., Osindero, S.: Conditional Generative Adversarial Nets. pp. 1–7 (2014). https://arxiv.org/abs/1411.1784
36. Arjovsky, M., Chintala, S., Bottou, L.: Wasserstein GAN (2017). Accessed: 17 Nov 2021. https://arxiv.org/abs/1701.07875v3

Computational Analysis of the Particles Matter in the Respiratory Tract of Children

Gustavo Suárez[1](✉) ⓘ, Juliana A. Niño[3] ⓘ, José D. Hoyos[1] ⓘ,
Camilo A. Paramo[2] ⓘ, Wuitman Garrafa[1] ⓘ, and Egidio Clavijo Gañan[4] ⓘ

[1] Grupo de Investigación Sobre Nuevos Materiales, Universidad Pontificia
Bolivariana, Medellín, Colombia
gustavo.suarez@upb.edu.co

[2] SENA, Centro de Servicios y Gestión Empresarial, Tecnoparque Medellín,
Medellín, Colombia

[3] Grupo de Investigación en Ingeniería Aeroespacial,
Universidad Pontificia Bolivariana, Medellín, Colombia

[4] Semillero de Matemáticas, Centro de Ciencia Básica,
Universidad Pontificia Bolivariana, Medellín, Colombia

Abstract. According to the World Health Organization, unhealthy air causes respiratory and cardiovascular diseases worldwide, moreover, children are particularly susceptible and vulnerable due to their accelerated metabolism, biological development among other factors. In this work, particle transport and deposition pattern were analyzed using a three-dimensional model of the trachea and bronchi of a child under inhalation condition. The phenomenon is computationally modeling employing fluid-dynamic laws coupled with particle theory to study the two-phase flow. The understanding of inhalation and transport phenomena of toxic particles from 0.5 to 10 μm of diameter through the human respiratory system is also important for investigations into dosimetry and respiratory health effects. From the results it is found that a higher number of particles are deposited at the bifurcation junctions for particles with 5 μm of diameter or higher because of the inertial effect and the shape of the bronchial branching, meanwhile the smaller particles are slightly more randomly attached to the inner walls of the bronchial system. In addition, the heavy particles tended to go to the lower bronchi, as fewer particles circulate to the aligned bronchi against gravity. The results obtained allow us to increase the knowledge of the affectation of the broncho-pulmonary system in young people and children due to air pollutants.

Keywords: Pollution particles · Pediatric airway · Brochi · Deposition · Computational fluid dynamics

© Springer Nature Switzerland AG 2022
F. R. Narváez et al. (Eds.): SmartTech-IC 2021, CCIS 1532, pp. 247–258, 2022.
https://doi.org/10.1007/978-3-030-99170-8_18

1   Introduction

The latest data from the World Health Organization (WHO) shows that deaths associated with respiratory diseases are the third leading cause of death [9]. Furthermore, one of the causes of unhealthy air is pollution, and air containing microbes and toxic particles, which are usually in the range of $0.5\,\mu m$ to $10\,\mu m$ of diameter. Moreover, epidemiological investigations showed that particulate matter (PM) 2.5 is associated with morbidity and mortality of heart failure. The concentration of PM2.5 rises 3 $\mu g/m^3$, the number of heart failure patients increases by 4.70% [4].

Several studies have established that children are particularly susceptible and vulnerable to unhealthy air [7, 16, 21]. Children have an accelerated metabolism which causes them to breathe more frequently and absorb a higher amount of pollutants relative to their body weight [7, 16]. Children also have a larger lung surface area per kilogram of body weight than adults [7, 21]. Moreover, stagnation points of toxic particles have been found in the airflow of the cities at locations where there is a greater population concentration [22], including educational institutions increasing the exposure of children to polluting factors.

As a particular case, in the city of Medellín, Colombia, there has been a serious problem of environmental unhealthiness affecting mainly the educational sectors. There are areas of the city with a high concentration of particles where a large number of schools and colleges are also located. The topography of Medellín has been a relevant factor in the determination of the points of environmental contamination.

Understanding particulate transport, movement, and deposition in airways is the main phase to predicting and helps to prevent respiratory diseases. Various human activities like the combustion of fossil fuels, industrial processes, and many other sources produce a significant amount of PM [3]. Most of the inhaled particles are expelled in the exaltation, however, a considerable number of particles are embedded in different zones of the airway with a specificity of particles according to the region. In order to study the mentioned patterns, computational simulation is performed to characterize the flow in a pediatric airway model.

Previously works have been carried out on the numerical analysis of the deposition of aerosol in an airway model [17]. Another previous work [10] covered the flow behavior through the lung and particle deposition in human airways. Moreover, particle clearance in the lungs has also been reviewed [18]. The present work contributes to analyzing the distribution of deposition and affected zones, including the impact of the particle size. Moreover, more bronchi generations and bifurcations are studied, along with the children-sized system.

The study of the deposition of the particles is also relevant for the effectiveness of inhaled drugs. Airway obstruction results in a reduction of the lumen, which consequently alters the flow characteristics, deposition pattern of the particles that are inhaled and the effectiveness of inhaled drugs [15].

2   Methods

2.1   Geometric Model and Mesh

To investigate the particle deposition in a pediatric airway, a respiratory model with a 6.67 mm of trachea diameter is generated, this value corresponds a child under 11 years old [14]. The model consists of the trachea and five-level bronchus, the representation of model is shown in Fig. 1. The model could incorporate alveoli to study the gas exchange that occur in these biological zones.

The high quality computational meshing has 5 structured layers from the wall and a total of 2.65×10^6 cells and 1.12×10^6 nodes. The mesh is shown in Fig. 2.

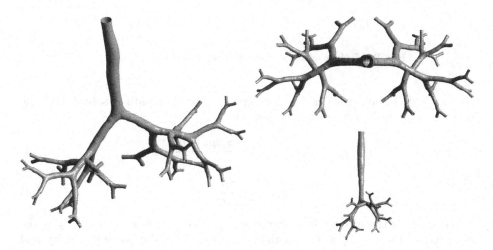

Fig. 1. Three-dimensional trachea and bronchi with six generations and five bifurcations.

2.2   Transport Equations

The air flow of respiratory system calculation is based on the incompressible Navier-Stokes,

$$\rho\frac{\partial \boldsymbol{v}}{\partial t} + \rho(\boldsymbol{v} \cdot \nabla)\boldsymbol{v} = -\nabla p + \mu\nabla^2\boldsymbol{v} \tag{1}$$

$$\nabla \cdot \boldsymbol{v} = 0 \tag{2}$$

where ρ is the air density, $\boldsymbol{v}$ is the fluid velocity, p is the pressure and μ is the dynamic viscosity.

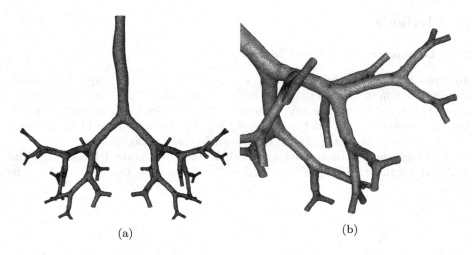

(a)   (b)

Fig. 2. Mesh frontal view (a) and right bronchis view (b).

The particles are described as a discrete phase. The path is solved with the force equilibrium equation and the particle drag,

$$\frac{dv_p}{dt} = F_D(v - v_p) + \frac{g_x(\rho_p - \rho)}{\rho_p} + F_x \tag{3}$$

$$F_D = \frac{18\mu}{d_p^2 \rho_p C_c} \tag{4}$$

where g_x is the gravity in x direction, v_p is the particle velocity, F_x is the other particle forces, d_p is the particle diameter, ρ_p is the particle density and C_c is the Cunningham correction for drag force.

In order to solve the governing equations, the *Simple* algorithm was employed for velocity and pressure couple [1].

2.3 Turbulence Model and Boundary Conditions

The RANS $k - \omega$ turbulence model is widely used in respiratory simulations [11,19,25]. Implicit unsteady simulation of 2 s of inhalation was implemented due to the fact that the deposition of particles occurs almost exclusively during inhalation [2], the time step was 0.003s with 20 inner iterations. The upper cross-section of the trachea was selected as the velocity inlet with 0.7 m/s. A 10% turbulent intensity was assigned at the inlet with the $k - \omega$ shear stress transport turbulence model with low Reynolds number correction was employed as recommended in [23].

The properties of air are the standard, density $\rho = 1.225 \frac{kg}{m^3}$ and dynamic viscosity $\mu = 1.789 \times 10^{-5} \frac{kg}{ms}$. For deposition phenomenon, the particles are trapped at the wall as soon as the particle touches the mucus surface as has been considered in a wide range of studies [6,8,11,12].

The particles that are transported by the unsteady flow are injected uniformly at the trachea with the same air velocity. Three different simulations are carried out employing spherical injected particles, the first one for diameter of 0.5 μm, the second one with 2.5 μm and the last one with different sizes from 0.5 μm to 10 μm of diameter. The density of particles was selected as in [23], $\rho_p = 1200\frac{kg}{m^3}$. Finally the mass flow rate is selected as $4.21 \times 10^{-8}\frac{kg}{s}$ from [20].

3   Results and Discussion

The results elucidated a higher circulation of particles of different sizes (0.5–10 μm) in the descending bronchial branches with an obstruction of the lumen. On the other hand, in the ascending bronchial system, a smaller quantity of particles was observed, predominating the smaller ones of 0.5 μm as is shown in Fig. 4. This biological behavior has been presented in other studies [13] (Fig. 3).

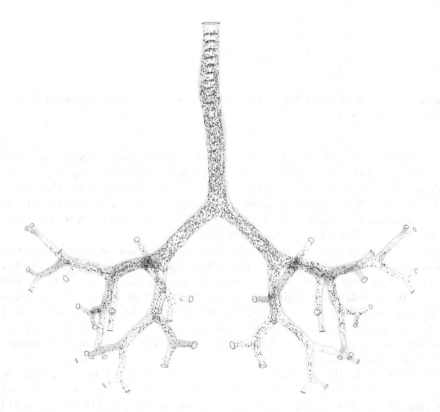

Fig. 3. Pollution particles distribution from 0.5 to 10 μm of diameter throughout the bronchi.

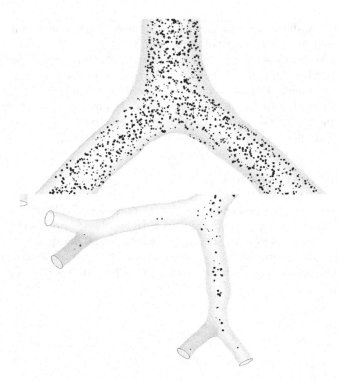

Fig. 4. Close view of pollution particles distribution from 0.5 to 10 μm of diameter throughout bronchioles.

The non-regular cross-section in the trachea reproduces a nonconstant velocity profile, the numerical values can be seen in Fig. 5, which can promote turbulence, this result due to scrubbing of the trachea is present in other studies [20]. Moreover there is a slight pressure difference between the trachea and the 5th generation bronchial as shown in Fig. 6. This phenomenon has been shown to reproduce realistic physiological flow [24].

The velocity gradients can generate a particle collision at bifurcations what promotes deposition. The behavior of the flow represented by the particles in the bronchial transport loses speed, passing the system from a convective regime to a convective-diffusive regime and ending in a diffusive one, for this reason there is a decrease in the speed and pressure in the branches of 5th and 6th level, which may be one of the reasons why the smallest particles in greater quantity are oriented towards the alvioli and end up in the transition phase to the cardiopulmonary system.

In addition to the movement of the particles, there are places where they brush the mucous wall and are trapped, these are the deposition maps. From the simulation with a range of different diameters, the deposition was found to occur mostly on the underside of the internal bronchi as is shown in Fig. 8. In

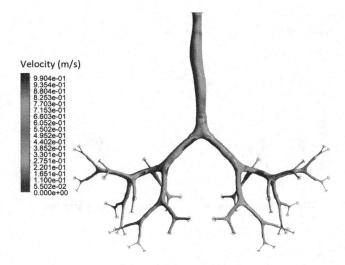

Fig. 5. Velocity distribution.

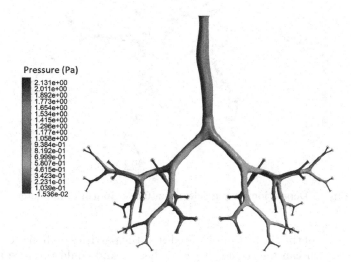

Fig. 6. Pressure distribution.

the case of particles with a diameter of 0.5 μm, the location of their deposition is found to be close to the bifurcations. This phenomenon has been observed before for cases of nano-sized particles [5] (Fig. 7).

The deposition for particles with 0.5 μm and 2.5 μm of diameter are evaluated in independent simulations. For both cases, the deposition zones are close to forks although with some randomness as is shown in Figs. 9 and 10.

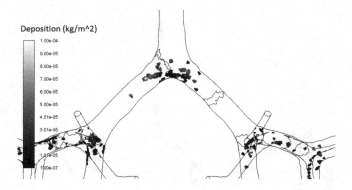

Fig. 7. Bifurcation deposition for 0.5 μm particles.

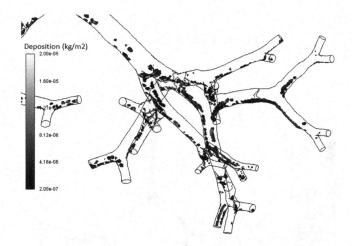

Fig. 8. Deposition for particles from 0.5 to 10 μm of diameter.

The analysis of the simulations showed that the particles of diameter 0.5 reach the alveoli, which can affect the children's health and could produce affections due to the air pollutants.

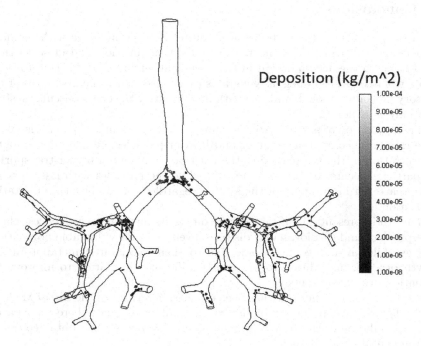

Fig. 9. Deposition for 0.5 μm diameter particles.

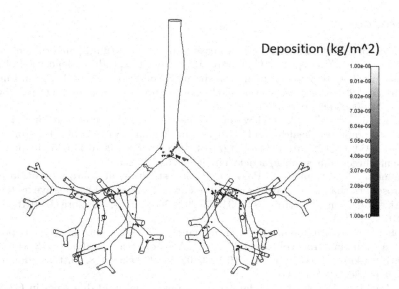

Fig. 10. Deposition for 2.5 μm diameter particles.

4   Conclusions

The results indicate the existence of pollutant deposition zones with diameter particles from 5 μm to 10 μm at the bifurcation junction and close to these in addition to the accumulation in the lower half of the bronchi. Due to being points where deposition begins, generates as a consequence the first cases of respiratory morbidity (cough and asthmã), further affect the cardiovascular system, especially in children.

The deposition of particles with a diameter from 0.5 μm to 5 μm is visualized more randomly compared to larger and heavier particles, even finding a higher concentration in the bifurcation of the trachea. Moreover, a higher transport of the particles occurs to the lower bronchi while the particles with less mass are easily scattered in any part of the system regardless of the bronchi orientation or location.

The study presents significant results due to its medical consequences related to respiratory and cardiovascular diseases, even more for vulnerable populations such as children and young people due to their accelerated metabolism and growth process, in addition to presents significant information to improve the inhalation drug treatments.

As a special case, the study has been oriented in an area of the city of Medellín where there is a high density of the educational sector and where information on the population of children with respiratory diseases is being obtained due to environmental unhealthiness.

This simulation methodology has obtained an interest in both medical and engineering due to its non-invasive method.

References

1. Ansys software 19.2. https://www.ansys.com/products/fluids/ansys-fluent
2. Augusto, L.L.X., Lopes, G.C., GonÃ, J.A.S.: A CFD study of deposition of pharmaceutical aerosols under different respiratory conditions. Braz. J. Chem. Eng. **33**, 549–558 (2016). http://www.scielo.br/scielo.php?script=sci_arttext&pid=S0104-66322016000300549&nrm=iso
3. Chen, J., et al.: A review of biomass burning: emissions and impacts on air quality, health and climate in China. Sci. Total Environ. **579**, 1000–1034 (2017). https://doi.org/10.1016/j.scitotenv.2016.11.025, http://www.sciencedirect.com/science/article/pii/S0048969716324561
4. Chueinta, W., Hopke, P., Paatero, P.: Investigation of sources of atmospheric aerosol at urban and suburban residential areas in Thailand by positive matrix factorization. Atmos. Environ. **34**, 3319–3329 (2000). https://doi.org/10.1016/S1352-2310(99)00433-1
5. Cohen, B.S., Sussman, R.G., Lippmann, M.: Ultrafine particle deposition in a human tracheobronchial cast. Aerosol Sci. Technol. **12**(4), 1082–1091 (1990). https://doi.org/10.1080/02786829008959418, https://doi.org/10.1080/02786829008959418
6. De Backer, J.W., et al.: Validation of computational fluid dynamics in CT-based airway models with SPECT/CT. Radiology **257**(3), 854–862 (2010). https://doi.org/10.1148/radiol.10100322, pMID: 21084417

7. For Europe, W.H.O.R.O., for Environment, E.C., Health: Effects of air pollution on children's health and development: a review of the evidence (2005)
8. Farkas, Á., Balásházy, I.S.K.: J. Aerosol Med. **19**, 329
9. FIRS: The Global Impact of Respiratory Disease. European Respiratory Society (2017)
10. Islam, M.S., Paul, G., Ong, H.X., Young, P.M., Gu, Y.T., Saha, S.C.: A review of respiratory anatomical development, air flow characterization and particle deposition. Int. J. Environ. Res. Public Health **17**(2), 380 (2020). https://doi.org/10.3390/ijerph17020380, https://www.mdpi.com/1660-4601/17/2/380
11. Islam, M.S., Saha, S.C., Sauret, E., Gu, Y.T.: Numerical investigation of diesel exhaust particle transport and deposition in up to 17 generations of the lung airway. In: Proceedings of the 20th Australasian Fluid Mechanics Conference 2016. Proceedings of the 20th Australasian Fluid Mechanics Conference, AFMC 2016, Australasian Fluid Mechanics Society, Australia, January 2016
12. Islam, M.S., Saha, S., Sauret, E., Gu, Y., Ristovski, Z.: Numerical investigation of aerosol particle transport and deposition in realistic lung airway. In: Liu, G.R., Das, R. (eds.) Proceedings of the 6th International Conference on Computational Methods, vol. 2, 2015, pp. 1–9. ScienTech Publisher, United States of America (2015). https://eprints.qut.edu.au/86704/
13. Islam, S., Saha, S., Gemci, T., Yang, I., Sauret, E., Gu, Y.: Polydisperse microparticle transport and deposition to the terminal bronchioles in a heterogeneous vasculature tree. Sci. Rep. **8**, 16387 (2018). https://doi.org/10.1038/s41598-018-34804-x
14. King, B.R., Baker, M.D., Braitman, L.E., Seidl-Friedman, J., Schreiner, M.S.: Endotracheal tube selection in children: a comparison of four methods. Ann. Emerg. Med. **22**(3), 530–534 (1993). https://doi.org/10.1016/s0196-0644(05)81937-7
15. Labiris, N.R., Dolovich, M.B.: Pulmonary drug delivery. part i: physiological factors affecting therapeutic effectiveness of aerosolized medications. Br. J. Clin. Pharmacol. **56**(6), 588–599 (2003). https://doi.org/10.1046/j.1365-2125.2003.01892.x, https://bpspubs.onlinelibrary.wiley.com/doi/abs/10.1046/j.1365-2125.2003.01892.x
16. Landrigan, P., Etzel, R.: Textbook of children's environmental health. OUP USA (2013). https://books.google.com.co/books?id=5dhBAgAAQBAJ
17. Longest, P.W., et al.: Use of computational fluid dynamics deposition modeling in respiratory drug delivery. Expert Opinion Drug Delivery **16**(1), 7–26 (2019). https://doi.org/10.1080/17425247.2019.1551875, pMID: 30463458
18. Majid, H., Madl, P.: Lung deposition predictions of airborne particles and the emergence of contemporary diseases Part-I. theHealth **2**, 51–56 (2011)
19. Matida, E., Finlay, W., Lange, C., Grgic, B.: Improved numerical simulation of aerosol deposition in an idealized mouth'throat. J. Aerosol Sci. **35**(1), 1–19 (2004). https://doi.org/10.1016/S0021-8502(03)00381-1, http://www.sciencedirect.com/science/article/pii/S0021850203003811
20. Rahimi-Gorji, M., Pourmehran, O., Gorji-Bandpy, M., Gorji, T.: CFD simulation of airflow behavior and particle transport and deposition in different breathing conditions through the realistic model of human airways. J. Mol. Liquids **209**, 121–133 (2015). https://doi.org/10.1016/j.molliq.2015.05.031, http://www.sciencedirect.com/science/article/pii/S016773221530101X
21. Schwartz, J.: Air pollution and children's health. Pediatrics **113**(Suppl. 3), 1037–1043 (2004). https://pediatrics.aappublications.org/content/113/Supplement_3/1037

22. Suárez, G., Niño, J.A., Chakir, R., Hoyos, J.D., Streichenberger, B.: Computational analysis of the behavior of atmospheric pollution due to demographic, structural factors, vehicular flow and commerce activities, pp. 427–434. CIMNE (2019). http://hdl.handle.net/2117/181708
23. Taherian, S., Rahai, H.R., Bonifacio, J., Gomez, B.Z., Waddington, T.: Particulate deposition in a patient with tracheal stenosis. J. Eng. Sci. Med. Diagn. Therapy **1**(1), 011005 (2017). https://doi.org/10.1115/1.4038260
24. Wang, X., Walters, K., Burgreen, G., Thompson, D.: Cyclic breathing simulations: pressure outlet boundary conditions coupled with resistance and compliance, July 2015. https://doi.org/10.1115/AJKFluids2015-26569
25. Zhang, Z., Kleinstreuer, C.: Airflow structures and nano-particle deposition in a human upper airway model. J. Comput. Phys. **198**(1), 178–210 (2004). https://doi.org/10.1016/j.jcp.2003.11.034, http://www.sciencedirect.com/science/article/pii/S0021999104000245

Diabetic Retinopathy: Detection and Classification Using AlexNet, GoogleNet and ResNet50 Convolutional Neural Networks

Jhonny Caicho[1] , Cristina Chuya-Sumba[1] , Nicole Jara[1] ,
Graciela M. Salum[1,2] , Andrés Tirado-Espín[3] , Gandhi Villalba-Meneses[1] ,
Omar Alvarado-Cando[4] , Carolina Cadena-Morejón[5] ,
and Diego A. Almeida-Galárraga[1(✉)]

[1] School of Biological Sciences and Engineering, Universidad Yachay Tech, San Miguel de Urcuquí, Ibarra 100119, Ecuador
dalmeida@yachaytech.edu.ec
[2] Carrera de Ingeniería Biomédica, Departamento de Rio Negro, Instituto Tecnológico Regional Suroeste, Universidad Tecnológica del Uruguay, 65000 Fray Bentos, Uruguay
[3] School of Mathematical and Computational Sciences, Universidad Yachay Tech, San Miguel de Urcuquí, Ibarra 100119, Ecuador
[4] Escuela de Electrónica, Universidad de Azuay, Cuenca, Ecuador
[5] Universidad de Zaragoza, 50018 Zaragoza, Spain

Abstract. Diabetic retinopathy (DR) is an ocular condition developed in diabetes patients. This eye disease is increasing worldwide and is considered one of the leading causes of blindness; for this reason, early detection and prompt treatment are essential. DR can be divided depending on its severity into five stages: i) no DR, ii) mild, iii) moderate, iv) severe, and v) proliferative. This pathology is almost undetectable in its early stages, and it can even take a long time for highly trained healthcare professionals to detect it. In this context, artificial intelligence has become a promising solution compared to manual detection methods. It offers an easy, fast, less expensive, and more efficient alternative. Convolutional Neural Networks (CNN) have been widely used for medical image analysis. This study used three CNN: AlexNet, GoogleNet, and ResNet50 to detect and classify the five different stages of DR. The best results were obtained using AlexNet getting an accuracy of 93.56%, and the lowest value was obtained using GoogleNet (89.43%).

Keywords: Diabetic retinopathy · CNN · Accuracy · Metrics classification

1 Introduction

Diabetes is one of the most severe health problems since it affects 425 million people worldwide and will affect 600 million people in 2040 [1]. Diabetes is a chronic disease characterized by high blood sugar levels due to the lack of insulin and causing many complications in different organs such as the heart, kidney, retina, and others. One of the most critical ocular complications is Diabetic Retinopathy (DR), which is considered the leading cause of blindness [2, 3].

© Springer Nature Switzerland AG 2022
F. R. Narváez et al. (Eds.): SmartTech-IC 2021, CCIS 1532, pp. 259–271, 2022.
https://doi.org/10.1007/978-3-030-99170-8_19

DR is an eye condition in which the blood vessels located behind the retina cause complications such as microaneurysms, hemorrhages, exudates, etc. [1, 2, 4, 5]. This disease is a major concern due to the lack of symptoms in the early stages that could provoke the irreversible and total loss of sight [6]. In Ecuador, one in every ten people (over 50 years) has diabetes, and approximately 30% develop impaired eyesight [7]. According to the International Clinical Diabetic Retinopathy (ICDR), DR is classified into five levels: no DR, mild, moderate, severe, and proliferative [8, 9]. This classification is advantageous for automated detection since each stage has characteristic lesions that can be identified using algorithms. For example, microaneurysm occurs in the early stages, while hemorrhages occur in advanced settings [2, 8, 10].

The automated methods for DR detection are faster, less expensive, and more efficient than manual detection methods [4, 11]. Generally, these methods use artificial intelligence models such as Machine Learning (ML) that involve Deep Learning (DL). Convolutional Neural Networks (CNN) is a type of DL method that is the most widely used for analyzing and classifying medical images without hand-crafted feature extraction [2, 12]. There are some architecture such as AlexNet, VGG, GoogleNet, ResNet50 which are used for developing more effective models [4, 13–15]. In this way, several authors have proposed systems for DR detection using CNN, Deep CNN, multi-channel CNN, and other models.

At present, developing countries have lagged in applying technology in the medical area. It is due to the lack of government support, cost, and limit access to ophthalmic services and highly skilled professionals [4, 11]. As a result, the incidence of DR has gradually increased. Thereby, the current work focuses on developing a CNN model for detecting and classifying DR depending on its severity. For this purpose, some image processing methods were first applied, and then the real-time classification of fundus images. Finally, the images were used for training and develop a high sensitivity, specificity, and accuracy model.

1.1 Related Works

CNN have been uses in several works to classify the retinal fundus image (see Table 1). Ratanapakorn et al. [16] developed automated software for screening and diagnose DR using 400 fundus images previously interpreted by an ophthalmologist. They obtained sensitivity, specificity, and precision of 98%, 67%, and 96.25%, respectively. First, they pre-process image extracting the characteristics of the eye, such as the optic disc, fovea, macula, and blood vessels. Second, they extract the characteristics related to DR (brightening pathologies, microaneurysm, dot/blot hemorrhages, venous beading, neovascularization). Finally, classified, but only in three levels: normal, no proliferative DR and proliferative DR.

Shaban et al. [11] proposed a deep CNN model based on the weights and biases of the VGG-19 network to classify in three stages (no DR, moderate DR, and severe DR). They used 4,648 high-resolution fundus images from the Kaggle dataset to train and test. The model has 18 convolutional layers and three fully connected layers, obtaining a precision, sensitivity, and specificity of 88–89%, 87–89%, and 94–95%, respectively. In addition, they also measured performance with 5-fold and 10-fold cross-validation, Quadratic Weighted Kappa Score, ROC, AUC, and confusion matrices methods.

Table 1. Diabetic retinopathy detection and classification studies found in literature

Deep learning method	Dataset (size)	Type of channels	Number of classes	Performance measure				Ref.
				Accuracy (%)	Sensitivity (%)	Specificity (%)	AUC	
CNN	Kaggle (80,000)	–	5	75.00	95.00	–	–	[17]
CNN	EyePACs (88,702)	Blue channel	5	97.08	–	–	–	[8]
CNN	MESSIDOR (1,200)	–	2	98.15	98.94	97.87	–	[18]
BiChannel Convolutional Neural Network	Kaggle (32,126)	Gray level, and green channel	2	87.83	93.88	77.81	0.93	[1]
Fully CNN	DRIVE (40), STARE (20), HRF (45), and CHASE DB1 (28)	Green and RGB	–	96.34	79.41	98.34	0.98	[19]
CNN (modified AlexNet)	Kaggle (22,700), and IDRID (516)	–	5	90.07	–	–	–	[20]
CNN (Inception, ResNet, Inception-ResNet, Exception)	EyePACs, and DIARETDB1 (35,126)	RGB	5	89.00–95.00	74.00–86.00	93.00–97.00	0.95–0.98	[21]
Fused CNN512, CNN299, and CNN (YOLOv3, EfficientNetB0)	DDR (13,673), and Kaggle (3,662)	RGB	5	89.00	89.00	97.30	0.97	[2]
GoogleNet	Messidor	RGB	5	66.03	–	–	–	[22]

Butt et al. [8] developed three neural network models with different filters for detecting and classifying diabetic retinopathy. They used 88,702 images from the EyePACs dataset divided in 0–4 according to the DR stage. They obtained an accuracy of 97.08% using Model 2 in the blue channel. Model 2 is composed of 3 MAX pooling layers with a kernel size 2 x 2, 3 convolution layers, and fully connected dense layers of 128 and 64 features. Similarly, Doshi et al. [23] developed three models for the DR diagnosis using a database of 35,126 images of the fundus obtained from EyePACs. Better results were obtained using model 3 with the green channel.

Pratt et al. [17] developed a convolutional neural network for DR using the Kaggle dataset. They classified into the different stages of DR with an accuracy of 75%. The images went through a preprocessing to establish homogeneous characteristics. CNN is composed of several convolution layers so that the network could learn more in-depth features, and thus the recognition of the images would be more accurate. As well, Mobeen-ur-Rehman et al. [18] used a MESSIDOR dataset with 1200 images of the fundus of the eye. The accuracy and sensitivity were 98.15% and 98.94%, respectively.

Pradhan et al. [4] developed a CNN-based DR detection method that categorizes fundus images according to their severity level (no DR, mild, moderate, severe, and proliferative). The authors used a Kaggle dataset and several image processing steps, including cropping, resizing, grayscaling, and normalization. The CNN architecture consisted of 13 layers integrated by convolution, pooling, fully connected, ReLu, Dropout, and Softmax layer. They obtained a training accuracy of 93.13% and a testing accuracy of 85.68% due to the disproportionate distribution of the dataset. However, the authors propose to use regularization techniques to have better precision, recall, and kappa score value.

2 Materials and Methods

2.1 Dataset Description

This work uses a dataset from Kaggle, which has 3662 fundus images. The images were obtained from the Asia Pacific Tele-Ophthalmology Society (APTOS) as part of the Blindness detection competition in 2019 [24]. The images are classified into five classes of DR and scored on a scale of 0 to 4. Where 0 is no DR, 1 is mild DR, 2 is moderate DR, 3 is severe DR, and 4 is proliferative DR (see Table 2). The images have varied sizes ranging between 474 x 358 and 4288 x 2848 pixels and unbalanced distribution.

2.2 Data Preprocessing

Resizing. The size of all images was changed to reduce the memory space and accelerate the process but preserve the intrinsic characteristics that want to identify. For this purpose, the network layers were explored, precisely the input size of the first layer, obtaining that AlexNet accepts 227 x 227 x 3 pixels while GoogleNet and ResNet50 allow 224 x 224 x 3 pixels.

Table 2. Overall dataset classification from Kaggle

Class	Name	Sample Size
0	no DR	1805
1	mild DR	370
2	moderate DR	999
3	severe DR	193
4	proliferative DR	295
	Total	**3662**

Enhancement. The method used to enhance images was Contrast Limited Adaptive Histogram Equalization (CLAHE). This method consists of improving the contrast of the images of the fundus of the eye. CLAHE is usually applied in the L channel of fundus images that have higher contrast [25].

Cropping. DR is a disease characterized by abnormalities of the blood vessels behind the retina. For this reason, it is necessary to extract the rectangular region of interest and discard the areas that contain less helpful information. The image will crop from the left, right top, and bottom side [2].

Color Normalization. The image dataset has high variability because this comes from patients with different ages and ethnicities and different lighting levels, which cause non-uniformly illuminated and local luminosity and contrast variability. Therefore, its condition changes the pixel intensity and variation in the image. To overcome this, each channel of RGB images was normalized. For that, it was calculated the mean and then divide to the variance of images [17, 26].

Data Augmentation. The Kaggle data set does not present a uniform classification, as shown in Table 2. To avoid an excessive adjustment for specific groups and inefficient for others, the dataset distribution was balanced as shows Table 3 using some techniques that include: flipping (horizontal, vertical), and translation for training group (see Fig. 1) [27, 28].

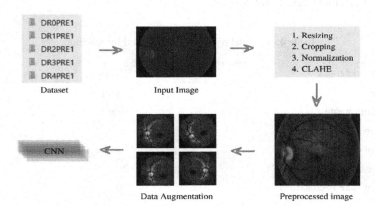

Fig. 1. Image preprocessing.

2.3 Training CNN

Transfer learning is a technique that used CNN to reduce time and effort in medical diagnosis. It transfers the hyperparameters from trained Neural Networks on extensive data instead of training from scratch [29, 30]. CNN comprises several layers, including convolutions, pooling, RELU, max-pooling, softmax, and fully connected layers. The output of a layer is an activation or feature map, which is the input of the next layer. At each layer, a set of filters is applied to extract different features such as curves, edges, blood vessels, etc. [11].

After data pre-processing and balancing the images of each category, the transfer learning process was carried out using three neural networks AlexNet, GoogleNet, and

Table 3. Augmentation dataset and distributed in training and validation.

Class	Name	Sample Size	Training	Validation
0	no DR	1672	854	214
1	mild DR	1074	854	214
2	moderate DR	1070	854	214
3	severe DR	1068	854	214
4	proliferative DR	1088	854	214
	Total	**5972**	4270	1070

ResNet50. For this, the category with the lowest number of images (Severe = 1068) was taken as the base. Later, the database was randomly divided into 80%t for training and 20% for validation, as shown in Table 3. To AlexNet, the last three layers were changed, fully connected (fc8), softmax (prob), and output classification (output) from 1000 categories to 5 categories. During the training process, hyperparameters were tuned until to get optimal ones, as shown in Table 4.

Table 4. Optimal hyperparameters used for training.

Hyper parameters	Values
Optimizer	sgdm
Initial learning rate	0,0001
Mini batch size	32
Number of epochs	24
Weight Learn Rate Factor (fc7)	20
Bias Learn Rate Factor (fc7)	20

Similarly, some GoogleNet layers were modified. For this, the last fully connected layers (loss3-classifier) and classification output (output) were automatically found first and replaced by new layers that adapt to the characteristics of the image in our database. Furthermore, the first ten layers were freeze to make training faster and also prevent overfitting. The exact process was followed with ResNet50 (see Fig. 2).

Performance Measure. There are many methods to measure deep learning classification performance. The measures that are commonly used are precision, specificity, and sensitivity values. These are obtained from the CNN confusion matrix. Precision is the percentage of images that are classified correctly, specificity is the percentage of images that are classified as normal, these images being normal, and sensitivity is the percentage of images that are classified as abnormal correctly [31–33]. These values

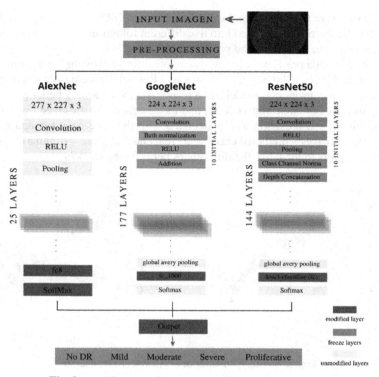

Fig. 2. Architecture of the three modified neural networks

were calculated from the following formulas:

$$Accuracy = \frac{TP + TN}{TP + FP + TN + FN} \tag{1}$$

$$Sensitivity = \frac{TP}{TP + FN} \tag{2}$$

$$Specificity = \frac{TN}{TN + FP} \tag{3}$$

The true positives (TP) are images classified correctly, that is, abnormal images classified as abnormal. True negatives (TN) are the number of normal images classified as normal. On the other hand, false positives (FP) are normal images classified as abnormal. Finally, false negatives (FN) are abnormal images classified as normal.

3 Results and Discussion

3.1 Results Description

The pre-processing, training, and validation of the Neural Networks were performed in MATLAB. This work used a Kaggle dataset with 3662 images, of which 854 (80%)

and 214 (20%) were for training and validation for each DR level, respectively. For this purpose, the database was classified into five different folders according to the DR level: no DR, mild, severe, moderate, and proliferative.

First of all, image pre-processing was developed for improving fundus image quality. Later, three CNNs (AlexNet, GoogleNet, and ResNet50) were used to compare the performance of the developed model. As a result, AlexNet shows a better performance according to the Confusion Matrix (CM) and its associated metrics (see Fig. 3). Sensitivity, specificity, and precision were calculated with the false positives and negatives outputs of the two axes: "predicted class" and "real class". Figure 4 summarizes the data into three box plots to visualize the differences between the models.

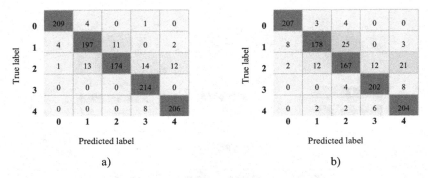

Fig. 3. Confusion matrix of a) AlexNet b) ResNet50

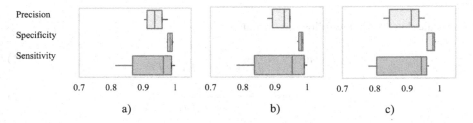

Fig. 4. Performance measure of a) AlexNet, b) ResNet50, and c) GoogleNet

3.2 Analysis Results

The Diabetic Retinopathy images of the Kaggle database were separated depending on their levels: no DR, mild, moderate, severe, and proliferative. Classifying the images in different folders was an essential starting point for the following steps (see Fig. 1). The image preprocessing was necessary to construct the detection and classification software; since this process highlighted and differentiated dark lesions (hemorrhages, abnormal blood vessels) and bright (exudates) of each level.

Image pre-processing included five steps: resizing, cropping, normalizing, CLAHE, and data augmentation. According to the literature, each step is essential to observe and differentiate ocular lesions. Moreover, it is demonstrated that using a pre-processed image improves the model performance compared to an original image [34–36]. The use of architectures such as AlexNet, GoogleNet, and other ones is a widely used practice in recent studies; it is due to its flexibility for different applications, including the development of disease detection and classification software [37, 38]. As a result, this study implied three architectures (AlexNet, GoogleNet, and ResNet50) that have been used in many articles for many diseases detection such as: glaucoma [39], skin lesions [40], breast cancer [41], and others; even prediction models for disorders like Parkinson [42–44].

In this work, modified AlexNet was the architecture with the most remarkable ability to detect and classify images according to their DR level. The accuracy obtained by AlexNet was 93.46% compared to 92.15% (ResNet50) and 89.53% (GoogleNet). This result was quite similar to the article by Harangi et al. [20] obtained 90.07% accuracy with modified AlexNet. Likewise, in other scientific papers, accuracies of around 90% were obtained with ResNet50 and AlexNet [43, 45] (see Table 5).

Table 5. Comparison between related studies

Method	Learning technique	Clinical Scale	Accuracy (%)	Ref
Image processing and CNN classification (**proposed method**)	CNN, transfer learning using AlexNet	DRSS	93.56	–
Automatic feature extraction and classification	Deep convolutional neural networks (DCNN)	DRSS	85.00	[33]
Entropy Images	CNN	N/A	86.10	[46]
Processing and classification	Deep Convolutional Neural Networks (DCNNs)	ETDRS	98.00	[47]

Another of the parameters used to evaluate the performance of the proposed models were the metrics associated with the CM. Specificity, sensitivity, and precision were calculated for each DR level, and the mean of each model was subsequently obtained (see Fig. 4). The mean obtained for these parameters was higher than 0.9 in all cases; however, modified AlexNet performed better. Based on the results obtained, the developed model shows a greater capacity to distinguish between healthy eyes images (high specificity) and DR images (sensitivity).

The limitations presented in this study were mainly related to the number of images per folder. Since the images representing the healthy eyes represented the higher number of images than the other levels, some images in the database were not good quality; thus, they were eliminated to avoid affecting the performance. Finally, data augmentation was performed to balance the number of images per folder.

4 Conclusions

To summarize, a software was developed to detect and classify fundus images at the five levels of DR. This study shows a simple and efficient method to detect ocular complication using a considerable number of data. The Kaggle database was successfully sorted and organized into folders according to their DR level. Image preprocessing was quite helpful to highlight and identify essential features in images and thus increase the performance measures of the model. The preprocessing of the images and the modification of specific layers of the used architecture allowed a high accuracy and classification for the different levels of DR. The precision records values of 89%, 91%, 93% for GoogleNet, ResNet50, and AlexNet, respectively.

From future perspectives, the authors intend to compare performance measures with a more significant number of CNNs to determine the model that best fits the detection and classification of DR. Moreover, they plan to reach the R, G, B, and grayscale channels because several authors disagree on the most appropriate channel for this type of application.

References

1. Pao, S.I., Lin, H.Z., Chien, K.H., Tai, M.C., Chen, J.T., Lin, G.M.: Detection of diabetic retinopathy using bichannel convolutional neural network. Journal of Ophthalmology. 2020, (2020). https://doi.org/10.1155/2020/9139713
2. Alyoubi, W.L., Abulkhair, M.F., Shalash, W.M.: Diabetic retinopathy fundus image classification and lesions localization system using deep learning. Sensors. **21**, 1–22 (2021). https://doi.org/10.3390/s21113704
3. Arcadu, F., et al.: Deep learning predicts OCT measures of diabetic macular thickening from color fundus photographs. Invest. Ophthalmol. Vis. Sci. **60**, 852–857 (2019). https://doi.org/10.1167/iovs.18-25634
4. Pradhan, A., Sarma, B., Nath, R.K., Das, A., Chakraborty, A.: Diabetic Retinopathy Detection on Retinal Fundus Images Using Convolutional Neural Network. In: Bhattacharjee, A., Borgohain, S.K., Soni, B., Verma, G., Gao, X.-Z. (eds.) MIND 2020. CCIS, vol. 1240, pp. 254–266. Springer, Singapore (2020). https://doi.org/10.1007/978-981-15-6315-7_21
5. Mookiah, M.R.K., et al.: Application of different imaging modalities for diagnosis of Diabetic Macular Edema: a review. Comput. Biol. Med. **66**, 295–315 (2015). https://doi.org/10.1016/j.compbiomed.2015.09.012
6. Chetoui, M., Akhloufi, M.A., Kardouchi, M.: Diabetic retinopathy detection using machine learning and texture features. 2018 IEEE Canadian Conference on Electrical & Computer Engineering (CCECE). 2018-May, 1–4 (2018). https://doi.org/10.1109/CCECE.2018.8447809
7. Sarrazin, L.: Retinopatía diabética: tercera causa de ceguera en Ecuador - Revista Vive, https://revistavive.com/retinopatia-diabetica-tercera-causa-de-ceguera-en-ecuador/ (2016)
8. Butt, M.M., Latif, G., Iskandar, D.N.F.A., Alghazo, J., Khan, A.H.: Multi-channel convolutions neural network based diabetic retinopathy detection from fundus images. Procedia Computer Science. **163**, 283–291 (2019). https://doi.org/10.1016/j.procs.2019.12.110
9. Ting, D.S.W., et al.: Development and validation of a deep learning system for diabetic retinopathy and related eye diseases using retinal images from multiethnic populations with diabetes. JAMA - Journal of the American Medical Association. **318**, 2211–2223 (2017). https://doi.org/10.1001/jama.2017.18152

10. Aleena, S.L., Prajith, C.A.: Retinal lesions detection for screening of diabetic retinopathy. 2020 11th International Conference on Computing, Communication and Networking Technologies, ICCCNT 2020. 65, 608–618 (2020). https://doi.org/10.1109/ICCCNT49239.2020. 9225617

11. Shaban, M., et al.: A convolutional neural network for the screening and staging of diabetic retinopathy. PLoS ONE **15**, 1–13 (2020). https://doi.org/10.1371/journal.pone.0233514

12. Bakator, M., Radosav, D.: Deep learning and medical diagnosis: a review of literature. Multimodal Technolo. Interac. **2**, 47 (2018). https://doi.org/10.3390/mti2030047

13. Kieffer, B., Babaie, M., Kalra, S., Tizhoosh, H.R.: Convolutional neural networks for histopathology image classification: Training vs. Using pre-trained networks. Proceedings of the 7th International Conference on Image Processing Theory, Tools and Applications, IPTA 2017. 2018-Janua, 1–6 (2018). https://doi.org/10.1109/IPTA.2017.8310149

14. Abdullah, Hasan, M.S.: An application of pre-trained CNN for image classification. 20th International Conference of Computer and Information Technology, ICCIT 2017. 2018-Janua, 1–6 (2018). https://doi.org/10.1109/ICCITECHN.2017.8281779

15. Arti, P., Agrawal, A., Adishesh, A., Lahari, V.M., Niranjana, K.B.: Convolutional neural network models for content based X-Ray image classification. 2019 5th IEEE International WIE Conference on Electrical and Computer Engineering, WIECON-ECE 2019 - Proceedings. 27–30 (2019). https://doi.org/10.1109/WIECON-ECE48653.2019.9019943

16. Ratanapakorn, T., Daengphoonphol, A., Eua-Anant, N., Yospaiboon, Y.: Digital image processing software for diagnosing diabetic retinopathy from fundus photograph. Clin. Ophthalmol. **13**, 641–668 (2019). https://doi.org/10.2147/OPTH.S195617

17. Pratt, H., Coenen, F., Broadbent, D.M., Harding, S.P., Zheng, Y.: Convolutional neural networks for diabetic retinopathy. Procedia Comp. Sci. **90**, 200–205 (2016). https://doi.org/10. 1016/j.procs.2016.07.014

18. Mobeen-Ur-Rehman, Khan, S.H., Abbas, Z., Danish Rizvi, S.M.: Classification of Diabetic Retinopathy Images Based on Customised CNN Architecture. Proceedings - 2019 Amity International Conference on Artificial Intelligence, AICAI 2019. 244–248 (2019). https:// doi.org/10.1109/AICAI.2019.8701231

19. Lu, J., Xu, Y., Chen, M., Luo, Y.: A coarse-to-fine fully convolutional neural network for fundus vessel segmentation. Symmetry. **10**, 1–16 (2018). https://doi.org/10.3390/sym101 10607

20. Harangi, B., Toth, J., Baran, A., Hajdu, A.: Automatic screening of fundus images using a combination of convolutional neural network and hand-crafted features. Proceedings of the Annual International Conference of the IEEE Engineering in Medicine and Biology Society, EMBS. 2699–2702 (2019). https://doi.org/10.1109/EMBC.2019.8857073

21. Reguant, R., Brunak, S., Saha, S.: Understanding inherent image features in CNN-based assessment of diabetic retinopathy. Sci. Rep. **11**, 9704 (2021). https://doi.org/10.1038/s41 598-021-89225-0

22. Gangwar, A.K., Ravi, V.: Diabetic Retinopathy Detection Using Transfer Learning and Deep Learning. In: Bhateja, V., Peng, S.-L., Satapathy, S.C., Zhang, Y.-D. (eds.) Evolution in Computational Intelligence. AISC, vol. 1176, pp. 679–689. Springer, Singapore (2021). https:// doi.org/10.1007/978-981-15-5788-0_64

23. Doshi, D., Shenoy, A., Sidhpura, D., Gharpure, P.: Diabetic retinopathy detection using deep convolutional neural networks. 2016 International Conference on Computing, Analytics and Security Trends (CAST). 261–266 (2016). https://doi.org/10.1109/CAST.2016.7914977

24. APTOS 2019 blindness detection, https://www.kaggle.com/c/aptos2019-blindness-detection/ data

25. Sonali, Sahu, S., Singh, A.K., Ghrera, S.P., Elhoseny, M.: An approach for de-noising and contrast enhancement of retinal fundus image using CLAHE. Optics and Laser Technology. 110, 87–98 (2019). https://doi.org/10.1016/j.optlastec.2018.06.061

26. Wan, S., Liang, Y., Zhang, Y.: Deep convolutional neural networks for diabetic retinopathy detection by image classification. Comput. Electr. Eng. **72**, 274–282 (2018). https://doi.org/10.1016/j.compeleceng.2018.07.042

27. Takahashi, R., Matsubara, T., Uehara, K.: Data augmentation using random image cropping and patching for deep CNNs. IEEE Trans. Circuits Syst. Video Technol. **30**, 2917–2931 (2020). https://doi.org/10.1109/TCSVT.2019.2935128

28. Araújo, T., et al.: Data augmentation for improving proliferative diabetic retinopathy detection in eye fundus images. IEEE Access. **8**, 182462–182474 (2020). https://doi.org/10.1109/ACCESS.2020.3028960

29. Litjens, G., et al.: A survey on deep learning in medical image analysis (2017)

30. Shin, H.C., et al.: Deep convolutional neural networks for computer-aided detection: CNN architectures, dataset characteristics and transfer learning. IEEE Trans. Med. Imaging **35**, 1285–1298 (2016). https://doi.org/10.1109/TMI.2016.2528162

31. Chen, W., Yang, B., Li, J., Wang, J.: An approach to detecting diabetic retinopathy based on integrated shallow convolutional neural networks. IEEE Access. **8**, 178552–178562 (2020). https://doi.org/10.1109/ACCESS.2020.3027794

32. Jayakumari, C., Lavanya, V., Sumesh, E.P.: Automated diabetic retinopathy detection and classification using ImageNet convolution neural network using fundus images. 2020 International Conference on Smart Electronics and Communication (ICOSEC). 577–582 (2020). https://doi.org/10.1109/ICOSEC49089.2020.9215270

33. Kwasigroch, A., Jarzembinski, B., Grochowski, M.: Deep CNN based decision support system for detection and assessing the stage of diabetic retinopathy. 2018 International Interdisciplinary PhD Workshop, IIPhDW 2018. 111–116 (2018). https://doi.org/10.1109/IIPHDW.2018.8388337

34. Ramasubramanian, B., Selvaperumal, S.: A comprehensive review on various preprocessing methods in detecting diabetic retinopathy. Inter. Conf. Commun. Sig. Proc. ICCSP **2016**, 642–646 (2016). https://doi.org/10.1109/ICCSP.2016.7754220

35. Swathi, C., Anoop, B.K., Dhas, D.A.S., Sanker, S.P.: Comparison of different image preprocessing methods used for retinal fundus images. 2017 Conference on Emerging Devices and Smart Systems, ICEDSS 2017. 175–179 (2017). https://doi.org/10.1109/ICEDSS.2017.8073677

36. Junjun, P., Zhifan, Y., Dong, S., Hong, Q.: Diabetic retinopathy detection based on deep convolutional neural networks for localization of discriminative regions. Proceedings - 8th International Conference on Virtual Reality and Visualization, ICVRV 2018. 46–52 (2018). https://doi.org/10.1109/ICVRV.2018.00016

37. Sabbir, M.M.H., Sayeed, A., Jamee, M.A.-U.-Z.: Diabetic retinopathy detection using texture features and ensemble learning. 2020 IEEE Region 10 Symposium (TENSYMP). 178–181 (2020). https://doi.org/10.1109/TENSYMP50017.2020.9230600

38. Wang, Z., Yin, Y., Shi, J., Fang, W., Li, H., Wang, X.: Zoom-in-Net: Deep Mining Lesions for Diabetic Retinopathy Detection. In: Descoteaux, M., Maier-Hein, L., Franz, A., Jannin, P., Collins, D.L., Duchesne, S. (eds.) MICCAI 2017. LNCS, vol. 10435, pp. 267–275. Springer, Cham (2017). https://doi.org/10.1007/978-3-319-66179-7_31

39. Almeida-Galarraga, D., et al.: Glaucoma detection through digital processing from fundus images using MATLAB. Proceedings - 2021 2nd International Conference on Information Systems and Software Technologies, ICI2ST 2021. 39–45 (2021). https://doi.org/10.1109/ICI2ST51859.2021.00014

40. Yanchatuña, O.P., et al.: Skin lesion detection and classification using convolutional neural network for deep feature extraction and support vector machine. Inter. J. Adv. Sci. Eng. Info. Technol. **11**, 1260–1267 (2021). https://doi.org/10.18517/ijaseit.11.3.13679

41. Pereira-Carrillo, J., Suntaxi-Dominguez, D., Guarnizo-Cabezas, O., Villalba-Meneses, G., Tirado-Espín, A., Almeida-Galárraga, D.: Comparison Between Two Novel Approaches in Automatic Breast Cancer Detection and Diagnosis and Its Contribution in Military Defense. In: Rocha, Á., Fajardo-Toro, C.H., Rodríguez, J.M.R. (eds.) Developments and Advances in Defense and Security. SIST, vol. 255, pp. 189–201. Springer, Singapore (2022). https://doi.org/10.1007/978-981-16-4884-7_15

42. Suquilanda-Pesántez, J.D., et al.: Prediction of Parkinson's Disease Severity Based on Gait Signals Using a Neural Network and the Fast Fourier Transform. In: Botto-Tobar, M., Cruz, H., Díaz Cadena, A. (eds.) CIT 2020. AISC, vol. 1326, pp. 3–18. Springer, Cham (2021). https://doi.org/10.1007/978-3-030-68080-0_1

43. Elswah, D.K., Elnakib, A.A., El-Din Moustafa, H.: Automated diabetic retinopathy grading using resnet. National Radio Science Conference, NRSC, Proceedings. 2020-Septe, 248–254 (2020). https://doi.org/10.1109/NRSC49500.2020.9235098

44. Chaki, J., Thillai Ganesh, S., Cidham, S.K., Ananda Theertan, S.: Machine learning and artificial intelligence based Diabetes Mellitus detection and self-management: a systematic review. J. King Saud Univ. Comp. Info. Sci. (2020). https://doi.org/10.1016/j.jksuci.2020.06.013

45. Shanthi, T., Sabeenian, R.S.: Modified alexnet architecture for classification of diabetic retinopathy images. Comput. Electr. Eng. **76**, 56–64 (2019). https://doi.org/10.1016/j.compeleceng.2019.03.004

46. Lin, G.M., et al.: Transforming retinal photographs to entropy images in deep learning to improve automated detection for diabetic retinopathy. Journal of Ophthalmology. 2018, (2018). https://doi.org/10.1155/2018/2159702

47. Hemanth, D.J., Deperlioglu, O., Kose, U.: An enhanced diabetic retinopathy detection and classification approach using deep convolutional neural network. Neural Comput. Appl. **32**(3), 707–721 (2019). https://doi.org/10.1007/s00521-018-03974-0

Convolutional Neural Network for Imagine Movement Classification for Neurorehabilitation of Upper Extremities Using Low-Frequency EEG Signals for Spinal Cord Injury

Mario G. Gualsaquí[1] , Alejandro S. Delgado[1] , Lady L. González[1] ,
Giovana F. Vaca[1] , Diego A. Almeida-Galárraga[1] , Graciela M. Salum[4] ,
Carolina Cadena-Morejón[3] , Andres Tirado-Espín[2] ,
and Fernando Villalba-Meneses[1(✉)]

[1] Escuela de Ciencias Biológicas e Ingeniería, Universidad Yachay Tech, Hacienda
San José s/n, San Miguel de Urcuquí 100119, Ecuador
gvillalba@yachaytech.edu.ec
[2] Escuela de Ciencias Matemáticas y Computacionales, Universidad Yachay Tech,
Hacienda San José s/n, San Miguel de Urcuquí 100119, Ecuador
[3] Universidad de Zaragoza, 50018 Zaragoza, Spain
[4] Instituto Tecnológico Regional Suroeste Carrera de Ingeniería Biomédica,
Universidad Tecnológica del Uruguay, Fray Bentos 65000, Departamento de Rio
Negro-Uruguay, Uruguay

Abstract. As a result of the improvement of digital signal processing
techniques and pattern recognition, it has been possible to relate brain
signals with motor actions. Indeed, there are many ongoing investigations
related to brain-computer interfaces that might be helpful for biomedical applications in rehabilitation procedures. This study proposes to
use delta electroencephalographic signal band (0.3 Hz–3 Hz) with a classification of imagine movements using a convolutional neural network
for neurorehabilitation assistant for upper limbs in patients with spinal
cord injuries. This was achieved through the classification of 5 classes of
movements to predict potential imaginary movement by the training of
a convolutional neural network with a specific architecture for electroencephalographic signals, EEGNet. Interpolation and independent component analysis was applied as well to optimize the training of a neural network which allowed to predict neurophysiological motor processes with
a 31% accuracy. Hence, the classification of movement-related cortical
potential with convolutional neural network model opens the possibility
for future Brain-Computer Interfaces applications in the biomedical field
for rehabilitation processes.

Keywords: Neurorehabilitation · Spinal cord ·
Electroencephalogram · Convolutional Neural Network

F. R. Narváez et al. (Eds.): SmartTech-IC 2021, CCIS 1532, pp. 272–287, 2022.
https://doi.org/10.1007/978-3-030-99170-8_20

1 Introduction

A spinal cord injury (SCI) is a permanent or temporary alteration of motor, sensory or autonomic function. This is generated since the existing damage causes neurological problems, being more frequent that it occurs at lower levels of the place where the injury occurs. This damage is called complete spinal cord injury, and the person has no control of their limbs or sensations. When the person has certain motor and sensory capacity, it is called incomplete spinal cord injury [32,45]. The complexity of the neurological deficit depends on the level and completeness of the injury, the transverse or longitudinal extension of the injured tissue, and the involvement of white or gray matter [25].

In addition, this type of pathology can be classified according to the factors that generated it. The injury is said to be traumatic when it is caused by external factors, for example, vehicular accidents, falls, injuries from weapons, etc. On the other hand, it is considered non-traumatic when the agents that produce it are some type of disease such as tumors, osteoporosis, sclerosis, etc. [1,20].

Worldwide, the global incidence of SCI ranges from 10.4 to 83 per million inhabitants per year, and the prevalence ranges from 223 to 755 per million inhabitants [7]. There are at least five types of complications that people with spinal cord injury experience over time, which are listed in Table 1.

Table 1. Overview of the common complications experienced by patients with spinal cord injury

Complication	Effects	Rehabilitation	Reference
Cardiovascular	Cardiac arrest, hemodynamic, instability, autonomic, dysfunction and thromboembolism	Management of autonomic, dysreflexia and chronic hemodynamic	[28]
Gastrointestinal	Fecal impaction, constipation, intestinal obstruction, gastric and duodenal ulcers	Elaborate a continence program for preventive gastrointestinal care	[28]
Dermatological	Pressure ulcers	Position should be change to prevent and manage pressure ulcers	[28]
Musculoskeletal	Osteoporosis, fractures, overuse symptoms, acute and chronic pain	Passive exercises to manage: contracture, spasticity and postural abnormalities	[28,31]
Respiratory	Respiratory failure, atelectasis and pneumonia	Preventing respiratory care and, respiratory conditioning programme	[28]

There is no definitive cure for patients with SCI, and current treatments only improve the symptoms and complications of complete SCI [11,47]. Stem cell implants [48] and tissue regeneration [22] attempt to repair damage to the spinal cord. However, studies in rodents with intentionally damaged marrow bones have shown to reconnect them, but these results cannot be verified in humans and/ or non-human primates yet [41]. Also, neuromodulatory approaches targeting surviving neural tissue have allowed patients with complete SCI to regain function after a rehabilitation process [31].

SCI has been described in two stages lesions: primary and secondary injuries, which explain the lesion progression. First, the initial events, or primary SCI, are caused by mechanical trauma which includes traction and compression forces on the spinal cord. Direct compression of neural components such as axons, blood vessels, and neural cells, by bone fragments, disc material, and ligaments, affecting both the central and peripheral nervous system. Therefore, microhemorrhages occur in the central grey area and, spreading out radially and axially, causing the spinal cord to swells blocking the spinal channel at the injured region. Secondary, ischemia occurs once the cord swelling exceeds venous blood pressure, aggravates ischemia caused the release of toxic chemicals triggering secondary injuries [28].

Secondary injuries, and ischemia caused a cascade of events which produced hypoperfusion, inadequate delivery of oxygen to tissues, blocking propagation of action potentials along axons that lead to a series of destructive events, including production of free radicals that damage neural elements at injury region as well as affecting neighboring cells [28].

For all these reasons the common symptoms for SCI patients include cardiovascular, respiratory, gastrointestinal, genitourinary, and musculoskeletal problems (see Table 1). Treatments focus on controlling the secondary injury progression by decompressing the swollen cords [28,49]. Because there is no definite cure for SCI, depending on where the lesion occurs and the severity, the injured patients might recover some functional activities or not. After the patients are stabilized, rehabilitation process aims to improve the quality of life of patients, protecting the integrity of muscle and articulations to prevent atrophy, contractions, and pain [42]. For instance, in paraplegic patients which suffer a loss of function in the lower part of the body rehabilitation consists of exercises of movement range in the inferior extremities and superior to maintain muscular functionality and prevent pain in the area [10].

Due to the fact that, currently, there are no therapies or surgical techniques that can totally repair the physiological damage, there is a need to establish a new channel of communication between the individual and its environment that does not depend on the action of the nervous or muscular pathways [34]. That is, a direct interface between the brain and the environment of the subject, in terms of current technology, this is equivalent to establishing a Brain-Computer Interface (BCI) [17]. This would allow the person connected to the BCI to send messages and commands to the external world, establishing communications with it.

BCIs are devices that allow us to capture electrical and magnetic signals produced by the brain, which are generated when it is trying to produce an action [2,17]. These stimuli are interpreted by computers or other devices that translate the brain signal and execute the voluntary command. These types of devices have been used more and more nowadays due to their great potential to restore motor functions in patients who have suffered some type of neuromotor injury [9,52].

There are several ways in which brain signals can be obtained [16], but this article is based on electroencephalography (EEG) signals which is the most commonly non-invasive method used. These signals are obtained through electrodes and are captured during stimulation of the patient or some mental and/or motor activity. The EEG activity is complex because of its wide variety of different rhythms identified by its localization, frequency, or amplitude [23,40]. After the EEG signals extraction, they are preprocessed to extract the characteristics and to emit an answer based on the intention of the patient in order to control an external device. Also, advanced systems use interesting and sophisticated classification techniques employing features extracted from signals [51]. Then, the system can be adapted to the requirements of the patient, and therefore, improve precision in EEG signal decoding [38,46]. In this study, EEGNet is used, which is a compact CNN for the classification and interpretation of BCI based on EEG. Concerning the design of a BCI system, some critical properties of these features presented in Table 2 must be considered:

Table 2. Critical properties

Property	Description	Reference
Noise and outliners	BCI features are noisy or contain outliners because EEG signals have a poor signal-to-noise ratio	[27,38]
High dimensionality	In BCI systems, feature vectors are often of high dimensionality	[27,38]
Time information	BCI features should contain time information as brain activity patterns are generally related to specific time variations of EEG	[27,38]
Non-stationarity	BCI features are non-stationary since EEG signals may rapidly vary over time and more especially over sessions	[27,38]
Small training sets	The training sets are relatively small since the training process is time-consuming and demanding for the subjects.	[27,38]

2   Methods

We propose to use only the delta band (0.3–3 Hz) of the EEG signal for movement classification [5,26]. In the state-of-the-art we found that several authors employ this methodology for the classification of movement intention using artificial intelligence, however, they have not employed the use of the EEGNet architecture [8,30,54].

Then, for the methodology, the BNI horizon database of a rehabilitation center (AUVA rehabilitation clinic, Tobelbad, Austria) was taken. During the study, 5 types of movements were executed: pronation, supination, palmar grip, lateral grip, and open hand. Subsequently, for the pre-processing of EEG signals with neural networks, the EEGLab tool in Matlab® was used to preprocess signals(filtering, remove bad channels, extract epochs). Finally, to proceed with the classification stage, the dataset with the epochs was uploaded to Google drive and a Convolutional Neural Network (CNN) was trained with specific parameters. All this process will be detailed in the following paragraphs.

2.1   Dataset Description

The dataset consisted of 10 subjects who were taken to the AUVA rehabilitation clinic ranged in age from 20 to 69 years and had a lesion between the C1–C7 vertebrae. The recording of EEG signals was obtained by seating each participant in front of a computer where instructions were displayed. The tests consisted of the emission of a sound indicating the beginning of the trial and the participants were asked to fix their gaze on a cross for 5 s. The beginning of the movement class started 2 s after the end of the sound and lasted 3 s.

As mentioned before five types of movements were performed: pronation, supination, palmar grip, lateral grip, and open hand. Signals were obtained with 61 electrodes for the EEG signal in VESA 5–10 configuration (Fig. 1). The total

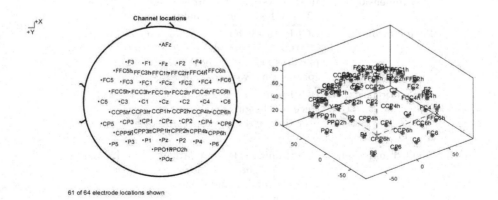

Fig. 1. Localization of each channel according to the VESA 10-5 system. Localization on two dimensional and three dimensional, from top to bottom respectively.

of electrodes were 64, 61 EEG and 3 EOG. In addition, 4 16-channel amplifiers were used. The sample was obtained with a sampling frequency 256 Hz and a bandpass filter from 0.01 Hz to 100 Hz. They also used 50 Hz Notch filter in order to eliminate power line interference. Finally, the signals were saved in GDF (General Data Format for Biosignals) format [36].

2.2   Classification of EEG Signals with Neural Networks

Later, signals were preprocessed with the EEGLab tool in Matlab®. MATLAB was chosen for preprocessing because it has powerful features and toolboxes for easy signal and image processing [3]. First, the signals were filtered with a bandpass filter (from 0.3 Hz to 70 Hz). Second, the bad channels were eliminated. Third, a decomposition of independent components was performed and the components that showed to be responsible for the artifacts were rejected. Fourth, a bandpass filter (from 0.3 Hz to 3 Hz) was accomplished, this in order to leave only the low-frequency delta band. Finally, the signal was segmented.

The filters implemented are detailed below:

Bandpass Filter (0.3 Hz–70 Hz). A minimum order FIR (finite impulse response) filter was used (Fig. 2(a)). The range that interests us for the classification of MCRP is between 0.3 Hz and 3 Hz [36], which is because the filter that we are using initially does not eliminate our band of interest and improves the visualization of bad channels for their respective elimination.

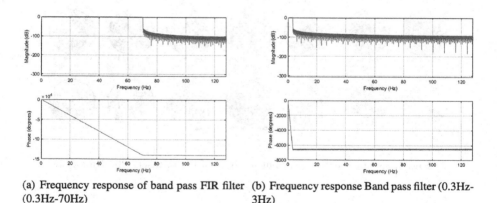

(a) Frequency response of band pass FIR filter (0.3Hz-70Hz)   (b) Frequency response Band pass filter (0.3Hz-3Hz)

Fig. 2. Dataset filtered with Bandpass filter (0.3 Hz–70 Hz) and (0.3 Hz–3 Hz).

Bad Channel Elimination. We eliminated the channels that presented a very high level of noise, and that is visually perceptible. In order to avoid reducing the dimension of the channels, the interpolation method was used. This was done since not all the recordings had the same noisy channels and it is not recommended to use datasets with different channels.

Independent Component Analysis. The independent component analysis of the 61 EEG channels was performed. The Runic algorithm was chosen for this purpose because provides identification of the independent components maximizing the difference of their kurtosis from Gaussian [4,29,37]. So since the number of channels was not large, the dimension reduction was disabled with a principal component analysis (PCA) (see Fig. 3). And components with a probability greater than 50% were marked as muscle, eye, heart, and noise channel stimuli. The marked components were removed to remove artifacts from the signal.

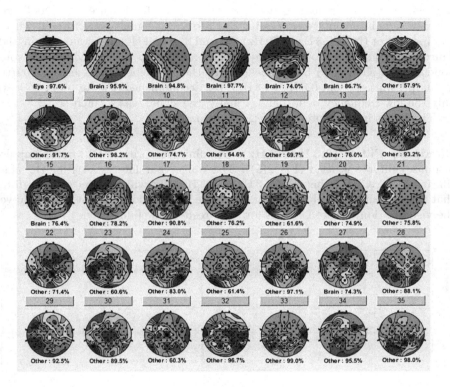

Fig. 3. Independent component analysis of the dataset. P02 Run 4

Bandpass Filter (0.3 Hz–3 Hz). A last bandpass filter (Fig. 2(b)) was performed in order to eliminate the signal bands that is not of our interest in the signal clean of artifacts [5,26,43].

Signal Segmentation. The signal was segmented into epochs of a length of 5 s that were extracted from marked events corresponding to the classes of movements. We extract 0.25 s of pre-stimulus, and 3 s of stimulus from each of the classes (pronation, supination, palmar grip, lateral grip and open hand). We then proceeded to combine all the trials from the datasets. The final number of epochs obtained is 1479 from 5 participants.

For the classification stage of neural network training, a Convolutional Neural Network (CNN) was trained. For this study, we used the EEGNet architecture obtained from https://github.com/vlawhern/arleegmodels. The architecture was not manipulated and only some parameters were set (see Table 3). The reason why this model was chosen is that EEGNet has been developed to decode brain states at Brain-Computer Interfaces (BCI), and it can be trained with limited data. The system input has a Channels(C) × Time(T) dimension [15]. The dataset was divided into 50% for training, 25% for validation and 25% for testing. The model was tuned with an Adam optimizer which has proven to be reliable as seen in the literature [6,21,40,53], keeping the settings provided by [23]. The training consisted of 1479 training interactions equivalent to the number of epochs obtained from the dataset.

Table 3. CNN architecture used for the training. It is used from the template of Lawhern et al. [23]

Block	Layer	N° filters	Size	N° Params	Output	Activation	Options
1	Input				(C, T)		
	Reshape				$(1, C, T)$		
	Conv2D	$F1$	$(1, 32)$	$32 * F1$	$(F1, C, T)$	Linear	mode = same
	BatchNorm			$2 * F1$	$(F1, C, T)$		
	DepthwiseConv2D	$D * F1$	$(C, 1)$	$C * D * F1$	$(D * F1, 1, T)$	Linear	mode = valid, depth = D, max norm = 1
	BatchNorm			$2 * D * F1$	$(D * F1, 1, T)$	ELU	
	Activation				$(D * F1, 1, T)$		
	AveragePool2D		$(1,4)$		$(D * F1, 1, T/4)$		
	Dropout*				$(D * F1, 1, T/4)$		$p = 0.25$ or $p = 0.5$
2	SeparableConv2D	$F2$	$(1, 64)$	$64 * D * F1 + F2 * (D * F1)$	$(F2, 1, T/4)$	Linear	mode = same
	BatchNorm			$2 * F2$	$(F2, 1, T/4)$		
	Activation				$(F2, 1, T/4)$	ELU	
	AveragePool2D		$(1, 8)$		$(F2, 1, T/32)$		
	Dropout				$(F2, 1, T/32)$		$p = 0.25$ or $p = 0.5$
	Flatten				$(F2, 1, T/32)$		
Classifier	Dense	$N * (F2 * T/32)$			N	Softmax	max norm = 0.25

The convolutional neural network consists of 2 blocks with specific parameters The parameters used were:

Block 1. Fit F1 2D-convolutional filters of size (1, 32), which is eighth fraction of the sampling frequency (256 Hz), a value suggested because it allows capturing information 2 Hz. Also, this model has Depthwise Convolution of dimension (C,1) which serves as a spatial filter, and provides direct information to the temporal filter. An additional parameter (D = 1) is a depth that controls the number of spatial filters. The Dropout probability is set to 0.5 in order not to give an over-fitting training on small samples.

Block 2. The convolutional network architecture applies is a separable convolution, specifically a depthwise convolution with length (1,16), which is equivalent to 250ms of EEG signal 64 Hz. The parameter F2 (1,64) pointwise convolution is also applied. This type of network architecture is used since it has fewer parameters to fit and allows decoupling of the relationship within and across feature maps. On the other hand, the Average Pooling layer was kept at length (1.8) for dimensional reduction [23].

The classification is configured for 5 classes of movements, which correspond to those mentioned in the dataset [36].

3   Results

3.1   Neural Network

Figure 4 shows the confusion matrix of the training performed, with probabilities of true positives (recall: ability of the algorithm to detect positive cases for each class) of 40%, 32.2%, 23.7%, 29.4% and 31.4%, for supination, pronation, open hand, palmar grip and lateral grip movements, respectively. On the other hand, additional criteria are shown in Table 4. Accuracy (ratio of number of correct predictions to total predictions) of 33%, 39%, 37%, 19%, and 29%; F1-score of 36%, 35%, 29%, 23% and 30% were obtained for supination, pronation, open hand, palmar grip and lateral grip movements, respectively. Finally, it was observed that the accuracy (indicating the closeness between the data provided by the model and the real data) of the model was 31%.

4   Discussion

4.1   Neural Networks

This work identifies neurophysiological correlation of motor processes features using EEGNet architecture which is a compact CNN, that in the existence of limited data has proved to present interpretable data and, less pre-processing needs compared to other models [13,23]. Pre-processing pipeline of the data with

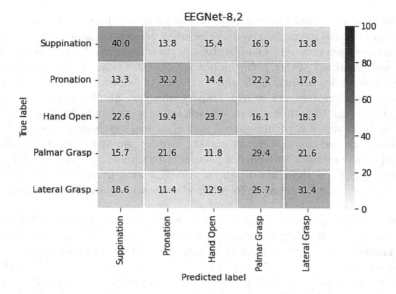

Fig. 4. Confusion matrix that show accuracy and sensitivity of the trained model

Table 4. Show the main results of the trained model for each class

	Precision	Recall	F1- score	Support
Suppination	0.33	0.40	0.36	65
Pronation	0.39	0.32	0.35	90
Hand Grasp	0.37	0.24	0.29	93
Palmar Grasp	0.19	0.29	0.23	51
Lateral Grasp	0.29	0.31	0.30	70
Accuracy			0.31	369
Macro avg	0.31	0.31	0.31	369
Weighted avg	0.33	0.31	0.31	369

low bandpass and interpolation methods showed high repeatability across class repetitions that improve performance during training with the neural network, thus enabling using all channels without losing dimensionality in the dataset and offering the best trade-off between input dimensionality and flexibility to discover relevant features [18, 23, 39, 40, 44].

Despite the CNN performance having shown promising accuracy results, the classification accuracy in this model for imagined movement is rather encouraging (31% accuracy) for this kind of classification compare with other classification results for imaginary movements, as shown in Table 4, in line with previous literature. For instance, Ofner et al. obtained with a binary classification for imagined and executed movements. For the imagined movement, in the movements versus movements binary classification accuracies around 27%, and for the movements versus rest classification accuracies around 72%. For executed movement obtained better performance for classifications in different windows lengths, accuracies around 55% and 84% was obtained for the movements vs movements and movements vs rest, respectively [35]. Similar studies as Schwarz et al. showed in their multi-class classification model moderate accuracies of 38.6% in their study with unimanual and bimanual reach and grasp action, for six movements and one rest condition [44]. Further, many studies have validated CNN high performance in terms of accuracy; to illustrate, a dataset for binary classification of the right hand palmar versus lateral movement was obtaining 70% mean accuracy compared to other classification models which performed below [44].

This research shows that EEGNet can classify different classes of MRCP on a single subject on single trials events. This was realized in 25% of the participants and, classification accuracy from the confusion matrix showed the average prediction accuracy of the EEGNet was 31%. Further, we observed that each class accuracy was classified as 32% pronation, 40% supination, 23% hand open, 29% palmar grasp and, 31% lateral grasp. Additionally, we measure the sensitivity or recall which is a metric that calculates the ability of our model to predict a result as actual positive, for each class having an average recall of 31%. Although, our values slightly differ from previous literature [13,23] mainly due to the length of the data used for this particular training. Perhaps with adding more participants to the model the training accuracy parameter might be improved. Moreover, in the case of imagined movement classification as reported in previous literature, low accuracies values might be caused because the imagined movement EEG signals were time-locked to a virtual movement rather than an actual movement as occur in executed movement [35]. Also, in executed movement, the brain pattern is more pronounced than imagined movement [19,33].

In contrast, this classification methodology showed promising results, and future studies could focus on improving performance by automating the preprocessing of the signal to work with more volume of data. And, these models can be used as interpretive models; in order words, it is not required to train the neural network in every rehabilitation session done by the therapist. Indeed, the present work found that the applied EEGNet is capable of creating reliable models from extracting signals obtained from the electrodes.

The relevance of the model developed in this work is that it can be used as a rehabilitation assistant when it is implemented in an assistant robot that executes the movements. According to [14] to develop a repetitive training which is based on active movements promoting motor recovery and brain plasticity after a stroke. This means that assisted therapy could reduce motor impairment. Some studies have worked with robotic assistance such as the publication [12], in which the rehabilitation of patients with incomplete SCI is carried out using a four degrees of freedom exoskeleton used for isolated rehabilitation of the elbow and the wrist. Another example is the study [24], which compares rehabilitation guided by an exoskeleton and an end-effector in chronic stroke patients with moderate to severe upper extremity impairment. Similarly, in [50] an adaptive admittance control of an upper extremity rehabilitation robot with neural-network-based disturbance observer, in order to find a functional rehabilitation training of the joints (shoulder, elbow, and wrist) of the upper limb and at the same time facilitate the physiotherapist the optimization of the clinical treatment.

4.2 Challenges

The artifacts or unwanted signals in the data obtained from the electrodes have to be excluded in the pre-processing stage. Then, this process is computationally expensive, because affects the performance of the neural network causing delays between the reading of the signal in the pre-processing stage and, the sending of the command to the training stage. Moreover, the time-consuming of the pre-processing step of the signal is an opportunity for future studies to develop an automated program for this step, to clean as much data as possible, and work the model with more volume of data improving accuracy particularly for imagine movement classification.

The cost of production of a single prototype is expensive, that is to say, the acquisition of a BCI system with the electrodes. For instance, only the cost of the plate is around 900 American dollars, depending on the number of channels to configure. Also, the cost of developing an assistant robot such as an exoskeleton, end-effector, or others has to be considered. However, this technology could be helpful for rehabilitation centers in terms of automatizing the rehabilitation process for patients with SCI.

5 Conclusion

In this study, we trained a promising classification model for predicting MRCP using EGGNet architecture on a dataset for five participants that the EEG signals were pre-processed with low frequency band-pass to include five movements or classes (supination, pronation, hand open, palmar grasp and, lateral grasp). Even though the number of participants was relatively short to train the model we obtain as a result of the, imagine movement, classifications a medium performance in terms of accuracy and sensibility of the CNN (average accuracy of 0.31 and sensibility of 0.31). However, we might expect better performance for both parameters by adding more participants to the model. Eventually, this deep learning model will become important to evolve BCI technology that could benefit the processes of neurorehabilitation for the upper extremities in patients with SCI.

Promising applications for the rehabilitation process have been approached, the exoskeleton that has been proposed in this work is a promising candidate to develop a rehabilitation platform for its ability to improve motor recovery and brain plasticity.

References

1. Ahuja, C.S., et al.: Traumatic spinal cord injury. Nat. Rev. Dis. Primers **3**(1), 1–21 (2017)
2. Albán-Cadena, A.C., et al.: Wearable sensors in the diagnosis and study of Parkinson's disease symptoms: a systematic review. J. Med. Eng. Technol. **45**(7), 532–545 (2021). https://doi.org/10.1080/03091902.2021.1922528
3. Almeida-Galarraga, D., et al.: Glaucoma detection through digital processing from fundus images using Matlab, pp. 39–45. Institute of Electrical and Electronics Engineers Inc., March 2021. https://doi.org/10.1109/ICI2ST51859.2021.00014
4. Benevides, A.B., Bastos Filho, T.F., Sarcinelli Filho, M.: Comparison of artifact removal techniques on single-trial event-related potentials for use in brain-computer interfaces. CEP **48**, 08 (2013)
5. Bibián, C., López-Larraz, E., Irastorza-Landa, N., Birbaumer, N., Ramos-Murguialday, A.: Evaluation of filtering techniques to extract movement intention information from low-frequency EEG activity. Annu. Int. Conf. IEEE Eng. Med. Biol. Soc. **2017**, 2960–2963 (2017)
6. Bock, S., Goppold, J., Weiß, M.: An improvement of the convergence proof of the ADAM-Optimizer, April 2018. http://arxiv.org/abs/1804.10587
7. Bolaños, C.D.F., Correa, H.L.: Interfaz cerebro-computador multimodal para procesos de neurorrehabilitación de miembros superiores en pacientes con lesiones de médula espinal: una revisión. Revista Ingeniería Biomédica **12**(24), 35–46 (2018)
8. Bressan, G., Cisotto, G., Müller-Putz, G.R., Wriessnegger, S.C.: Deep learning-based classification of fine hand movements from low frequency EEG. Future Internet **13**, 103 (2021). https://doi.org/10.3390/fi13050103
9. Cossio, E.G., Gentiletti, G.G.: Interfaz cerebro computadora (ICC) basada en el potencial relacionado con eventos p300: AnÁlisis del efecto de la dimensiÓn de la matriz de estimulaciÓn sobre su desempeño. Revista Ingeniería Biomédica, vol. 2 (2008). https://doi.org/10.24050/19099762.n4.2008.51
10. Diong, J., et al.: Incidence and predictors of contracture after spinal cord injury-a prospective cohort study. Spinal Cord **50**(8), 579–584 (2012)
11. Donati, A.R., et al.: Long-term training with a brain-machine interface-based gait protocol induces partial neurological recovery in paraplegic patients. Sci. Rep. **6**(1), 1–16 (2016)
12. Frullo, J.M., et al.: Effects of assist-as-needed upper extremity robotic therapy after incomplete spinal cord injury: a parallel-group controlled trial. Front. Neurorobotics **11**, 26 (2017). https://doi.org/10.3389/fnbot.2017.00026
13. Gramfort, A., et al.: MEG and EEG data analysis with MNE-Python. Front. Neurosci. **7**, 1–13 (2013). https://doi.org/10.3389/fnins.2013.00267
14. Grosmaire, A.G., Duret, C.: Does assist-as-needed upper limb robotic therapy promote participation in repetitive activity-based motor training in sub-acute stroke patients with severe paresis? NeuroRehabilitation **41**, 31–39 (2017). https://doi.org/10.3233/NRE-171454
15. Hassan, M., Shamas, M., Khalil, M., Falou, W.E., Wendling, F.: EegNet: an open source tool for analyzing and visualizing M/EEG connectome. PLoS ONE **10**, e0138297 (2015). https://doi.org/10.1371/journal.pone.0138297
16. Herrera-Romero, B., Villalba-Meneses, G., Almeida-Galárraga, D., Echeverría-Ortíz, P., Salum, G., Villalba-Meneses, C.: Procesamiento y análisis de imágenes digitales para el diagnóstico de enfermedades oftalmológicas: análisis descriptivo actual de la investigación científica (2021)

17. Hornero, R., Corralejo, R., Álvarez González, D.: Brain-computer interface (BCI) aplicado al entrenamiento cognitivo y control domótico para prevenir los efectos del envejecimiento. Lychnos (2012)
18. Huang, W., Xue, Y., Hu, L., Liuli, H.: S-EEGNet: electroencephalogram signal classification based on a separable convolution neural network with bilinear interpolation. IEEE Access **8**, 131636–131646 (2020). https://doi.org/10.1109/ACCESS.2020.3009665
19. Ieracitano, C., Mammone, N., Hussain, A., Morabito, F.C.: A novel explainable machine learning approach for EEG-based brain-computer interface systems. Neural Comput. Appl. 1–14 (2021). https://doi.org/10.1007/s00521-020-05624-w
20. Jain, N.B., et al.: Traumatic spinal cord injury in the United States, 1993–2012. JAMA **313**(22), 2236–2243 (2015)
21. Jais, I.K.M., Ismail, A.R., Nisa, S.Q.: Adam optimization algorithm for wide and deep neural network. Knowl. Eng. Data Sci. **2**, 41 (2019). https://doi.org/10.17977/um018v2i12019p41-46
22. Joosten, E.A.: Biodegradable biomatrices and bridging the injured spinal cord: the corticospinal tract as a proof of principle. Cell Tissue Res. **349**(1), 375–395 (2012)
23. Lawhern, V.J., Solon, A.J., Waytowich, N.R., Gordon, S.M., Hung, C.P., Lance, B.J.: EEGNet: a compact convolutional neural network for EEG-based brain-computer interfaces. J. Neural Eng. **15**(5), 056013 (2018). http://stacks.iop.org/1741-2552/15/i=5/a=056013
24. Lee, S.H., et al.: Comparisons between end-effector and exoskeleton rehabilitation robots regarding upper extremity function among chronic stroke patients with moderate-to-severe upper limb impairment. Sci. Rep. **10**, 1806 (2020). https://doi.org/10.1038/s41598-020-58630-2
25. Lema, C.P.H., Parra, J.E.P.: Lesiones medulares y discapacidad: revisión bibliográfica. Aquichan **10**(2), 157–172 (2010)
26. Li, T., Xue, T., Wang, B., Zhang, J.: Decoding voluntary movement of single hand based on analysis of brain connectivity by using EEG signals. Front. Human Neurosci. **12**, 381 (2018). https://doi.org/10.3389/fnhum.2018.00381
27. Lotte, F., et al.: A review of classification algorithms for EEG-based brain-computer interfaces: a 10 year update. J. Neural Eng. **15**(3), 031005 (2018)
28. McDonald, J.W., Sadowsky, C.: Spinal-cord injury. The Lancet **359**(9304), 417–425 (2002)
29. Melnik, A., Hairston, W.D., Ferris, D.P., König, P.: EEG correlates of sensorimotor processing: Independent components involved in sensory and motor processing. Sci. Rep. **7**, 1–15 (2017). https://doi.org/10.1038/s41598-017-04757-8
30. Mondini, V., Kobler, R.J., Sburlea, A.I., Müller-Putz, G.R.: Continuous low-frequency EEG decoding of arm movement for closed-loop, natural control of a robotic arm. J. Neural Eng. **17**, 046031 (2020). https://doi.org/10.1088/1741-2552/aba6f7
31. Nas, K., Yazmalar, L., Şah, V., Aydın, A., Öneş, K.: Rehabilitation of spinal cord injuries. World J. Orthop. **6**(1), 8 (2015)
32. Nayduch, D.A.: Los fundamentos: identificación y tratamiento de la lesión medular aguda. Nursing (Ed. española) **29**, 8–15 (2011). https://doi.org/10.1016/S0212-5382(11)70160-1, https://linkinghub.elsevier.com/retrieve/pii/S0212538211701601
33. Niazi, I.K., Jiang, N., Tiberghien, O., Nielsen, J.F., Dremstrup, K., Farina, D.: Detection of movement intention from single-trial movement-related cortical potentials. J. Neural Eng. **8**(6), 066009 (2011)

34. Nicolas-Alonso, L.F., Gomez-Gil, J.: Brain computer interfaces, a review. Sensors **12**(2), 1211–1279 (2012)
35. Ofner, P., Schwarz, A., Pereira, J., Müller-Putz, G.R.: Upper limb movements can be decoded from the time-domain of low-frequency EEG. PLoS ONE **12**(8), e0182578 (2017)
36. Ofner, P., Schwarz, A., Pereira, J., Wyss, D., Wildburger, R., Müller-Putz, G.R.: Attempted arm and hand movements can be decoded from low-frequency EEG from persons with spinal cord injury. Sci. Rep. **9**(1), 1–15 (2019). https://doi.org/10.1038/s41598-019-43594-9
37. Popescu, T.D.: Artifact removing from EEG recordings using independent component analysis with high-order statistics. Int. J. Math. Models Meth. Appl. Sci. 15, 76–85 (2021). https://doi.org/10.46300/9101.2021.15.11
38. Raza, H., Chowshury, A., Bhattacharyya, S., Samothrakis, S.: clasificación de eeg de ensayo único con eegnet y aprendizaje estructurado neuronal para mejorar el rendimiento de BCI, pp. 1–8. Conferencia conjunta internacional de 2020 sobre redes neuronales (IJCNN) (2020)
39. Raza, H., Chowdhury, A., Bhattacharyya, S., Samothrakis, S.: Single-trial EEG classification with EEGNet and neural structured learning for improving BCI performance. https://github.com/vlawhern/arl-eegmodels
40. Riyad, M., Khalil, M., Adib, A.: INCEP-EEGNet: a convnet for motor imagery decoding. Image Signal Process. **12119**, 103–111 (2020)
41. Sahni, V., Kessler, J.A.: Stem cell therapies for spinal cord injury. Nat. Rev. Neurol. **6**(7), 363–372 (2010)
42. Aguiar Salazar, E.D., et al.: Design of a glove controlled by electromyographic signals for the rehabilitation of patients with Rheumatoid Arthritis. In: Rodriguez Morales, G., Fonseca C., E.R., Salgado, J.P., Pérez-Gosende, P., Orellana Cordero, M., Berrezueta, S. (eds.) TICEC 2020. CCIS, vol. 1307, pp. 3–11. Springer, Cham (2020). https://doi.org/10.1007/978-3-030-62833-8_1
43. Schwarz, A., Ofner, P., Pereira, J., Sburlea, A.I., Müller-Putz, G.R.: Decoding natural reach-and-grasp actions from human EEG. J. Neural Eng. **15**, 016005 (2018). https://doi.org/10.1088/1741-2552/aa8911
44. Schwarz, A., Pereira, J., Kobler, R., Müller-Putz, G.R.: Unimanual and bimanual reach-and-grasp actions can be decoded from human EEG. IEEE Trans. Biomed. Eng. **67**(6), 1684–1695 (2019)
45. Strassburguer, K.: Lesión medular: Guía para el manejo integral del paciente con lm crónica. ASPAYM Madrid, vol. 4 (2013)
46. Suquilanda-Pesántez, J.D., et al.: Prediction of Parkinson's disease severity based on gait signals using a neural network and the Fast Fourier Transform. In: Botto-Tobar, M., Cruz, H., Díaz Cadena, A. (eds.) CIT 2020. AISC, vol. 1326, pp. 3–18. Springer, Cham (2021). https://doi.org/10.1007/978-3-030-68080-0_1
47. Thuret, S., Moon, L.D., Gage, F.H.: Therapeutic interventions after spinal cord injury. Nat. Rev. Neurosci. **7**(8), 628–643 (2006)
48. Tsuji, O., et al.: Therapeutic potential of appropriately evaluated safe-induced pluripotent stem cells for spinal cord injury. Proc. Natl. Acad. Sci. **107**(28), 12704–12709 (2010)
49. Vásquez-Ucho, P.A., Villalba-Meneses, G.F., Pila-Varela, K.O., Villalba-Meneses, C.P., Iglesias, I., Almeida-Galárraga, D.A.: J. Med. Eng. Technol. Analysis and evaluation of the systems used for the assessment of the cervical spine function: a systematic review **45**(5), 380–393 (2021). https://doi.org/10.1080/03091902.2021.1907467

50. Wu, Q., Chen, B., Wu, H.: Adaptive admittance control of an upper extremity rehabilitation robot with neural-network-based disturbance observer. IEEE Access **7**, 123807–123819 (2019). https://doi.org/10.1109/ACCESS.2019.2938566

51. Yanchatuña, O.P., et al.: Skin lesion detection and classification using convolutional neural network for deep feature extraction and support vector machine. Int. J. Adv. Sci. Eng. Inf. Technol. **11**, 1260–1267 (2021). https://doi.org/10.18517/ijaseit.11.3.13679

52. Yger, F., Berar, M., Lotte, F.: Riemannian approaches in brain-computer interfaces: a review. IEEE Trans. Neural Syst. Rehabil. Eng. **25**(10), 1753–1762 (2016)

53. Zou, F., Shen, L., Jie, Z., Zhang, W., Liu, W., Tencent AI Lab: A sufficient condition for convergences of Adam and RMSProp (2019)

54. Úbeda, A., Azorín, J.M., Chavarriaga, R., del R Millán, J.: Classification of upper limb center-out reaching tasks by means of EEG-based continuous decoding techniques. J. Neuroeng. Rehabil. **14**, 1–14 (2017). https://doi.org/10.1186/s12984-017-0219-0

Smart Trends and Applications

A New Handwritten Number Recognition Approach Using Typical Testors, Genetic Algorithms, and Neural Networks

Eddy Torres-Constante[1] , Julio Ibarra-Fiallo[1] ,
and Monserrate Intriago-Pazmiño[2]($\boxtimes$)

[1] Colegio de Ciencias e Ingenierías, Universidad San Francisco de Quito,
Cumbayá, Ecuador
eatorresc@estud.usfq.edu.ec, jibarra@usfq.edu.ec
[2] Departamento de Informática y Ciencias de la Computación, Escuela Politécnica
Nacional, Quito, Ecuador
monserrate.intriago@epn.edu.ec

Abstract. In this paper, a method combining three techniques is proposed in order to reduce the amount of features used to train and predict over a handwritten data set of digits. The proposal uses typical testors and searches through evolutionary strategy to find a reduced set of features that preserves essential information of all the classes that compose the data set. Once found it, this reduced subset will be strengthened for classification. To achieve it, the neural network prediction accuracy plays the role of fitness function. Thus, when a subset reaches a threshold prediction accuracy, it is returned as a solution of this step. Evolutionary strategy makes this intense search of features viable in terms of computing complexity and time. The discriminator construction algorithm is proposed as a strategy to achieve a smaller feature subset that preserves the accuracy of the overall data set. The proposed method is tested using the public MNIST data set. The best result found a subset of 171 features out of the 784, which only represents 21.81% of the total number of characteristics. The accuracy average was 97.83% on the testing set. The results are also contrasted with the error rate of other reported classifiers, such as PCA, over the same data set.

Keywords: Evolutionary strategy · Fitness function · Genetic algorithms · Handwritten number classification · Multi-layer neural network · Typical testors

1 Introduction

Handwritten text recognition presents significant challenges, such as the different types of handwriting, the quality of images or input devices. Because of this, each specific software needs that users train their accounts to improve the recognition of their digital handwriting. In this research work, a handwritten digit

© Springer Nature Switzerland AG 2022
F. R. Narváez et al. (Eds.): SmartTech-IC 2021, CCIS 1532, pp. 291–305, 2022.
https://doi.org/10.1007/978-3-030-99170-8_21

recognition method is proposed to minimize the number of image descriptors (pixels sample). For this purpose, the theory of typical testors, artificial neural networks and genetic algorithms have been combined.

The objective of reducing the dimensionality of the feature space is to find a minimum set that preserves the essential information and allows to distinguish and identify the compared classes. As result, it facilities the models' training for areas of pattern recognition or data mining [1–4].

A testor is a reduced set of features that provides the same capability to differentiate between objects as the entire set of features does. This is why it has been used in supervised pattern recognition as in [5–8]. When the cardinality set of the testors is enormous, a subspace is searched among all possible subsets of cells in a matrix, where every cell is a feature [9–11]. Some state-of-the-art algorithms include: LEX [12], YYC [13], all-NRD [14], CUDA based hill-climbing [15], Fast-BR [16], FAST-CT-EXT [17] which focuses on returning the whole set of typical testors. An algorithm that manages to find minimum length typical testors is reported in [18]. It has been reported that heuristic algorithms like UMDA [19], PHC [20], and HC [21] perform better over large data sets. It could be possible to compare the accuracy of prediction over all testors on these algorithms if it guarantees to find the whole set of typical testors. Nevertheless, in most real cases, the exponential complexity does not allow it.

The output of all types of algorithms focus on trying to reach the highest cardinality of the returned subset of the typical testor or the minimum-length subset of them. Therefore, the effort is to answer how effectively a testor can be built since there have been issues the entire features set [21]. In [22], testors are used to improve the diagnosis of breast cancer cells. Furthermore, there are several problems in which there is a necessity to find an optimal discriminator (or close to it), that allows maximizing the performance of the classification and reducing the number of features. For example, in the fields of diagnostic diseases [23], feature selection for text classification [5], and categorization [6]. Unlike other techniques developed for feature selection, testors have been focused on this purpose, especially a certain type known as irreducible or typical [24,25], [26–28]. The time complexity increases as the number of features grow. Finding testors with previous algorithms does not provide measures of over how useful one testor is compared to another, or even the whole set when using it for prediction.

Furthermore, considering how a testor can be used in practice, is why we propose to build one. In fact, [19] considers that each typical testor can be recognized as a local optimum for discrimination. To achieve it we start from evolutionary strategy to reach typicality as near as possible. The objective function is also defined in terms of accuracy on testing. Over a trained only with selected features multi-layer feed-forward back-propagation neural network. Thus, each result can be compared in terms of its efficiency in a reasonable computer time under given conditions of structure of the testor like the number of features desired in it. In this sense, prediction accuracy plays the roll of fitness function over the evolution strategy. It selects not only the typical features but also the ones that increases the prediction accuracy of the model.

Typical testor research gives an initial subset of features which has discrimination properties. Evolution allows to find this initial subset so when reached, it can be improved using accuracy over prediction as a new fitness function. This is how this three techniques interact.

Considering the important aspects mentioned, in this paper, we propose a method for classifying handwritten number using a small set of features. The small set is obtained using the testors' theory, evolutionary techniques and neural networks. Hence, the main contribution of the proposed approach is to reduce the amount of features used to train and predict over classification models. The main difference with other methods is that this subset of features is developed from a theoretical optimum which is strengthened specially for classification allowing to keep only the most relevant features.

The rest of this paper is organized as follows. In Sect. 2, we formally describe the typical testor for a boolean matrix, multi-layer feed-forward neural networks, and genetic algorithm strategy used to achieve an equal or close enough typical testor with Univariate Marginal Distribution Algorithm's fitness function; the dataset MNIST is also described. Section 3 provides the results and analysis of the study. Finally, conclusions and future works are presented in Sect. 4.

2 Materials and Methods

2.1 Typical Testor

Let U be a collection of objects, that are described by a set of n features and are grouped into l classes. By comparing feature to feature, each pair of objects belonging to different classes, we obtain a matrix $M = [m_{ij}]_{pxn}$ where $m_{ij} \in \{0,1\}$. $m_{ij} = 0$ and $m_{ij} = 1$ means that the objects of pairs denoted by i are similar or different in the feature j, respectively. Let $I = \{i_1, ..., i_p\}$ be the set of the rows of M and $J = \{j_1, ..., j_n\}$ the set of labels of its columns.

Let a and b two rows of M.

Definition 1 [29]: We say that $a < b$ if $\forall i$, $a_i \leq b_i$, and $\exists j$ such that $a_j \neq b_j$.

Definition 2 [29]: a is a basic row of M if there is no other row less than a in M.

Definition 3 [29]: The *basic matrix* of M is the matrix B, only containing all different basic rows of M. Let $T \subseteq J$, B^T be a subset of features obtained from B, eliminating all columns not belonging to the set T.

Definition 4 [15]: Let p be a row of B^T; we say that p is a zero row if it contains only zeros.

Definition 5 [15]: A set $T = \{j_{k_s}, ..., j_{k_s}\} \subseteq J$ is a testor of M if no zero row in B^T exists.

Definition 6 [15]: The feature $x_i \in T$ is called a non-removable feature of T if there exists a row p in B^T such that when the column corresponding to x_i is eliminated from B^T, the remaining row p is a zero row of $B^{T-\{x_i\}}$. Otherwise, x_i is called a removable feature.

Definition 7 [15]: A set $T = \{j_{k_s}, ..., j_{k_s}\} \subseteq J$ is called typical with respect to the M matrix and of the collection U if it is a testor and each feature $x_i \in T$ is a non-removable feature of T.

Proposition 1 [10]: The set of all typical testors of M is equal to the set of all typical testors from the basic matrix B.

Let $\Psi^*(M)$ be the set of all typical testors of the matrix M. According to proposition 1, to search over the set $\Psi^*(M)$ it is very convenient to find the matrix B. Taking into account that B has equal or less number of rows than M, the efficiency of the algorithms should improve with B than with M [10].

2.2 Multi-layer Feed-Forward Back-Propagation Neural Networks (FFBP)

FFBP neural networks have been positioned as the most used type of neural networks [30]. They have been applied in several fields like prediction as in [31], image recognition as in [32], chemistry problems as in [33], among others [34, 35], [36, 37]. A FFBP is built by neurons, which are ordered by layers. The first layer is the input layer and the last is called the output layer. All the layers in between are called hidden layers.

Let Γ be the mapping function that relates for each neuron i a subset $\Gamma(i) \subseteq V$ which consists of all ancestors of the given neuron.

The subset $\Gamma^{-1}(i) \subseteq V$ consists of all predecessors of the ith neuron.

Each neuron in a specific layer is connected with all the neurons of the next layer.

The connection between the ith and jth neuron is characterised by the weight coefficient w_{ij} and the ith neuron by the bias coefficient θ_i.

The weight coefficient measures the degree of significance of the given connection in the neural network.

The output value also called as activity of the ith neuron x_i holds that:

$$x_i = h(\xi_i)$$
$$\xi_i = \theta_i + \sum_{j \in \Gamma^{-1}(i)} w_{ij} x_j$$

where ξ_i is the potential of the ith neuron and function $h(\xi_i)$ is the transfer function or activation function.

The supervised adaptation process varies the threshold coefficients θ_i and weight coefficients w_{ij} to minimize the objective function which relates computed and required output values. The back-propagation algorithm disperses the output error from the output layer through the hidden layers to the input layers so that the connection between the neurons can be recurrently calculated on training in an attempt to minimize the loss function in each training iteration [38].

2.3   Genetic Algorithms (GA)

Genetic Algorithms (GA) are heuristic-based search approaches, specially applicable to optimization problems. These algorithms are useful in practice because of their flexibility over a wide range of problems [39].

GAs begin with an initial population (set of initial points) and select a set of potential points to generate a new population. This operation is repeated until a stop criteria is reached. Thus, it works by creating new populations of points (usually called chromosomes or individuals), by applying a set of genetic operators to the previous population of selected points [19].

Classical genetic operators are selection, crossover, and mutation. Crossover recombines the genetic information contained in the parents of two individuals picked from the selection set, and mutation applies modifications to certain values (alleles) of variables (genes) in the points [40].

2.4   Database MNIST

The MNIST is a database of handwritten numbers. It is a widely used data set in machine learning. Handwriting recognition is a difficult problem and a good test for learning algorithms. The MNIST database has become a standard test. It collects 60,000 training images and 10,000 test images, taken from a previous database, simply called NIST1. These are black-and-white, normalized images centered at 28 pixels per side [41].

2.5   Proposed Method

This section introduces an algorithm that searches for an optimal solution as a subset of features, in terms of efficiency over discrimination between classes of a collection U, based on a desired reduction of the total number of features.

Depending on the density of the elements of each class l of the collection U, n objects of each class is chosen up; this sub-collection is called U'. The first step is to obtain the basic matrix B over the collection $U' \subseteq U$. If needed, previous image prepossessing is recommended to reduce noise. The second step is to remove all the columns of B where all the rows are 0. We do this because this features do not help to discriminate. If a testor contains any of them, we can remove the feature since it will not generate a zero row by removing it. Furthermore, removing columns reduces the complexity on searching over the subspace of all possible combination of features.

Before introducing the Discriminator Construction Algorithm, we present its components. For this purpose, we will divide them in two parts.

Let P be a set of N randomly chosen subsets of features of B of size nxm such that $x_k = \{x_{k1}, ..., x_{km}\} \in P$ with $x_{ki} \in \{0, 1\}$, $k = 1, ..., N$ and $i = 1, ..., m$. x_k is called a *chromosome*.

1) *Genetic Components (Evolutionary Strategy)*

As in [42], we use Univariate Marginal Distribution Algorithm (UMDA). The fitness function is defined as:

$$f(x_k) = \alpha \frac{t(x_k)}{n} + (1 - \alpha) \frac{p(x_k)}{\sum_{v=1}^{m} x_{kv}} \tag{1}$$

We define $T \subseteq x_k$ by eliminating all columns in x_k where $x_{ki} = 0$.
Where, $t(x_k)$ is the number of non-zero rows in B^T, $p(x_k)$ is the number of typical features of B^T and α is a weighting coefficient.
Recall that for any chromosome x_k, $0 \leq f(x_k) \leq 1$ where x_k is a typical testor if $f(x_k) = 1$.
For initial and next generations we used a population size of 20 *chromosomes*.

2) *FFBP Components* The components for FFBP selected for the modeling testor performance during evolution has one input layer, two hidden layers, and one output layer. Let m' be the total number of test cases. We explicit define the accuracy of a chromosome as:

$$g(x_k) = \frac{\delta(x_k)}{m'} \tag{2}$$

where $\delta(x_k)$ is the number of correct predictions of the trained neural network over a common test set. Recall that for any chromosome x_k, $0 \leq g(x_k) \leq 1$ where $f(x_k)$ approaching to 1 means a better performance on discriminating between the classes of U'. Finally, we are able to describe the Discriminator Construction Algorithm (DCA). Figure 1 describes graphically the algorithm. To begin, DCA selects uniformly random a subset of features based on a selected percentage. In this first stage it starts searching for a typical testor by evolution using as fitness function $f(x_k)$. Once the threshold is reached for typical testor search, we change evolution objective function to $g(x_k)$ so the subset returned of typical testor search can be improved on its prediction accuracy. Finally, once prediction accuracy threshold is reached and the subset of features is reported as a solution. This solution is named *discriminator*.

2.6 Experimental Setup

For $U' \subseteq U$ we decided to choose 50 random objects of each class from training MNIST data set proceeding to binarize them to calculate B. With B calculated we removed all the zero columns in it, keeping record of the original indexes.

For the Genetic Components we settled α to 0.2 as we have higher probability of finding testors of large length [42]. We set the maximum number of iterations to 100 and the solution length to 1 as stop conditions. We searched only for one

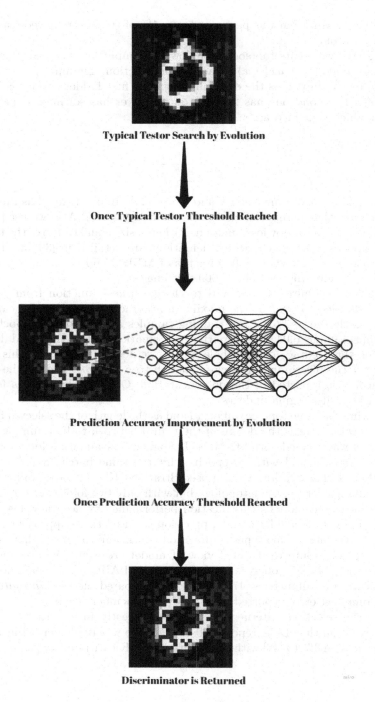

Fig. 1. Discriminator construction algorithm

discriminator. Mutation was performed over 1% of the non-removed features in every generation.

For FFBP we set its topology as follows: the input layer and all the hidden layers has $relu(x) = max\{0, x\}$ as activation function. The input layer has the same number of inputs as the discriminator. The first hidden layer has 52 neurons, and the second one has 26. The output layer has softmax as activation function which is defined as:

$$\sigma(z)_j = \frac{e^{z_j}}{\sum_{k=1}^{K} e^{z_k}}$$

where z is a vector of dimension k and $j = 1, ..., k$. In our case z has dimension 10 as we have that number of classes (digits from 0 to 9). Also we used Sparse Categorical Cross-entropy loss function, set batch size equal to 1/5 of the training samples and used 10 epochs which definitions are detailed in [30, 43]. Training is performed over the whole 60000 images of MNIST and the accuracy value is returned by evaluating over the 10000 test images.

Since DCA requires a threshold to change fitness function from $f(x_k)$ to $g(x_k)$ we decided to set t as the maximum accuracy that the model can reach under a batch size of 1/5 of the training samples and the double epochs than used in $g(x_k)$ minus 0.04. It is important to remark that this threshold does not depend on the accuracy of the whole model, we decided to do it in this way to ensure that the discriminator is close enough to a known value for the model, which in fact is reported in the documentation. Once a solution was found it was translated its original indexes.

Following the same topology of $g(x_k)$ and as the length of the selected features of *discriminator* turns the design of the neural network to be a unique model. This model was trained with Stratified K-Folds cross-validation for 5 folds over the train set each fold with 20 epochs whit the same batch size. For one-vs-all multi-class classification we also used Stratified K-Folds cross-validation for model training over the same topology but with only two folds over the train set [44]. We measured model's classification performance by accuracy, loss, multi-class precision. For calculate model precision we used three approaches: micro, macro and weighted. This types of precision contribute to present how samples and classes contribute to detailed view of model precision. We also measured multi-class log loss [45], one-vs-all ROC curves and AUC scores [46], and one vs all precision vs recall metrics [47]. Finally, we compared the *discriminator* error rate to some test error reported on the MNIST documentation.

Since the selection criteria was developed directly in evolution we choose the first solution that DCA report. All source code was implemented in *Python* language version 3.7.10 [48] with the scikit-learn (SKlearn) library [49] and Keras [50].

3   Results and Discussion

In this section we discuss assessment metrics calculated over the model proposed using the testing data set of the MNIST database. In Fig. 2 we present some evolution steps with the corresponding feature selection for each generation. A total of 50 generations that were needed to build a discriminator with a 21.81% of the total features.

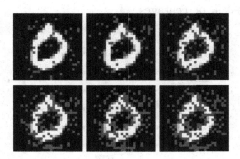

Fig. 2. Generations 0, 10, 20, 30, 40, 50 (With left right up down direction respectively)

3.1   Performance Evaluation

The *discriminator* reported from DCA has a length of 171 features which represents a 21.81% of the total amount of features. By reducing data sets matrices to those only containing the selected features and training a FFBP as described before we end up with the an accuracy on training of 99.65% and a validation accuracy of 97.83% on testing. In addition, the model reported a loss of 0.0191 on training and a loss of 0.081 on testing. Detailed view of this metrics versus epochs for each fold are presented below in Figs. 3 and 4.

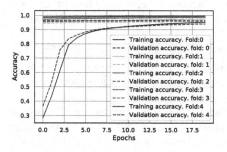

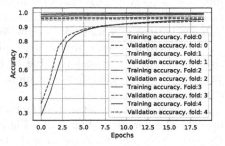

Fig. 3. Accuracy vs Epochs   **Fig. 4.** Loss vs Epochs

As we can see training and validation almost converge later on, even though at the beginning the curves are slightly different. This means any variation between the training and validation curves is going to be statistical rather than systematic so the model fits the data properly. From Fig. 2 and 3 we can also mention that the model is not over-fitted.

The confusion matrix shows how the model performs on classifying between multiple classes. As seen below in Fig. 5, almost the whole diagonal is almost highlighted. This describes a high rate between predicted labels and true labels. Results are presented in percentages.

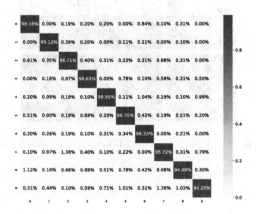

Fig. 5. Confusion matrix for *discriminator* in percentage.

The global prediction shows that in most of the time the model classifies correctly between all the classes but more than that it also shows in which classes it has problem. The errors in prediction of the model with the highest percentages are those made between 4 and 2 classes, 5 and 8 classes, and 8 and 3. However this error is not greater that 0.1% so it is not considered relevant. On the other hand, as mentioned, the diagonal is highlighted which means in most cases every class is correctly identified. Furthermore, every class prediction rate is near 10% of the total amount, and since there are ten classes it also show balance between data and its prediction.

For micro-averaged precision we obtained a precision value of 97.15%. For macro-averaged a precision value of 97.14%. For weighed-average a precision value of 97.15%. Therefore the model is consistent and predicts accurate for distinct classes.

To show in more detail this fact we plotted the ROC curves for all one-vs-all with the corresponding AUC. Figure 6 shows an area under the curve closer to 1 for every one versus all cases. This means that the model has an strong performance in distinguish between all classes. This scenario allows interpreting that those points chosen by discriminator are good enough to be able to clearly classify between all classes. The precision measures the ability of the model

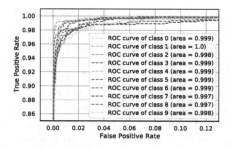

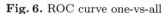

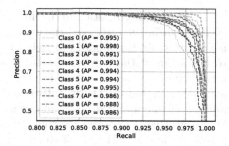

Fig. 6. ROC curve one-vs-all

Fig. 7. Precision versus Recall one-vs-all

to predict each of the classes; since the higher precision and recall scores, the better performance of the model, with an average precision closer to 1, the model presented can distinguish between all classes with precision as seen in Fig. 7.

Finally, we calculate multi-class log loss with a value of 0.2240 which means the model assigns a high probability for each class to predict correctly. For this value in particular the fact of having 10 classes makes the reported value a positive measure.

3.2 Comparison Based on the State of the Art

Despite the fact that there is no other discriminator in the literature, we can evaluate the performance of the model against the error rate reported in the MNIST documentation over other models. The results presented show how the features selected by DCA play an essential roll as in every model the error rate was almost preserved.

Table 1. Comparison of the different classifiers reported on the literature against the error rate of the same model trained only with the features selected by the discriminator

Classifier	Reported test error rate (%) considering all the features	Replicated test error rate (%) considering all the features	Replicated test error rate (%) considering the selected features by the discriminator
Linear classifier (1-layer NN) [51]	12.00%	12.70%	14.23%
K-nearest-neighbors, Euclidean (L2) [51]	5.00%	3.35%	4.62%
40 PCA + quadratic classifier [51]	3.30%	3.74%	5.60%
SVM, Gaussian Kernel [41]	1.40%	3.34%	3.32%
2-layer NN, 800 HU, Cross-Entropy Loss [52]	1.60%	1.86%	2.14%
3-layer NN, 500 + 300 HU, softmax, cross entropy, weight decay [41]	1.53%	1.79%	2.60%

It is possible to notice in Table 1, all models that used the features selected by *discriminator* preserved the error rates in a small range as when all the data is used to train the models; in either case the difference is greater than 2%. Due to the state of the art-based comparisons we are going to focus on test error rate defined as the difference between 1 and the model accuracy. Furthermore, all models based on DCA feature selection, could be considered less complex and faster in computational time, since it selects some features of the entire set. We would like to emphasize that DCA method reported an error rate of only 2.14% while using 21.81% of the features in the two layer neural network which is the closest model from where it was built. Other models such as SVM when trained with the features selected by *discriminator* preserved the error rate with a difference of only 0.02% compared with the same model trained with all the features. We see that this features are enough for truly classify and preserve accuracy and error rates of some reported models.

4 Conclusions and Future Work

This work proposed an algorithm to build a discriminator for a group of classes. With the knowledge of testors, we were able to establish a starting point for an intelligent search. With the evolution strategy, we searched for some features with properties of testors and typicality. Once the features were found, we changed the fitness value to reach the accuracy goal for this reduced featured set. In this point, FFBP played the role of fitness function with their accuracy on predicting. With this strategy, we built a discriminator with 21.81% of the total amount of features. Considering that all calculated assessment metrics and their interpretation, with the discriminator we can build a model that predicts with a precision over 97% and can distinguish between all the classes. Therefore, we conclude that DCA algorithm is able to build a reduced features discriminator for training and testing over MNIST data set.

Furthermore, experimentation shows that the computational cost represented by calculating testors is worth the results; the substantial reduction in the number of variables that can be used confirms that not all the information is necessary when classifying objects. Also, the successful coordination of algorithms, evolutionary, and neural networks is important, as proven by the coherence of the classification results. Finally, interleaving two optimization functions, one for the selection of a discriminator and the other for training the network, sheds light on the way forwards to obtain robust discriminators with a substantially lower number of characteristics.

As potential for future work, we propose: (1) to use typical testors properties to look for a minimum-length optimal discriminator, (2) to explore other feature selection techniques to compare their ability to preserve accuracy over prediction models, as well as (3) to reduce complexity over calculations to search over bigger spaces.

References

1. Mafarja, M.M., Mirjalili, S.: Hybrid binary ant lion optimizer with rough set and approximate entropy reducts for feature selection. Soft Comput. **23**(15), 6249–6265 (2018). https://doi.org/10.1007/s00500-018-3282-y
2. Saxena, A., Saxena, K., Goyal, J.: Hybrid technique based on DBSCAN for selection of improved features for intrusion detection system. In: Rathore, V.S., Worring, M., Mishra, D.K., Joshi, A., Maheshwari, S. (eds.) Emerging Trends in Expert Applications and Security. AISC, vol. 841, pp. 365–377. Springer, Singapore (2019). https://doi.org/10.1007/978-981-13-2285-3_43
3. Wang, M., Chunming, W., Wang, L., Xiang, D., Huang, X.: A feature selection approach for hyperspectral image based on modified ant lion optimizer. Knowl.-Based Syst. **168**, 39–48 (2019)
4. Zhou, H.F., Zhang, Y., Zhang, Y.J., Liu, H.J.: Feature selection based on conditional mutual information: minimum conditional relevance and minimum conditional redundancy. Appl. Intell. **49**(3), 883–896 (2018). https://doi.org/10.1007/s10489-018-1305-0
5. Carrasco-Ochoa, J.A., Martínez-Trinidad, J.F.: Feature selection for natural disaster texts classification using testors. In: Yang, Z.R., Yin, H., Everson, R.M. (eds.) IDEAL 2004. LNCS, vol. 3177, pp. 424–429. Springer, Heidelberg (2004). https://doi.org/10.1007/978-3-540-28651-6_62
6. Pons-Porrata, A., Gil-García, R., Berlanga-Llavori, R.: Using typical testors for feature selection in text categorization. In: Rueda, L., Mery, D., Kittler, J. (eds.) CIARP 2007. LNCS, vol. 4756, pp. 643–652. Springer, Heidelberg (2007). https://doi.org/10.1007/978-3-540-76725-1_67
7. Lopez-Perez, S., Lazo-Cortes, M., Estrada-Garcia, H.: Medical electro-diagnostic using pattern recognition tools. In: Proceedings of the Iberoamerican Workshop on Pattern Recognition (TIARP 1997), pp. 237–244 (1997)
8. Valev, V., Zhuravlev, J.I.: Integer-valued problems of transforming the training tables in k-valued code in pattern recognition problems. Pattern Recogn. **24**(4), 283–288 (1991)
9. Alba-Cabrera, E., Godoy-Claderon, S., Ibarra-Fiallo, J.: Generating synthetic test matrices as a benchmark for the computational behavior of typical testor-finding algorithms. Pattern Recogn. Lett. **80**, 46–51 (2016)
10. Alba-Cabrera, E., Lazo-Coréz, M., Ruiz-Shulcloper, J.: An overview of the concept of testor. Pattern Recogn. J. **34**, 753–762 (2000)
11. Valev, V., Asaithambi, A.: On computational complexity of non-reducible descriptors, pp. 208–211 (2003)
12. Alganza, Y.S., Porrata, A.P.: Lex: a new algorithm for calculating typical testors. Revista Ciencias Matematicas, Cuba **21**(1), 85–95 (2003)
13. Alba-Cabrera, E., Ibarra-Fiallo, J., Godoy-Calderon, S., Cervantes-Alonso, F.: YYC: a fast performance incremental algorithm for finding typical testors. In: Bayro-Corrochano, E., Hancock, E. (eds.) CIARP 2014. LNCS, vol. 8827, pp. 416–423. Springer, Cham (2014). https://doi.org/10.1007/978-3-319-12568-8_51
14. Asaithambi, A., Valev, V.: Construction of all non-reducible descriptors. Pattern Recogn. **37**(9), 1817–1823 (2004)
15. Piza-Davila, I., Sanchez-Diaz, G., Lazo-Cortes, M.S., Rizo-Dominguez, L.: A CUDA-based hill-climbing algorithm to find irreducible testors from a training matrix. Pattern Recogn. Lett. **95**, 22–28 (2017)

16. Lias-Rodriguez, A., Sanchez-Diaz, G.: An algorithm for computing typical testors based on elimination of gaps and reduction of columns. Int. J. Pattern Recogn. Artif. Intell. **27**(08), 1350022 (2013)
17. Sanchez-Diaz, G., Piza-Davila, I., Lazo-Cortes, M., Mora-Gonzalez, M., Salinas-Luna, J.: A fast implementation of the CT_{EXT} algorithm for the testor property identification. In: Sidorov, G., Hernández Aguirre, A., Reyes García, C.A. (eds.) MICAI 2010. LNCS (LNAI), vol. 6438, pp. 92–103. Springer, Heidelberg (2010). https://doi.org/10.1007/978-3-642-16773-7_8
18. Piza-Dávila, I., Sánchez-Díaz, G., Lazo-Cortés, M.S., Villalón-Turrubiates, I.: An algorithm for computing minimum-length irreducible testors. IEEE Access **8**, 56312–56320 (2020)
19. Diaz-Sanchez, G., et al.: Typical testors generation based on an evolutionary algorithm. In: Yin, H., Wang, W., Rayward-Smith, V. (eds.) IDEAL 2011. LNCS, vol. 6936, pp. 58–65. Springer, Heidelberg (2011). https://doi.org/10.1007/978-3-642-23878-9_8
20. Piza-Davila, I., Sanchez-Diaz, G., Aguirre-Salado, C.A., Lazo-Cortes, M.S.: A parallel hill-climbing algorithm to generate a subset of irreducible testors. Appl. Intell. **42**(4), 622–641 (2014). https://doi.org/10.1007/s10489-014-0606-1
21. Sanchez-Diaz, G., et al.: An evolutionary algorithm with acceleration operator to generate a subset of typical testors. Pattern Recogn. Lett. **41**, 34–42 (2014)
22. Gallegos, A., Torres, D., Álvarez, F., Soto, A.T.: Feature subset selection and typical testors applied to breast cancer cells. Res. Comput. Sci. **121**, 151–163 (2016)
23. Ortíz-Posadas, M.R., Martínez-Trinidad, J.F., Ruiz-Shulcloper, J.: A new approach to differential diagnosis of diseases. Int. J. Biomed. Comput. **40**(3), 179–185 (1996)
24. Becht, E., et al.: Dimensionality reduction for visualizing single-cell data using UMAP. Nat. Biotechnol. **37**(1), 38–44 (2019)
25. Fernandez, D., Gonzalez, C., Mozos, D., Lopez, S.: FPGA implementation of the principal component analysis algorithm for dimensionality reduction of hyperspectral images. J. Real-Time Image Proc. **16**(5), 1395–1406 (2019)
26. Lazo-Cortés, M.S., Martínez-Trinidad, J.F., Carrasco-Ochoa, J.A., Sanchez-Diaz, G.: On the relation between rough set reducts and typical testors. Inf. Sci. **294**, 152–163 (2015)
27. Sayed, G.I., Hassanien, A.E., Azar, A.T.: Feature selection via a novel chaotic crow search algorithm. Neural Comput. Appl. **31**(1), 171–188 (2017). https://doi.org/10.1007/s00521-017-2988-6
28. Singh, D., Singh, B.: Hybridization of feature selection and feature weighting for high dimensional data. Appl. Intell. **49**(4), 1580–1596 (2018). https://doi.org/10.1007/s10489-018-1348-2
29. Ruiz-Shulcloper, J., Soto, A., Fuentes, A.: A characterization of the typical testor concept in terms of a notable set of columns. Rev Cien Mat (in Spanish) **1**(2), 123–134 (1980)
30. Haykin, S.: Neural Networks - A Comprehensive Foundation (2008)
31. Weytjens, H., Lohmann, E., Kleinsteuber, M.: Cash flow prediction: MLP AND LSTM compared to ARIMA and Prophet. Electron. Commer. Res. **21**, 371–391 (2019)
32. Dosovitskiy, A., et al.: An image is worth 16 × 16 words: transformers for image recognition at scale. arXiv preprint arXiv:2010.11929 (2020)
33. Abdi-Khanghah, M., Bemani, A., Naserzadeh, Z., Zhang, Z.: Prediction of solubility of n-alkanes in supercritical CO_2 using RBF-ANN and MLP-ANN. J. CO_2 Util. **25**, 108–119 (2018)

34. Ghorbani, M.A., Deo, R.C., Karimi, V., Yaseen, Z.M., Terzi, O.: Implementation of a hybrid MLP-FFA model for water level prediction of Lake Egirdir, Turkey. Stoch. Env. Res. Risk Assess. **32**(6), 1683–1697 (2018)
35. Orrù, P.F., Zoccheddu, A., Sassu, L., Mattia, C., Cozza, R., Arena, S.: Machine learning approach using MLP and SVM algorithms for the fault prediction of a centrifugal pump in the oil and gas industry. Sustainability **12**(11), 4776 (2020)
36. Jia, X., et al.: Mapping soil pollution by using drone image recognition and machine learning at an arsenic-contaminated agricultural field. Environ. Pollut. **270**, 116281 (2021)
37. Auer, A., Strauss, M.T., Strauss, S., Jungmann, R.: nanoTRON: a Picasso module for MLP-based classification of super-resolution data. Bioinformatics **36**(11), 3620–3622 (2020)
38. Svozil, D., Kvasnicka, V., Pospichal, J.: Introduction to multi-layer feed-forward neural networks. Chemom. Intell. Lab. Syst. **39**(1), 43–62 (1997)
39. Kramer, O.: Genetic Algorithms. Springer, New York (2017). https://doi.org/10.1007/978-1-4471-0577-0
40. Muhlenbein, H., Manhnig, T., Ochoa-Rodriguez, A.: Schemata, distributions and graphical models in evolutionary optimization. J. Heuristics **5**(2), 215–247 (1999)
41. LeCun, Y., Cortes, C.: MNIST handwritten digit database (2010)
42. Eduardo, A.-C., Roberto, S., Alberto, O.-R., Manuel, L.-C.: Finding typical testors by using an evolutionary strategy. In: Proceedings of the 5th Ibero American Symposium on Pattern Recognition, p. 267 (2000)
43. Liu, W., Wen, Y., Zhiding, Yu., Yang, M.: Large-margin softmax loss for convolutional neural networks. ICML **2**(3), 7 (2016)
44. Ramezan, C.A., Warner, T.A., Maxwell, A.E.: Evaluation of sampling and cross-validation tuning strategies for regional-scale machine learning classification. Remote Sens. **11**(2), 185 (2019)
45. Hazan, E., Kale, S.: Newtron: an efficient bandit algorithm for online multiclass prediction. In: NIPS, vol. 11, pp. 891–899. Citeseer (2011)
46. Wandishin, M.S., Mullen, S.J.: Multiclass ROC analysis. Weather Forecast. **24**(2), 530–547 (2009)
47. Powers, D.M.W.: Evaluation: from precision, recall and F-measure to ROC, informedness, markedness and correlation. arXiv preprint arXiv:2010.16061 (2020)
48. Van Rossum, G., Drake, F.L.: Python 3 Reference Manual. CreateSpace, Scotts Valley (2009)
49. Pedregosa, F., et al.: Scikit-Learn: machine learning in Python. J. Mach. Learn. Res. **12**, 2825–2830 (2011)
50. Chollet, F., et al.: Keras (2015). https://github.com/fchollet/keras
51. LeCun, Y., Bottou, L., Bengio, Y., Haffner, P.: Gradient-based learning applied to document recognition. Proc. IEEE **86**(11), 2278–2324 (1998)
52. Simard, P.Y., Steinkraus, D., Platt, J.C., et al.: Best practices for convolutional neural networks applied to visual document analysis. In: ICDAR, vol. 3. Citeseer (2003)

Land Cover Classification Using CNN and Semantic Segmentation: A Case of Study in Antioquia, Colombia

Juan C. González-Vélez[✉][iD], Juan D. Martinez-Vargas,
and Maria C. Torres-Madronero[iD]

MIRP Lab - Instituto Tecnológico Metropolitano - ITM, Medellín, Colombia
juancgonzalez@itm.edu.co
https://www.itm.edu.co

Abstract. Human pressures on the environment have drastically accelerated in the last decades, risking biodiversity and ecosystem services. Monitoring the locations and distributions of Land use and land cover change (LULCC) is vital. In Colombia, Corine land cover maps are the primary source of information for researchers and governmental institutes responsible for managing and conserving natural areas. However, these maps are made mainly by a visual classification of multi-temporal satellite imagery. This paper presents an adapted methodology for the land cover classification in a highly intervened area in Colombia using state-of-the-art convolutional networks with a semantic segmentation approach with transfer learning techniques. We tested two decoders (Unet and PSPNet) with five different architectures (Resnet 18, 50, 101, 152, and inceptionresnetv2). The tests showed that the Unet encoder with Resnet 18 had the highest Jaccard index (mIoU = 0.806) and a pixel accuracy of 0.933 on the validation dataset. These results improve the previous attempts to make a deep learning-based model for the land cover classification in the Colombian context. This ongoing work is set to evaluate Deep learning-based algorithms to analyze multi-temporal LULCC in Colombia using high-resolution imagery. Developing a semi-supervised algorithm infused with SAR imagery for LULCC classification is expected to contribute to this work.

Keywords: Land cover classification · Deep learning · Unet · PSPNET · Semantic segmentation

1 Introduction

Human pressures on the environment have drastically accelerated in the last decades, risking biodiversity and providing goods and ecosystem services [29]. Direct impacts of human activities on natural systems include habitat loss and degradation [6], fragmentation [12], deforestation [14], extinctions of species[8]. Because of this, it is imperative to understand the spatio-temporal relationships between natural and anthropogenic changes in ecosystems, necessary for

© Springer Nature Switzerland AG 2022
F. R. Narváez et al. (Eds.): SmartTech-IC 2021, CCIS 1532, pp. 306–317, 2022.
https://doi.org/10.1007/978-3-030-99170-8_22

planning, managing, and monitoring natural resources. Studies of land use and land cover change require the adequate characterization of different natural vegetation types.

Monitoring the locations and distributions of Land use and land cover change (LULCC) is vital. Remote sensing has revolutionized the ability to characterize and monitor urban land change. Data and information about changes in urban land structure, form and extent that were once only available through ground surveys and traditional mapping techniques are now routinely collected and produced through a constellation of government and commercial airborne and satellite sensors [25]. In recent years, it has become apparent that there are growing user communities studying LULCC, coming from three broad categories: 1) scientists and researchers, 2) policy- and decision-makers, and 3) practitioners and the public. These communities operate at different geographic and temporal scales and thus require different types of land change information [25].

In Colombia, the LULCC has been mainly studied by the Institute of Hydrology, Meteorology, and Environmental Studies (IDEAM), a scientific institute of the Ministry of Environment and Sustainable Development. The IDEAM has developed a series of CORINE land cover maps for the geography of Colombia (2000-2002, 2005-2009, and 2010-2012). These maps are the primary source of information for researchers and other governmental institutes responsible for managing and conserving the country's natural areas. The CORINE Land Cover methodology used by the IDEAM relies on the visual classification of multitemporal satellite imagery, making this approach highly costly in terms of workforce and time.

Remotely sensed datasets have proven to be more helpful, economical, and convenient. They also can be used for LULC mapping and assessment. Data integration of remote sensing and GIS have been used for LULC classification. GIS data, i.e., census data, topography, and GPS points, have been combined with remote sensing images for LULC classification. Traditionally, GIS environments have been used for LULC classification and mapping based on image interpretation [21].

Several computational methods seek to improve the performance and accuracy of land cover classification from remotely sensed datasets. Some of the previously used methods for LULCC include but are not limited to decision trees [26], Markov chains [13], image differencing, and change of the analysis vector spectral signatures and vegetation indices [3]. However, convolutional neural networks have proven to surpass the results obtained by machine learning techniques for satellite image classification. For instance, in [17] the authors propose to use convRNN to tackle land cover classification from a Sentinel-2 modelling the task as semantic segmentation.

Several studies reveal that the classification capability of remotely sensed data depends on the types of input data and landscape complexity. Many publications have explored the robustness and achievements of classifiers fitted with different datasets. However, the most appropriate classifier for mapping is still in question. Popular supervised classifiers include Maximum Likelihood Classifier (MLC), Spectral Angle Mapper (SAM), Support Vector Machine (SVM),

Random Forest (RF), Decision Tree (DT), Minimum Distance (MD), etc. and unsupervised classifiers (k-means and ISODATA). Usually categorized into pixel-based (MLC, SVM) algorithms and object-based methods [23].

The performance of the classifiers depends on the number of user-defined parameters, the number of training samples, and the time for classification accuracy. Several techniques such as MLC, SAM, SVM, ANN, decision tree have been used on Landsat TM, data to assess and evaluate the LULC cover [9,28]. Based on their results, researchers suggested that both ANN and SVM outperform MLC on ETM [9]. SVM performed well with TM data while ANN performed well against SVM, MLC with TM/ETM [16].

This paper presents an adapted methodology for the land cover classification in a highly intervened area in Colombia, using state-of-the-art convolutional networks. This methodology differs from previous methodologies by using transfer learning techniques. An evaluation of different state-of-the-art architectures for a semantic segmentation approach is included.

2   Methods

2.1   Study Area and Remote Sensing Information

The study area is approximately 1500 (km^2) including La Ceja, El Carmen de Viboral, La Union, Guarne, El Retiro, and Rionegro in the San Nicolas Valley (Colombia). This region presents temperatures between 9 to 24C. It is characterized by secondary vegetation areas with agricultural mosaics, pastures, forest plantations, and open forests in constant changes due to the urban sprawl. According to the Green Growth and Climate Compatible Development Plan for Eastern Antioquia, the area has high soil productivity that allows it to be considered a food pantry; various productive sectors (energy, industry, transportation) contribute significantly to the national GDP (Zapata et al. 2017).

To further improve the amount of information available from the different land cover patterns present in the study area, a set of high-resolution imagery was obtained for an area of approximately 9000 square kilometres between the municipalities of Yarumal, Betulia, Abejorral, and El Santuario. This vast area includes many thermal floors and a great diversity of land cover patterns resulting from the changes in Altitude. The images were obtained through the Planet explorer platform (Planet Team 2017). These were captured by the Rapid Eye MSI constellation between January 2013 and April 2014. The selected images have 5 spectral bands (Blue, Red, Green, Red Edge and NIR) and were downloaded with the radiometric, sensor and geometric correction. These images were sampled with a 256 × 256 kernel, resulting in 4762 individual images with a spatial resolution of 5 m/px.

We increased the dimensionality of the images, including multispectral indexes such as Normalized Difference Vegetation Index - NDVI [19], and Green Normalized Difference Vegetation Index - GNDVI [11]. Finally, we used the first level of the IDEAM Land Cover map for 2012 as the ground truth for the training phase of our convolutional networks. This level has five classes: urban areas, open plains, forests, coastal areas, and water surfaces. The labels defined by the IDEAM institute have been thoroughly validated by on-site visits, as well as by UAV photographs were taken in randomly selected areas [1].

2.2 Semantic Segmentation Approach

Semantic segmentation is the task of determining a semantic label (land-cover or land-use class) to every pixel of an image through a computational model. Most state-of-the-art methods have relied on supervised classifiers trained on specific hand-crafted feature sets (appearance descriptors when processing high-resolution data). Some authors have used autoencoders trained to reconstruct PCA-compressed hyperspectral signals, then optimize the neural networks by a softmax loss stacked on top of the encoders, providing the final classification of the pixels [4]. Other authors have trained a sparse convolutional autoencoder to perform object detection in remote sensing images [10], among other applications applied to remote sensing.

Several convolutional neural networks (CNN) architectures have been developed to perform segmentation tasks for different applications in recent years. In this work, we use a state-of-the-art architecture proposed by [35], iin which a feature map of the last convolutional layer is extracted. Then, a pyramid parsing module is applied to harvest different subregion representations. The pyramid parsing module is followed by upsampling and concatenating layers to form the final feature representation, which carries local and global context information. Finally, the representation is fed into a convolution layer to get the final per-pixel prediction. An overview of the PSPNet proposed by [35] can be seen in Fig. 1.

On the other hand, the U- Neural Network (U-Net) is a convolutional neural network proposed by [27]. It was initially proposed for segmentation tasks of biomedical images; however, it has proven helpful for a wide range of different areas. The Unet Architecture is characterized by an initial set of 3×3 convolutions with downsampling through 2×2 max pool operations, increasing the number of dimensions of the output image. Then, an upsampling phase allows the network to propagate context information to higher resolution layers. The network does not have any fully connected layers and only uses the valid part of Each convolution, i.e., the segmentation map only contains the pixels, for which the entire context is available in the input image ([27]. An overview of the Unet can be seen in Fig. 2.

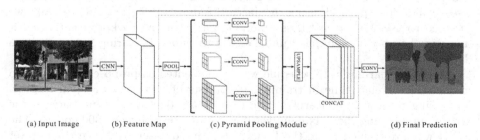

(a) Input Image   (b) Feature Map   (c) Pyramid Pooling Module   (d) Final Prediction

Fig. 1. Overview of the PSPNet proposed by [35]

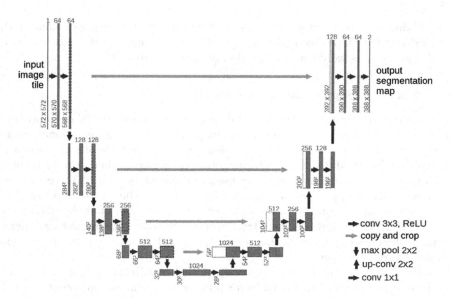

Fig. 2. Overview of the Unet proposed by [27]

2.3 Implementation

Each of these architectures is implemented using the Segmentation Models library [34]. This library is implemented both in PyTorch and TensorFlow ecosystems. It consists of a pipeline made of an encoder, also called a feature extractor, which consists of an initial down-sampling section; a decoder, an up sampling convolutional structure of predefined dimensions fusing the extracted features, and finally, a segmentation head which reduces the number of channels and up to sample the ground truth mask to preserve input-output spatial resolution identity. This library also enables pre-trained encoders with publicly available image databases to perform transfer learning [32,33].

We compared five architectures to identify the best encoder for land cover classification: Resnet 18, Resnet 50, Resnet 101, Resnet 152, and inceptionresnetv2. The decoder was fixed into a simple array of 5 convolutional layers with depths of 16, 32, 64, 128, 256 square pixels [15,30]. Each of these architectures is used as the segmentation pipeline's encoder and validated through a cross-validation approach using the Jaccard Index - mIoU [18]. Additionally, we decided to use the Jaccard Loss function metric for the backpropagation optimization because of an implicit unbalance of the labels favouring the open plains label.

A 1Cycle learning rate schedule was implemented as proposed by [29,21] to reduce convergence time in training. It consists of two steps of equal lengths, one going from a lower learning rate to a higher one, then going back to the minimum, defining the maximum learning rate to 1e-3 between 300 epochs. The CNN was pre-trained using the ImageNet image dataset [7]. Since the dataset contains RGB 3 channel images, the first three dimensions of the CNN were fitted to the dataset, the rest of the dimensions were randomly initiated.

Due to the different depths of each CNN, different VRAM requirements were needed for the training. Each CNN was fitted with the maximum number of images per training batch. The minimum batch size was 40 images with 256×256 pixels and seven depth layers.

The experiments were implemented using an NVIDIA GTX 3060 GPU with 12 GB of GPU RAM and took between 8 and 25 h to train each CNN. Finally, it is known that Deep learning requires large amounts of data and significant computation times to bring satisfactory results [24]. This is particularly difficult for remote sensing data since there is a limited number of sensors and images. We implemented data augmentation techniques during the training of the neural networks.

A cross-validation methodology was applied to ensure a good fit from the algorithm. Our cross-validation approach split our image dataset into three groups: train, test, and validation datasets. We then load the train images and augment them using a Horizontal flip and Gaussian Filter, yielding 7286 images. The algorithm does not know which is the original image and the noisy image.

3 Results

Table 1 presents the overall accuracies, mIoU indexes, and training time for the encoders PSPNET and UNET and the five architectures: Resnet 18, Resnet 50, Resnet 101, Resnet 152, and inceptionresnetv2.

Table 1 shows that the performance of the models is directly correlated with the depth of the CNN, except for the Unet CNN with the Resnet 18 encoder. This last architecture obtained the best result for the least depth encoder architecture. Unet architecture and the inceptionv4 encoder presented the highest performance in the test set, yielding a mean accuracy of 0.91 and a Jaccard index of 0.812. Figure 3 shows the Jaccard index yielded by the Unet CNN with the inceptionv4 encoder during the training phase.

Table 1. Experimental results

Encoder type	Encoder	Val Acc	Train Acc	Test acc	Train mIoU	Val mIoU	Test mIoU
PSPNET	Resnet 18	0.892	0.899	0.881	0.727	0.694	0.681
PSPNET	Resnet 50	0.883	0.886	0.871	0.701	0.688	0.657
PSPNET	Resnet 101	0.888	0.896	0.877	0.727	0.754	0.669
PSPNET	Resnet 152	0.905	0.923	0.906	0.792	0.773	0.729
PSPNET	inceptionresnetv2	0.915	0.934	0.911	0.8	0.791	0.75
Unet	Resnet 18	0.934	0.973	0.933	0.843	0.806	0.804
Unet	Resnet 50	0.917	0.944	0.9154	0.77	0.789	0.765
Unet	Resnet 101	0.908	0.904	0.947	0.769	0.739	0.746
Unet	Resnet 152	0.916	0.949	0.917	0.788	0.794	0.774
Unet	**inceptionv4**	**0.92**	**0.936**	**0.91**	**0.778**	**0.793**	**0.812**

Finally, Fig. 4 presents the performance of the Unet CNN with the inceptionv4 encoder compared against the ground truth. We can note that the model fits the general form of the label area, especially detecting borders and the general shape of the objects (e.g. Forests, rivers, etc.). It is worth noting that the mIoU value reported in Table 1 is the mean mIoU reported for the whole test dataset, composed of 477 images.

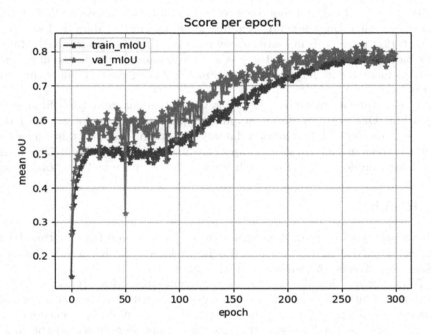

Fig. 3. Jaccard index yielded by the Unet CNN with the inceptionv4 encoder during the Training phase

It is important to note that the IDEAM Land Cover map contains errors, as shown in Fig. 5 in which the purple area at the right is classified as an open area and not as a forest. However, CNN learns the general pattern of each label and classify it by that patter, making a visually acceptable segmentation, although in terms of the Jaccard index, even if the CNN is doing a good classification the mIoU is not perfect.

4   Discussion

This research has successfully adapted a land cover classification methodology for a highly intervened area in the Colombian Andes region. This methodology uses a state-of-the-art deep learning architecture previously trained with the ImageNet dataset. This methodology has yielded the highest accuracy for the currently known DL experiments for the Colombian region [20,22]. Likewise, it has achieved higher accuracy than other works presented with ML techniques. i.e., [5] presented SVM, RF and KNN approaches which in terms of overall accuracy have been surpassed by the proposed DL models. Additionally, this work has been done with a limited amount of images, which are set to be further increased in future iterations, which will surely impact positively the performance of the trained models.

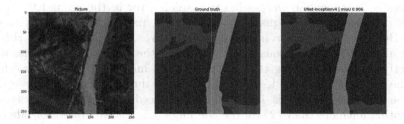

Fig. 4. Ground truth comparison against the predicted mask. Purple: open areas, Teal: forests, Yellow: water surface (Color figure online)

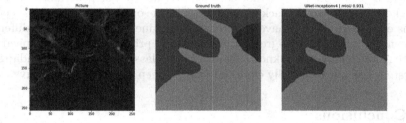

Fig. 5. Ground truth comparison against the predicted mask. Purple: open areas, Teal: forests, Yellow: water surface (Color figure online)

The described methodology took up to 28 h to complete in terms of computational costs. We consider this a cost-efficient methodology, especially considering that this could be replicated easily using cloud-based solutions for scalability. Furthermore, we can see in Table 1 that the time needed for the training of each CNN is affected by the depth of its architecture, especially in the case of the Unet CNN, which presents a strong correlation between time and the number of layers present in the CNN $r^2 = 0.7526$, which is expected behavior of this type of architectures.

Additionally, in Fig. 3, we see the Jaccard index yielded by the inceptionv4 for each training epoch. We can see a non-overfitted behavior, having close values between train and validation mIoU values. This also shows that our validation of splitting data into three groups adequately fits the CNN, ensuring the validation data is completely unknown to the model. Finally, regarding the model's performance, in Fig. 4, we present the results of a classification performed on a highly intervened area with the presence of dry forest. This area usually presents challenges to machine-learning-based models due to the area's dry conditions, which are similar in terms of reflectance to a fragmented forest or an open area [2]. Our results show that CNN has a good performance, as shown by the 0.906 Jaccard index, even in the difficult conditions for the classification.

The good fit of the model is also shown in Fig. 5. In it, we can see the ground truth comparison of a conserved area near the Guatapé hydroelectric reservoir. We wanted to show this image due to a small error in the ground truth label image. The ground truth image shows the right part of the image as an open area. However, at a closer inspection of the area, it is visible that the area is populated by a continuous forest bordering the reservoir, which the model correctly classifies, showing that the predictions made by it are not overfitted, but the result of a pattern learned by the model during the fitting phase.

The training dataset is inherently unbalanced towards open areas label, accounting for more than 72% of the training area, followed by forest label with 16% of the pixels, followed by urban area label with 10% and, lastly, the water surfaces with 2% of the total pixels, which must be taken into account for the future works made in this study area.

Although this experiment uses images from warm areas with the presence of Tropical Dry Forest, this was not considered. Since it was generalized as Forest label, however, due to the lack of reflectance in the optical bands of the spectrum of this ecosystem, it may have resulted in noise due to the significant difference between the high-altitude-green forest and the primarily brown Tropical Dry forest. Additionally, we acknowledge that the classification of this endangered ecosystem has not been fully explored from a Deep Learning perspective.

5   Conclusions

The objective of this paper has been successfully achieved, having systematically revised the proposed architectures of deep learning models with its corresponding results by using transfer learning techniques from RGB databases such as ImageNet. The results presented in this work have improved those presented previously by comparable methodologies [20].

Due to the high amount of data being constantly captured by remote sensing satellites, deep learning models are emerging as an alternative for the classification of LULC, surpassing the performance of machine learning models. However, due to its unique geography and atmospheric conditions, Colombia is usually covered by clouds, reducing the number of image samples available for training these algorithms [31]. Because of that, Synthetic aperture radar (SAR) imagery should be further explored as a complementary tool to mix with optical sensors. However, the interaction of this kind of mixed dataset has not been sufficiently explored.

Although the results are promising, this work is set to improve the results by mixing high-resolution optical images with Synthetic aperture radar (SAR) imagery for the study area, as presented by [5]. which is considered the future of this work. Additionally, semi-supervised techniques will be evaluated to reduce the number of images needed for the training phase.

The methodology presented in this work has limitations, such as excluding clouds from the training images and a time-consuming training phase that can exponentially increase by introducing more data. A low cost-effective labeling method requires a human-based classification and a natural imbalance in class labels due to the proliferation in the study area of open areas. These limitations are set to be resolved in future works by including clouds, recurring to time-optimized methods for training such as GPU-parallelization techniques, the design and implementation of a semi-supervised technique for the classification of land cover based on deep learning algorithms, and the use of synthetic balance methods such as ADASYN and SMOTE.

Acknowledgments. This work was financed with resources from the Patrimonio autónomo fondo nacional de financiamiento para ciencia, tecnología e innovación Francisco José de Caldas through RC 80740-475-2020, supported by the Ministerio de Ciencia, Tecnologia e Innovación - Minciencias, Instituto Tecnológico Metropolitano - ITM, Corporación Colombiana de Investigación Agropecuaria - AGROSAVIA, and BLACK-SQUARE S.A.S.

References

1. METODOLOGÍA CORINE LAND COVER - IDEAM (2021). http://www.ideam. gov.co/web/ecosistemas/metodologia-corine-land-cover. Accessed 15 Nov 2021
2. Andrade, J., Cunha, J., Silva, J., Rufino, I., Galvão, C.: Evaluating single and multi-date landsat classifications of land-cover in a seasonally dry tropical forest. Remote Sens. Appl. Soc. Environ. **22**, 100515 (2021)
3. Backoulou, G.F., Elliott, N.C., Giles, K.L., Mirik, M.: Processed multispectral imagery differentiates wheat crop stress caused by greenbug from other causes. Comput. Electronics in Agriculture **115**, 34–39 (2015)
4. Chen, Y., Lin, Z., Zhao, X., Wang, G., Gu, Y.: Deep learning-based classification of hyperspectral data. IEEE J. Sel. Topics Appl. Earth Observ. Remote Sens. **7**, 2094–2107 (2014). https://doi.org/10.1109/JSTARS.2014.2329330
5. Clerici, N., Valbuena Calderón, C.A., Posada, J.M.: Fusion of sentinel-1a and sentinel-2a data for land cover mapping: a case study in the lower Magdalena region, Colombia. J. Maps **13**(2), 718–726 (2017). https://www.doi.org/ 10.1080/17445647.2017.1372316. https://www.tandfonline.com/doi/pdf/10.1080/ 17445647.2017.1372316?needAccess=true
6. Crooks, K.R., Burdett, C.L., Theobald, D.M., Rondinini, C., Boitani, L.: Global patterns of fragmentation and connectivity of mammalian carnivore habitat. Philos. Trans. R. Soc. B: Biol. Sci. **366**, 2642–2651 (2011)
7. Deng, J., Dong, W., Socher, R., Li, L., Kai, L., Li, F.F.: ImageNet: a large-scale hierarchical image database, pp. 248–255. https://doi.org/10.1109/CVPR.2009. 5206848
8. Dirzo, R., Young, H.S., Galetti, M., Ceballos, G., Isaac, N.J.B., Collen, B.: Defaunation in the anthropocene. Science **345**, 401 (2014)

9. Dixon, B., Candade, N.: Multispectral landuse classification using neural networks and support vector machines: one or the other, or both? Int. J. Remote Sens. **29**(4), 1185–1206 (2008)
10. Firat, O., Can, G., Vural, F.T.Y.: Representation learning for contextual object and region detection in remote sensing, pp. 3708–3713. https://doi.org/10.1109/ICPR.2014.637
11. Gitelson, A.A., Kaufman, Y.J., Merzlyak, M.N.: Use of a green channel in remote sensing of global vegetation from EOS-MODIS. Remote Sens. Environ. **58**, 289–298 (1996)
12. Haddad, N.M., et al.: Habitat fragmentation and its lasting impact on earth's ecosystems. Sci. Adv. **1**, e1500052 (2015)
13. Halmy, M.W.A., Gessler, P.E., Hicke, J.A., Salem, B.B.: Land use/land cover change detection and prediction in the north-western coastal desert of Egypt using Markov-CA. Appl. Geogr. **63**, 101–112 (2015)
14. Hansen, M.C., et al.: High-resolution global maps of 21st-century forest cover change. Science **342**, 850–853 (2013)
15. He, K., Zhang, X., Ren, S., Sun, J.: Deep residual learning for image recognition. IEEE (2016). https://doi.org/10.1109/CVPR.2016.90
16. Huang, C., Davis, L.S., Townshend, J.R.G.: An assessment of support vector machines for land cover classification. Int. J. Remote Sens. **23**(4), 725–749 (2002)
17. Ienco, D., Interdonato, R., Gaetano, R., Minh, D.H.T.: Combining Sentinel-1 and Sentinel-2 satellite image time series for land cover mapping via a multi-source deep learning architecture. ISPRS J. Photogrammetry Remote Sens. **158**, 11–22 (2019)
18. Jaccard, P.: The distribution of the flora in the alpine zone.1. New Phytol. 11, 37–50 (1912). https://doi.org/10.1111/j.1469-8137.1912.tb05611.x
19. Jackson, R.D.: Spectral indices in n-space. Remote Sens. Environ. **13**, 409–421 (1983)
20. Londoño, A.S.S., Jimenez, A., Castro-Franco, M., Cruz-Roa, A.: Clasificación y mapeo automático de coberturas del suelo en imágenes satelitales utilizando redes neuronales convolucionales. ORINOQUIA **21**, 64–75 (2017). http://www.scielo.org.co/scielo.php?script=sci_arttext&pid=S0121-37092017000300064&nrm=iso
21. Lillesand, T., Lillesand, T., Kiefer, R., Kiefer, R.: Remote Sensing and Image Interpretation. Wiley (1994). https://books.google.com.co/books?id=BU3uAAAAMAAJ
22. Martínez, P.C.M.: Análisis de cambio en la cobertura boscosa en el municipio de cartagena del chairá a través de imágenes satelitales de 2016 y 2019 por medio de algoritmos de machine learning (2020). http://hdl.handle.net/10654/37354
23. Pandey, P.C., Koutsias, N., Petropoulos, G.P., Srivastava, P.K., Ben Dor, E.: Land use/land cover in view of earth observation: data sources, input dimensions, and classifiers-a review of the state of the art. Geocarto Int. **36**(9), 957–988 (2021)
24. Rani, K.S., Kumari, M., Singh, V.B., Sharma, M.: Deep learning with big data: an emerging trend, pp. 93–101. https://doi.org/10.1109/ICCSA.2019.00005
25. Reba, M., Seto, K.C.: A systematic review and assessment of algorithms to detect, characterize, and monitor urban land change. Remote Sens. Environ. **242**, 111739 (2020)
26. Rodriguez-Galiano, V.F., Ghimire, B., Rogan, J., Chica-Olmo, M., Rigol-Sanchez, J.P.: An assessment of the effectiveness of a random forest classifier for land-cover classification. ISPRS J. Photogrammetry Remote Sens. **67**, 93–104 (2012)
27. Ronneberger, O., Fischer, P., Brox, T.: U-Net: convolutional networks for biomedical image segmentation (2015). http://arxiv.org/abs/1505.04597

28. Srivastava, P.K., Han, D., Rico-Ramirez, M.A., Bray, M., Islam, T.: Selection of classification techniques for land use/land cover change investigation. Adv. Space Res. **50**(9), 1250–1265 (2012)
29. Steffen, W., Broadgate, W., Deutsch, L., Gaffney, O., Ludwig, C.: The trajectory of the Anthropocene: the great acceleration. Anthropocene Rev. **2**, 81–98 (2015)
30. Szegedy, C., Ioffe, S., Vanhoucke, V., Alemi, A.: Inception-v4, inception-resnet and the impact of residual connections on learning. arXiv (2016). https://arxiv.org/pdf/1602.07261v2.pdf
31. Sánchez-Cuervo, A.M., Aide, T.M., Clark, M.L., Etter, A.: Land cover change in Colombia: surprising forest recovery trends between 2001 and 2010. PLOS ONE **7**(8), e43943 (2012). https://www.doi.org/10.1371/journal.pone.0043943. https://doi.org/10.1371/journal.pone.0043943
32. Wen, S., Tian, W., Zhang, H., Fan, S., Zhou, N., Li, X.: Semantic segmentation using a GAN and a weakly supervised method based on deep transfer learning. IEEE Access **8**, 176480–176494 (2020). https://doi.org/10.1109/ACCESS.2020.3026684
33. Xu, J., Feng, G., Zhao, T., Sun, X., Zhu, M.: Remote sensing image classification based on semi-supervised adaptive interval type-2 fuzzy c-means algorithm. Comput. Geosci. **131**, 132–143 (2019)
34. Yakubovskiy, P.: Segmentation models (2019). https://github.com/qubvel/segmentation_models
35. Zhao, H., Shi, J., Qi, X., Wang, X., Jia, J.: Pyramid scene parsing network, pp. 6230–6239. https://doi.org/10.1109/CVPR.2017.660

Towards the Recommendation of Time for Physical Activities Based on Air Pollution and Meteorological Variables

Juan Calle, Emilio Guzmán, Juan-Fernando Lima⬤, Andrés Patiño⬤,
Marcos Orellana$^{(\boxtimes)}$ ⬤, and Priscila Cedillo⬤

Laboratorio de Investigación Y Desarrollo en Informática – LIDI, Universidad del Azuay,
Cuenca, Ecuador
{juancarlos11,emilio43415}@es.uazuay.edu.ec, {flima,andpatino,
marore,icedillo}@uazuay.edu.ec

Abstract. Exercising outdoors, in a polluted environment, can cause adverse health effects for people. Therefore, it is important to know the levels of pollutants in the environment in which the exercise is carried out. This article applies the Clustering technique to generate a recommendation system of hours of the day in which it is possible to perform physical activities, reducing the damage to health, considering the levels of pollutants present in the environment. A dataset provided by the Monitoring Network of the Public Mobility, Transit and Transport Company (EMOV EP) of Cuenca, Ecuador, was used. The results show that through an unsupervised learning data mining technique such as clustering, a recommendation system can be implemented. This system generates a range of time within physical activities are suggested to be performed, reducing the negative impact on people's health of high levels of pollutants and meteorological variables present in the environment.

Keywords: Physical activities · Clustering · Atmospheric pollutants · Recommendation system

1 Introduction

Nowadays, air pollution is a highly important problem due to it reduces air quality, therefore, it has a negative impact on the people's health. There are several mechanisms that help monitor the different pollutants found in the atmosphere, the most common of which are sensors. In this context, Sellers et al. [1] used passive sensors to monitor air quality of Cuenca, Ecuador; this project was carried out using a system that collects data in real time to get information about atmospheric pollutants. It is important to consider the air quality to which people are exposed while performing their daily activities outdoors. The World Health Organization (WHO) inform that 91% of the world's population stays on places that don't meet established air quality standards, which could have future consequences on health [2–4]. Air quality is measured in different scales: good, moderate, unhealthy, harmful, very harmful, and dangerous [5]. The variables that directly

© Springer Nature Switzerland AG 2022
F. R. Narváez et al. (Eds.): SmartTech-IC 2021, CCIS 1532, pp. 318–331, 2022.
https://doi.org/10.1007/978-3-030-99170-8_23

affects are: ozone (O3), nitrogen dioxide (NO2), carbon monoxide (CO), particulate matter (PM2.5), and sulfur dioxide (SO2). These pollutants together with atmospheric variables such as: temperature, humidity, precipitation, among others, deteriorate the air quality index (AQI) [1, 3, 6, 7]. The daily activities that take place during prolonged exposure to a polluted environment should be considered, especially for athletes affect significantly their performance and have negative impact on their subsequent performance [8]. A tool focused on help athletes to consider the levels of pollutants to which they will be exposed when exercising is a recommender system. A recommender or recommendation system analyzes and processes data from a user with respect to an item or field and returns an output with information that the same user is interested in to help them make decisions [9]. Related works in which recommender systems have been developed for aspects of daily life, such as exercise routines within gyms or a recommender system to complement health videos [10, 11].

In some cases, a recommender system often uses data mining techniques for its operation. Data mining is the process by which large data sets are analyzed to find relevant information that is hidden in plain sight. This information cannot be obtained using conventional statistical methods [12]. In the evaluation of the air quality index, various techniques were used, for example: clustering, association rule and sequential pattern mining, obtaining results mainly through correlation patterns [1, 13–15]. There are recommender systems that use data mining for their operation, through the implementation of techniques such as collaborative filtering, matrix factorization or clustering [9, 16]. In this work, the clustering method will be used to develop the recommender system of a time range for the performance of exercises. Clustering is a data mining technique to perform the division of data into groups of similar objects, which helps in data modeling along with mathematics and statistics [17].

This work aims to generate a system for recommending physical activities based on the time of day and the concentration of pollutants in the environment. Data mining techniques are used to prepare the recommender, taking as a base the discretization of data and the technique of clustering for grouping variables that affect air quality. The data for the recommender's operation will be obtained from the Monitoring Network of the Public Mobility, Transit and Transport Company (EMOV EP) [18, 19].

The structure of this paper is the following: Section 2 presents the related works to recommender systems that have addressed the problem of the air quality index. Section 3 explains the methodology used to implement the recommender and the experimentation to obtain results. Finally, in Section 4 the results obtained in the previous section are displayed and the discussion is carried out to evaluate the hypothesis raised, thus providing the conclusions of the operation of the recommender.

2 Related Work

The analysis of the related works allowed to obtain two topics: the first part refers literature about atmospheric and pollutant variables that have a strong impact on people's health and, specifically on people who perform physical activity abroad. And, the second, it addresses the recommender systems that use data mining techniques for their implementation, from decision trees to clustering, the latter being the most important and related to the present work.

2.1 Pollutants and the Effect on People's Health

When performing physical activities outdoors, two types of variables are considered: atmospheric and meteorological, they influence the performance of people's activities [3, 21]. The main atmospheric pollutants that affect the AQI, and consequently, people's health: ozone (O3), nitrogen dioxide (NO2), carbon monoxide (CO), sulfur dioxide (SO2) and fine particles (PM2.5) [6, 21–23]. These pollutants can have adverse effects on the health of people when exposed to them in the open air, causing respiratory and cardiovascular diseases and other complications in the future such as problems in lung functions [3, 4].

The level of air saturation is represented by relative humidity (RH), it quantifies the proximity of the air to its saturation. RH is higher when air is closer to saturation. This mainly occurs in the early morning and in winter, causing adverse effects on people's health [23, 24]. Davis, et al. [24] concluded that HR can cause adverse effects after physical activity outdoors in asthmatic patients.

Temperature, on the other hand, is directly related to people's health, Lee, et al. [23] state that different types of ailments such as: headache, sneezing, menstrual pain, etc., have a direct relationship with temperature. In the same way, temperature directly influences when exercising, being a determining factor in the performance of athletes. Prolonged exposures to non-optimal temperature conditions can result in future problems such as those mentioned above [24].

The correlation between different atmospheric pollutants occurs due to the constant emission of fossil fuels, secondary aerosols, among others, where meteorological variables such as temperature and humidity intervene in its constant growth. Correlations between pollutants are also affected by temporal variations [25]. Liu et al [22] mention that, annually and temporarily, the low relative humidity and long duration of sunlight accumulate PM2.5, on the other hand, the high limited relative humidity increases the levels of PM10, raising the chances of exceeding the range that affects people's health.

2.2 Recommender Systems Based on Data Mining Techniques

Kuzelewska [26] presents a recommender system solution to help users in selecting an interesting product, using grouping methods to find similarities between users. The research uses the cluster-only technique, and this algorithm was divided into two phases: construction of an offline data model of user profiles; and online generation of recommended articles by grouping the user's profile with the profiles built offline. The grouping was carried out using the k-means method, in this way, the most similar objects are placed in a group described by their representative values and the representatives of each group are obtained in relation to the frequency of the evaluation of the belonging users to the group. The research result showed that the cluster-only algorithm is faster than the cluster-based methods. Recommendations are generated based solely on the selected representative and for this reason the procedure for calculating the representative is of high importance. This approach has a lower precision, but a higher speed, which, says the author, is important in an online recommender system.

Alzu'Bi, et al. [27] implemented a recommender system for the elicitation of requirements. Using the a-priori algorithm, and the rules are extracted for user requirements.

These can be used to suggest new requirements. In its development, it was shown that the algorithm is efficient in execution time and was able to extract the rules quickly. However, the authors affirm that this technique is an alternative of several algorithms that can be equal to or even more efficient than the one used for the extraction of correlational requirements.

The aforementioned research addresses the implementation of recommender systems through the use of data mining techniques in different areas such as: marketing, commerce, health, etc. [26–29]. In particular, it was possible to denote the use of the clustering technique for the implementation of recommender systems [27, 30–33], through the use of data mining techniques in a correct way and with an adequate approach, taking advantage of the use of different algorithms. However, unlike the studies analyzed, this research uses the agglomerative clustering technique for the implementation of a recommendation system, the basis is the grouping of atmospheric pollutants to suggest hourly ranges to carry out physical activities in the open air, minimizing the impact it has on people's health.

3 Methods and Materials

This section shows how the information is collected in the EMAC and the description of the variables involved in the research. In addition, it addresses the issue of the necessary pre-processing techniques that must be applied to data to discard any type of anomalous data, and finally transform the data, and get data on the same scale allowing to work and process without inconvenience. The phases used in the methodology for this work is showed in Fig. 1.

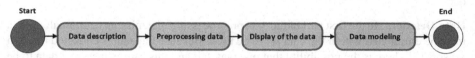

Fig. 1. SPEM diagram of the methodology

3.1 Data Description

According to the latest EMOV 2019 technical report, the data is collected through the Cuenca Air Quality Monitoring Network, it has 20 surveillance points located in different parts of the city. This network has an automatic station which records the concentrations of the different air pollutants in real time. A 19-station sampling subnetwork measures pollutants using the passive technique which is based on the principle of gas diffusion. By selection, the sampling devices capture the contaminants in a chemical substrate and the passive collectors are placed in order to minimize the influence of external factors that alter the results. Finally, quantification is carried out, a technique that allows determining the mean concentration of contaminants [19].

Table 1. Data information

Variable	Unit of measurement	Mean	SD	p_value
Ozone (O3)	ug/m^3	22.020261	12.436496	2.2e−16
Carbon monoxide (CO)	mg/m^3	0.730349	0.274170	2.2e−16
Nitrogen dioxide (NO2)	ug/m^3	11.811261	9.219506	2.2e−16
Sulfur dioxide (SO2)	ug/m^3	14.728704	8.403353	2.2e−16
Fine particles (PM2.5)	ug/m^3	8.343817	4.847673	2.2e−16
Temperature	°C	14.124141	2.730022	0.1052
RH	%	61.176064	14.239142	6.645e−12
Dew point	°C	6.333214	2.134538	2.2e−16
Atmospheric pressure	hPa	752.444518	5.053323	2.2e−16
Global radiation	w/m^2	165.631727	241.422521	2.2e−16
Precipitation	Mm	0.002537	0.051147	2.2e−16
UVA	w/m^2	10.476273	14.607943	2.2e−16
UVE	w/m^2	0.005783	0.004271	2.2e−16

3.2 Data Pre-processing

The first part is to debug the dataset obtained by removing anomalous data. Next, the normalization of the data is carried out using the Jarque-Bera normality test. Finally, a correlation test between variables is carried out to eliminate data that is highly correlated data.

Data Deletion. In the first part of the data preprocessing, the missing or anomalous data must be eliminated within the data set to be used. Because the data is collected through sensors [5], there is the possibility that one may fail and this causes incorrect data to be stored, which when processed will generate empty knowledge. Then, a selection stage was made of the data to be used since not all the data captured by the sensors are useful or relevant for the present investigation. At this stage, working with wind direction and speed was ruled out because they do not directly influence the main objective of the research.

Data Normalization. The distribution test was performed to verify the normality of the data. A test of goodness of fit was used to contrast the used data has a certain distribution, therefore, allowing to verify what type of distribution the data has [35]. In the first instance, the Shapiro method was used for normality tests, however, it was decided to use the Jarque-Bera due to the amount of data that is being processed in the investigation is more than three thousand and, therefore, the Jarque-Bera test is better adapted to that amount of data [36]. The formula is:

$$JB = n\left(\frac{\left(\sqrt{b_1}\right)^2}{6} + \frac{(b_2 - 3)^2}{24}\right) \tag{1}$$

The Jarque-Bera normality test follows a chi-square distribution with two degrees of freedom. The null hypothesis is that skewness is zero and kurtosis was 3, with the advantage of a larger amount of data [37].

The data was normalized using the scale technique, which performs a transformation according to the characteristics, so that they all share the same mean value and the same mean deviation. This method allows keeping the shape of the data; however, it must be considered that it is very sensitive to outliers and it is the responsibility of the data scientist to know how to correctly apply the method [37].

Correlation Data. Due to the non-existence of normality evidenced in the p_value value of Table 1, therefore, non-parametric statistical techniques must be used to find the correlation between variables. Through correlation tests, it was possible to observe the redundancy of data among three variables that were collected. In this case, the Pearson correlation method [34] was used. Figure. 2 shows the correlation table between the variables.

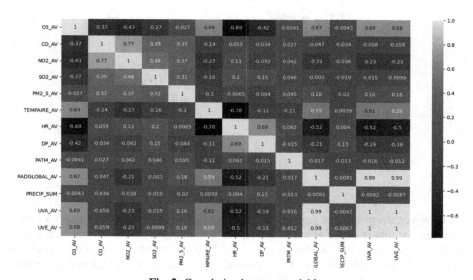

Fig. 2 Correlation between variables

As is presented in Fig. 2, the correlation between UVA and UVE with global radiation is 0.99, which allows eliminating both variables and keeping only one variable, in this case global radiation is the variable maintained.

3.3 Data Inspection

It was plotted in two dimensions using the principal component analysis (PCA). This is because there are 13 columns, each one reflects a pollutant or atmospheric variable. Then, it is necessary to represent in some way for a better human understanding, since it is impossible to graph 13 dimensions in the plane. Here, the PCA is used to transform the initial 13 dimensions to a 2-Dimensional chart that is easy for people to understand. On the other hand, the solver parameter was used to execute the complete singular value decomposition (SVD) and select the components through post-processing. SVD is another way to factor a matrix into vectors and singular values. The main advantage of using the PCA method is the ability to reduce dimensions for a better understanding of problems [38, 39].

Based on the data dispersion observed in the Fig. 3, it is possible to use grouping methods in order to create groups that share similar characteristics and it is possible to forecast and make decisions based on the processed information. The grouping technique based on the figure is the agglomerative clustering, since the information is found in clusters and this technique helps to make a hierarchy of them in order to merge equivalent data.

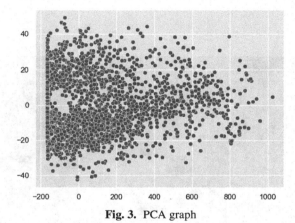

Fig. 3. PCA graph

However, the process of going from 13 dimensions to 2 dimensions implies a loss of accuracy, for this reason it is necessary to obtain the degree of confidence of applying the PCA algorithm, allowing the point that can be used for the reduction of dimensions and verify if it is useful to do it. In the present investigation, the confidence percentage of applying the PCA algorithm is 99.24%.

3.4   Data Modeling

This phase has been divided into two parts for a better understanding. In the first part, the specification of the ranges of the variables is presented, this is on relation to the thresholds that they have to accept for performing the exercise. In the second section, the methodology for the implementation of the recommender system is developed.

Variable Ranges. At this stage of the research, the data was discretized to be placed on a categorical scale. Thus, it is determined if under these levels of pollutants, it is possible to exercise: to perform the recommender system an additional column was added in which denotes the possibility of exercising with exposure to outside air.

In the first instance, air pollutants were divided into six scales based on the risk they represent to people's health, associated with the air quality index, as presented on Table 2 [22].

Table 2. Discretization of atmospheric pollutants

SO2	NO2	CO	O3	PM2.5	Quality	Exercise
0–50	0–40	0.0–2.0	0–100	0–35	Excellent	Yes
51–150	41–80	2.1–4.0	101–160	35–75	Moderate	Yes
151–475	81–180	4.1–14.0	161–215	75–115	Regular	Yes
476–800	181–280	14.1–24.0	216–265	116–150	Bad	No
801–1600	281–565	24.1–36.0	266–800	151–250	Very bad	No
1601–2620	566–940	36.1–60.0	–	251–500	Dangerous	No

On the other hand, the meteorological variables were categorized with the same objective. Temperature and relative humidity have a significant effect on the performance and health of people who exercise in exposure to these variables, having a high relationship with each other and being the most important at the time of the decision to exercise outdoors. [23, 24, 40].

Table 3. Discretization of weather variables

Temperature (°C)	Scale	Exercise	RH(%)	Scale	Exercise
< 5	Bad	No	< 40	Danger	No
5–15	Excellent	Yes	40–59	Excellent	Yes
16–23	Good	Yes	60–84	Danger	Yes
24–29	Regular	Yes	> 85	Regular	No
> 30	Danger	No	–	–	–

However, data collected in Cuenca, Ecuador does not satisfy the necessary pollutant ranges to perform an analysis referring to the ranges shown in Tables 2 and 3. For this reason, this proposal works with the minimum values to find results that are the closest to the reality of our country. However, in this research the values and ranges reviewed through the literature are emphasized, providing the possibility of generating recommendation algorithms when the variables to be analyzed are within the previously established ranges.

Recommender for Minimum Values. As a consequence of not being able to use the ranges of the variables in the research, an alternative technique was used. In this technique the minimum value and the first quartile are used, so the recommender system can specify whether it is possible to exercise at certain hours of the day. For this, clustering technique is applied, which allows the necessary grouping which provides the desired results.

As its name indicates, the minimum value technique uses the minimum value of each variable in the data set, working with the first or second quartile and obtaining a specific range that allows physical activities to be carried out. A new column was created for each variable or contaminant and in this way to locate if the examined variable is in the previously established range. Subsequently, each piece of data in the data set was compared, with the range established between the minimum and the first quartile for each variable, thus determining if the data being evaluated falls within the range or exceeds it.

With the data set obtained by combining the initial data with the columns created from the acceptance of the ranges, a PCA is again carried out to reduce the dimensionality of the new data set, which is presented on Fig. 4.

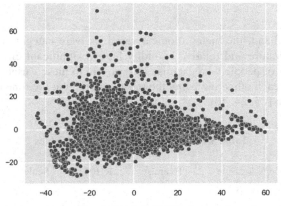

Fig. 4. Updated PCA chart

With the data set obtained by combining the initial data with the columns created from the acceptance of the ranges, a PCA is again carried out to reduce the dimensionality of the new data set, which is presented on Fig. 4.

The agglomerative clustering this grouping process is carried out in a direction from bottom to top, in each step two nearby clusters generate a fusion with each other until being able to leave only one, which generates a hierarchy of clusters. Said clusters turn out to be a large accumulation of material or immaterial things, the hierarchy for two different clusters A and B of different levels of the hierarchy has to be $A \cap B = \emptyset, A \subset B, B \subset A$. The few results of the computed clustering of the algorithm formed a certain metric distance function, thus the algorithm computes a clustering K with an approximation factor Ω (log k) [40]

In some initial groups, the closest neighbor fusion algorithm, as a first step in each sample together with the nearest neighbor form a cluster and likewise n clusters are obtained, each of which has two samples, as a next step the clusters are merge to remove duplicate samples [41]. The use of the algorithm is complemented with structural graphs allowing the fusion of two clusters with maximum affinity within a directed graph, for the construction of the graph a set of vectors is generated $X = \{x_1, x_2, \ldots\ldots\ldots, x_n\}$, building a graph where $G = (V, E)$, where V is the number of vertices corresponding to a vector and E is the set of edges that connect with the vertices. The graph is associated with an adjacency matrix $W = [w_{ij}]$, where w_{ij} is the similarity of pairs between x_i and x_j and is defined as:

$$w_{ij} = \begin{cases} \exp\left(-\frac{dist(i,j)^2}{\sigma^2}\right), & ifX_j \in N_i^K, \\ 0, & otherwise. \end{cases} \qquad (2)$$

As can be seen from Fig. 4, the massive amount of data demonstrates the use of clustering function as a technique for data fusion. In Fig. 5, the application of the Agglomerative Clustering technique to the research data is evidenced, separating them into two clusters, one red and the other purple. Here, one contains the hours that exercise can be performed and the other the hours in which cannot be exercised, depending on the location of its variables within the range between the minimum and the first quartile.

Through a visual analysis, a review of the values found in each cluster was carried out in order to identify in which cluster the minimum values are located and relate them to the hours of said values. Through this method, it was possible to obtain the corresponding hours of the values that are in the range between the minimum and the first or second quartile to determine the hours in which people can exercise according to the least square's method.

Finally, due to the dimension of the data in the research, which exceeds three thousand data, the unique values were obtained, thus discarding repeated hours for a better visualization of the results.

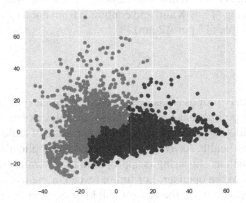

Fig. 5. Agglomerative clustering

The previously exposed methodology refers to its application, contrasting the variables with the range between the minimum value and the first quartile of the data. However, for a better contrast of results, the use of the same methodology was added with a variant in the range using the second quartile to contrast the data found with the first quartile.

4 Results

This section presents the results of the application of the minimum value method proposed for the research, using the minimum and the first and second quartiles to compare the results obtained in both cases, based on atmospheric pollutants and methodological variables of the city of Cuenca (Table 4).

Table 4. Selection of hours according to the cluster with minimum values

	SO2	NO2	CO	O3	PM2.5	°C	RH
Min-Q1	7.77-9.96	0.001-5.20	0.26-0.55	4.74-11.40	0.46-5.29	5.3-12.2	24-1251.0
Hour	1am-7am	1am-7am	1am-7am	1am-7am	1am-7am	1am-7am	1am-7am
Min-Q2	7.77-11.68	0.001-10.01	0.26-0.67	4.74-20.30	0.46-7.3	5.3-14.0	24-61.0
Hour	1am-8am / 12pm-12am	1am-8am / 12pm-12am	1am-8am / 12pm-12am	1am-8am / 12pm-12am	1am-8am / 12pm-12am	1am-8am / 12pm-12am	1am-8am / 12pm-12am

By means of the elimination method, the hours found in both clusters were discarded, in this way only the hours found in the cluster that evidence the possibility of exercising were obtained.

According to the minimum values detected in cluster 0 for the first quartile, the linked hours in which exercise can be performed are between one in the morning and seven in the morning (1 am–7 am), excluding the other hours. On the other hand, for the second quartile a reduced restriction is obtained that goes between one in the morning and eight in the morning (1 am–8 am) and continues from noon to midnight with a range of twelve hours available (12 pm–12 am).

5 Conclusions

In this article, an hourly proposal has been presented for carrying out outdoor exercise based on the level of pollutants and atmospheric variables existing in the environment. This will allow considering the air quality for the exposure of athletes to it, reducing the harmful effect it has on health. As it has been observed, the application of an unsupervised learning technique such as clustering is appropriate to generate a recommender system of physical activities in the open air. For future research, the use of other techniques is planned, such as: decision trees, the nearest neighbor method or collaborative filtering; in order to find more accurate data to the reality of the geographic space where the research has been raised and observe if there is an improvement in the results obtained.

References

1. Arce, D., Lima, F., Orellana, M., Ortega, J., Sellers, C., Ortega, P.: Descubriendo patrones de comportamiento entre contaminantes del aire: Un enfoque de minería de datos (Discovering

behavioral patterns among air pollutants : a data mining approach). Catalog **9**(4), 168–179 (2018), [Online]. Available: http://scielo.senescyt.gob.ec/pdf/enfoqueute/v9n4/1390-6542-enfoqueute-9-04-00168.pdf

2. Calidad del aire ambiente (exterior) y salud. https://www.who.int/es/news-room/fact-sheets/detail/ambient-(outdoor)-air-quality-and-health. (Accessed 25 Nov. 2020)

3. Giles, L., Koehle, M.: The health effects of exercising in air pollution. Sport. Med. **44**(2), 223–249 (2013). https://doi.org/10.1007/s40279-013-0108-z

4. An, R., Zhang, S., Ji, M., Guan, C.: Impact of ambient air pollution on physical activity among adults: a systematic review and meta-analysis. Perspect. Public Health **138**(2), 111–121 (2018). https://doi.org/10.1177/1757913917726567

5. Walden, C.A.S.: Publicación de contaminantes atmosféricos de la estación de monitoreo de la ciudad de Cuenca, utilizando servicios estándares OGC. ACI Av. en Ciencias e Ing. **9**(15), 94–103 (2017). https://doi.org/10.18272/aci.v9i15.300

6. Kargarfard, M., et al.: Effects of polluted air on cardiovascular and hematological parameters after progressive maximal aerobic exercise. Lung **193**(2), 275–281 (2015). https://doi.org/10.1007/s00408-014-9679-1

7. Tai, A.P.K., Mickley, L.J., Jacob, D.J.: Correlations between fine particulate matter (PM2.5) and meteorological variables in the United States: implications for the sensitivity of PM2.5 to climate change. Atmos. Environ. **44**(32), 3976–3984 (2010). https://doi.org/10.1016/j.atmosenv.2010.06.060

8. Rundell, K.W.: Effect of air pollution on athlete health and performance, pp. 407–413 (2012). https://doi.org/10.1136/bjsports-2011-090823

9. Zahra, S., Ghazanfar, M.A., Khalid, A., Azam, M.A., Naeem, U., Prugel-Bennett, A.: Novel centroid selection approaches for KMeans-clustering based recommender systems. Inf. Sci. (Ny) **320**, 156–189 (2015). https://doi.org/10.1016/j.ins.2015.03.062

10. Bocanegra, C.L.S., Ramos, J.L.S., Rizo, C., Civit, A., Fernandez-Luque, L.: HealthRecSys: a semantic content-based recommender system to complement health videos. BMC Med. Inform. Decis. Mak. **17**(1), 1–10 (2017). https://doi.org/10.1186/s12911-017-0431-7.

11. Guzmán-Luna, J., Torres Pardo, I.D., Sebastián Vallejo, J.: Un sistema recomendador móvil de rutinas de ejercicio basado en el perfil del usuario. Res. Comput. Sci. **94**(1), 137–149 (2015). https://doi.org/10.13053/rcs-94-1-11

12. Ballesteros, H.F.V., Iñiguez, E.G., Velasco, S.R.M.: Minería de Datos. Recimundo **2**(Esp), 339–349 (2018). https://doi.org/10.26820/recimundo/2.esp.2018.339-349

13. Zhang, C., Yuan, D.: Fast fine-grained air quality index level prediction using random forest algorithm on cluster computing of spark. In: Proc. – 2015 IEEE 12th Int. Conf. Ubiquitous Intell. Comput. 2015 IEEE 12th Int. Conf. Adv. Trust. Comput. 2015 IEEE 15th Int. Conf. Scalable Comput. Commun. **20**, 929–934 (2016). https://doi.org/10.1109/UIC-ATC-ScalCom-CBDCom-IoP.2015.177

14. Represa, N.S., Fernández-Sarría, A., Porta, A., Palomar-Vázquez, J.: Data mining paradigm in the study of air quality. Environ. Processes **7**(1), 1–21 (2019). https://doi.org/10.1007/s40710-019-00407-5

15. Chowdhury, A.S., Uddin, M.S., Tanjim, M.R., Noor, F., Rahman, R.M.: Application of data mining techniques on air pollution of Dhaka City. In: 2020 IEEE 10th Int. Conf. Intell. Syst. IS 2020 – Proc., pp. 562–567 (2020). https://doi.org/10.1109/IS48319.2020.9200125

16. Thai-Nghe, N., Drumond, L., Krohn-Grimberghe, A., Schmidt-Thieme, L.: Recommender system for predicting student performance. Procedia Comput. Sci. **1**(2), 2811–2819 (2010). https://doi.org/10.1016/j.procs.2010.08.006

17. Pande, S.R., Sambare, M.S.S., Thakre, V.M.: Data Clustering Using Data Mining Techniques, vol. 1, no. 8, pp. 494–499 (2012)

18. Parra, R., Espinoza, C.: Insights for air quality management from modeling and record studies in Cuenca, Ecuador. Atmosphere (Basel) **11**(9) (2020). https://doi.org/10.3390/atmos1109 0998
19. EMOV – monitoreo.
20. Meehan, K., Lunney, T., Curran, K., McCaughey, A.: Context-aware intelligent recommendation system for tourism. In: 2013 IEEE Int. Conf. Pervasive Comput. Commun. Work. PerCom Work. 2013, no. March, pp. 328–331 (2013). https://doi.org/10.1109/PerComW. 2013.6529508
21. Lichter, A., Pestel, N., Sommer, E.: Productivity effects of air pollution: evidence from professional soccer. Labour Econ. **48**(June 2016), 54–66 (2017). https://doi.org/10.1016/j.lab eco.2017.06.002
22. Liu, Y., Wu, J., Yu, D., Hao, R.: Understanding the patterns and drivers of air pollution on multiple time scales: the case of northern China. Environ. Manage. **61**(6), 1048–1061 (2018). https://doi.org/10.1007/s00267-018-1026-5
23. Lee, M., Ohde, S., Urayama, K.Y., Takahashi, O., Fukui, T.: Weather and health symptoms. Int. J. Environ. Res. Public Health **15**(8) (2018). https://doi.org/10.3390/ijerph15081670
24. Davis, R.E., McGregor, G.R., Enfield, K.B.: Humidity: a review and primer on atmospheric moisture and human health. Environ. Res. **144**, 106–116 (2016). https://doi.org/10.1016/j.env res.2015.10.014
25. Ma, T., et al.: Air pollution characteristics and their relationship with emissions and meteorology in the Yangtze River Delta region during 2014–2016. J. Environ. Sci. (China) **83**, 8–20 (2019). https://doi.org/10.1016/j.jes.2019.02.031
26. Kuzelewska, U.: Clustering algorithms in hybrid recommender system on MovieLens data. Stud. Logic, Gramm. Rhetor. **37**(50), 125–139 (2014). https://doi.org/10.2478/slgr-2014-0021
27. Alzu'Bi, S., Hawashin, B., Eibes, M., Al-Ayyoub, M.: A novel recommender system based on apriori algorithm for requirements engineering. In: 2018 5th Int. Conf. Soc. Networks Anal. Manag. Secur. SNAMS 2018, pp. 323–327 (2018). https://doi.org/10.1109/SNAMS. 2018.8554909
28. Golbandi, N., Koren, Y., Lempel, R.: Adaptive bootstrapping of recommender systems using decision trees. In: Proceedings of the fourth ACM international conference on Web search and data mining – WSDM '11, 2011, vol. 1, no. 2, p. 595. https://doi.org/10.1145/1935826. 1935910
29. Sharif, M.A., Raghavan, V.V.: A clustering based scalable hybrid approach for web page recommendation. In: Proc. 2014 IEEE Int. Conf. Big Data, IEEE Big Data 2014, pp. 80–87 (2015). https://doi.org/10.1109/BigData.2014.7004360
30. Luo, Y., Hu, J., Wei, X.: Blog recommender based on hypergraph modeling clustering algorithm. In: Proc. – 2013 4th World Congr. Softw. Eng. WCSE 2013, pp. 231–235 (2013). https://doi.org/10.1109/WCSE.2013.42
31. Renaud-Deputter, S., Xiong, T., Wang, S.: Combining collaborative filtering and clustering for implicit recommender system. In: Proc. – Int. Conf. Adv. Inf. Netw. Appl. AINA, pp. 748–755 (2013). https://doi.org/10.1109/AINA.2013.65
32. Hassan, M.T., Karim, A., Javed, F., Arshad, N.: Self-optimizing a clustering-based tag recommender for social bookmarking systems. In: Proc. – 9th Int. Conf. Mach. Learn. Appl. ICMLA 2010, pp. 601–606 (2010). https://doi.org/10.1109/ICMLA.2010.93
33. Wasid, M., Ali, R.: An improved recommender system based on multi-criteria clustering approach. Procedia Comput. Sci. **131**, 93–101 (2018). https://doi.org/10.1016/j.procs.2018. 04.190
34. Bishara, A.J., Hittner, J.B.: Testing the significance of a correlation with nonnormal data: comparison of Pearson, Spearman, transformation, and resampling approaches. Psychol. Methods **17**(3), 399–417 (2012). https://doi.org/10.1037/a0028087

35. Cerron, J.C.P.: Comparación De Pruebas De Normalidad Multivariada. An. Científicos **77**(2), 141 (2016). https://doi.org/10.21704/ac.v77i2.483
36. Pedrosa, I., Juarros-Basterretxea, J., Robles-Fernández, A., Basteiro, J., García-Cueto, E.: Pruebas de bondad de ajuste en distribuciones simétricas, no. 1, pp. 245–254 (2015). https://doi.org/10.11144/Javeriana.upsy13-5.pbad
37. Yap, B.W., Sim, C.H.: Comparisons of various types of normality tests. J. Stat. Comput. Simul. **81**(12), 2141–2155 (2011). https://doi.org/10.1080/00949655.2010.520163
38. Randolph, T.W.: Scale-based normalization of spectral data. Cancer Biomarkers **2**(3–4), 135–144 (2006). https://doi.org/10.3233/CBM-2006-23-405
39. Xu, H., Caramanis, C., Sanghavi, S.: Robust PCA via outlier pursuit. In: Adv. Neural Inf. Process. Syst. 23 24th Annu. Conf. Neural Inf. Process. Syst. 2010, NIPS 2010, vol. 58, no. 5, pp. 3047–3064 (2010)
40. Park, J.E., Son, W.S., Ryu, Y., Choi, S.B., Kwon, O., Ahn, I.: Effects of temperature, humidity, and diurnal temperature range on influenza incidence in a temperate region. Influenza Other Respi. Viruses **14**(1), 11–18 (2020). https://doi.org/10.1111/irv.12682
41. Ackermann, M., Blömer, J., Kuntze, D., Sohler, C.: Analysis of agglomerative clustering. Algorithmica **69**(1), 184–215 (2012). https://doi.org/10.1007/s00453-012-9717-4

Analysis of the Generation of a Synthetic Response to the Application of Contrast Agents in Breast Medical Images Using Generative Adversarial Networks

Jaider Stiven Rincón[1]📷, Carlos Mera[1(✉)]📷, Rubén Fonnegra[2]📷,
and Gloria M. Díaz[1]📷

[1] Facultad de Ingenierías, Instituto Tecnológico Metropolitano, Medellín, Colombia
`jaiderrincon204297@correo.itm.edu.co`, {`carlosmera,gloriadiaz`}`@itm.edu.co`
[2] Facultad de Ingenierías, Institución Universitaria Pascual Bravo,
Medellín, Colombia
`ruben.fonnegra@pascualbravo.edu.co`

Abstract. Since different studies alerted about deposits of contrast medium in the brain after conducting contrast-enhanced magnetic resonance examinations, developing strategies to reduce or avoid the use of those contrast agents has become a highly relevant research topic. In this work, we propose the use of a conditional generative adversarial network model (cGAN) for generating a synthetic response to the application of contrast agents in medical images, specifically magnetic resonance images of the breast. A large MRI data set with 30527 images corresponding to 163 examinations were used to train and validate the model. The results show a successful generation of the spatial structure of images; however, a large variability in the results is observed, especially when the breast tissue is high density. A detailed analysis shows an average error of 8% for regions of diagnostic interest, which is a promising result.

Keywords: Breast cancer · Magnetic resonance image (MRI) ·
Generative adversarial networks (GANs)

1 Introduction

Breast cancer is the most common type of cancer in the world and is considered one of the leading causes of cancer death [24]. This cancer has the highest prevalence rate (5 years). However, it is well-known that breast cancer can have a good prognosis if it is diagnosed early and treated appropriately.

Among the methods for cancer diagnosis, Contrast Enhanced Magnetic Resonance Imaging (MRI) [6,10] is one of those that report the highest sensitivity rate [16], showing significant potential in the detection, characterization, and discrimination of tumors associated with the development of soft tissue cancer, such as breast cancer. Moreover, the diagnosis through this type of image has

© Springer Nature Switzerland AG 2022
F. R. Narváez et al. (Eds.): SmartTech-IC 2021, CCIS 1532, pp. 332–344, 2022.
https://doi.org/10.1007/978-3-030-99170-8_24

shown the most significant sensitivity in the detection and characterization of cancer in cases where other methods fail, such as patients with dense tissue or breast prostheses [13].

It is a method for acquiring a series of MR images in rapid succession following the administration of contrast agent, which is usually a gadolinium-containing molecule that is injected intravenously into the patient [7]. It is performed by obtaining sequential magnetic resonance images before, during, and following the injection of a contrast agent [7]. First, one unenhanced fat-suppression T1 sequence is acquired; then, the contrast medium (gadolinium based) is injected intravenously, and a sequence of images are acquired, allowing to analyze hemodynamic and morphological tumor characteristics based on the estimation of the rate of change of the concentration of contrast agent in blood plasma (AIF) [25].

Even that, the implementation of this type of study in clinical settings is restricted by both the limited availability of the acquisition equipment, and the cost associated with the image acquisition and the radiology time interpretation [4]. On the other hand, in recent past, several studies has warned about the deposition of gadolinium in the base of the brain when it is used as a contrast agent for magnetic resonance imaging, without ruling out the appearance of side effects. Therefore, the development of strategies to reduce or avoid contrast agents and to reduce image acquisition costs are highly relevant research topics [3].

Recently, computational models have been proposed to generate synthetic information or pseudo-information from known information, such as other images or signs. These techniques have shown promising results for the generation of medical pseudo-images, allowing generate images that offer relevant information for diagnosis. In state-of-the-art, the use of generative models based on artificial neural networks, known as generative adversarial networks (GANs), has been highlighted. Among these, Li et al. [14] recently proposed cycleGan, a model to synthesize MRIs of the brain through computed tomography images (CT). Similarly, Chong and Ho [1] used GANs to generate synthetic 3D magnetic resonance images of the brain. In [15], a combination of a cycleGAN with conditional GANs (cGANs) are used to generate high-resolution MRIs of the brain. Also, in [22], the authors used generative models for this task, but this time using a 3D GAN. Results in those tasks are promising; however, breast MRI synthesis proposes new challenges due to the variability of the tissues.

On the other hand, although the DCE-MRI examination requires the acquisition of the sequence of post-contrast images, recent studies have demonstrated the feasibility of using only the early response to the contrast medium, i.e. the image acquired 2 or 3 min after the injection, for screening, staging, recurrence assessing, and problem-solving or lesion clarification. Thus, in this work, we evaluate the feasibility of generating a synthetic image of early contrast medium response from the unenhanced image using a computational model, specifically, one based on the generative model known as Pix to Pix [9]. This architecture has already shown great potential for transforming images between two different domains, including: cityscapes labels to photo, black and white to color, edges to photo, day to night, among many others. Recently has shown its usefulness in the synthesis of mammograms for the detection of breast cancer [2].

2   Materials and Methods

The Pix to Pix model was modified to evaluate the synthetic generation of early contrast agent response in breast MRIs. Specifically, the architecture of the generator and the discriminator were modified to adapt them to our purpose. The description of the model and its operation are detailed below.

2.1   Model

Pix to Pix is a conditional generative adversarial network (cGAN) that aims to map a data set from a domain x and a random noise vector z to a new domain y, that is, $G : \{x, z\} \rightarrow y$. In this case, the x domain corresponds to a magnetic resonance image acquired before applying the contrast agent. These images are known as "conditional" images since they condition the learning of the model. The new domain y is the objective domain and corresponds to the magnetic resonance images after injection of the contrast agent. These images are known as objective images or "real" images.

The model uses a generator G and a discriminator D, where both architectures are based on convolutional neural networks. G aims to create a "false" sample starting from a conditional image. Therefore, it is trained so that false or generated samples cannot be distinguished from real ones. The goal of D is to discriminate between real samples and fake samples. Mathematically the loss function of the Pix to Pix model is drawn in Eq. (1).

$$L_{cGAN}(G, D) = E_{x,y}[log D(x, y)] + E_{x,z}[log(1 - D(x, G(x, z)))] \qquad (1)$$

where G tries to minimize this objective function, while its adversary D tries to maximize it, that is:

$$G^* = arg\ min_G max_D\ L_{cGAN}(G, D) \qquad (2)$$

In [9] the authors show the benefit of using the objective function of cGAN with the traditional loss L1 scaled by a factor λ. Therefore, the objective function that was used in this work is given in Eq. (3).

$$G^* = arg\ min_G max_D\ L_{cGAN}(G, D) + \lambda \mathcal{L}_{L1}(G) \qquad (3)$$

On the other hand, the architectures used for the generator and the discriminator are shown in Fig. 1. Specifically, for the generator, a U-net [20] like architecture was adopted. It has seven convolutional layers in which a "down-sampling" of the input image is performed from the third convolution. Also, it consists of six deconvolutional layers to perform an "up-sampling" and a last convolutional layer which returns the image to its original dimensions through a sigmoid function. The discriminator consists of four convolutional layers and an output layer that reduces the number of channels and applies the sigmoid activation function. A batch normalization [8] was used in both the generator and the discriminator, except for the first convolutional layer. A Leaky rectified linear unit (ReLU) [19], with $\alpha = 0.2$, was used as the activation function for all layers in the generator and discriminator, except for the output layer. The kernel size for the convolutions was fixed to 3×3. For both architectures Adam [12] was used as optimizer with the following parameters: $\alpha = 0.0001$, $\beta_1 = 0.5$, $\beta_2 = 0.999$ for the generator, while for the discriminator, the value of LR was set to 0.0005. We trained the model for at least 100 epochs, training first the discriminator and then the generator during each iteration of the epoch. The parameter λ of L_1 regularization was set at 100 as suggested in the original architecture. The model was implemented on the TensorFlow and Keras framework using a NVIDIA GeForce RTX 2070 GPU.

The difficulty of training cGANs is well known. For this reason, various techniques were tested in order to stabilize the model and its convergence. Spectral normalization [17] was used in both the discriminator and the generator. Pixel shuffle [23] was also tested to perform deconvolutions in the generator. Different learning rates were tested for the discriminator and the generator based on the Two Time-Scale Update Rule (TTUR) [5]. The value of the learning rate appropriate for each case were described above. To achieve the same goal, soft and noisy labels and label smoothing [21] were used. In this work, the best results are reported.

2.2 Dataset

A database with 30527 magnetic resonance images of the breast, belonging to 163 examinations, was used to carry out the training and validation of the model. Specifically, 27791 images from 146 examinations of different patients were used to train the model, and 2736 images from other 17 patients were used to evaluate its performance.

The sequences of the MRI protocol [16] to perform the experiment were unenhanced image, which corresponds to the conditional image or image before the application of the contrast agent, and post-contrast image, i.e. the acquired 90 s after applying the contrast agent. Figure 2 shows an example of each of these images corresponding to the training image set.

From the validation studies, 15 of those contain annotations made by expert radiologists. The annotations include the localization of the regions of interest (ROIs), as well as their classification according to the Breast Imaging Reporting And Data System (BIRADS) [18]. Thus, were identified 66 ROIs distributed as follows: 8 ROIs categorized as BIRADS 1 or normal tissues, 37 as BIRADS 2 or benign lesions, one as BIRADS 3, which mean that it has a small probability to be malignant (<2%), eight were classified as BIRADS 5 (with a high probability of being malignant) and 12 were classified as BIRADS 6 due that malignancy was

Generator

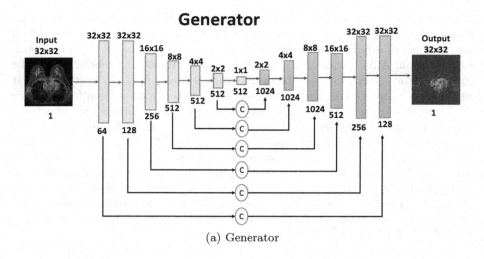

(a) Generator

Discriminator

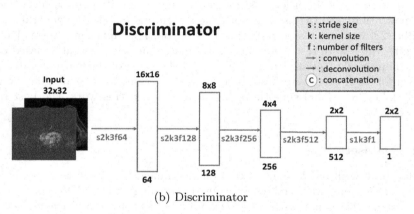

s : stride size
k : kernel size
f : number of filters
→ : convolution
⇀ : deconvolution
Ⓒ : concatenation

(b) Discriminator

Fig. 1. Architectures for the generator and the discriminator of the cGAN model used.

biopsy proven. As an example, Fig. 3 shows an MRI image with its corresponding annotated ROI, which is BIRADS 2.

2.3   Training and Validation

Figure 4 shows the general training scheme of the model using the generator and discriminator components. First, a batch of real-conditional images and a batch of generated-conditional images are shown to the discriminator so that it learns to discriminate them. Then, the generator learns to generate false samples from conditional images aiming to fool the discriminator.

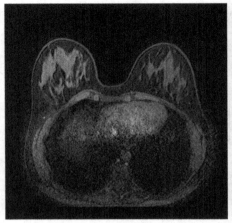
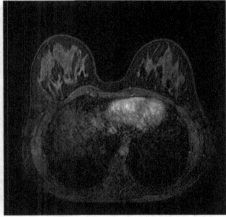

(a) Conditional image - unenhanced precontrast image.

(b) Real image - contrast enhanced image.

Fig. 2. An example of the MRI images contained in the database is shown. The images correspond to one of the studies used to train the model.

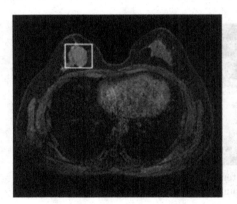
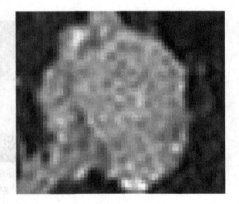

Fig. 3. On the left, one of the MRI images with its proper region of interest demarcated by an expert radiologist is shown. On the right, this region is zoomed in to appreciate it in detail. ROI corresponds to a finding classified as BIRADS 2 or benign lesion.

At the training stage, patches with a spatial resolution of 32×32 pixels were used instead of the complete image. This was done mainly for two reasons, first for removing the image background by cutting the patches from places where tissue that provided information was found, such as the breast or the thoracic cavity. Second, to try to improve the resolution in the parts of the image that contain dense tissue. The size of 32×32 pixels was chosen based on the average size of the ROIs.

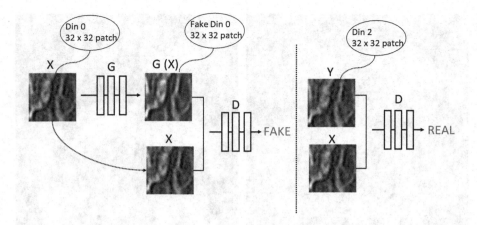

Fig. 4. The general operation of the implemented model is shown.

Figure 5 shows the algorithm used for the generation of patches to train the model. First, a mask is applied to the image filtering the background and leaving

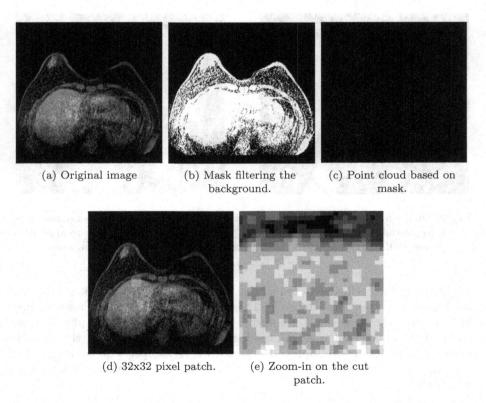

(a) Original image

(b) Mask filtering the background.

(c) Point cloud based on mask.

(d) 32x32 pixel patch.

(e) Zoom-in on the cut patch.

Fig. 5. Algorithm with which the 32×32 pixel random patch cut was performed to train the model.

only the tissue of interest. After this, a random point cloud is generated on the mask. Taking these points as the center, patches of 32 × 32. Pixels are cut over the original image.

Although the model was trained using randomly extracted patches, the complete image was generated instead of generating it by patches. This was done to avoid discontinuities in the image, especially at the edges where two consecutive patches join. The model performance was calculated base on the mean absolute error (MAE) and the mean squared error (MSE) among the generated and real images. Equations (4) and (5) describe these metrics, where X_i is the i-th pixel of the real image, $\hat{X}_i$ is the i-th pixel of the generated image, and n is the number of pixels in the image.

$$MAE = \frac{1}{n} \sum_{1}^{n} |X_i - \hat{X}_i| \tag{4}$$

$$MSE = \frac{1}{n} \sum_{1}^{n} (X_i - \hat{X}_i)^2 \tag{5}$$

3   Results and Discussion

Figure 6 shows one of the images generated by the trained model. On the left, there is the corresponding conditional image, which corresponds to the

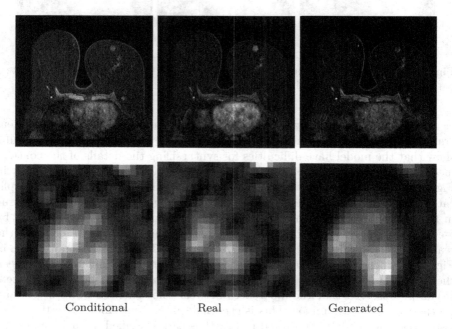

| Conditional | Real | Generated |

Fig. 6. On the left unenhanced pre-contrast image, on the center real post-contrast and on the right synthetic post-contrast generated. Its corresponding ROI is shown below each image. In this case, the ROI correspond to a patient with BIRADS 5 classification.

pre-contrast unenhanced image. In the center, the objective or real image (post-contrast), which was acquired 90 s after the contrast agent has been applied. Finally, on the right is the image generated by the model, which is the synthesized post-contrast image. Below, ROI classified as BIRADS 5 (malignant) is extracted from each image. Figures 7, 8 and 9 are structured in the same way, but ROIs are classified as BIRADS 6 (Malignant), BIRADS 2 (Benign), and BIRADS 1 (Normal tissue), respectively.

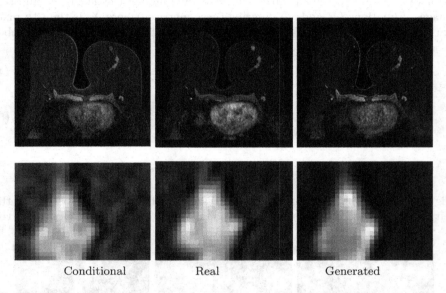

Conditional   Real   Generated

Fig. 7. The Figure is shown analogous to Fig. 6. In this case the ROI correspond to a patient with BIRADS 6 classification.

According to these visual results, in all cases, the computational model generate the shape and spatial structure of the image correctly. However, results show that the model have difficulties for synthesizing the details of the contrast medium uptake, which are observed as micro textures in the tissue. Thus, in Fig. 6 it can be observed that the spatial shape and normal tissues are replicated correctly by the model. However, it misses in generating the densest tissue in the thoracic region or inside the ROI. This difficulty is especially shown by focusing on the region of interest as the corresponding contrasts between the real and generated ROI are not entirely generated. This fail is less noticeable in Fig. 7, in which it is observed that although there are slight differences between the images in the thoracic region, the region of interest was better generated. It can be observed that the differences between the contrasts of both real and synthesized ROIs are minor. This is especially important since these two studies correspond to BIRADS 5 and 6, i.e., those are classified as malignant, and their response to the contrast agent must be greater. This shows that the model correctly generates the response to the contrast agent in some cases but does

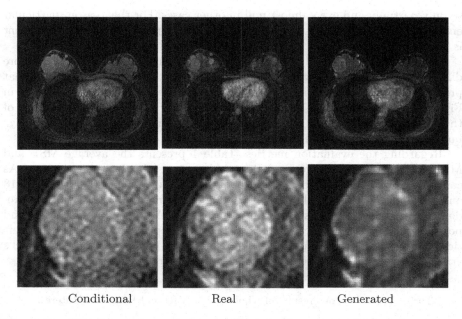

| | | |
| Conditional | Real | Generated |

Fig. 8. The Figure is shown analogous to Fig. 6. In this case the ROI correspond to a patient with BIRADS 2 classification.

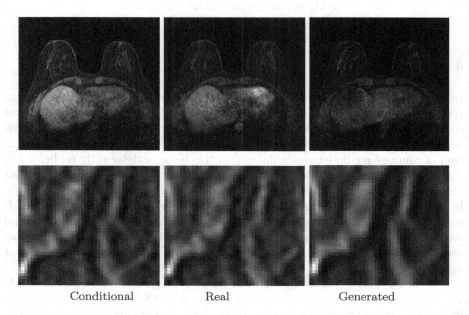

| | | |
| Conditional | Real | Generated |

Fig. 9. The Figure is shown analogous to Fig. 6. In this case the ROI correspond to a patient with BIRADS 1 classification, that is, normal tissue.

so only partially and even almost null in other cases. For this reason, particular emphasis should be placed on cases in which the response to the contrast agent is not as expected.

It can also be observed in Figs. 6, 7, 8 and 9 that the algorithm has more difficulty synthesizing irregular contrast enhancing; however, the tissues that present a highlighted contrast enhancement are generated satisfactorily. ROI in Fig. 9, which was classified as normal tissue by the radiologist, is an example of that: the model reproduces not only the structural or spatial shape of the image but also the contrasts in this one.

Regarding the evaluation metrics, Table 1 presents the average MSE and MAE for both whole images and Regions of interest in the validation set. As can be observed, very low errors are reported to whole images (0.0047 ± 0.0018 and 0.0335 ± 0.0057), which is expected due to the normal tissue, which is predominant in the image, is successfully synthesized. Also, the image background positively influences the metrics because it is fully replicated. However, the metrics computed only over the ROIs give us a better perspective on the model's error, being around 8% when the images are compared Pixel to Pixel.

Table 1. Evaluations results of whole breast MRI and Regions of Interest.

	Images	ROIs
MSE	0.0047 ± 0.0018	0.0146 ± 0.0163
MAE	0.0335 ± 0.0057	0.0806 ± 0.0478

4   Conclusion

In this work, a model based on conditional generative adversarial networks (cGAN) was proposed to generate a synthetic response to the application of contrast agent in breast MRIs. The model successfully replicates the spatial structure of images and normal tissues. However, the response to the application of contrast media has variable results, this being satisfactorily replicated in some cases but unsatisfactory in others. The generation of tissues with irregular or low contrast enhancement presents more difficulty than tissues with a highlighted enhancement. Regarding the evaluation metrics, the MSE and the MAE have relatively small values when evaluating the set of both whole images and ROIs. It can be explained since normal tissue's spatial structure and intensities are satisfactorily replicated, similar to many tissues that enhance with contrast agent.

As future work, it is proposed to evaluate new models of deep neural networks, specifically generative models such as cycle-GAN [27] or GAN-Circle [26], in order to improve the synthesis of dense breast tissue and, in turn, improve the response to the application of contrast agent in the cases where this does not have a satisfactory answer. It has also been recently shown that the use of attention mechanisms, as well as the implementation of local discriminators in GANs architectures [11], helps to improve the response to the application of contrast agents, therefore we propose to evaluate these new mechanisms in the architectures already implemented and in the new ones to be implemented.

It is also proposed to use other evaluation metrics that allow measuring the behavior of the response to the contrast agent. The current evaluation metrics are computed pixel by pixel over all the images and are biased by the background and normal tissues.

Acknowledgment. This work was supported by COLCIENCIAS (RC830-2020), Instituto Tecnológico Metropolitano (research grant P20213), and the Institución Universitaria Pascual Bravo (research grant CE-007-2020).

References

1. Chong, C.K., Ho, E.T.W.: Synthesis of 3d mri brain images with shape and texture generative adversarial deep neural networks. IEEE Access **9**, 64747–64760 (2021). https://doi.org/10.1109/ACCESS.2021.3075608
2. Guan, S.: Breast cancer detection using synthetic mammograms from generative adversarial networks in convolutional neural networks. J. Med. Imaging **6**(03), 1 (2019). https://doi.org/10.1117/1.jmi.6.3.031411
3. Guo, B.J., Yang, Z.L., Zhang, L.J.: Gadolinium deposition in brain: current scientific evidence and future perspectives. Frontiers in molecular neuroscience **11**, 335 (2018). https://doi.org/10.3389/fnmol.2018.00335
4. Hernández, M.L., Osorio, S., Florez, K., Ospino, A., Díaz, G.M.: Abbreviated magnetic resonance imaging in breast cancer: a systematic review of literature. Eur. J. Radiol. Open **8**, 100307 (2021). https://doi.org/10.1016/j.ejro.2020.100307
5. Heusel, M., Ramsauer, H., Unterthiner, T., Nessler, B., Hochreiter, S.: GANs trained by a two time-scale update rule converge to a local Nash equilibrium (2018)
6. Heywang, S.H., et al.: MR imaging of the breast using gadolinium-DTPA. Journal of Computer Assisted Tomography **10**(2), 199–204 (1986). https://doi.org/10.1097/00004728-198603000-00005
7. Hylton, N.: Dynamic contrast-enhanced magnetic resonance imaging as an imaging biomarker. Journal of Clinical Oncology **24**(20), 3293–3298 (2006). https://doi.org/10.1200/jco.2006.06.8080
8. Ioffe, S., Szegedy, C.: Batch normalization: accelerating deep network training by reducing internal covariate shift (2015)
9. Isola, P., Zhu, J.Y., Zhou, T., Efros, A.A.: Image-to-image translation with conditional adversarial networks. In: Proceedings of the IEEE Conference on Computer Vision and Pattern Recognition, pp. 1125–1134 (2017)
10. Kaiser, W.A., Zeitler, E.: MR imaging of the breast: fast imaging sequences with and without Gd-DTPA. Preliminary observations. Radiology **170**(3), 681–686 (1989). https://doi.org/10.1148/radiology.170.3.2916021
11. Kim, E., Cho, H.h., Ko, E., Park, H.: Generative adversarial network with local discriminator for synthesizing breast contrast-enhanced MRI. In: 2021 IEEE EMBS International Conference on Biomedical and Health Informatics (BHI), pp. 1–4 (2021). https://doi.org/10.1109/BHI50953.2021.9508579
12. Kingma, D.P., Ba, J.: Adam: a method for stochastic optimization (2017)

13. Leithner, D., et al.: Clinical role of breast MRI now and going forward. Clin. Radiology **73**(8), 700–714 (2018). https://doi.org/10.1016/j.crad.2017.10.021
14. Li, W., et al.: Magnetic resonance image (MRI) synthesis from brain computed tomography (CT) images based on deep learning methods for magnetic resonance (MR)-guided radiotherapy. Quan. Imaging Med. Surg. **10**(6), 1223–1236 (2020). https://doi.org/10.21037/qims-19-885. 32550132[pmid]
15. Lyu, Q., You, C., Shan, H., Wang, G.: Super-resolution MRI through deep learning (2018)
16. Mann, R.M., Cho, N., Moy, L.: Breast MRI: state of the art. Radiology **292**(3), 520–536 (2019). https://doi.org/10.1148/radiol.2019182947
17. Miyato, T., Kataoka, T., Koyama, M., Yoshida, Y.: Spectral normalization for generative adversarial networks (2018)
18. Morris, E., Comstock, C., Lee, C., Lehman, C., Ikeda, D., Newstead, G., et al.: ACR BI-RADS® magnetic resonance imaging. ACR BI-RADS® Atlas, Breast imaging reporting and data system **5** (2013)
19. Nair, V., Hinton, G.E.: Rectified linear units improve restricted Boltzmann machines. In: ICML (2010)
20. Ronneberger, O., Fischer, P., Brox, T.: U-Net: Convolutional networks for biomedical image segmentation (2015)
21. Salimans, T., Goodfellow, I., Zaremba, W., Cheung, V., Radford, A., Chen, X.: Improved techniques for training GANs (2016)
22. Sanchez, I., Vilaplana, V.: Brain MRI super-resolution using 3D generative adversarial networks (2018)
23. Shi, W., et al.: Real-time single image and video super-resolution using an efficient sub-pixel convolutional neural network (2016)
24. Sung, H., et al.: Global cancer statistics 2020: GLOBOCAN estimates of incidence and mortality worldwide for 36 cancers in 185 countries. CA: Cancer J. Clin. **71**(3), 209–249 (2021). https://doi.org/10.3322/caac.21660
25. Yankeelov, T., Gore, J.: Dynamic contrast enhanced magnetic resonance imaging in oncology: theory, data acquisition, analysis, and examples. Current Med. Imaging Rev. **3**(2), 91–107 (2007). 10.2174/157340507780619179
26. You, C., et al.: CT super-resolution GAN constrained by the identical, residual, and cycle learning ensemble (GAN-circle). IEEE Transactions on Medical Imaging **39**(1), 188–203 (2020). https://doi.org/10.1109/TMI.2019.2922960
27. Zhu, J.Y., Park, T., Isola, P., Efros, A.A.: Unpaired image-to-image translation using cycle-consistent adversarial networks (2020)

Brain Tumor Segmentation Based on 2D U-Net Using MRI Multi-modalities Brain Images

Daniela Tene-Hurtado[1] , Diego A. Almeida-Galárraga[1(✉)] ,
Gandhi Villalba-Meneses[1] , Omar Alvarado-Cando[2] ,
Carolina Cadena-Morejón[3] , Valeria Herrera Salazar[4] , Onofre Orozco-López[5] ,
and Andrés Tirado-Espín[6]

[1] School of Biological Sciences and Engineering, Universidad Yachay Tech, San Miguel de Urcuquí 100119, Ecuador
dalmeida@yachaytech.edu.ec
[2] Escuela de Electrónica, Universidad de Azuay, Cuenca, Ecuador
[3] Universidad de Zaragoza, 50018 Zaragoza, Spain
[4] Facultad de La Energía, CIS, Universidad Nacional de Loja, Av. Pío Jaramillo Alvarado, Loja 100111, Ecuador
[5] Centro Universitario de los Lagos, Universidad de Guadalajara, Enrique Díaz de León 1144, Lagos de Moreno 47460, México
[6] School of Mathematical and Computational Sciences, Universidad Yachay Tech, San Miguel de Urcuquí 100119, Ecuador

Abstract. Glioblastoma is the most common malignant primary brain tumor, making up approximately 80% of all malignant primary brain tumors and 48.6% of all malignant tumors. Regardless of the diagnosis, the morbidity and mortality associated with a brain tumor are significant. They have a 5-year relative survival rate of around 7.2% and an average survival time of roughly 8 months. It's a difficult but vital endeavor to detect the existence of brain tumors utilizing magnetic resonance images in a quick, precise, and repeatable manner. The delineation of different tumor locations, such as peritumoral edema, enhancing tumor, and tumor core, is a critical aspect in the analysis of gliomas. Various approaches in the literature now use the tumor segmentation methodology to improve diagnosis and treatment plans. The suggested methodology entails using neural networks, specifically U-Net and Attention U-Net, to automate the segmentation of brain tumors. In this study, the BraTS 2020 dataset is used to evaluate the segmentation performance of the proposed approach. The accuracy of 0.9950 was obtained for both models, and a sensitivity of 0.9931 and 0.9891 for the U-Net and Attention U-Net models. A peritumoral edema, enhancing tumor, and tumor core dice similarity coefficient of 0.8453, 0.6950, and 0.7429 respectively has been achieved, for the U-Net model. For the Attention U-Net model, a dice score of 0.8829, 0.7233, and 0.8090 was obtained. Results show that both approaches have considerable potential and can be employed in clinical practice in the segmentation of various sub-regions of brain tumors.

Keywords: Glioma · Brain tumor segmentation · U-net · Multimodal MRI · BraTS dataset

© Springer Nature Switzerland AG 2022
F. R. Narváez et al. (Eds.): SmartTech-IC 2021, CCIS 1532, pp. 345–359, 2022.
https://doi.org/10.1007/978-3-030-99170-8_25

1   Introduction

A brain tumor is a mass of abnormal cells in the brain or central spine that grows uncontrollably. These tumors might be benign or cancerous. Non-cancerous tumors, also known as benign tumors, are homogenous formations that lack malignant cells. Non-cancerous tumors, unlike malignant tumors, grow slowly and have clear borders that do not spread to neighboring tissues [1]. Neurological symptoms vary in severity based on the size, location, and organs involved; nevertheless, they can grow to be quite large before causing any symptoms. It should be noted that some benign brain tumors can change and transform into malignant tumors [2]. Malignant tumors are cancerous heterogeneous masses with no clear borders that frequently include active cancer cells [3]. They have the ability to proliferate quickly, skip crucial regulatory mechanisms, and infiltrate other tissues, with the potential to spread to other vital organs in the body. MRI scans of a healthy brain, a brain with a benign tumor, and a brain with a malignant tumor are shown in Fig. 1. All brain tumors have the potential to destroy normal brain tissue, which can be both detrimental and lethal.

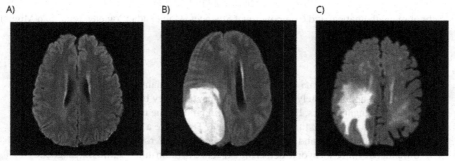

Fig. 1. MRI scans of (a) a healthy brain, (b) a brain with a benign tumor, and (c) a brain with a malignant tumor. The images were obtained from BraTS dataset [4].

Neuroimaging is useful for a variety of purposes, including diagnosis, therapy planning, tumor progression evaluation, and monitoring [5, 6]. The most common procedures for evaluating this disease are computed tomography (CT) and magnetic resonance imaging (MRI). Magnetic resonance imaging is the most widely used technique for the detection of brain tumors. MRI can be used to determine the location of the tumor, the level of tissue involvement, and the mass effect [7]. It can also be used to gather information about cellular, vascular, metabolic, and functional aspects of brain tumors [8]. Images of various tumor substructures, such as the tumor core, enhancing tumor, and peritumoral edema, can be obtained using a combination of MR modalities. Only having one modality makes it difficult for these substructures to be studied, and it does not provide entire information on abnormally-shaped tumors. As a result, T1-weighted (T1), T1-weighted contrast-enhanced (T1ce), fluid-attenuated inversion recovery (FLAIR), and T2-weighted (T2) are routinely utilized to segment brain tumors and provide an accurate diagnosis [9].

Glioma analysis relies heavily on brain tumor segmentation [10]. Because manual segmentation can become exceedingly uneven, an automatic technique for brain tumor segmentation is essential. Glioma segmentation in multimodality MRI scans is one of the most difficult tasks in medical image processing due to their highly varied appearance and structure of brain tumors. There has been an overflow of interest in brain tumor segmentation in recent years, allowing for a lot of research in this field which brings benefits for the biomedical industry [11]. The authors' numerous methodologies for automating the segmentation of brain tumors, and new deep learning methodology and implementations are expected to improve segmentation techniques and produce more accurate and reliable findings [12, 13].

Jiang et al. [14] proposed a brain tumor segmentation approach based only on a cascade strategy. The authors used a two-stage cascade U-Net. The first stage's purpose was to train a coarse prediction. U-Net was employed at this stage, with the 4 modalities of the MR images as input. The first stage's neural network architecture has a big encoding path and a short decoder path. The encoder path's task is to extract all of the complex semantic features. On the other hand, the decoder path must recover the segmentation map while keeping the input dimensions. To extend the network width, they used a second-stage network architecture. The first stage's raw images and coarse segmentation map are fed into the second stage's U-net. The second stage can produce a more precise segmentation with additional network parameters. The two-stage cascaded network is used for end-to-end training.

Another study proposes a deep learning system for tumor segmentation which consist of the application of a Cascade Convolutional Neuronal Network (C-CNN). Ranjbarzadeh et al. [15] propose a model that begins with image pre-processing to remove all unnecessary elements. This C-CNN model takes data from a variety of MRI modalities, both local and global. The local route is used to detect each pixels of tumor, whereas the global route is utilized to label each pixel within the tumor. All experiments performed by Ranjbarzadeh et al. were developed on the BraTS 2018 dataset, obtaining promising result. The dice scores achieved were as follows: mean whole tumor 0.9203, enhancing tumor 0.9113 and tumor core 0.8726 [15].

Another study presents an Enhanced Convolutional Neuronal Network (ECNN) for automatic segmentation with loss function optimization using the BAT algorithm. Thaha et al. [16] designed a method that is divided into two components. Skull stripping, cortex stripping, and image enhancing procedures. Following that, a patch extraction and patch pre-processing were completed before moving on to the second phase, which involved using ECNN to segment the brain image. The Enhanced Convolutional Neuronal Network employs small kernels to ensure a deep architecture while also avoiding overfitting due to the network's smaller weights. The ECNN model produces results of higher precision, recall and accuracy obtaining 87%, 90% and 92% respectively, while the CNN methods only produce 82%, 85% and 89% respectively [16].

The proposed methodology entails using neural networks, specifically U-Net and Attention U-Net, to automate the segmentation of brain tumors, so it can differentiate tumor regions including enhancing tumor, tumor core, and peritumoral edema regions.

These networks are commonly utilized for quick and accurate segmentation of biomedical images [17]. The effectiveness of the technique was evaluated using the freely available BraTS 2020 dataset.

Several ideas relating to brain tumor segmentation were discussed in this paper. The following section summarizes the methodology of the proposal for brain tumor segmentation, which is based on the U-Net and Attention U-Net architecture. Finally, all the results obtained by both models are represented, and these results are compared with those obtained by other state-of-the-art methodologies. The paper concludes with a discussion of the project's findings as well as some of our directions for future research works.

2 Proposed Methodology

The implementation of this project was performed on Google Colaboratory which offers free GPUs with better features than a conventional computer. The resources provided by colaboratory was NVIDIA Tesla P100-PCIE GPU and a RAM of 12 GB.

2.1 Dataset

The BraTS dataset is one of the most extensive and commonly utilized for segmenting brain tumors, primarily in low- and high-grade glioma patients [18]. The 2020 edition incorporates data from 19 different institutes, as well as the cancer imaging archive (TCIA) collections; however, unlike previous versions, this edition exclusively includes pre-therapy scans [19]. Furthermore, all MRI scans were brain extracted prior to public distribution, in compliance with institutional requirements for anonymity; and the images were aligned to the same brain anatomical template for normalization of different resolutions and orientations.

As shown in Fig. 2, every MRI data comprises the following fundamental structural imaging sequences:

- Fluid Attenuated Inversion Recovery (FLAIR): T2-weighted FLAIR image, axial, coronal, or sagittal 2D acquisitions, 2–6 mm slice thickness.
- T1-weighted (T1): Native image, sagittal, or axial 2D acquisitions, with 1–6 mm slice thickness.
- Post-contrast T1 weighted (T1ce): T1-weighted, contrast-enhanced (Gadolinium) image, with 3D acquisition and 1 mm isotropic voxel size for most patients.
- T2-weighted (T2): T2-weighted image, axial 2D acquisition, with 2–6 mm slice thickness [20, 21].

Implementation of the Dataset. In this study, the BraTS 2020 dataset is used to evaluate the segmentation performance of our proposed approach. The clinical image data consists of a training set and a validation set. The validation set has 125 images, while the training set contains 369 MRI scans for each participant with the four imaging modalities previously described. The ground truth is only available in the training set and was manually segmented by one to four raters using the same annotation technique.

Tumor segmentation annotations are Background (label 0), Non-enhancing Tumor (label 1), Edema (label 2), and Enhancing Tumor (label 4) [22]. Despite this, as seen in Fig. 3, the labels that were used for this work were:

- Whole Tumor (label 0): consists of all tumoral structures.
- Tumor Core (label 1): it includes the necrosis and non-enhancing tumor structures.
- Edema (label 2): consisting of an abnormal accumulation of fluid in the affected tissue surrounding the tumor core.
- Enhancing Tumor (label 3): comprises only the enhancing tumor class [23].

We randomly divided the training set into two parts: 80% for network training and 20% for validation and testing. There are 249 subjects for training and 119 individuals for validation and testing.

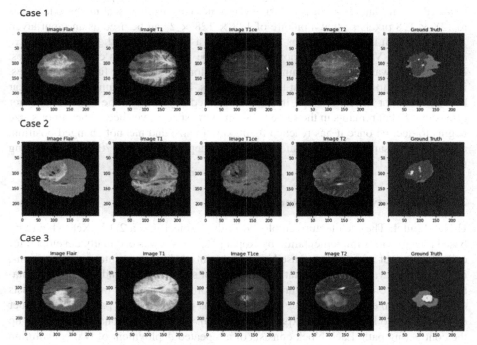

Fig. 2. Three cases from the BraTS 2020 dataset, showing the different types of image modalities: Flair, T1, T1ce, T2, and the Ground Truth.

2.2 Imaging Processing

The volume of each MR scan is $240 \times 240 \times 155$ voxels. We separated the dataset into slices because the dataset provided for the BraTS challenge is 3D volume data and our proposed methodology is a 2D U-Net, therefore there are 155 axial slices available

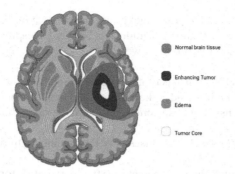

Fig. 3. Schematic diagram of brain tumor structures.

for brain tumor segmentation. Although a large amount of image preprocessing is not required for this dataset, some processing was done. This involves scaling the axial slices to 128 × 128 pixels so that a picture of 128 × 128 × 2 can be used as an input layer. All images with no tumor regions visible or with a vaguely defined ground truth were also discarded. Variations in tumor size and shape were evident in each of the slices. Because there was usually no brain structure, let alone tumor, in the first and last slices, it was decided to discard the first and last 5 slices. Normally, the tumor would appear between the first 22 slices, small in size and located anywhere in the brain. The tumor grows in size but remains in the same location in the successive slices. The tumor's size begins to decline once it has reached its maximum size and has not changed position, until it fully disappears. The greatest tumors are depicted in slices 70 to 80, according to the findings.

2.3   Neural Network Architecture

U-Net Model. The architecture employed in this project was a 2D U-Net, which was based on a previous implementation by Kopál [24]. U-Net was originally developed for cell tracking, but it is now being used in a number of medical segmentation applications, including brain vascular segmentation, brain tumor segmentation, and retinal segmentation [25]. The complete architecture used for this project is detailed in Fig. 4. It consists of two paths: an encoder (left side), also known as the contracting path, and a decoder (right side), also known as the expansive path [26]. Five convolutional blocks make up the contracting path. Each block consists of a repeated deployment of two convolution layers with a kernel size of 3 × 3, a Rectified Linear Unit (RELU) activation function, and zero-padding of all convolution operations to maintain the input image dimensions. After the first block's convolutional layers were finished, the image was downsampled using a 2 × 2 max-pooling operation, thereby reducing the dimension to half. This technique was continued until the base curve of the "U" which is where the expanded path begins, was reached. Each of the five convolutional blocks can extract a broad variety of rich and diversified feature components. The data processed by these five blocks was concatenated via skip connections with the blocks of the expansive path, which has a similar structure to the contracting path but uses a 2 × 2 up-sampling layer to process data from the bottom to the top. In addition, dropout between convolutional steps was used in 20% of the pixels to avoid overfitting [27]. Finally, the final segmentation map and an output layer with dimensions of 128 × 128 × 4 are created using a 1 × 1 convolution with a softmax activation function. In total, the network has 23 convolutional layers. In each block of the contracting path, the number of filters doubles (32, 64, 128, 256, and 512). In the expanded path, on the other hand, the number of convolutional filters is cut in half (512, 256, 128, 64, and 32). Our model has a total of 7,759,908 trainable parameters.

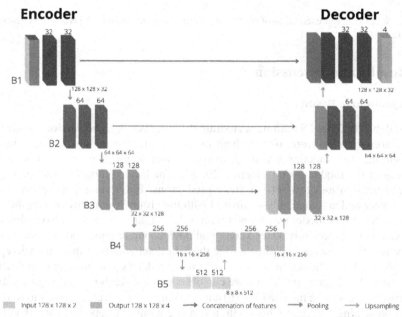

Fig. 4. Structure of the 2D U-Net used for the segmentation of brain tumors from multi-modal brain images.

Attention U-Net Model. The attention model has a very similar architecture to the previously discussed U-Net, with the exception that this model employs attention gates (AGs). By assigning big weights to the relevant parts and small weights to the less relevant parts, AGs causes the model to highlight only relevant activations during training. The Attention U-Net model does this by using AGs at each skip connection in the network. The model's design was based on the implementation that was performed by Bhattiprolu [28]. The composition of an attention block is depicted in Fig. 5. This block basically has two inputs, × and g. × comes from the skip connections, which provide greater special information, and g is the gating signal, which comes from the network's deeper layers and provides richer feature representation. Figure 5 depicts the attention gate implemented in the B2 of the U-Net neural network as an example. Our model had a total of 9,336,848 trainable parameters, and there are 7,816 non-trainable parameters.

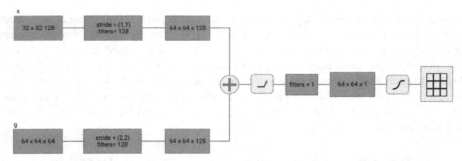

Fig. 5. Schematic representation of the attention block implemented in the B2 of the U-Net neural network.

3 Results and Discussion

3.1 Qualitative Results

We used the 2020 BraTS training set to train the models using two versions of the U-Net deep learning architecture, one of them including attention modules. The categorical cross-entropy loss function was used, with this function it was possible to measure the accuracy of the model during training [29, 30]. The trained models were then applied to the validation and test sets to make predictions. Furthermore, these results were immediately and automatically compared with the ground truth provided by the BraTS dataset. The U-Net model was trained with 5, 15, 25, and 35 epochs also called model A, B, C, and D respectively. Due to computational resources and good outcomes already observed with 35 epochs, we did not train the neural network with more than 35 epochs.

Figure 6 shows the segmentation results using a deep convolutional neural network using the U-Net architecture. Here we can observe the different visual segmentation of our proposed model on the BraTS 2020 data training set. Figure 6 is split into four rows, each representing a trained model with a variable number of epochs, and six columns, each containing one image: The original picture flair is the first, and the manually segmented ground truth mask is the second, both acquired directly from the dataset. The third image shows the brain tumor's predicted segmentation, which shows all of the tumor regions merged together. The fourth, fifth, and sixth images are distinct predictions for each of the tumor regions, i.e., peritumoral edema, enhancing tumor, and tumor core, respectively. Figure 7 depicts the segmentation accomplished by the Attention U-Net model after 35 epochs of training. We may say that there is no significant difference between the results generated from this model and the results given in Fig. 6 (D) because there is no substantial difference that highlights one model over the other.

3.2 Quantitative Results

We used the most generally used metrics for brain tumor segmentation to evaluate our method and its experimental results: Dice Similarity Coefficient, Mean IoU, Accuracy, Loss, Precision, Sensitivity, and Specificity. All of these metrics were tested in U-Net models A, B, C, and D, which correspond to epochs of 5, 15, 25, and 35, respectively.

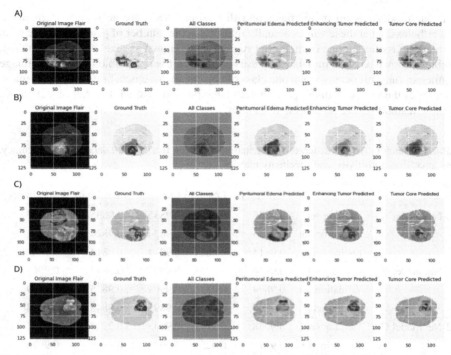

Fig. 6. The segmentation visual results of proposed method U-Net on the BraTS 2020 datasets. Row (A), (B), (C), and (D) are the model trained with 5, 15, 25, 35 epochs, respectively. The color codes for prediction are as follows: Peritumoral edema (green), enhancing tumor (blue), tumor core (red), and for ground truth: Peritumoral edema (sky-blue), enhancing tumor (blue), tumor core (white).

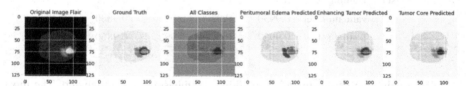

Fig. 7. The segmentation visual results of proposed Attention U-Net model on the BraTS 2020 datasets. The color codes for prediction are as follows: Peritumoral edema (green), enhancing tumor (blue), tumor core (red), and for ground truth: Peritumoral edema (sky-blue), enhancing tumor (blue), tumor core (white).

The same metrics were calculated for the Attention U-Net model after 35 epochs of training.

Table 1, lists all the metrics that are generally used for the evaluation of any method. These metrics, however, are of minimal interest to us because they are not very accurate for semantic segmentation. The values obtained are high, as indicated in Table 1, and there are no significant differences between them. We may conclude from these statistics that our model has no major flaws and that around 98% are accurately segmented. Nevertheless, what these values actually interpret is the number of pixels that have been correctly classified in one of the tumor regions, also known as pixel accuracy. Due to a problem known as class imbalance, these results aren't very reliable for medical image segmentation. This occurs when one class of objects, in this case a brain or tumor region, dominates the image in disproportionately large proportions, while other objects make up only a small percentage of the MRI scan.

Table 1. Quantitative evaluation of segmentation results on BraTS 2020 dataset using accuracy, loss, precision, sensitivity, and specificity metrics.

Model		Accuracy	Loss	Precision	Sensitivity	Specificity
U-Net model A	Training set	0.9836	0.0698	0.9835	0.9835	0.9945
	Validation set	0.9824	0.0798	0.9824	0.9824	0.9941
	Testing set	0.9814	0.0824	0.9814	0.9814	'0.9938
U-Net model B	Training set	0.9874	0.0411	0.9907	0.9842	0.9968
	Validation set	0.9894	0.0371	0.9909	0.9875	0.9969
	Testing set	0.9870	0.0427	0.9891	0.9848	0.9963
U-Net model C	Training set	0.9938	0.0177	0.9943	0.9921	0.9981
	Validation set	0.9915	0.0255	0.9922	0.9899	0.9974
	Testing set	0.9933	0.015	0.9938	0.9918	0.9979
U-Net model D	Training set	0.9950	0.0152	0.9948	0.9931	0.9982
	Validation set	0.9926	0.0232	0.9931	0.9912	0.9977
	Testing set	0.9940	0.0183	0.9943	0.9927	0.9981
Attention U-Net	Training set	0.9950	0.0131	0.9940	0.9891	0.9882
	Validation set	0.9930	0.0200	0.9930	0.9880	0.9880
	Testing set	0.9927	0.0183	0.9922	0.9860	0.9810

In the evaluation of our model, two additional measures were included. The most important parameters for brain tumor segmentation are the dice similarity coefficient and mean IoU. Both measures have a better degree of reliability. The dice coefficients and mean IoU for the U-Net models, as well as the Attention U-Net model, are shown in Table 2. These data were only acquired from the testing set. These data, unlike the metrics in the previous table, demonstrate considerable differences between models. Model A, with a dice coefficient of 0.26 and a mean IoU of 0.37, is a model with a low effectiveness in terms of tumor segmentation. Model D, on the other hand, gets a dice coefficient of 0.63 and a mean IoU of 0.83. This demonstrates a very good segmentation that is similar to other state-of-the-art approaches.

Table 2. Quantitative evaluation of segmentation results on BraTS 2020 dataset using dice similarity coefficient and Mean IoU metrics.

Testing set	Dice coefficient	Mean IoU
U-Net model A	0.2643	0.3757
U-Net model B	0.4372	0.3807
U-Net model C	0.5960	0.8095
U-Net model D	0.6313	0.8310
Attention U-Net model	0.7420	0.8836

Figure 8 and Fig. 9 illustrate the individual visual segmentation results of the U-Net and Attention U-Net models, respectively. In both figures the model performance (a), model loss (b), dice coefficient model curve (c), and the intersection over union model curve (d) are illustrated, it can be see that these results are consistent with those shown in the previous tables.

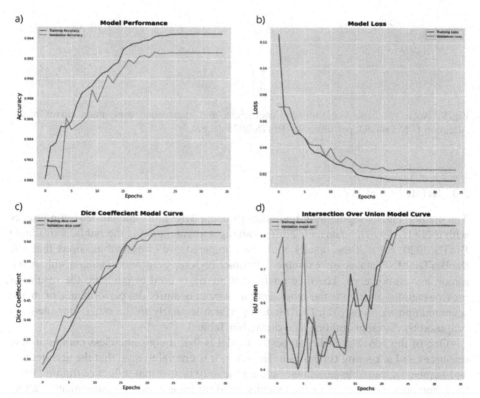

Fig. 8. Accuracy, loss, dice similarity coefficient, and intersection over union curves of the model D, performed on BraTS 2020 dataset.

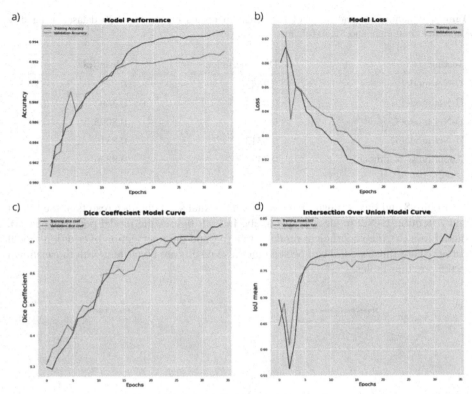

Fig. 9. Accuracy, loss, dice similarity coefficient, and intersection over union curves of the Attention U-Net model, performed on BraTS 2020 dataset.

3.3 Related Work

The method entails segmenting brain tumors using MRI multi-modalities brain images with a 2D U-Net. The dataset used for training and validation is the publicly available BraTS 2020. So that the results could be compared, we chose submissions that test the BraTS 2020 dataset and examined all tumor regions: peritumoral edema, enhancing tumor, and tumor core. The dice coefficient metric is used to compare the results of previous studies since it is the most accurate way to quantify the performance of image segmentation methods [31]. Our models perform similarly to the other four methods proposed by different authors, as indicated in Table 3.

One of the benefits of the suggested model is that it consumes less computational resources and a training time of 3 h. However, it is crucial to note that the architecture and number of trainable parameters are not the only factors that influence training time; the computational capacity of the machine used for training is also a significant factor.

Table 3. Quantitative results of our proposed methodology for brain tumor segmentation compared to the performance of other recently published deep learning-based methods.

Method	Dataset	Dice similarity coefficient		
		Edema	Enhancing tumor	Tumor core
Proposed U-Net	BraTS 2020	0.8453	0.6950	0.7429
Proposed attention U-Net	BraTS 2020	0.8829	0.7233	0.8090
Asymmetric U-Net – EfficientNet [32]	BraTS 2020	0.8413	0.6537	0.6804
3D U-Net model [33]	BraTS 2020	0.8893	0.6980	0.7835
Volumetric deep network (VDN) [34]	BraTS 2020	0.7800	0.6600	0.7000
V-Net [35]	BraTS 2020	0.8760	0.6702	0.7687

4 Conclusion

The qualitative and quantitative evaluations of the suggested method demonstrate that our results are remarkably similar to those obtained utilizing other state-of-the-art approaches. Furthermore, it was demonstrated that our suggested method's visual segmentation is comparable to the ground truth produced by expert manual segmentation. The evaluation findings demonstrate that U-Net model D performs better than models A, B, and C. Furthermore, the proposed methods more precisely segment the peritumoral edema region, the tumor core, and lastly the enhancing tumor. Multiple models and hierarchical architectures are not required because a single forward run through the suggested model can successfully segment the three tumor regions in a relatively short time. This will substantially facilitate practical application in real-life circumstances where processing time and ease of use are critical. Both strategies, we believe, are extremely acceptable and promising models. More implementations and functions, on the other hand, can be added to improve its performance.

References

1. Wadhwa, A., Bhardwaj, A., Verma, V.S.: A review on brain tumor segmentation of MRI images. Magn. Reson. Imaging **61**, 247–259 (2019). https://doi.org/10.1016/j.mri.2019.05.043
2. Community, C.S.: Frankly Speaking About Cancer: Brain Tumors (2013)
3. Bahadure, N.B., Ray, A.K., Thethi, H.P.: Image analysis for MRI based brain tumor detection and feature extraction using biologically inspired BWT and SVM. Int. J. Biomed. Imag. (2017). https://doi.org/10.1155/2017/9749108
4. Menze, B.H., et al.: The multimodal brain tumor image segmentation benchmark (BRATS). IEEE Trans. Med. Imag. **34**(10), 1993–2024 (2015). https://doi.org/10.1109/TMI.2014.2377694
5. Almeida-Galárraga, D., et al.: Glaucoma detection through digital processing from fundus images using MATLAB. In: 2021 Second International Conference on Information Systems and Software Technologies (ICI2ST), pp. 39–45. IEEE (2021). https://doi.org/10.1109/ICI2ST51859.2021.00014

6. Pereira-Carrillo, J., Suntaxi-Dominguez, D., Guarnizo-Cabezas, O., Villalba-Meneses, G., Tirado-Espín, A., Almeida-Galárraga, D.: Comparison between two novel approaches in automatic breast cancer detection and diagnosis and its contribution in military defense. In: Rocha, Á., Fajardo-Toro, C.H., Rodríguez, J.M.R. (eds.) Developments and Advances in Defense and Security. SIST, vol. 255, pp. 189–201. Springer, Singapore (2022). https://doi.org/10.1007/978-981-16-4884-7_15

7. Suquilanda-Pesántez, J.D., et al.: Prediction of Parkinson's disease severity based on gait signals using a neural network and the fast Fourier transform. In: Botto-Tobar, M., Cruz, H., Díaz Cadena, A. (eds.) CIT 2020. AISC, vol. 1326, pp. 3–18. Springer, Cham (2021). https://doi.org/10.1007/978-3-030-68080-0_1

8. Villanueva-Meyer, J.E., Mabray, M.C., Cha, S.: Current clinical brain tumor imaging. Neurosurgery **81**, 397–415 (2017). https://doi.org/10.1093/neuros/nyx103

9. Zhang, J., Chen, K., Wang, D., Gao, F., Zheng, Y., Yang, M.: Advances of neuroimaging and data analysis. Front. Neurol. (2020). https://doi.org/10.3389/fneur.2020.00257

10. Bhandari, A., Koppen, J., Agzarian, M.: Convolutional neural networks for brain tumour segmentation. Insights Imag. **11**(1), 1–9 (2020). https://doi.org/10.1186/s13244-020-00869-4

11. Alvarado-Cando, O., Torres-Salamea, H., Almeida, D.A.: UDA-μBioLab: teaching micro-controllers with bioinstrumentation. In: Lhotska, L., Sukupova, L., Lacković, I., Ibbott, G.S. (eds.) World Congress on Medical Physics and Biomedical Engineering 2018. IP, vol. 68/1, pp. 877–880. Springer, Singapore (2019). https://doi.org/10.1007/978-981-10-9035-6_163

12. Havaei, M., et al.: Brain tumor segmentation with deep neural networks. Med. Image Anal. **35**, 18–31 (2017). https://doi.org/10.1016/j.media.2016.05.004

13. Almeida-Galárraga, D.A., Ros Felip, A., Marco Martínez, F., Serrano-Mateo, L.: Photoelastic Analysis of Shoulder Arthroplasty: Current Descriptive Analysis of Research in Scientific Journals. In: Lhotska, L., Sukupova, L., Lacković, I., Ibbott, G.S. (eds.) World Congress on Medical Physics and Biomedical Engineering 2018. IP, vol. 68/2, pp. 713–717. Springer, Singapore (2019). https://doi.org/10.1007/978-981-10-9038-7_132

14. Jiang, Z., Ding, C., Liu, M., Tao, D.: Two-stage cascaded U-net: 1st place solution to BraTS challenge 2019 segmentation task. In: Crimi, A., Bakas, S. (eds.) BrainLes 2019. LNCS, vol. 11992, pp. 231–241. Springer, Cham (2020). https://doi.org/10.1007/978-3-030-46640-4_22

15. Ranjbarzadeh, R., Kasgari, A.B., Ghoushchi, S.J., Anari, S., Naseri, M., Bendechache, M.: Brain tumor segmentation based on deep learning and an attention mechanism using MRI multi-modalities brain images. Sci. Rep. **11**, 1–17 (2021). https://doi.org/10.1038/s41598-021-90428-8

16. Thaha, M.M., Kumar, K.P.M., Murugan, B.S., Dhanasekeran, S., Vijayakarthick, P., Selvi, A.S.: Brain tumor segmentation using convolutional neural networks in MRI images. J. Med. Syst. **43**(9), 1 (2019). https://doi.org/10.1007/s10916-019-1416-0

17. Al-Masni, M.A., Kim, D.-H.: CMM-Net: contextual multi-scale multi-level network for efficient biomedical image segmentation. Sci. Rep. **11**, 1–18 (2021). https://doi.org/10.1038/s41598-021-89686-3

18. Kumar, D.D., Vandhana, S., Priya, K.S., Subashini, S.J.: Brain Tumour Image Segmentation using MATLAB (2015)

19. Menze, B., et al.: Analyzing magnetic resonance imaging data from glioma patients using deep learning. Comput. Med. Imag. Graph. (2021). https://doi.org/10.1016/j.compmedimag.2020.101828

20. Karayegen, G., Aksahin, M.F.: Brain tumor prediction on MR images with semantic segmentation by using deep learning network and 3D imaging of tumor region. Biomed. Signal Process. Control **102458** (2021). https://doi.org/10.1016/j.bspc.2021.102458

21. Luo, Y., et al.: Edge-preserving MRI image synthesis via adversarial network with iterative multi-scale fusion. Neurocomputing **452**, 63–77 (2021). https://doi.org/10.1016/j.neucom.2021.04.060

22. Saleem, H., Shahid, A.R., Raza, B.: Visual interpretability in 3D brain tumor segmentation network (2021). https://doi.org/10.1016/j.compbiomed.2021.104410
23. Puch, S.: Multimodal brain tumor segmentation in magnetic resonance images with deep architectures. Ph.D. Thesis (2019)
24. Kopál, R.: 3D MRI Brain Tumor Segmentation (2021). https://www.kaggle.com
25. Ronneberger, O., Fischer, P., Brox, T.: U-Net: convolutional networks for biomedical image segmentation. In: Navab, N., Hornegger, J., Wells, W.M., Frangi, A.F. (eds.) MICCAI 2015. LNCS, vol. 9351, pp. 234–241. Springer, Cham (2015). https://doi.org/10.1007/978-3-319-24574-4_28
26. Nguyen, T., Bui, V., Lam, V., Raub, C.B., Chang, L.-C., Nehmetallah, G.: Automatic phase aberration compensation for digital holographic microscopy based on deep learning background detection. Opt. Express 25, 15043–15057 (2017)
27. Brito-Loeza, C., Espinosa-Romero, A., Martin-Gonzalez, A., Safi, A.: Intelligent Computing Systems: Third International Symposium, ISICS 2020 on Proceedings. Springer Nature, Sharjah, United Arab Emirates (2020)
28. Bhattiprolu, S.: Mitochondria semantic segmentation using U-net, attention Unet and Att ResUnet (2021). https://github.com/bnsreenu/python_for_microscopists/blob/master/224_225_226_mito_segm_using_various_unet_models.py
29. Yanchatuñaa, O., et al.: Skin lesion detection and classification using convolutional neural network for deep feature extraction and support vector machine. Int. J. Adv. Sci. Eng. Inf. Technol. (2020)
30. Vásquez-Ucho, P.A., Villalba-Meneses, G.F., Pila-Varela, K.O., Villalba-Meneses, C.P., Iglesias, I., Almeida-Galárraga, D.A.: Analysis and evaluation of the systems used for the assessment of the cervical spine function: a systematic review. J. Med. Eng. Technol., 1–14 (2021). https://doi.org/10.1080/03091902.2021.1907467
31. Takahashi, S., et al.: Fine-tuning approach for segmentation of gliomas in brain magnetic resonance images with a machine learning method to normalize image differences among facilities. Cancers 13, 1415 (2021). https://doi.org/10.3390/cancers13061415
32. Messaoudi, H., et al.: Efficient embedding network for 3D brain tumor segmentation. arXiv preprint arXiv:2011.11052 (2020)
33. Tang, J., Li, T., Shu, H., Zhu, H.: Variational-autoencoder regularized 3D MultiResUNet for the BraTS 2020 brain tumor segmentation. In: Crimi, A., Bakas, S. (eds.) BrainLes 2020. LNCS, vol. 12659, pp. 431–440. Springer, Cham (2021). https://doi.org/10.1007/978-3-030-72087-2_38
34. Soltaninejad, M., Pridmore, T., Pound, M.: Efficient MRI Brain Tumor Segmentation Using Multi-resolution Encoder-Decoder Networks (2020)
35. Fang, Y., et al.: Nonlocal convolutional block attention module VNet for gliomas automatic segmentation. Int. J. Image Syst. Technol. (2021). https://doi.org/10.1002/ima.22639

Automatic Identification of COVID-19 in Chest X-Ray Images Based on Deep Features and Machine Learning Models

Rubén D. Fonnegra[1]([envelope]) [ID], Fabián R. Narváez[3] [ID], and Gloria M. Díaz[2] [ID]

[1] Institución Universitaria Pascual Bravo, Medellín, Colombia
ruben.fonnegra@pascualbravo.edu.co
[2] Instituto Tecnológico Metropolitano, Medellín, Colombia
[3] Universidad Politécnica Salesiana, Quito, Ecuador

Abstract. In 2020, the novel coronavirus (COVID-19), spread around the world and became a pandemic. It is diagnosed by a Real-Time Reverse Transcriptase Polymerase Chain reaction (RT-PCR) test, which requires a specialized laboratory to confirm the presence of the virus. Due to the insufficient availability of these labs, medical images have been used as an alternative diagnosis, being the most easily available and least expensive option the Chest X-Ray. As COVID-19 infected patients display very similar respiratory affections like other kinds of pneumonia, distinguish them is difficult even for experienced radiologists. In this paper, two popular deep learning architectures are used to extract deep features, which are then used for training multi-class classification machine learning models to distinguish COVID-19 from healthy, bacterial, and other viral pneumonia infections. The evaluation was performed on a dataset of 7732 images, including 1575 healthy patients, 2801 diagnosed with bacterial pneumonia, 1493 with a viral (no COVID) infection, and 1863 subjects with COVID-19 confirmed diagnosis. The general area under the ROC curve was between $93\% \pm 2\%$ for general categories; and $99\% \pm 1\%$ with a sensitivity of $83\% \pm 2\%$ to identify COVID-19 infected patients.

Keywords: COVID-19 · Deep learning · Machine learning

1 Introduction

COVID-19 is a disease caused by SARS Cov-2, a coronavirus subtype that was discovered in Wuhan, China, in December 2019. Despite the fact that it is not a particularly fatal virus, it is characterized by a high level of infection, with 230 million infections and 4.7 million deaths worldwide as of September 21, 2021 [23]. As a consequence, The World Health Organization (WHO) declared the disease a pandemic on March 11, 2020 based on its behavior [16].

COVID-19 causes issues in the elderly and those with a history of medical problems. SARS-CoV 2 is reported to accumulate in the body to a higher level,

© Springer Nature Switzerland AG 2022
F. R. Narváez et al. (Eds.): SmartTech-IC 2021, CCIS 1532, pp. 360–369, 2022.
https://doi.org/10.1007/978-3-030-99170-8_26

resulting in a longer incubation period and being more infectious than SARS. Furthermore, as a wholly novel virus, it was impossible to identify a distinct prognosis or treatment for the condition early on. Moreover, despite the fact that the creation of a vaccine has slowed the spread of the coronavirus, new sub-groups of the virus have evolved. As a result, the WHO continues to advocate the use of medical resources, including vaccination, to control it, and healthcare systems around the world remain on high alert. Given this, the scientific community has focused its efforts on developing a variety of techniques to combat the disease on a daily basis, including the application of machine learning. However, there are a number of limitations and downsides to COVID-19, including a lack of data, protocol variability, simplicity of use, and new emergent sub-groups.

To tackle data availability, mainly from patients diagnosed with COVID-19 and other pulmonary diseases in an easily accessible medical image type (chest x-ray), we build a rich dataset containing images from normal patients, patients with different bacterial lung disease, patients with different viral lung disease and different patients with COVID-19. This dataset was build using a combination of two different datasets, Chest X-ray images database (CXRI) [14] and COVID saves lives dataset from HM Hospitals. In this point, it is important to remark that this proposal does not include a data augmentation algorithm, as COVID saves lives dataset from HM hospitals contains plenty of information about patients diagnosed with the disease, including the chest x-ray images. From each image sample, we extracted deep features using the ChexNet model [18] and then, classification using different machine learning algorithms is performed to distinguished between the classes. The model distinguish efficiently between COVID-19 and other lung pathologies, as shown in results. Besides, deep features and the original data joints will be shared to perform further analysis during the worldwide health emergency.

The rest of this work is organized as follows: Sect. 3 mentioned the construction of the database, the extraction of deep features, the characterization and the description of the machine learning models, Sect. 4 presents the most relevant results for the detection of the disease, and Sect. 5 presents the conclusions and future perspectives from this work.

2   Previous Works

Computer aided models for clinical applications have been widely used in various medical areas including risk of pulmonary failure or mortality caused by pneumonia [7,24], mortality risk in critical care [5,9], among others.

Due to the rapid spread of the disease, some problems arose in the health sector, one of these being the collapse of the hospitals [2,6,26]. This was due in some cases to a misdiagnosis at the time of the patients' first admission to a healthcare systems and hospitals. For this reason, most of the studies initially focused on early detection of the disease, since this is a decisive stage for carriers of the [25] virus. These works emphasize that this is the main and decisive action against the saturation of hospitals. As a consequence, scientific community has responded to these needs by developing computational aid systems for tackling the pandemic around the world

Therefore, the early diagnosis of the disease could establish early the needs of usage of healthcare resources such intensive care units (ICU) and different diagnostic tools or imaging modalities. As COVID-19 have shown similar symptoms to pneumonia, there exist a differential features among patients clinical history and lung failure caused by the virus in comparison with other viral pneumonia. As a consequence, previous works in the state of the art have conducted the detection of COVID-19 using computational intelligence tools [4]. However, the main limitation for most of these works lies in the lack of information available for the time they were developed, as most hospitals and healthcare systems have not released the data from patients with the disease, and reducing the possibilities for contribution to a limited portion of the community.

Other works have treated the problem for detecting COVID-19 from computed tomography images (CT) obtaining promising results in the diagnosis [22,28]. However, their main limitation is the ease of usage massively and the availability of the imaging sources. Despite CT remains as an accurate manner to detect pulmonary diseases, other imaging modalities (such chest X-ray) can be extended easily to supplement PCR in combating the virus from spreading; as they might require lower ionizing radiation dose and result cheaper or more available, in spite of imaging sources are also limited [21].

In this sense, deep learning approaches have displayed efficient performance for detecting pulmonary disease. Deep learning is mainly boosted by stacked convolutions with randomly assigned filters optimized iteratively during multiple epochs. The filters are able to extract high dimensional abstract features contained in input images describing different phenomenon in them. For this reason, deep features have been used to estimate different applications including medical imaging, displaying promising results. Nevertheless, one of the main drawbacks concerning deep learning in medical setups is the lack of objective interpretability [19].

The diagnosis using deep learning have been mainly employed to estimate patient's current state [8]. Some of the proposed or presented works have obtained promising results to detect the disease from x-ray images [13,27]. Nevertheless, two main drawbacks can be evidenced in most of the existing works. First, as clinical data from patients diagnosed with COVID-19 have not been widely shared for security reasons with patients data or privacy, data availability is low. For this reason, proposed models have used small subsets of data, even from the same patient or manually retrieved or annotated before implementing abrupt data augmentation strategies to force models to learn [3]. Second, deep learning models tend to a high bias as data augmentation is more severe and naturally acquired data becomes significantly less or limited. Then, proposed models might be biased and they cannot be effectively used or validated in real-world scenarios as there is still limited source of information and their usage might result medically unethical.

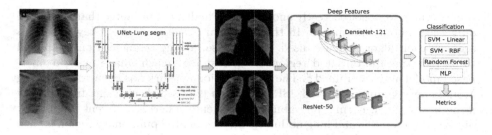

Fig. 1. Proposed methodology

Despite, deep features from medical imaging are still used in medical imaging analysis, and their availability might ease the research for specific purposes, such the detection of COVID-19 using an adequate source of information. For all these reasons, this work is intended to use deep learning to detect COVID-19 in a differentiate setup and using a rich dataset containing images from multiple patients diagnosed with the disease. From the complete dataset, deep features are extracted and might be shared to ease and motivate the research on the detection of the disease.

3   Proposed Methodology

3.1   Recombined Dataset

As there is not an homogeneous and consistent dataset currently published to differentiate among covid and other kind of diseases, it was required to build a dataset containing different lung pathologies and covid images. For this purpose, 4 different classes of patients were established: Normal (patients without any kind of disease), bacterial (patients with any kind of bacterial lung disease), viral (patients with any kind of viral lung disease) and covid (patients with any kind of covid variant). The dataset was collected from a combination of the Chest X-ray images database (CXRI) [14] and the Covid saves lives (CSL) dataset from HM Hospitals[1]. It is important to remark, that images from the CSL datasets are confirmed patients with COVID-19, and they were take from the first stage or progression of the disease after detection. Images were relabeled according to their respective class name. As images from both datasets where acquired and converted in different data format (jpg for CXRI and dicom CSL), images from CSL dataset were normalized and converted to 8 bits data format and compressed to jpg to avoid discrepancies per differences in changes of intensities in both collections. Besides, all personal information contained in the metadata from the dicom file was discarded to guarantee anonimization of patients; as

---

[1] FulldetailsandinformationofHMhospitalsandCOVIDDataSaveLivescanbefoundin
https://www.hmhospitales.com/coronavirus/covid-data-save-lives/english-version
https://www.hmhospitales.com/coronavirus/covid-data-save-lives/english-version

some of them were not correctly anonimized. Finally, to guarantee that the model only learn about information in the pulmonary regions of the x-ray images; a segmentation algorithm was used. In our case, a lung segmentation is applied to extract the appropriated region of interest from each image using a unet-based model already trained [2]. The segmentation network has been trained using Montgomery County [12] and JSRT datasets [20]; which contains frontal-view x-ray images from normal and abnormal patients suffering different pulmonary disease (tuberculosis and lung nodules). The segmented pulmonary region is then passed to the deep characterization models described below.

3.2 Deep Characterization Models

For the proposed architecture, two different deep characterization models were employed. First, a DenseNet-121 model [11] was used to extract deep features from images. The deep features were extracted from the last convolutional layer of the last Dense block. Additionally, a ResNet50 model [10] was also used to extract deep features as well with comparative purposes. In both cases, transfer learning was performed from the ChexNet model [18]. ChexNet was selected for transfer learning as it was trained using the ChestX-ray 14 dataset, which contains x-ray imaging screening of lungs in front-view to detect 14 different pathologies (Atelectasis, Cardiomegaly, Consolidation, Edema, Effusion, Emphysema, Fibrosis, Hernia, Infiltration, Mass, Nodule, Pleural Thickening, Pneumonia, and Pneumothorax). In case of both characterization models, the last layer extracts 1024 filters with sizes 7×7 per sample; which means 50176 features in total. Despite all features and kernels might not be required to obtain best performance in the classification task; we pretend to determine the validity of deep features to effectively characterize the types of pulmonary disease, including COVID-19. Nevertheless, it might be an interesting approach to study the relevance of deep features to optimize model performance. These 50176 features are given to the classification models to perform classification among different types of diseases and metrics are reported.

3.3 Deep Feature Classification

To perform classification, three different models were selected. First, a support vector machine (SVM) with radial basis function (RBF) and liner kernels in a one-versus-one configuration. According to the amount of deep features per image extracted, *gamma* was selected as $1/num\_deep\_features$ and $C = 1.0$. On the other hand, a random forest was employed as well to classify among categories. Finally, a multilayer perceptron (MLP) was used containing 3 densely connected layers with rectified linear units (RelU) [17] and softmax activation for the output. For the MLP, Adam was selected for parameter optimization

---

[2] Full details and results on the segmentation network can be found in https://github.com/imlab-uiip/lung-segmentation-2dhttps://github.com/imlab-uiip/lung-segmentation-2d

Table 1. Data distribution for train and validation subsets

Train distribution

Normal
Bacterial
Viral
Covid

1341 (19,5%)
1623 (23,7%)
1345 (19,6%)
2553 (37,2%)

Test distribution

Normal
Bacterial
Viral
Covid

240 (27,6%)
234 (26,9%)
148 (17,0%)
248 (28,5%)

[15] using a learning rate of $1e-5$, $\beta_1 = 0.9$ and $\beta_2 = 0.999$. All models were trained using deep features extracted by ResNet and DenseNet individually. Then, performance metrics were estimated, reported and compared. A diagram showing the full proposed strategy can be found in Fig. 1.

3.4 Experimental Setup

To perform the experiments data was split in train and validation subsets. Train subset was composed by a total of 6862 images distributed similarly for all available categories. This subset is employed to adjust parameters of the models. On the other hand, test samples was composed by 870 images distributed to avoid great class unbalance. Besides; as similar works in the state of the art use aggressive data augmentation techniques in COVID-19 patients given the lack of available data; it is important to remark that no data augmentation was perform and all images are real screenings from different patients. The validation subset is employed to estimate predictions an compare performance using metrics such the receiver operating characteristics (AUROC), accuracy, specificity, recall, f1 score and confusion matrix. To implement the models and perform the experiments, we used a Ubuntu system with an CPU Intel Xeon with 16 cores @3.8GHz and a GPU Nvidia Quadro P2000 using CUDA 10 software. To train the models, Python 3.6 was used with libraries for this purpose such TensorFlow and Keras; and other useful libraries such as Numpy, Scipy, Pandas, and Matplotlib. The data distribution for each data subset is shown in Table 1.

4 Results and Discussion

4.1 Detecting Pneumonia from Deep Feature Characterization

Results for all models can be found in Table 2, which portrays confusion matrix per classification and image characterization models. As shown in figure, all classification models obtained high performance to detect COVID-19, which is the

Table 2. Results for Deep features using Random forest for all normal, bacterial, viral and COVID-19 patients. From left to right, MLP, Random Forest, SVM (RBF), SVM (Linear). Top, results for DenseNet. Bottom, results for ResNet.

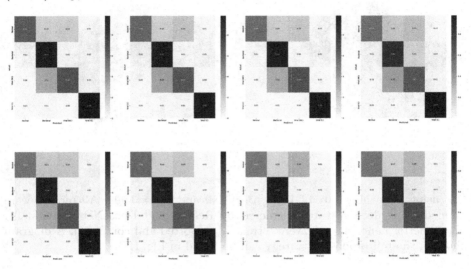

most interesting individual category given the worldwide emergency. This might show efficiency for deep feature to model the disease. However, all models show similar variations in confusion for normal patients; causing some false positive cases. This aspect regards a limitation on our work. However, We believe this difference might be given for the individual variability of bacterial and viral categories, as both of them contains different pathologies that might causes different symptoms, visualizations and consequences. This limitation could be tackled by extending the model to more specific types of pneumonia found in lungs; but that migh be conducted in future works as our main interest is finding COVID-19 in patients. Besides, as this tool is intended to provide a compliment to the RT-PCR test; in combination might denote an increase y the diagnosis. In our case specifically; this was not performed in our work since no data from patients were available to estimate result of RT-PCR test per patients; but this could be considered in future validation stages.

On the other hand, obtained average AUROC per characterization and classification model is reported in Fig. 2. As shown, MLP obtained best performance; and the combination with ResNet show higher rates. This is supposed as both ResNet and MLP are boosted by back-propagation optimization; which might denote a better minimization in parameters in comparison with the other conventional machine learning models. Obtained results are similar (99) in comparison to [27] and [1] that obtained 96% and 98% in accuracy for the detection of COVID-19 cases. However, there are several limitations that might outperform results of this work. First, content of images could beimproved during the acquisition since chest x-ray might cause some false positive or negative cases

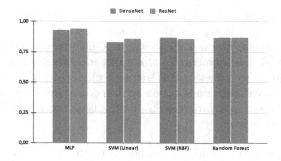

Fig. 2. Summarized average AUROC per characterization and classification models.

for the protocol, the movement in patients or their position, etc. This might cause limits or occlusion of lungs regions from soft tissues or bones. Despite this was not addressed in this work, an enhancement in the images using non-computational techniques could outperform results. Second, as deep features are able to characterize the disease; it is also known that all features are not strictly required to estimate the presence of the disease. For this reason, as classification algorithms have similar performance, further analysis on the deep features (e.g. the use of different feature selection, transformation or scaling) might improve performance. This might be realized in future works to outperform results in comparison with this model.

5   Conclusions and Future works

In this work, an implementation to detect COVID-19 from an easily accessible medical imaging modality (chest x-ray) is proposed. Due to the COVID-19 pandemic, this tool is presented as an alternative to increase detection rates in combination to RT-PCR test. In the first stage, a dataset from the combination of different subsets is compiled containing normal patients and different types of pneumonia (bacterial, viral and COVID-19). In this sense, as other works in the state of the art perform aggressive data augmentation techniques from few COVID-19 patients due to the lack of data availability, it is important to remark that no data augmentation was used and images belong to screenings from different patients. Then, images are given to the framework that extracts the pulmonary region to discard possible noise or other non-interesting image regions. Afterwards, images are uses two different deep learning architectures (DenseNet and ResNet) to characterize x-rays through their convolutions. As a consequence, 1024 filters with size 7×7 are extracted from each image. The deep feature dataset is then compiled and given to different machine learning algorithms to detect among different categories. Results demonstrate efficiency to detect pneumonia in general; and high accuracy to detect COVID-19. Despite the work shows a limitation detecting normal patients (significant confusion rate); this work is designed as a complementary tool to already existent tests to detect COVID-19.

To outperform results from this work, it is intended to realize further analysis of the deep features using selection, transformation or scaling algorithms to increase performance on the reported metrics. On the other hand; we will implement the advanced developments in this work including other data modalities that report efficiency to detect COVID-19 such clinical trials and information. In this sense, we believe that combination with medical imaging processing might increase the detection and progression of the disease in comparison with independent data modalities.

Acknowledgements. This work was supported by the Agencia de Educación Superior de Medellín - Sapiencia, the Universidad Politécnica Salesiana, Ecuador and the Institución Universitaria Pascual Bravo, Colombia and the Instituto Tecnológico Metropolitano, Colombia. We also want to give special thanks to the HM Hospitals, Spain for providing access to the COVID-19 data employed to develop this work.

References

1. Akter, S., Shamrat, F., Chakraborty, S., Karim, A., Azam, S.: COVID-19 detection using deep learning algorithm on chest x-ray images. Biology **10**(11), 1174 (2021)
2. Assaf, D., et al.: Utilization of machine-learning models to accurately predict the risk for critical COVID-19. Intern. Emerg. Med. **15**(8), 1435–1443 (2020)
3. Berrimi, M., Hamdi, S., Cherif, R.Y., Moussaoui, A., Oussalah, M., Chabane, M.: COVID-19 detection from Xray and CT scans using transfer learning. In: 2021 International Conference of Women in Data Science at Taif University (WiDSTaif), pp. 1–6. IEEE (2021)
4. Chiu, W.H.K., et al.: Detection of COVID-19 using deep learning algorithms on chest radiographs. J. Thorac. Imaging **35**(6), 369–376 (2020)
5. Clermont, G., Angus, D.C., DiRusso, S.M., Griffin, M., Linde-Zwirble, W.T.: Predicting hospital mortality for patients in the intensive care unit: a comparison of artificial neural networks with logistic regression models. Crit. Care Med. **29**(2), 291–296 (2001)
6. Condes, E., Arribas, J.R., et al.: Impact of COVID-19 on Madrid hospital system. Enfermedades Infecciosas Y Microbiologia Clinica (2020)
7. Cooper, G.F., et al.: An evaluation of machine-learning methods for predicting pneumonia mortality. Artif. Intell. Med. **9**(2), 107–138 (1997)
8. Degerli, A., et al.: COVID-19 infection map generation and detection from chest x-ray images. Health Inf. Sci. Syst. **9**(1), 1–16 (2021)
9. Ghassemi, M., et al.: Unfolding physiological state: mortality modelling in intensive care units. In: Proceedings of the 20th ACM SIGKDD International Conference on Knowledge Discovery and Data Mining, pp. 75–84 (2014)
10. He, K., Zhang, X., Ren, S., Sun, J.: Deep residual learning for image recognition. In: Proceedings of the IEEE Conference on Computer Vision and Pattern Recognition, pp. 770–778 (2016)
11. Huang, G., Liu, Z., Van Der Maaten, L., Weinberger, K.Q.: Densely connected convolutional networks. In: Proceedings of the IEEE Conference on Computer Vision and Pattern Recognition, pp. 4700–4708 (2017)
12. Jaeger, S., Candemir, S., Antani, S., Wáng, Y.X.J., Lu, P.X., Thoma, G.: Two public chest x-ray datasets for computer-aided screening of pulmonary diseases. Quant. Imaging Med. Surg. **4**(6), 475 (2014)

13. Kassania, S.H., Kassanib, P.H., Wesolowskic, M.J., Schneidera, K.A., Detersa, R.: Automatic detection of coronavirus disease (COVID-19) in X-ray and CT images: a machine learning based approach. Biocybern. Biomed. Eng. **41**(3), 867–879 (2021)

14. Kermany, D.S.: Identifying medical diagnoses and treatable diseases by image-based deep learning. Cell **172**(5), 1122–1131 (2018)

15. Kingma, D.P., Ba, J.: Adam: a method for stochastic optimization. arXiv preprint arXiv:1412.6980 (2014)

16. Mahase, E.: China coronavirus: who declares international emergency as death toll exceeds 200. BMJ: British Med. J. (Online) **368** (2020)

17. Nair, V., Hinton, G.E.: Rectified linear units improve restricted Boltzmann machines. In: ICML (2010)

18. Rajpurkar, P., et al.: CheXNet: radiologist-level pneumonia detection on chest x-rays with deep learning. arXiv preprint arXiv:1711.05225 (2017)

19. Razzak, M.I., Naz, S., Zaib, A.: Deep learning for medical image processing: overview, challenges and the future. In: Dey, N., Ashour, A.S., Borra, S. (eds.) Classification in BioApps. LNCVB, vol. 26, pp. 323–350. Springer, Cham (2018). https://doi.org/10.1007/978-3-319-65981-7_12

20. Shiraishi, J., et al.: Development of a digital image database for chest radiographs with and without a lung nodule: receiver operating characteristic analysis of radiologists' detection of pulmonary nodules. Am. J. Roentgenol. **174**(1), 71–74 (2000)

21. Shorten, C., Khoshgoftaar, T.M., Furht, B.: Deep learning applications for COVID-19. J. Big Data **8**(1), 1–54 (2021). https://doi.org/10.1186/s40537-020-00392-9

22. Song, Y., et al.: Deep learning enables accurate diagnosis of novel coronavirus (COVID-19) with CT images. IEEE/ACM Trans. Comput. Biol. Bioinform. **18**, 2775–2780 (2021)

23. World Health Organization (WHO): COVID-19 Weekly Epidemiological Update. Technical report (2021). https://covid19.who.int/

24. Wu, C., Rosenfeld, R., Clermont, G.: Using data-driven rules to predict mortality in severe community acquired pneumonia. PLoS ONE **9**(4), e89053 (2014)

25. Wu, Q., et al.: Radiomics analysis of computed tomography helps predict poor prognostic outcome in COVID-19. Theranostics **10**(16), 7231 (2020)

26. Yan, L., et al.: An interpretable mortality prediction model for COVID-19 patients. Nat. Mach. Intell. **2**, 1–6 (2020)

27. Zhang, J., Xie, Y., Li, Y., Shen, C., Xia, Y.: COVID-19 screening on chest x-ray images using deep learning based anomaly detection. arXiv preprint arXiv:2003.12338 27 (2020)

28. Zhou, T., Canu, S., Ruan, S.: Automatic COVID-19 CT segmentation using u-net integrated spatial and channel attention mechanism. Int. J. Imaging Syst. Technol. **31**(1), 16–27 (2021)

COVID-19 Pulmonary Lesion Classification Using CNN Software in Chest X-ray with Quadrant Scoring Severity Parameters

Denisse N. Niles[1] ⓘ, Daniel A. Amaguaña[1](✉) ⓘ, Alejandro B. Lojan[1] ⓘ,
Graciela M. Salum[1,2] ⓘ, Gandhi Villalba-Meneses[1] ⓘ, Andrés Tirado-Espín[3] ⓘ,
Omar Alvarado-Cando[4] ⓘ, Adriana Noboa-Jaramillo[5] ⓘ,
and Diego A. Almeida-Galárraga[1] ⓘ

[1] School of Biological Sciences and Engineering, Universidad Yachay Tech, San Miguel de
Urcuquí 100119, Ecuador
dalmeida@yachaytech.edu.ec

[2] Instituto Tecnológico Regional Suroeste, Carrera de Ingeniería Biomédica, Universidad
Tecnológica del Uruguay, 65000 Fray Bentos, Departamento de Rio Negro, Uruguay

[3] School of Mathematical and Computational Sciences, Universidad Yachay Tech, San Miguel
de Urcuquí 100119, Ecuador

[4] Escuela de Electrónica, Universidad de Azuay, Cuenca, Ecuador

[5] Nuclear Medicine World, Quito 170135, Ecuador

Abstract. The Sars-Cov2 virus has caused the worst health emergency of the last
decade. Furthermore, new strains make the fight against COVID-19 appear far
from over. The virus causes a severe acute respiratory syndrome that can lead to
death. Effective identification of lung damage by chest radiography using deep
learning methods could be advantageous for imaging physicians in differentiating
people who need to be admitted to an intensive care unit (ICU) from people that
don't require medical attention, to avoid the collapse of health systems. This article
describes the development of a deep learning model to classify and assess lung
injuries with a protocol for lung injury quantification. The model is based on U-
Net segmentation and injury classification according to the RALE score system.
Kaggle platform was used to obtain the chest radiography dataset and MATLAB to
generate the mask dataset for training. Finally, each lung is divided in 4 quadrants
for lesion quantification. An accuracy of 92.86% was obtained in the segmentation
process and 100% in the process of classifying levels of lung lesions.

Keywords: COVID-19 · Chest X-ray · CNN · Machine learning · U-Net · Lung
lesion

1 Introduction

COVID-19 is the disease caused by the SARS-Cov2 virus from Nidovirales order, family
Coronaviridae [1], this beta coronavirus is transmitted via zoonosis [2] and has spread
from human to human contact [3]. Although COVID-19 has less than 2% mortality

F. R. Narváez et al. (Eds.): SmartTech-IC 2021, CCIS 1532, pp. 370–382, 2022.
https://doi.org/10.1007/978-3-030-99170-8_27

rate [4] is a rapid transmission disease, on January 30th of 2020 the World Health Organization (WHO) declared COVID-19 a Public Health Emergency of International Concern [5]. The main initial symptoms of COVID-19 include fever, myalgia, dyspnea, cough and fatigue. Furthermore, in later stages of COVID-19 acute respiratory distress syndrome (ARDS) or multiple organ failure (MOF) may occur [6]. The main death cause is respiratory failure, mechanical ventilation is used to stabilize patients [7] but the increasing transmission rate makes the situation complicated for hospitals [8].

Chest X-ray is used in chronic lung disease detection, such as emphysema or cystic fibrosis, as well as lung complications [9]. The most frequent allegations on chest X-rays are: nodulillary reticular opacities (52–47%) and ground glass opacity (48–33%) [10]. As the disease progresses, multiple bilateral opacities [11] can be detected in the lower and peripheral lobes, the latter are the most common findings. Radiological findings are commonly found between the 6th–14th day [12] and the peak of radiological severity occurs between the 10th–12th day from the onset of symptoms [13].

Thoracic radiography has gained importance during the pandemic for pulmonary lesion diagnosis and prognosis studies [14]. Oftentimes COVID-19 patients do not present clinical symptoms [15], thoracic X-ray is a non-invasive way to evaluate pulmonary lesions in the form of a frosted glass pattern and an increased vascular network; it can also find condensations or consolidations that will depend on the injury or the degree of COVID-19 [16].

It is important to remark that chest X-ray is not a virus detection method but rather a lung lesion detection procedure, that is why chest X-rays can be crucial for mortality rate prevention [17]. Some advantages of this method include: it can be done in a matter of minutes, is a cheap technique and emits less radiation than other imaging methods [18]. In addition, since X-ray machines are found in most medical centers, it has a feasible implementation [19]. The severity of lung lesions can be quantified with Radiographic Assessment of Lung Edema (RALE) which employs a 1–8 point score system divided in quadrants [20]. It has been found that patients with a higher RALE score have less chance of survival [21].

According to the Royal College of Radiologists, in the last years the amount of biomedical information has increased drastically while the amount of radiologist has stayed practically the same [22], since X-rays can be used for COVID-19 identification this numbers have grown exponentially during the pandemic, and radiologist have to face the increasing clinical demands [23]. The situation has worsen in developing countries with higher transmission rate [24], the medical personnel and ICUs are insufficient, the need for a tool that facilitates the lung lesion identification produced by SARS-Cov 2, given the scarce qualified radiologist specialists number in relationship to the increasing workload [24].

The development of software to help manage radiologist workload have been actively studied in recent years [25], deep learning applications with convolutional neural networks (CNN) have severely increased performance in comparison with previous state of the art rule based and model based methods [26].

The detection of pathologies through artificial intelligence (AI) presents a significant advance in current medicine. The detection of pathologies through artificial intelligence (AI) presents a significant advance in current medicine. Through neural networks that are one of the main axes of AI, it has been possible to make smart decisions when diagnosing diseases such as glaucoma, skin lesion, cancer, and Parkinson's disease [27–30]. Furthermore, artificial neural networks have proved to process various kinds of medical data and improve the way health professionals diagnose. There is a diverse range of CNN with potential biomedical applications. Minaee et al. review the application of 4 types of CNN (DenseNet-161, SqueezeNet, ResNet18 and ResNet50) in COVID-19 prediction with average results of 90% sensitivity and 98% specificity [16]. Inspired by significant discoveries in neural networks [31], the present project is based on a ten layer U-Net type of convolutional network [32], with the purpose of detecting pneumonia patterns of chest X-ray in COVID-19 patients with potential clinical applications [33]. The current work aims to automatically detect lung lesions in thoracic radiography and provide quantification of the severity of the lesion with the RALE scoring system dividing each lung in four different quadrants [34], using open-source software and public databases of COVID-19 affected and normal thoracic radiography for neural network training to make front to the COVID-19 pandemic and prevent future public health emergencies.

2 Methodology

In order to predict the degree of severity of COVID-19 based on chest X-rays, semantic segmentation was used as a starting point, to detect the area of the lung lesion and subsequently obtain a diagnosis corresponding to the COVID-19 degree of severity, see Fig. 1.

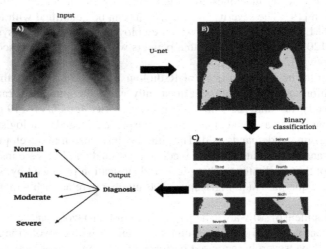

Fig. 1. Proposed model. A) corresponds to the input (COVID-19 radiography image). B) predicted mask corresponding to the COVID-19 lesions from the U-Net network. C) quadrant chart used to predict the diagnosis; the final output could be: normal, mild, moderate, severe.

2.1   Dataset Pre-processing

To create the database for this study a sample of 3000 images of COVID-19 chest radiographs were used. The sample was obtained and validated from the COVID-19 Radiography Database [35, 36]. For each image of the sample there was created a mask containing the lung lesions. COVID-19 lesion masks were generated in grayscale with MATLAB, for this reason each mask image has 1 channel, see Fig. 1. Ground truths segmentations were validated by Dr. Adriana Paola Noboa Jaramillo radiologist and CEO of Nuclear Medicine World. All kind of lung lesions caused by COVID-19 were included in the ground truths segmentations. The database was divided in a group of training, corresponding to the random assignment of 80% of the total sample, and a group of testing; corresponding to the random assignment of 20% of the total sample. (Table 1).

The aim of image pre-processing is to improve the quality of the image, suppress unwilling distortions and enhance some image features important for further processing. Pre-processing is a group of operations with images at the lowest level of abstraction [37]. In this study, for image pre-processing there were used a normalization of the data followed by a conversion of the dataset images into grayscale and a resizing of 128 × 128 × 1 pixels. This result into and advantage in computational and time cost. Once the pre-processing was completed, the image segmentation was carried out (Fig. 2).

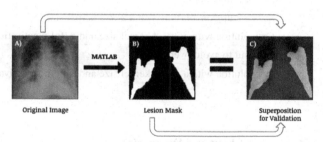

Fig. 2. Example of mask image generated. A) Original COVID-19 radiography image. B) Author's segmentation. C) Superposition of A and B images for validation of the segmentation.

Table 1. Dataset information description and distribution.

COVID-19 radiography images		COVID-19 lesion masks	
3000		3000	
Training	Testing	Training	Testing
2400	600	2400	600

2.2   U-Net Segmentation Model

In order to automatically detect the lung lesions in patients with COVID-19 through the analysis of chest X-rays a U-Net convolutional neural network was used because U-Net networks needs few training images and yields more precise segmentations [26].

U-Net framework in terms of architecture is divided into two sections the contracting path and extensive path, U-Net has the same amount of down-sampling and up-sampling layers producing the characteristic "U" design architecture [32].

After image pre-processing with the resized inputs of $128 \times 128 \times 1$ pixels (width, height, channels) a U-Net architecture was constructed (Fig. 3). The implemented network has a total of 10 convolutional layers: 5 convolutional layers corresponding to the contraction path, 4 convolutional layers corresponding to the expansion path and 1 final convolution layer to adjust the output dimension (Table 2).

Table 2. Proposed U-Net architecture

U-Net layers	Characteristics
Contraction	2 convolutions with a 3×3 Kernel size and a ReLu activation
	Dropout to avoid overfitting
	A 2×2 max pooling
Expansion	A 2×2 up convolution with a 2×2 kernel size
	Convolution with a 3×3 kernel size and a ReLu activation
	Dropout to avoid overfitting
Final	Convolution with a 1×1 kernel size and a sigmoid activation

2.3   Process of Quadrant Chart and Diagnosis

To provide better visualization of COVID-19 lung lesions in thoracic X-rays. The U-Net predicted mask was divided into eight quadrants; four quadrants corresponding to each lung. The division of the imagen was based on the indications for RALE score; each lung is divided into four quadrants. RALE score has been proved to be an effective quantitative method for COVID-19 severity diagnosis and it is highly correlated with an increased risk of ICU admission [38].

2.4   RALE Score

In order to obtain the final output corresponding to the diagnosis of COVID-19 severity a binary classification was carried out to each quadrant obtained from the U-Net output (mask). Through an algorithm a value of zero or one was assigned to each quadrant (lesion present = 1, no lesion = 0). In the last step the value resulting of the sum of all quadrant values of a single mask was used to calculate the severity degree of COVID-19 according to the RALE score (Table 3). RALE score is measured by dividing the lungs

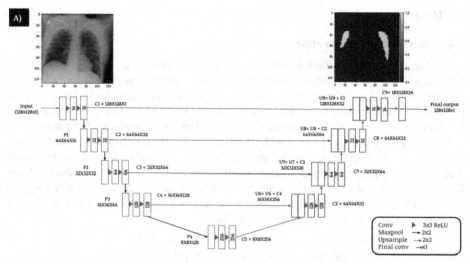

Fig. 3. U-Net implemented architecture. A) Represents the applied U-Net in a diagram. The number of channels is denoted on top of the boxes. The turquoise boxes represent the contraction path formed by 5 layers that reduce dimension to a half each time. The magenta boxes represent the expansion path formed by 4 layers that increase the dimension in a factor of 2 each time. In this figure is easy to observe the concatenation of each layer in the contraction path with each layer of the expansive path, which forms the U-like structure.

in 4 quadrants each one, having a total number of quadrants equal. According to the RALE scale every quadrant that presents a lesion is going to represent a point for the final score. The final score of the RALE scale is calculated as the sum of the value of every quadrant, being 8 the maximum score that can be achieved.

Table 3. Parameters for the final predicted output, where "FV" is the sum of the binary predicted outputs for every quadrant of a single predicted mark.

Final output	
Values	Output
$FV = 0$:	Diagnosis: normal
$0 < FV \leq 2$:	Diagnosis: mild
$2 < FV \leq 6$	Diagnosis: moderate
$FV > 6$	Diagnosis: severe

3   Results

3.1   Parameter Configuration

The parameters of the neural network were adjusted to optimize the processing of the X-ray images. In the segmentation model, the most important parameters were: the learning rate, the batch size, and the number of epochs, whose values are detailed in Table 4. These parameters were essential to creating an efficient and reliable segmentation process [35]. Regarding the output of the segmentation model, the characteristics of the mask were a 2D image of 128 × 128 × 1, with a batch size of 164, with a 3 × 3 kernel, and a ReLu activation function. For the quadrant process, an impression of the lesions in their respective quadrant was generated based on the Radiographic Assessment of Lung Edema score. Subsequently, to quantify the percentage of damage in each lung, an algorithm was generated capable of generating a counter-type output that will classify the degree of severity of lung damage in levels.

Table 4. Parameters of the applied networks

Segmentation model (U-Net)		RALE algorithm	
Parameter	Value	Parameter	Value
Learning rate	1 × e−4	Contour area	500
Batch-size	164	*Contour retrieval mode*	*RETR-EXTERNAL*
Number of epochs	8		

3.2   Performance Evaluation for Prediction and Evaluation

The performance of learning algorithms has accepted Performance Evaluation Measures ways of evaluating their results[39]. For this reason, parameters such as accuracy as a metric and predictive quality indicator for the output images (1). In addition, Sensitivity and specificity (2), (3) regarding recognized examples registered correctly and incorrectly for each class. These parameters use the confusion matrix that reflects the correct answers that the algorithm prediction had in comparison with the actual value and are helpful in biomedicine, especially in algorithms with images [39].

Accuracy:
Is the ratio of the correct class of samples to the total number of samples.

$$Accuracy = \frac{TP + FN}{TP + FN + TN + F} \tag{1}$$

Sensitivity:
Which defines probability of positive results in case of correct class of sample.

$$Sensitivity = \frac{TP}{TP + FN} \tag{2}$$

Specificity: Gives the probability of negative result in case of incorrect class of sample.

$$Specificity = \frac{TN}{TN + FP} \qquad (3)$$

Table 5. U-net detection and learning results.

Segmentation	
Parameter	Value
Accuracy	0.9286
Sensitivity	1.0000
Specificity	0.9286

For training, the neural network data was divided into 80:20 for training and testing, respectively. Figure 4 A), B) shows that after eight epochs, a precision of 0.9286 and a training loss relative to the epoch number of 0.2235 were obtained. This precision shows us a great capacity for learning on the U-Net, an important point to take into account when implanting for the detection of pathologies in chest radiographs. On the other hand, a sensitivity of 1,000 was obtained, which shows us that the radiographs that present lesions are correctly identified by the neural network (true positive rate). Finally, with a specificity of 0.9286, we deduce a high identification of true negatives, thus avoiding false negatives. These results are shown in Table 5.

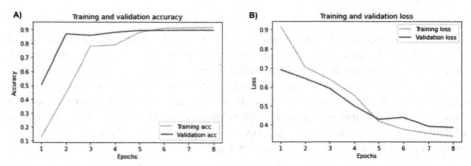

Fig. 4. A) Train & validation accuracy with respect to number of epochs of U-Net. B) Train & validation loss with respect to number of epochs

3.3 Output Evaluation

In summary, the process by which the output image is obtained using the actual model: A conventional chest X-ray image does select from the data set. Subsequently, a mask is produced with MATLAB where the lung lesion can be isolated. After that, the prediction of the segmentation network originated. Then, RALE algorithm was applied to obtain the level of damage in the lungs. This process is shown in Fig. 5. U-Net detection and learning outcomes.

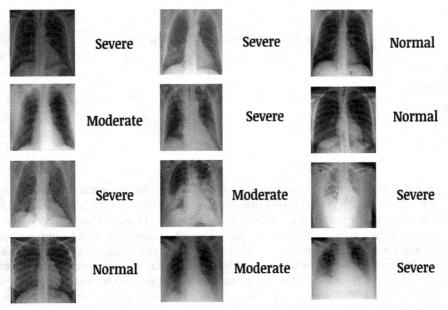

Fig. 5. The random input of images and their output with classification based on the RALE scale's normal, moderate, and severe levels.

For the final result of Fig. 6, an image divided into eight quadrants is generated, with four quadrants destined for each lung. Subsequently, the lesions were located in each lung, and weight was assigned to them. In this injury, a score of 6 quadrants was obtained with a weighting of 1 point for each affected quadrant (presence of lung damage), which in the weighted sum would mean $\sum quadrant = n$ with n affected quadrants out of a total value of 8 quadrants. This result will be quantified to determine if the percentage of damage is: normal, mild, moderate, severe. The process was repeated for each of the images in the current database, as shown in Fig. 6.

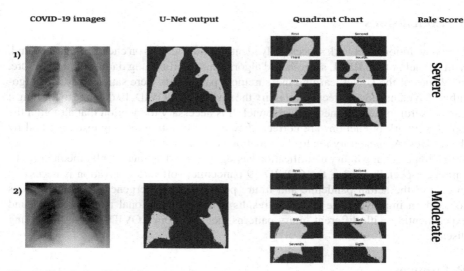

Fig. 6. The random input of images and their output with classification based on the RALE scale's normal, moderate, and severe levels.

4 Discussion

4.1 Comparison with Similar Models

The method presented in this project has promising results in arresting lung injuries caused by COVID-19. Since it is based on an efficient method for pulmonary assessment and the results it shows are high compared to similar studies that use machine learning and chest radiographs to assess lung injury shown in Table 6. In which was collected information on investigations that are in the same of CNN presented.

Table 6. Comparison with similar models.

Paper	Study	Model	Performance	Dataset
Present work	Application of CNN in Software assisted pulmonary lesion detection due to COVID-19 using cheperfost X-ray	U-Net	0.9286	3000
[40]	Divergent Nets: medical image segmentation by network ensemble	TriU-Net	0.796	1000
		Divergent Nets	0.823	
		U-Net++	0.917	
		Tri U-Net	0.925	
[41]	Few-shot 3D multi-modal medical image segmentation using generative adversarial learning	Basic U-Net	0.8200	3500

5 Conclusions

The convolutional network successfully identifies lung lesions on chest radiography and, with the help of the RELE score-based algorithm, classifies lung damage. Furthermore, the values of the U-Net learning measurement parameters were satisfactory. The algorithm also managed to detect and classify the severity of COVID-19 damage to the lungs; this is useful to support medical personnel. It is necessary to mention that although the neural network predictions are correct, they do not constitute a diagnostic method by themselves. A mandatory medical evaluation is necessary.

Automated lung injury identification has significant advantages for biomedical applications, especially during the COVID-19 pandemic; software innovation is necessary to control the actual pandemic and future public health emergencies. Future work is focused on improving the precision results of the convolutional neural network and experimenting with different injury patterns, not just from COVID-19. But also, lung diseases.

References

1. Malik, Y.A.: Properties of coronavirus and SARS-CoV-2. In: Malays. J. Pathol. (ed.) Immune Responses in COVID-19 and Potential Vaccines: Lessons Learned from SARS and MERS Epidemic, pp. 3–11. Elsevier, Boston (2021)
2. Prompetchara, E., Ketloy, C., Palaga, T.: Allergy and Immunology Immune Responses in COVID-19 and Potential Vaccines: Lessons Learned from SARS and MERS epidemic. https://doi.org/10.12932/AP-200220-0772
3. Chowdhury, M.A., Hossain, N., Kashem, M.A., Shahid, M.A., Alam, A.: Immune response in COVID-19: a review. J. Infect. Public Health 13, 1619–1629 (2020). https://doi.org/10.1016/J.JIPH.2020.07.001
4. Ong, E.Z., et al.: A dynamic immune response shapes COVID-19 progression. Cell Host Microbe 27, 879-882.e2 (2020). https://doi.org/10.1016/J.CHOM.2020.03.021
5. Sohrabi, C., et al.: World Health Organization declares global emergency: a review of the 2019 novel coronavirus (COVID-19). Int. J. Surg. 76, 71–76 (2020). https://doi.org/10.1016/J.IJSU.2020.02.034
6. Huang, C., et al.: Clinical features of patients infected with 2019 novel coronavirus in Wuhan, China. Lancet (London, England) 395, 497–506 (2020). https://doi.org/10.1016/S0140-6736(20)30183-5
7. Vincent, J.-L., Taccone, F.S.: Understanding pathways to death in patients with COVID-19. Lancet Respir. Med. 8, 430–432 (2020). https://doi.org/10.1016/S2213-2600(20)30165-X
8. Van Wees, J.-D., et al.: Forecasting hospitalization and ICU rates of the COVID-19 outbreak: an efficient SEIR model. https://doi.org/10.2471/BLT.20.251561
9. Wielpütz, M.O., et al.: Imaging of cystic fibrosis lung disease and clinical interpretation. RöFo – Fortschritte auf dem Gebiet der Röntgenstrahlen und der Bildgeb Verfahren 188, 834–845 (2016). https://doi.org/10.1055/S-0042-104936
10. Collins, J., Stern, E.J.: Ground-glass opacity at CT: the ABCs. AJR 169 (1997)
11. Funama, Y., et al.: Detection of nodules showing ground-glass opacity in the lungs at low-dose multidetector computed tomography: Phantom and clinical study. J. Comput. Assist. Tomogr. 33, 49–53 (2009). https://doi.org/10.1097/RCT.0B013E31815E6291
12. Rousan, L.A., Elobeid, E., Karrar, M., Khader, Y.: Chest X-ray findings and temporal lung changes in patients with COVID-19 pneumonia. BMC Pulm. Med. 20, 1–9 (2020). https://doi.org/10.1186/S12890-020-01286-5/FIGURES/5

13. Shaw, B., Daskareh, M., Gholamrezanezhad, A.: The lingering manifestations of COVID-19 during and after convalescence: update on long-term pulmonary consequences of coronavirus disease 2019 (COVID-19). Radiol. Med. (Torino) **126**(1), 40–46 (2020). https://doi.org/10.1007/s11547-020-01295-8
14. Monaco, C.G., et al.: Chest X-ray severity score in COVID-19 patients on emergency department admission: a two-centre study. Eur. Radiol. Exp. **4**(1), 1–7 (2020). https://doi.org/10.1186/s41747-020-00195-w
15. Lu, S., et al.: Alert for non-respiratory symptoms of coronavirus disease 2019 patients in epidemic period: a case report of familial cluster with three asymptomatic COVID-19 patients. J. Med. Virol. **93**, 518–521 (2021). https://doi.org/10.1002/JMV.25776
16. Minaee, S., Kafieh, R., Sonka, M., Yazdani, S., Jamalipour Soufi, G.: Deep-COVID: predicting COVID-19 from chest X-ray images using deep transfer learning. Med. Image Anal. **65**, 101794 (2020). https://doi.org/10.1016/J.MEDIA.2020.101794
17. Hasan, M.J., Alom, M.S., Ali, M.S.: Deep learning based detection and segmentation of COVID-19 pneumonia on chest X-ray image. In: 2021 Int. Conf. Inf. Commun. Technol. Sustain. Dev. ICICT4SD 2021 – Proc., pp. 210–214 (2021). https://doi.org/10.1109/ICICT4SD50815.2021.9396878
18. Dong, D., et al.: The role of imaging in the detection and management of COVID-19: A Review. IEEE Rev. Biomed. Eng. **14**, 16–29 (2021). https://doi.org/10.1109/RBME.2020.2990959
19. Kong, W., Agarwal, P.P.: Chest imaging appearance of COVID-19 infection. Radiol. Cardiothoracic Imag. **2**, e200028 (2020). https://doi.org/10.1148/ryct.2020200028
20. Warren, M.A., et al.: Severity scoring of lung oedema on the chest radiograph is associated with clinical outcomes in ARDS. Thorax **73**, 840–846 (2018). https://doi.org/10.1136/THORAXJNL-2017-211280
21. Bisso, I.C., et al.: Caracteristicas clinicas de los pacientes criticos con COVID-19. Med. (Buenos Aires) **81**, 527–535 (2021)
22. Kwee, T.C., Kwee, R.M.: Workload of diagnostic radiologists in the foreseeable future based on recent scientific advances: growth expectations and role of artificial intelligence. Insights Imaging **12**(1), 1–12 (2021). https://doi.org/10.1186/s13244-021-01031-4
23. Veerasuri, S., Vekeria, M., Davies, S.E., Graham, R., Rodrigues, J.C.L.: Impact of COVID-19 on UK radiology training: a questionnaire study. Clin. Radiol. **75**, 877.e7-877.e14 (2020). https://doi.org/10.1016/J.CRAD.2020.07.022
24. Salluh, J.I.F., Lisboa, T., Bozza, F.A.: Challenges for the care delivery for critically ill COVID-19 patients in developing countries: the Brazilian perspective. Crit. Care **241**(24), 1–3 (2020). https://doi.org/10.1186/S13054-020-03278-7
25. Hira, S., Bai, A., Hira, S.: An automatic approach based on CNN architecture to detect Covid-19 disease from chest X-ray images. Appl. Intell. **51**(5), 2864–2889 (2020). https://doi.org/10.1007/s10489-020-02010-w
26. Ronneberger, O., Fischer, P., Brox, T.: U-Net: convolutional networks for biomedical image segmentation. Lect. Notes Comput. Sci. (including Subser Lect. Notes Artif. Intell. Lect. Notes Bioinformatics) **9351**, 234–241 (2015)
27. Pereira-Carrillo, J., Suntaxi-Dominguez, D., Guarnizo-Cabezas, O., Villalba-Meneses, G., Tirado-Espín, A., Almeida-Galárraga, D.: Comparison Between Two Novel Approaches in Automatic Breast Cancer Detection and Diagnosis and Its Contribution in Military Defense. In: Rocha, Á., Fajardo-Toro, C.H., Rodríguez, J.M.R. (eds.) Developments and Advances in Defense and Security. SIST, vol. 255, pp. 189–201. Springer, Singapore (2022). https://doi.org/10.1007/978-981-16-4884-7_15
28. Yanchatuña, O.P., et al.: Skin lesion detection and classification using convolutional neural network for deep feature extraction and support vector machine. Int. J. Adv. Sci. Eng. Inf. Technol. **11**, 1260–1267 (2021). https://doi.org/10.18517/IJASEIT.11.3.13679

29. Almeida-Galarraga, D., et al.: Glaucoma detection through digital processing from fundus images using MATLAB. In: Proc – 2021 2nd Int. Conf. Inf. Syst. Softw. Technol. ICI2ST 2021, pp. 39–45 (2021). https://doi.org/10.1109/ICI2ST51859.2021.00014

30. Suquilanda-Pesántez, J.D., et al.: Prediction of Parkinson's Disease Severity Based on Gait Signals Using a Neural Network and the Fast Fourier Transform. In: Botto-Tobar, M., Cruz, H., Díaz Cadena, A. (eds.) CIT 2020. AISC, vol. 1326, pp. 3–18. Springer, Cham (2021). https://doi.org/10.1007/978-3-030-68080-0_1

31. Wu, X., et al.: Deep learning-based multi-view fusion model for screening 2019 novel coronavirus pneumonia: a multicentre study. Eur. J. Radiol. **128**, 109041 (2020). https://doi.org/10.1016/J.EJRAD.2020.109041

32. Weng, Y., Zhou, T., Li, Y., Qiu, X.: NAS-Unet: neural architecture search for medical image segmentation. IEEE Access **7**, 44247–44257 (2019). https://doi.org/10.1109/ACCESS.2019.2908991

33. Rahman, T., et al.: Vol 10. Page **3233**(10), 3233 (2020). https://doi.org/10.3390/APP10093233

34. Setiawati, R., et al.: Modified chest X-ray scoring system in evaluating severity of COVID-19 patient in Dr. Soetomo General Hospital, Surabaya, Indonesia. Int. J. Gen. Med. **14**, 2407–2412 (2021). https://doi.org/10.2147/IJGM.S310577

35. Rahman, T., et al.: Exploring the effect of image enhancement techniques on COVID-19 detection using chest X-ray images. Comput. Biol. Med. **132**, 104319 (2021). https://doi.org/10.1016/J.COMPBIOMED.2021.104319

36. Chowdhury, M.E.H., et al.: Can AI help in screening viral and COVID-19 pneumonia? IEEE Access **8**, 132665–132676 (2020). https://doi.org/10.1109/ACCESS.2020.3010287

37. Sonka, M., Hlavac, V., Boyle, R.: Image pre-processing. In: Image Processing, Analysis and Machine Vision, pp. 56–111. Springer US, Boston, MA (1993)

38. Cozzi, D., et al.: Chest X-ray in new coronavirus disease 2019 (COVID-19) infection: findings and correlation with clinical outcome. Radiol. Med. (Torino) **125**(8), 730–737 (2020). https://doi.org/10.1007/s11547-020-01232-9

39. Sokolova, M., Japkowicz, N., Szpakowicz, S.: Beyond Accuracy, F-Score and ROC: A Family of Discriminant Measures for Performance Evaluation. In: Sattar, A., Kang, B.-h (eds.) AI 2006. LNCS (LNAI), vol. 4304, pp. 1015–1021. Springer, Heidelberg (2006). https://doi.org/10.1007/11941439_114

40. Thambawita, V., Hicks, S.A., Halvorsen, P., Riegler, M.A.: DivergentNets: medical image segmentation by network ensemble. CEUR Workshop Proc. **2886**, 27–38 (2021)

41. Mondal, A.K., Dolz, J., Desrosiers, C.: Few-shot 3D Multi-modal Medical Image Segmentation using Generative Adversarial Learning (2018)

HJ-Biplot and Clustering to Analyze the COVID-19 Vaccination Process of American and European Countries

Lenin Riera-Segura$^{(\boxtimes)}$, Guido Tapia-Riera , Isidro R. Amaro ,
Saba Infante , and Harvey Marin-Calispa

Yachay Tech University, Hacienda San José, Urcuquí 100119, Ecuador
{lenin.riera,guido.tapia,iamaro,sinfante,harvey.marin}@yachaytech.edu.ec

Abstract. HJ-Biplot and Cluster Analysis are used in a data set that contains variables related to the impact of COVID-19 and vaccination in American and European countries. The variables considered are total cases per million, total tests per thousand, total deaths per million, total vaccinations per hundred, and people fully vaccinated per hundred. The purpose of this paper is to analyze the time evolution of the COVID-19 vaccination process in the aforementioned region during March, April, May, June, July, and August 2021. The results obtained provide a straightforward way of determining each country's status with respect to the variables considered, which could be useful for policymakers to understand the evolution of their country throughout the pandemic.

Keywords: COVID-19 · Cluster analysis · HJ-Biplot · Vaccination

1 Introduction

A new coronavirus called SARS-CoV-2 is the cause of the disease COVID-19, which was communicated through a report for the first time to the World Health Organization (WHO) in December 2019, where cases of viral pneumonia were mentioned in Wuhan, China [1]. Due to the rapid expansion rate of COVID-19, on March 11th, 2020, the WHO announced that COVID-19 became a pandemic. Even more, this disease continues to affect almost all countries around the world. Also, this virus has infected more than 229 million people and killed more than 4.7 million people up to September 20th, 2021, according to Worldometers [2].

Fortunately, it took no more than a year for the world to announce the development of vaccines capable of fighting COVID-19. Since then, at least 43.3% of the world population has been vaccinated with one dose up to September 20th, 2021 [3].

In the early stage of the pandemic, the impact of COVID-19 was measured through several variables such as the number of intensive care units, hospital beds, tests, and economic-related ones. To illustrate, we can mention the work done by Pozo et al. [4], where they studied the relationship between public

F. R. Narváez et al. (Eds.): SmartTech-IC 2021, CCIS 1532, pp. 383–397, 2022.
https://doi.org/10.1007/978-3-030-99170-8_28

health damages and economic impact of COVID-19 in South American countries. When countries began their vaccination programs, new data became available for researchers to study the impact of COVID-19. This work makes use of such data.

The purpose of this paper is to analyze the time evolution of the COVID-19 vaccination process in the aforementioned region during March, April, May, June, July, and August 2021 by means of multivariate statistical techniques such as HJ-Biplot and Cluster Analysis. The results obtained provide a straightforward way of determining each country's status with respect to the variables considered, which could be useful for policy makers to understand the evolution of their countries throughout the pandemic.

The present work is organized as follows. Section 2 is dedicated to describe the data and method used. Section 3 reports the graphical results obtained, which consist of six graphs representing the clusters for each month. Besides, a discussion in view of the results is presented. Section 4 concludes the results and provides policy implications. Additional visual material to Sects. 2 and 3 are presented in Appendices A and B.

2   Materials and Methods

2.1   Data Description

The data set considered in this work was obtained from a GitHub public repository (https://github.com/owid/covid-19-data/tree/master/public/data) maintained by Our World in Data [3,5,6]. It consists of several variables that characterize COVID-19 related issues such as the number of vaccinated people, number of confirmed deaths, number of confirmed cases, number of tests, as well as other variables of potential interest.

The data set covers the majority of countries and territories in the world for which public data is available. For this work, the following American and European countries (observations) are considered: Argentina, Bolivia, Canada, Chile, Colombia, Costa Rica, Ecuador, The United States of America (USA), Guatemala, Mexico, Panama, Paraguay, Peru, Dominican Republic, Uruguay, Germany, Belgium, Spain, Italy, Netherlands, Portugal, and The United Kingdom (UK). The most important filtering criterion for selecting both American and European countries is the availability of data and its update frequency. This is why countries such as Brazil and France are not considered. Of the remaining countries, we choose those with the largest population to better interpret and visualize the results. This is also why countries belonging to other regions were not initially considered.

To study the 22 countries described above, we consider 5 variables from the previously mentioned GitHub public repository. The description of these variables is given below. They are given with respect to the entire population of each country.

1. total cases per million (V_1): This variable measures the number of confirmed cases of COVID-19 per one million people.

2. total deaths per million (V_2): This variable quantifies the number of deaths caused by COVID-19 per one million people.
3. total tests per thousand (V_3): This variable counts the number of tests for COVID-19 per one thousand people.
4. total vaccinations per hundred (V_4): This variable measures the number of COVID-19 vaccination doses administered per one hundred people.
5. people fully vaccinated per hundred (V_5): This variable keeps track of the number of people who received all vaccine doses per one hundred people

The data set is updated daily. However, for the purpose of this paper, a Python [7] script is used to organize it on a monthly basis. The data is also arranged cumulatively. That is, it takes into account all of the available historical data until the last day of each month.

2.2   HJ-Biplot

Biplots are a useful data visualization method proposed by Gabriel [8]. This multivariate analysis technique allows the representation of a $n \times p$ data matrix Y in a low dimensional space, which helps its interpretation. For a geometric interpretation of a Biplot representation, see Fig. 1. The Biplot technique is based on the decomposition of Y as the product of two matrices A and B of dimension $n \times s$ and $p \times s$, respectively. In this way, $Y = AB^T$, and any element y_{ij} can be written as the inner product $a_i^T b_j$, where $a_1, \ldots, a_n$ are the rows of A and $b_1, \ldots, b_p$ are the rows of B. Vectors a_i and b_j are called row markers and column markers, respectively. For a detailed explanation about the properties of the markers of a Biplot, the reader is referred to [9].

The matrices A and B are usually obtained by the singular value decomposition (SVD) of Y, that is,

$$Y = AB^T = U\Lambda V^T, \tag{1}$$

where the columns of matrix U are orthonormal eigenvectors of YY^T, Λ is a diagonal matrix that has the singular values λ_s of Y which are sorted in descending order, and the columns of matrix V are orthonormal eigenvectors of Y^TY [9]. It is easy to note that the elements y_{ij} can also be written as

$$y_{ij} = \sum_{s=1}^{\min(n,p)} \lambda_s u_{is} v_{js}. \tag{2}$$

The most common classical Biplots are GH-Biplot and JK-Biplot, and the difference between the two is the choice of A and B. In the GH-Biplot, $A = U$ and $B = V\Lambda$ while in the JK-Biplot, $A = U\Lambda$ and $B = V$ [9,10]. The former better represents the columns of Y and the latter the rows. A third alternative introduced by Galindo [11] depicts rows and columns simultaneously with a high quality of representation [12]. This alternative is called HJ-Biplot, for which, $A = U\Lambda$ and $B = V\Lambda$. The quality of representation indicates how accurately a row/column marker is represented in the low dimensional space.

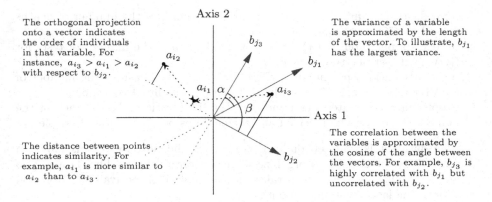

Fig. 1. Geometric meaning of the HJ-Biplot representation on plane 1–2. Source: [10].

HJ-Biplot technique has been used by several authors to study a wide range of problems. For instance, Díaz-Faes et al. [13] used HJ-Biplot as a tool to inspect a bibliometric data matrix. Recently, Carrasco et al. [10] evaluated the water quality in Panama Canal by means of HJ-Biplot. In the context of COVID-19, Tenesaca-Chillogallo et al. [14] studied the relationship between COVID-19 and severe health complications using HJ-Biplot. This paper uses HJ-Biplot as well.

2.3   Cluster Analysis

Cluster analysis is a multivariate statistical technique that allows looking patterns in a data set intending to achieve a grouping of observations with similar characteristics into clusters based mainly on some dissimilarity measure. However, the clusters are heterogeneous among them [15].

Agglomerative Clustering. It is a hierarchical method that allows grouping the two closest clusters in each step that is executed. To know what clusters group a dissimilarity measure is used; usually, a distance metric is employed as this measure [15]. In short, this works as in the following steps:

Step 1: Assume that every observation is a cluster.
Step 2: Choose the two closest clusters based on distance and put them together as a new cluster.

Step 2 is repeated until getting only a single cluster. For this work, average linkage is used, which computes the distance between two clusters C_1 and C_2 through the average of nm distances, where n and m denote the observations of the cluster C_1 and C_2, respectively [15]. That is,

$$D(C_1, C_2) = \frac{1}{nm} \sum_{i=1}^{n} \sum_{j=1}^{m} d(y_i, y_j), \tag{3}$$

where d is a distance between the observations $y_i \in C_1$ and $y_j \in C_2$. Euclidean distance is employed for the present work.

K-Means. This is a non-hierarchical method that allows dividing the data into k clusters minimizing the intra-cluster distance [16], that is,

$$\sum_{i=1}^{k} \sum_{y \in C_i} d^2(y - \mu_i), \tag{4}$$

where μ_i is the mean of the C_i cluster and d denotes the distance employed. This method is performed in the following steps:

Step 1: Choose the number of k cluster.
Step 2: Randomly select the centroids. These are not necessarily observations from the data set. However, in the simplest case they are.
Step 3: Assign each observation to the nearest centroid. Notice that in this step, clusters are constructed.
Step 4: Compute and assign the new centroid of each cluster.
Step 5: Reassign each observation to the nearest centroid. Repeat step 4 if new assignments are observed (i.e., an observation changes of the cluster where it was assigned previously); otherwise, stop.

Notice that in Step 3 to assign an observation to the nearest centroid, a distance is used. Commonly Euclidean distance is chosen. Nevertheless, other distances such as squared Euclidean and manhattan, are employed according to the case studied. For this work, squared Euclidean distance is used.

In fields such as data analysis, information retrieval, and machine learning, K-Means is one of the most used algorithm. However, it presents some restrictions, such as define the optimal number of clusters, the presence of outliers, and others [17]. A widely used technique to determine the optimal number of clusters is to combine information obtained from hierarchical and non-hierarchical methods such as dendrograms and the elbow method. In this sense, the present work uses the average linkage approach as the hierarchical method and K-Means as the non-hierarchical method.

2.4   Methodology

The following methodology is applied to each month considered in this work.

The first step was to standardize the data. What we did next was to compute the determinant of the correlation matrix to check whether or not it is appropriate to use multivariate statistical techniques. It turned out to be suitable for all the months. The next step was to apply the HJ-Biplot using the software Mult-Biplot developed by Vicente-Villardón [18] to get a representation of the data in the plane 1–2 along with the quality of representation of countries/variables and the total variance explained. Then hierarchical clustering with Biplot coordinates was used in order to find the highest cophenetic correlation for each method available in MultBiplot. In general, the highest cophenetic correlation was achieved when using the average linkage method. This method was then used to plot a dendrogram for each month see Appendix A).

The large changes in distances approach is employed in the aforementioned dendrograms to determine the appropriate number of clusters. Nevertheless, the number of clusters was ultimately determined by combining the mentioned approach and the elbow method (using original standardized data). Both approaches conclude that 5 clusters are the appropriate choice to describe the data each month. For plotting the elbow graph, we conducted several tests, which allowed us to determine that the Hartigan-Wong version [19] of K-Means algorithm yields the largest distance inter-cluster. After selecting the optimal number of clusters and the best algorithm, we apply K-Means (squared Euclidean, Hartigan-Wong) using Biplot coordinates to get the clusters in plane 1-2.

3   Results and Discussion

Before displaying and interpreting the graphical results, we first evaluate the goodness of the fit and the quality of representation. We find out that the goodness of the fit is above 80% for all months and the quality of representation is at least 65% for all variables in all months (see Appendix B). We therefore conclude that the two dimensional projection of the data is acceptable and that all the variables are suitable to draw conclusions. With respect to the quality of representations of the countries, conclusions are not immediate. As a general rule, we can say that the large majority are suitable to draw conclusions. The ones excepting the rule are listed in Table 1. These countries are not be interpreted. To determine whether a country/variable can be interpreted or not, the following rule was used: a country/variable is interpretable if its quality of representation is larger than half the largest, see [20] for more details.

Table 1. Countries that are not interpretable.

March	April	May	June	July	August
Netherlands	Netherlands	Netherlands	Netherlands	Netherlands	Costa Rica
Panama	Panama	Panama	Panama	Panama	Panama
	Canada	Argentina			

Bearing in mind the previous remarks, we now are able to report our findings.

According to the two approaches described in Subsect. 2.4 for choosing the optimal number of clusters, five clusters are plotted in the HJ-Biplot representation on plane 1–2 for each month. This is done with the software MultBiplot, in which K-Means on the Biplot coordinates was used to perform the clustering. Along with the HJ-Biplot, a histogram showing the quality of representation of the countries and some brief comments on the most notable changes are provided (the complete analysis is reserved at the end of this section). A lighter turquoise tone in the histograms indicates a high quality of representation.

The HJ-Biplot representation in Fig. 2 explains 82.6% of variance corresponding March. The most notable observations of this month are the location of Canada and Germany and the marked isolation of Peru.

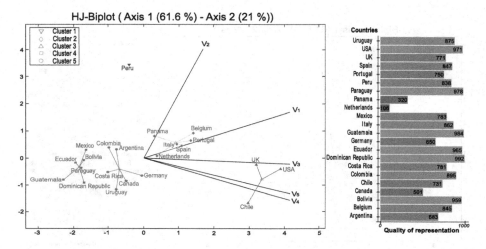

Fig. 2. HJ-Biplot, clustering, and quality of representation March.

The HJ-Biplot representation in Fig. 3 explains 82.6% of variance corresponding to April. In this month, it is remarkable the new location of Uruguay, which has migrated at a high rate.

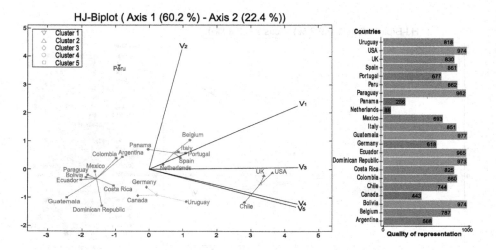

Fig. 3. HJ-Biplot, clustering, and quality of representation April.

The HJ-Biplot representation in Fig. 4 explains 83.5% of variance corresponding to May. Uruguay also changes clusters this month. In fact, no other country, except Uruguay, has significantly changed its relative position until May.

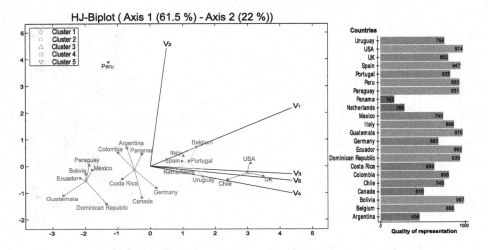

Fig. 4. HJ-Biplot, clustering, and quality of representation May.

The HJ-Biplot representation in Fig. 5 explains 82.7% of variance corresponding to June. It is noticeable how Clusters 1 and 3 in Fig. 4 come together to become one in this month.

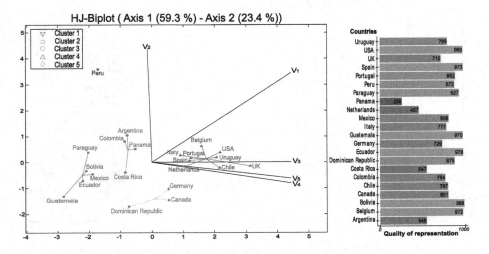

Fig. 5. HJ-Biplot, clustering, and quality of representation June.

The HJ-Biplot representation in Fig. 6 explains 81.3% of variance corresponding to July. In this month, no country has changed clusters. However, it is interesting how Ecuador, Mexico, and Bolivia become indistinguishable.

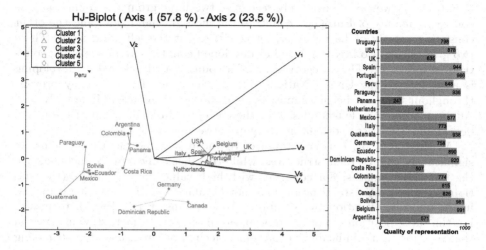

Fig. 6. HJ-Biplot, clustering, and quality of representation July.

The HJ-Biplot representation in Fig. 7 explains 80.5% of variance corresponding to August. This month, Ecuador has moved considerably to the right and has abandoned Mexico and Bolivia, which still overlap.

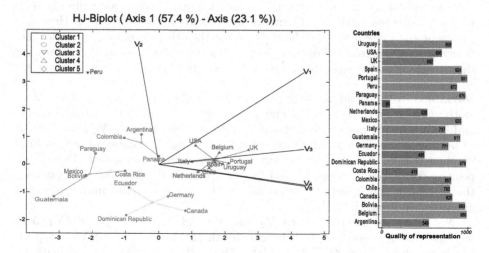

Fig. 7. HJ-Biplot, clustering, and quality of representation August.

The remainder of this section provides an interpretation of the graphical results.

Countries. If a vertical line is drawn along the origin in all Biplots in Figs. 2, 3, 4, 5, 6 and 7, we can immediately recognize two large groups of countries. One consisting mainly of European countries (at the right-hand side) and the other consisting mostly of Latin American countries (at the left-hand side). These two groups can also be categorized as developed countries and developing countries, respectively. The categorization of a country as developed or developing is according to the United Nations [21] classification. This tendency prevails throughout time but becomes more evident in the last months (June, July, and August), where the left-hand side of the corresponding Biplot consists of only developing countries spotlighting the gap between the two groups.

As time goes by, clusters stabilize. In the first three months, all clusters significantly change their structures, while they basically remain unchanged in the last three months. For countries with high values in V_4 and V_5 (vaccination variables), this stabilization may not be alarming. However, for countries in the opposite situation (for example, those in cluster 1 in Fig. 7), maintaining the same position is not an appropriate indicator. In fact, staying stuck in that position would indicate that national vaccination programs are not making progress.

Ecuador, Bolivia, Mexico, Paraguay, and Guatemala stay together all the time, except in August when Ecuador changes cluster. Italy, Portugal, Spain, and Belgium never separate as well. As mentioned prior to Fig. 2, Peru always forms a cluster by itself. Chile, USA, and UK constitute a cluster from the beginning and remain together even when later they form a larger cluster. It is also noticeable how Germany, Canada and Dominican Republic slowly separate from their initial clusters and form a cluster by themselves (in August, Ecuador joins this cluster). It is surprising the location of Germany and Canada in the first month. However, as time goes by, they move to the right, where the other developed countries are. Uruguay starts surrounded by developing countries and moves rapidly towards the right reaching a better-positioned cluster, where developed countries enclose it.

Variables. We now advocate to provide information about the variables. Most of the time, the variable with largest variance is V_1. In all months, V_3, V_4, and V_5 are highly positive correlated. Indeed, as time goes by, V_4 and V_5 tend to become equal. This result is expected since a higher number of people fully vaccinated is related to a higher number of vaccines administered. The highly positive correlation between V_3 and $\{V_4, V_5\}$ reflects the fact that the countries that are most concerned about testing are those that are also most concerned about vaccination.

Note how the angle between V_2 and V_3 and between V_2 and $\{V_4, V_5\}$ increases as time goes by. On the one hand, in March, V_2 and V_3 are positively correlated since $\angle(V_2, V_3) < 90°$[1]. In April, $\angle(V_2, V_3)$ increases without reaching $90°$. In the remaining months, it becomes evident that V_2 and V_3 are

---

[1] $\angle(V_2, V_3) < 90$ is a short way of saying: the angle between V_2 and V_3 is less that $90°$.

uncorrelated because $\angle(V_2, V_3) \approx 90°$. On the other hand, in the first three months, $\angle(V_2, \{V_4, V_5\})$ indicates that V_2 and $\{V_4, V_5\}$ are uncorrelated. However, in the last three months, $\angle(V_2, \{V_4, V_5\}) > 90°$, which means that V_2 and $\{V_4, V_5\}$ are negatively correlated. This discussion shows that between May and June, V_2 changes from being positively related by testing to be negatively influenced by vaccination. Therefore, vaccination has prevented the mortality rate from continuing to rise.

Countries and Variables. An interpretation of both countries and variables is presented in the sequel. We start noticing that Latin American countries, specifically, those constituting the red cluster in all months has always the lowest values in V_1. This means that the number of cases per million is relatively low in comparison with countries appearing in the right hand side (mostly European countries) of the corresponding Biplot. UK has the largest value in V_1 (except in March). USA is also one of the leading countries with respect to V_1 in the first months. Oppositely, Guatemala has always the smallest value. Chile is one of the Latin American countries with largest value in V_1. The case of Uruguay is interesting. In March, Uruguay has a small value in V_1. However, as time goes by, Uruguay migrates and increases its V_1 value in the subsequent months. The performance of Ecuador in terms of V_1 is poor.

We now move into analyzing the behaviour of countries with respect to V_2. The most evident and worrying observation is the high value of Peru in V_2 during the whole time frame. This unparalleled high value in V_2 explains why Peru always forms a cluster by itself. We note that Argentina increases its V_2 value as time goes by. In June, it becomes the second worst country in terms of deaths. This position is maintained the subsequent months. Uruguay and Chile also increases its V_2 as time goes by.

In average, we can say that European and Latin American countries perform equally in terms of V_2. In the first three months, the European countries have higher values in V_2 while in the last three months the trend is reversed. Most of the time, the best performing countries with respect to V_2 are Guatemala, Dominican Republic, Canada, and Germany.

With respect to V_3 we notice that Chile, USA, and UK are the leading countries in the first four months. In August, Belgium, Uruguay, and Portugal surpasses them (except to UK). It is evident that most of Latin American countries are the worst in terms of V_3 during the whole time frame.

Finally, we devote to study V_4 and V_5. In general, European countries are the best performing in these variables. Chile, USA, and UK are the leading countries in these variables during the whole time frame (except in August, where Belgium and Portugal surpass USA and Chile). In April, we notice how Ecuador, Bolivia, Paraguay, Mexico, Colombia, Guatemala, and Argentina are aligned in these variables, which means that their performance is similar in terms of vaccination.

4   Conclusions

Understanding the time evolution of the COVID-19 vaccination process provides governments and policymakers with tools to better manage the pandemic.

To that end, this paper used HJ-Biplot and Cluster Analysis. These visualization tools led to the following conclusions. Despite having 5 clusters, the variables considered in this study reveal that countries divide into two underlying groups: developing and developed countries.[2] This can be verified by looking at the orthogonal projections of countries on V_4 and V_5 in Fig. 7. The formation of these two groups shows two issues. The first is that facing the pandemic is not a matter of global collaboration. The second one is that there is no need to be a developed country to quickly vaccinate people as Chile and Uruguay demonstrate.[3] The evolution of Uruguay in terms of vaccination is impressive during the whole time frame. The case of Ecuador also exhibits that a rapid vaccination is a matter of political will. In fact, things started to change in August 2021, just right after three months since a new government took office in Ecuador.

Another important conclusion is related to the positive impact of vaccination in reducing the number of deaths. This began to be evident in May (see Fig. 4), when the number of deaths and vaccination variables (V_4 and V_5) became inversely correlated, which means that as long as vaccination progress, the number of deaths will reduce.

Appendix A   – Dendrograms Using HJ-Biplot Coordinates

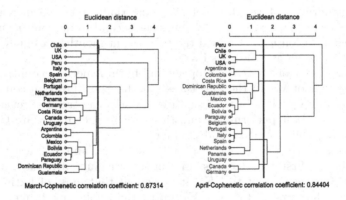

Fig. 8. Dendrograms using HJ-Biplot coordinates of March and April.

---

[2] Being the Dominican Republic and Germany the border of the two groups, respectively.

[3] As of September 15th 2021, Chile and Uruguay has vaccinated over 73% of their population [3].

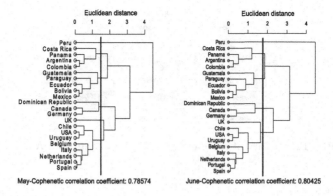

Fig. 9. Dendrograms using HJ-Biplot coordinates of May and June.

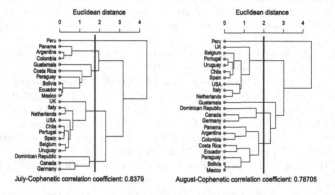

Fig. 10. Dendrograms using HJ-Biplot coordinates of July and August.

Appendix B — Quality of Representation for Months

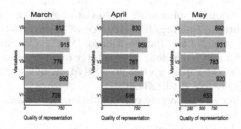

Fig. 11. Quality of representation for March, April, and May.

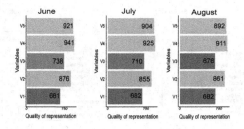

Fig. 12. Quality of representation for June, July, and August.

References

1. World Health Organization: Report of the who-china joint mission on coronavirus disease 2019 (covid-19) (2020). https://www.who.int/publications/i/item/report-of-the-who-china-joint-mission-on-coronavirus-disease-2019-(covid-19)/, Accessed 20 Sept 2021
2. Worldometer: Covid-19 coronavirus pandemic (2020). https://www.worldometers.info/coronavirus/, Accessed 20 Sept 2021
3. Mathieu, E., et al.: A global database of COVID-19 vaccinations. Nat. Human Behav. **5**(7), 947–953 (2021). https://doi.org/10.1038/s41562-021-01122-8
4. Pozo, S., Carrillo, G., Amaro, I.R.: An exploratory analysis of COVID-19 in South America. In: Iano, Y., Saotome, O., Kemper, G., Mendes de Seixas, A.C., Gomes de Oliveira, G. (eds.) BTSym 2020. SIST, vol. 233, pp. 266–280. Springer, Cham (2021). https://doi.org/10.1007/978-3-030-75680-2_31
5. Ritchie, H., et al.: Coronavirus Pandemic (COVID-19). Our World in Data (2020). https://ourworldindata.org/coronavirus, Accessed 18 Sept 2021
6. Hasell, J., et al.: A cross-country database of COVID-19 testing. Sci. Data **7**(1), 345 (2020). https://doi.org/10.1038/s41597-020-00688-8
7. Van Rossum, G., Drake Jr, F.L.: Python reference manual. Centrum voor Wiskunde en Informatica Amsterdam (1995)
8. Gabriel, K.R.: The biplot graphic display of matrices with application to principal component analysis. Biometrika **58**(3), 453–467 (1971). https://doi.org/10.1093/biomet/58.3.453
9. Nieto, A.B., Galindo, M.P., Leiva, V., Vicente-Galindo, P.: A methodology for biplots based on bootstrapping with R. Revista colombiana de estadística **37**(2), 367–397 (2014). https://doi.org/10.15446/rce.v37n2spe.47944
10. Carrasco, G., Molina, J.L., Patino-Alonso, M.C., Castillo, M.D.C., Vicente-Galindo, M.P., Galindo-Villardón, M.P.: Water quality evaluation through a multivariate statistical HJ-Biplot approach. J. Hydrol. **577**, 123993 (2019). https://doi.org/10.1016/j.jhydrol.2019.123993
11. Galindo, M.P.: Una alternativa de representacion simultanea: HJ-Biplot. Qüestiió **10**(1), 13–23 (1986)
12. Gallego-Alvarez, I., Vicente-Galindo, M.P., Galindo-Villardón, M.P., Rodríguez-Rosa, M.: Environmental performance in countries worldwide: determinant factors and multivariate analysis. Sustainability **6**(11), 7807–7832 (2014). https://doi.org/10.3390/su6117807

13. Díaz-Faes, A.A., González-Albo, B., Galindo, M.P., Bordons, M.: HJ-Biplot como herramienta de inspección de matrices de datos bibliométricos. Revista Española de Documentación Científica **36**(1), e001 (2013). https://doi.org/10.3989/redc.2013.1.988
14. Tenesaca-Chillogallo, F., Amaro, I.R.: COVID-19 data analysis using HJ-Biplot method: a study case. Bionatura **6**(2), 1778–1784 (2021). https://doi.org/10.21931/RB/2021.06.02.18
15. Rencher, A., Christensen, W.: Methods of multivariate analysis. In: Wiley Series in Probability and Statistics. Wiley, New Jersey (2012)
16. Omran, M.G.H., Engelbrecht, A.P., Salman, A.: An overview of clustering methods. Intell. Data Anal. **11**, 583–605 (2007). https://doi.org/10.3233/IDA-2007-11602
17. Chetty, N., Shukla, S.: A review on K-means data clustering approach. Int. J. Inf. Comput. Technol. **4**(17), 1847–1860 (2014)
18. Vicente-Villardón, J.L.: Multbiplot: a package for multivariate analysis using biplots. Universidad de Salamanca, Departamento de Estadística (2010)
19. Hartigan, J.A., Wong, M.A.: Algorithm AS 136: a k-means clustering algorithm. J. R. Stat. Soc. Ser. C (Appl. Stat.) **28**(1), 100–108 (1979). https://doi.org/10.2307/2346830
20. Cabrera, J.G., Martínez, M.F., Mateos, E.M., Tavera, S.V.: Study of the evolution of air pollution in Salamanca (Spain) along a five-year period (1994–1998) using HJ-Biplot simultaneous representation analysis. Environ. Model. Softw. **21**(1), 61–68 (2006). https://doi.org/10.1016/j.envsoft.2004.10.009
21. United Nations Department of Economic and Social Affairs: World Economic Situation and Prospects 2020. United Nations, 2020 edn. (2020). https://www.un-ilibrary.org/content/books/9789210046169

Epidemic Models and Estimation of the Spread of SARS-CoV-2: Case Study Portoviejo-Ecuador

Sánchez Luis[1] and Infante Saba[2]

[1] Universidad Técnica de Manabí, Portoviejo, Ecuador
luis.sanchez@utm.edu.ec
[2] Universidad Yachay Tech., Urcuqui, Ecuador
sinfante@yachaytech.edu.ec

Abstract. The mathematical models can help to characterize, quantify, summarize, and determine the severity of the outbreak of the Coronavirus, the estimation of the dynamics of the pandemic helps to identify the type of measures and interventions that can be taken to minimize the impact by classified information. In this work, we propose four epidemiological models to study the spread of SARS-CoV-2. Specifically, two versions of the SIR model (Susceptible, Infectious, and Recovered) are considered, the classical Crank-Nicolson method is used with a stochastic version of the Beta-Dirichlet state-space models. Subsequently, the SEIR model (Susceptible, Exposed, Infectious, and Recovered) is fitted, the Euler method and a stochastic version of the Beta-Dirichlet state-space model are used. In the results of this study (Portoviejo-Ecuador), the SIR model with the Beta-Dirichlet state-space form determines the maximum point of infection in less time than the SIR model with the Crank-Nicolson method. Furthermore, the maximum point of infection is shown by the SEIR model, that is reached during the first two weeks where the virus begins to spread, more efficient is shown by this model. To measure the quality of the estimation of the algorithms, we use three measures of goodness of fit. The estimated errors are negligible for the analyzed data. Finally, the evolution of the spread is predicted, that can be helpful to prevent the capacity of the country's health system.

Keywords: SARS-CoV-2 · Stochastic epidemic model · SIR model · SEIR model · Portoviejo-Ecuador

1 Introduction

All dynamic biological systems under stochastic forces are evolved. For example, when the physiological characteristics of an individual are analyzed, many factors are found that cannot be controlled, such as hormonal oscillations, variations in blood pressure, respiration, neuronal control, the variability of muscular activity, enzymatic processes, chemical reactions, genes, cellular metabolism, among

© Springer Nature Switzerland AG 2022
F. R. Narváez et al. (Eds.): SmartTech-IC 2021, CCIS 1532, pp. 398–411, 2022.
https://doi.org/10.1007/978-3-030-99170-8_29

others. In [13] an epidemiological stochastic model is studied, and a method determines the probability of an epidemic reaching, a specific size is proposed to extinction, and also, a partial differential equation model by age-structured populations models is obtained in continuous time. In [11] a deterministic epidemic model and an equation for the extinct size of the epidemic are studied, and a threshold for population density is considered. In [5] a stochastic version of the McKendrick model is developed. In [4] the version of a deterministic and stochastic epidemiological model is unified. Also, the statistical models are presented to make an inference. Others deterministic models of great impact are proposed, by [2,3,5,7] among others. Recent research on the subject is shown in [6], that is a mathematical model for the spread of infectious diseases, a homogeneous population with spreads of a communicable disease is shown that is during a short outbreak. In [1] some mathematical methods for numerical simulation of stochastic epidemic models are proposed, and the models in terms of a continuous-time Markov chain and stochastic differential equations are formulated. The methodology are illustrated to use well-known examples, such as the SIR epidemic model and a vector-host malaria model. Some analytical methods are discussed to approximate the probability of a disease outbreak. In [10] proposes two statistical models by systems of stochastic differential equations to model the dynamics of population growth and to understand the relationships between variables. In [15] a model in the space-state form by susceptible infectious-recovered (SIR) deterministic mathematical model is proposed, seasonal influenza is forecasted, simultaneously, multiple sources of uncertainties are explained. A stochastic model of transmission of diseases of the SEIR model is proposed in [14], a nonlinear system of stochastic differential equations is formulated. Numerical simulations by the Euler-Maruyama algorithm are performed, and the parameters by an adaptive Markov Monte Carlo chain and an extended Kalman filter algorithm are estimated. Finally, the parameters by the proposed methodology are identified. In [18] proposes a susceptible-exposed-infectious-recovered deterministic model (SEIR), that is based on a dependent dynamic system on the time, that considers clinical progression of the disease, that is dependent on epidemiological status of individuals, and mobility restrictions.

The contribution of this paper is based on the estimation of the two classical and stochastic versions of the SIR/SEIR models. In addition, an adaptation of the Dirichlet-Beta state-space model is performed. Crank-Nicolson, Euler, and Gibbs algorithms are used to estimate the parameters and solution of the states of the differential equations.

The rest of the article continues, as follows: In Sect. 2, the models are formulated; In Sect. 3, the methodology is described, In Sect. 4, the results are discussed, In Sect. 5 a discussion and conclusions are established.

2   Models Formulation

2.1   SIR Model

In the SIR model, three compartments or categories are defined: Susceptible: are individuals without immunity to the infection, those individuals, if they are exposed, they can become infected. Infectious: are infected individuals and they can transmit the infection to susceptible individuals. Recovered: when individuals are immune to infection, therefore those individuals do not affect transmission dynamics. A basic transmission model for a directly transmitted infectious disease is presented, the SIR model [11]. Consider a closed population of individuals, that is divided into three categories: Susceptible (S), Infectious (I), and Recovered (R). At any time $t = 0.1, \ldots, T$. Each individual belongs to one of these three categories. The proportion of the population as Susceptible, Infectious, and Recovered is defined:

$$s(t) = \frac{S(t)}{N}, \quad i(t) = \frac{I(t)}{N}, \quad r(t) = \frac{R(t)}{N} \tag{1}$$

respectively, $S(t) + I(t) + R(t) = N$, and $s(t) + i(t) + r(t) = 1$. The SIR model by a deterministic representation is described, that is, the dynamics of the infection by a set of ordinary differential equations are modeled.

$$\frac{dS}{dt} = -\beta si, \quad \frac{dI}{dt} = \beta si - \gamma i, \quad \frac{dR}{dt} = \gamma i \tag{2}$$

where: $\beta > 0$ is the rate of transmission of a disease, and $\gamma > 0$ is the recovery rate. The stochastic version of the SIR model is shown:

$$\begin{pmatrix} dx_1 \\ dx_2 \end{pmatrix} = \begin{pmatrix} -\beta x_1 x_2 \\ \beta x_1 x_2 - \gamma x_2 \end{pmatrix} dt + \frac{1}{\sqrt{N}} \begin{pmatrix} \sqrt{\beta x_1 x_2} & 0 \\ -\sqrt{\beta x_1 x_2} & \sqrt{\gamma x_2} \end{pmatrix} \begin{pmatrix} dB_1 \\ dB_2 \end{pmatrix}$$

where $x_1 = s$ and $x_2 = i$ denote the fractions of susceptible and infectious individuals in the population, B_1 and B_2 are independent Brownian motion, that represents the stochastic part in the transmission and recovery of the disease.

2.2 Fokker-Planck-Kolmogorov Equation (FPK)

Suppose the transition density $p(x, t)$ of an Itô diffusion process $x(t)$:

$$dX_i(t) = \mu_i(t; X_i(t), \theta)dt + \Sigma_i(t; X_i(t), \theta)dB_i \tag{3}$$

where $B_1, \ldots, B_N$ denotes independent Brownian motion, $\mu_i(t; X_i(t), \theta) \in \mathbb{R}^N$, and $\Sigma_i(t; X_i(t), \theta) \in \mathbb{R}^{N \times N}$. The probability density $p(x, t)$ of the solution of the SDE in Eq. (3) solves the partial differential equation (FPK):

$$\frac{\partial p_\theta(t; x_0, x)}{\partial t} = -\frac{\partial (\mu_1(x, \theta)p_\theta(t; x_0, x))}{\partial x_1} - \frac{\partial (\mu_2(x, t)p_\theta(x, t))}{\partial x_2} + \frac{1}{2}\frac{\partial^2 (\Sigma_{11}(x, \theta)p_\theta(t; x_0, x))}{\partial x_1^2}$$

$$+ \frac{1}{2}\frac{\partial^2 (\Sigma_{22}(x, \theta)p_\theta(t; x_0, x))}{\partial x_2^2} + \frac{\partial^2 (\Sigma_{21}(x, \theta)p_\theta(t; x_0, x))}{\partial x_2 \partial x_1}$$

The discrete version of the FPK equation is given by:

$$\left(1 - \frac{\kappa}{2}c_1(x, \theta)\frac{\partial^2 p_\theta(t; x_0, x)}{\partial x_1^2}\right) p_{j,l}^{i+0.5} = \left(1 + \frac{\kappa}{2}c_2(x, \theta)\frac{\partial^2 p_\theta(t; x_0, x)}{\partial x_2^2}\right)$$

$$\times p_{j,l}^i + \kappa c_3(x, \theta)\frac{\partial^2 p_\theta(t; x_0, x)}{\partial x_2 \partial x_1}p_{j,l}^i \tag{4}$$

and

$$\left(1 - \frac{\kappa}{2} c_2(x, \theta) \frac{\partial^2 p_\theta(t; x_0, x)}{\partial x_2^2}\right) p_{j,l}^{i+1} = \left(1 + \frac{\kappa}{2} c_1(x, \theta) \frac{\partial^2 p_\theta(t; x_0, x)}{\partial x_1^2}\right) p_{j,l}^{i+0.5}$$
$$+ \kappa c_3(x, \theta) \frac{\partial^2 p_\theta(t; x_0, x)}{\partial x_2 \partial x_1} p_{j,l}^{i+0.5} \tag{5}$$

2.3   The SEIR Model

We investigate the SEIR epidemic model [11] for application to data of COVID-19 incidence. The model assumes S, E, I, and R compartments that is representing: susceptible, exposed, infectious, and recovered individuals. The equations for the population change of each warehouse that are established as following:

$$\frac{dS}{dt} = -\beta SI, \quad \frac{dE}{dt} = \beta SI - \omega E, \quad \frac{dI}{dt} = \omega E - \gamma I, \quad \frac{dR}{dt} = \gamma I \tag{6}$$

where: $\beta = \beta_0 k$, β denotes the coefficient of the rate of infection, β_0 denotes the probability of exposure of infection, k denotes the frequency of exposure; $\omega = \frac{1}{T_e}$, ω denotes the coefficient of the latency of the rate of migration, T_e denotes the average of latency; and $\gamma = \frac{1}{T_i}$, γ denotes the coefficient of the migration rate, T_i denotes the average time of recovery. In [18] transmission dynamics by the system of differential equations is modeled:

$$\frac{dS}{dt} = - \left(\beta + c(t)q\left(1 - \beta\right)S\left(I + \theta A\right) + \lambda S_q\right), \quad \frac{dE}{dt} = \beta c(t)\left(1 - q\right)S\left(I + \theta A\right) - \sigma E$$
$$\frac{dI}{dt} = \sigma \varrho E - \left(\delta_I(t) + \alpha + \gamma_I\right)I, \quad \frac{dA}{dt} = \sigma\left(1 - \varrho\right)E - \gamma_A A$$
$$\frac{dS_q}{dt} = \left(1 - \beta\right)cqS\left(I + \theta A\right) - \lambda S_q, \quad \frac{dE_q}{dt} = \beta c(t)qS\left(I + \theta A\right) - \delta_q E_q$$
$$\frac{dH}{dt} = \delta_I(t)I + \delta_q E_q - \left(\alpha + \gamma_H\right)H, \quad \frac{dR}{dt} = \gamma_I I + \gamma_A A + \gamma_H H \tag{7}$$

where: $c(t)$ is contacted rate, β is probability of transmission per contact, q is quarantined rate of exposed individuals, σ is rate of transition of exposed individuals to the infected class, λ is the rate of uninfected individuals in quarantine they are released into the wider community, ϱ is the probability of symptoms among infected individuals, δ_I is the rate of transition of symptomatic infected individuals to the quarantined infected class, δ_q is the rate of transition of quarantined exposed individuals to the quarantined infected class. $\gamma_I(t)$ is the rate of recovery of symptomatic infected individuals, δ_A is the rate of recovery of asymptomatic infected individuals, γ_H is the rate of recovery of quarantined infected individuals, α is the rate of disease-induced death.

2.4   Dirichlet-Beta State-Space SIR Model

Let $X_i = X(t_;; \theta)$, and $X_{0:N} = (X_0, \dots, X_N)^T$. The process $X_{0:N}$ is only observed through another process $Y_{1:N} = (Y_1, \dots, Y_N)^T$ with $Y_n \in \mathbb{R}^r$. The conditionally observed random variables $Y_{1:N}$ are given by $X_{0:N}$. The Dirichlet-Beta state-space model is defined as:

$$X(t_0) \sim p_0(x(t_0)|\theta), \quad Y(t_i)|\eta(t_i) \sim p_1\left(y(t_i)|\eta(t_i)\right), \quad \eta(t_i)|X(t_i) = f(x_t)$$
$$X(t_{i+1})|X(t_i) \sim p_2\left(x(t_{i+1})|x(t_i);\theta\right), \quad \theta \sim p_3(\theta_0) \tag{8}$$

where: $Y(t_i)$ are the observations in time t_i; $Y(t_i)|\eta(t_i)$ is the distribution of the observation; $X(t_i)$ is an unobserved state of the process. The states are governed by a Markov process with a transition distribution $p_1\left(x(t_{i+1})|x(t_i);\theta\right)$, that may not be generally treatable; $p_2(x(t_0|\theta)$ is an initial distribution; $p_3(\theta_0)$ is a prior distribution of the parameter θ; and $f : \mathbb{R} \longrightarrow \mathbb{R}$ is a linked function, that is allowed by a non-linear transformation of the observations. An equivalent way of representing the Dirichlet-Beta state-space SIR model is followed

$$y(t_i)|\eta(t_i) \sim Beta(\mu(t), \nu(t)), \quad \eta(t_i)|x(t_i) \sim Beta(UV; (1-U)V)$$

$$U = \frac{\mu(t)}{\mu(t) + \nu(t)}, \quad V = \mu(t) + \nu(t), \quad x(t_i)|x(t_{i-1}) \sim Dirichlet\left(\kappa f(x_{t-1}, \beta, \gamma)\right)$$

$$x(t_0) \sim unif(L_i, L_s), \quad \kappa \sim Gamma(a, b) \tag{9}$$

where: $y(t_i) = (y_{t_i}^S, y_{t_i}^I, y_{t_i}^R)^T$, the data with errors over time is measured: $x(t_i) = (x_{t_i}^S, x_{t_i}^I, x_{t_i}^R)^T$, $i = 1, \ldots, N$ represent the true proportion (unknown) of the states of the susceptible, infected and recovered population, respectively, $\Theta = (\theta_0, \beta, \gamma, \kappa)^T$ where $\gamma > 0$ is the rate of the recovery, $\beta > 0$ is the rate of disease transmission, and $f(x_{t-1}, \beta, \gamma) \in \mathbf{R}^3$ is the solution of the system of ordinary differential equations

$$\frac{dx^S(t)}{dt} = -\beta x^S(t)x^I(t), \quad \frac{dx^I(t)}{dt} = \beta x^S(t)x^I(t) - \gamma x^I(t), \quad \frac{dx^R(t)}{dt} = \gamma x^R(t) \tag{10}$$

where $x_t^S + x_t^I + x_t^R = 1$, and $x_t^S = x^S(t), x_t^I = x^T(t), x_t^R = x^R(t) > 0$. The system (10) is transformed by a system of stochastic differential equations.

$$\frac{dx^S(t)}{dt} = -\beta x^S(t)x^I(t) + dB_1^S, \quad dB_1^S \sim N(0, \sigma^2)$$

$$\frac{dx^I(t)}{dt} = \beta x^S(t)x^I(t) - \gamma x^I(t) + dB_2^I, \quad dB_2^I \sim N(0, \sigma^2)$$

$$\frac{dx^R(t)}{dt} = \gamma x^R(t) + dB_3^R, \quad dB_3^R \sim N(0, \sigma^2) \tag{11}$$

2.5   Dirichlet-Beta State-Space SEIR Model

Consider the Eq. (9), let:

$$y(t_i) = (y_{t_i}^S, y_{t_i}^E, y_{t_i}^I, y_{t_i}^A, y_{t_i}^{Sq}, y_{t_i}^{Eq}, y_{t_i}^H, y_{t_i}^R)^T, \quad t = 1, \ldots, T \tag{12}$$

and the observations with errors in time are measured:

$$x(t_i) = (x_{t_i}^S, x_{t_i}^E, x_{t_i}^I, x_{t_i}^A, x_{t_i}^{S_q}, x_{t_i}^{E_q}, x_{t_i}^H, x_{t_i}^R, x_{t_i}^{I_q})^T \quad , \quad i = 1, \ldots, N \qquad (13)$$

is a vector to respectively represent proper proportion (unknown) of the states of the susceptible, exposed, infected, symptomatic, quarantine, exposed isolated, hospitalized, recaptured, and infected isolates. The system of stochastic differential Eq. (7) defines the Dirichlet-Beta state-space SEIR model:

$$\frac{dS}{dt} = -(\beta + c(t)q(1-\beta)S(I+\theta A) + \lambda S_q) + dB_1^S, \quad dB_1^S \sim N(0, \sigma^2)$$

$$\frac{dE}{dt} = \beta c(t)(1-q)S(I+\theta A) - \sigma E + dB_1^E, \quad dB_1^E \sim N(0, \sigma^2)$$

$$\frac{dI}{dt} = \sigma \varrho E - (\delta_I(t) + \alpha + \gamma_I)I + dB_1^I, \quad dB_1^I \sim N(0, \sigma^2)$$

$$\frac{dA}{dt} = \sigma(1-\varrho)E - \gamma_A A + dB_1^A, \quad dB_1^A \sim N(0, \sigma^2)$$

$$\frac{dS_q}{dt} = (1-\beta)cqS(I+\theta A) - \lambda S_q + dB_1^{S_q}, \quad dB_1^{S_q} \sim N(0, \sigma^2)$$

$$\frac{dE_q}{dt} = \beta c(t)qS(I+\theta A) - \delta_q E_q + dB_1^{E_q}, \quad dB_1^{E_q} \sim N(0, \sigma^2)$$

$$\frac{dH}{dt} = \delta_I(t)I + \delta_q E_q - (\alpha + \gamma_H)H + dB_1^H, \quad dB_1^H \sim N(0, \sigma^2)$$

$$\frac{dR}{dt} = \gamma_I I + \gamma_A A + \gamma_H H + dB_1^A, \quad dB_1^A \sim N(0, \sigma^2) \qquad (14)$$

3   Methodology

The solutions of the FPK equation are approximated, the Peaceman-Rachford scheme [17] in conjunction with the Crank Nicolson algorithm are used that is a very effective method, and that guarantees stability in the solutions, ([8,12,16], among others). A tridiagonal system of equations is obtained, that can be solved in an interactive way, i.e., 5.

The SIR epidemic model can be written in the form of space-state models, and that is considered a partially observed process; that is interesting to infer about the solutions of the unknown states $x_{0:t} = (x_0, \ldots, x_t)$ where the states are given the observations $y_{1:t} = (y_1, \ldots, y_t)$. Then if θ is known, and $x_{0:k}$ is unknown, the joint distribution of the states is given:

$$p(x_{0:t}) = p(x_t|x_{t-1})p(x_{t-1}|x_{t-2}), \ldots, p(x_1|x_0)p(x_0) = p(x_0)\prod_{i=1}^{t} p(x_i|x_{i-1}) \quad (15)$$

where $p(x_0)$ is a prior initial density. The likelihood of the data is given:

$$p(y_{1:t}|x_{0:t}) = p(y_1|x_1)p(y_2|x_2)\ldots p(y_t|x_t) = \prod_{i=1}^{t} p(y_i|x_i) \qquad (16)$$

Then a posterior distribution is given:

$$p(x_{0:t}|y_{1:t}) = \frac{p(y_{1:t}|x_{0:t})p(x_{0:t})}{p(y) = \int p(y_{1:t}|x_{0:t})p(x_{0:t})dx_{0:t}} \tag{17}$$

In most applications, that is complicated to implement the algorithm for the Eq. (17) since the marginal density $p(y)$ is generally not available in the closed-form. Therefore, algorithm is based in methods to approximate values. A Markov chain Monte Carlo (MCMC) method is used. Specifically, the Gibbs sampler [9] simulates the samples of the posterior distribution. The algorithm is:

1. For $m = 1, 2, \ldots, M$,
2. $\theta^{(m)} \sim p(\theta)$ is sampled from (8).
3. For $t = 1, 2, \ldots, T$,
4. $x_t^{(m)} \sim p\left(x_t|x_{t-1}^{(m)}, \theta^{(m)}\right)$ is sampled from (8).
5. $y_t^{(m)} \sim p\left(y_t|x_t^{(m)}, \theta^{(m)}\right)$ is sampled from (8).

The predictions for future observations $y_{t+1:T} = (y_{t+1}, y_{t+2}, \ldots, y_T)$ are based on a posterior predictive distributions, that are obtained from

$$p\left(y_{t+1:T}|y_{1:t}\right) = \int \int p\left(y_{t+1:T}, x_{1:t}, \theta|y_{1:t}\right) dx_{1:T} d\theta \tag{18}$$

The algorithm is followed to sample from $y_{t+1:T}|y_{1:T}$ by the Eq. (18)

1. Given M is sampled from $x_{1:t}, \theta|y_{1:t}$
2. For $m = 1, 2, \ldots, M$,
3. For $t = 1 = t + 1, t + 2, \ldots, T$
4. $x_t^{(m)} \sim p\left(x_t|x_{t-1}^{(m)}, \theta^{(m)}\right)$ is sampled from (8).
5. $y_t \sim p\left(x_t^{(m)}|x_t^{(m)}, \theta^{(m)}\right)$ is sampled from (8).
6. Return:

$$y_{t+1:T}^{(m)} = \left(y_{t+1}^{(m)}, y_{t+2}^{(m)}, \ldots, y_T^{(m)}\right) \tag{19}$$

3.1 The Goodness of Fit Measures

The goodness of fit measures are presented, the accuracy of the estimation of the proposed models is validated. The error is the difference between the actual value and the predictive value that is corresponding period: $\epsilon_t = y_t - \hat{y}_t$, where ϵ_t is the error, y_t is the actual value, and $\hat{y}_t$ is the predicted value in the period t. Then, the error measures are considered:

1. The MAE or mean absolute error: measures the average of the sum of differences of absolute value between observed values and predicted values: $MAE = \frac{1}{N}\sum_{t=1}^{N}|y_t - \hat{y}_t|$
2. The mean square error (MSE) of a predicted value $\hat{y}$ and current value y is defined by: $MSE = \frac{1}{N}\sum_{t=1}^{N}(y_t - \hat{y}_t)^2$
3. The RMSE is the root of the mean square error that is defined by: $RMSE = \sqrt{\frac{1}{N}\sum_{t=1}^{N}(y_t - \hat{y}_t)^2}$ where N represents the number of used observations for analysis.

4   Results

The SARS-CoV-2 data is obtained from the National Health Commission of the Republic of Ecuador and the project: Evaluation of the progress of the pandemic in the Portoviejo canton of the Province of Manabí, that corresponds to series from $15 - 03 - 2020$ to $01 - 05 - 2020$, that is considering a sample of 60 days in the province of Potoviejo. The estimated population is of 329.144 inhabitants, where there are 444 cases are confirmed.

Four epidemiological models are estimated to understand the dynamics of the pandemic. First: the SIR model (5), a numerical method of estimation is known as C-N, the algorithm is incorporated; Second: a second Bayesian model is proposed to base on the Beta-Dirichlet state-space model (9), specifically a Gibbs algorithm allows to approximate solutions in on-line, the vector of states $x(t_i)$ of the model is defined in the Eq. (11); Third: the classic model [18] is used, an Euler discretization is carried out, the solutions of the model (7) are approximated. Finally, a stochastic version of the [18] model is adjusted, that is defined in the Eq. (7). An adaptation of the SEIR model is performed to estimate the solutions the form of Beta-Dirichlet state-space models (9) is used. The stochastic version of the [18] model is given (14). The prior distributions of the parameters are:

1. The Beta-Dirichlet state-space SIR model:
   (a) $x^S(t_0) \sim Beta(0.00899, 8.98101)$, $x^I(t_0) \sim Beta(73.37198, 0.55817)$,
   (b) $x^R(t_0) \sim Beta(0.25278, 0.00003)$, $\kappa \sim Gamma(241, 10)$,
   (c) $\nu(t) \sim Unif(1, 1000)$, $\mu(t) \sim Gamma(241, 1)$.
2. The Beta-Dirichlet state-space SEIR model:
   (a) $x^S(t_0) \sim Beta(0.00899, 8.98101)$, $x^E(t_0) \sim Beta(48.50625, 0.24375)$,
   (b) $x^I(t_0) \sim Beta(73.37198, 0.55817)$, $x^R(t_0) \sim Beta(0.25278, 0.00003)$,
   (c) $x^A(t_0) \sim Beta(23.87765625, 0.05984375)$, $x^{S_q}(t_0) \sim Beta(0.8, 7.2)$,
   (d) $x^{E_q}(t_0) \sim Beta(0.25278, 0.00003)$, $x^H(t_0) \sim Beta(5.99090343, 0.00419657)$,
   (e) $\kappa \sim Gamma(89.9, 809.1)$, $\nu(t) \sim Unif(1, 1000)$, $\mu(t) \sim Gamma(89.9, 809.1)$.

Table 1, the required values for the initialization of the algorithms are defined, the solution states and the parameters of the SIR model are estimated. A closed population of individuals of size $N = 319.185$ is considered, that is without any restrictions, the population is partitioned into three states: Susceptible S, Infectious I, and Recovered R, where each individual is a member of exactly one of

Table 1. Initial values and parameters of the SIR model

$dt = 0.01$	$\gamma = 0.2$	$\beta = 1.75$
$I_0 = 7.550e - 4$	$S_0 = 0.999$	$R_0 = 1.253e - 5$
$\mu(t) = 1$	$\nu(t) = 0.729$	$U = 0.578$
$V = 1.307$	$\sigma^2 = 1$	$T = 6000$

those three categories. For a time $t = 0, 1, \ldots, T$, the trajectories $S(t), I(t), R(t)$ of the solutions of the stochastic differential equation system are estimated by Fokker-Planck-Kolmogorov. The graphs of the temporal evolution of the number of susceptible, infected, and recovered individuals in the population are shown. The graphs are obtained by a numerical computational scheme that is known as the C-N algorithm. In the graph of the infected, a maximum outbreak point is approximately reached at day 25. In Figs. 1(a), 1(b), 2(a), see appendix A, the solutions by the SIR model is obtained. The second proposed model is a Beta-Dirichlet state-space SIR model, that is defined in the Eq. (9). In Figs. 2(b), 3(a), 3(b) the curves for the susceptible, infectious, and recovered states are shown, the infected pick on the day 22 is shown. The third considered model is a deterministic model, that is defined in Eq. (7). In the first instance, a numerical discretization of Euler's algorithm is implemented when the system of differential equations in a deterministic way is solved. The model is allowed to reflect the flow of people between the four states: susceptible S, exposed E, infected I, and recovered R. The model includes restrictions in the population such as quarantine, isolation, hospitalization, treatment, reduced mobility flow. This model is used to understand the dynamics of the pandemic. In the Figs. 4(a), 4(b), 5(a), 5(b), 6(a), and 6(b) are shown, see appendix A, the solution states $S(t)$, $E(t)$, $I(t)$, $A(t)$, $Sq(t)$, $Eq(t)$, $H(t)$ and $R(t)$ are estimated. Finally, the fourth model as a stochastic version of the [18] is adjusted, that is defined in Eq. (14). The parameters of the model are established in Table 2. That is seen/observed that when there are control policies by the government then the curve of the population of susceptible is slightly decreased, the maximum peak of the infected population by less time is reached, that represents an asymmetric curve that gets full height in the first week around day 7 and then that decreases and to tend to zero after day 30. In non-symptomatic (pre-symptomatic) patients, a decreased curve tends to zero that is approximately starting after day 50; the graph of the exposed individuals is decreased, that is approximately tending to zero after day 20; in the recovery curve, an increased function can be observed that tends to stabilize from day 40; in the hospitalized patients can notice an asymmetric curve, a maximum peak around 10 is reached, that tends to decrease. In Figs. 8(a), 8(b), 9(a), 9(b), 10(a), 10(b), 11(a), and 11(b) are shown, see appendix A. Now the Beta-Dirichlet state-space SEIR model is defined in (14). In the obtained Figures, a very similar behavior to the model (7) can be observed. An earlier

Table 2. Initial values of the parameters of the SEIR model

$S_0 = 0.999$	$E_0 = 0.005$	$I_0 = 7.550e - 4$	$A_0 = 0.0025$
$S_{q0} = 1$	$E_{q0} = 0.0052$	$H_{q0} = 7.55.10^{-4}$	$R_0 = 1.253e - 5$
$\alpha = 0.000017826$	$\beta = 0.000000021$	$\gamma_A = 0.13978$	$\gamma_I = 0.33029$
$\gamma_H = 0.11624$	$\lambda = 0.07142857$	$\delta_{IO} = 0.86834$	$\frac{1}{\delta_{If}} = 0.13266$
$\delta_q = 0.1259$	$\sigma = 0.14285714$	$\sigma = 0.142857$	$\varrho = 1$
$c_0 = 14.781$	$c_b = 2.9253$	$r_1 = 1.3768$	$q = 0.000012$

warning in time is shown, i.e., in the case of the infected individuals, the maximum peak is reached at the end of the first week, and the convergence to zero is accelerated faster than the model (7).

In Tables 3 and 4 are shown three measures of goodness of fit: the MSE, RMSE and MAE measure the quality estimation of the models, that are defined in (9) and (14), insignificant estimation errors are respectively shown. Table 5 shows the predictions of the third model (7) and the Beta-Dirichlet state-space model (14). Expected values for days from $01 - 05 - 2020$ can be observed.

Table 3. Estimation of the MSE, RMSE and MAE, model (9)

States	MSE	RMSE	MAE
S	$1.92e^{-07}$	$4.39e^{-04}$	$5.66e^{-05}$
E	$8.81e^{-10}$	$9.39e^{-05}$	$1.21e^{-07}$
R	$1.14e^{-07}$	$3.38e^{-04}$	$4.36e^{-06}$

Table 4. Estimation of the MSE, RMSE and MAE, model (14)

States	MSE	RMSE	MAE
S	$2.33e^{-07}$	$3.53e^{-04}$	$4.76e^{-06}$
E	$7.85e^{-11}$	$8.46e^{-06}$	$3.25e^{-07}$
I	$2.14e^{-07}$	$2.21e^{-04}$	$3.52e^{-06}$
A	$2.14e^{-07}$	$5.48e^{-04}$	$4.67e^{-06}$
S_q	$9.95e^{-09}$	$2.46e^{-06}$	$2.21e^{-07}$
E_q	$3.32e^{-07}$	$44.41e^{-05}$	$5.54e^{-06}$
H	$7.88e^{-08}$	$3.55e^{-06}$	$3.26e^{-07}$
R	$4.44e^{-07}$	$3.33e^{-05}$	$4.41e^{-06}$

Table 5. Prediction of models (7) and (14)

Days	Model (7)	Model (14)	Data Real
0	444	444	444
1	822	819	786
2	1099	1095	1016
3	1195	1192	1208

5   Discussions and Conclusions

Four epidemiological models are proposed to estimate the solutions of the differential equations SARS-CoV-2. Two versions of the SIR models and two versions of the SEIR model are fitted. Several strategies of the estimation are used: two numerical methods, Cank-Nicolson and Euler are used. In addition, two versions of the SIR and SEIR models are included in the form of Beta-Dirichlet state-space models. In addition, a Gibbs algorithm is used to find the solutions. As partial conclusions are obtained from this empirical study, that is possible to point out that the proposed models allow to find the satisfactory solution of the states. When the SIR model is fitted by the C-N algorithm, the maximum point of infected $I(t)$ is reached in the day 25, the susceptible $S(t)$ tends to zero after day 30, and the recovered $R(t)$ stabilizes after day 40. In the case of the SIR model fits in the Beta-Dirichlet state-space form, that has similar behaviors, $S(t) = 38$, $I(t) = 22$, and $R(t) = 35$, the only difference is in determining the maximum peak of infected. When the SEIR model is fitting by the Euler method, the maximum point of infected $I(t)$ is reached in the first week, the pre-symptomatic $A(t)$ shows to tend to zero from day 40, the susceptible $S_q(t)$ in quarantine tends to zero from day 50, those exposed individuals in isolation $E_q(t)$ tend towards zero from day 30, hospitalized $H(t)$ reaches the maximum around day 10. Finally, the recovered $R(t)$ stabilizes from day 40. Thus, the fit of the SEIR model in the Beta-Dirichlet state-space form has a behavior quite similar to the Euler method. Theoretically, that is known that the SIR model is free of restrictions on the population, that implies that is controlling the peak points of pandemic, outbreaks is much more complicated to handle due to the lack of control in the population. The SEIR model incorporates restrictions such as quarantine, isolation, treatment, and other stratifications in the population. The restriction of measures in this study can explain how to detect the outbreak of infections in two weeks, that is concerning much less time than free models of restrictions that is compared by the values of the predictions for the considered models, that shows all reasonable estimates. Finally, three goodness-of-fit measures are used to validate the performance of the models, insignificant errors of estimation are obtained.

Appendix A: Supporting Information

Figures

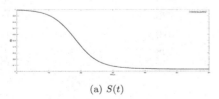
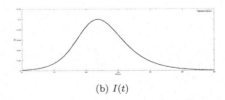

(a) $S(t)$ (b) $I(t)$

Fig. 1. Estimate of $S(t)$ and $I(t)$, SIR model by the C-N algorithm

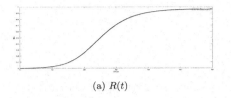
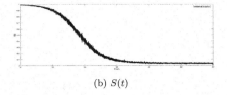

(a) $R(t)$

(b) $S(t)$

Fig. 2. Estimate of $R(t)$, SIR model by the C-N algorithm, and $S(t)$ SIR model, Gibbs algorithm

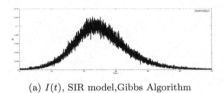
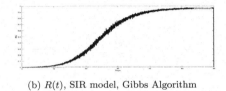

(a) $I(t)$, SIR model,Gibbs Algorithm

(b) $R(t)$, SIR model, Gibbs Algorithm

Fig. 3. Estimate of $I(t)$ and $R(t)$, SIR model, Gibbs Algorithm.

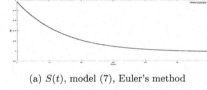
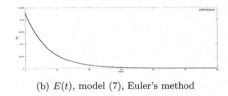

(a) $S(t)$, model (7), Euler's method

(b) $E(t)$, model (7), Euler's method

Fig. 4. Estimate of $S(t)$ and $E(t)$, model (7), Euler's method

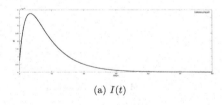
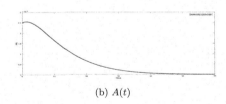

(a) $I(t)$

(b) $A(t)$

Fig. 5. Estimate of $I(t)$ and $A(t)$, model (7), Euler's method

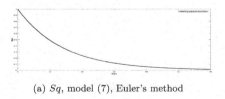
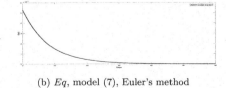

(a) Sq, model (7), Euler's method

(b) Eq, model (7), Euler's method

Fig. 6. Estimate of Sq and Eq, model (7), Euler's method

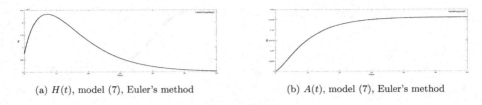

(a) $H(t)$, model (7), Euler's method   (b) $A(t)$, model (7), Euler's method

Fig. 7. Estimate of $H(t)$ and $A(t)$, model (7), Euler's method

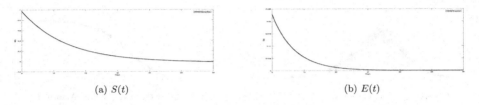

(a) $S(t)$ (b) $E(t)$

Fig. 8. Estimate of $S(t)$ and $E(t)$, model (14), Gibbs algorithm

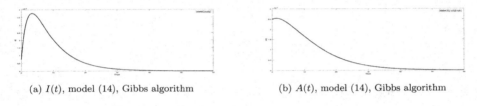

(a) $I(t)$, model (14), Gibbs algorithm   (b) $A(t)$, model (14), Gibbs algorithm

Fig. 9. Estimate of $I(t)$ and $A(t)$, model (14), Gibbs algorithm

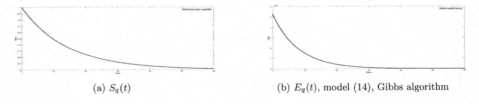

(a) $S_q(t)$ (b) $E_q(t)$, model (14), Gibbs algorithm

Fig. 10. Estimate of $S_q(t)$ and $E_q(t)$, model (14), Gibbs algorithm

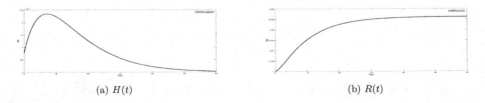

(a) $H(t)$ (b) $R(t)$

Fig. 11. Estimate of $H(t)$ and $R(t)$, model (14), Gibbs algorithm

References

1. Allen, L.: A primer on stochastic epidemic models: formulation numerical simulation and analysis. Infect. Dis. Model. **2**(2), 128–142 (2017)
2. Anderson, R., May, R.: Infectious Diseases of Humans; Dynamic and Control. Oxford University Press, Oxford (1991)
3. Andersson, H., Britton, T.: Stochastic Epidemic Models and their Statistical Analysis. Springer Lecture Notes in Statistics, Springer, New York (2000). https://doi.org/10.1007/978-1-4612-1158-7
4. Bailey, N.: The mathematical theory of infectious diseases and its applications. London, Griffin (1975)
5. Bartlett, M.: Some evolutionary stochastic processes. J. R. Stat. Soc. Ser. B **11**(2), 211–229 (1949)
6. Britton, T.: Stochastic Epidemic Models with Inference. Springer, Heidelberg (2019). https://doi.org/10.1007/978-3-030-30900-8
7. Daley, D., Gani, J.: Epidemic Modelling: An Introduction. Cambridge University Press, Cambridge (1999)
8. Fuchs, C.: Inference for Diffusion Processes with Applications in Life Sciences. Springer, Heidelberg (2013). https://doi.org/10.1007/978-3-642-25969-2
9. Geman, S., Geman, D.: Stochastic relaxation Gibbs distributions and the Bayesian restoration of images. IEEE Trans. Pattern Anal. Mach. Intell. **6**, 721–741 (1984)
10. Infante, S., Sánchez, L., Hernández, A.: Stochastic models to estimate population dynamics. Stat. Optim. Inf. Comput. **7**, 311–328 (2019)
11. Kermack, W., McKendrick, A.: A contribution to the mathematical theory of epidemics. Proc. R. Soc. Lond. **115**, 700–721 (1927)
12. Lux, T.: Inference for systems of stochastic differential equations from discretely sampled data: A numerical maximum likelihood approach. Kiel Working Paper. Kiel Institute for the World Economy (IfW) (1781) (2012)
13. McKendrick, A.: Applications of mathematics to medical problems. Proc. Edinb. Math. Soc. **13**, 98–130 (1926)
14. Ndanguza, D., Mbalawata, I., Nsabimana, J.: Analysis of SDEs applied to SEIR epidemic models by extended Kalman filter method. Appl. Math. **7**, 2195–2211 (2016)
15. Osthus, D., Hickmann, K., Caragea, P., Higdon, D., Valle, S.D.: Forecasting seasonal influenza with a state-space sir model. Ann. Appl. Stat. **11**(1), 202–224 (2017)
16. Poulsen, R.: Approximate maximum likelihood estimation of discretely observed diffusion processes. Manuscript. University of Aarhus (1999)
17. Strikwerda, J.: Finite Difference Schemes and Partial Differential Equations, 2nd edn. Society for Industrial and Applied Mathematics, Philadelphia (2004)
18. Tang, B., et al.: Estimation of the transmission risk of the 2019-nCoV and its implication for public health interventions. J. Clin. Med. **9**(462) (2020)

Hand Gesture Recognition Using Leap Motion Controller, Infrared Information, and Deep Learning Framework

Bryan Toalumbo[1]([✉]) [iD] and Rubén Nogales[1,2] [iD]

[1] Universidad Técnica de Ambato, Ambato, Ecuador
{btoalumbo7749,re.nogales}@uta.edu.ec
[2] Escuela Politécnica Nacional, Quito, Ecuador
ruben.nogales@epn.edu.ec

Abstract. Hand gesture recognition (HGR) systems are the current topic, attracting interest in many fields. This broad interest is because people use hand movements to communicate and interact with the physical world. HGR systems are overgrowing, and the reason is that they have applications for different fields of study. Fields can be human-computer interaction (HIC), augmented and virtual reality, robotics, medicine, and video games. Recognizing the frames to correspond to the hand gesture from a frames sequence is essential to developing HIC systems. Thus, this paper presents algorithms to detect the images corresponding to a hand gesture from a frame sequence acquired by the Leap Motion Controller. The frames sequence contains non-gestures images because the movement follows a video pattern in which the initial and final images correspond to the transition of the gesture. Therefore, this paper develops an automatic (AID) and manual (MID) images discriminator. Every algorithm returns a dataset with images corresponding to the hand gesture. To validate the algorithms, we present an HGR model with every algorithm. The models take as input the new dataset and feed an architecture based on convolutional neural networks (CNN). Our models recognize five static gestures: open hand, fist, wave in, wave out and pinch. The results show a classification accuracy of 92.31% with MID and 94.70% with AID.

Keywords: Hand gesture recognition · Convolutional neural network · Leap motion controller

1 Introduction

Hand gesture recognition (HGR) systems are active research. This wide interest is because, with hands, people can communicate and interact with the physical world [1, 2]. Likewise, HGR systems are a challenge for researchers because they seek to obtain high accuracy values in classification and recognition using machine learning (ML) models. ML models can fall into overfitting scenarios caused by data sparsity and the high dimensionality of the problem. Moreover, the applications of HGR systems are adaptable to different fields of study. The areas can be human-computer interaction (HCI), robotics,

© Springer Nature Switzerland AG 2022
F. R. Narváez et al. (Eds.): SmartTech-IC 2021, CCIS 1532, pp. 412–426, 2022.
https://doi.org/10.1007/978-3-030-99170-8_30

sign language interpreting, virtual and augmented reality, medicine, and video games [3, 4]. In [5] presents a rehabilitation application for improving upper extremity activity and mobility. Similarly, in [6], an application for the control of electronic devices in operating rooms is presented. In [7] offers an application for the management of a robot in rescue operations. Likewise, in [8], an analysis of human behavior in an instructional and learning scenario in a classroom is presented. The previous applications changed the way people and computers interact with each other due to non-invasive sensor technology.

In [9], the authors classify non-invasive sensors for HGR systems into two categories. The first category includes wearable sensors like Myo Armband and Smart Gloves using inertial sensors, for example: accelerometers, magnetometers, and gyroscopes. These sensors improve the way of interaction. Nevertheless, it presents some limitations in sensitivity measurements, signals noise level, device calibration, discomfort, and sweating due to prolonged use. The second category is non-contact sensors, and it is generally used in 3D depth cameras. Some of them are Microsoft Kinect, Intel RealSense Camera, and Leap Motion Controller (LMC). Sensors to the second category generate more excellent safety and comfort for the user. It also presents problems with sensitivity to lighting conditions, occlusion, complex backgrounds, and especially the interaction in front of the sensor [9, 10]. On the other hand, it provides hand movement in two types of data as spatial position data and images [9].

The spatial position hand gesture is mentioned in papers [9–15]. These papers present HGR models with classifiers as Long-Short-Term Memory (LSTM), Support Vector Machine (SVM), K-Nearest Neighbor (KNN). Whereas, the papers [8, 16–21] use non-contact sensor images to develop HGR models. These HGR models apply pre-processing and feature extraction techniques to the images and use classifiers like Random Forest (RF), Dynamic Time Warping (DTW), SVM, KNN, CNN to classify hand gestures. Similarly, the papers [22, 23] use a CNN architecture to learn the features and classify the image automatically. However, only the papers [24–27] use CNN architecture with LMC's images to develop HGR models.

In [11, 13], the authors mention that the LMC is a low-cost, accurate and dedicated device for capturing hand movements. In addition, LMC can be tracking the hand in a range of 150° vast and 60 cm high, with an accuracy of 0.01 mm [28]. The LMC uses infrared cameras to retrieve images, spatial positions of the hand and fingers. This estimation is about the 3D coordinate axes, whose origin is in the sensor's center. The LMC returns a sequence of grayscale images $f(h, w, 1), ..., f(h, w, T)$, where the image $f(h, w, t)$ contains a snapshot of the hand movement at time t, with $t = 1, 2, 3, ..., T$. The position of the fingertips at time t is represented using the matrix $P_t = [p_{(1,t)}^{(x)}, p_{(1,t)}^{(y)}, p_{(1,t)}^{(z)}; ...; p_{(5,t)}^{(x)}, p_{(5,t)}^{(y)}, p_{(5,t)}^{(z)}]_t^{(leap)}$, being $\left[p_{(i,t)}^{(x)}, p_{(i,t)}^{(y)}, p_{(i,t)}^{(z)}\right]$ the vector with the spatial positions of the i-th finger concerning the sensor coordinate axes.

This paper aims to recognize five static gestures: open hand, fist, wave in, wave out, and pinch using images captured by the LMC. According to the literature review, these gestures are the most commonly used in HCI applications. For this reason, we use the dataset from [29]. The dataset contains frame sequences that describe the five hand gestures mentioned. In this context, our paper is divided into two parts. The *first* part is an automatic (AID) and manual (MID) image discriminator to recognize images containing the hand gesture from frames sequences. Every algorithm returns a dataset with images corresponding to the hand gesture. The **second** part is the creation of a CNN architecture to validate AID and MID algorithms. We generate two HGR models. MID dataset trains the first model, and the AID dataset train the second model. Then, we test every model and compare the results. The results are very close, but the second model classifies better than the first model. It is because the AID algorithm discriminates the images in a better way.

AID uses P_t Signals to recognize the block of frames $f(h, w, t_i), ..., f(h, w, t_j)$ that contain hand gestures. The t_i is the starts zone, and t_j is the ends zone of a gesture. Then, every element from $f(h, w, t_i), ..., f(h, w, t_j)$ is pre-processing to remove the background and noise. Finally, we use the Point Feature Matching (PFM) algorithm to discriminate spullier images from $f(h, w, t_i), ..., f(h, w, t_j)$.

MID involves the researchers, and they select and discriminate the images that correspond to a gesture-based on their perception. Then, we remove the background and noise from the image through a pre-process.

2   Related Works

This section proposes review literature about the HGR problem using a Convolutional Neural Network and images acquired by the LMC. We use scientific databases like Science Direct, Springer, ACM digital library, IEEE Xplorer, and a scientific journal, Plos ONE. In the same sense, we used a search string that includes all problem keywords and logic operators. The keywords are Hand Gesture Recognition, Leap Motion Controller, Images, Infrared images, infrared imagery, Convolutional Neural Network. The search string is (hand gesture recognition) AND (leap motion controller OR ("LMC")) and (images OR ("infrared imagery")) AND (convolutional neural network OR ("CNN")). The results obtained filterer by the inclusion and exclusion criteria defined in Table 1.

The inclusion and exclusion criteria showed the works described below.

In [24] proposed an HGR system using images captured by the LMC. The dataset has 800 images of four gestures from five users. The images are segmented using the Gray Threshold technique, and they perform several experiments on the Speeded-Up Robust Features (SURF), Local Binary Pattern (LBP), and Geometric Structure feature extractors. The system uses the Radial Base Function (RBF) neural network as a classifier and reports 99.5% recognition. They mention that LBP performs poorly when the size of the image changes. This paper does not report the amount of data to train, test, and evaluate the neural network.

In [25] proposed a hand gesture recognition system based on infrared images acquired by the LMC. This system characterizes the hand gesture by calculating Depth Spatiograms of Quantized Patterns (DSQP). However, DSQP is an improved modification of LBP, but with too large a feature vector [30]. They use a Compressive Sensing framework to cope with the high dimensionality of the image descriptor by reducing the number of features. They employ an SVM for gesture recognition applying a One-vs-All strategy. The dataset has 2000 images of 10 gestures from 10 users, and it divides into 50/50 for training and testing the system. They report a high accuracy value of 99% to the system.

Table 1. Inclusion and exclusion criteria to filter related works according to our research

Type	Description
Inclusion	Publications from January 2016 to January 2021
	Only work from the databases previously described
	Papers and scientific publications focus on hand gesture recognition models through infrared imaging of the LMC with a CNN architecture
	Papers and scientific publications include the keywords in the abstract, even if they are not in the title
Exclusion	Publications before 2016
	Papers and scientific publications that don't include the use of infrared imaging to recognize hand gestures
	Non-English papers and scientific publishes
	Papers and scientific publishes based on applications but not in the proposed model

A real-time hand gesture recognition system proposes in [26]. The authors build a dataset with 15 gestures, 11 static, and four dynamics from 25 users. The authors annotate the user's distance in front of the LMC and calculate the standard deviation. This calculation is combined with the Otsu algorithm to segment the images. Then, the system extract features from images using Histogram Oriented Gradients (HOG) and LBP. The system uses two layers of SVM classifiers; the first layer is multiclass classifiers using a one-vs-all binary classifier configuration; the second layer implements each previous binary classifier as a bank of binary SVMs. Dataset is divided 80% for training and 20% for testing. They report an average recognition accuracy value of 96.02%. However, in [31], it is mentioned that HOG shows the occurrences of a specific gradient orientation, but the histogram can change considerably due to image rotation or resizing.

In [27], the authors present a system to recognize hand gestures to manipulate 3D objects interactively with images captured from the LMC. The dataset contains 12000 images from 6 gestures. This work does not mention the number of users. Each image is processed by three Feature Extraction Unit (FEU). An FEU has a convolution layer, a ReLU layer, and a max-pooling layer. They report a training and validation accuracy of 98% and 99% for the proposed system. However, the dataset is small and does not guarantee a generalization to recognize hand gestures of different users.

The papers [24–27] use LMC images to recognize hand gestures. However, their datasets are composed of static images perfectly recorded in laboratory environments, with the same light intensity, no noise, and no missing parts. But in fact, the gesture follows a video pattern with images subject to complex background, noise, variable lighting environments, and the interaction zone between the LMC sensor and the user's hand.

3   Methods

The present work uses infrared information from the LMC sensor to recognize the open hand, fist, wave in, wave out, and pinch hand gestures. To develop this work, we use a dataset from [29]. This dataset has frames sequences that represent the hand gestures mentioned above. The frames sequences include non-gesture images because the movement follows a video pattern in which the initial and final images correspond to the transition of the gesture. For this reason, we create AID and MID algorithms to recognize the hand gestures images from a frames sequence. Every algorithm returns a dataset with the hand gesture images. Then, we create a CNN architecture to validate the AID and MID algorithms. The CNN feds with the newly generated datasets and classify the hand gestures.

3.1   Dataset

This paper uses the dataset from [29], which describes a data acquisition protocol. The protocol specifies performing 30 repetitions for every hand gesture during a sampling time of 5 s. The dataset contains nine gestures, five static, and four dynamics from 56 people. Every gesture includes positions spatial sequence P_t, and a images sequence $f(h, w, 1), \ldots, f(h, w, T)$, and every element is labeled with $c_t \in \{1, 2, 3, \ldots, 9\}$. The images have a dimension of 320×120 pixels.

The dataset presents challenges as different behavior from data per user, hand gesture frame sequences, varying lighting environments, and the different interaction zone between the LMC and the user's hand. Also, the dataset has a variable frame sampling that ranges between 16 to 225 fps. The variation is from computer data processing. These challenges approximate how a user performs the gesture in real life when interacting with a HIC system. But also, these challenges are difficult for the process of classifying and recognizing hand gestures.

3.2   Manual Image Discriminator (MID)

MID constructs a new dataset with the hand gesture images. In this algorithm, the researchers perform the process of recognizing and discriminating the images manually. Frames sequence $f(h, w, 1), \ldots, f(h, w, T)$ contains non-gesture images because the movement follows a video pattern. Figure 1 illustrates the video pattern to the fist gesture. The video starts and ends with the open hand; this shows the gesture is at the i-th time instant of the acquired frames.

The researchers save every image in folders and subfolders structure that identifies the user, the gesture, and repetition, as illustrated in Fig. 2. Images recognized by researchers are different in every repetition, and this causes images distribution in each gesture to be different, resulting in an unbalanced dataset.

An unbalanced dataset causes a classifier to be biased towards a specific class and produces lower efficiency in the classifier. To balance our dataset, we establish a limit n on the number of images selected by the researcher in every repetition. When the number of images that the researchers recognize is less than n, a random image is chosen from the

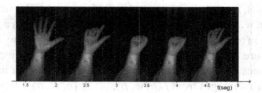

Fig. 1. Example to video pattern in fist gesture

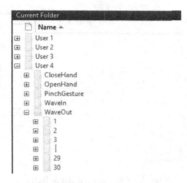

Fig. 2. Folders and subfolders structures according to the user, gesture, and repetition.

selected images and doubled until complete limit n. To calculate n, we use the Hoeffding inequality formula.

$$1 - \delta = 2e^{-2\varepsilon^2 N} \tag{1}$$

Where $1 - \delta$ is confidence level, ε is margin error, and N is the sample size to test the model.

$$N = \frac{\log\left(\frac{2}{1-\delta}\right)}{2\varepsilon^2} \tag{2}$$

With $\delta = 0.05$ y $\varepsilon = 0.05$; N is ≈738, N is the minimum sampling number in every gesture to test the model and minimize the overfitting risk. For this reason, we stablish empirically n value in 4. Thus, every gesture train with 5400 images and tests with 1320 images. In this sense, the dataset has 33600 images, close to the amount of data required to avoid falling into an overfitting scenario. Then, the images go through pre-processing, and it consists of applying a Laplacian filter with sigma 0.4 and gamma 0.5 to accentuate the edges. Then each image is segmented by the Gray Threshold level 2 technique to remove the background and eliminate the image's noise.

3.3 Automatic Image Discriminator (AID)

AID algorithm generates a new dataset with images corresponding to the hand gesture automatically. AID algorithm composes by Zone Values, Image Selector, Image Pre-processing, and Point Feature Matching. The Zone Values uses P_t signals to recognize and return the starts (t_i) and ends (t_j) zone values of a gesture. The Image Selector select block of frames $f(h, w, t_i), \ldots, f(h, w, t_j)$ from frames sequence of a gesture. Image Pre-processing consists in remove the background and noise from $f(h, w, t_i), \ldots, f(h, w, t_j)$. Finally, Point Feature Matching (PFM) algorithm detects an object based on finding point correspondences between the reference image and the target image. We use PFM to discriminate spullier images from $f(h, w, t_i), \ldots, f(h, w, t_j)$. Figure 3 shows the AID schema.

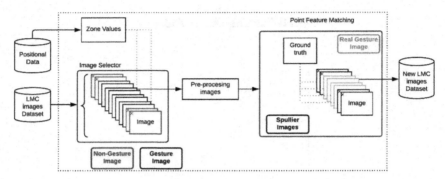

Fig. 3. AID algorithm schema

Zone Values. This algorithm receives the P_t signal as input and returns the i-th time instants where user performs gesture. The i-th time instants of a gesture are represented to t_i and t_j. Where t_i corresponds to a time instant where the user starts the gesture and t_j corresponds to a time instant where the user ends the gesture. To calculate the values for t_i and t_j. We pre-process P_t at k time instants using interpolation and extrapolation techniques. Through experimentation, we empirically defined the value for k in 70. The pre-processed P_t signal is divided into Windows of 18 with a step of 15. In every window, the pre-processed P_t signal is represented by 15 channels. The spatial positions [X, Y, Z] of each finger form the channels. Empirically, we observe that gesture representation occurs at the same time instants in all channels. In this sense, we take only one channel for processing. For every window, we calculate the spectrogram with a Short-time Fourier transform (STFT). STFT returns a matrix where the columns represent the time instants and the rows are frequencies starting at zero. From this matrix, we obtain an average vector, and we calculate the standard deviation. A standard deviations vector is getting at the end of sliding the window over the whole signal. From the standard deviations vector, we take the index of the maximum value. This index defines the corresponding window to the gesture. Figure 4 describes Zone Values process.

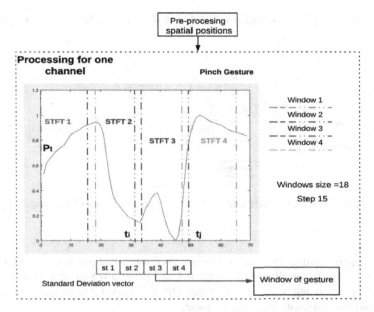

Fig. 4. Zone values process to the pinch gesture.

Image Selector. This algorithm uses the images sequence $f(h, w, 1), \ldots, f(h, w, T)$ of a gesture where the image $f(h, w, t)$ contains a snapshot of the hand movement at time t, with $t = 1, 2, 3, \ldots, T$. To extract the block of frames that containing the gesture, we use the t time instants. We normalize t whenever $T > k$. If the condition is met, T divides into k, and the quotient (Q) is round. Every t element divides into Q whenever $Q > 0$. The results obtained from this operation are new time instants $f(h, w, t_i), \ldots, f(h, w, t_j)$. Figure 5 describe the process to standardization in 70 time instants.

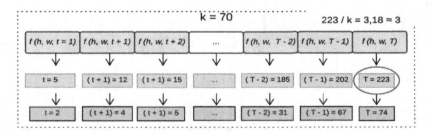

Fig. 5. Example to standardization in k time instants of a gesture.

The new time instants and the values returned by the Zones Value allow obtaining the block of images corresponding to the gesture. For example, in Fig. 4, the third window contains the hand gesture between $t_{i=33}$ and $t_{j=48}$. Then, the images between

$f(h, w, t_{i=33})$ and $f(h, w, t_{j=48})$ are taken. Figure 6 illustrates the process of Image Selector.

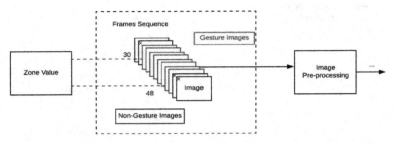

Fig. 6. Example to image selector with $t_{i=33}$ and $t_{j=48}$ in a frames sequence.

Image Pre-processing. The selected images go through pre-processing, and it consists of applying a Laplacian filter with sigma 0.4 and gamma 0.5 to accentuate the edges. Then each image is segmented by the Gray Threshold level 2 technique to remove the background and eliminate the image's noise.

Point Feature Matching. The newly generated dataset contains two problems: spullier images and the unbalanced images distribution in each gesture. To solve these problems, we use object detection using Point Feature Matching (PFM). This algorithm detects an object in an image by extracting the most characteristic points of the object and searches for matching points in the image using SURF. The operation of SURF consists of three parts: feature extraction, feature description, and feature matching. SURF detects objects despite a change of scale or rotation in the plane and is resistant to small amounts of out-of-plane rotation and occlusion [32].

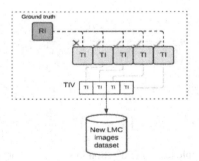

Fig. 7. PFM algorithm to discriminate spullier images

In the PFM, a Ground Truth image of each user's gesture establish as a reference image (RI) and the pre-processed images as target images (TI). From each TI, the strengths are extracted and compared with the IR strengths number. When TI strengths number is equal to the number of RI strengths (TI corresponds to an image containing the gesture), we save TI in a temporary image vector (TIV). When TIV length is less than n, and there are no more ID images, RI is added to TIV until the length of TIV equals n. In this way, the dataset obtains the images corresponding to the gesture, and the classes are balanced. Figure 7 shows the PFM algorithm.

3.4 Convolutional Neural Network

The CNN architecture is defined according to the specific problem that wishes resolved. The CNN is usually composed of two stages: feature learning and classification layers. The feature learning to our CNN architecture is composed of 6 convolutional layers, three pooling layers, six normalization layers, 6 ReLU layers, and two dropout layers. Likewise, the classification layer contains a fully connected layer, a SoftMax layer, and a pixel layer. Figure 8 shows our CNN architecture.

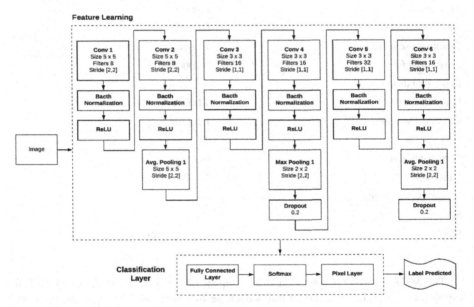

Fig. 8. CNN architecture

Conv 1 and Conv 2 convolutional layers have 8 filters with a size of 5 × 5 and use a stride of 2. The following convolutional layer has a size of 3 × 3 with a stride of 1. Conv 3, Conv 4, and Conv 6 convolutional layer have 16 filters and Conv 5 has 32 filter. All pooling layers have a stride of 2. The first pooling layer has a size of 5 × 5, and the following pooling layers have a size of 2 × 2.

In [33], the authors mentioned there should be multiple convolutional layers before each pooling layer to extract enough features from an image. But, on the other hand, the high dimensionality of the feature vector increases the complexity of the problem and can fall into an overfitting scenario. For this reason, we add the Dropout regularization technique to CNN to avoid falling into this problem.

4   Experimentation and Results

The experiments used an Alienware computer with Windows 10 operating System and Matlab Software version R2019B. The machine has an Intel Core i7-6800K processor and 16 Gb memory ram. To develop the CNN architecture, we use Deep Learning Toolbox with hyperparameters described in Table 2.

Table 2. CNN hyperparameters

Option	Value
Optimizer	Sgdm
Momentum	0.9000
Initial learn rate	0.0100
Learn rate schedule	Piecewise
Learn drop factor	0.2000
Learn rate drop period	5
l2 regularization	1.0000e-4
Gradient threshold method	L2norm
Max epochs	15
Mini-batch size	64
Validation data	1×2 cell
Validation frequency	50
Shuffle	Once
Plots	Training-progress

The MID and AID dataset is divided empirically into 80% for train and 20% for testing the model, i.e., the model trains each gesture with 5400 images and tests with 1320 images. The MID and AID models execute three times. In each run, the model obtains different images for training and testing.

Table 3 shows the training and testing accuracy values for each run of the MID model. MID model reports the average test accuracy for MID model is 92.31% with a standard deviation of 0.56%. On other hand, Table 4 shows the training and testing accuracy values for each run of the AID model. AID model reports the average test accuracy is 94.70% with a standard deviation of 2.55%.

The CNN is also used to classify hand gestures from the dataset of [25]. This dataset is available at the following link: https://www.kaggle.com/gti-upm/leapgestrecog, and the images are entered directly into the CNN. Also, the dataset of [25] is divided empirically

Table 3. Accuracy results to MID dataset.

Execution	Train accuracy	Test accuracy	Time
1	97.34%	92.92%	00:34:43
2	98.44%	92.17%	00:33:11
3	98.44%	91.83%	00:35:56

Table 4. Accuracy results to AID dataset.

Execution	Train accuracy	Test accuracy	Time
1	98.72%	97.50%	00:36:40
2	96.20%	92.50%	00:36:59
3	98.80%	94.11%	00:35:40

Table 5. Accuracy results to [25] dataset with our CNN architecture.

Execution	Train accuracy	Test accuracy	Time
1	100%	99.97%	00:16:39
2	100%	99.99%	00:15:59
3	100%	99.95%	00:16:12

into 80% for training and 20% for testing; this model executes three times. Table 5 shows the training and testing accuracy values for each run.

The average test accuracy for the dataset in [25] is high with our CNN architecture. We report to this dataset the average test accuracy is 99.97%, with a standard deviation of 0.20%. This dataset confirms the robustness of our CNN. Accuracy results for this dataset demonstrate the images were recorded in laboratory environments without noise or missing parts.

Our accuracy results obtained for MID and AID are comparable to the accuracy results reported in related works. Table 6 shows a comparative table of the results of our work compared to related works. However, our work is different from related work. Our work takes frames to correspond to the gesture from a frames sequence. The frames sequence has varying lighting environments; the user's hand gesture is at different interaction distances with the LMC. Moreover, related works take static images flawlessly executed and recorded in laboratory environments without noise or missing parts. Because of the above observations, the related works guarantee high results. On the other hand, our work has high classification accuracies, although our dataset presents different challenges for the researchers.

Table 6. Comparative table of test accuracy result of our work compares to related works.

Dataset	Classifier	Test accuracy
[24]	RBF	99.50%
[25]	SVM	99.00%
[26]	SVM	96.02%
[27]	CNN	99.00%
MID	**CNN**	**92.31%**
AID	**CNN**	**94.70%**

5 Conclusions

Recognizing the frames to correspond to the hand gesture from a frames sequence is essential for the development of real-time HIC systems. This paper presents a hand gesture recognition model using infrared information from the LMC with a CNN architecture. Our dataset contains frame sequences that describe five static gestures: open hand, fist, wave in, wave out, and pinch. The frames sequences include non-gesture images because the hand gesture follows a video pattern.

We recognize the hand gesture images from a frames sequence with AID and MID algorithms. These algorithms generate a new dataset with images corresponding to the gesture. We create the MID algorithm to verify the efficiency of the AID results. Our results are high, the AID model has accuracy of 94.70%, and the MID model has accuracy of 92.31%.

The results of MID and AID are similar, but AID has better results; this shows that the AID algorithm recognizes, selects, and discriminates the images that correspond to the hand gesture from frame sequence in a better way. Because the Zone Values and PFM algorithms perform the image recognition and discrimination process. In comparison, the images in the MID dataset are selected and discriminated by the researchers based on their perception.

The results obtained for MID and AID are comparable to the results reported in related works. However, we have challenges with our dataset like different behavior of the data per user, the sequence of frames of a gesture, variable lighting environments, different distances between the LMC and the user's hand. Moreover, related works have static images of the hand gesture, are flawlessly executed, and are recorded in laboratory environments without noise or missing parts. Because of the related works observations, their model has a good class separation and high classification accuracy. It is demonstrated in experiment executed with dataset of [25] in our CNN architecture. The results with our CNN architecture are superior to results of [25].

In this sense, the accuracy of our models tends to decrease because the users have different interaction zone with the LMC sensor in every gesture. Also, the frames sequences have images with a gesture, not recorded perfectly, noise, and complex background.

References

1. Lupinetti, K., Ranieri, A., Franca, G., Monti, M.: 3D dynamic hand gestures recognition using the Leap Motion sensor and convolutional neural networks (2020) [Online]. Available: https://manus-vr.com/. Accessed 4 Jan 2021

2. Yang, Q., Ding, W., Zhou, X., Zhao, D., Yan, S.: Leap motion hand gesture recognition based on deep neural network. In: Proceedings of the 32nd Chinese Control and Decision Conference, CCDC 2020, pp. 2089–2093 (Aug. 2020). https://doi.org/10.1109/CCDC49329.2020.9164723

3. Hoang, V.T.: HGM-4: a new multi-cameras dataset for hand gesture recognition. Data Br. **30**, 105676 (2020). https://doi.org/10.1016/j.dib.2020.105676

4. Wang, Q., Wang, Y., Liu, F., Zeng, W.: Hand gesture recognition of Arabic numbers using leap motion via deterministic learning. In: Chinese Control Conference, CCC, pp. 10823–10828 (Sept. 2017). https://doi.org/10.23919/ChiCC.2017.8029083

5. Niechwiej-Szwedo, E., Gonzalez, D., Nouredanesh, M., Tung, J.: Evaluation of the leap motion controller during the performance of visually-guided upper limb movements. PLoS ONE **13**(3), 1–25 (2018). https://doi.org/10.1371/journal.pone.0193639

6. Nasr-Esfahani, E., Karimi, N., Soroushmehr, S.M.R.: Hand Gesture Recognition for Contactless Device Control in Operating Rooms (2017). https://doi.org/10.1007/s11548-017-1588-3

7. Shang, W., Cao, X., Ma, H., Zang, H., Wei, P.: Kinect-based vision system of mine rescue robot for low illuminous environment. J. Sens. **2016** (2016). https://doi.org/10.1155/2016/8252015

8. Wang, J., Liu, T., Wang, X.: Human hand gesture recognition with convolutional neural networks for K-12 double-teachers instruction mode classroom. Infrared Phys. Technol. **111**, 103464 (2020). https://doi.org/10.1016/j.infrared.2020.103464

9. Ameur, S., Ben Khalifa, A., Bouhlel, M.S.: Chronological pattern indexing: an efficient feature extraction method for hand gesture recognition with Leap Motion. J. Vis. Commun. Image Represent. **70**, 102842 (2020). https://doi.org/10.1016/j.jvcir.2020.102842

10. Raman, B., Kumar, S., Roy, P.P., Sen, D. (eds.): Proceedings of International Conference on Computer Vision and Image Processing. AISC, vol. 460. Springer, Singapore (2017). https://doi.org/10.1007/978-981-10-2107-7

11. Nogales, R., Benalcazar, M.: Real-Time Hand Gesture Recognition Using the Leap Motion Controller and Machine Learning (Nov. 2019). https://doi.org/10.1109/LA-CCI47412.2019.9037037

12. Xue, Y., Gao, S., Sun, H., Qin, W.: A Chinese sign language recognition system using leap motion. In: Proceedings – 2017 International Conference on Virtual Reality and Visualization, ICVRV 2017, pp. 180–185 (Jul. 2017). https://doi.org/10.1109/ICVRV.2017.00044

13. Ameur, S., Ben Khalifa, A., Bouhlel, M.S.: A novel hybrid bidirectional unidirectional LSTM network for dynamic hand gesture recognition with leap motion. Entertain. Comput. **35**, 100373 (2020). https://doi.org/10.1016/j.entcom.2020.100373

14. Nogales, R., Benalcázar, M.E.: A Survey on Hand Gesture Recognition Using Machine Learning and Infrared Information. In: Botto-Tobar, M., Zambrano Vizuete, M., Torres-Carrión, P., Montes León, S., Pizarro Vásquez, G., Durakovic, B. (eds.) ICAT 2019. CCIS, vol. 1194, pp. 297–311. Springer, Cham (2020). https://doi.org/10.1007/978-3-030-42520-3_24

15. Gopinath, N., Anuja, J., Anusha, S., Monisha, V.: A Survey on Hand Gesture Recognition Using Machine Learning, pp. 3003–3008 (2020)

16. Huang, Y., Yang, J.: A multi-scale descriptor for real-time RGB-D hand gesture recognition. Pattern Recognit. Lett. (2020). https://doi.org/10.1016/j.patrec.2020.11.011

17. Sharma, A., Mittal, A., Singh, S., Awatramani, V.: Hand gesture recognition using image processing and feature extraction techniques. Procedia Comput. Sci. **173**, 181–190 (2020). https://doi.org/10.1016/j.procs.2020.06.022
18. Lazo, C., Sanchez, Z., del Carpio, C.: A Static Hand Gesture Recognition for Peruvian Sign Language Using Digital Image Processing and Deep Learning. In: Iano, Y., Arthur, R., Saotome, O., Vieira Estrela, V., Loschi, H.J. (eds.) BTSym 2018. SIST, vol. 140, pp. 281–290. Springer, Cham (2019). https://doi.org/10.1007/978-3-030-16053-1_27
19. Liao, B., Jing, L., Zhaojie, J., Gaoxiang, O.: Hand Gesture Recognition with Generalized Hough Transform and DC-CNN Using RealSense, pp. 84–90 (2018)
20. Pinto, R.F., Borges, C.D.B., Almeida, A.M.A., Paula, I.C.: Static hand gesture recognition based on convolutional neural networks. J. Electr. Comput. Eng., **2019** (2019). https://doi.org/10.1155/2019/4167890
21. Islam, M.R., Mitu, U.K., Bhuiyan, R.A., Shin, J.: Hand gesture feature extraction using deep convolutional neural network for recognizing American sign language. In: Proc. 2018 4th Int. Conf. Front. Signal Process. ICFSP 2018, pp. 115–119 (2018). https://doi.org/10.1109/ICFSP.2018.8552044
22. Li, G., et al.: Hand gesture recognition based on convolution neural network. Clust. Comput. **22**(2), 2719–2729 (2017). https://doi.org/10.1007/s10586-017-1435-x
23. Chang, C.-M., Tseng, D.-C.: Loose Hand Gesture Recognition Using CNN (2019)
24. Zhang, R., Ming, Y., Sun, J.: Hand gesture recognition with SURF-BOF based on Gray threshold segmentation, pp. 118–122 (2016)
25. Blanc-Talon, J., Distante, C., Philips, W., Popescu, D., Scheunders, P. (eds.): ACIVS 2016. LNCS, vol. 10016. Springer, Cham (2016). https://doi.org/10.1007/978-3-319-48680-2
26. Mantecón, T., Del Blanco, C.R., Jaureguizar, F., García, N.: A real-time gesture recognition system using near-infrared imagery, pp. 1–17 (2019). https://doi.org/10.1371/journal.pone.0223320
27. Tripathy, S.: Natural gestures to interact with 3d virtual objects using deep learning framework. In: TENCON 2019 – 2019 IEEE Reg. 10 Conf., pp. 1363–1368 (2019). https://doi.org/10.1109/TENCON.2019.8929637
28. Weichert, F., Bachmann, D., Rudak, B., Fisseler, D.: Analysis of the accuracy and robustness of the leap motion controller. Sensors (Switzerland) **13**(5), 6380–6393 (2013). https://doi.org/10.3390/s130506380
29. Nogales, R., Benalcazar, M.E., Toalumbo, B., Palate, A., Martinez, R., Vargas, J.: Construction of a Dataset for Static and Dynamic Hand Tracking Using a Non-invasive Environment. In: García, M.V., Fernández-Peña, F., Gordón-Gallegos, C. (eds.) Advances and Applications in Computer Science, Electronics and Industrial Engineering. AISC, vol. 1307, pp. 185–197. Springer, Singapore (2021). https://doi.org/10.1007/978-981-33-4565-2_12
30. Mantecón, T., Mantecón, A., Del-Blanco, C.R., Jaureguizar, F., García, N.: Enhanced gesture-based human-computer interaction through a compressive sensing reduction scheme of very large and efficient depth feature descriptors (Oct. 2015). https://doi.org/10.1109/AVSS.2015.7301804
31. Cheon, M.-K., Lee, W.-J., Hyun, C.-H., Park, M.: Rotation invariant histogram of oriented gradients. Int. J. Fuzzy Log. Intell. Syst. **11**(4), 293–298 (2011). https://doi.org/10.5391/ijfis.2011.11.4.293
32. Feature Extraction Using SURF – MATLAB & Simulink – MathWorks América Latina. https://la.mathworks.com/help/gpucoder/ug/feature-extraction-using-surf.html. Accessed 29 Jul. 2021
33. Bao, P., Maqueda, A.I., Del-Blanco, C.R., Garciá, N.: Tiny hand gesture recognition without localization via a deep convolutional network. IEEE Trans. Consum. Electron. **63**(3), 251–257 (2017). https://doi.org/10.1109/TCE.2017.014971

Author Index

Printed in the United States
by Baker & Taylor Publisher Services